T0205818

Lecture Notes of the Institute for Computer Sciences, Social Informatics and Telecommunications Engineering

More information about this series at http://www.springer.com/series/8197

Honghao Gao · Zhiyong Feng ·
Jun Yu · Jun Wu (Eds.)

Communications and Networking

14th EAI International Conference, ChinaCom 2019
Shanghai, China, November 29 – December 1, 2019
Proceedings, Part II

 Springer

Editors
Honghao Gao
Shanghai University
Shanghai, China

Jun Yu
Hangzhou Dianzi University
Hangzhou, China

Zhiyong Feng
School of Computer Software
Tianjin University
Tianjin, China

Jun Wu
Tongji University
Shanghai Shi, China

ISSN 1867-8211   ISSN 1867-822X (electronic)
Lecture Notes of the Institute for Computer Sciences, Social Informatics
and Telecommunications Engineering
ISBN 978-3-030-41116-9   ISBN 978-3-030-41117-6 (eBook)
https://doi.org/10.1007/978-3-030-41117-6

This Springer imprint is published by the registered company Springer Nature Switzerland AG
The registered company address is: Gewerbestrasse 11, 6330 Cham, Switzerland

Preface

We are delighted to introduce the proceedings of the 14th European Alliance for Innovation (EAI) International Conference on Communications and Networking in China (ChinaCom 2019). This conference brought together researchers, developers, and practitioners from around the world, who are interested in the field of communications, networks, image processing, and internet applications.

The technical program of ChinaCom 2019 consisted of 92 papers, including 80 full papers and 12 workshop papers in oral presentation sessions at the main conference tracks. The conference sessions were: Session 1 - Internet of Things, Edge and Fog; Session 2 - Antenna, Microwave and Cellular Communication; Session 3 - Wireless Communications and Networking; Session 4 - Network and Information Security; Session 5 - Communication QoS, Reliability & Modeling; Session 6 - Pattern Recognition and Signal Processing; Session 7 - Information Processing; and Session 8 - DISA Workshop. Apart from high quality technical paper presentations, the technical program also featured four keynote speeches which were delivered by Prof. Jun Yu from Hangzhou Dianzi University, Prof. Yang Yang from Shanghai Tech University, Prof. Xinheng Wang from Xi'an Jiaotong - Liverpool University, and Prof. Haijun Zhang from the University of Science and Technology Beijing.

Coordination with the steering chair, Prof. Imrich Chlamtac, and honorary chairs, Prof. Changjun Jiang, Prof. Qing Nie, and Prof. R. K. Shyamasundar, was essential for the success of the conference. We sincerely appreciate their constant support and guidance. It was also a great pleasure to work with such an excellent Organizing Committee and we thank them for their hard work in organizing and supporting the conference. In particular we would like to thank, the Technical Program Committee (TPC), led by our TPC co-chairs, Honghao Gao, Guangjie Han, Jun Wu, and Wei Xi, who completed the peer-review process of technical papers and made a high-quality technical program. We are also grateful to conference manager, Kristina Lappyova, for her support, and all the authors who submitted their papers to the ChinaCom 2019 conference and workshops.

We strongly believe that the ChinaCom conference series provides a good forum for all researcher, developers, and practitioners to discuss all science and technology aspects that are relevant to communications and networking. We also expect that the future ChinaCom conferences will be as successful and stimulating, as indicated by the contributions presented in this volume.

November 2019

Honghao Gao
Jizhong Zhao
Zhiyong Feng
Jun Yu

Organization

Steering Committee

Chair

Imrich Chlamtac   Bruno Kessler Professor, University of Trento, Italy

Honorary Co-chairs

Changjun Jiang	Tongji University, China
Qing Nie	Shanghai University, China
R. K. Shyamasundar	Indian Institute of Technology, India

Organizing Committee

General Chairs

Jizhong Zhao	Xi'an Jiaotong University, China
Zhiyong Feng	Tianjin University, China
Jun Yu	Hangzhou Dianzi University, China

Technical Program Chairs

Honghao Gao	Shanghai University, China
Guangjie Han	Hohai University, China
Jun Wu	Tongji University, China
Wei Xi	Xi'an Jiaotong University, China

International Advisory Committee

Zhenhua Duan	Xidian University, China
Vladimir Zwass	Fairleigh Dickinson University, USA
Mohammad S. Obaidat	Fordham University, USA
Han-Chieh Chao	National Dong Hwa University, Taiwan
Tai-Wei Kuo	National Taiwan University, Taiwan
Minho Jo	Korea University, South Korea

Publicity Chairs

Congfeng Jiang	Hangzhou Dianzi University, China
Zijian Zhang	Beijing Institute of Technology, China

Social Media Chair

Jiang Deng   Shanghai University, China

Workshops Chairs

Yuyu Yin   Hangzhou Dianzi University, China
Xiaoxian Yang   Shanghai Polytechnic University, China

Sponsorship and Exhibits Chair

Honghao Gao   Shanghai University, China

Publications Chairs

Youhuizi Li   Hangzhou Dianzi University, China
Wenmin Lin   Hangzhou Dianzi University, China

Demos Chair

Rui Li   Xidian University, China

Posters and PhD Track Chairs

Yueshen Xu   Xidian University, China
Zhiping Jiang   Xidian University, China

Local Arrangement Chairs

Yihai Chen   Shanghai University, China
Yuan Tao   Shanghai University, China

Web Chair

Qiming Zou   Shanghai University, China

Conference Manager

Kristina Lappyova   European Alliance for Innovation, Belgium

Technical Program Committee

Amjad Ali   Korea University, South Korea
An Liu   Zhejiang University, China
Anand Nayyar   Duy Tan University, Vietnam
Anwer Al-Dulaimi   University of Toronto, Canada
Ao Zhou   Beijing University of Posts and Telecommunications,
                              China
Bin Cao   Zhejiang University of Technology, China
Buqing Cao   Hunan University of Science and Technology, China
Changai Sun   University of Shanghai for Science and Technology,
                              China
Congfeng Jiang   Hangzhou Dianzi University, China
Cui Ying   Shanghai Jiao Tong University, China
Dongjing Wang   Hangzhou Dianzi University, China

Tao Huang   Silicon Lake University, China
Wenda Tang   Lancaster University, UK
Wenmin Lin   Hangzhou Dianzi University, China
Xiaobing Sun   Yangzhou University, China
Xiaoliang Fan   Fuzhou University, China
Xiaolong Xu   Nanjing University of Information Science
                             and Technology, China
Xiaoxian Yang   Shanghai Polytechnic University, China
Xihua Liu   Nanjing University of Information Science
                             and Technology, China
Xuan Liu   Southeast University, China
Xuan Zhao   Nanjing University, China
Yanmei Zhang   Central University of Finance and Economics, China
Yihai Chen   Shanghai University, China
Ying Chen   Beijing University of Information Technology, China
Yiping Wen   Hunan University of Science and Technology, China
Yirui Wu   Hohai University, China
Yiwen Zhang   Anhui University, China
Youhuizi Li   Hangzhou Dianzi University, China
Yu Weng   Minzu University of China, China
Yu Zheng   Nanjing University of Information Science
                             and Technology, China
Yuan Yuan   Michigan State University, USA
Yu-Chun Pan   University of West London, UK
Yucong Duan   Hainan University, China
Yueshen Xu   Xidian University, China
Yunni Xia   Chongqing University, China
Yutao Ma   Wuhan University, China
Yuyu Yin   Hangzhou Dianzi University, China
Zhe Xing   Sichuan University, China
Zhixhi Xu   Tongji University, China
Zhongqin Bi   Shanghai University of Electric Power, China
Zhuofeng Zhao   North China University of Technology, China
Zijian Zhang   Beijing Institute of Technology, China

Contents – Part II

Pattern Recognition and Signal Processing

Integrity-Preserving Image Aesthetic Assessment 3
  Xin Sun and Jun Zhou

Near-Field Source Localization by Exploiting the Signal Sparsity 20
  Huan Meng, Hongqing Liu, Yi Zhou, and Zhen Luo

Layer-Wise Entropy Analysis and Visualization of Neurons Activation 29
  Longwei Wang, Peijie Chen, Chengfei Wang, and Rui Wang

Analog Images Communication Based on Block Compressive Sensing 37
  Min Wang, Bin Tan, Jiamei Luo, and Qin Zou

Tier-Based Directed Weighted Graph Coloring Algorithm
for Device-to-Device Underlay Cellular Networks.................... 47
  Yating Zhang and Tao Peng

Iterative Phase Error Compensation Joint Channel Estimation
in OFDM Systems 62
  Qian Li, Hang Long, and Mingwei Tang

A Practical Low Latency System for Cloud-Based VR Applications 73
  Shuangfei Tian, Mingyi Yang, and Wei Zhang

A Panoramic Video Face Detection System Design and Implement........ 82
  Hang Zhao, Dian Liu, Bin Tan, Songyuan Zhao, Jun Wu, and Rui Wang

Coherence Histogram Based Wi-Fi Passive Human Detection Approach 95
  Zengshan Tian, Xiaoya Zhang, and Lingxia Li

Information Processing

A Convolutional Neural Network Decoder for Convolutional Codes 113
  Zhengyu Zhang, Dongping Yao, Lei Xiong, Bo Ai, and Shuo Guo

A Classifier Combining Local Distance Mean and Centroid
for Imbalanced Datasets..................................... 126
  Yingying Zhao and Xingcheng Liu

Content Recommendation Algorithm Based on Double Lists
in Heterogeneous Network.................................... 140
  Jianing Chen, Xi Li, Hong Ji, and Heli Zhang

Research on High Precision Location Algorithm of NB Terminal
Based on 5G/NB-IoT Cluster Node Information Fusion   154
   Wei Ju, Di He, Xin Chen, Changqing Xu, and Wenxian Yu

A Novel Indoor Positioning Algorithm Based on IMU.   168
   Bi He, Hui Wang, Minshuo Li, Kozyrev Yury, and Xu Shi

Service Delay Minimization-Based Joint Clustering and Content Placement
Algorithm for Cellular D2D Communication Systems   180
   Ahmad Zubair, Pengfei Ma, Tao Wei, Ling Wang, and Rong Chai

T-HuDe: Through-The-Wall Human Detection with WiFi Devices   192
   Wei Zeng, Zengshan Tian, Yue Jin, and Xi Chen

Legitimate Eavesdropping with Multiple Wireless Powered Eavesdroppers . . .   205
   Qun Li and Ding Xu

WiHlo: A Case Study of WiFi-Based Human Passive Localization
by Angle Refinement.   216
   Zengshan Tian, Weiqin Yang, Yue Jin, and Gongzhui Zhang

An Integrated Processing Method Based on Wasserstein Barycenter
Algorithm for Automatic Music Transcription.   230
   Cong Jin, Zhongtong Li, Yuanyuan Sun, Haiyin Zhang, Xin Lv,
   Jianguang Li, and Shouxun Liu

Spinal-Polar Concatenated Codes in Non-coherent UWB
Communication Systems   241
   Qianwen Luo, Zhonghua Liang, and Yue Xin

Dynamic Programming Based Cooperative Mobility Management in Ultra
Dense Networks   252
   Ziyue Zhang, Jie Gong, and Xiang Chen

Low-Latency Transmission and Caching of High Definition
Map at a Crossroad.   264
   Yue Gu, Jie Liu, and Long Zhao

Gradient-Based UAV Positioning Algorithm for Throughput
Optimization in UAV Relay Networks.   278
   Xiangyu Li, Tao Peng, and Xiaoyang Li

DISA Workshop

Multi-convex Combination Adaptive Filtering Algorithm
Based on Maximum Versoria Criterion (Workshop).   297
   Wenjing Wu, Zhonghua Liang, Yimeng Bai, and Wei Li

Secure *k*-Anonymization Linked with Differential
Identifiability (Workshop) 307
  Zheng Zhao, Tao Shang, and Jianwei Liu

Energy Management Strategy Based on Battery Capacity
Degradation in EH-CRSN (Workshop)............................ 317
  Errong Pei, Shan Liu, and Maohai Ran

Multipath and Distorted Detection Based on Multi-correlator (Workshop) ... 328
  Rongtao Qin

Delay Optimization-Based Joint Route Selection and Resource Allocation
Algorithm for Cognitive Vehicular Ad Hoc Networks (Workshop) 338
  Changzhu Liu, Rong Chai, Shangxin Peng, and Qianbin Chen

Energy Efficiency Optimization-Based Joint Resource Allocation
and Clustering Algorithm for M2M Communication
Networks (Workshop)... 351
  Changzhu Liu, Ahmad Zubair, Rong Chai, and Qianbin Chen

Latency-Reliability Analysis for Multi-antenna System (Workshop)........ 364
  Zhichao Xiu, Hang Long, and Yixiao Li

Cost Function Minimization-Based Joint UAV Path Planning
and Charging Station Deployment (Workshop) 378
  Tao Wei, Rong Chai, and Qianbin Chen

Energy Efficient Computation Offloading for Energy Harvesting-Enabled
Heterogeneous Cellular Networks (Workshop) 391
  Mengqi Mao, Rong Chai, and Qianbin Chen

Wi-Fi Gesture Recognition Technology Based on Time-Frequency
Features (Workshop)... 402
  Zengshan Tian, Mengtian Ren, Qing Jiang, and Xiaoya Zhang

Accompaniment Music Separation Based on 2DFT and Image
Processing (Workshop) 414
  Tian Zhang, Tianqi Zhang, and Congcong Fan

Average Speed Based Broadcast Algorithm for Vehicular
Ad Hoc Networks (Workshop).................................. 425
  Qichao Cao, Yanping Yu, and Xue Su

Author Index 437

Contents – Part I

Internet of Things, Edge and Fog

Pricing-Based Partial Computation Offloading in Mobile Edge Computing. . .   3
  Lanhui Li and Tiejun Lv

Dynamic Resource Allocation in High-Speed Railway Fog Radio Access
Networks with Delay Constraint   15
  Rui Wang, Jun Wu, and Jun Yu

Distributed Task Splitting and Offloading in Mobile Edge Computing   33
  *Yanling Ren, Zhihui Weng, Yuanjiang Li, Zhibin Xie, Kening Song,
  and Xiaolei Sun*

Evolution Computation Based Resource Allocation for Hybrid
Visible-Light and RF Femtocell   43
  Yuan Zhang, Yang Li, Liang Chen, Ning Wang, and Bo Fan

Deep Reinforcement Learning Based Computation Offloading
for Mobility-Aware Edge Computing.   53
  Minyan Shi, Rui Wang, Erwu Liu, Zhixin Xu, and Longwei Wang

Priority EDF Scheduling Scheme for MANETs.   66
  *Abel Mukakanya Muwumba, Godfrey Njulumi Justo,
  Libe Valentine Massawe, and John Ngubiri*

Joint Collaborative Task Offloading for Cost-Efficient Applications
in Edge Computing   77
  Chaochen Ma, Zhida Qin, Xiaoying Gan, and Luoyi Fu

Energy-Efficient Coded Caching and Resource Allocation
for Smart Grid-Supported HetNets.   91
  Fangfang Yin, Junyi Lyu, Danpu Liu, Zhilong Zhang, and Minyin Zeng

Task-Aware Joint Computation Offloading for UAV-Enabled Mobile Edge
Computing Systems.   102
  Junshi Hu, Heli Zhang, Xi Li, and Hong Ji

Burst Traffic Awareness WRR Scheduling Algorithm in Wide Area
Network for Smart Grid.   117
  Xin Tan, Xiaohui Li, Zhenxing Liu, and Yuemin Ding

Joint Task Offloading, CNN Layer Scheduling and Resource Allocation
in Cooperative Computing System   129
  Xia Song, Rong Chai, and Qianbin Chen

A Resource Scheduling Algorithm with High Task Request Acceptance
Rate for Multi-platform Avionics System   143
  Kui Li, Qing Zhou, Guonan Cui, and Liang Liu

DPTM: A UAV Message Transmission Path Optimization Method Under
Dynamic Programming   167
  Pingyu Deng, Qing Zhou, Kui Li, and Feifei Zhu

Antenna, Microwave and Cellular Communication

Orbital Angular Momentum Microwave Generated by Free Electron Beam   179
  Pengfei Xu and Chao Zhang

MmWave-NOMA-Based Semi-persistent Scheduling
for Enhanced V2X Services   193
  Fanwei Shi, Bicheng Wang, Ruoqi Shi, Jian Tang, and Jianling Hu

Underwater Acoustic Channel Estimation Based on Signal Cancellation.   207
  Junkai Liu, Yangze Dong, Gangqiang Zhang, and Junqing Zhang

A Novel Spectrum Correlation Based Energy Detection
for Wideband Spectrum Sensing   220
  Bo Lan, Tao Peng, PeiLiang Zuo, and Wenbo Wang

Spread Spectrum Audio Watermark Based on Non-uniform Quantization. . . .   235
  MeiJun Ning, Tao Peng, YueQing Xu, and QingYi Quan

DBS: Delay Based Hierarchical Downlink Scheduling for Real-Time
Stream in Cellular Networks.   246
  Wenjin Fan, Yu Liu, and Yumei Wang

Combination of Multiple PBCH Blocks in 5G NR Systems   258
  Fang Wang, Hang Long, and Wenxi He

A Channel Threshold Based Multiple Access Protocol for Airborne
Tactical Networks   269
  Bo Zheng, Yong Li, Wei Cheng, and Wei-Lun Liu

Multi-service Routing with Guaranteed Load Balancing for LEO
Satellite Networks   283
  Cui-Qin Dai, Guangyan Liao, P. Takis Mathiopoulos, and Qianbin Chen

Wireless Communications and Networking

Mode Identification of OAM with Compressive Sensing
in the Secondary Frequency Domain   301
   Jin Li and Chao Zhang

Improved Incremental Freezing HARQ Schemes Using Polar Codes over
Degraded Compound Channels   316
   Tianze Hu, Lei Xie, Huifang Chen, Hongda Duan, and Kuang Wang

Maximum Ergodic Capacity of Intelligent Reflecting Surface Assisted
MIMO Wireless Communication System   331
   Chang Guo, Zhufei Lu, Zhe Guo, Feng Yang, and Lianghui Ding

Trajectory Optimization for UAV Assisted Fog-RAN Network   344
   Qi Qin, Erwu Liu, and Rui Wang

A Design of D2D-Clustering Algorithm for Group D2D Communication   356
   Ruoqi Shi, Bicheng Wang, Fanwei Shi, Dongming Piao, and Jianling Hu

Cluster and Time Slot Based Cross-Layer Protocol for Ad Hoc Network   368
   Yifan Qiu, Xiandeng He, Qingcai Wang, Heping Yao, and Nan Chen

A Cluster-Based Small Cell On/Off Scheme for Energy Efficiency
Optimization in Ultra-Dense Networks   385
   Cui-Qin Dai, Biao Fu, and Qianbin Chen

A DASH-Based Peer-to-Peer VoD Streaming Scheme   402
   Pingshan Liu, Yaqing Fan, Kai Huang, and Guimin Huang

A Generic Polynomial-Time Cell Association Scheme in Ultra-Dense
Cellular Networks   417
   Chao Fang, Lusheng Wang, Hai Lin, and Min Peng

Deep Q Network for Wiretap Channel Model with Energy Harvesting   433
   Zhaohui Li and Weijia Lei

Building Gateway Interconnected Heterogeneous ZigBee and WiFi
Network Based on Software Defined Radio   445
   Shuhao Wang, Yonggang Li, Chunqiang Ming, and Zhizhong Zhang

A Cross-Layer Protocol for Mobile Ad Hoc Network Based on Hexagonal
Clustering and Hybrid MAC Access Approach   457
   *Longchao Wang, Xiandeng He, Qingcai Wang, Heping Yao,
   and Yifan Qiu*

On SDN Controllers Placement Problem in Wide Area Networks   471
   Firas Fawzy Zobary and ChunLin Li

Network and Information Security

Performance Analysis of Consensus-Based Distributed System Under False
Data Injection Attacks   483
    Xiaoyan Zheng, Lei Xie, Huifang Chen, and Chao Song

Trajectory Clustering Based Oceanic Anomaly Detection Using
Argo Profile Floats   498
    Wen-Yu Cai, Zi-Qiang Liu, and Mei-Yan Zhang

DICOM-Fuzzer: Research on DICOM Vulnerability Mining Based
on Fuzzing Technology   509
    *Zhiqiang Wang, Quanqi Li, Qian Liu, Biao Liu, Jianyi Zhang, Tao Yang,
    and Qixu Liu*

Secure Communication with a Proactive Eavesdropper Under Perfect CSI
and CDI.   525
    Qun Li and Ding Xu

GNSS Spoofing Detection Using Moving Variance of Signal Quality
Monitoring Metrics and Signal Power   537
    Lixuan Li, Chao Sun, Hongbo Zhao, Hua Sun, and Wenquan Feng

Towards a Complete View of the SSL/TLS Service Ports in the Wild   549
    Peipei Fu, Mingxin Cui, and Zhenzhen Li

Secrecy Precoder Design for k-User MIMO Interference Channels   564
    Bing Fang and Wei Shao

Communication QoS, Reliability and Modeling

Wireless Channel Pattern Recognition Using k-Nearest Neighbor
Algorithm for High-Speed Railway   579
    Lei Xiong, Huayu Li, Zhengyu Zhang, Bo Ai, and Pei Tang

Price-Based Power Control in NOMA Based Cognitive Radio Networks
Using Stackelberg Game   589
    *Zhengqiang Wang, Hongjia Zhang, Zifu Fan, Xiaoyu Wan,
    and Xiaoxia Yang*

Deep Learning Based Single-Channel Blind Separation of Co-frequency
Modulated Signals.   607
    Chen Chen, Zhufei Lu, Zhe Guo, Feng Yang, and Lianghui Ding

Personalized QoS Improvement in User-Centered Heterogeneous V2X
Communication Networks   619
    *Mo Zhou, Chuan Xu, Guofeng Zhao,
    and Syed Mushhad Mustuzhar Gilani*

A Lightweight Interference Measurement Algorithm for Wireless
Sensor Networks.. 631
  Bo Zeng, Gege Zhang, Zhixue Zhang, and Shanshan Li

Dynamic Network Change Detection via Dynamic Network
Representation Learning... 642
  Hao Feng, Yan Liu, Ziqiao Zhou, and Jing Chen

Robust RSS-Based Localization in Mixed LOS/NLOS Environments........ 659
  Yinghao Sun, Gang Wang, and Youming Li

Primary Synchronization Signal Low Complexity Sliding
Correlation Method... 669
  Huahua Wang, Dongfeng Chen, and Juan Li

Analysis of Frequency Offset Effect on PRACH in 5G NR Systems....... 679
  Wenxi He, Yifan Du, and Hang Long

Energy-Efficient Mode Selection for D2D Communication
in SWIPT Systems.. 693
  Jingjing Cui and Jun Huang

Research on OTFS Performance Based on Joint-Sparse Fast Time-Varying
Channel Estimation.. 707
  Wenjing Gao, Shanshan Li, Lei Zhao, Wenbin Guo, and Tao Peng

Load Balancing Mechanism Based on Sparse Matrix Prediction
in C-RAN Networks.. 720
  Yang Liu, Zhanjun Liu, Ling Kuang, and Xinrui Tan

A Signaling Analysis Algorithm in 5G Terminal Simulator............. 729
  Yu Duan, Wanwan Wang, and Zhizhong Zhang

Design and Implementation of Assembler for High Performance Digital
Signal Processor (DSP)... 741
  Peng Ding, Haoqi Ren, Zhifeng Zhang, Jun Wu, Fusheng Zhu,
  and Wenru Zhang

Author Index 753

Pattern Recognition and Signal Processing

Integrity-Preserving Image Aesthetic Assessment

Xin Sun$^{(\boxtimes)}$ and Jun Zhou

Institute of Image Communication and Network Engineering,
Shanghai JiaoTong University, Shanghai 200240, China
379349408@qq.com
zhoujun@sjtu.edu.cn

Abstract. Image aesthetic assessment is a challenging problem in the field of computer vision. Recently, the input size of images is often limited by the network of aesthetic problems. The methods of cropping, wrapping and padding unify images to the same size, which will destroy the aesthetic quality of the images and affect their aesthetic rating labels. In this paper, we present an end-to-end deep Multi-Task Spatial Pyramid Pooling Fully Convolutional Neural NasNet (MTP-NasNet) method for image aesthetic assessment that can directly manipulate the original size of the image without destroying its beauty. Our method is developed based on Fully Convolutional Network (FCN) and Spatial Pyramid Pooling (SPP). In addition, existing studies regards aesthetic assessment as a two-category task, a distribution predicting task or a style predicting task, but ignore the correlation between these tasks. To address this issue, we adopt the multi-task learning method that fuses two-category task, style task and score distribution task. Moreover, this paper also explores the reference of information such as variance in the score distribution for image reliability. Our experiment results show that our approach has significant performance on the large-scale aesthetic assessment datasets (AVA [1]), and demonstrate the importance of multi-task learning and size preserving. Our study provides a powerful tool for image aesthetic assessment, which can be applied to photography and image optimization field.

Keywords: Multi-task learning · Image aesthetic assessment · Fully convolutional neural networks · Spatial pooling layer

1 Introduction

Image aesthetic assessment is a challenging issue in the field of computer vision in recent years, and has a wide range of application scenarios. For example, image aesthetic quality assessment can give certain guidance and help to photography [2]; it can be used as a loss function for image beautification or optimization [3]; iterative artificial intelligence can make pictures and optimization [4].

© ICST Institute for Computer Sciences, Social Informatics and Telecommunications Engineering 2020
Published by Springer Nature Switzerland AG 2020. All Rights Reserved
H. Gao et al. (Eds.): ChinaCom 2019, LNICST 313, pp. 3–19, 2020.
https://doi.org/10.1007/978-3-030-41117-6_1

Recently, the most models for aesthetic assessment have to fix the size of the input image, thus destroying the aesthetic elements of the image, affecting its aesthetic score, and affecting the subsequent training. Figure 1 shows the three common methods that divert images to the fixed size. The original image (640 × 480) is taken by three operations: cropping, wrapping and padding that transforms the image to the specified size (224 × 224). These operations will obviously damage the beauty of the picture. To address this problem, this paper proposes the MTP-NasNet for images of arbitrary size input, which has achieved outstanding experimental results. The main work are introducing the modified FCN of image segmentation and the SPP layer of image classification to our aesthetic models. In addition, for the convenience and efficiency of training, three different treatments were performed to speed up the training and increase the convergence speed for three different aspect ratio pictures.

(a) cropping to (224 x 224)   (b) padding to (224 x 224)

(c) the original image (640 x 480)   (d) wrapping to (224 x 224)

Fig. 1. The original image and three images that transformed to (224 × 224)

In addition, early image aesthetic assessments were judged based on two classifications, that is, the image was divided into high and low quality according to the threshold of the rating score (usually 5 points). Usually, a single and simple label (i.e.,good or bad) is attached to image to indicate its aesthetic quality [5]. However, due to the subjectivity of aesthetic assessment, a simple label might be insufficient to indicate the divergence among different rater' aesthetic. In recent years, the researches on aesthetic assessment have gradually changed from simple two-category prediction to complex score distribution prediction and image style prediction [6–9]. Nevertheless, the correlation between these tasks is ignored. In fact, these tasks can promote each other and learn together.

In this paper, we introduce a method based on multi-task learning that learned score distributed prediction, two-category prediction and style prediction at the same time. The two classification of images reflects the overall aesthetic quality of a photo, but for aesthetic problems, the amount of information in training times is too small, it is difficult for computer learning to get better results, and it cannot reflect the difference of human views. At present, the relationship between the two-category prediction task and the score distribution prediction task is not effectively utilized. In addition, style prediction is also helpful for the two-category prediction tasks and score distribution prediction tasks. Above all, multi-task learning is an inductive migration mechanism that uses additional sources of information to improve the learning performance of current tasks [10–12]. Based on the above points, this paper proposes a new multi-task method combining distributed prediction, two-category prediction and style prediction.

Furthermore, we discovery that the distribution of each image rating score of our AVA dataset has different variances. Figure 2 is the variance histogram and standard deviation histogram of all the image scores distributions of the AVA dataset. The abscissa is the magnitude of the variance and the standard deviation, and the ordinate is the number of images. The large variance distribution indicates that the scorers' opinions have large divergence and therefore its reference is quite doubtful. So the significance of such training data onto predicting the high and low quality binary classification is relative smaller. Based on this problem, this paper provides a corresponding weight for each training data to indicate its reliability.

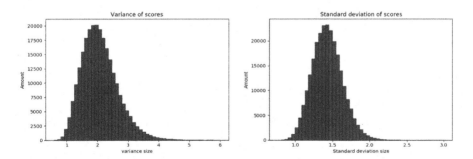

Fig. 2. Variance and Standard deviation histogram of the score distribution.

Our main contributions can be summarized as the following three points:

In order to solve the problem that the picture input into the network is unified to a fixed size and thus the image aesthetics is damaged, we introduce the full convolutional network and the spatial pyramid pooling layer, and propose a new aesthetic evaluation network that can process image input of any size.

In order to improve the experimental results, we adopted the multi-task learning method, and jointly studied the three tasks of two-category prediction, style prediction and score distribution prediction.

Finally, considering the variance information in the score distribution to help determine the reliability of the score, we added the weight of the distribution variance to each image to optimize the learning efficiency.

The rest of this paper is organized as follows: The second part reviews the related work in this field in recent years, and the third part elaborates the details and implementation details of the new model proposed in this paper. The fourth part shows the experimental results and experimental analysis. The final fifth section summarizes the overall work and looks ahead to future work.

2   Related Work

In this section, we first review the existing research on image aesthetic assessment and then demonstrate a short overview of two interrelated of our work: multi-task learning and our MTP-NasNet.

2.1   Image Aesthetic Assessment

Detecting and measuring different distortions, e.g. block, noise and blur to measure image quality might be the earliest methods for the image quality assessment [13]. Although these methods always have an outstanding effect on those issues caused by storage, transmission and acquisition, they often reflect people's subjective perception of image aesthetic quality not well [14].

Image aesthetic quality evaluation has attracted the attention of many researchers because of its wide application [4]. The common image aesthetic quality evaluation system is divided into two stages: feature extraction and decision making. Feature extraction is divided into manual design features and deep learning automatic learning features [3]. Classifiers or regressions such as Bayesian classifiers, support vector regression or convolutional neural networks are generally used in the decision process. Initial research often designs aesthetic features that match it by analyzing some of the adopted photography rules and common perceptual criteria. Datta et al. [15] was the first to start researching this aspect. Sun et al. [16] estimates the distribution of the focus of the visual person based on the global significance region. Luo et al. [5] extracts geometric composition, color harmony, texture definition, illumination and other features in the extracted target area to represent the image. Most of the subsequent manual extraction features are based on content and significantly improve the accuracy of image aesthetic quality assessment.

With the development of deep learning the research work on image aesthetic classification and scoring has entered a new era: the aesthetic characteristics of images are automatically extracted. The researchers applied a variety of volumes and neural networks for image recognition to aesthetic scores, and the accuracy was much higher than that of hand-designed features. Peng et al. [17] proposed to improve the network structure of AlexNet for emotional classification, style classification and other tasks.

But most deep neural network models require fixed-size inputs, and recent studies have tried to solve this problem. Lu et al. [8] proposes the method that the images of the same picture with different cuts are input into the network in order to obtain global features and local features. Argyriou et al. [18] implements the prediction of any size input by applying a full convolutional neural network, but the training is still fixed in two sizes. Although some recent studies want to eliminate the effects of fixed size, their improvement actually hasn't sufficient effect.

For this issue, we propose our MTP-NasNet method for image aesthetic assessment that can directly manipulate the original size of the image without destroying its beauty. In addition, we introduced multitasking and variance weights into our model to improve predictions. Specifically, our approach modified the NasNet to a double-column CNN that one column handle the full-convolution network and another column adopts the spatial pyramid pooling layer. In order to improve accuracy, we adopted multi-task learning, joint learning of two-category prediction task, style prediction task and scoring distribution prediction task. Furthermore, we consider the influence of variance information on the distribution reliability, and add variance weights to each group of distributions. The experimental results also illustrate the effectiveness of our work.

2.2 Multi-task Learning

For complex problems, they can be divided into simple and independent sub-problems, and then merged to finally get the results of complex problems. But in the real world, many problems cannot be broken down into multiple sub-problems. In addition, if we treat a real problem as a stand-alone single task, we will ignore the rich information between the questions. Multitasking is born to solve this problem [19]. The associated multitasking learning is better than the single task learning. Since all tasks have more or less noise, for example, when we train the model on task A, our goal is to get a good representation of task A, ignoring data-related noise and generalization performance [19–21]. Since different tasks have different noise modes, learning different tasks at the same time can get a more general representation. Tang et al. [12] proposes a deep identification-verification features for joint training of face recognition loss and face classification loss. Lu et al. [8] has found that there is a close relationship between style and image classification. In this paper, we propose to use multi-task learning to learn the two-category, score distribution and style simultaneously and achieved good results.

2.3 FCN and SPP

In order to avoid the influence of image sizes change, this paper proposes a deep MTP-NasNet method that can handle the issue of different pixel images, thus retain the quality of original images. The design of our MTP-NasNet is inspired by the success of the FCN [13,22] in image semantic segmentation filed and SPP [23] in visual recognition filed.

At present, FCN [13] in the field of image segmentation and SPP [23] in the field of image recognition can theoretically process images of any size input, but they all have their own problems. By increasing the deconvolution layer of the data size, the FCN can output fine results and can feel the details of the picture. However, since FCN only classifies individual pixels and does not fully consider the relationship between pixels and pixels, it lacks spatial consistency. Since SPP uses a plurality of windows to extract features, it is possible to effectively consider spatial information of an image. However, since SPP divides the image from the fine space to the coarse space, it is easy to lack the perception of the detailed information of the image (the theoretical division is very fine and the detailed information can be perceived, but the calculation amount is too large to be realized [22]). In this paper, in order to achieve arbitrary size input and at the same time take into account the spatial information and detail information of the image, we propose a new two-column aesthetic network. Both column can receive image input of any size, one column network uses FCN to extract detail information of the image, and the other column network uses SPP to extract spatial information. We refer to the idea of the two-column network in [8], but our work is very different from his work: first, although their network and our network are both two-column network, but their network input still fixed size to compromise the aesthetics of the image. Second, the network structure inside each channel is different totally. The network proposed in this paper uses SPP to extract spatial information and uses FCN to extract other information.

3 Framework

3.1 Multi-task Learning

we adopts the multi-task learning method to improve our tasks' performance, where each level of the supervised information is formulated as a learning task. This allows our model to share learned features between multiple tasks, making it possible to learn more deep image features by using the additional low-level supervision [19]. This greatly facilitates convergence of the task for aesthetic quality prediction.

The method of multi-task learning we propose is shown in Fig. 3. We share hidden layers between image two-category prediction tasks, score distribution prediction tasks, and style prediction tasks, and retain their respective output layers. By sharing parameters between shared layers, the risk of overfitting can be reduced, and individual parameters of different specified tasks can be trained by separate training of specific output layers. In this experiment, because the current research gradually shifts from the two-category prediction to the score distribution prediction, we pay more attention to the effect of the score distribution prediction. We refer to the classical method [24–26], taking the score distribution prediction as the core task. In the experiment, three tasks are jointly trained. During the test, only the two-category prediction and the score distribution prediction were tested. The three tasks of our model have a certain hierarchy and range from simple two-category prediction to complex rating distribution prediction. This hierarchy essentially follows the basic procedures of the person to judge the beauty of the picture. People should first be able to have an intuitive judgment of the style of the image, and then have a high or low judgment on its aesthetics, which in turn can have a rough division of the specific score distribution.

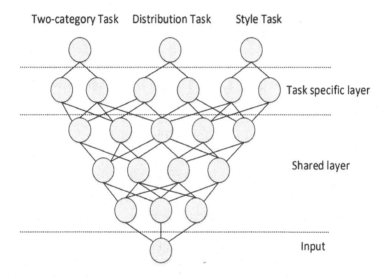

Fig. 3. Our multi-task learning method.

In the jointly training of three tasks, we use the implicit sharing of hidden layer parameters. The most important problem in the specific implementation is the loss function. In the traditional multi-task learning's training process, the importance of all tasks is considered the same [27], but in this model, it is obvious that the importance of the three tasks is different. For example, the aesthetic quality two-category prediction is much more complicated than the style prediction, which leads to learning difficulty and convergence rate are different. We initially tried to add different losses simply. But soon we found that although one task would converge to get good result, others would perform poorly. We found a good method [27], which proposes to introduce uncertainty to determine the weight loss in multi-task learning: learn another noise parameters in the loss function of each task. In this way, we can directly add up to the total loss as before. In addition, we refer to the proposed multitasking loss function by Liu et al. [28]. Finally our multitasking total loss function and their separate loss functions are as follows:

$$Loss_{total} = \frac{1}{2\sigma_1^2} \cdot L_{dis} + \frac{1}{2\sigma_2^2} \cdot \lambda_1 L_{two} + \frac{1}{2\sigma_3^2} \cdot \lambda_2 L_{sty} + \log \sigma_1 + \log \sigma_2 + \log \sigma_3 \quad (1)$$

where L_{dis}, L_{two} and L_{sty} are the distribution functions of fractional distribution prediction, two-category prediction and style prediction. σ_1, σ_2 and σ_3 are the observation noises of three task scalars respectively, and the range of values is $-1.0 < \log \sigma < 2.5$. λ_1 and λ_2 are the weighting factor of the auxiliary task respectively. After a lot of experiments and repeated tests, their values are finally set as: $\lambda_1 = 0.15, \lambda_2 = 0.06, \log \sigma_1 = 0.5, \log \sigma_2 = 0.9, \log \sigma_3 = 0.6$.

$$L_{dis}(y, \widehat{y}) = \left(\frac{1}{N} \sum_{k=1}^{N} \left| CDF_y(k) - CDF_{\widehat{y}}(k) \right|^r \right)^{1/r} \quad (2)$$

where y and $\hat{y}$ are the truth distribution and predictive distribution, with N ordered classes of distance $\|s_i - s_j\|_r$, $CDF_\mathbf{y}(k)$ is the cumulative distribution function as $\sum_{i=1}^{k} \mathbf{y}_{s_i}$

$$L_{two}(y_i, \hat{y}_i) = -\log | Softmax(y_i, \hat{y}_i)) | \quad (3)$$

$$L_{sty}(y_i, \hat{y}_i) = -\log | Softmax(y_i, \hat{y}_i)) | \quad (4)$$

Adjusting the learning rate in a neural network is one of the most important hyper parameters. So we try to adjust the learning rate. However, there is a particularly suitable learning rate for task A, while the rate of learning is different for another task B. If the learning rate is too large, the gradient will disappear in training. We adjust the learning rate separately in the sub-network of each task, and use another learning rate in the shared network part. In the specific experiment, we set the learning rate to 0.01 in the shared network part, and set the learning rate to 0.001 for the specific task part.

3.2   Double-Column Network

In order to solve the problem of different size input, we have proposed a double-column MTP network to directly manipulate input images of any size without having to change to a fixed size. Figure 4 are our double-column network structure. The first column of the network draws on the ideas of the FCN network. CNN usually consists mainly of two types of layers with weight parameters: convolutional layer and fully connected layer. Among them, the convolutional layer uses the filter sliding serial port to obtain the convolution, and does not require a fixed-size input. However, the fully connected layer requires a fixed length vector as input, resulting in constraints on the fixed size input of the CNN. Inspired by this, for the first column, we removed the fully connected layer in the original networks, transformed it into a full convolutional network structure, and then replaced the original full layer with a convolution layer with filters that size of 1×1.

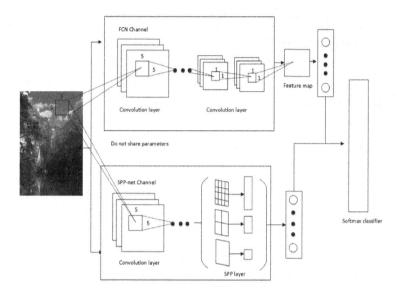

Fig. 4. Our double-column NasNet structure.

Another column of networks refers to the idea of SPP. We add the spatial pyramid pooling layer behind the feature map of the convolutional layer output and use the softmax classifier to get the final probability distribution. Specifically, our experiment uses 1×1, 3×3, and 4×4 three pooling windows to pool the convolved feature maps, merge the results, and then pass the fully connected layer to get the output. Then we combine the outputs of the two columns of channels and get the final prediction result through the softmax classifier. We identify the improved networks based on the original Nasnet as MTF-Nasnet. It is worth noting that in the experiment we used the pre-trained weights on Imagenet as the initial weights. This is because the weight of the original network and the new network we proposed are the same, which makes our training easier and more efficient.

3.3   Variance and Distribution-Aware

In the previous work, we treated all sample images fairly. In reality, however, the score distribution for each image has different variances and medians to indicate the degree of score divergence and the concentration score for most scores, respectively [39]. For the distribution prediction task, if the variance of the score distribution of a picture is larger, the difference of the score is larger, which indicates that the aesthetic distribution is less credible. Conversely, the smaller the variance, the higher the credibility. For the high and low quality two-category classification task, if the score of a picture is more concentrated at about 5 points, it means that most people think that the aesthetic quality of this picture is medium, then the importance of this image for the classification task is small. Based on the above two points, we add corresponding weights to the training samples in the distributed prediction task and the two-category prediction task to indicate their referability.

4   Experiment

We conducted the tasks of aesthetic distribution prediction and aesthetic quality classification, and compared them with the existing learning methods in these two fields. For the aesthetic distribution prediction task, we mainly compare with the kNN [29], LDSVR [30], SANE [7], IIS-LDL [31] and SVDR [32] methods. The aesthetic distribution prediction task mainly evaluates the performance of different methods by measuring the distance between the predicted distribution and the true distribution of all images. In this experiment, we used several measures: Probability of Euclidean Distance (PED), Chebyshev distance (Cheb), cosine distance (Cos), Probability of Kullback-Leibler divergence (PKL) and Earth Mover's Distance EMD. For the aesthetic quality classification task, we mainly compare with DCNN [8], DMA-Net [6], MNA-CNN [43], and SANE [7]. The measure of performance is the accuracy of the two classifications. Based on the NasNet network, we modified it and obtain the Multi-tasking NasNet (MT-Nasnet) that only adopt the multi-tasking method, Spatial pooling and Fully-convolutional NasNet (SF-NasNet) that only adopt the two column convolutional NasNet, Variance and Distribution-aware NasNet (VD-NasNet) that add corresponding weights and Multi-Task Spatial Pooling Fully Convolutional Neural NasNet (MTP-NasNet) respectively. The experimental results and corresponding comparative analysis are described in detail below.

PED: The loss function using the Euclidean distance of the two probability distribution functions is defined as:

$$l^{PED}(y, \hat{y}) = \sum_{i=1}^{Z} (y(i) - \hat{y}(i))^2 \tag{5}$$

PKL (Wang et al. [23]): The loss function using the symmetrical version of the KullbackLeibler divergence of the two probability distribution functions is defined as:

$$l^{PKL}(y, \hat{y}) = \frac{1}{2}\left[\sum_{i=1}^{Z} y(i) \log \frac{y(i)}{\hat{y}(i)} + \sum_{i=1}^{Z} \hat{y}(i) \log \frac{\hat{y}(i)}{y(i)}\right] \tag{6}$$

Cheb: The Chebyshev distance is a measure derived from a uniform norm (or upper bound norm) and is also a type of injective metric space. It is defined as:

$$l^{Cheb}(y, \hat{y}) = \max_i \left(|y(i) - \hat{y}(i)|\right) \tag{7}$$

Cos: For two n-dimensional sample points a (y1, y2, ..., yn) and b ($\hat{y}1$, $\hat{y}2$, ..., $\hat{y}n$), a similarity to the cosine of the angle can be used to measure the degree of similarity between them. It is defined as:

$$\text{sim}(y, \hat{y}) = \cos\theta = \frac{\boldsymbol{y} \cdot \hat{\boldsymbol{y}}}{\|y\| \cdot \|\hat{y}\|} \tag{8}$$

EMD [9]: EMD is defined as the minimum cost to move the mass of one distribution to another. Given the ground truth and estimated probability mass functions y and $\hat{y}$, with N ordered classes of distance $\|s_i - s_j\|_r$, the normalized Earth Mover's Distance can be defined as:

$$\text{EMD}(\mathbf{y}, \hat{\mathbf{y}}) = \left(\frac{1}{N} \sum_{k=1}^{N} \left|\text{CDF}_{\mathbf{y}}(k) - \text{CDF}_{\hat{\mathbf{y}}}(k)\right|^r\right)^{1/r} \tag{9}$$

where $\text{CDF}_{\mathbf{y}}(k)$ is the cumulative distribution function as $\sum_{i=1}^{k} \mathbf{y}_{s_i}$.

4.1 Datasets

We trained our different models on the AVA dataset. The AVA dataset is a large-scale image aesthetic quality dataset from Murray, which contains 255,530 images downloaded from the online image sharing scoring website (dpchallenge.com). This datasets is a recognized benchmark set in the field of image aesthetic evaluation. In this experiment, 200,000 picture were randomly selected as the training sets, the 25,000 of rest pictures were value sets and the rest 25,000 pictures were test sets. So it is set to 80% training, 10% valuing and 10% testing.

4.2 Distribution Predicting Results

On the basis of NasNet [33], we have proposed the MT-NasNet, SF-NasNe, VD-NasNet and the MTP-NasNet. Our improved models were tested on the AVA dataset and compared with the work related to the distribution prediction. The experimental results are shown in Table 1. The evaluation indicators evaluated were PED, Cheb, Cos, PKL and EMD. Among them, the smaller the PED, Cheb, PKL and EMD, the better the performance of the distribution prediction, and the larger the Cos, the better the performance of the distribution prediction.

It can be seen that, obviously, the network we designed is superior to other competitors in all evaluations. The best-performing MTP-NasNet increased by 18.11%, 17.44%,26.6% 12.77%, 1.57%, and 39.24% on PED, Cheb, PKL, Cos, and EMDrespectively. Therefore, we can confirm that MTP–NasNet has achieved the best results on the aesthetic distribution forecast. In addition, through observation, it can be found that SANE has also achieved good results as a method that can also accept multi-scale input. SVDR performs poorly in most cases, indicating that its defined loss function does not effectively distinguish the aesthetic distribution of images. This finding suggests that this computationally complex structured learning is less suitable for aesthetic distribution prediction. IIS-LDL is not very effective due to its difficulty in convergence. Recent studies have also shown that this algorithm is an extremely low-efficiency entropy model in parameter estimation. KNN directly minimizes the distance between the predicted distribution and the real distribution, and has achieved good results, but is not effective than LDSVR.

Table 1. The result of different methods for aesthetic distribution prediction on AVA datasets

Model	PED	Cheb	PKL	Cos	EMD
IIS-LDL	0.215	0.154	0.213	0.886	0.132
KNN	0.172	0.113	0.176	0.918	0.095
LDSVR	0.153	0.100	0.139	0.934	0.083
SVDR	0.381	0.294	0.143	0.820	0.126
SANE	0.127	0.086	0.094	0.958	0.079
MT-NasNet	0.118	0.081	0.091	0.963	0.064
SF-NasNet	0.116	0.079	0.086	0.966	0.057
VD-NasNet	0.123	0.084	0.092	0.959	0.072
MTP-NasNet	**0.104**	**0.071**	**0.082**	**0.973**	**0.048**

4.3   Two-Category Prediction

Our improved models were tested on the AVA dataset and compared with the work related to the two-category quality prediction. The experimental results are shown in Table 2. The evaluation index of the evaluation is the two-category accuracy rate. We use the trained model to predict the aesthetic distribution of the image, and then use the average of the aesthetic distribution as its quality score. In our work, we judge photos with scores less than $5 - \delta$ points as low-quality photos and photos above $5 + \delta$ as high-quality photos. In our experiment, δ is set to 1. By comparing the prediction category with the category of the real distribution, we can get the accuracy of data sets.

It can be seen that, obviously, the network we designed is also slightly better than other competitors in the accuracy evaluation. It can be seen that the current methods have achieved quite high accuracy, and the method proposed in this paper has only achieved a small improvement. The network structure of SANE

Table 2. The result of different methods for aesthetic two-category prediction on AVA datasets

Model	Accuracy
DMA-Net	80.12%
DCNN	88.01%
SANE	96.71%
MNA-CNN	95.76%
MT-NasNet	96.84%
SF-NasNet	96.95%
VD-NasNet	96.79%
MTP-NasNet	**97.34%**

Fig. 5. Images predicted with the higher and lower aesthetic rating in the testing set.

and MNA-CNN still has high reference value. Figure 5 shows examples of high-quality images and low-quality images of our proposed model on the test set. It can be seen that high-quality images have finer quality and more aesthetic layout than low-quality images. It also illustrates the effectiveness of our model.

4.4 Effect of Input Size Reserving

In our experiments, we used NasNet as the initial network and get our new MTP-NasNet by transforming it. In order to evaluate the effectiveness of our network structure for any size input, we compared the network with three operations of cropping, warpping and padding. Among them, the input of the NasNet-crop network is clipped to a fixed size of 224×224; the input of the NasNet-wrap network is scaled to a fixed size of 224×224. The input to the NasNet-pad network is scaled down to 224 on the long side and then zeroed to 224×224. Table 3 shows the comparison between our experimental results and these three methods. The experimental results show that these three operations do have a certain negative effect on the experimental results. In addition, we found that the effect of NasNet-wrap is the best of the three networks, probably because direct scaling does not reduce the information of the original image, and the retention is relatively complete.

Table 3. Compare between our method and the baseline methods with fixed-sized inputs

Model	Euc	Cheb	KL	Cos	EMD
NasNet-Crop	0.137	0.097	0.131	0.933	0.089
NasNet-Wrap	0.134	0.092	0.125	0.949	0.087
NasNet-Pad	0.141	0.101	0.136	0.930	0.094
MTP-NasNet	**0.104**	**0.071**	**0.082**	**0.973**	**0.048**

4.5 Implementation Details

We used the deep learning platform Keras to implement network training and testing. Our network uses the original Nasnet to pre-train the weights on Imagenet for initialization. All experiments were performed on a workstation equipped with a 16-core 2.8 GHz Intel Xeon processor, two Nvidia GTX 1080Ti GPUs, and 256 G RAM. The implementation details is below:

Training size: In theory, our method can accept images of any size as input, but in fact, one is too much calculation for training, and the other is not easy to optimize and parameter transfer. Therefore, we have adopted a multi-scale training method for training to simulate original results. We counted the aspect ratios of all the images in the dataset and found that they can be roughly divided into 1:1.5, 1.5:1, and 1:1. Therefore, we have selected 224×336, 336×224, and 224×224 as the predetermined sizes. Different epoch turns to unify the pictures to different sizes in training, so that the network can also learn the concept of variable size. In the test phase, we handle images of any size directly.

Regularization: In our experiment, Adam was used as the optimization function, and the batch size was set to 128. The baseline NasNet weights are initialized by training on the ImageNet [34], and the last fully-connected layer is randomly initialized. Mostly, the learning rate was set to 0.001. In the experiment, our training generally converged around 70 epoches and took nearly 3 days.

Data enhancement: At the beginning we did not adopt a data enhancement method and produced an overfitting. Later, we adopted a data enhancement method of horizontal flipping, vertical flipping, and rotation, which expanded the scale of the data set and achieved better results.

5   Conclusion

Transforming the input image to a fixed size that causes aesthetic damage is an important issue in the field of aesthetic quality evaluation. To solve this problem, this paper proposes a new end-to-end deep double-column network structure. Through this double-column network structure based on SPP and FCN, we can not only operate input images of any size, but also extract spatial information and detailed information of images at the same time. In addition, we have effectively improved the prediction effect through multi-task learning. Further, we consider the information such as the variance in the score distribution, and enhance the learning effect by weighting the samples. The results on AVA's large datasets illustrate the effectiveness of our improvements and the importance of arbitrary size input and multitasking learning. Next we will delve into the important factors that affect the aesthetics of the image and introduce it into our network to optimize the model.

Acknowledgment. The paper was supported by NSFC under Grant 61471234, 61771303, and Science and Technology Commission of Shanghai Municipality (STCSM) under Grant 18DZ1200102

References

1. Murray, N., Marchesotti, L., Perronnin, F.: Ava: a large-scale database for aesthetic visual analysis. In: 2012 IEEE Conference on Computer Vision and Pattern Recognition, pp. 2408–2415. IEEE (2012)
2. Marchesotti, L., Perronnin, F., Larlus, D., Csurka, G.: Assessing the aesthetic quality of photographs using generic image descriptors. In: 2011 International Conference on Computer Vision, pp. 1784–1791. IEEE (2011)
3. Larson, E.C., Chandler, D.M.: Most apparent distortion: full-reference image quality assessment and the role of strategy. J. Electron. Imaging **19**(1), 011006 (2010)
4. Yin, W., Mei, T., Chen, C.W., Li, S.: Socialized mobile photography: learning to photograph with social context via mobile devices. IEEE Trans. Multimed. **16**(1), 184–200 (2013)
5. Luo, Y., Tang, X.: Photo and video quality evaluation: focusing on the subject. In: Forsyth, D., Torr, P., Zisserman, A. (eds.) ECCV 2008. LNCS, vol. 5304, pp. 386–399. Springer, Heidelberg (2008). https://doi.org/10.1007/978-3-540-88690-7_29
6. Lu, X., Lin, Z., Shen, X., Mech, R., Wang, J.Z.: Deep multi-patch aggregation network for image style, aesthetics, and quality estimation. In: Proceedings of the IEEE International Conference on Computer Vision, pp. 990–998 (2015)

7. Cui, C., Fang, H., Deng, X., Nie, X., Dai, H., Yin, Y.: Distribution-oriented aesthetics assessment for image search. In: Proceedings of the 40th International ACM SIGIR Conference on Research and Development in Information Retrieval, pp. 1013–1016. ACM (2017)
8. Lu, X., Lin, Z., Jin, H., Yang, J., Wang, J.Z.: Rating image aesthetics using deep learning. IEEE Trans. Multimed. **17**(11), 2021–2034 (2015)
9. Talebi, H., Milanfar, P.: Nima: Neural image assessment. IEEE Trans. Image Process. **27**(8), 3998–4011 (2018)
10. Huang, G.B., Mattar, M., Berg, T., Learned-Miller, E.: Labeled faces in the wild: a database for studying face recognition in unconstrained environments (2008)
11. Zhang, Z., Luo, P., Loy, C.C., Tang, X.: Facial landmark detection by deep multi-task learning. In: Fleet, D., Pajdla, T., Schiele, B., Tuytelaars, T. (eds.) ECCV 2014. LNCS, vol. 8694, pp. 94–108. Springer, Cham (2014). https://doi.org/10.1007/978-3-319-10599-4_7
12. Sun, Y., Chen, Y., Wang, X., Tang, X.: Deep learning face representation by joint identification-verification. In: Advances in Neural Information Processing Systems, pp. 1988–1996 (2014)
13. Long, J., Shelhamer, E., Darrell, T.: Fully convolutional networks for semantic segmentation. In: Proceedings of the IEEE Conference on Computer Vision and Pattern Recognition, pp. 3431–3440 (2015)
14. Brandão, T., Queluz, M.P.: No-reference quality assessment of H. 264/AVC encoded video. IEEE Trans. Circuits Syst. Video Technol. **20**(11), 1437–1447 (2010)
15. Datta, R., Joshi, D., Li, J., Wang, J.Z.: Studying aesthetics in photographic images using a computational approach. In: Leonardis, A., Bischof, H., Pinz, A. (eds.) ECCV 2006. LNCS, vol. 3953, pp. 288–301. Springer, Heidelberg (2006). https://doi.org/10.1007/11744078_23
16. Sun, X., Yao, H., Ji, R., Liu, S.: Photo assessment based on computational visual attention model. In: Proceedings of the 17th ACM International Conference on Multimedia, pp. 541–544. ACM (2009)
17. Peng, K.C., Chen, T.: Toward correlating and solving abstract tasks using convolutional neural networks. In: 2016 IEEE Winter Conference on Applications of Computer Vision (WACV), pp. 1–9. IEEE (2016)
18. Cui, C., Liu, H., Lian, T., Nie, L., Zhu, L., Yin, Y.: Distribution-oriented aesthetics assessment with semantic-aware hybrid network. IEEE Trans. Multimed. **21**(5), 1209–1220 (2018)
19. Evgeniou, T., Pontil, M.: Regularized multi-task learning. In: Proceedings of the tenth ACM SIGKDD International Conference on Knowledge Discovery and Data Mining, pp. 109–117. ACM (2004)
20. Jebara, T.: Multitask sparsity via maximum entropy discrimination. J. Mach. Learn. Res. **12**, 75–110 (2011)
21. Argyriou, A., Evgeniou, T., Pontil, M.: Convex multi-task feature learning. Mach. Learn. **73**(3), 243–272 (2008)
22. Springenberg, J.T., Dosovitskiy, A., Brox, T., Riedmiller, M.: Striving for simplicity: the all convolutional net. arXiv preprint arXiv:1412.6806 (2014)
23. He, K., Zhang, X., Ren, S., Sun, J.: Spatial pyramid pooling in deep convolutional networks for visual recognition. IEEE Trans. Pattern Anal. Mach. Intell. **37**(9), 1904–1916 (2015)
24. Liu, X., Gao, J., He, X., Deng, L., Duh, K., Wang, Y.Y.: Representation learning using multi-task deep neural networks for semantic classification and information retrieval (2015)

25. Girshick, R.: Fast R-CNN. In: Proceedings of the IEEE International Conference on Computer Vision, pp. 1440–1448 (2015)
26. Yang, Y., Hospedales, T.M.: Trace norm regularised deep multi-task learning. arXiv preprint arXiv:1606.04038 (2016)
27. Kendall, A., Gal, Y., Cipolla, R.: Multi-task learning using uncertainty to weigh losses for scene geometry and semantics. In: Proceedings of the IEEE Conference on Computer Vision and Pattern Recognition, pp. 7482–7491 (2018)
28. Liu, P., Qiu, X., Huang, X.: Adversarial multi-task learning for text classification. arXiv preprint arXiv:1704.05742 (2017)
29. Geng, X.: Label distribution learning. IEEE Trans. Knowl. Data Eng. **28**(7), 1734–1748 (2016)
30. Geng, X., Hou, P.: Pre-release prediction of crowd opinion on movies by label distribution learning. In: Twenty-Fourth International Joint Conference on Artificial Intelligence (2015)
31. Geng, X., Yin, C., Zhou, Z.H.: Facial age estimation by learning from label distributions. IEEE Trans. Pattern Anal. Mach. Intell. **35**(10), 2401–2412 (2013)
32. Mai, L., Jin, H., Liu, F.: Composition-preserving deep photo aesthetics assessment. In: Proceedings of the IEEE Conference on Computer Vision and Pattern Recognition, pp. 497–506 (2016)
33. Wu, O., Hu, W., Gao, J.: Learning to predict the perceived visual quality of photos. In: 2011 International Conference on Computer Vision, pp. 225–232. IEEE (2011)
34. Krizhevsky, A., Sutskever, I., Hinton, G.E.: Imagenet classification with deep convolutional neural networks. In: Advances in Neural Information Processing Systems, pp. 1097–1105 (2012)

Near-Field Source Localization
by Exploiting the Signal Sparsity

Huan Meng[1(✉)], Hongqing Liu[2], Yi Zhou[1], and Zhen Luo[2]

[1] School of Communication and Information Engineering,
Chongqing University of Posts and Telecommunications, Chongqing, China
menghuan1308343329@outlook.com, zhouy@cqupt.edu.cn
[2] Chongqing Key Lab of Mobile Communications Technology,
Chongqing University of Posts and Telecommunications, Chongqing, China
hongqingliu@outlook.com, luozhen@cqupt.edu.cn

Abstract. This work aims to study the source localization problem using a symmetric array in a near-field environment. To reduce the computational complexity, in this work, two spatial correlation signals are created in which each signal only depends on one parameter of direction of arrival (DOA) or range. In the development process, the each resulting signal still possesses the array spatial structure, and therefore, the atomic norm minimization is utilized to obtain the corresponding solutions. The utilization of atomic norm also allows one to avoid the off-grid problem when the sparse reconstruction concept is employed. The numerical studies demonstrate the proposed method provides a superior performance compared with other approaches.

Keywords: Near-field localization · Sparse reconstruction · Basis mismatch · Atomic norm

1 Introduction

Source localization plays a important role in a wide range of applications such as radar, sonar, oceanography, and seismology, to name a few [8–10,15]. In terms of the distance of the source signal, the localization technique is divided into two categories of far-field and near-field source localizations. In the far-field source localization, the wave front is assumed to be a plane wave, where only the direction of arrival (DOA) of the source is estimated. To estimate the DOA, in the past decades, many techniques have been developed, for example, multiple signal classification (MUSIC) algorithm [10], estimation of signal parameters via rotational invariance techniques (ESPRIT) [9], and source localization approaches based on compressed sensing (CS) [1,2,4,5].

For the near-field source localization, the signal wave is considered as a spherical wave front, and hence the DOA and range of the source need to be estimated to achieve localization [7]. By extending the original MUSIC algorithm into two-dimensional (2-D), 2-D MUSIC algorithm is developed to perform the near-field

© ICST Institute for Computer Sciences, Social Informatics and Telecommunications Engineering 2020
Published by Springer Nature Switzerland AG 2020. All Rights Reserved
H. Gao et al. (Eds.): ChinaCom 2019, LNICST 313, pp. 20–28, 2020.
https://doi.org/10.1007/978-3-030-41117-6_2

source localization, but this algorithm is known to be computationally intensive. Some suboptimal subspace-based methods with second-order statistics (SOS) are subsequently proposed for the mixed incident signals [6,13], but their estimation performances are inferior.

The objective of this work is to jointly estimate the DOA and range of the source signal to complete the near-field localization based on the sparse reconstruction concept. To do so, an over-complete dictionary can be constructed based on the DOA and range gridding, and then the sparse reconstruction method can be utilized to estimate the position parameters of the source signal. However, since this dictionary is 2-D, the computational complexity is high. Besides that, this gridding technique also creates the so-called off-grid issue. In this work, a special spatial relationship of the array outputs and the Fresnel approximation are explored to transform the 2-D problem into two one-dimensional (1-D) problems, where each 1-D problem is solved by atomic norm minimization. In doing so, the joint estimation of DOA and range is achieved, and the off-gird problem is also avoided.

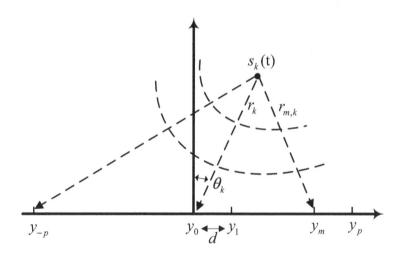

Fig. 1. Array geometry and signal illustration.

2   Signal Model

In Fig. 1, it is assumed that K near-field sources impinge on a symmetrical uniform linear array (ULA) with $M = 2p + 1$ sensors along the x-axis, where d is the sensor spacing, and θ_k, r_k respectively denote DOA and range of the k-th source, $k = 1, 2, \ldots, K$. The received signal of the m-th, $m = -p, \ldots, -1, 0, 1, \ldots, p$, sensor is

$$y_m(t) = \sum_{k=1}^{K} s_k(t) \exp(j\frac{2\pi}{\lambda}(r_{m,k} - r_k)) + w_m(t), \tag{1}$$

where $s_k(t)$ denotes the signal from the k-th source with power $\sigma_{s,k}^2$, $w_m(t)$ denotes the additive Gaussian white noise of the m-th sensor with variance σ_w^2 and zero mean, λ is the wavelength. In (1), $r_{m,k}$ represents the distance from the k-th source signal to the m-th sensor, and according to the cosine theorem, it is

$$r_{m,k} = \sqrt{r_k^2 + (md)^2 - 2mdr_k \sin(\theta_k)}. \tag{2}$$

In a matrix form, the received signal is rewritten as

$$\mathbf{y}(t) = \mathbf{A}(\theta, r)\mathbf{s}(t) + \mathbf{w}(t), \tag{3}$$

where $\mathbf{y}(t) = [y_{-p}(t), \ldots, y_0(t), \ldots, y_p(t)]^T$, $\mathbf{s}(t) = [s_1(t), \ldots, s_K(t)]$, and $\mathbf{w}(t) = [w_{-p}(t), \ldots, w_0(t), \ldots, w_p(t)]$. In (3) $\mathbf{A}(\theta, r) = [\mathbf{a}(\theta_1, r_1), \ldots, \mathbf{a}(\theta_K, r_K)]$ is the direction matrix, and steering vector is given by $\mathbf{a}(\theta_k, r_k) = [e^{(j\frac{2\pi}{\lambda}(r_{-p,k}-r_k))}, \ldots, e^{(j\frac{2\pi}{\lambda}(r_{0,k}-r_k))}, \ldots, e^{(j\frac{2\pi}{\lambda}(r_{p,k}-r_k))}]^T$.

3   The Proposed Algorithm

3.1   Signal Reformulation

The Fresnel approximation [11,14] is based on the second order Taylor expansion, and using that, (2) is approximated by

$$r_{m,k} \approx r_k - md \sin \theta_k + m^2 d^2 \left(\frac{\cos^2 \theta_k}{2r_k} \right). \tag{4}$$

Substituting (4) into (1) yields

$$y_m(t) \approx \sum_{k=1}^{K} s_k(t)e^{j(m\omega_k + m^2 \beta_k)} + w_m(t), \tag{5}$$

where $\omega_k = -\frac{2\pi d}{\lambda} \sin(\theta_k)$ and $\beta_k = \frac{\pi d^2}{\lambda r_k} \cos^2(\theta_k)$.

From (5), using the symmetric property of the array, a special spatial correlation is calculated by

$$Y_{1(-m,m)} = \sum_{k=1}^{K} e^{j((-m-m)\omega_k + ((-m)^2 - m^2)\beta_k)} \sigma_{s,k}^2$$

$$+ \sigma_w^2 \delta(-m - m) \tag{6}$$

$$= \sum_{k=1}^{K} e^{j(-2m)\omega_k} \sigma_{s,k}^2 + \sigma_w^2 \delta(-2m),$$

where $\sigma_{s,k}^2 = \mathbb{E}\{s_k(t)s_k^*(t)\}$ is the signal power of the k-th source and $\sigma_w^2 = \mathbb{E}\{\sigma_w(t)\sigma_w^*(t)\}$ represents the noise power at m-th sensor, and $\delta(\cdot)$ denotes the Dirac function.

Collecting all the spatial correlations at different sensor pairs, one obtains

$$\mathbf{Y}_1 = \mathbf{A}_\omega(\theta)\boldsymbol{\sigma}_s + \sigma_\omega^2 \mathbf{e}, \tag{7}$$

where $\mathbf{Y}_1 = [Y_{1(0,0)}, \ldots, Y_{1(p,-p)}]$,   and $\mathbf{A}_\omega(\theta) = [1, \ldots, e^{j(-2p)\omega_1}, 1, \ldots,$
$e^{j(-2p)\omega_2}, \ldots, 1, \ldots, e^{j(-2p)\omega_K}]$, $\boldsymbol{\sigma}_s = [\sigma_{s,1}^2, \ldots, \sigma_{s,K}^2]$, and $\mathbf{e} = [1, 0, \ldots, 0]^T$. From
both (6) and (7), it is seen that the correlation signals only involve one parame-
ter ω_k, which depends on the DOA. This is to say that DOA estimation can be
obtained by using (7).

3.2 Sparse Reconstruction

DOA Estimation of Near-Field Signals. From (6), it is now a 1-D problem.
By gridding the angle space, a dictionary $\mathbf{A}_\omega(\bar{\theta})$, where $\bar{\theta} = [\bar{\theta}_1, \ldots, \bar{\theta}_{N_\theta}]$ and
the interval size is Δ_θ, can be constructed. Based on sparse reconstruction, the
following ℓ_1-regularized minimization problem can be utilized to obtain the DOA
estimation

$$\hat{\mathbf{x}} = \arg\min_{\mathbf{x}} \|\mathbf{Y} - \mathbf{A}_\omega(\bar{\theta})\mathbf{x}\|_2^2 + \mu\|\mathbf{x}\|_1, \tag{8}$$

where μ is the penalty factor. The solution of $\mathbf{x}$ provides the DOA estimation.

It is the same as all the grid-based approaches, the solution in (8) suffers
from off-grid problem. To circumvent this issue, in this work, the atomic norm
minimization is utilized to produce the DOA estimation. With that spirit, (7) is
rewritten as

$$\mathbf{Y} = \sum_{k=1}^{K} A_k \boldsymbol{\omega}_k + \sigma_w^2 \mathbf{e}, \tag{9}$$

where $\boldsymbol{\omega}_k = [1, e^{-j\omega_k}, \cdots, e^{j(-2p)\omega_k}]^T$. To estimate $\boldsymbol{\omega}$, based on atomic norm,
the following optimization is devised

$$\text{minimize}_{\mathbf{i}} \|\mathbf{Y} - \mathbf{i}\|_2^2 + \tau\|\mathbf{i}\|_{\mathcal{A}}, \tag{10}$$

where $\mathbf{i} = \sum_{k=1}^{K} A_k \boldsymbol{\nu}_k$ and $\|\cdot\|_{\mathcal{A}}$ is the atomic norm, which is defined by

$$\|\mathbf{i}\|_{\mathcal{A}} = \inf\left\{\sum_l c_l : \mathbf{i} = \sum_l c_l \boldsymbol{\nu}(f_l), c_l > 0, \boldsymbol{\nu}(f_l) \in \mathcal{A}\right\}, \tag{11}$$

where $\mathcal{A}$ is a collection of atoms and $\boldsymbol{\nu}(f_l) = [1, e^{-jf_l}, \cdots, e^{-j(2p)f_l}]^T$. To efficiently solve the atomic norm, it can be transformed into the following semidef-
inite programming (SDP) [12].

$$\|\mathbf{i}\|_{\mathcal{A}} = \text{minimize}_{t,\mathbf{u}} \frac{1}{2}(t + u_1)$$

$$\text{subject to } \begin{bmatrix} T(\mathbf{u}) & \mathbf{i} \\ \mathbf{i}^H & t \end{bmatrix} \succeq \mathbf{0}, \tag{12}$$

where $T(\mathbf{u})$ is an $N \times N$ Toeplitz matrix, given by

$$T(\mathbf{u}) = \begin{bmatrix} u_1 & u_2 & \cdots & u_N \\ u_2^* & u_1 & \cdots & u_{N-1} \\ \vdots & \vdots & \vdots & \vdots \\ u_N^* & u_{N-1}^* & \cdots & u_1 \end{bmatrix}, \tag{13}$$

where u_i is the ith component of $\mathbf{u}$.

By utilizing the SDP formulation in (12), the optimization problem (10) is

$$\text{minimize}_{t,\mathbf{u},\mathbf{i}} \; \tau(t + u_1) + \|\mathbf{r} - \mathbf{i}\|_2^2$$
$$\text{subject to} \; \begin{bmatrix} T(\mathbf{u}) & \mathbf{i} \\ \mathbf{i}^{\mathrm{H}} & t \end{bmatrix} \succeq \mathbf{0}. \tag{14}$$

Range Estimation of Near-Field Signals. From (5), another spatial correlation sequence can be constructed by utilizing different sensor outputs. That is,

$$Y_{2(m+1,m-1)} = \sum_{k=1}^{K} \sigma_{s,k}^2 \exp(j2\omega_k + j4m\beta_k). \tag{15}$$

Using the matrix representation, (15) is rewritten as

$$\mathbf{Y}_2 = \mathbf{A}_\vartheta(\vartheta)\mathbf{r}_s + \sigma_w^2 \mathbf{e}, \tag{16}$$

where $\mathbf{Y}_2 = [Y_{2(1,-1)}, Y_{2(2,0)}, \cdots, Y_{2(p,p-2)}]^{\mathrm{T}}$, $\mathbf{r}_s = \mathrm{diag}(\sigma_1^2 e^{j2\omega_1}, \cdots, \sigma_K^2 e^{j2\omega_K})$, and the array manifold $\mathbf{A}_\vartheta(\vartheta) = [\mathbf{a}_\vartheta(\vartheta_1), \cdots, \mathbf{a}_\vartheta(\vartheta_K)]$ with the steering vector $\mathbf{a}_\vartheta(\vartheta_k) = [1, e^{j\vartheta_k}, \cdots, e^{jp\vartheta_k}]^{\mathrm{T}}$ with $\vartheta_k = 4\beta_k$.

It is seen from (16) that the signal structure is the same as the DOA estimation in (7) and it only depends on the unknown parameter β. Therefore, the atomic norm minimization can be applied to eliminate the off-grid issue.

4 Simulation Results

To access the performance of the proposed method, the simulations are conducted in this section and comparisons with popular methods are also provided. The root mean square error (RMSE) as a performance indicator is utilized. In the experiment, $d = \frac{\lambda}{4}$ is set and the number of sensor is $M = 15$, unless stated otherwise.

In the first experiment, three near-field narrowband sources are located at $(-36°, 6\lambda)$, $(6°, 10\lambda)$, $(40°, 20\lambda)$, and the estimation results are provided in Fig. 2. To utilize the sparse construction idea, the DOA of $[-90°, 90°]$ and the range of $[5\lambda, 24\lambda]$ are uniformly gridded with the interval sizes of $\Delta_\theta = 1°$ and $\Delta_r = 0.5\lambda$, respectively. From Fig. 2a, when there is no off-grid, the estimations match the

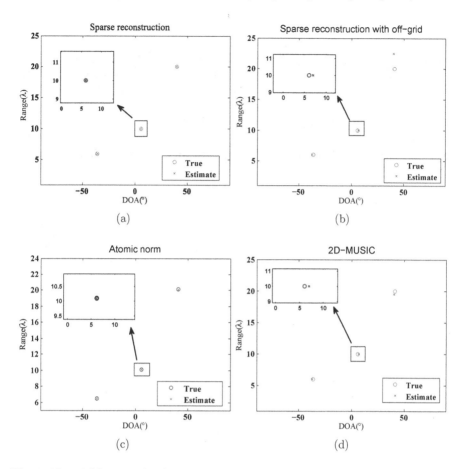

Fig. 2. Near-field source localization with snapshot 100 and SNR = 20 dB. (a) sparse reconstruction, (b) basis mismatch, (c) proposed method, (d) 2D-MUSIC.

true values perfectly, whereas when there is a off-grid, the performance deteriorates, demonstrated in Fig. 2b. The proposed atomic norm minimization approach achieves the full sparse reconstruction performance, regardless the off-gird, shown in Fig. 2c. It is seen that 2D-MUSIC algorithm also cannot perfectly estimate the source locations, depicted in Fig. 2d.

In Fig. 3, the RMSEs of DOA and range estimations of the proposed method with different number of sensors M versus SNR are provided. As expected, in the case where the number of sensors M is constant, the performance improves as SNR increases. However, the proposed method outperforms other methods. Specifically, Fig. 4 displays that the RMSEs vary from the numbers of sources. Although the performance of algorithms has degraded with the increase of K, the proposed algorithm is better than other algorithms. Finally, in Fig. 5, the performances of different methods are plotted versus the number of snapshots.

It is noticed that the estimation error of the proposed method is the lowest and approaches the CRB [3].

Finally, the proposed algorithm is analyzed for complexity. The running time of different methods is provided in Table 1, using a Intel Dual Core i3 with CPU 2.4 GHz and MATLAB. The results show that running time of all the Methods increases as the number of sensors increases. In particular, compared with Sparse reconstruction based method, the proposed Atomic norm based approach is faster than the Sparse one. Since Atomic norm method does not require grid search, the method greatly reduces time consumption.

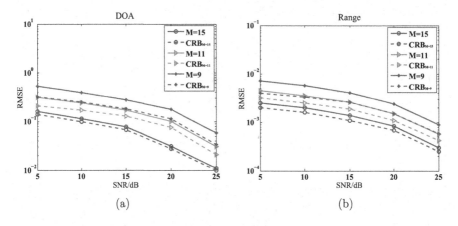

Fig. 3. Performance evaluations of the proposed method versus SNR.

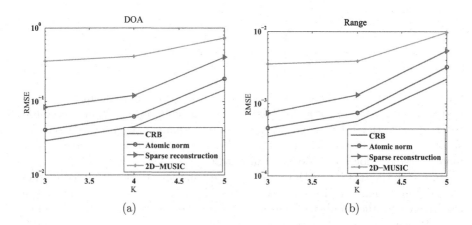

Fig. 4. Performance comparisons versus K.

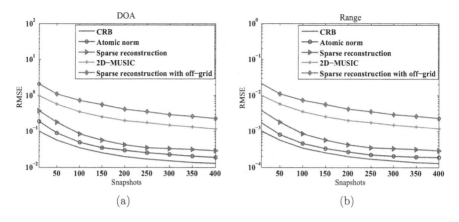

Fig. 5. Performance comparisons versus snapshots.

Table 1. Running times of different methods versus number of sensors (seconds).

M	3	5	7	9
2D-MUSIC	1.012	1.536	2.563	4.807
Sparse reconstruction	3.917	5.773	7.088	7.296
Atomic norm	1.503	1.761	2.153	2.721

5   Conclusion

In this work, the near-field source localization problem is investigated, designed to estimate DOA and range. By exploiting the symmetric property of the array, two special spatial correlation sequences are constructed. With that, near-field source localization problem is separated into two subproblems, where each subproblem is solved by atomic norm minimization. Because of this decouple operation, the computational complexity is obviously reduced since the search only confines to one parameter. In doing so, the off-grid problem is eliminated, and the numerical results indicate the effectiveness of the proposed method.

Acknowledgment. This work was jointly supported by the National Natural Science Foundation of China under Grants 61501072 and 61801066.

References

1. Cevher, V., Gurbuz, A.C., McClellan, J.H., Chellappa, R.: Compressive wireless arrays for bearing estimation. In: 2008 IEEE International Conference on Acoustics, Speech and Signal Processing, pp. 2497–2500 (2008). https://doi.org/10.1109/ICASSP.2008.4518155

2. Fallon, M.F., Godsill, S.: Acoustic source localization and tracking using track before detect. IEEE Trans. Audio Speech Lang. Process. **18**(6), 1228–1242 (2010). https://doi.org/10.1109/TASL.2009.2031781

3. Grosicki, E., Abed-Meraim, K., Hua, Y.: A weighted linear prediction method for near-field source localization. IEEE Trans. Signal Process. **53**(10), 3651–3660 (2005). https://doi.org/10.1109/TSP.2005.855100

4. Gurbuz, A.C., McClellan, J.H., Cevher, V.: A compressive beamforming method. In: 2008 IEEE International Conference on Acoustics, Speech and Signal Processing, pp. 2617–2620 (2008). https://doi.org/10.1109/ICASSP.2008.4518185

5. Hu, K., Chepuri, S., Leus, G.: Near-field source localization: sparse recovery techniques and grid matching. In: IEEE 8th Sensor Array and Multichannel Signal Processing Workshop (SAM), pp. 369–372 (2014)

6. Jiang, J., Duan, F., Chen, J., Li, Y., Hua, X.: Mixed near-field and far-field sources localization using the uniform linear sensor array. IEEE Sens. J. **13**(8), 3136–3143 (2013). https://doi.org/10.1109/JSEN.2013.2257735

7. Johnson, R.C.: Antenna Engineering Handbook. McGraw-Hill, New York (1993)

8. Liu, H.Q., Li, D., Zhou, Y., Truong, T.K.: Simultaneous radio frequency and wideband interference suppression in SAR signals via sparsity exploitation in time-frequency domain. IEEE Trans. Geosci. Remote Sens. **56**(10), 5780–5793 (2018)

9. Roy, R., Kailath, T.: Esprit-estimation of signal parameters via rotational invariance techniques. IEEE Trans. Acoust. Speech Signal Process. **37**(7), 984–995 (1989). https://doi.org/10.1109/29.32276

10. Schmidt, R.: Multiple emitter location and signal parameter estimation. IEEE Trans. Antennas Propag. **34**(3), 276–280 (1986). https://doi.org/10.1109/TAP.1986.1143830

11. Swindlehurst, A.L., Kailath, T.: Passive direction-of-arrival and range estimation for near-field sources. In: Fourth Annual ASSP Workshop on Spectrum Estimation and Modeling, pp. 123–128 (1988). https://doi.org/10.1109/SPECT.1988.206176

12. Tang, G., Bhaskar, B.N., Shah, P., Recht, B.: Compressed sensing off the grid. IEEE Trans. Inf. Theory **59**(11), 7465–7490 (2013)

13. Wang, B., Zhao, Y., Liu, J.: Sparse recovery method for far-field and near-field sources localization using oblique projection. J. China Univ. Posts Telecommun. **20**(3), 90–96 (2013)

14. Weiss, A.J., Friedlander, B.: Range and bearing estimation using polynomial rooting. IEEE J. Ocean. Eng. **18**(2), 130–137 (1993). https://doi.org/10.1109/48.219532

15. Yassin, A., et al.: Recent advances in indoor localization: a survey on theoretical approaches and applications. IEEE Commun. Surv. Tutor. **19**(2), 1327–1346 (2017). https://doi.org/10.1109/COMST.2016.2632427

Layer-Wise Entropy Analysis and Visualization of Neurons Activation

Longwei Wang[1(✉)], Peijie Chen[1], Chengfei Wang[1], and Rui Wang[2]

[1] Department of Computer Science and Software Engineering,
Auburn University, Auburn, USA
{lzw0070,pzc0018,czw0078}@auburn.edu
[2] Department of Information and Communications,
Tongji University, Shanghai, China
ruiwang@tongji.edu.cn

Abstract. Understanding the inner working mechanism of deep neural networks (DNNs) is essential and important for researchers to design and improve the performance of DNNs. In this work, the entropy analysis is leveraged to study the neurons activation behavior of the fully connected layers of DNNs. The entropy of the activation patterns of each layer can provide an efficient performance metric for the evaluation of the network model accuracy. The study is conducted based on a well trained network model. The activation patterns of shallow and deep layers of the fully connected layers are analyzed by inputting the images of a single class. It is found that for the well trained deep neural networks model, the entropy of the neuron activation pattern is monotonically reduced with the depth of the layers. That is, the neuron activation patterns become more and more stable with the depth of the fully connected layers. The entropy pattern of the fully connected layers can also provide guidelines as to how many fully connected layers are needed to guarantee the accuracy of the model. The study in this work provides a new perspective on the analysis of DNN, which shows some interesting results.

Keywords: Entropy analysis · Visualization · Neurons activation

1 Introduction and Motivation

For the past decade, deep learning has been proposed as an efficient way to realize the general artificial intelligence [2,3]. There have been significant progresses on the design of neural network architectures [3,4]. Deep learning algorithms have made great improvement in all kinds of applications.

Although deep learning has achieved significant success in a wide range of applications, there are few works that can fully illustrate the internal working mechanisms of the deep neural networks (DNN). They are often treated as black box and the optimization process is ignored in the applications [5].

© ICST Institute for Computer Sciences, Social Informatics and Telecommunications Engineering 2020
Published by Springer Nature Switzerland AG 2020. All Rights Reserved
H. Gao et al. (Eds.): ChinaCom 2019, LNICST 313, pp. 29–36, 2020.
https://doi.org/10.1007/978-3-030-41117-6_3

Understanding the inner working mechanism of deep neural networks (DNNs) is essential and important for researchers to design and improve the performance of DNNs. One effective way to explain how neurons work internally is to study what kind of features can activate certain neurons, which is known as the feature visualization in the deep learning community [1]. One such method is called activation maximization, which synthesizes an image that highly activates a neuron.

The idea of using information theoretic methods for investigating deep neural networks was proposed by Tishby (2015) [6]. However, they did not conduct any experimental result. In the work, they propose that the neural network layers can be seen as a successive Markov chain. The mutual information of the input layer X with the inner layers Y are studied in the information plane. The theoretical base for this study is the invariance of mutual information to re-parameterization along the Markov chain of the layers. They also show that the optimal neural networks can approach the Information Bottleneck bound of the optimal achievable representations of the input X [8,9].

The mutual information study of the layers does not fully characterize the working mechanisms of the deep neural networks. In this work, we adopt the entropy analysis to study the behavior of the fully connected layers. The entropy of the activation patterns of each layer can provide a performance metric for the evaluation of the network model accuracy.

1.1 Contribution

In this work, the neuron activation pattern is studied by inputting the images of an individual class and the statistical activation pattern differences between shallow and deep layers' neurons is investigated.

Entropy analysis is used to quantify the statistical property of neuron activation patterns. The study is conducted based on a well trained network model. The activation patterns of shallow and deep layers of the fully connected layers are analyzed by inputting the images of a single class, which can provide some useful insights as to the design and optimization of deep convolutional neural networks. By analyzing the activation patterns for different layers, it can not only help us understand the behavior of CNN, but also give us a way to improve the CNN. The entropy pattern of the fully connected layers can provide some guidelines as to how many fully connected layers are needed to guarantee the accuracy of the model. The method provides a new perspective on the analysis of deep CNN, which shows some interesting results.

2   Visualization Methods

2.1 How to Visualize the Neurons Activation of a Layer?

The visualization method for the neuron activation pattern is depicted in Fig. 1. The experiment is conducted based on a well trained neural network model.

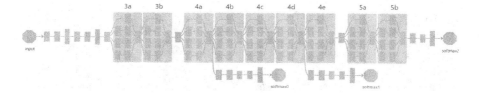

Fig. 1. Neuron activation pattern extraction

The images of an individual class are inputted to the network, and we first extract the representation of the layer and let it go through the softmax function, then the activation probabilities of the layer are obtained. In this way we can visualize the neuron activation pattern.

2.2   How to Quantify the Activation Patterns of Each Layer

The data used in this work are MNIST and CIFAR. We study the internal neuron patterns for different classes by visualizing the neuron activations in the fully connected layers (Figs. 2, 3 and 4).

We take advantage of the entropy tool in information theory to quantify the randomness of the neuron activation of different layers. For a fixed class, we first use those test images as input and calculate the output of each neurons in each fully connected layer. And then we average the output over all test images of all neurons in every fully connected layer. By using softmax function, we can derive the activation pattern of the neurons (probability of the neuron will be shown). Finally, we use the formal entropy definition to compute the entropy of each layer.

The entropy in information theory is used to characterize the uncertainty of the random phenomenons. The definition of the information entropy is quite general, and is expressed in terms of a discrete set of probabilities p_i so that

$$H(X) = -\sum_{i=1}^{n} p(x_i) \log p(x_i) \tag{1}$$

where the probabilities p_i are the activation probabilities after softmax functions. The entropy can be used as a measure of the activation pattern of the neurons in the network model.

For the fair comparison of the entropy among layers with different number of neurons, normalization of the layer-wise entropy is performed for each layer.

$$H(X) = -\frac{1}{f(n)} \sum_{i=1}^{n} p(x_i) \log p(x_i) \tag{2}$$

where the term $f(n)$ is the normalization factor, which is function of the number of neurons in each layer.

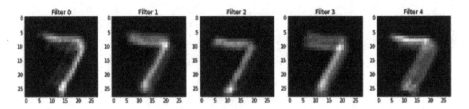

Fig. 2. Visualization of hidden layer 1

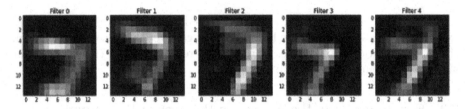

Fig. 3. Visualization of hidden layer 2

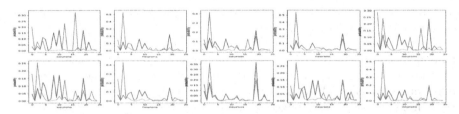

Fig. 4. Neuron activation of fully connected layer 1

3   Results 1: MNIST

3.1   Visualization of the Convolution Layers' Neuron Activation

The figures of hidden layer neurons show that as the convolutional layer getting deeper, only abstract features remain in the images. Such kind of feature is hard to understand by human, so we move forward to the following layers, which are fully connected layers, to analyze how these kinds of features activate the neurons of the CNN.

3.2   Visualization of the Fully Connected Layers' Neuron Activation

(1) Direct visualization: By looking at the output of different classes, we can see that the activation of the shallower layer is more unstable compare to the deeper layer. In Figs. 5, 6 and 7, blue and orange represent two different classes. The x-axis is neurons, y-axis is the probability that the neuron will activate. In Fig. 5, it seems that in layer 1, multiple neurons are activated with high probability.

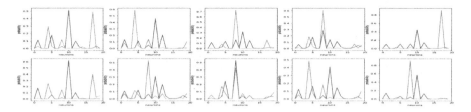

Fig. 5. Neuron activation of fully connected layer 2

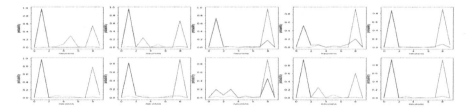

Fig. 6. Neuron activation of fully connected layer 3

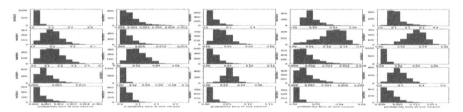

Fig. 7. Statistical neuron activation of fully connected layer 1

However, in layer 2 (Fig. 6), only one or two neurons are activated with high probability. In the last layer, the activation seems very stable expect when the error occurs.

(2) Statistical visualization: In this section, we study the statistical activation of the neurons in the neural network (Figs. 8, 9 and 10, are the histograms of the activation probabilities of the neurons of 1000 samples for a fixed class. The x-axis is the probability of activation and the y-axis is the number of samples). We found that in shallower layer, combinations of neurons will be activated for

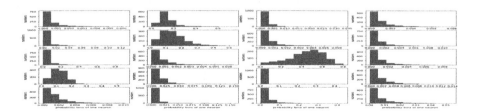

Fig. 8. Statistical neuron activation of fully connected layer 2

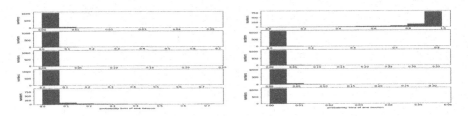

Fig. 9. Statistical neuron activation of fully connected layer 3

a fixed class. But as the layer goes deeper, only fewer neurons will be activated. And the activation combinations become more and more stable.

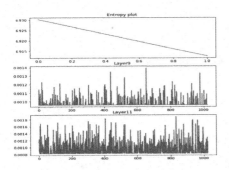

Fig. 10. 2 fully connected layers   **Fig. 11.** 4 fully connected layers

4   Results 2: CIFAR

4.1   Entropy Reduction

The CIFAR data is studied in this section. By looking at the representations of different fully connected layers, we can see that the activation of the shallower layer is more unstable compared with the deeper layer. In Figs. 11, 12 and 13, the entropy plot (first plot of each figure) shows that the entropy of the neuron activations pattern is monotonically reduced with depth of the fully connected layers. And the activation become more and more stable as the layer goes deeper. Another interesting phenomenon is that if the entropy plot is pretty "flat", that is, the gradient of the entropy is very small, then these fully connected layers don't make significant contributions to the network. (The accuracy of these three models from 2 fully connected layers to 6 fully connected layers are 0.774, 0.7686 and 0.7187 respectively.)

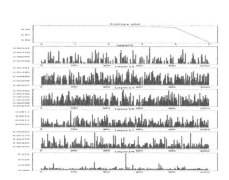

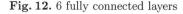

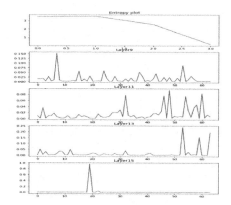

Fig. 12. 6 fully connected layers

Fig. 13. 4 fully connected layers, accuracy = 0.3935

4.2 Relationship Between Entropy and How Many Fully Connected Layers Are Needed

As we can see in the experiment results, the entropy in Fig. 14 increases a little bit and then decrease, which is not the expected "entropy reduction" phenomenon. However, this abnormality somewhat means that there's shortcoming in our model (The accuracy is roughly 0.39). By simply deleting the corresponding layer (the second fully connected layer), we can get a much better result as Fig. 15 shows. But There is still an abnormality in the entropy. Last by deleting the corresponding layer (fully connected layer 3), we actually get a better result as Fig. 15 shows.

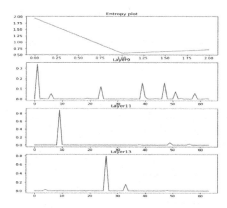

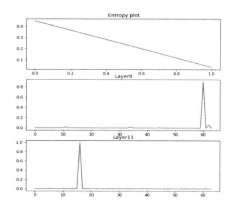

Fig. 14. 3 fully connected layers, accuracy = 0.6283

Fig. 15. 2 fully connected layers, accuracy = 0.6626

5   Conclusion

In this work, we found that for the well trained deep neural networks model, the entropy of the neuron activation pattern is monotonically reduced with the depth of the layers. That is, the neuron activation patterns become more and more stable with the depth of the fully connected layers. Furthermore, if the entropy of the first few fully connected layers are almost the same, such a layer do not have a significant contribution to the overall neural network classification accuracy. So we tried to remove some of the fully connected layers, and the prediction accuracy is almost the same.

Our experiments also indicate that when the neural networks is well trained, the entropy of the fully connected layers are monotonically reduced, while for the not-so-well-trained network model, the entropy of the fully connected layer neurons activation is sort of random.

References

1. Olah, C., Mordvintsev, A., Schubert, L.: Feature visualization. Distill **2**(11), e7 (2017)
2. Szegedy, C., et al.: Intriguing properties of neural networks. arXiv preprint arXiv:1312.6199 (2013)
3. LeCun, Y., Bengio, Y., Hinton, G.: Deep learning. Nature **521**, 436–444 (2015)
4. He, K., Zhang, X., Ren, S., Sun, J.: Deep residual learning for image recognition. CoRR, abs/1512.03385 (2015)
5. Alain, G., Bengio, Y.: Understanding intermediate layers using linear classifier probes (2016)
6. Tishby, N., Pereira, F.C., Bialek, W.: The information bottleneck method. In: Proceedings of the 37th Annual Allerton Conference on Communication, Control and Computing (1999)
7. Wang, L., Liang, Q.: Representation learning and nature encoded fusion for heterogeneous sensor networks. IEEE Access **7**, 39227–39235 (2019)
8. Moshkovich, M., Tishby, N.: Mixing complexity and its applications to neural networks (2017). URL https://arxiv.org/abs/1703.00729
9. Tishby, N., Zaslavsky, N.: Deep learning and the information bottleneck principle. In: Information Theory Workshop (ITW), pp. 1–5. IEEE (2015)
10. Mohamed, S., Rezende, D.V.: Variational information maximisation for intrinsically motivated reinforcement learning. In: NIPS, pp. 2125–2133 (2015)
11. Wang, L., Liang, Q.: Partial interference alignment for heterogeneous cellular networks. IEEE Access **6**, 22592–22601 (2018)
12. Achille, A., Soatto, S.: Information dropout: learning optimal representations through noisy computation (2016). URL http://arxiv.org/abs/1611.01353
13. Bau, D., Zhou, B., Khosla, A., Oliva, A. and Torralba, A.: Network dissection: quantifying interpretability of deep visual representations. In: Proceedings of the IEEE Conference on Computer Vision and Pattern Recognition, pp. 6541–6549 (2017)
14. Agostinelli, F., Hoffman, M., Sadowski, P., Baldi, P.: Learning activation functions to improve deep neural networks. arXiv preprint arXiv:1412.6830 (2014)

Analog Images Communication Based on Block Compressive Sensing

Min Wang[1,3], Bin Tan[2], Jiamei Luo[1], and Qin Zou[1(✉)]

[1] School of Mathematics and Computer Science,
Gannan Normal University, Ganzhou, China
{wangmin,zouqin}@gnnu.edu.cn, JiameiLuo325@qq.com
[2] College of Electronics and Information Engineering,
Jinggangshan University, Ji'an, China
tanbin@jgsu.edu.cn
[3] Key Laboratory of Jiangxi Province for Numerical
Simulation and Emulation Techniques, Ganzhou, China

Abstract. Recently, owing to graceful performance degradation for various wireless channels, analog visual transmission has attracted considerable attention. The pioneering work about analog visual communication is SoftCast, and many advanced works are all based on the framework of SoftCast. In this paper, we propose a novel analog image communication system called CSCast based block compressive sensing. Firstly, we present the system framework and detailed design of CSCast, which consists of discrete wavelet transform, power scaling, compressive sampling and analog modulation. Furthermore, we discuss how to determine the appropriate value of scaling factor α in power allocation, and block size of measurement matrix in compressive sampling. Simulations show that the performance of CSCast better than Softcast in all SNR range, and better than Cactus in high SRN range. In particular, CSCast outperforms over Softcast about 1.72 dB. And CSCast achieves the maximum average PSNR gain 1.8 dB over Cacuts and 2.03 dB over SoftCast when SNR = 25 dB, respectively. In addition, our analyses shows CSCast can save about 75% overhead comparing to SoftCast and Cactus.

Keywords: Analog images communication · Block compressive sensing · Wireless image multicast

1 Introduction

Nowadays, digital image/video transmission technologies serve as an important role in modern wireless multimedia networks. However, these traditional transmissions methods of image/video include quantization and entropy coding, it lacks of scalability and robustness [1]. Especially, since traditional image/video transmission systems suffer high bit error, the received images/videos appear mosaic when the quality of channel below a certain threshold.

© ICST Institute for Computer Sciences, Social Informatics and Telecommunications Engineering 2020
Published by Springer Nature Switzerland AG 2020. All Rights Reserved
H. Gao et al. (Eds.): ChinaCom 2019, LNICST 313, pp. 37–46, 2020.
https://doi.org/10.1007/978-3-030-41117-6_4

Recently, analog visual transmission has attracted considerable attention owing to its graceful performance degradation for various wireless channels. Jakubczak et al. [1] firstly proposed a cross-layer analog visual communications system SoftCast. This pioneering work changes the network stack to act like a linear transform, and the conventional quantization and entropy coding are all skipped. SoftCast is very robust and efficient in unicast and multicast because it avoids the cliff effect in digital communications. Subsequently, a lot of research work based on softcast are emerged [2–8]. A lot of these work reconstruct images with the help of size information. This undoubtedly will increase the overhead of those communication system. Especially, Cui et al. [5] designed a visual transmission system named Cactus, which adopts temporal filtering at the sender and denoising techniques at the receiver to fully exploit the tempospatial redundancy. Cactus is the state of the art analog visual communication schemes without using side information.

Compressive sensing (CS) is a novel sampling theory that challenges the traditional data acquisition. It states that an n-dimensional signal $x \in R^n$ having a sparse or compressible representation can be reconstructed form m linear measurements even if $m < n$. A few work are on wireless visual communications based on CS [9–11]. These work use the entire image as input of CS encoder. To save memory storage and reduce computation time, references [12,13] introduce block compressive sensing (BCS) to implement wireless image transmission system.

However, the above work is either based on softCast framewok, or the performance needs to be improved. In this paper, we propose an another analog image communication framework named CSCast, based on block compressive sensing. CSCast consists of discrete wavelet transform, power scaling, compressive sampling and analog modulation. We adopt the Cohen Daubechies Feauveau 9/7 (CDF 9/7) wavelet transform [14] to de-correlating for input images signal. In power allocation, we set scaling factor $\alpha = -1/4$ to achieve good performance. And, we adopt block compressive sensing [15] to encode DWT coefficients, and use compressive reconstructed algorithm named CS-SPL-DCT [16,17] to decoding. Simulations show that the performance of CSCast better than Softcast in all SNR range, and better than Cactus in high SRN range. On test iamges, CSCast outperforms over Softcast about 1.72 dB. And CSCast achieves the maximum average PSNR gain 1.8 dB over Cacuts and 2.03 dB over SoftCast when SNR = 25 dB, respectively. Comparing to SoftCast and Cactus, CSCast can save 75% overhead.

The rest of this paper is organized as follows. Section 2 presents the proposed novel analog image communication system. The simulation evaluations of our proposed system are included in Sect. 3. Finally, Sect. 4 concludes this paper.

2   System Design

2.1   Overview of System Model

Figure 1 describes the system framework of CSCast. Transmitter of this system includes discrete wavelet transform (DWT), power allocation, compressive sampling, and analog modulation. Receiver performs contrary operators of

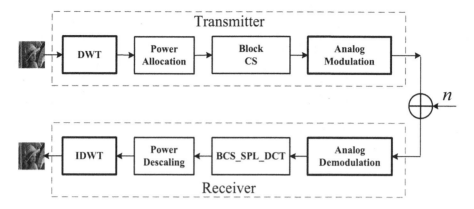

Fig. 1. System framework of CSCast.

transmitter, includes analog demodulation, compressive sensing decoding, power descaling and invert discrete wavelet transform (IDWT).

From the blocks diagram of CSCast, we can find that our proposed system is different from Softcast. In Softcast, 2-dimensional discrete cosine transform (DCT) and power scaling are performed in the transmitter, and power descaling and 2-dimensional discrete cosine invert transform (IDCT) transforming are performed in the receiver. It is should be note that power descaling in Softcast uses linear least squares estimator (LLSE) to estimate coefficients in receiver. In CSCast, power scaling and power descaling are only multiplied a factor corresponding to a block coefficients.

2.2 Transmitter

In transmitter of CSCast, to remove the spatial correlation in the original natural image, the original signal in pixel domain is converted to wavelet domain by discrete wavelet transform. This operator is similar to that used in JPEG2000 standard [18]. In this paper, we adopt the Cohen Daubechies Feauveau 9/7 (CDF 9/7) wavelet transform [14] to de-correlate for an input image, and set the decomposition layer number $L = 5$.

$$X_{dwt} = f_{dwt}(X, L). \tag{1}$$

where X is a input image, X_{dwt} is the discrete wavelet coefficients, its schematic diagram is described by Fig. 2. From the diagram, we can observe L subband coefficients, and the l-th subband includes three blocks, i.e., X_{Hl}, X_{Vl}, X_{Dl}. In L-th subband, there are four coefficients blocks X_{HL}, X_{VL}, X_{DL} and X_{AL}. Because of $L = 5$, we can get $N = 3L + 1 = 16$ coefficients blocks.

If we use analog modulation to send these discrete wavelet coefficients, the energy carried by each coefficient determines its anti-noise ability in wireless

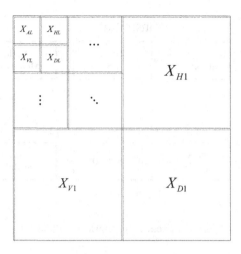

Fig. 2. Schematic diagram of wavelet coefficients.

channel. In other word, power allocation directly affects the quality of reconstructing image at the receiver. As Fig. 2, these wavelet coefficients are divided into N blocks, and the coefficient of power allocation in each block is calculated by

$$g_i = C \cdot \left(\sigma_i^2\right)^\alpha. \tag{2}$$

where $\sigma_i^2, i = 1, 2, ..., N$ is the variance information of i'th block, C is a constant number to ensure all allocated powers satisfy the constraint of total transmitting power, and α is a power scaling factor. According to the channel protection, a larger value of α can provides better protection for the low frequency band coefficients. On the contrary, smaller value of α provides protection for the high frequency band coefficients. So, we should choose the right value to make the system achieves better performance. Like Softcast, we also set $\alpha = -1/4$, and it can achieve the best performance. Section 3 gives the evaluation results of choosing different value of α. We can get the power allocated coefficients.

$$X_{pa} = G. * X_{dwt}. \tag{3}$$

where G is a power allocation matrix which consists of different sub-matrices, and the elements of each sub-matrix are all g_i, .* is dot product operator in matrix.

Next, our proposed system performs compressive sampling. Consider the high computational load of full-signal compressed sensing, we adopt block-based compressed sensing (BCS) [15]. In BCS framework, X_{pa} is decomposed into non-overlapping blocks of $B \times B$ pixels, and each block is compressively sensed independently. Assume that the dimensions of the block sensing matrix Φ_B are $B^2R \times B^2$, and the measurement vector of i'th block is given by

$$X_{cs_i} = \Phi_B X_{B_i}. \tag{4}$$

where $X_{B_i} \in \mathbb{R}^{B^2}$ is the i'th coefficients block, and Φ_B is an orth-normalized independent identically distributed (i.i.d) Gaussian matrix.

Finally, our proposed system performs analog modulations. To save wireless resource, every two adjacent coefficients make up a complex symbol.

$$X_{am_k} = X_{cs_{(2k-1)}} + jX_{cs_{(2k)}}, k = 1, 2, \ldots \qquad (5)$$

2.3 Receiver

Assume that the channel is additive white Gaussian noise (AWGN), the receiver receives signals $Y_n = X_{am} + \mathbf{n}$, where $\mathbf{n}$ is a complex vector whose entries are obey i.i.d. Gaussian distribution. The operators performed at receiver are as follows.

Firstly, receiver performs analog demodulations. The system separates the real and imaginary part from received complex signal, and we get Y_{am}.

Secondly, to improve the performance of reconstructed image, we use (BCS_SPL_DCT) [16,17] method to implement CS decoding. After this operator, we get the reconstructed blocks coefficients Y_{B_i}.

Thirdly, according to the g_i transmitted from sender, the system performs power de-scaling, i.e., $Y_{dwt_i} = Y_{B_i}/g_i$. It should be note that Softcast implements power descaling by using LLSE, while the power de-scaling in CSCast is done by multiplying a coefficient.

Finally, receiver performs the operator of reconstructing image by invert discrete wavelet transform.

$$\hat{X} = f_{idwt}(Y_{dwt}, -L). \qquad (6)$$

3 Simulation Results

In this section, the performance of proposed scheme is evaluated by comparison with reference schemes. We develop and implement CSCast on a personal computer. This PC was equipped with an i7 CPU with 2.4 GHz and 16 GB DDR4 memory.

3.1 Evaluation Metric

In our evaluation, peak signal-to-noise ratio (PSNR) is used to assess image quality. PSNR is computed by

$$PSNR = 10log_{10}\frac{255^2}{MSE}, \qquad (7)$$

where $MSE = \frac{1}{mn}\sum_{x=0}^{m-1}\sum_{y=0}^{n-1}\left(f(x,y) - \tilde{f}(x,y)\right)^2$. In addition, we set the SNR region from 5 to 25 dB.

Table 1. Performance comparison among different value of α.

α/SNR	5 dB	10 dB	15 dB	20 dB	25 dB
$\alpha = -1/8$	25.9418	30.8872	35.9572	40.9012	45.8202
$\alpha = -1/5$	27.9094	32.8866	37.8345	42.8075	47.8097
$\alpha = -1/4$	**28.1969**	**33.2814**	**38.1153**	**43.2551**	**48.1432**
$\alpha = -1/3$	27.0085	32.1548	37.0848	41.8705	46.6731

3.2   Parameters Selection

In this subsection, we first evaluate how much the size of sampling matrix Φ_B affects the performance of CSCast. Then, we give out how to choose the value of α to achieve better performance. The two problem are discussed as follows.

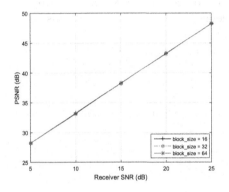
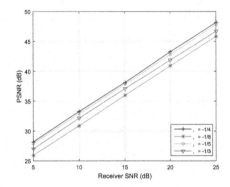

Fig. 3. PSNR comparison among different size of Φ.

Fig. 4. PSNR comparison among different α.

How to set up the size of measurement matrix Φ_B? Given a fixed $\alpha = -1/4$, Fig. 3 shows the result of comparison among three size of Φ_B through simulation experiments. We can find that the size of Φ_B isn't affect the performance of CSCast. We know that the computation complexity will increase with the increasing of size of Φ_B. Therefore, we set the size of Φ_B equals 16×16.

How to choose the value of α? In simulation, we set $\alpha = \{-1/8, -1/5, -1/4, -1/3\}$, respectively. Figure 4 shows the PSNR comparison among these schemes, and Table 1 gives out the detailly PSNR value of different schemes in all SNR. we can observe that the system achieves the best performance when $\alpha = -1/4$.

3.3   Performance Comparison

(1) Reference Schemes

The first reference scheme is Softcast [1], which is the most typical joint source and channel coding based scheme. Softcast is pioneering work to act like linear transform, and skips the conventional quantization and entropy coding. In Soft-Cast, 2D-DCT transforming and power scaling are performed in the transmitter, and power descaling and 2D-IDCT transforming are performed in the receiver.

The second reference scheme is Cactus [5] based on Softcast. In the implemented Cactus, to utilize efficiently the BM3D algorithm [19], transmitter performs IDCT on the spatial data after power allocation, and receiver performs DCT on the denoising data after BM3D. Except operators in Softcast, Cactus needs additional IDCT, DCT, and BM3D operators.

(2) Performance Comparison

In this simulation, we choose *boat, lena, cameraman,* and *peppers* as test images. For fair comparison, we set the compression ratio $R = 1$ in experiments. Given a fixed image, all schemes transmit the same size of data.

Table 2. Performance comparison among reference schemes.

Images	Schemes	5 dB	10 dB	15 dB	20 dB	25 dB
Boat	CSCast	29.3029	34.3619	**39.4057**	**44.3888**	**49.3655**
	SoftCast	27.9161	32.8640	37.8047	42.7524	47.5299
	Cactus	**30.9983**	**34.5501**	38.1904	43.0946	47.6810
Cameraman	CSCast	26.3936	31.1772	36.1703	**41.1463**	**46.0907**
	SoftCast	25.0142	29.7584	34.7358	39.7218	44.5371
	Cactus	**29.4773**	**32.8349**	**36.5414**	40.2382	44.6729
Lena	CSCast	28.2160	33.1329	**38.2140**	**43.1397**	**48.1949**
	SoftCast	26.3322	31.3363	36.1510	41.0875	45.9312
	Cactus	**29.5158**	**33.2710**	37.0620	41.2568	46.4771
Peppers	CSCast	30.4984	**35.4353**	**40.3915**	**45.3343**	**50.3805**
	SoftCast	28.2635	33.1763	38.1407	43.2035	47.8751
	Cactus	**31.5800**	34.9598	38.5314	43.4345	47.9992

Table 2 gives out the PSNR performance comparison among different schemes on test images. The bold numbers are the best performance of test images at a SNR. We can observe that CSCast achieves better performance over Softcast in all SNR range, and achieves better performance over Cactus in high SNR range.

Based on Table 2, we calculate the average PSNR for every scheme. Figure 5 shows the PSNR performance comparison results. From Fig. 5, we can observe that the performance of CSCast and Cactus better than Softcast. With the

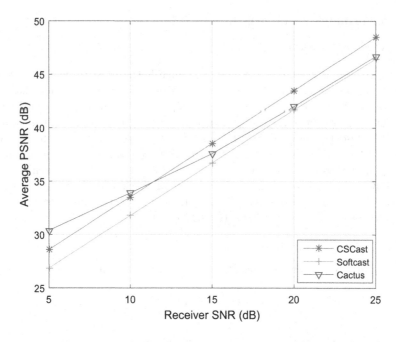

Fig. 5. Average PSNR comparison among different schemes.

Fig. 6. Visual quality comparison.

increasing of SNR, the gain of CSCast over Softcast is increase, while the gain of Cactus over Softcast is decrease. When SNR >12 dB, the performance of CSCast better then Cactus. Specially, when SNR = 25 dB, CSCast achieves a maximum gain 1.8 dB over Cactus, and achieves a maximum gain 2.03 dB over Softcast, respectively.

The visual results with a 25 dB AWGN channel are shown in Fig. 6. It is easy to see that our proposed scheme achieves better visual quality than the reference schemes.

(3) Overhead Comparison

In Softcast and Cactus, it needs to transmit the power scaling factors with reliable digital method as in our scheme. Since the DCT block size is 8×8 in the two schemes, there are 64 metadata per image. In CSCast, we use CDF97 with level $L = 5$ to de-correlate. Therefore, there are only 16 metadata sent to receiver by using digital method. In addition, receiver needs generate the measurement matrix Φ from a pseudo random number, which negotiated with transmitter. Therefore, CSCast only needs 17 metadata, while others schemes need 64 meatdata. Comparing to SoftCast and Cactus, CSCast can save about 75% overhead.

4   Conclusion

We present an analog images communications system called CSCast which adopts CDF 9/7 to perform decorrelation transform and BCS to resist channel noise. We give out the appropriate value of power scaling factor α. According to our analysis, CSCast can save about 75% overhead by comparing with schemes based on Softcast. Simulation shows that the performance of CSCast outperforms over Softcast in all SNR range, and better than Cactus in high SNR range.

Acknowledgment. This work was supported in part by the National Nature Science Foundation of China (No. 61601128, 61762053, 61962003), the Science and Technology Plan Funding of Jiangxi Province of China (No. 20151BBE50076), the Research Foundations of Education Bureau of Jiangxi Province (No. GJJ151001, No. GJJ150984), and the Open Project Funding of Key Laboratory of Jiangxi Province for Numerical Simulation and Emulation Techniques, China.

References

1. Jakubczak, S., Katabi, D.: A cross-layer design for scalable mobile video. In: Proceedings of the 17th Annual International Conference on Mobile Computing and Networking, MobiCom 2011, pp. 289–300. ACM, New York (2011)
2. Fan, X., Wu, F., Zhao, D., Au, O.C., Gao, W.: Distributed soft video broadcast (DCAST) with explicit motion. In: 2012 Data Compression Conference, pp. 199–208, April 2012

3. Liu, X.L., Hu, W., Pu, Q., Wu, F., Zhang, Y.: ParCast: soft video delivery in MIMO-OFDM WLANs. In: Proceedings of the 18th Annual International Conference on Mobile Computing and Networking, Mobicom 2012, pp. 233–244. ACM, New York (2012)

4. Wu, F., Peng, X., Xu, J.: LineCast: line-based distributed coding and transmission for broadcasting satellite images. IEEE Trans. Image Process. **23**(3), 1015–1027 (2014)

5. Cui, H., Song, Z., Yang, Z., Luo, C., Xiong, R., Wu, F.: Cactus: a hybrid digital-analog wireless video communication system. In: Proceedings of the 16th ACM International Conference on Modeling, Analysis and Simulation of Wireless and Mobile Systems, MSWiM 2013, pp. 273–278. ACM, New York (2013)

6. Wu, J., Wu, J., Cui, H., Luo, C., Sun, X., Wu, F.: DAC-mobi: data-assisted communications of mobile images with cloud computing support. IEEE Trans. Multimed. **18**(5), 893–904 (2016)

7. Song, X., Peng, X., Xu, J., Shi, G., Wu, F.: Distributed compressive sensing for cloud-based wireless image transmission. IEEE Trans. Multimed. **19**(6), 1351–1364 (2017)

8. Liu, H., Xiong, R., Fan, X., Zhao, D., Zhang, Y., Gao, W.: CG-cast: scalable wireless image softcast using compressive gradient. IEEE Trans. Circuits Syst. Video Technol. **29**(6), 1832–1843 (2019)

9. Xiang, S., Cai, L.: Scalable video coding with compressive sensing for wireless videocast. In: 2011 IEEE International Conference on Communications (ICC), pp. 1–5, June 2011

10. Chen, H., Wang, A., Ma, X.: An improved wireless video multicast based on compressed sensing. In: 2013 Ninth International Conference on Intelligent Information Hiding and Multimedia Signal Processing, pp. 582–585, October 2013

11. Karishma, S.N., Srinivasarao, B.K.N., Chakrabarti, I.: Compressive sensing based scalable video coding for space applications. In: 2016 Twenty Second National Conference on Communication (NCC), pp. 1–6, March 2016

12. Yami, A.S., Hadizadeh, H.: Visual attention-driven wireless multicasting of images using adaptive compressed sensing. In: 2017 Artificial Intelligence and Signal Processing Conference (AISP), pp. 37–42, October 2017

13. Ming, X., Shu, T., Xianzhong, X.: An energy-efficient wireless image transmission method based on adaptive block compressive sensing and softcast. In: 2017 International Conference on Security, Pattern Analysis, and Cybernetics (SPAC), pp. 712–717, December 2017

14. Feauveau, J.C., Cohen, A., Daubechies, I.: Biorthogonal bases of compactly supported wavelets. Commun. Pure Appl. Math. **45**, 245–267 (1992)

15. Gan, L.: Block compressed sensing of natural images. In: 2007 15th International Conference on Digital Signal Processing, pp. 403–406, July 2007

16. Mun, S., Fowler, J.E.: Block compressed sensing of images using directional transforms. In: 2010 Data Compression Conference, pp. 547–547, March 2010

17. Fournasier, M., Daubechies, I., De Vore, R., Gunturk, C.S.: Iteratively reweighted least squares minimization for sparse recovery. Commun. Pure Appl. Math. **63**(1), 1–38 (2010)

18. Unser, M., Blu, T.: Mathematical properties of the JPEG2000 wavelet filters. IEEE Trans. Image Process. **12**(9), 1080–1090 (2003)

19. Dabov, K., Foi, A., Katkovnik, V., Egiazarian, K.: Image denoising by sparse 3-D transform-domain collaborative filtering. IEEE Trans. Image Process. **16**(8), 2080–2095 (2007)

Tier-Based Directed Weighted Graph Coloring Algorithm for Device-to-Device Underlay Cellular Networks

Yating Zhang$^{(\boxtimes)}$ and Tao Peng

Wireless Signal Processing and Networks Laboratory (WSPN),
Key Laboratory of Universal Wireless Communications, Ministry of Education,
Beijing University of Posts and Telecommunications, Beijing, China
{zhangyating,pengtao}@bupt.edu.cn

Abstract. Device-to-Device (D2D) communication has been recognized as a promising technology in 5G. Due to its short-range direct communication, D2D improves network capacity and spectral efficiency. However, interference management is more complex for D2D underlaying cellular networks compared with traditional cellular networks. In this paper, we study channel allocation in D2D underlaying cellular networks. A tier-based directed weighted graph coloring algorithm (TDWGCA) is proposed to solve cumulative interference problem. The proposed algorithm is composed of two stages. For the first stage, the tier-based directed weighted graph is constructed to formulate the interference relationship among users. For the second stage, the maximum potential interference based coloring algorithm (MPICA) is proposed to color the graph. Different from the hypergraph previously investigated in channel allocation, our proposed graph reduces the complexity of graph construction significantly. Simulation results show that the proposed algorithm could better eliminate cumulative interference compared with the hypergraph based algorithm and thus the system capacity is improved.

Keywords: Device-to-Device communication · Channel allocation · Graph coloring

1 Introduction

Data traffic in cellular network increases significantly in recent years, which gives large pressure to base stations (BS). Device-to-Device communication, where two communication devices in proximity communicate directly with each other without relaying by the base station, has been recognized as a promising technique in 5G. D2D could offload data traffic of base stations. A D2D pair could transmit data on a dedicated channel in the overlay mode or reuse the spectrum of

This work is supported in part by the National Natural Science Foundation of China (No. 61631004) and the National Science and Technology Major Project of China under Grant 2016ZX03001017.

H. Gao et al. (Eds.): ChinaCom 2019, LNICST 313, pp. 47–61, 2020.
https://doi.org/10.1007/978-3-030-41117-6_5

cellular user equipment (CUE) in the underlay mode [1]. In this approach, cellular devices can coexist with D2D devices in the same licensed channel. D2D communication increases overall spectral efficiency, network capacity and energy efficiency due to its short-range direct data transmission and spectrum reusing gain. However, underlay D2D causes severe interference to both cellular devices and other D2D devices sharing the same channel [2]. Interference management is a challenging problem in D2D underlaying cellular networks. Many existing researches aim to decrease the mutual interference between devices using the same channel.

Stackelberg game model was used in [3], where power allocation is modeled as a noncooperative game. Authors in [4] proposed a channel allocation algorithm which enables collision-free concurrent transmission. Channel allocation is formulated as one-to-one and many-to-one matching games in [5]. The algorithm proposed in [6] adopts VGG auction model to sell channels under the constraint of interference. The authors in [7] changed the resource allocation problem into a maximum weighted independent set (MWIS) problem and proposed a low complexity and distributed greedy approximation algorithm, called DistGreedy algorithm to solve MWIS problem. The DistGreedy algorithm can better exploit the opportunistic gains under fading channels. The authors in [8] formulate a multiobjective optimization problem (MOOP) to maximize the energy efficiency. The MOOP maximizes the rate and minimize the total transmit power of D2D transmitters simultaneously.

Graph theory is a practical tool in resource allocation. The authors in [9] used weighted bipartite graph and proposed an interactive algorithm to solve channel assignment problem. In [10], the authors proposed a heuristic graph-coloring resource allocation (GOAL) algorithm. An interference graph-based resource allocation (inGRA) algorithm is proposed in [11]. The authors proposed a novel greedy-based coloring algorithm based on interference graph in [12].

Traditional graph coloring algorithms only consider pair-wise interference model. It cannot well model cumulative interference caused by multiple devices. Hypergraph interference model is adopted in [13] and [14] to formulate cumulative interference relationship. A hypergraph based coloring algorithm was proposed in [13]. It first recognizes weak interferers and strong interferers to construct the graph and then colors the graph in a greedy manner. A directed hypergraph based algorithm in [14] takes asymmetric interference into account and used a centralized-distributed learning algorithm for channel allocation. In [13] and [14], the complexity of the algorithms increases significantly as the number of users increases.

In this paper, we study channel allocation for D2D underlaying cellular networks and present a novel tier-based directed weighted graph coloring algorithm. The algorithm is composed of two stages. For the first stage, a tier-based directed weighted graph (TDWG) is constructed to formulate interference relationship between user equipments (UEs). Since the structure of our proposed graph is similar to the traditional graph, the complexity of graph construction is greatly reduced compared with the hypergraph in [13]. For the second stage, the maximum potential interference based coloring algorithm (MPICA) is proposed to color the graph which considers cumulative interference elimination. We calculate each UE's maximum potential interference in different channels and select the UE which might be interfered most severely in the unchecked set to color. Then we color the UE in a greedy manner. Cumulative interference is eliminated better compared with the hypergraph algorithm and thus the network capacity increases.

The following sections are organized as follows. We introduce the system model and formulate the problem in Sect. 2. The proposed algorithm is presented in Sect. 3. Theoretical analysis are presented in Sect. 4. Simulation results are provided in Sect. 5 and conclusions are drawn in Sect. 6.

2   System Model and Problem Formulation

2.1   System Model

As shown in Fig. 1, we consider an isolated cellular network. The base station (BS) is located at the center. There are M D2D pairs and K cellular user equipments (CUEs) randomly located in the network. The set of D2D pairs is denoted by $D = [D_1, D_2, ..., D_M]$. The set of CUEs is denoted by $C = [C_1, C_2, ..., C_K]$. D_i^t and D_i^r represent the transmitter and receiver of D_i respectively. There are a total of N RBs, denoted by $RB = [RB_1, RB_2, ..., RB_N]$. Each RB occupies the same number of subcarriers. For simplicity, we use D_i or $i \in D$ to both denote the same D2D pair, C_k or $k \in C$ to denote the same CUE and channel n to denote RB_n.

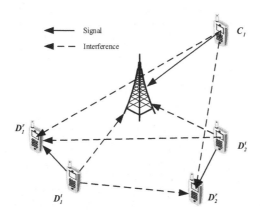

Fig. 1. System model for D2D communications underlaying cellular networks when sharing uplink resource.

If RB_n is allocated to C_k, the instantaneous signal-to-interference-plus-noise Ratio (SINR) of C_k on RB_n is denoted by

$$\gamma_{k,n}^c = \frac{P_{k,n}^c h_{k,b}^c}{\sum\limits_{i \in \phi_n, i \in D} P_{i,n}^d h_{i,b}^d + \sigma^2} \tag{1}$$

where $P_{k,n}^c$ represents the transmit power of C_k on RB_n, $h_{k,b}^c$ represents the channel gain of the cellular communication link from C_k to BS, ϕ_n represents the set of UEs which RB_n is allocated to, $P_{i,n}^d$ represents the transmit power of D_i^t and $h_{i,b}^d$ represents the channel gain of the interference link from D_i^t to BS. The thermal noise satisfies independent Gaussian distribution with zero mean and variance σ^2.

If RB_n is allocated to D_i, the instantaneous SINR of D_i on RB_n is denoted by

$$\gamma_{i,n}^d = \frac{P_{i,n}^d h_{i,i}^d}{\sum\limits_{k \in \phi_n, k \in C} P_{k,n}^c h_{k,i}^c + \sum\limits_{j \in \phi_n, j \in D, j \neq i} P_{j,n}^d h_{j,i}^d + \sigma^2} \tag{2}$$

where $h_{i,i}^d$ represents the channel gain of D2D communication link from D_i^t to D_i^r, $h_{k,i}^c$ represents the channel gain of interference link from C_k to D_i^r and $h_{j,i}^d$ represents the channel gain of interference link from D_j^t to D_i^r.

2.2   Problem Formulation

We assume that a CUE could utilize at most one RB and different CUEs could not share the same RB. CUEs wouldn't interfere with each other due to the characteristic of OFDM system. Consider the scenario where the number of D2D pairs is greater than that of CUEs. We investigate the case where a D2D pair could occupy at most one RB, but one RB could be allocated to multiple D2D pairs. Denote $\beta_{k,n}$ and $x_{i,n}$ as

$$\beta_{k,n} = \begin{cases} 1 & when\ RB_n\ is\ allocated\ to\ C_k \\ 0 & otherwise \end{cases} \tag{3}$$

$$x_{i,n} = \begin{cases} 1 & when\ RB_n\ is\ allocated\ to\ D_i \\ 0 & otherwise \end{cases} \tag{4}$$

Our objective is to maximize the network capacity by designing efficient algorithm with low complexity. Shannon capacity formula is used here to evaluate the network capacity.

$$max \sum_{n \in N} [\sum_{i \in D} log_2(1 + x_{i,n} \gamma_{i,n}^d) + \sum_{k \in C} log_2(1 + \beta_{k,n} \gamma_{k,n}^c)] \tag{5}$$

$$C1: \sum_{n \in N} x_{i,n} \leq 1 \quad for\ \forall i \in D$$

$$C2 : \sum_{n \in N} \beta_{k,n} \leq 1 \quad for \; \forall k \in C$$

$$C3 : \sum_{k \in C} \beta_{k,n} \leq 1 \quad for \; \forall n \in RB$$

where $\gamma_{k,n}^c$ and $\gamma_{i,n}^d$ are given in (1) and (2) respectively. $C1$ and $C2$ implies that one D2D pair and one CUE could occupy at most one RB respectively. $C3$ means that one RB could be allocated to at most one CUE.

Note that the problem in (5) is NP-hard, which means we could not obtain the optimal result in polynomial time. We need to design an approximate algorithm with low complexity to solve the problem. In the following section, an improved graph coloring algorithm is presented.

3   Tier-Based Directed Weighted Graph Coloring Algorithm

In this section, we formulate the channel allocation problem as a coloring problem and propose a tier-based directed weighted graph coloring algorithm. We first present how to construct the tier-based directed weighted graph to recognize weak interferers with low complexity. Then we color the graph in a greedy manner which considers cumulative interference elimination. We assume that each UE only has local information.

3.1   Tier-Based Directed Weighted Graph Construction

The first step is to construct a tier-based directed weighted graph which corresponds to the network interference condition.

The graph is denoted by $G(V, E, W)$. Each CUE or D2D pair is represented by a vertex in the graph, the set of vertices is denoted by V. $E = [e_{i,j}]$ is the set of edges and $e_{i,j}$ denotes the directed edge from v_i to v_j. W is defined as $W = [w_{i,j}]$, where $w_{i,j}$ is the weight of $e_{i,j}$. Note that $w_{i,j}$ and $w_{j,i}$ might have different values due to the asymmetric interference effect.

It is assumed that C_k have local information and D_i is within its sensing range.

$$\eta_c q \leq \frac{P_k^c h_{k,b}^c}{P_i^d h_{i,b}^d} < \eta_c(q+1) \quad for \; i \in D \tag{6}$$

where η_c denotes the SINR threshold of CUE. P_k^c is the transmit power of C_k and P_i^d is the transmit power of D_i^t.

$q = floor(\frac{P_k^c h_{k,b}^c}{P_i^d h_{i,b}^d \eta_c})$ is derived from (6). If $q \in [0, Q-1]$, let $D_i \in L_q^k$ and form a directed edge $e_{i,k}$ from v_i to v_k with weight $w_{i,k} = \frac{1}{q+1}$. L_q^k is defined as interference q-tier. If we randomly select $(q+1)$ UEs from L_q^i and let them share the same channel with C_k, they together would cause strong cumulative interference to C_k.

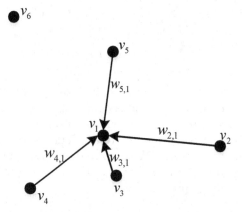

Fig. 2. A demonstration of directed edge formulation between UE1 and its neighboring nodes

Two CUEs could not share the same channel. For $\forall l \in C, l \neq k$, always form an edge from v_l to v_k with weight $w_{l,k} = 1$ and let $C_l \in L_0^k$.

Define $L^k = \bigcup_q L_q^k$. The set of neighboring nodes of vertex v_i is defined as $N(i) = \{j | w_{i,j} > 0\} \bigcup \{j | w_{j,i} > 0\}$.

For the receiver of a D2D pair, denoted by D_i^r, we define the following equations,

$$\eta_d q \leq \frac{P_i^d h_{i,i}^d}{P_j^d h_{j,i}^d} < \eta_d(q+1) \quad for \ j \in D \tag{7}$$

$$\eta_d q \leq \frac{P_i^d h_{i,i}^d}{P_k^c h_{k,i}^c} < \eta_d(q+1) \quad for \ k \in C \tag{8}$$

where η_d denotes the SINR threshold of a D2D pair.

From (7), we could calculate $q = floor(\frac{P_i^d h_{i,i}^d}{P_j^d h_{j,i}^d \eta_d})$. If $q \in [0, Q-1]$, let $D_j \in L_q^i$, and form a directed edge $e_{j,i}$ from v_j to v_i with weight $w_{j,i} = \frac{1}{q+1}$.

Likewise, $q = floor(\frac{P_i^d h_{i,i}^d}{P_k^c h_{k,i}^c \eta_d})$ is derived from (8). If $q \in [0, Q-1]$, let $C_k \in L_q^i$, and form a directed edge $e_{k,i}$ from v_k to v_i with weight $w_{k,i} = \frac{1}{q+1}$.

Figure 2 shows an example of edge formulation between UE1 and its neighboring nodes v_2, v_3, v_4, v_5. Neighboring nodes of v_1 are the strong interferers or weak interferers to v_1. v_6 is out of the sensing range of v_1.

It is worth mentioning that Q is a constant and the value of Q is optional. The network capacity will increase as Q increases. Different from the hypergraph based algorithm in [13], which goes through all the combinations of Q UEs to determine whether they cause cumulative interference to the specific UE, the proposed graph has a similar structure as the traditional graph. The complexity of graph construction wouldn't increase significantly as Q increases, thus reduces the complexity. Detailed complexity analysis is presented in Sect. 4.

Algorithm 1. Tier-based Directed Weighted Graph Construction

1: Initialize $L^i = \varnothing$, for $\forall i \in C \bigcup D$.
2: **for** each $c_k \in C$ **do**
3:      **for** each $d_j \in D$ **do**
4:          Calculate $q = floor(\frac{P_k^c h_{k,b}^c}{P_j^d h_{j,b}^d \eta_c})$
5:          **if** $q \in [0, Q-1]$ **then**
6:              Let $D_j \in L_q^k$ and form an edge $e_{j,k}$ with weight $w_{j,k} = \frac{1}{q+1}$.
7:          **end if**
8:      **end for**
9:      Let $l \in L_0^k$, for$\forall l \neq k, l \in C$ and form an edge $e_{l,k}$ with weight $w_{l,k} = 1$.
10: **end for**
11: **for** each $d_i \in D$ **do**
12:      **for** each $d_j \in D$ **do**
13:          Calculate $q = floor(\frac{P_i^d h_{i,i}^d}{P_j^d h_{j,i}^d \eta_d})$
14:          **if** $q \in [0, Q-1]$ **then**
15:              Let $D_j \in L_q^i$ and form an edge $e_{j,i}$ with weight $w_{j,i} = \frac{1}{q+1}$.
16:          **end if**
17:      **end for**
18:      **for** each $c_k \in C$ **do**
19:          Calculate $q = floor(\frac{P_i^d h_{i,i}^d}{P_k^c h_{k,i}^c \eta_d})$
20:          **if** $q \in [0, Q-1]$ **then**
21:              Let $C_k \in L_q^i$ and form an edge $e_{k,i}$ with weight $w_{k,i} = \frac{1}{q+1}$.
22:          **end if**
23:      **end for**
24: **end for**

3.2 Coloring Algorithm

After the tier-based directed weighted graph being constructed, we present the coloring algorithm to color $G(V, E, W)$. The set of $RB = [RB_1, RB_2, ..., RB_N]$ is represented by a set of colors $\zeta = [c_1, c_2, ..., c_N]$. Each RB_n is represented by a color c_n. Coloring vertex v_i in c_n is equivalent to allocating RB_n to UE i. Some definitions are formulated below.

Definition 1. $WP_{i,n}$ is defined as

$$WP_{i,n} = \sum_{j \in L^i \bigcap (\Phi \bigcup \psi_n)} w_{j,i} \tag{9}$$

where Φ is the set of UEs which are waiting to be colored and ψ_n is the set of UEs which have been allocated to RB_n. $WP_i = [WP_{i,1}, WP_{i,2}, ..., WP_{i,N}]$ is the vector that stores $WP_{i,n}$.

$\Phi \bigcup \psi_n$ is the set of UEs which might cause interference to v_i on channel n. The vertex with higher $WP_{i,n}$ has higher probability of being strongly interfered by its neighboring nodes on channel n.

After constructing the graph, initialize $WP_{i,n} = \sum\limits_{j \in L^i} w_{j,i}$, for $\forall n \in RB$. If v_i's neighboring node v_j is colored in c_n before coloring v_i, v_i updates

$$WP_{i,ch} = WP_{i,ch} - w_{j,i}, for \ \forall ch \neq n, ch \in RB \tag{10}$$

Definition 2. *Available color set (ACS) is represented by* $A_i = [a_{1,i}, a_{2,i}, ..., a_{N,i}]$. $a_{n,i} \in [0,1]$ *represents the availability of channel n on* v_i.

$a_{n,i} = 0$ means v_i would suffer strong cumulative interference if RB_n is allocated to UE i. Thus c_n is not available to v_i. $a_{n,i} = 1$ means v_i is not interfered by its neighboring nodes on channel n. Before coloring, initialize $a_{n,i} = 1$. If v_i's neighboring node v_j is colored in c_n before v_i, v_i updates

$$a_{n,i} = max(0, a_{n,i} - max(w_{i,j}, w_{j,i})) \tag{11}$$

The pseudo code of the proposed algorithms are presented in Algorithm 1 and Algorithm 2.

In the graph construction stage, each UE senses it's neighboring nodes and uses (6), (7) or (8) to determine L^i. A tier-based directed weighted graph could be constructed using Algorithm 1.

For each vertex in the graph, initialize $a_{n,i} = 1$ and use (9) to calculate $WP_{i,n}$, for $\forall i \in C \bigcup D, \forall n \in RB$.

Algorithm 2. Maximum Potential Interference based Coloring Algorithm

---
1: Initialize $a_{n,i} = 1$, for $\forall i \in C \bigcup D, n \in RB$.
2: **for** each $i \in C \bigcup D$ **do**
3:    Calculate $WP_{i,n}$ using (9), for $\forall n \in RB$
4: **end for**
5: Initialize $r = 1$, $\varphi_r = \varnothing$.
6: **repeat**
7:    **if** $\varphi_r \neq \varnothing$ **then**
8:       Use (12) to determine x_r
9:    **else**
10:       Use (13) to determine x_r
11:    **end if**
12:    **if** $A_{x_r} == 0_{1*N}$ **then**
13:       leave vertex x_r uncolor.
14:    **else**
15:       $n = \underset{n}{\text{argmax}}(a_{n,x_r})$.
16:       Color vertex x_r in c_n.
17:    **end if**
18:    Use (10) to update WP_i and use (11) to update A_i, for $i \in N(x_r)$
19:    Update $\varphi_r = \bigcup\limits_{h=1}^{r-1} N(x_h) - \bigcup\limits_{h=1}^{r-1} x_h$.
20:    r=r+1
21: **until** $r > M + K$

Let x_r denotes the rth vertex to be colored. Different from the hypergraph based algorithm in [13] or the traditional graph-based algorithm which chooses the node having maximum degree in the subgraph as the next node to be colored, we select the node which might receive maximum potential interference to color. Define $\varphi_r = \bigcup_{h=1}^{r-1} N(x_h) - \bigcup_{h=1}^{r-1} x_h$. φ_r is the set of unchecked neighboring nodes of the previously colored vertices.

When $\varphi_r \neq \varnothing$, x_r is determined by

$$x_r = \underset{i \in \varphi_r}{\operatorname{argmax}}(\max_{n \in \alpha_i} WP_{i,n}) \tag{12}$$

When $\varphi_r = \varnothing$, x_r is selected from the rest of the unchecked vertices.

$$x_r = \underset{i \in D \cup C - \bigcup_{h=1}^{r-1} x_h}{\operatorname{argmax}} (\max_{n \in \alpha_i} WP_{i,n}) \tag{13}$$

where $\alpha_i = \{n|a_{n,i} > 0\}$ is denoted as the available channel of v_i.

When vertex x_r is chosen, check A_{x_r}. If $a_{n,x_r} = 0$, for $\forall n \in N$, leave vertex x_r uncolor. Otherwise, select the color with maximum value in A_{x_r}. If A_{x_r} has multiple maxima, randomly select one of them and color vertex x_r using the corresponding color. If vertex x_r is colored in c_n, the neighboring nodes of vertex x_r update their ACS vectors and WP vectors. For example, assume vertex x_r and v_j are neighbors, then update $a_{n,j} = \max(0, a_{n,j} - max(w_{j,x_r}, w_{x_r,j}))$ and $WP_{j,ch} = WP_{j,ch} - w_{x_r,j}$, for $ch \neq n, ch \in \forall RB$.

After x_r is checked. Let $r = r + 1$. Repeat the process until all the vertices are checked.

4   Theoretical Analysis

The tier-based directed weighted graph coloring algorithm is processed in a greedy manner. There is no accurate complexity analysis for greedy based graph coloring algorithm. We focus on the worst case complexity of the algorithm.

The algorithm is composed of two stages, i.e. the graph construction stage and the coloring stage.

For graph construction stage, each UE calculates the SIR with its neighboring UEs. Note that two CUEs could not share the same channel and any two CUEs automatically form an edge. It's unnecessary for a CUE to calculate the interference from other CUEs. The complexity is proportional to $O(MK + M^2)$.

For graph coloring stage, we first need to initialize each vertex's A_i vector and WP_i vector. The time complexity is $O(M + K)$. When a specific vertex is colored in c_n, its neighboring node should update $a_{i,n}$ and $WP_{i,n}$. The time complexity is proportional to the number of edges. The worst case is that any two vertices form two directed edges. The maximum number of edges is $(M + K)(M + K - 1)$. In the coloring process, the complexity is proportional to $O((M + K)^2)$.

The overall complexity of the proposed algorithm is $O((M + K)^2)$.

Our proposed algorithm takes quadratic polynomial time, which is similar to the graph based channel allocation algorithm. This is because the structure of our proposed graph is similar to the traditional graph. The complexity of the hypergraph based channel allocation algorithm in [13] is cubic given by $O((M + K)^3)$ when $Q = 2$, and the complexity increases significantly as Q increases. While the time complexity of the proposed algorithm is still $O((M + K)^2))$ when Q increases. The proposed algorithm reduces the complexity significantly compared with hypergraph based algorithm.

5   Simulation Results

Table 1. Simulation parameters

Cellular layout	Isolated cell
Cell radius	500 m
D2D pair distance	20 m–60 m
D2D pair transmit power	13 dBm
CUE transmit power	23 dBm
Noise power spectral density	−174 dBm/Hz
Channel bandwidth per RB	1.25 MHz
Pathloss model (UE to UE)	$148 + 40 \lg(d(km))$
Pathloss model (UE to BS)	$128.1 + 37.6 \lg(d(km))$
Threshold η_c	10 dB
Threshold η_d	20 dB

To evaluate the performance of the proposed tier-based directed weighted graph coloring channel allocation algorithm, we conduct the simulations in this section. Consider an isolated cell. D2D pairs and CUEs are randomly distributed in the cell. Each D2D pair or CUE has a fixed transmit power. The distance between the transmitter and receiver of one D2D pair is uniformly distributed between 20 m to 60 m. The channel is frequency flat. The simulation parameters are presented in Table 1.

In Fig. 3, we show the network capacity as a function of D2D pairs M with $K = 10$ CUEs and $N = 20$ channels. The hypergraph based resource sharing method (HBRSM) in [13] is evaluated with $Q = 2$, while our proposed algorithm is evaluated with both $Q = 2$ and $Q = 10$. The network capacity increases as M grows. When $Q = 2$, our proposed algorithm and the hypergraph based algorithm could both eliminate the independent interference generated by one neighboring UE and cumulative interference generated by two neighboring UEs. The network capacity gain of our proposed algorithm is due to the change of coloring order. In our proposed algorithm, the UE chosen to be allocated next

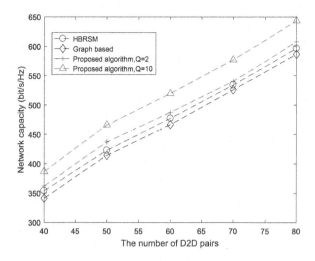

Fig. 3. The network capacity with the number of D2D pairs, K = 10, N = 20

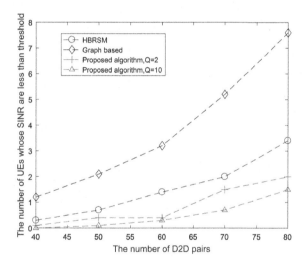

Fig. 4. The number of UEs whose SINR are below η, K = 10, N = 20

is selected from the neighboring set of the previously allocated UEs and the UE who might be interfered most in the set is colored. Further growth of network capacity when $Q = 10$ is due to cumulative interference being eliminated more accurately.

In Fig. 4, we show the number of UEs whose SINR are less than SINR threshold η after channel allocation. For our proposed algorithm, the number of UEs whose SINR are less than η is approximate zero when $M < 60$. Graph based algorithm has the worst performance, because it doesn't consider cumulative interference. When $M > 70$, the number of UEs which receive strong cumulative

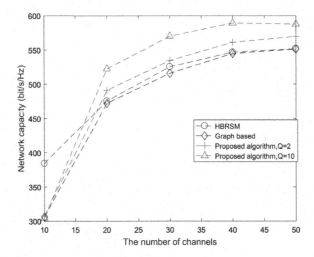

Fig. 5. Network capacity with the number of channels, K = 10, M = 60

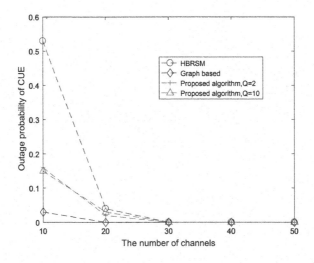

Fig. 6. Outage probability Of CUE with the number of channels, K = 10, M = 60

interference using the hypergraph based algorithm increases rapidly. Our proposed algorithm shows better performance due to better cumulative interference elimination method.

In Fig. 5, the network capacity as a function of the number of channels N is presented. As the number of channels grows, cumulative interference decreases. The capacity gap between the hypergraph based method and graph based algorithm is decreased. When $N > 40$, the performance of the hypergraph based algorithm and graph based algorithm is nearly the same. When $N = 40$, the

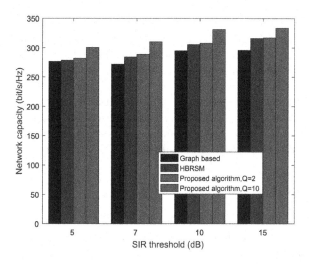

Fig. 7. The network capacity with η, K = 10, N = 20, $\eta = \eta_c = \eta_d$

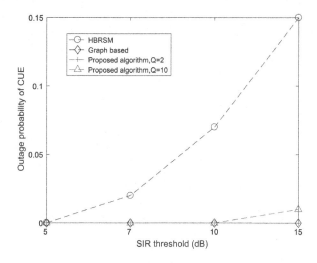

Fig. 8. Outage probability Of CUE with η, K = 10, N = 20, $\eta = \eta_c = \eta_d$

network capacity of our proposed algorithm with $Q = 2$ is 16.4 bit/s/Hz higher than the hypergraph based algorithm, the gap increases to 44.5 bit/s/Hz when $Q = 10$.

Figure 6 shows the outage probability of CUEs as a function of the number of channels. The outage probability of CUEs decreases as the number of channels increases. The hypergraph based algorithm has the highest CUE outage probability when few channels are available. Combine Figs. 5 and 6, when few channels are available in the network, the CUEs in the hypergraph based method are least likely to be allocated a channel compared with the other two algorithms. D2D pairs usually contribute more to the network capacity compared with CUEs because of its short-range direct communication. The hypergraph based algorithm sacrifices some of the CUEs in exchange for DUEs in order to gain high network capacity. While the proposed algorithm guarantees that most of the CUEs would be allocated a channel.

In Figs. 7 and 8, when η_c and η_d increase simultaneously, the network capacity first increases then becomes saturated using the graph based method and the proposed method. Network capacity increases as η grows using the hypergraph based method, but the outage probability of CUEs also increases.

6 Conclusion

In this paper, we studied channel allocation in D2D underlaying cellular networks. The neighborhood interference was formulated as a tier-based directed weighted graph. We proposed maximum potential interference based coloring algorithm to color the graph in a greedy manner. The proposed algorithm aims to eliminate cumulative interference and thus increases network capacity. Complexity of the proposed algorithm also reduce significantly compared with the hypergraph based algorithm. Simulation results showed that our proposed algorithm has better performance compared with the graph based algorithm and the hypergraph based algorithm.

References

1. Asadi, A., Wang, Q., Mancuso, V.: A survey on device-to-device communication in cellular networks. IEEE Commun. Surv. Tutor. **16**(4), 1801–1819 (2014)
2. Doppler, K., Rinne, M., Wijting, C., Ribeiro, C.B., Hugl, K.: Device-to-device communication as an underlay to LTE-advanced networks. IEEE Commun. Mag. **47**(12), 42–49 (2009)
3. Yin, R., Zhong, C., Yu, G., Zhang, Z., Wong, K.K., Chen, X.: Joint spectrum and power allocation for D2D communications underlaying cellular networks. IEEE Trans. Veh. Technol. **65**(4), 2182–2195 (2016)
4. Zhao, H., Ding, K., Sarkar, N.I., Wei, J., Xiong, J.: A simple distributed channel allocation algorithm for D2D communication pairs. IEEE Trans. Veh. Technol. **67**(11), 10960–10969 (2018)
5. Kazmi, S.M.A., et al.: Mode selection and resource allocation in device-to-device communications: a matching game approach. IEEE Trans. Mob. Comput. **16**(11), 3126–3141 (2017)
6. Zhang, F., Zhou, X., Sun, M.: Constrained VCG auction for spatial spectrum reuse with flexible channel evaluations. In: 2017 IEEE Global Communications Conference (GLOBECOM 2017), pp. 1–6, Singapore (2017)
7. Joo, C., Lin, X., Ryu, J., Shroff, N.B.: Distributed greedy approximation to maximum weighted independent set for scheduling with fading channels. IEEE/ACM Trans. Netw. **24**(3), 1476–1488 (2016)
8. Mili, M.R., Tehrani, P., Bennis, M.: Energy-efficient power allocation in OFDMA D2D communication by multiobjective optimization. IEEE Wirel. Commun. Lett. **5**(6), 668–671 (2016)

9. Zhang, H., Wang, T., Song, L., Han, Z.: Graph-based resource allocation for D2D communications underlaying cellular networks. In: 2013 IEEE/CIC International Conference on Communications in China - Workshops (CIC/ICCC), pp. 187–192, Xi'an (2013)
10. Cai, X., Zheng, J., Zhang, Y.: A graph-coloring based resource allocation algorithm for D2D communication in cellular networks. In: 2015 IEEE International Conference on Communications (ICC), pp. 5429–5434, London (2015)
11. Zhang, R., Cheng, X., Yang, L., Jiao, B.: Interference graph-based resource allocation (InGRA) for D2D communications underlaying cellular networks. IEEE Trans. Veh. Technol. **64**(8), 3844–3850 (2015)
12. Zhao, L., Wang, H., Zhong, X.: Interference graph based channel assignment algorithm for D2D cellular networks. IEEE Access **6**, 3270–3279 (2018)
13. Zhang, H., Song, L., Han, Z.: Radio resource allocation for device-to-device underlay communication using hypergraph theory. IEEE Trans. Wirel. Commun. **15**(7), 4852–4861 (2016)
14. Sun, Y., Du, Z., Xu, Y., Zhang, Y., Jia, L., Anpalagan, A.: Directed-hypergraph-based channel allocation for ultradense cloud D2D communications with asymmetric interference. IEEE Trans. Veh. Technol. **67**(8), 7712–7718 (2018)

Iterative Phase Error Compensation Joint Channel Estimation in OFDM Systems

Qian Li[✉], Hang Long, and Mingwei Tang

Wireless Signal Processing and Network Lab,
Key Laboratory of Universal Wireless Communication, Ministry of Education,
Beijing University of Posts and Telecommunications, Beijing, China
lq9603@icloud.com

Abstract. Orthogonal frequency division multiplexing (OFDM) system is very sensitive to the phase noise especially in high frequency since the orthogonality between sub-carriers is easily destroyed. It is very important to estimate and compensate the phase noise in the research of 5G systems. The influence of phase noise on OFDM systems is manifested in two aspects: introducing common phase error (CPE) and causing inter-carrier interference (ICI). In this paper, we propose a new joint channel and CPE estimation algorithm to obtain more accurate channel and CPE estimates through iterations. In each iteration, we update the channel and CPE estimates to make them closer to the true value. Besides, the performance improvement brought by the algorithm under the simplified system model is analyzed. Simulation results show that this algorithm has a great impact on improving the accuracy of channel and CPE estimation.

Keywords: Phase noise · CPE compensation · Channel estimation

1 Introduction

Higher demands will be put on wireless communication systems when it comes to the service requirements of mobile Internet and Internet of Things in the future. In the 5G (5th-Generation) wireless communication system, it is especially important to suppress the influence of phase noise. Therefore, phase noise research was included in the 3GPP work items in Ref. [1]. The phase noise is caused by the instability of the local RF circuit crystal oscillator. When the frequency is higher than 6 GHz, the influence of phase noise cannot be ignored [2]. The impact of phase noise on OFDM systems receivers is manifested in two aspects, namely CPE (Common Phase Error) and ICI (Inter-Carrier Interference) [3]. The CPE causes the rotation of the phase of the received signal, while the ICI increases the system noise that will lead system performance degradation. Especially when the OFDM system adopts a high modulation order

Supported by China Unicom Network Technology Research Institute and project 61302088 which was supported by National Science Foundation of China.

H. Gao et al. (Eds.): ChinaCom 2019, LNICST 313, pp. 62–72, 2020.
https://doi.org/10.1007/978-3-030-41117-6_6

(such as 64 QAM, etc.), the phase noise has an increasing impact on the performance of the system. Hence, at the 3GPP RAN1#87 conference, a reference signal for phase tracking is specified by PTRS (Phase Tracking Reference Signal) [4].

At present, there are a lot of literatures on phase noise estimation and compensation. In Ref. [5], the authors propose a joint channel and data symbol phase estimation algorithm that includes estimation and correction of CPE and ICI. And the exact data model of phase noise is given in the paper. However, a large number of pilot signals is required to be placed on the transmitting end in the algorithm, which will affect the system performance. In Ref. [6], the authors consider an iterative feedback correction method to estimate the phase noise. In the iterative process, the received signal is first corrected by the CPE estimated by the pilot signal, and then enters the feedback system to continuously correct by estimating the log likelihood ratio of the reliability. In Ref. [7], the author introduces the least-mean-square (LMS) adaptive filter to estimate CPE, calculate the receiver tap weight vector and correct CPE by minimizing the MSE. However, the performance of the algorithm depends on the system step size. To obtain a more accurate phase estimation, the system step size must be reduced, which will inevitably lead to slower system convergence. In Ref. [8], the author proposes a non-data-aided phase noise compensation algorithm which means there is no pilot needed, and shows that it works well for high-order constellation CO-OFDM systems.

In this paper, we propose a new joint channel and CPE estimation algorithm, and analyze the performance improvement brought by the algorithm under the simplified system model. In this algorithm, we use reference signals to perform channel estimation and CPE compensation and then correct the estimates iteratively. An iterative process with more prior information is also considered. It can be seen from the theoretical analysis and simulation results that the joint channel and CPE estimation algorithm can bring good performance improvement.

This paper is organized as follows. Section 2 introduces the system model with phase noise and the basic algorithm for CPE estimation. Section 3 introduces the joint channel and CPE estimation algorithm and gives the algorithm flows. Section 4 analyzes the performance of the algorithm under two simplified conditions. Simulation results are given in Sect. 5.

2 System Model and CPE Estimation

In OFDM systems, the received signal after removing the CP (Cyclic Prefix) in the frequency domain can be expressed as

$$y_{k,n} = x_{k,n} h_{k,n} \varphi_{0,n} + \sum_{i=0,i\neq k}^{P-1} x_{i,n} h_{i,n} \varphi_{(k-i)_{[P]},n} + w_{k,n}, \qquad (1)$$

where $x_{k,n}$ denotes the transmitted data in the frequency domain, $h_{k,n}$ denotes the frequency domain channel, $\varphi_{0,n}$ represents the CPE, k means the k-th subcarrier where the reference signals are placed, n means the n-th OFDM symbol.

The second term in the formula denotes the ICI due to phase noise where P indicates the number of FFT points and subscript $[P]$ indicates modulo P operation. $w_{k,n}$ represents the additive white Gaussian noise.

It can be seen from (1) that the influence of phase noise on the received OFDM signals consists of two parts:

1. CPE, which scales and rotates the ideal received signal and can be expressed as

$$\varphi_{0,n} = \frac{1}{P} \sum_{i=0}^{P-1} e^{j\phi_i} \approx e^{j\theta_n}, \qquad (2)$$

   where ϕ_i indicates the phase noise. In general, the magnitude of the CPE is close to 1, mainly as a phase error.
2. ICI, which breaks the orthogonality between subcarriers in OFDM systems.

Since the common phase error is the main influencing factor, and it is same for all subcarriers on an OFDM symbol which can be estimated and eliminated, this article only analyzes the impact of CPE. Considering ICI as a part of Gaussian noise, (1) can be simplified to

$$y_{k,n} = x_{k,n} h_{k,n} e^{j\theta_n} + w_{k,n}'. \qquad (3)$$

To estimate and eliminate the CPE, a new reference signal named PTRS (Phase Tracking Reference Signal) is proposed in the 5G systems. For the convenience of subsequent formula derivation, we assume that one DMRS symbol and $(N-1)$ PTRS symbols are placed on each sub-carrier. We also define n_d as the OFDM symbol index for placing DMRS, and $\{n_{p_i}\}, i = 0, 1, ..., N-2$ is the set of OFDM symbols for placing PTRS.

Therefore, the received signals of the DMRS and PTRS can be expressed as

$$y_{k,n_d} = x_{k,n_d} h_{k,n_d} e^{j\theta_{n_d}} + w_{k,n_d}', \qquad (4)$$

$$y_{k,n_p} = x_{k,n_p} h_{k,n_p} e^{j\theta_{n_p}} + w_{k,n_p}'. \qquad (5)$$

Since the radio channel changes slowly, the channel at n_d and n_p OFDM symbol can be considered equal and we defined it as h_{kn_d}. Divided by the known reference signal, Eqs. (4) and (5) becomes

$$h_{k,n_d}' = h_{k,n_d} e^{j\theta_{n_d}} + n_{k,n_d} = \hat{h}_{k,n_d} + n_{k,n_d}, \qquad (6)$$

$$h_{k,n_p}' = h_{k,n_p} e^{j\theta_{n_p}} + n_{k,n_p} = \hat{h}_{k,n_p} + n_{k,n_p}, \qquad (7)$$

where $\hat{h}_{k,n_d} = h_{k,n_d} e^{j\theta_{n_d}}$, $\hat{h}_{k,n_p} = h_{k,n_d} e^{j\theta_{n_p}} = \hat{h}_{k,n_d} e^{j\theta_\tau}$, $\theta_\tau = \theta_{n_p} - \theta_{n_d}$, here θ_τ is the difference of CPE between two OFDM symbols. When there are multiple sub-carriers in the frequency domain to place PTRS, θ_τ is usually estimated by [4].

$$\theta_\tau = \frac{1}{K} \sum_{k=1}^{K} \text{angle}\{y_{k,n_d}{}^* y_{k,n_p}\}. \qquad (8)$$

Equation (8) estimates the difference of the CPE between the PTRS and DMRS. Therefore, the channel estimate of PTRS $\hat{h}_{k,n_p}$ can be obtained by performing a phase rotation operation on the channel estimate of the DMRS $\hat{h}_{k,n_d}$.

However, the amplitude of $y_{k,n_d}{}^*y_{k,n_p}$ is ignored in (8) which means that the magnitude of each complex has the same effect during the merge. In fact, the larger the amplitude, the closer the estimated CPE is to the true value. Therefore, we introduce a better solution to obtain θ_τ [9]

$$\theta_\tau = \text{angle}\{\sum_{k=1}^{K} y_{k,n_d}{}^*y_{k,n_p}\}, \tag{9}$$

where angle $\{*\}$ represents the operation of taking the angle of the complex, y^* represents the conjugation of y. On this basis, continue to perform operations such as equalization and data demodulation, more accurate source data can be obtained.

3 Joint Estimation of CPE and Channel

When the Gaussian noise is large, the CPE estimated by (9) is not accurate enough. y_{k,n_d} in (9) can be replaces by $\hat{h}_{k,n_d}$ if the channel estimate $\hat{h}_{k,n_d}$ is accurate enough. Thus (9) becomes

$$\theta_\tau = \text{angle}\{\sum_{k=1}^{K} \hat{h}^*_{k,n_d}y_{k,n_p}\}. \tag{10}$$

In this way, the influence of Gaussian noise can be eliminated and the CPE estimate is more accurate. In order to estimate CPE by using PTRS, Fig. 1 gives an example of reference signals pattern.

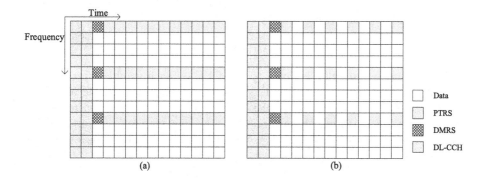

Fig. 1. Distribution of reference signal

In Fig. 1(a), the PTRS are located on the OFDM symbols where all datas are located, and cooperate with the DMRS on the same sub-carrier to estimate the phase error on each OFDM symbol. In Fig. 1(b), the PTRS is separated by one OFDM symbol in the time domain. CPE at the position where the PTRS is not placed can be obtained by the interpolation of adjacent CPE estimates.

We assume that the pattern of the reference signals is the same as shown in Fig. 1, and there is 1 DMRS and $N-1$ PTRS on each sub-carrier. Since only DMRS and PTRS are considered, DMRS is defined as the starting OFDM symbol. For the sake of simplicity, we abbreviate $\hat{h}_{k,n_d}$ as $\hat{h}_k$.

Since the distribution of channel and phase errors to be estimated is unknown, the optimal estimation criterion is ML (Maximum Likelihood) criterion. This problem can be expressed as

$$(\{\hat{h}_k\}, \{\hat{\theta}_n\}) = \underset{\{h_k\},\{\theta_n\}}{\arg\min} \sum_k \sum_n |y_{k,n} - h_k e^{j\theta_n}|^2, \tag{11}$$

where $\{h_k\}$ is the channel to be sought and $\{\theta_n\}$ is the CPE to be sought, $y_{k,n}$ is the received signal on the n-th symbol of the k-th subcarrier.

For the optimization problem in (11), if $\{\theta_n\}$ is determined, we can get

$$\hat{h}_k = \frac{1}{N} \sum_{n=1}^{N} y_{k,n} e^{-j\theta_n}. \tag{12}$$

When $\{h_k\}$ is determined, we can get (9). Therefore, the optimization problem in (11) can be solved in an iterative manner. If there is more prior information about $\{h_k\}$, we will discuss it separately.

3.1 No Prior Information

In this part, we assume that there is no prior information about the channel. Through the above analysis, the iterative process can be given as

0: Initialize the estimated CPE: $\theta_1 = 0, \theta_n = angle\{\sum_{k=1}^{K} y_{k,1}^* y_{k,n}\}$;
1: Update $\{h_k\}$ according to (12);
2: Update $\{\theta_n\}$ according to (10);
3: Repeat step 1 and 2 until there is no significant improvement in the objective function $|y_{k,n} - h_k e^{j\theta_n}|^2$.

At first, an initial value is given to the CPE on each symbol where PTRS is placed, then we obtain the channel estimate through the CPE according to (12), and then update the CPE based on the channel estimate according to (10). Finally, by repeating the above steps, the gap between $y_{k,n}$ and $h_k e^{j\theta_n}$ is continuously narrowed, more accurate CPE and channel estimates can be obtained.

3.2 With Known Delay Power Spectrum

If the delay power spectrum is known at the receiver, the channel correlation matrix r_{hh} can be obtained. The channel estimation based on LMMSE is

$$\hat{h} = r_{hh}\left[r_{hh} + \sigma^2(x*x)^{-1}\right]^{-1} h_{LS}, \tag{13}$$

where $r_{hh} = E(\mathbf{h} \cdot \mathbf{h}^*), \mathbf{h} = [h_1, h_2, \cdots, h_K]^T$, x denotes the known reference signal, σ^2 indicates Gaussian noise variance, h_{LS} represents LS channel estimate which can be replaced during the iteration. Hence, the iterative process is given as

1: Through frequency domain filtering, we can get $\{h_k\}$ according to (13);
2: Update $\{\theta_n\}$ according to (10);
3: Update $\{h_k\}$ according to (12);
4: Repeat steps 1,2 and 3 until there is no significant improvement in the objective function $|y_{k,n} - h_k e^{j\theta_n}|^2$.

Different from scheme one, we first obtain the channel estimate by frequency domain filtering, then obtain the CPE through channel estimate, and then update the channel estimation based on the CPE.

At the first iteration, channel estimation is performed by LMMSE if the delay power spectrum is known, otherwise LS channel estimation is used. Also, when the channel delay power spectrum is known, the frequency domain filtering to update $\{h_k\}$ is added in the iterative process. If there is any other prior information about $\{h_k\}$, you can add it to the process.

4   MSE Analysis of Proposed Joint Estimation

Due to the complexity of the objective function, an analytical expression cannot be derived in theoretical analysis. Therefore, we will analyze the MSE of channel under the following two conditions.

4.1 $K=1$, $N=2$

Assuming that there is only one sub-carrier and the number of DMRS and PTRS is both 1, the optimization problem in (11) becomes

$$(\hat{h}, \hat{\theta}) = \underset{h,\theta}{\arg\min} \left(|y_1 - h|^2 + |y_2 - he^{j\theta}|^2 \right), \tag{14}$$

where $\hat{h}$, $\hat{\theta}$ are the channel to be sought and the CPE to be sought, y_1 and y_2 are the received signals of the DMRS and PTRS. The problem in (14) can be equivalently converted to another minimization problem:

$$(\hat{a}, \hat{\varphi}_1, \hat{\varphi}_2) = \underset{a,\varphi_1,\varphi_2}{\arg\min} \left(|y_1 - ae^{j\varphi_1}|^2 + |y_2 - ae^{j\varphi_2}|^2 \right), \tag{15}$$

where $a = |h|$, $\varphi_1 = \text{angle}(h)$, $\varphi_2 = \varphi_1 + \theta$, Eq. (15) can be broken down into 3 separate problems for solving:

$$\begin{cases} \hat{\varphi}_1 = \underset{\varphi_1}{\arg\min} \left(|y_1 - ae^{j\varphi_1}|^2 \right) = \text{angle}(y_1), \\ \hat{\varphi}_2 = \underset{\varphi_2}{\arg\min} \left(|y_2 - ae^{j\varphi_2}|^2 \right) = \text{angle}(y_2), \\ \hat{a} = \underset{a}{\arg\min} \left[(|y_1| - a)^2 + (|y_2| - a)^2 \right]. \end{cases} \tag{16}$$

Then we can get

$$\begin{cases} \hat{a} = \frac{|y_1|+|y_2|}{2}, \\ \hat{\theta} = \hat{\varphi}_2 - \hat{\varphi}_1 = \text{angle}(y_2) - \text{angle}(y_1) = \text{angle}(y_1^* y_2). \end{cases} \tag{17}$$

It can be seen that according to the ML criterion, the optimal estimation result of the CPE in (14) is consistent with the existing method in (9). According to (17), the performance of the MSE can be analyzed:

$$\begin{aligned} MSE_{channel} &= \tfrac{1}{2} E \left| h - \hat{a} e^{j\,\text{angle}(y_1)} \right|^2 + \tfrac{1}{2} E \left| h e^{j\theta} - \hat{a} e^{j\,\text{angle}(y_2)} \right|^2 \\ &= \tfrac{1}{2} E \left| h - \tfrac{|y_1|+|y_2|}{2} e^{j\,\text{angle}(y_1)} \right|^2 + \tfrac{1}{2} E \left| h e^{j\theta} - \tfrac{|y_1|+|y_2|}{2} e^{j\,\text{angle}(y_2)} \right|^2. \end{aligned} \tag{18}$$

The two terms in (18) should be equal, so only the first item is analyzed. Assuming that $h = 1, \theta = 0$:

$$\begin{aligned} MSE_{channel} &= E \left| 1 - \tfrac{|1+n_1|+|1+n_2|}{2} e^{j\,\text{angle}(1+n_1)} \right|^2 \\ &= \tfrac{1}{4} E \left| 1 - |1 + n_2| e^{j\,\text{angle}(1+n_1)} - n_1 \right|^2, \end{aligned} \tag{19}$$

where $e^{j\,\text{angle}(1+n_1)} \approx 1 + j\text{Im}(n_1)$, $|1 + n_2| \approx 1 + \text{Re}(n_2)$, then we have

$$\begin{aligned} MSE_{channel} &= \tfrac{1}{4} E \left| 1 - [1 + \text{Re}(n_2)][1 + j\text{Im}(n_1)] - n_1 \right|^2 \\ &= \tfrac{1}{4} E \left| \text{Re}(n_1) + \text{Re}(n_2) + j\text{Im}(n_1)[2 + \text{Re}(n_2)] \right|^2 \\ &\approx \tfrac{1}{4} E \left| \text{Re}(n_1) + \text{Re}(n_2) + j2\text{Im}(n_1) \right|^2 \\ &= \tfrac{3}{4} \sigma^2. \end{aligned} \tag{20}$$

It can be seen from (20) that the MSE of the joint CPE and channel estimation is reduced compared to the no joint situation. However, since the CPE estimate is not accurate enough due to the small number of sub-carriers, the effect of LS channel estimation combining the two reference signals is not achieved.

4.2 $N=2$

Assuming that the number of DMRS and PTRS is both 1 on each sub-carrier, the optimization problem in (11) becomes

$$(\{\hat{h}_k\}, \hat{\theta}) = \arg\min_{\{h_k\},\theta} \sum_k \left(|y_{k,1} - h_k|^2 + |y_{k,2} - h_k e^{j\theta}|^2 \right), \tag{21}$$

where $y_{k,1}$ and $y_{k,2}$ are the received signals of the DMRS and PTRS on the k-th subcarrier. When θ is determined, each item in $\{h_k\}$ affects only one of the additions, so problem (21) can be broken down into K independent optimization problems:

$$\begin{aligned} \hat{h}_k &= \arg\min_{h_k} \left(|y_{k,1} - h_k|^2 + |y_{k,2} - h_k e^{j\theta}|^2 \right) \\ &= \arg\min_{h_k} \left(|y_{k,1} - h_k|^2 + |y_{k,2} e^{-j\theta} - h_k|^2 \right) \\ &= \frac{y_{k,1} + y_{k,2} e^{-j\theta}}{2}. \end{aligned} \tag{22}$$

As can be seen from (22), $\hat{h}_k$ can be represented by θ. Bringing (22) into (21), the problem is reduced to

$$\hat{\theta} = \arg\min_{\theta} \sum_k \left(|y_{k,1}e^{j\theta} - y_{k,2}|^2 \right). \tag{23}$$

Equation (23) can be represented in vector form $\arg\min_{e^{j\theta}} \left\| \mathbf{y}_2 - \mathbf{y}_1 e^{j\theta} \right\|_F^2$, where

$$\begin{aligned}
\mathbf{y}_1 &= [y_{1,1}, y_{2,1}, y_{3,1}, \cdots, y_{K,1}]^T, \\
\mathbf{y}_2 &= [y_{1,2}, y_{2,2}, y_{3,2}, \cdots, y_{K,2}]^T.
\end{aligned} \tag{24}$$

Then, the problem in (23) can be transformed into a merger problem with one transmit and multiple receive, so we can get

$$\hat{\theta} = \text{angle}\left(\mathbf{y}_1^H \mathbf{y}_2 \right) = \text{angle}\left(\sum_k y_{k,1}^* y_{k,2} \right). \tag{25}$$

When $K \gg 1$, the estimate of CPE is relatively accurate, and the combination in (22) can reduce the MSE to half of the noise power.

After the above theoretical analysis, we can see that this joint channel and CPE estimation algorithm can significantly improve system performance, and the performance is related to the number of sub-carriers. When the number of sub-carriers is large enough, the MSE can be reduced to the theoretical value.

5   Simulation Results and Analysis

In this section, we make simulations for comparison and analysis. Main assumptions are shown in Table 1.

Table 1. Simulation assumption

Parameters	Assumptions
Carrier frequency	30 GHz
Channel model	CDL-B
Subcarrier spacing	120 kHz
Allocated bandwidth	100 MHz
Number of RB	4
Coding scheme	Turbo
Channel estimation	LMMSE
SNR	13

5.1 No Prior Information

In this part, we compare the proposed joint estimation effects of different PTRS time domain densities. 1 DMRS and 3, 6 or 11 PTRS every sub-carrier in time domain are placed and three sub-carriers of the above pattern are placed in each RB. The simulation results are given in Fig. 2 where abscissa 0 represents without iteration. In Fig. 2, 1:3 represents the ratio of the number of DMRS and PTRS. It can be seen from the Fig. 2 that by the iteration, the MSE of the channel estimation is decreasing. However, what really works is the first iteration. That is, after the iterative process is called once, its MSE performance is basically stabilized. Also, we can see that the more the number of PTRS, the more the MSE declines since the number of PTRS will affect the accuracy of CPE estimate.

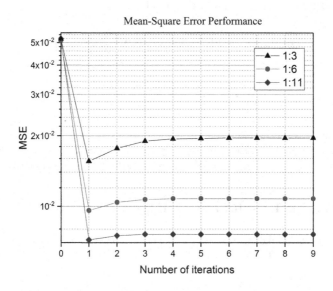

Fig. 2. Simulation result of joint estimation with no prior information

5.2 With Known Delay Power Spectrum

In this part, frequency domain filtering is added in the iterative process and the simulation results are given in Fig. 3. In order to get the system gain brought by each step in the iterative process, we do not use the iteration number as the abscissa, but the step in one iteration proposed in Sect. 3.2. It can be seen that every three steps is an iteration, step 1 is the beginning of the first iteration and step 3 is the end of the first iteration.

In Fig. 3, it can be seen that in each iteration, MSE is significantly reduced after frequency domain filtering, and MSE does not change much after other steps which shows the importance of frequency domain filtering. After the second iteration, the MSE is basically stabilized. We can see that after adding the

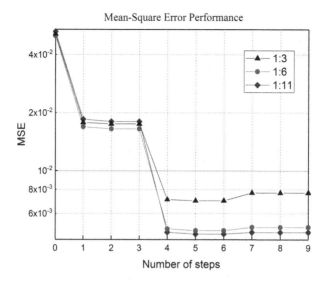

Fig. 3. Simulation result of joint estimation with known delay power spectrum

frequency domain filtering, the difference in system gain between the three cases is not as obvious as before. This is because after the first frequency domain filtering, we can get a more accurate channel estimate. Then we obtain CPE based on channel estimate instead of random assignment in Sect. 3.1. Therefore, the impact of the number of PTRS will be smaller.

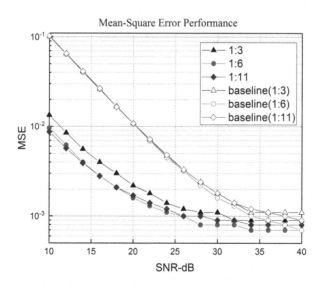

Fig. 4. Simulation result of the comparison between the joint estimation and the baseline

Then a set of baselines are added to make comparison, that LS was used for channel estimation and Eq. (8) for CPE estimation. As can be seen from the Fig. 4, the MSE decreases with increasing SNR under both algorithms. And under different SNR, the performance of the joint estimation algorithm is better than the traditional algorithm, especially when the SNR is small.

6   Conclusion

In this paper, an iterative algorithm is proposed to estimate CPE and channel. In this algorithm, a simplified system model which treats ICI as part of Gaussian noise is used to iteratively obtain more accurate channel and CPE estimates. We present the algorithm flow in two cases, one with no prior information and the other with known delay power spectrum. In addition, the system gain brought by the algorithm under two simplified conditions is analyzed. One condition is that the number of PTRS and DMRS is both 1, and the other condition is that the number of PTRS, DMRS and sub-carriers is all 1. The simulation results show that when there is more prior information about the channel, such as the delay power spectrum, the joint estimation of CPE and channel algorithm will perform much better. Meanwhile, the simulation results show that the proposed algorithm performs better than the traditional algorithm, especially when the SNR is small. Therefore, it can be concluded that this algorithm has a great impact on improving the accuracy of the estimation of channel and CPE.

References

1. R1-162885: On the phase noise model for 5G new radio evaluation, Nokia, Alcatel-Lucent Shanghai Bell, 3GPP TSG-RAN WG1 Meeting #84bis, Busan, Korea (April 2016)
2. 3GPP TS 38.214: 3rd generation partnership project, technical specification group radio access network, NR, Physical layer procedures for data, Release 15 (2018)
3. R1-164041: Phase noise model for above 6 GHz, Huawei, HiSilicon, 3GPP TSG-RAN WG1 Meeting #85, Nanjing, China (May 2016)
4. R1-1611981: On phase tracking for NR, Intel Corporation, 3GPP TSG-RAN WG1 Meeting #87, Reno, USA (November 2016)
5. Zou, Q., Tarighat, A., Sayed, A.H.: Compensation of phase noise in OFDM wireless systems. IEEE Trans. Signal Process. **55**(11), 5407–5424 (2007)
6. Bibi, A., Shah, A.A., Khattak, S.: Iterative common phase error correction in OFDM systems. In: 2011 Frontiers of Information Technology, pp. 258–262, Islamabad (2011)
7. Cheng, C., Chen, K., Lee, G., Huang, Y.: Phase error cancellation for OFDM systems using adaptive filters. In: 2010 International Conference on Broadband, Wireless Computing, Communication and Applications, pp. 643–647, Fukuoka (2010)
8. Ha, Y., Chung, W.: Non-data-aided phase noise suppression scheme for CO-OFDM systems. IEEE Photonics Technol. Lett. **25**(17), 1703–1706 (2013)
9. Gu, S., Long, H., Li, Q.: Phase noise estimation and compensation algorithms for 5G systems. In: Liu, X., Cheng, D., Jinfeng, L. (eds.) ChinaCom 2018. LNICST, vol. 262, pp. 551–561. Springer, Cham (2019). https://doi.org/10.1007/978-3-030-06161-6_54

A Practical Low Latency System for Cloud-Based VR Applications

Shuangfei Tian, Mingyi Yang[✉], and Wei Zhang

State Key Laboratory of ISN, Xidian University, Xi'an, China
myyang_96@stu.xidian.edu.cn

Abstract. With the development of multimedia technologies, VR services have quickly gained popularity at an accelerating speed. To reduce the high cost of purchasing high-performance VR terminals for end users and to enhance the user experience, recently, the concept of cloud-based VR was proposed which brings the cloud computing technologies to VR services. On-cloud GPU clusters and multi-core servers are expected to be used for simplifying VR terminals at the users' side. This idea, however, arises several challenges in deploying such cloud-based VR system for practical applications, among which the cloud-to-end latency is mainly concerned. In this paper, we designed a practical solution for bearing cloud-based VR applications. We aim at reducing the cloud-to-end latency to improve the experience of end users. In our system, a frame splitting technique was proposed to fulfill the goal. Specially designed algorithms including reference frame determination and rate control strategies were also included to limit the computational complexity and improve the coding efficiency while obtaining promising user experience. Experimental results showed that the proposed system can significantly reduce the cloud-to-end latency.

Keywords: Cloud-based VR · Cloud-to-end latency · H.264 coding scheme · Rate control

1 Introduction

Recent years have witnessed tremendous progress in the development of virtual reality (VR) technologies, which are now widely applied in many fields including education [6], entertainment [13], medicine [11] and gaming [9]. It is predicted that VR services will have a global user base of more than 275 million by 2025 [5]. A recent report foresaw that the VR business will grow into an $80 billion market by 2025 [1]. Currently, VR ecosystems is progressing in an accelerate pace in various aspects including the design of VR terminals (e.g., Head-Mounted Display (HMD)), coding and rendering schemes as well as transmission strategies.

This research was supported by the National Nature Science Foundation of China (Grant No. 61801364) and the Fundamental Research Funds for the Central Universities (Grant No. JB180105).

H. Gao et al. (Eds.): ChinaCom 2019, LNICST 313, pp. 73–81, 2020.
https://doi.org/10.1007/978-3-030-41117-6_7

Current VR terminals can be generally classified into three categories including mobile phone-based VR terminals, all-in-one VR terminals and PC-based VR terminals. The rather limited computing capability of the mobile phone-based and all-in-one VR terminals restrict their application to mainly VR videos services (i.e., 360-degree video streaming). In contrast, PC-based VR terminals are usually used to perform more demanding VR applications such as interactive VR gaming. However, most PC-based VR terminals are tethered to PCs using HDMI cables, which limits the movements range of end users and brings inconvenience. Moreover, to bring users with better sense of immersion and presence, visual scenes are expected to be rendered in higher resolution, e.g., 12K/24K with at 30/60 fps [8]. However, the capability of existing hardware fails to meet these challenging requirements. Additionally, mainstream PC-based VR manufacturers reported that the minimum configuration requirements for a basic VR experience will cost at least USD 1,500 including the purchase of a PC and an HMD [8]. This price will significantly arise if better visual experience is expected. The heavy cost of entry surely retard the popularity of VR applications among potential users. In this regard, it is of fundamental importance to design more portable, affordable and practical VR solutions for end users.

Very recently, the concept of cloud-based VR was proposed which brings the cloud computing technologies to VR services. The so-called VR cloudification aims at reducing the burden of logical computing and rendering process of VR terminals. The on-cloud GPU cluster and multi-core servers are used to compensate the deficiency of VR terminals. Figure 1 shows the basic system. The logic computing and rendering modules that have required high performance requirements for the terminal are placed in the cloud. VR terminals at the users' side only needs perform less demanding tasks such as sensor data transmission, video decoding and interaction control commands transmission. Such a change reduces the performance requirements of the VR terminal under the premise of ensuring the user experience, making it possible for VR to truly enter our daily life. Investigating the potential challenge as well as development practical cloud-based VR systems become a new research topic in both academia and industry.

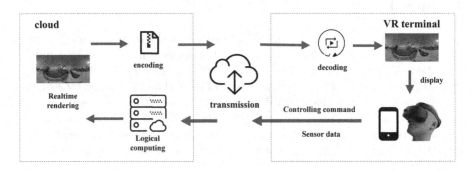

Fig. 1. An overview of the basic cloud-based VR system.

In September 2018, Huawei released the Cloud VR Solution White Paper which expressed its vision on the cloud-pipe-terminal Cloud VR [8]. Challenges of deploying such cloud-based VR system, e.g., the cloud-to-end latency, are discussed. Likewise, in [4], the authors discussed difficulties in improving the accessibility of interactive VR gaming experience by utilizing cloud techniques. They pointed out that cloud-to-end latency is the main issue to be solved before the successful deployment of cloud-based interactive VR gaming system. In [12], an implementation of an interactive VR game with the capability to move game servers across the world was demonstrated. However, end users reported a latency to different extent according to their distance to the server. Similarly, research in [7] investigated the challenges for enabling the cloud-based VR applications in wireless networks. They also analysed the challenging bitrate and latency requirements to enable wireless VR.

From the research above, we can see that solving the issue of cloud-to-end latency is the key factor in designing cloud-based VR system. In this paper, we designed a practical solution for bearing cloud-based VR application. More specifically, we aim at reducing the cloud-to-end latency to enhance the user experience. A frame splitting technique was first proposed to reduce the latency. Other algorithms including reference frame determination and rate control strategies were also included to limit the computational complexity and improve the coding efficiency while obtaining promising user experience. Experimental results showed that the proposed system can significantly reduce the cloud-to-end latency.

2   The Design of the Low Latency System

2.1   Overview of the Proposed System

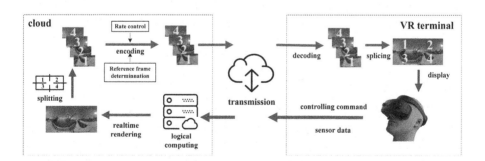

Fig. 2. An overview of the proposed system.

Figure 2 shows an overview of the proposed system. The entire VR rendering process was re-allocated where the logical computing, real-time rendering and encoding process are performed by the cloud server. In the original cloud-based

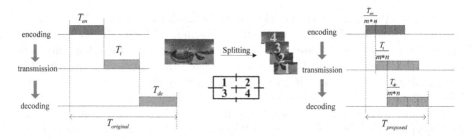

Fig. 3. The comparison of the cloud-to-end latency between no splitting and M × N splitting. M and N are set to be 2 for illustration.

VR system, the transmission of each frame should only begin after the codec has finished encoding that entire frame. Similarly, the decoding process only begin after the client receive the complete stream of one frame. Its corresponding cloud-to-end latency is denoted as $T_{original}$ in Fig. 3. To reduce the cloud-to-end latency, we proposed a frame splitting module in our system. As shown in Fig. 2, the cloud rendering platform first split each frame into M × N (e.g., 2 × 2 as illustrated) sub-frames. The obtained M × N sub-frames are then arranged to form a new temporal sequence in lower resolution. In this setup, once a part (e.g., a sub-frame) of the entire frame is encoded, it can be sent for transmission without waiting for the rest part to be encoded. Besides, as long as the client receive the stream of a sub-frame, the decoding process can be started. The cloud-to-end latency $T_{proposed}$ in our proposed system is shown in Fig. 3 which is clearly shorter. The reduction of cloud-to-end latency depends on the number of sub-frames divided.

When the sub-frame sequence are encoded, the temporal relativity between them is different from that of normal sequences, so a reference frame selection strategy is proposed. Moreover, as each frame is split into multiple sub-frames and each sub-frame is encoded separately, it is therefore important to make sure the sub-frames that belongs to the same original frame are consistent in their coding quality. To do so, a rate control module was further proposed in our system to keep that consistency. As current multimedia devices are compatible with H.264 coding scheme, our system thus used X264 codec as the basis.

2.2   Reference Frame Determination

After the frame splitting process, temporally adjacent sub-frames do not possess high relativity. Instead, this temporal relativity appears in every M × N sub-frames. Since the efficient prediction in temporal domain is a key technique for improving the coding efficiency, how to effectively use the temporal correlation is of fundamental importance.

The H.264/AVC video coding scheme [14] supports multi-reference frame in the temporal domain. More specifically, the encoder stores a number of reconstructed video frames as reference. Motion prediction is performed in these reference frames to find a more accurate match. However, X264 codec needs to

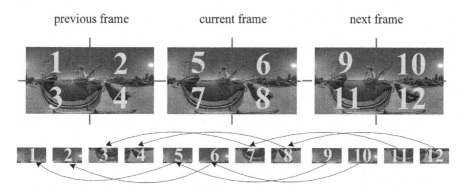

Fig. 4. Illustration of the prediction dependency of the sub-frames generated by the 2×2 splitting.

perform motion prediction in all reference frames when using multiple reference frames, which greatly increases the computational complexity compared to using a single reference. Especially, in the proposed system, it is no meaningful to perform motion prediction in those candidate reference sub-frames that have no temporal relativity with current sub-frame. As the sequence to be coded in our system has a fixed temporal structure, we hope to directly use single reference frame that is adjacent in temporal domain to control the computational complexity while ensuring sufficient coding efficiency. The expected prediction dependency between sub-frames just like Fig. 4 shows. With this in mind, we proposed an algorithm which can be achieved by setting the related syntax utilizing the H.264/AVC reference frame modification technique:

(1) Setting the reference frame list re-ordering flag:

$$ref\_pic\_list\_reordering\_flag\_10 = 1 \tag{1}$$

(2) Setting the type of modification process to be short-term reference frame modification where the re-ordered reference frame precedes the current frame:

$$reordering\_of\_pic\_nums\_idc = 0 \tag{2}$$

(3) Setting the distance between the current frame and the re-ordered frame to be m × n:

$$abs\_diff\_pic\_num\_minus1 = m * n \tag{3}$$

As the X264 codec supports no more than 16 reference frames, m × n must less than 16. That is to say, our splitting module thus allows several spatial partitions that generates less than 16 sub-frames.

By using the technique above, the reference frame list will be re-ordered. So that the right frame can be referred when just using single reference frame.

2.3   Rate Control for Quality Consistency

In our system, a frame will be divided into a number of sub-frames for encoding, and displayed after the client spliced them together. If the quality of the sub-frames that belong to the same original frame is significantly different, the user experience will be drastically reduced. To ensure the quality consistency among the splitted sub-frames, we designed a rate control algorithm as shown in Algorithm 1 based on the averaged bit rate (ABR) method [10] of X264 scheme.

Algorithm 1. Rate control for quality consistency

Input:

$SATD$: the sum of absolute transformed difference of the current sub-frame[10];

$cplxsum$: iterative quantities initialized according to the number of macroblocks[10];

$cplxcount$: iterative quantities initialized to be 0;

$qcompress$: the compression control parameter which equals to 0.6;

$rate\_factor$: the ratio of the summation of all coded bits to the complexity of current sub-frame;

$overflow$: the deviation between the total target bits and the actual generated bit;

$preQP$: quantification parameter of the previous sub-frame;

a, b, c : parameters which empirically set to be 12, 6 and 0.85 respectively;

Output: QP : quantification parameter;

1: $cplxsum \leftarrow cplxsum * 0.5 + SATD$
2: $cplxcount \leftarrow cplxcount * 0.5 + 1$
3: $blurred\_complexity \leftarrow cplxsum/cplxcount$
4: **if** current sub-frame is the first one in that frame **then**
5:     $qscale \leftarrow blurred\_complexity^{(1-qcompress)}$
6:     $qscale = qscale/rate\_factor$
7:     $qscale = qscale * overflow$
8:     $QP \leftarrow a + b \cdot log_2(qscale/c)$
9: **else**
10:     $QP \leftarrow preQP$
11: **end if**
12: $preQP \leftarrow QP$
13: **return** QP

In Algorithm 1, the step 4 to step 11 calculate the QPs of each sub-frame. The QPs of all sub-frames in one frame are set to be equal to that of the first sub-frame, To do so, we can ensure the quality consistency of the entire frame. However, the $blurred\_complexity$ of each sub-frame should always be calculated to ensure the correct calculation of $qscale$ for the following sub-frames. In step 5 the $qscale$ is firstly calculated according to $blurred\_complexity$, then the step 6 and 7 revise it according $rate\_factor$ and $overflow$.

3   Performance of the System

To benchmark the performance of the proposed system, we measured the coding efficiency as well as the cloud-to-end latency. The test sequences are four standard omnidirectional videos provided by Joint Video Exploration Team [3].

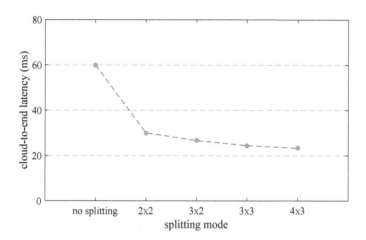

Fig. 5. Illustration of the cloud-to-end latency under different splitting mode.

3.1   Cloud-to-End Latency

The proposed system is designed to reduce the cloud-to-end latency by including the frame splitting module. As already shown in Fig. 3, when no splitting is used, the cloud-to-end latency can be calculated as:

$$T_{original} = T_{en} + T_t + T_{de} \tag{4}$$

where T_{en} is the encoding time of the entire frame, T_t is the transmission delay, T_{de} is the decoding time. In contrast, when a frame is divided into M × N subframes, the cloud-to-end latency can be calculated as:

$$T_{proposed} = \frac{T_{en}}{m*n} + \frac{T_t}{m*n} + T_{de} \tag{5}$$

To provide numeric evidence on to what extent can the proposed method reduce latency, we empirically set the encoding time, transmission delay and the decoding time for a single 4 K frame as 20 ms each. Note that the time of 20 ms was empirically set based on typical statistics in [8] to show the varying tendency of the cloud-to-end latency for different splitting mode. Real-world processing time in each step may be different according to specific methods used. Figure. 5 plots the cloud-to-end latency with different splitting mode. It shows that the latency reduces from 60 ms in no splitting mode to 23.3 ms in 4 × 3 mode. In the case of 4 × 3 splitting mode, the cloud-to-end latency is mainly occupied by the decoding time (i.e., 20 ms out of 23.3 ms) which is mainly determined by the client.

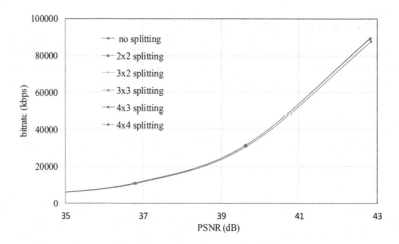

Fig. 6. Illustration of RD curves for encoding the sequence called PoleVault_le.

3.2 Coding Efficiency

Table 1 lists the performance of the proposed system in terms of Bjøntegaar Delta-rate (BD-rate) criterion [2] between no splitting mode and various possible partitions. Figure 6 further shows the RD curve for encoding the sequence called PoleVault_le. They showed that the coding efficiency of the proposed system experiences a slight drop since the spatial correlation of frames are affected due to the frame splitting. However, even at the largest 4×3 splitting mode, the BD-rates for different video content are controlled to be smaller than 4%, indicating that the coding efficiency of the proposed system can be relatively maintained.

Table 1. Performance in terms of the BD-rate of the proposed system with different $M \times N$ splitting mode

	2×2	3×2	3×3	4×3
AerialCity	1.42%	1.86%	3.13%	3.93%
Harbor	2.23%	2.36%	3.34%	3.89%
PoleVault_le	2.62%	2.75%	3.01%	3.15%
KiteFlite	2.57%	2.81%	2.94%	3.25%

4   Conclusion

This paper presents a practical cloud-based VR system to reduce the cloud-to-end latency for VR applications. A frame splitting technique was proposed to reduce the latency. To make sure the perceived quality of each sub-frame after splitting is consistent, a rate control method was further proposed. Experimental results showed that the cloud-to-end latency can be significantly reduced by almost three times in our implementations. In the meanwhile, the video quality only experiences a slight drop in terms of BD-rate. Experimental results showed that the proposed system can significantly reduce the cloud-to-end latency.

References

1. Bellini, H.: The real deal with virtual and augmented reality (January 2016). http://www.goldmansachs.com/our-thinking/pages/virtual-and-augmented-reality.html

2. Bjontegaard, G.: Calculation of average PSNR differences between RD-curves. VCEG-M33 (2001)

3. Boyce, J., Alshina, E., Abbas, A., Ye, Y.: JVET common test conditions and evaluation procedures for 360 video. Joint Video Explor. Team ITU-T SG **16** (2017)

4. Chan, K., Ichikawa, K., Watashiba, Y., Iida, H.: Cloud-based VR gaming: our vision on improving the accessibility of VR gaming. In: Proceedings of the International Symposium on Ubiquitous Virtual Reality, pp. 24–25 (June 2017)

5. Espelien, J.: The future of consumer VR and its impact on video viewing, 2016–2025 (January 2016). http://tdgresearch.com/report/the-future-of-consumervr-and-its-impact-on-video-viewing-2016-2025/

6. Freina, L., Ott, M.: A literature review on immersive virtual reality in education: state of the art and perspectives. eLearning Softw. Educ. (1), 133–141 (2015)

7. Hou, X., Lu, Y., Dey, S.: Wireless VR/AR with edge/cloud computing. In: Proceedings of the 26th International Conference on Computer Communication and Networks, pp. 1–8 (July 2017)

8. Ltd., H.T.C.: Cloud VR solution white paper (September 2018). https://www.huawei.com/en/press-events/news/2018/9/cloud-vr-solution-white-paper

9. McMahan, R.P., Bowman, D.A., Zielinski, D.J., Brady, R.B.: Evaluating display fidelity and interaction fidelity in a virtual reality game. IEEE Trans. Visual. Comput. Graph. **18**(4), 626–633 (2012)

10. Merritt, L., Vanam, R.: X264: a high performance H. 264/AVC encoder (2006). http://neuron2.net/library/avc/overview_x264_v8_5.pdf

11. Moglia, A., Ferrari, V., Morelli, L., Ferrari, M., Mosca, F., Cuschieri, A.: A systematic review of virtual reality simulators for robot-assisted surgery. Eur. Urol. **69**(6), 1065–1080 (2016)

12. Schmoll, R., Pandi, S., Braun, P.J., Fitzek, F.H.P.: Demonstration of VR/AR offloading to mobile edge cloud for low latency 5G gaming application. In: Proceedings of the 15th IEEE Annual Consumer Communications Networking Conference, pp. 1–3 (January 2018)

13. Sreedhar, K.K., Aminlou, A., Hannuksela, M.M., Gabbouj, M.: Viewport-adaptive encoding and streaming of 360-degree video for virtual reality applications. In: Proceedings of the IEEE International Symposium on Multimedia, pp. 583–586 (December 2016)

14. Wiegand, T.: Draft ITU-T recommendation and final draft international standard of joint video specification (ITU-T Rec. H. 264— ISO/IEC 14496-10 AVC). JVT-G050 (2003)

A Panoramic Video Face Detection System Design and Implement

Hang Zhao[1], Dian Liu[1], Bin Tan[2], Songyuan Zhao[1], Jun Wu[1(✉)], and Rui Wang[1]

[1] Tongji University, No. 4800 Caoan Road, Jiading District, Shanghai, People's Republic of China
{1730792,wujun,1830835,ruiwang}@tongji.edu.cn, liudian622@163.com
[2] College of Electronics and Information Engineering, Ji'an University, Jiangxi, China
1310499@tongji.edu.cn

Abstract. A panorama is a wide-angle view picture with high-resolution, usually composed of multiple images, and has a wide range of applications in surveillance and entertainment. This paper presents a end-to-end real-time panoramic face detection video system, which generates panorama video efficiently and effectively with the ability of face detection. We fix the relative position of the camera and use the speeded up robust features (SURF) matching algorithm to calibrate the cameras in the offline stage. In the online stage, we improve the parallel execution speed of image stitching using the latest compute unified device architecture (CUDA) technology. The proposed design fulfils high-quality automatic image stitching algorithm to provide a seamless panoramic image with 6k resolution at 25 fps. We also design a convolutional neural network to build a face detection model suitable for panorama input. The model performs very well especially in small faces and multi-faces, and can maintain the detection speed of 25 fps at high resolution.

Keywords: Panorama · Face detection · SURF · CUDA

1 Introduction

Traditional surveillance video, which can only display video from 40 to 50° of view usually in a larger scene, is unable to monitor the entire scene, thus multiple cameras need to be installed for monitoring. The panoramic video can provide 360° of video information without blind angle as Fig. 1. There is no need to install multiple cameras to cover the entire monitored area, saving hardware and installation costs. Face detection can make monitoring more intelligent and provide a technical basis for target recognition and tracking. It can greatly reduce the number of staff required, and the cost of manual operation, thus greatly reduce their labor intensity.

H. Gao et al. (Eds.): ChinaCom 2019, LNICST 313, pp. 82–94, 2020.
https://doi.org/10.1007/978-3-030-41117-6_8

(a) traditional surveillance   (b) panoramic surveillance

Fig. 1. Comparison of panoramic video and traditional surveillance

The key technology in the panoramic video is image stitching, which is to stitch multiple low-resolution images taken at different angles into a high-resolution image with a large field of view. Panorama video has an important applications in sports live broadcast, video entertainment, security surveillance, medical imaging, and other fields. Brown proposed AutoStitch [1] to make automatic recognition matching a step forward in panorama stitching, which allowed the panorama to be built without any user input. The previous generation of stitching algorithms based homography transformation, cylinder or spherical projection and multi-band combination is very mature.

However, with the development of head-mounted devices and liquid crystal displays, and the current 4k liquid crystal display has become the mainstream in the market while providing a better display platform for the panorama video. The pursuit of high-resolution video poses a higher challenge to panorama stitching. The panorama must be seamlessly and perfectly stitched to avoid misalignment, ghosting, and other issues in order to get good visual effects, especially at 360°, so the parallax problem in the panorama must be resolved. Parallax is the difference in direction caused by observing the same target from two points with a certain distance. Therefore, the same object captured by two adjacent cameras must have a certain difference. Directly stitching the combined image will produce ghosting. Therefore, the impact of parallax must be eliminated. In addition, the high-resolution output doubles the amount of computation. To provide high-resolution real-time panoramic video, the existing algorithms must be optimized to meet the demand.

Face detection is an important part of computer vision. With the continuous development of face detection technology, it is widely used in access control, surveillance systems and other kinds of security applications. Face detection research has made great progresses in the past two decades Viola and Jones proposed a groundbreaking algorithm [2], they trained the cascade classifier through Haar-Like features [3] and [4]. A face detector with good real-time performance is obtained. However, the research indicates that the algorithm has a very poor detection performance when the face is in an unconstrained environment. The unconstrained environment mentioned here is compared with the ideal conditions such as single face, simple background. With the large-scale application of face recognition, face tracking, etc., face detection is proposing higher and higher requirements. With the development of convolutional neural networks and the object detection algorithms such as RCNN and SSD, face detection has been greatly improved in accuracy. However, the detection speed is still a bottleneck. Most algorithms cannot guarantee 25 frames under VGA resolution. The resolution of panoramic video is generally 4K or higher, and 360-degree video contains more information and is more likely to contain more faces, Therefore, it is still challenging to perform face detection on panoramic video real-time.

This paper proposes an end-to-end real-time panoramic video face detection system, which integrates face detection technology into panoramic video, which will undoubtedly have a huge improvement on surveillance video technology, making up the shortcomings of traditional surveillance video.

2   Relate Works

Image stitching and face detection are the key issues in computer vision research in recent years which is the key points of panoramic video face detection systems. Pritam [5] extracted a panoramic video processing solution that can achieve 25 fps processing, but it only uses 4 cameras to shoot wide-angle images instead of 360 panorama. In 2016, [6] introduced Rich360 is a new system for creating and viewing 360-degree panoramic video. First, Rich360 utilizes a deformable spherical projection surface to minimize parallax from multiple cameras. The surface deforms in space and time based on the depth constraints estimated from the overlapping video regions. This enables fast and efficient non-parallax stitching without being affected by the number of views. Next, non-uniform spherical ray sampling is performed, the sampling density depending on the importance of the image area. Finally, for interactive viewing, a non-uniformly sampled video is mapped onto a unified viewing sphere using a UV map. [7] proposes a real-time 360 video stitching and stream processing method that focuses on GPU. This solution creates a scalable solution for large resolutions. This method uses a set of deformable meshes, processed using OpenGL (GLSL), and the final image uses a powerful pixel shader to combine the inputs. In addition, nVEnc GPU encoding can be used to stream results to cloud services using h.264 encoding.

With the development of artificial intelligence and machine learning technology, LeNet and AlexNet [8, 9], using the Convolutional Neural Network (CNN) to process images has become a research hotspot and future development direction. In the R-CNN proposed by Ross Girshick in CVPR 2014 [10], a convolutional neural network was used for target detection [9]. Then, about 2000 areas to be detected are proposed for SVM classification on the picture, and the size of the target bounding box is adjusted by a bounding box regression. The emergence of R-CNN has subverted the traditional target detection scheme, but it still has major deficiencies, such as long time spent and too many training modules. Then, fast-rcnn and faster-rcnn were proposed respectively, but even with the latest results, the time for target detection can only be maintained at around 5 fps. 2016 You Only Look Once (YOLO) was proposed by Redmon [11]. YOLO turned the detection problem into a regression problem, which greatly improved the speed of target detection, but reduced the accuracy. Single Shot MultiBox

Detector (SSD) [12] was proposed in 2016, using the idea of YOLO and the idea of Faster R-CNN's anchor box to satisfy the real-time performance while taking into account the accuracy rate [13]. MTCNN has a framework for deep convolutional multitasking [14], which takes advantage of the inherent relationship between detection and alignment to enhance their performance [15], but the detection time increases with the number of faces.

3   System Design

The panoramic face detection system is divided into two main modules, as shown in Fig. 2, panoramic video module and face detection module. The panoramic video system is also divided into the offline stage and the online stage. The offline stage is responsible for cameras design and geometric calibration and the online stage is in charge of image stitching, optical removal and image blending. The face detection module restores the data stream into panoramic images and detect face on panoramic video.

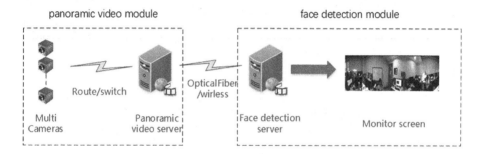

Fig. 2. System block diagram

3.1   Panoramic Video Module

In this section, We will introduce our designed panoramic stitching system. Our system is based on Facebook Surround360. Surround360 is a high-quality, production-ready 3D-360 hardware and software video capture system. It uses 17 high-precision industrial cameras and powerful processing workstations for post-processing. The time to render 4k video is 30 s per frame, and real-time processing is completely impossible. We improve the hardware design and software algorithms of surround360 to enable to stitch panoramas in real time on the personal computer. In particular, we make the following contributions:

(1) We redesign the hardware, reducing the number of cameras while maintaining stitching quality.
(2) We improve Surround360 feature extraction algorithm. Using the feature information to calculate intrinsic parameter and extrinsic parameters of cameras.
(3) We build a processing pipeline to render panoramas in real time using CUDA based on Surround360.

Hardware Design. The Surround360 has 14 side cameras with the resolution of
2048 * 2048. A camera's vertical and horizontal field of view is 90°. Surround360
is designed to render omnidirectional stereo panoramas, but we only need to
generate 2D panoramas. So we can reduce the number of cameras. In order to
obtain good stitching quality, the area of the overlap needs to be larger than
half of the image (Figs. 3 and 4).

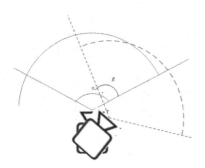

Fig. 3. Camera model α is the horizontal field of camera view. β is the angle of overlap area

Fig. 4. Unit sphere in the world coordinate system

After many experiments, we found N = 6, $\alpha = 120$ can stitch the panoramas
without distortion. Reducing the number of cameras greatly decrease the amount
of computation.

Feature Extraction. Although we reduced the number of cameras, Sur-
round360 still cannot stitch panoramas in real time. We improve software algorithms to meet real-time requirements. Surround360 use the scale-invariant feature transform (SIFT) features to register images. We use the SURF algorithm
which is an improvement of the SIFT algorithm. Its basic structure is similar to
SIFT, but the specific implementation process is different. The advantage of the
SURF algorithm is that it is much faster than SIFT and has good stability. In
order to generate panoramas in real time, we do not use the extracted features
to transform the image directly but used the features to calculate the camera
intrinsic parameter and extrinsic parameters. Establish the mapping relation
between the world coordinate system and the pixel coordinate. We called this
process is offline stage. The offline stage only runs once at program startup.

As the Fig. 4, we assume that the captured images are on a spherical surface
in the world coordinate system. The sphere can be sampled with longitude (ϕ)
and latitude (θ). The longitude ϕ in the range of $[-\pi, \pi]$ is called yaw, and the
latitude θ in the range of $[-\pi/2, \pi/2]$ is called pitch in aviation.

Spherical coordinates and latitude and longitude have the relations as follows:

$$X = \cos(\theta)\cos(\phi)$$
$$Y = \sin(\theta)$$
$$Z = -\cos(\theta)\sin(\phi)$$

We can get the longitude and latitude according to the angle of the camera, and then calculate the world coordinates of the image. So far, we can get the world coordinate through the longitude and latitude, but we want to get the pixel coordinate. It can be seen from the followed formula that we need to know the intrinsic and extrinsic parameters of the camera to complete the conversion of world coordinates to pixel coordinates.

$$
\begin{bmatrix} X_w \\ Y_w \\ Z_w \\ 1 \end{bmatrix} = \begin{bmatrix} R & T \\ 0 & 1 \end{bmatrix} \begin{bmatrix} \frac{Z_c}{f} & 0 & 0 \\ 0 & \frac{Z_c}{f} & 0 \\ 0 & 0 & Z_c \\ 0 & 0 & 1 \end{bmatrix} \begin{bmatrix} dx & 0 & -u_0 dx \\ 0 & dy & -v_0 dy \\ 0 & 0 & 1 \end{bmatrix} \begin{bmatrix} u \\ v \\ 1 \end{bmatrix}
\tag{1}
$$

R and T are the extrinsic parameters of the camera. R is the rotation and T is the translation transformation of the camera position to the world coordinate system. f is the focal length of the camera. dx and dy represent the actual size of the pixels on the sensor chip. u_0, and v_0 are the center of the image plane. These are the intrinsic parameters of the camera. We use the SURF algorithm to extract features. Then we use the features to register images, which is a non-linear regression problem. According to the position of the camera, a set of initial parameters are manually set, and the parameters are iteratively optimized by nonlinear least squares, and relative optimal results are obtained. Specific steps are as follows:

(1) Calibrate the camera to get the camera intrinsic parameters.
(2) Place a set of cameras in a designed position for calculating their extrinsic parameters.
(3) Capture a single frame as reference frame in a scene with plenty of features that is, containing objects with sharp edges and corners of different sizes. Using SURF to extract features.
(4) The reference frame is registered using the initial parameters, and the camera parameters are iteratively optimized with the Ceres Solver nonlinear optimization library and feature matching results.
(5) Finally, more accurate camera intrinsic parameters and extrinsic parameters are obtained, and a complete mapping of the world coordinate system to the pixel coordinate system is established.

The offline stage is performed only once, and the camera parameters are stored to the configuration file, and each frame of the acquired image is directly transmitted to the GPU for subsequent operations.

Pipeline Design. Because Surround360 is an offline stitching system. It only uses the CPU to perform the following steps serially: projection, parallax removal and image combination. We redesigned the images stitching pipeline with CUDA technology. Image processing has a high degree of parallelization. We pass the captured images to the GPU for parallelization called online stage. Compared with CPU, GPU has more powerful parallel processing capability. The online processing stage uses the camera coordinate system to perform spherical projection on the picture in each frame and then uses the optical flow method to combine the picture to generate a panoramic image. The next operation is performed in the spherical coordinate system and finally converted into a rectangular panorama (Fig. 5).

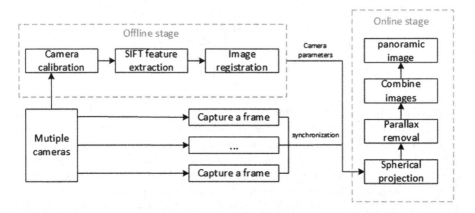

Fig. 5. Pipeline of panoramic video module

We put all the online stage operations on the GPU, and a lock-free single-producer-single-consumer circular queue is established to transmit the images. At first, the images data transfer to GPU was the largest bottlenecks for our algorithm. If we follow Surround360 algorithm, the images data will be transferred between CPU and GPU many times per frame. It will cost a lot of time and the real-time processing is completely impossible. We adjusted the algorithm structure and designed a pipeline that all the operations are performed on the GPU, so we just transfer the data to the device once per frame. In order to reduce the transmission time of data between the host and the device, we use the pinned memory to store the received images.

The pipeline we designed achieves full parallelization. The parallel optimization is mainly divided into two parts, global optimization, and local optimization. After analysis, we found the captured images are projected, parallax removed, and combined step by step. These operations are repeated on each image without data transfer, so we can process each image at the same time. This is the global optimization. For each image, it can also be pixel-level parallelized we called local optimization.

Surround360 does not directly generate a panorama, but it is performed by pasting together strips taken from the centers of the overlap images. Each strip is independent, so we can process each image in parallel to get the respective strip. We use 6 cameras to capture images, and there will be 6 streams concurrently executing. Each stream executes the operations as follows:

(1) Projection: remap each image to pixel coordinate so each image can be processed in the same coordinate system
(2) Parallax removal: calculate the optical flow in overlapping areas between adjacent images. Calculate the parallax map through the optical flow.
(3) Combination: combine the overlapping areas between adjacent images using parallax map.

The main operations contained in each stream are remapping, optical flow calculation, and fusion. These operations all can perform pixel-level parallel optimization using CUDA technology. We programmed kernel functions to implement the above operation. The kernel function is a function that executes in parallel in a thread on the GPU. In CUDA, each thread must execute a kernel function, and each thread will be assigned a unique thread number thread ID. We sent each pixel to a CUDA core, and got a unique thread ID. According the thread ID we can determine the pixel index. So we can do the operations on all the pixels of an image at the same time (Fig. 6).

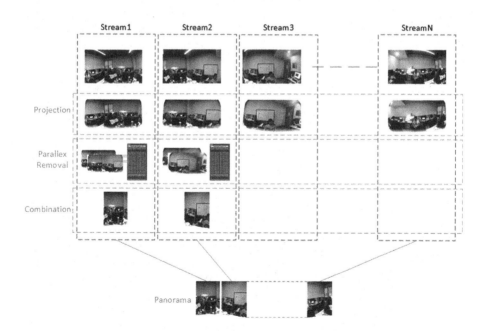

Fig. 6. Parallel processing

Now we have improved the Surround360 on hardware and software. Increase algorithm degree of parallelism while reducing data computation. So far, we can get the panoramic video in real time.

3.2   Face Detection Module

This module is detecting face performed on the panoramic video. With the development of the convolutional neural networks (CNN) and the target detection, people have achieved a high accuracy rate for the Face Detection Data Set and Benchmark (FDDB) dataset, but the scene under the real application is not as simple as the FDDB. Light, occlusion, size and resolution are also key issues to be addressed in face detection. Although there are many network models available today, there are still challenges in face detection. Our system uses the latest proposed Darknet-53 network structure in YOLOv3, with 53 convolution layers. The Darknet-53 is comparable to the most advanced classifiers, but with fewer floating point operations and faster speeds. The Darknet-53 performs better than the ResNet-101 and is 1.5 times faster. The Darknet-53 has similar performance to the ResNet-152, with a 2x speed increase. YOLOv3 draws on FPN and uses multiple scales to make predictions. Detect on multiple scale feature maps and predict 3 bounding boxes in each grid. This has a significant improvement in the detection of small faces. However, YOLOv3 has 9 anchor boxes clustered on Common Objects in Context (COCO) dataset. Among the COCO 91 classes targets, bicycles, big bus, birds, cats, the target size is very different. If use the anchor boxes to train the detection face, some of the anchors are not reasonable. We have adjusted the size of the anchors to meet the needs of face detection. Next, we will introduce the changed network structure:

(1) Feature Extraction Layer: Use the darknet-53 network proposed in YOLO removed the final fully connected layer. Therefore, it is a full convolutional network structure that adapts to image input at different resolutions. YOLOv3 the input image size is 416 * 416. The panorama resolution is very large if resize to 416 * 416 will loss lots of information. We change the input resolution as 832 * 832. Keep more information while meeting real-time conditions.

(2) Face detection layer: Using feature pyramid networks (FPN) to detect targets of different sizes by multi-scale. Select the last three different scale feature maps on darknet-53 as output. Using the upsampling concatenate two different scale feature maps are stitched together to realize predictions across scales. So we have 3 different scale feature maps, and each feature map needs 3 different scale anchor boxs. We did the k-means clustering on the WIDER FACE dataset and resized it to 832 * 832 resolution. Then we have 9 anchor boxes to detect the face.

(3) Loss function: Using the loss function calculation method in YOLO, first determine several key information in the detection: (x, y), (w, h), class, confidence. According to the characteristics of key information, it can be divided into the above four categories, and the loss function should be determined

by its own characteristics. Finally added together to form the final loss function, which is a loss function to get end-to-end training. The loss function of (w, h) uses the total square error, and the loss function of the other part uses the binary cross entropy. Finally added together (Fig. 7).

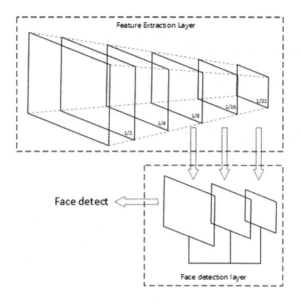

Fig. 7. Network structure

Then we have built the panoramic video module and face detection module. We use the RTSP protocol to transfer data between two modules.

4   Evaluation

4.1   Experiments

We designed and implemented a complete panoramic face detection system. In our system, we use 64 MP wide-angle industrial cameras as side cameras, through 2 PCI-e 1G Quad-Port PoE server adapter to connect to PC. Fix the cameras together using 3D printing technology. The graphics card is GTX1080Ti. The stitch system provides panoramic video with 6144 * 3160@25 fps as shown in Fig. 8. The stitched video stream is compressed and H265 encoded using NvEncoder and transmitted using the RTSP protocol. The video receiving end performs the decoding operation after receiving the RTSP video stream. Then the decoded video stream is input into the face detection network model.

We implemented the face detection model by PyTorch, First, using the WIDER FACE dataset to do pre-training, and the model input is performed

Fig. 8. Image of panoramic video

at a size of 416 * 416. Three different sizes of anchor boxes are used for the three different sizes of feature map, and a total of 9 different sizes of anchor boxes are used to cope with different sizes of face detection. Then using the panoramic images dataset to refine the model. The panorama resolution is 6144 * 3160, and the model input is 832 * 832.

Table 1. Comparison of render times

Panorama image resolution	Surround360 (ms)	This paper (ms)
2048 * 1024	961.50	20.77
4096 * 2048	1687.33	29.09
6144 * 3160	5614.07	38.15

4.2   Performance

Table 1 provides stitching times required for different resolution panorama. Our CUDA based panoramic image stitching system offers better results with more than hundred times faster than the Surround360 (using 6 cameras) system. The time for stitching one frame of 6k image is about 40 ms, so that the panoramic video can be played at a frame rate of 25 fps. As shown in Fig. 9. Face detection model mAP is 0.83, The YOLOv3 which input size 416 * 416 mAP is 0.66. YOLOv3 input images size are too small to detect face accurately. In the same scene, our panoramic face detection model has better performance as Fig. 10. Our face detection model frame rate is 28 fps. Although the speed is slower than YOLOv3, the accuracy is higher.

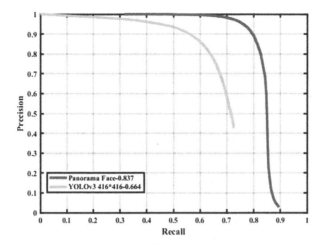

Fig. 9. P-R curve

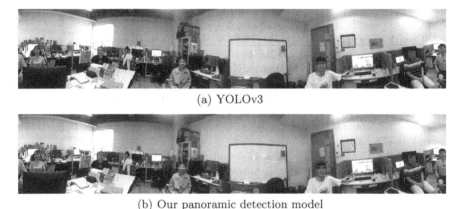

(a) YOLOv3

(b) Our panoramic detection model

Fig. 10. Face detection result

5 Conclusion

We design and build a panoramic video face detection system. The processing capability satisfies the requirements of the panoramic video, and it can improve surveillance video technology. In the future work, we will enhance the accuracy of face detection and improve panoramic video performance.

Acknowledgment. The authors thank the editors and the anonymous reviewers for their invaluable comments to help to improve the quality of this paper. This work was supported in part by the National Natural Science Foundation of China under Grant Nos. 61762053, 61831018, 61571329, Guangdong Province Key Research and Development Program Major Science and Technology Projects under Grant 2018B010115002, Key Laboratory of Embedded System and Service Computing (Tongji University), Ministry of Education, Shanghai (ESSCKF 2018-06).

References

1. Brown, M., Lowe, D.G.: Automatic panoramic image stitching using invariant features. Int. J. Comput. Vis. **74**, 59–73 (2007)
2. Viola, P., Jones, M.: Rapid object detection using a boosted cascade of simple features. In: IEEE Computer Society Conference on Computer Vision & Pattern Recognition, p. 511 (2001)
3. Papageorgiou, C.P., Oren, M., Poggio, T.: A general framework for object detection. In: Sixth International Conference on Computer Vision, pp. 555–562 (1998)
4. Freund, Y., Schapire, R.E.: A desicion-theoretic generalization of on-line learning and an application to boosting. In: Vitányi, P. (ed.) EuroCOLT 1995. LNCS, vol. 904, pp. 23–37. Springer, Heidelberg (1995). https://doi.org/10.1007/3-540-59119-2_166
5. Shete, P.P., Sarode, D.M., Bose, S.K.: Real-time panorama composition for video surveillance using GPU. In: International Conference on Advances in Computing. IEEE (2016)
6. Lee, J., Kim, B., Kim, Y., et al.: Rich360: optimized spherical representation from structured panoramic camera arrays. ACM Trans. Graph. **35–63**, 1–11 (2016)
7. Silva, R.M.A., Monteiro, D., Monteiro, D., et al.: Real time 360 video stitching and streaming. In: ACM SIGGRAPH, p. 70. ACM (2016)
8. LéCun, Y., Bottou, L., Bengio, Y., Haffner, P.: Gradient-based learning applied to document recognition. Proc. IEEE **26**, 2278–2324 (1998)
9. Krizhevsky, A., Sutskever, I., Hinton, G.E.: ImageNet classification with deep convolutional neural networks. In: International Conference on Neural Information Processing Systems, pp. 1097–1105. Curran Associates Inc. (2012)
10. He, K., Zhang, X., Ren, S., et al.: Deep residual learning for image recognition. In: Proceedings of the IEEE Conference on Computer Vision and Pattern Recognition, pp. 770–778 (2016)
11. Redmon, J., Divvala, S., Girshick, R., et al.: You only look once: unified, real-time object detection. In: Computer Vision and Pattern Recognition, pp. 779–788. IEEE (2016)
12. Liu, W., et al.: SSD: single shot multibox detector. In: Leibe, B., Matas, J., Sebe, N., Welling, M. (eds.) ECCV 2016. LNCS, vol. 9905, pp. 21–37. Springer, Cham (2016). https://doi.org/10.1007/978-3-319-46448-0_2
13. Everingham, M., Gool, L.V., Williams, C.K.I., et al.: The pascal visual object classes (VOC) challenge. Int. J. Comput. Vis. **88**, 303–338 (2010)
14. Zhang, K., Zhang, Z., Li, Z., et al.: Joint face detection and alignment using multitask cascaded convolutional networks. IEEE Sig. Process. Lett. **23**, 1499–1503 (2016)
15. Xiong, X., De La Torre, F.: Supervised descent method and its applications to face alignment. In: Proceedings of the IEEE Conference on Computer Vision and Pattern Recognition, pp. 532–539 (2013)

Coherence Histogram Based Wi-Fi Passive Human Detection Approach

Zengshan Tian$^{(\boxtimes)}$, Xiaoya Zhang, and Lingxia Li

School of Communication and Information Engineering, Chongqing University
of Posts and Telecommunications, Chongqing 400065, China
1159824866@qq.com

Abstract. Some traditional Wi-Fi indoor passive human detection systems only extract the coarse-grained statistical information such as the variance, which leads to low detection accuracy and poor adaptability. To solve the problem, we propose a new coherence histogram for Wi-Fi indoor passive people detection. In the histogram construction process, the method leverages time continuity relationship between received signal strength (RSS) measurements. The coherence histogram captures not only the occurrence probability of signals but also the time relationship between adjacent measurements. Compared to statistical features, the coherence histogram has more effective fine-grained information. The feature vector consists of coherence histograms is used to train the classifier. To eliminate the position drift problem, the Allen time logic helps to establish the transfer relationship between the sub-areas, we correct the results to improve the location accuracy. Compared with the classic passive human detection technology, the F1-measure is improved by nearly 5%.

Keywords: Wi-Fi · Passive human detection · Coherence histogram

1   Introduction

Nowadays, the device-free human detection system has been rapidly developed, such as ultra-wideband radar [1], computer vision [2], sensor networks [3] and radio tomography [4], which can achieve real-time human detection. However, in daily application scene, ultra-wideband radar requires special hardware support, which limits the application range; the monitoring environment under conditions of smoke, lowlight, etc., computer vision fails to detect people accurately, and the technology also has great limitation in smart home which involves privacy issues of users; sensor networks and radio tomography both require to deploy high-density tags, it is difficult for those systems to be used widely in the commercial market due to the expensive equipment costs. As wireless is widely deployed in our daily life, people are almost inseparable from the wireless. The study found

---

Supported by organization x.

that in the wireless environment, the appearance and movement of the human body can absorb, reflect and diffract part of the signal energy [5]. Using the characteristics of the wireless signal, received signal strength (RSS) based Wi-Fi passive people detection technology became a research hotspot. The technology does not require additional detection equipment carried by people. The characteristics of wide coverage, easy deployment, and low cost are helpful to applicate in the public safety field, commercial field, etc.

2   Related Work

The researchers conducted a variety of research on the original signal to extract the disturbance information. There are three typical detection methods: first of all, the statistical characteristics based system such as moving average (MA) [6] and moving variance (MV) [7] can obtain higher detection performance in a short time, but as time goes by and the environment changes, the performance gradually decreases. Secondly, the researchers have established systems such as RASID [8] and Ichnaea [9] by setting an environment anomaly index. The advantages of the system are efficient and fast when utilizing a single-link to detect the target. However, in the multi-link joint detection, due to the difference between links, it is necessary to adjust the abnormality index of each link to achieve better performance, which increases the system workload.

To solve the above problems, the support vector machine (SVM) [10] based on pattern recognition extracts the statistical features of the signal, such as variance, mean, extreme value, etc. However, the statistical features only reflect the coarse-grained information of the original signal. In contrast, if we use the distribution of the signal to characterize continuous RSS values, we must get more comprehensive and effective information than statistical features. For the people detection problem, wireless links react differently to environment condition, we should make full use of the received signal strength values to independently estimate the distribution of each wireless link in the monitoring environment, so a lightweight and efficient method must be used to find such a distribution. The histogram [11] meets the above requirements. It can estimate the probability distribution and reflect the fluctuation of continuous variables. Although the histogram can reflect the distribution of the signal, the ability of the histogram to obtain data time information is insufficient. Since the time relationship between RSS measurements is useful, the system adds it to the process of the histogram construction. We propose a Wi-Fi passive human detection approach based on coherence histogram.

3   Coherence Histogram Based Detection System

3.1   System Overview

The system overview of the proposed Wi-Fi passive people detection system is shown in Fig. 1. The system consists of three phases: signal collection and processing phase, model training phase and real-time detection phase.

(1) Signal collection and processing

We place some wireless access points (APs) and monitoring points (MPs) in the monitoring area. Secondly, the monitoring area is divided into several sub-areas, the MPs collect RSS measurements when the monitoring area with people and area without people, respectively. Finally, the RSS measurements will be filtered and normalized.

(2) Model training

To characterize all RSS streams received by MPs under different location status of people, the system constructs the coherence histogram for each link and merges them to form the feature vector. Then, the softmax classification model is trained by the feature vector to identify the movement and location of people.

(3) Real-time detection

The classification model classifies the RSS measurements received by the MPs. After that, the Allen-time logic is used to establish the transfer relationship of people movement in sub-areas. At last, the system outputs the final location result that is corrected by the transfer relationship.

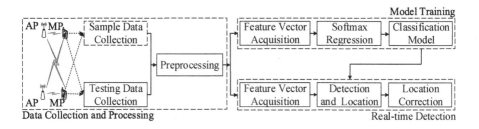

Fig. 1. System model.

3.2 Signal Collection and Processing

In the monitoring area, the number of placed AP and MP is X and Y, respectively. Altogether $J = X \times Y$ wireless links traveling through the monitoring area. The RSS measurements set of the $jth(= 1, 2, \cdots, J)$ wireless link is $RSS^j = [R_1^j, R_2^j, \cdots, R_K^j]$, where R_k^j indicates the kth RSS measurements. Since the noise in the monitoring environment affects the construction of the feature vector, the paper draws on the idea of outlier detection method [12] to design a filter to eliminate those extreme RSS measurements. For every link j, the mean D^j of the RSS^j is determined by

$$D^j = \frac{\sum_{k=1}^{K} R_k^j}{K} \tag{1}$$

and the maximum effective distance B^j from the mean is calculated as follows

$$B^j = 4\sqrt{\frac{\sum_{k=1}^{K} \left(R_k^j - D^j\right)^2}{K}} \tag{2}$$

The filtered outcome $\hat{R}_k^j(k = 1, 2, \cdots, K)$ of R_k^j is obtained by

$$\hat{R}_k^j = \begin{cases} D^j + B^j, & R_k^j > D^j + B^j \\ D^j - B^j, & R_k^j < D^j - B^j \\ R_k^j, & otherwise \end{cases} \quad (3)$$

After filtering all values in the RSS^j, we can get $R\hat{S}S^j = [\hat{R}_1^j, \hat{R}_2^j, \cdots, \hat{R}_K^j]$.

Because the signal distribution needs to be consistent during the construction process of the signal coherence histogram, the filtered $R\hat{S}S^j$ is normalized as $R\tilde{S}S^j = [\tilde{R}_1^j, \tilde{R}_2^j, \cdots, \tilde{R}_k^j]$, where $\tilde{R}_k^j = (\hat{R}_k^j - \hat{R}_{min}^j)\big/(\hat{R}_{max}^j - \hat{R}_{min}^j)$, $\hat{R}_{max}^j$ and $\hat{R}_{min}^j$ are the maximum and minimum values of $R\hat{S}S^j$, respectively.

3.3   Model Training

3.3.1   Feature Vector Construction

Figure 2 shows the fluctuation of the MP-side RSS signal of three wireless links when the monitoring area with people and without people. The wireless link RSS measurements change over a wide range. Therefore, it is possible to judge whether there are people in the monitoring area based on the fluctuation condition of the MP-side RSS signal.

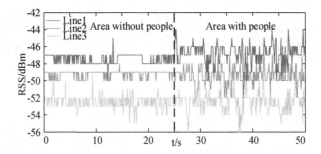

Fig. 2. Fluctuation of three wireless links.

The variance and histogram of three wireless links RSS measurements are shown in Figs. 3 and 4, respectively. From Fig. 3, we see the variance can characterize data features, but the expression is not obvious. Although histogram has a better ability to represent signal features than variance, signal information extracted by histogram is incomprehensive. This paper fully uses the time information of RSS measurements and constructs the coherence histogram.

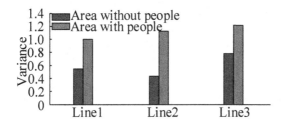

Fig. 3. RSS variances of three links.

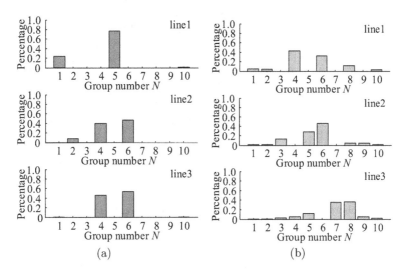

Fig. 4. RSS histograms of three links in different state of the monitoring area. (a) Area without people. (b) Area with people.

We divide $R\tilde{S}S^j$ into N groups of equal length. For the proceed RSS measurements of a link, if there no less than c consecutive measurements falling into the nth group, then we say the RSS measurements that belong to the same group are the c coherence, where c is termed as the degree of coherence. Then, the total number of RSS measurements in the nth group that meets the coherence degree requirement is recorded as s_n. Finally, the height of the nth group $\hat{s}_n^c$ is defined as

$$\hat{s}_n^c = \frac{s_n}{K} \tag{4}$$

where K is the total number of RSS measurements. Based on that, the coherence histogram of the jth link is calculated as $\hat{H}^j = [\hat{s}_1^c, ..., \hat{s}_n^c, ..., \hat{s}_N^c]$, where $n = 1, ..., N$. When the degree of coherence $c = 1$, we observe that the traditional histogram is a special case of coherence histogram.

Coherence histograms of three wireless links are shown in Fig. 5. The degree c of coherence directly reflects the change condition of RSS measurements, which means the more continuous the time of RSS measurements of the same group is, the bigger the group height is. It reflects that the change speed of the signal is slow in a short time and the signal fluctuation is stable.

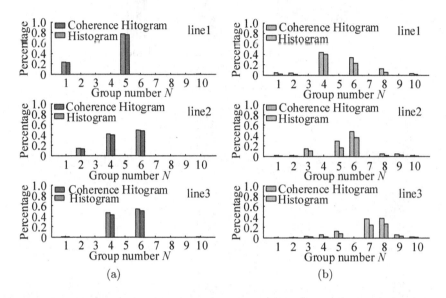

Fig. 5. RSS coherence histograms of three links in different state of the monitoring area. (a) Area without people. (b) Area with people.

To meet the real-time needs of the detection system, the entire samples should be divided into smaller samples. The sliding window mechanism [7] of length L divides different location status data. Samples of each location status of people are both $I = \lceil (K - L)/f \rceil$ for every wireless link, where f is the sampling frequency. There are total M kinds of samples in every sub-area and one type of sample corresponds to one location status. The coherence histogram of the ith samples of link j is calculated as $\hat{H}_{m,i}^{j} = [\hat{s}_{m,1}^{c}, \cdots, \hat{s}_{m,n}^{c}, \cdots, \hat{s}_{m,N}^{c}]$, $m = 1, \cdots, M, i = 1, \cdots, I$.

With the coherence histogram of all wireless links for every sub-area, the feature vector $F_{m,a}^{i}$ is formed by merging them

$$F_{m,a}^{i} = [\hat{H}_{m,i}^{1}, ..., \hat{H}_{m,i}^{j}, ..., \hat{H}_{m,i}^{J}]^{T} \tag{5}$$

where a denotes the sub-area number. The feature vector $F_{m,a}^{i}$ is a $NJ \times 1$ vector and the feature map is built as follows

$$\Lambda = \left\{ F_{m,a}^{i} | a = 1, ..., A; m = 1, ..., M; i = 1, ..., I \right\} \tag{6}$$

3.3.2   Classification Model Construction

The paper trains the classification model based on the feature vector $F_{m,a}^{i}$ of each location status samples to classify the RSS measurements in real-time detection phase. Let I be the number of classifiers, for the ith classifier, the training process is as follows.

In the real-time detection phase, the RSSt denotes the tested RSS measurements whose feature vector is F, the detection problem can be formulated as the following minimization problem

$$(\hat{m}, \hat{a}) = \arg \min_{m,a} \left\| F - F^i_{m,a} \right\| \tag{7}$$

where $\hat{m}$ and $\hat{a}$ are the estimated index of status and location of the target, respectively.

The monitoring area is divided into A sub-areas and each sub-area has M possible states. Therefore, there are total $Q = M \times A$ types of location states and RSSt can be any one of them, it is a typical multiple classes problem. This paper utilizes the softmax regression method which can convert the input feature vector into a probability [13]. As is shown in Fig. 6, the softmax regression model converts the input feature vector of every class into a probability $p(y_{m,a} = r|F^i_{m,a}, \theta)$ for $r = 1, ..., Q$. That is, it estimates the output probability of the class label y taking on Q classes.

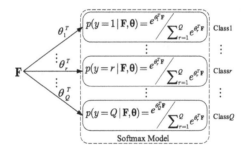

Fig. 6. Softmax regression model.

The output of the softmax regression model formulates as follows

$$h(F^i_{m,a}) = \begin{bmatrix} p(y_{m,a} = 1|F^i_{m,a}, \theta) \\ \vdots \\ p(y_{m,a} = r|F^i_{m,a}, \theta) \\ \vdots \\ p(y_{m,a} = Q|F^i_{m,a}, \theta) \end{bmatrix} = \frac{1}{\sum_{r=1}^{Q} e^{\theta_r^T F^i_{m,a}}} \begin{bmatrix} e^{\theta_1^T F^i_{m,a}} \\ \vdots \\ e^{\theta_r^T F^i_{m,a}} \\ \vdots \\ e^{\theta_Q^T F^i_{m,a}} \end{bmatrix} \tag{8}$$

where θ_r is a $NJ \times 1$ vector that indicates the model parameter for the rth output. All the system parameters of regression model are recorded as $\theta = [\theta_1, ..., \theta_Q]^T$, which is a $Q \times NJ$ matrix.

Firstly, the cost function of the regression model is defined as follows

$$\varphi_i(\theta) = -\frac{1}{Q}\left[\sum_{a=1}^{A}\sum_{m=1}^{M}\sum_{r=1}^{Q} 1\{y_{m,a} = r\}\log\frac{\theta_r^T F_{m,a}^i}{\sum_{l=1}^{Q} e^{\theta_l^T F_{m,a}^i}}\right] + \frac{\lambda}{2}\sum_{r=1}^{Q}\sum_{q=1}^{NJ} \theta_{rq}^2 \quad (9)$$

where $1\{\cdot\}$ represents an indicator function. When $y_{m,a} = r$, then $\{y_{m,a} = r\} = 1$, otherwise, $\{y_{m,a} = r\} = 0$. θ_{rq} represents the rth row and qth column element of the parameter matrix θ and λ is the proportion of the weight decay term.

After that, the cost function $\varphi_i(\theta)$ is strictly convex and its derivative is determined as follows

$$\nabla\theta_r\varphi_i(\theta) = -\frac{1}{Q}\sum_{a=1}^{A}\sum_{m=1}^{M} F_{m,a}^i[1\{y_{m,a} = r\} - p(y_{m,a} = r|F_{m,a}^i, \theta)] + \beta\theta_r \quad (10)$$

Finally, it is straightforward to solve the parameter matrix θ with the gradient descent algorithm using the feature vectors of training samples.

3.4   Real-Time Detection

3.4.1   Target Detection and Location

In the real-time detection phase, we use the sliding window mechanism that is the same as the data collection and processing phase to get the tested RSS measurements. Then, with the coherence histogram feature vector F extracted from the tested data, the probabilities of location status of people can be calculated as follows

$$h(F) = \theta \times F \quad (11)$$

The classification $(\hat{m}, \hat{a})$ of the element with the largest value in the $Q \times 1$ probability vector $h(F)$ is the current estimated location status of the target.

3.4.2   Physical Connection Relationship Construction

The connection relationship between the actual physical structures can constrain the movement behavior of people, hence, the movement pattern of people in

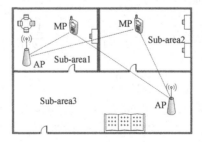

Fig. 7. Division of the monitoring area.

each sub-area is determined with the Allen Time Logic [14]. Figure 7 shows the divided sub-area for the monitoring area and Fig. 8 shows the Allen Time Logic that defines 8 time-order relationships between different events.

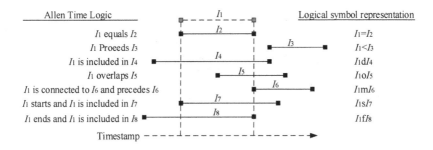

Fig. 8. Allen linear temporal logic.

All the motion modes are obtained by observing human behaviors in the monitoring area, Fig. 9 shows four of them and BP is the breakpoint which separates every event. Based on that, according to the Allen Time Logic, Fig. 10 shows the event map, the nodes represent events and the dotted path is the longest path. In each event graph, there is one and only one longest path, which satisfies two relationships: the first one is the happening order of events and the event nodes are connected by the operator 'm'; the second one is the end of movement and the operator 'f' connects the last event node to the movement node. According to each longest path associated with the sub-areas, the connection relationship of sub-areas can be constructed. Figure 11 shows the movement map that is the physical logic diagram of the monitoring area.

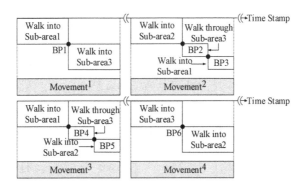

Fig. 9. People movement mode of the monitoring area.

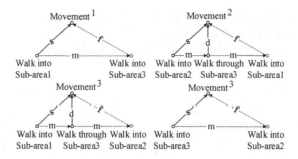

Fig. 10. Event map.

Fig. 11. Movement map.

3.4.3   Sub-area Transfer Weight Determination

According to the analysis of people behaviors in paper [15], the pedestrian movement rate distribution is shown in Table 1. This paper explores the distribution of actual walking distances of people during the sampling interval and uses the information to determine the transfer weight of sub-areas. Let d_{ab}^{min} and d_{ab}^{max} represent the minimum and maximum walking distance from sub-area a to sub-area b (a and b can be the same sub-area), respectively. The transfer probability W_{ab} from a to b is calculated by the cumulative distribution function (CDF)

$$f(v) = \begin{cases} \frac{1}{\sigma\sqrt{2\pi}} \exp\left(-\frac{(v-\mu)^2}{2\sigma^2}\right) & v_{min} \leq v \leq v_{max} \\ 0 & \text{otherwise} \end{cases}$$
$$W_{ab} = \int_{d_{ab}^{min}}^{d_{ab}^{max}} f(v) \cdot t dv \tag{12}$$

where μ and σ are the mean and variance of pedestrian movement rate. Then, we normalize the W_{ab} and get $\tilde{W}_{ab} = W_{ab}/\sum_{b=1}^{A} W_{ab}$.

Table 1. Pedestrian movement rate law.

Mean velocity (m/s)	Standard deviation (m/s)	Minimum (m/s)	Maximum (m/s)
1.127	0.5324	0.007	2.499

3.4.4   Location Correction

Since the motion state of people is continuous, the sliding window mechanism with the length G is used to filter the location at the current moment.

The transferred score that the target walks from the location obtained in the previous second to each location in the window is calculated as follows

$$Q_{ab} = n_b \times \tilde{W}_{ab} \tag{13}$$

where $n_b (\sum n_b = G)$ is the number of sub-area b in the window and $\tilde{W}_{ab}$ is the transition probability of sub-area a to sub-area b. In the end, the filtered result of the target location corresponds to the sub-area b when the score is the largest.

4   Experiment Evaluation

4.1   Experiment Setting

The layout of the experimental scene is shown in Fig. 12, we establish a prototype network to evaluate the performance of the proposed scheme in a typical complex home scene. The indoor area is $59.48\,\mathrm{m}^2$. Considering the limited number of available access points (APs) in the actual indoor environment, the network consists of 5 nodes, node 1 (Huawei Honor Router, WS851) is the access point that coordinates the operation of the network, while nodes 2 to 5 are the monitoring points (Samsung Mobile Phones, GT-S7568) that collect RSS measurements. A total of 4 wireless links cover the monitoring area. The AP uses the transmission over the frequency of 2.45 GHz and the sampling frequency of the MP is 10 Hz. MPs collect RSS measurements of all location states of people and the collection time for each kind of sample is 10 min. After that, the system performs multiple tests and each test lasts 5 min. According to the received RSS measurements, the system determines the location status of the target uniquely. The default parameters of the system are summarized in Table 2.

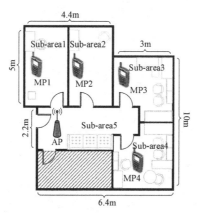

Fig. 12. Experimental scene.

Table 2. System default parameter values.

Parameter	Default value	Meaning
L	10	Sliding window size
N	5	Group number
C	3	Coherence degree
G	5	Filter window size

4.2 Parameter L, N and C for System Performance

As is shown in Fig. 13, when the L is restively short, the insufficient number of samples leads to the lack of discrimination of the feature vector, which makes the system performance is bad; however, when the L is restively long, due to the continuity of the movement of the target, there are lots of previous RSS measurements in the window. If the location status of the target changes at the current time, the previous data may cause misjudgment of the system. When the L is 20 or 30, the overall system performance is excellent, but considering the real-time needs of the system, we choose $L = 20$.

The next step is to confirm the influence caused by N and C on the system performance. In Fig. 13, we can see that relatively smaller C leads to the RSS values time continuity requirement is extremely low. A large number of motion RSS measurements fall into the same group due to the insufficient number of groups N. Hence, both of them can cause the inaccuracy judgment of motion status. In contrast, the restively larger C or the excessive N can result in misjudgment when there is no target walking around the monitoring area. Therefore, this paper chooses $L = 20$, $N = 10$, $C = 4$.

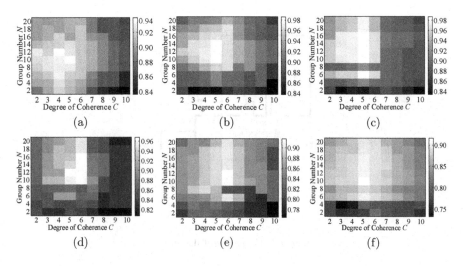

Fig. 13. F1-measure of different parameter. (a) $L = 10$. (b) $L = 20$. (c) $L = 30$. (d) $L = 40$. (e) $L = 50$. (f) $L = 60$.

4.3   Parameter G for System Performance

The sub-area location accuracy and average location accuracy are shown in Figs. 14 and 15, respectively. As we can see, the sub-area location accuracy increases as the filter window size increases, but when the window size reaches a certain size, the extension of the G makes the location accuracy decrease. Combining the results of the two graphs, the selection of the G is preferably between 5 and 10. The filter window $G = 10$ in this paper.

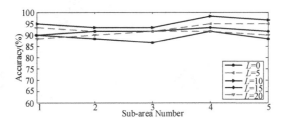

Fig. 14. Location accuracy.

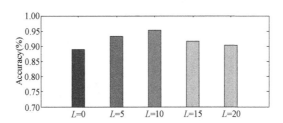

Fig. 15. Average location accuracy.

4.4   Performance Analysis

This section compares the proposed method with the MV system, the MA system, the histogram-based system, and the RASID system, the results are shown in Table 3. It can be seen that the F1-measure can reach 98%, the false positive rate (FP) and the false negative rate (FN) of the proposed algorithm are much lower. The confusion matrix is shown in Fig. 16, we can see the location accuracy is significantly improved after being filtered. As is shown in Fig. 17, filtered location accuracy of the detected target is at least 92%, the performance is higher than both Inchead system and Multi-feature PNN system [16]. To sum up, the proposed system has obvious advantages in the field of passive people detection.

Table 3. Comparison of detection performance with existing detection technologies.

Performance	MA	MV	RASID	Histogram	Coherence histogram
FN	0.1042	0.1174	0.0498	0.0687	0.0361
FP	0.1352	0.0962	0.0652	0.0997	0.0106
F1-measure	0.8799	0.8952	0.9303	0.9145	0.9769

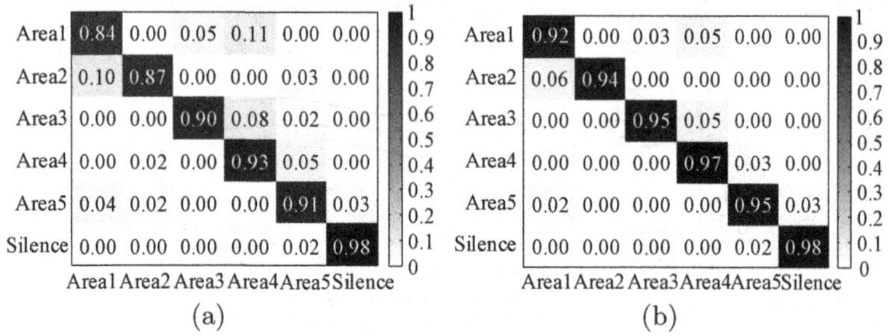

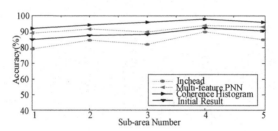

(a)   (b)

Fig. 16. Confusion matrix of location. (a) Initial location result. (b) Filtered location result.

Fig. 17. Comparison with existing locating technology.

5   Conclusion

To detect and locate people in an indoor environment, this paper proposes a people detection approach based on coherence histogram after comprehensively analyzing the advantages and disadvantages of the variance and histogram that are used to represent the original signal characteristics. On the one hand, the coherence histogram contains more fine-grained information which is related to the time relationship of RSS measurements. Therefore, the classification accuracy rate is been effectively improved. On the other hand, the proposed system has excellent tracking performance because the transfer relationship between different sub-areas is helpful to correct the location results. Therefore, the proposed method has more excellent performance.

References

1. Daim, T.J., Lee, R.M.A.: Indoor environment device-free wireless positioning using IR-UWB Radar. In: 2018 IEEE International Conference on Artificial Intelligence in Engineering and Technology (IICAIET), pp. 1–4. IEEE, Kota Kinabalu (2018)
2. Yasar, F.G., Kusetogullari, H.: Underwater human body detection using computer vision algorithms. In: 2018 26th Signal Processing and Communications Applications Conference (SIU), pp. 1–4. IEEE, Izmir (2018)
3. Wang, Q., Yiğitler, H., Jäntti, R., Huang, X.: Localizing multiple objects using radio tomographic imaging technology. IEEE Trans. Veh. Technol. **65**(5), 3641–3656 (2016)
4. Alippi, C., Bocca, M., Bopacchi, G., Patwari, N., Roveri, M.: RTI Goes Wild: radio tomographic imaging for outdoor people detection and localization. IEEE Trans. Mob. Comput. **15**(10), 3641–3656 (2016)
5. Pirzada, N., Nayan, M., Hassan, M., Subhan, F.: Filters for device-free indoor localization system based on RSSI measurement. In: 2014 International Conference on Computer and Information Sciences (ICCOINS), pp. 1–5. IEEE, Kuala Lumpur (2014)
6. Lv, J.G., Yang, W., Man, D.P., Du, X.J.: Wii: device-Free passive identity identification via WiFi signals. In: 2017 IEEE Global Communications Conference, pp. 1–6. IEEE, Singapore (2017)
7. Youssef, M., Moussa, M., Agrawala, A.: Challenges: device-free passive localization for wireless environments. In: Proceedings of the 13th Annual International Conference on Mobile Computing and Networking, pp. 222–229. ACM, Canada (2007)
8. Kosba, A.E., Saeed, A., Youssef, M.: RASID: a robust WLAN device-free passive motion detection system. In: 2012 IEEE International Conference on Pervasive Computing and Communications, pp. 180–189. IEEE, Lugano (2012)
9. Saeed, A., Kosba, A.E., Youssef, M.: Ichnaea: a low-overhead robust WLAN device-free passive localization system. IEEE J. Sel. Top. Sig. Process. **8**(5), 5–15 (2014)
10. Ilao, J., Cordel, M.: Crowd estimation using region-specific HOG With SVM. In: 2018 15th International Joint Conference on Computer Science and Software Engineering (JCSSE), pp. 1–5. IEEE, Nakhonpathon (2012)
11. Koray, K.: Histogram-based contextual classification of SAR images. IEEE Geosci. Remote Sens. Lett. **12**(1), 33–37 (2014)
12. Han, J., Kamber, M., Pei, J.: Data Mining Concepts and Techniques, 3rd edn. Elsevier, Amsterdam (1999)
13. Heckerman, D., Meek, C.: Models and selection criteria for regression and classification. In: 13th Conference on Uncertainty in Artificial Intelligence (UAI), pp. 223–228. Morgan Kaufmann, San Francisco (2009)
14. Roşu, G., Bensalem, S.: Allen linear (interval) temporal logic – translation to LTL and monitor synthesis. In: Ball, T., Jones, R.B. (eds.) CAV 2006. LNCS, vol. 4144, pp. 263–277. Springer, Heidelberg (2006). https://doi.org/10.1007/11817963_25
15. Azevedo, T.S., Bezerra, R.L., Campos, A.V.C., Moraes de, L.F.M.: An analysis of human mobility using real traces. In: 2009 IEEE Wireless Communications and Networking Conference, pp. 1–6. IEEE, Budapest (2009)
16. Tian, Z.S., Zhou, X.D., Zhou, M., Li, S.S.: Indoor device-free passive localization for intrusion detection using multi-feature PNN. In: 2015 10th International Conference on Communications and Networking in China (ChinaCom), pp. 272–277. IEEE, Shanghai (2015)

Information Processing

A Convolutional Neural Network Decoder
for Convolutional Codes

Zhengyu Zhang[1(✉)], Dongping Yao[1], Lei Xiong[1], Bo Ai[1], and Shuo Guo[2]

[1] State Key Laboratory of Rail Traffic Control and Safety,
Beijing Jiaotong University, Beijing 100044, China
18120185@bjtu.edu.cn
[2] Shanghai Gezhi High School, Shanghai 200001, China

Abstract. The convolutional neural network (CNN) decoder for general convolutional decoding is proposed. The parameters of CNN are determined by the initial state of each input block and the constraint relationship between adjacent bits is extracted by the convolutional layer as the constraint features. Then CNN decoder realizes decoding process through the extracted constraint feature instead of codewords directly. The result shows that, without changing the structure of decoder, the decoding performance of CNN decoder on different convolutional codes is equivalent to Viterbi soft decoding algorithm. Compared with Viterbi decoding, the larger constraint length or the lower SNR, the greater gain can be obtained in CNN decoder. Besides, we consider CNN trained by the two kinds of training sets in order to further investigate the potential and limitations of CNN decoder with respect to decoding performance, analysing the advantages and factors of these two kinds of training sets.

Keywords: Deep learning · Convolutional code · Viterbi decoding
algorithm · Neural network

1 Introduction

Convolutional codes are linear codes with a very distinct algebraic structure, which assign code bits to an incoming information bit stream continuously in a stream-oriented fashion. As an important channel coding technology, convolutional codes have been widely used in communication systems such as GSM, WCDMA, CDMA2000, and broadcasting.

In recent years, deep learning methods have developed rapidly and applied to all layers of communication systems to greatly improve the performance, including channel decoding. In [1] the author revisits the idea of using deep neural networks for one-shot decoding of random and structured codes. It provides that neural networks can learn a form of decoding algorithm, rather than a simple classifier. In [2] the author proposes a deep learning method for improving the belief propagation algorithm. The method generalizes the standard belief propagation algorithm by assigning weights to the edges of the Tanner graph.

© ICST Institute for Computer Sciences, Social Informatics and Telecommunications Engineering 2020
Published by Springer Nature Switzerland AG 2020. All Rights Reserved
H. Gao et al. (Eds.): ChinaCom 2019, LNICST 313, pp. 113–125, 2020.
https://doi.org/10.1007/978-3-030-41117-6_10

In [3] it introduces a recurrent neural decoder architecture based on the method of successive relaxation. The results demonstrate that the neural belief propagation decoder can be used to improve the performance, or alternatively reduce the computational complexity, of a close to optimal decoder of short BCH codes. In [4] it shows that the conventional iterative decoding algorithm for polar codes can be enhanced when sub-blocks of the decoder are replaced by neural network (NN) based components. In [5] the author proposes an iterative belief propagation convolutional neural network (BP-CNN) architecture for channel decoding. The results show that this architecture Iterating between BP and CNN can improve the decoding signal to noise ratio (SNR) and result in better decoding performance. [6] and [7] discuss an improved Viterbi soft decision method based on artificial neural network, which can improve the efficiency of decision making in comparison with other methods of decision making, in term of bit error rate (BER). The [8–10] discuss the structure of convolutional code decoder based on recurrent neural network. The results show that the neural network decoder has lower complexity and better performance than Viterbi decoding.

However, most of the current research about convolutional decoding focus on the a certain convolutional code, which cannot adapt to different convolutional codes. With the rapid development of mobile communication, different communication systems use different convolutional coding schemes (such as different code rates and constraint length). The traditional decoder, such as Viterbi decoder, needs to be designed separately, which seriously increases the design difficulty and cost at the terminal. In order to solve these problems, it is urgent to consider a convolutional decoder with general architecture to autonomously adapt to different convolutional codes.

In this paper, we propose a general convolutional decoder based on neural network and analyze the decoding performance. Inspired by the receptive field of convolution kernels, we consider CNN to realize convolutional decoding process where the parameters of CNN decoder is determined by the initial state of each coding block, thus ensuring the integrity of adjacent bits between two coding block. Besides, the convolutional layer is adopted to learn the constraint relationship of the convolutional code, so the CNN decoder realizes decoding process on the basis of learned constraint features, instead of directly the received sequence. The results show that the CNN decoder can adapt to different convolutional codes without changing the structure, and decoding performance is better than Viterbi soft decoding. Besides, we analyse the advantages and factors of received-sequence training sets and error-pattern training sets.

The rest of this paper is organized as follows. Section 2 proposes the scheme of decoder, which is carried out from four aspects: system model, training set generation, decoding process and convolutional neural network design. Section 3 presents the performance comparison of the CNN decoder trained by different training sets and simulation about general decoding capability. Conclusions are drawn in Sect. 4.

2   Neural Network Decoder

This section introduces the neural network decoding system model, training set generation, decoding process and the CNN decoder structure design. The principle of decoding process and implementation of CNN decoder are also explained in this section.

2.1   System Model

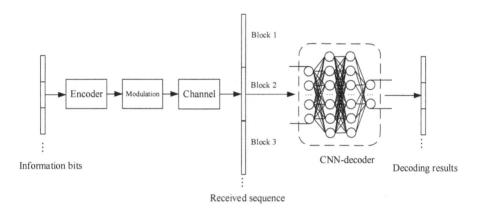

Fig. 1. System model.

This section introduces the system model from the perspective of neural networks. System model is shown as Fig. 1. The information bits sequence m is sent to the receiver via the encoder, modulation and channel. At receiver, the decoding results can be expressed as:

$$\hat{m} = D(R) \tag{1}$$

where R denotes the received sequence, $D(\cdot)$ denotes mapping of the decoder, and $\hat{m}$ denotes the output of the decoder. In the neural network decoder, decoding mapping is learned from the training sets, which is stored as the weight parameters in the neural network. The received sequence R is segmented into blocks of fixed length that decided by the window size of decoder. One block denoted as $r = [r_1, r_2, \ldots, r_k]^T$ is an input vector for neural network, where k is the window size of decoder. For neural nodes in the input layer, the net input, written as v, representing the weighted sum of the input vector, can be expressed as:

$$v = \sum_{i=1}^{k} w_i r_i + b = w^T r + b \tag{2}$$

where $\boldsymbol{w} = [w_1, w_2, \ldots, w_k]^T$ is a k-dimensional weight vector, and b denotes bias. The activation value of the neural node is generated via passing v through the activation function $f(\cdot)$. In order to learn the complex decoding mapping, the neural network decoder connects many neural nodes by a certain hierarchical structure. Given the parameter of the neural network decoder is θ, the decoding mapping of neural network can be expressed as:

$$\hat{m} = f(R; \theta) = f^{(L-1)}(f^{(L-2)}(\ldots f^{(0)}(R))) \quad (3)$$

where L is the number of layers in the neural network, and is also called *depth*.

2.2   Training Set

This section presents the generation of two kinds of training sets. The neural network decoder learns decoding mapping from the training sets and the training sets decide the upper limit of the decoding capability. The reasonable selection and processing of the training set, for example adding error patterns, can enhance the decoding capability of the neural network. Besides, the neural network decoder can learn error correction capability from reasonable training set to correct errors caused by transmission. For convolutional decoding, there are two kinds of training sets: the error-pattern training set and the received-sequence training set. The generation of them is shown in Fig. 2.

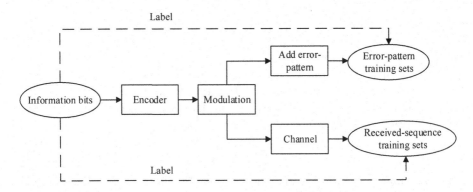

Fig. 2. The generation of the error-pattern training sets and the received-sequence training sets.

The generation of the error-pattern training set is described as follows. Suppose the length of information bits is p, then there are 2^p kinds of codewords without errors, and the length of codeword is q ($q > p$). In the *1*-error pattern training set, we consider all cases where only one bit error occurs in each block and there are $2^p \times (C_q^0 + C_q^1)$ kinds of samples in this training set. In the *2*-errors pattern training set, we consider all cases where one bit or two bits error occur in each block, and there are $2^p \times (C_q^0 + C_q^1 + C_q^2)$ samples in this training set. In the

r-errors pattern training set, the size of the training set is $2^p \times (\sum_{i=0}^{r} C_q^i)$. Each encoded block is used as the input of the neural network, and the corresponding uncoded information bits are used as the label.

The generation of the received-sequence training set is described as follows. Each encoded block impacted by the channel is used as the input of the neural network, and the corresponding uncoded information bits are used as the label.

The error-pattern training set considers all the correct cases and error cases, and the difference between the error samples and correct samples is obvious and clear. The learned decoding capability can reach to higher upper limit. In the received-sequence training set, samples are labeled vaguely, where failing to label correct and error samples clearly. But the generation of the received-sequence training set does not require additional computational cost, which can reduce the training cost. The neural network interface trained by these two training sets is shown in Fig. 3, the color depth represents the probability of decoding results, yellow means the decoding result is *1* and blue means the decoding result is *0*.

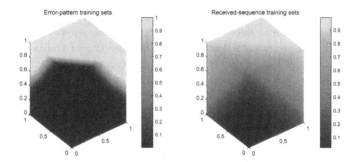

Fig. 3. Neural network interface trained by the error-pattern training sets (left) and the received-sequence training sets (right). (Color figure online)

2.3 Decoding Process

This section presents the decoding process of the neural network decoder. In the process of convolutional code encoding, due to the existence of the shift register, the convolutional code has strong constrained relationship between adjacent bits. If the continuous convolutional code is directly grouped into the neural network, the first and last bits of each block will lose the constrained information, resulting in a very poor decoding capability. Therefore, decoding process is required to realize the integrity of the input information between adjacent bits during convolutional decoding.

The decoding process is shown in Fig. 4. Taking the (2,1,3) convolutional code as the example, the size of shift registers in the encoder is 2, and there are four initial states 00, 01, 10, and 11 during encoding. When encoding, the initial state of the block is decided by the last two bits of the previous block. We train various neural network models corresponding the different initial states.

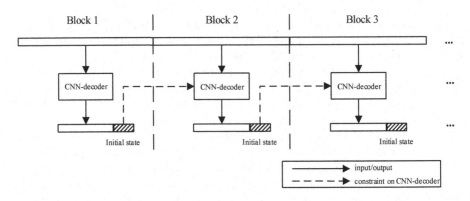

Fig. 4. The decoding process.

In (2,1,3) convolutional code, there are four neural network models corresponding four initial states. At the decoding process, we select the reasonable neural network model according to the previous decoding result and determine this model to complete convolutional decoding. Then repeat these operation in the next decoding block. These operation can ensure the integrity of the input information between adjacent bits of different blocks, and can also ensure the continuity of the decoding result without repeated decoding or missing decoding. Besides, every neural network model only corresponds to an initial state, thus the learning pressure for decoding mapping can be reduced, avoiding the neural network model being too complicated and redundant.

2.4   Convolutional Neural Network Design

This section presents the advantage of the CNN in convolutional decoding and the design of the CNN decoder. During the decoding process, the feature of codeword is firstly extracted by the convolutional layer, which is affected by the constraint relationship, named *Constraint feature*. Then CNN learns the decoding mapping from the extracted constraint feature. Compared with learning from codewords directly, it can ensure the integrity of continuous information preferably and does not cut the constraint relationship between adjacent bits.

In convolutional code, there is a certain constraint relationship between adjacent bits because of the shift register. The decoding process is equivalent to return the codeword to original information bits through the constraint relationship. Figure 5 shows the constraint feature of the (2,1,3) convolutional code. The bit that affects a batch of codewords is named as the *key bit* of corresponding sequence. In Fig. 5, the constraint length is 3, the key bit affects 6 continuous bits of codewords at most and we regard these 6 bits as the receptive field of the convolution kernel. The convolution kernel can learn the mapping between the key bit and the codeword. For decoding, the convolution kernel extracts the constraint feature from codewords via a certain receptive field range, and the constraint feature determines the value of the key bit, outputting as the decoding result.

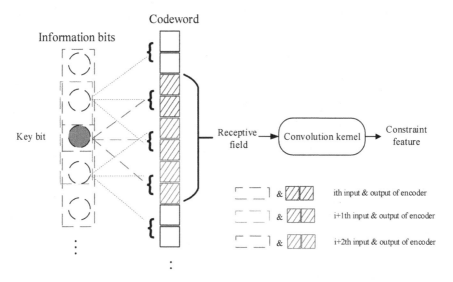

Fig. 5. The constraint feature learned from the codeword by the convolutional kernel.

The structure of CNN decoder is designed as Fig. 6, including an input layer, a convolutional layer, a flatten layer, a fully connected layer and an output layer. The size of input vector is 1×24, i.e., the window size of CNN decoder is 24. In the convolutional layer, the convolution kernel realizes feature-extraction by one-dimensional convolutional operation with size 1×10 and number 150. Feature maps, with size 1×15 and number 150, can be obtained via the convolutional layer. The single feature map represents the learned constraint feature. The flatten layer converts the multidimensional feature maps to one-dimensional. Through the fully connected layer and output layer, the size of vector changes to 1×12, which represents the decoding results. In addition, the RMSProp (root mean square prop) algorithm is used to update the parameters to accelerate the convergence. The Dropout and Early-Stopping strategies are adopted to avoid over-fitting problems.

3 Performance

This section compares the training results of different training sets and simulates the general decoding capability of the CNN decoder for different convolutional codes. The measure of decoding performance is BER.

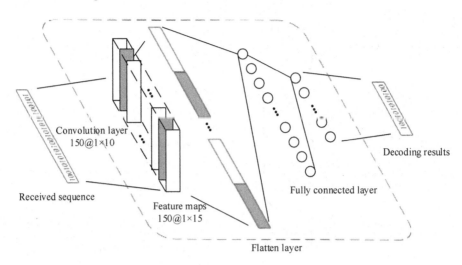

Fig. 6. The structure of CNN decoder.

3.1 Parameter Setting

In the simulation, we consider the error-pattern training sets including *1*-error, *2*-errors, *3*-errors and the received-sequence training sets affected by the SNR from 2 dB to 7 dB. The specific simulation parameters are shown in Table 1.

3.2 Simulation Result

This section gives the comparison of different training sets based on (2,1,3) convolutional code and the decoding performance of CNN decoders on (2,1,3), (2,1,5), (2,1,7), (2,1,9) convolutional codes, which are compared with the Viterbi decoding algorithm. Besides, the influence of constraint lengths on the decoding capability is considered.

Figure 7 shows the performance of the decoder trained by received-sequence sets with different SNR and Fig. 8 shows the performance of the decoder trained by error-pattern training sets with different error numbers. The results show that the received-sequence training sets with lower SNR can lead to better performance of CNN decoder and too many errors lead to confusion in the error-pattern training set, resulting in the poor performance of CNN decoder. For received-sequence training sets, there are less errors of received sequence during the transmission with higher SNR, therefore the error correction capability learned from the training sets will be weaker, causing the higher BER. For convolutional codes, because of the fixed constraint length, their error correction capability is limited. Too many errors have exceeded the error correction capability and lead to confusion in the training sets, resulting in the poor performance. For (2,1,3) code, the CNN decoder trained by *2*-errors pattern sets has better decoding performance.

Table 1. Simulation parameter

Parameters	Value
Training set	Error-pattern training set
	Received-sequence training set
Training set size[a]	100,000
Test set size	1,000,000
Modulation	BPSK
Channel	AWGN
Convolutional code	(2,1,3), (2,1,5), (2,1,7), (2,1,9)
Generator polynomial	[5,7], [23,33], [133,65], [753,561]
Decoder window size	24
Convolution kernel size	1×10
Convolution kernel number	150
Fully connected neural nodes	1,000
Decoder output size	12
Batch-size	1,000
Dropout rate	0.3
Early-Stopping steps	2

[a]Only list the received-sequence training set size. The error-pattern training set size depends on the number of errors.

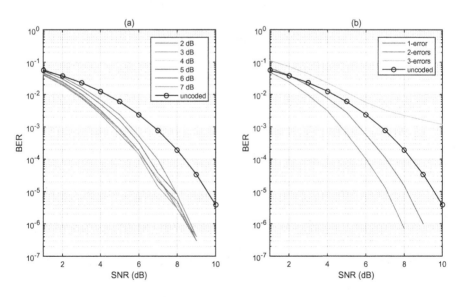

Fig. 7. Decoding performance of the CNN decoder trained by received-sequence training sets (a) and error-pattern training sets (b).

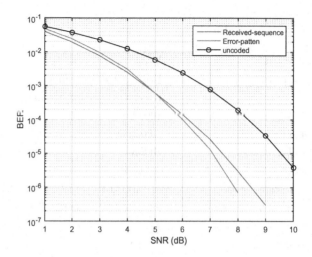

Fig. 8. Decoding performance comparison of the two training sets.

The comparison of the two kinds of training sets is shown as Fig. 8, where the 2 dB received-sequence training set and the 2-errors pattern training set are selected as representative, which perform better based on the previous analysis. The results show that the received-sequence training sets perform better in lower SNR environment and the error-pattern training sets perform better in higher SNR environment. It is caused by the interface of trained CNN decoder. The interface trained by the received-sequence training set is vague, bringing better noise tolerance capability in low SNR environment. The interface trained by the error-pattern training set is clear, bringing the more accurate decoding result in high SNR environment. In order to analyze the upper limit of the decoding performance, the error-pattern training set is considered in the subsequent simulation.

Figure 9 shows the BER of the (2,1,3), (2,1,5), (2,1,7) and (2,1,9) convolutional decoding. The results prove that the CNN decoder can learn general decoding capability, performing better than Viterbi decoding algorithm for different convolutional codes. Besides, the longer constraint length or lower SNR, the greater degree of improvement can be obtained on CNN decoder. In order to compare easily, we set the each block on the initial state of all-zero, and ignore these known bits information when calculating BER. For (2,1,3) code, the decoding performance of CNN decoder trained by 2-errors pattern training set is between Viterbi hard and soft decoding algorithm. It should be noted that the performance of CNN decoder trained by 3-errors pattern training set is poor because of the limited error correction

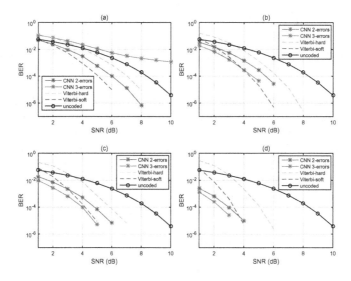

Fig. 9. Decoding performance for (2,1,3) Convolutional Code (a), (2,1,5) Convolutional Code (b), (2,1,7) Convolutional Code (c) and (2,1,9) Convolutional Code (d).

capability in (2,1,3) code. The performance of CNN decoder trained by the *2*-errors pattern training set is between Viterbi hard and soft decoding algorithm. For (2,1,5) code, the decoding performance of CNN decoder trained by *3*-errors pattern training set is better than Viterbi soft decoding when SNR < 4 dB, and slightly worse than Viterbi soft decoding when SNR > 4 dB. The performance of CNN decoder trained by the *2*-errors pattern training set is between Viterbi hard and soft decoding algorithm. For (2,1,7) code, the CNN decoder trained by the *3*-errors pattern training set can obtain the better performance all over SNR. About 0.2 dB gain can be obtained compared to Viterbi soft decoding algorithm when BER = 10^{-4}. The CNN decoder trained by *2*-errors pattern training set performs better than Viterbi soft decoding algorithm when SNR < 3 dB. For (2,1,9) code, the degree of improvement on CNN decoder trained by the *3*-errors pattern training set becomes greater. We can obtain gain of about 1 dB compared to Viterbi soft decoding when BER = 10^{-4}. And the CNN decoder trained by the *2*-errors pattern training set performs better than Viterbi soft decoding algorithm when SNR < 3.5 dB. In summary, the CNN decoder has better general decoding capability for different convolutional codes. When the structure of decoder is fixed, CNN decoder can realize decoding of different convolutional codes without structure changed, and the decoding performance is equivalent to Viterbi soft decoding algorithm, even better. Especially with the constraint length long enough or under the low SNR environment, the performance gain of the CNN decoder is greater.

4   Conclusion

In our work, the CNN decoder for general convolutional decoding is proposed. The parameters of CNN are determined by the initial state of each input block and the constraint relationship between adjacent bits is extracted by the convolutional layer as the constraint features. Then CNN decoder realizes decoding process through the extracted constraint feature rather than codewords directly. We analyse the advantages and factors of two kinds of training sets, knowing that the CNN decoder trained by received-sequence training sets obtains better noise tolerance capability, performing better in low SNR, and the CNN decoder trained by error-pattern training sets obtains better decoding capability, performing better in high SNR. Besides, the simulation shows that the decoding performance on different convolutional codes is equivalent to Viterbi soft decoding algorithm without changing the structure of CNN decoder. Compared with Viterbi soft decoding, the larger constraint length or the lower SNR, the greater gain can be obtained in CNN decoder.

Acknowledgments. This work was supported by the National Key Research and Development Program under Grant 2016YFE0200900, the Fundamental Research Funds for the Central Universities (2018JBM079), Beijing Natural Haidian Joint Fund under Grant L172020, Major Projects of Beijing Municipal Science and Technology Commission under Grant Z181100003218010, and the Royal Society Newton Advanced Fellowship (Grant no. NA191006).

References

1. Gruber, T., Cammerer, S., Hoydis, J.: On deep learning-based channel decoding. In: 2017 51st Annual Conference on Information Sciences and Systems (CISS), Baltimore, MD, pp. 1–6 (2017)
2. Nachmani, E., Be'ery, Y., Burshtein, D.: Learning to decode linear codes using deep learning. In: 2016 54th Annual Allerton Conference on Communication, Control, and Computing (Allerton), Monticello, IL, pp. 341–346 (2016)
3. Nachmani, E., Marciano, E., Lugosch, L., Gross, W.J., Burshtein, D., Beery, Y.: Deep learning methods for improved decoding of linear codes. IEEE J. Sel. Top. Sig. Process. **12**(1), 119–131 (2018)
4. Cammerer, S., Gruber, T., Hoydis, J., ten Brink, S.: Scaling deep learning-based decoding of polar codes via partitioning. In: GLOBECOM 2017 - 2017 IEEE Global Communications Conference, Singapore, pp. 1–6 (2017)
5. Liang, F., Shen, C., Wu, F.: An iterative BP-CNN architecture for channel decoding. IEEE J. Sel. Top. Sig. Process. **12**(1), 144–159 (2018)
6. Berber, S.M.: Soft decision output decoding (SONNA) algorithm for convolutional codes based on artificial neural networks. In: 2004 2nd International IEEE Conference on 'Intelligent Systems'. Proceedings (IEEE Cat. No.04EX791), Varna, Bulgaria, vol. 2, pp. 530–534 (2004)
7. Charei, Q.N., Aghamalek, H.F., Razavi, S.M., Golestanian, M.: An improved soft decision method in Viterbi decoder using artificial neural networks. In: 2013 First Iranian Conference on Pattern Recognition and Image Analysis (PRIA), Birjand, pp. 1–4 (2013)

8. Hamalainen, A., Henriksson, J.: A recurrent neural decoder for convolutional codes. In: 1999 IEEE International Conference on Communications (Cat. No. 99CH36311), Vancouver, BC, vol. 2, pp. 1305–1309 (1999)

9. Hamalainen, A., Henriksson, J.: Convolutional decoding using recurrent neural networks. In: International Joint Conference on Neural Networks. Proceedings (Cat. No.99CH36339), IJCNN 1999, Washington, DC, USA, vol. 5, pp. 3323–3327 (1999)

10. Hueske, K., Gotze, J., Coersmeier, E.: Improving the performance of a recurrent neural network convolutional decoder. In: 2007 IEEE International Symposium on Signal Processing and Information Technology, Giza, pp. 889–893 (2007)

A Classifier Combining Local Distance Mean and Centroid for Imbalanced Datasets

Yingying Zhao[1] and Xingcheng Liu[1,2(✉)]

[1] School of Electronics and Information Technology, Sun Yat-sen University,
Guangzhou 510006, China
isslxc@mail.sysu.edu.cn
[2] School of Information Science, Xinhua College of Sun Yat-sen University,
Guangzhou 510520, China

Abstract. The K-Nearest Neighbor (KNN) algorithm is widely used in practical life because of its simplicity and easy understanding. However, the traditional KNN algorithm has some shortcomings. It only considers the number of samples of different classes in k neighbors, but ignores the distance and location distribution of the unknown sample relative to the k nearest training samples. Moreover, classes imbalance problem is always a challenge faced with the KNN algorithm. To solve the above problems, we propose an improved KNN classification method for classes imbalanced datasets based on local distance mean and centroid (LDMC-KNN) in this paper. In the proposed scheme, different numbers of nearest neighbor training samples are selected from each class, and the unknown sample is classified according to the distance and position of these nearest training samples. Experiments are performed on the UCI datasets. The results show that the proposed algorithm has strong competitiveness and is always far superior to KNN algorithm and its variants.

Keywords: K-Nearest Neighbor (KNN) · Local distance mean · Centroid · Classes imbalance · Classifier

1 Introduction

Many algorithms of machine learning, such as support vector machine [1], decision tree [2], Bayesian classification [3], etc, train a model from training samples, and then use the model to classify unknown samples. Unlike these model-based algorithms, the KNN algorithm [4] has no training process. It makes statistic on

Supported by the National Natural Science Foundation of China (Grant Nos. 61572534 and 61873290), the Special Project for Promoting Economic Development in Guangdong Province (Grant No. GDME-2018D004), and the Opening Project of Guangdong Province Key Laboratory of Information Security Technology under Grant 2017B030314131.

H. Gao et al. (Eds.): ChinaCom 2019, LNICST 313, pp. 126–139, 2020.
https://doi.org/10.1007/978-3-030-41117-6_11

the number of each class in k training samples nearest to the unknown sample, and assigns unknown sample to the class that occupies the largest number in the k neighbours. The KNN method is not only easy to understand, simple to implement, but also has remarkable classification performance, which has been widely used in real life and has been rated as one of the top ten data mining algorithms [5]. However, there are some problems with the standard KNN algorithm, so researchers proposed a series of improved algorithms to overcome these shortcomings of KNN algorithm.

Firstly, sensitivity problem of k value. Different values of k have a great impact on the classification effect. Generally speaking, the method of cross validation is used to get an optimal k value. By introducing the training stage, a local k value is learned for each testing sample to improve the effect of k in these classifiers [6,7]. However, their complex training stages make the KNN algorithm lose its advantages of simplicity and convenience. Secondly, the relative distance between different samples are ignored and all samples within k neighboring training samples are treated equally in traditional KNN algorithm. Zeng et al. [8] weighted the distance, so that the neighbours who are closer get more weight. Similarly, the simple majority voting principle also ignores the spatial distribution of samples and fails to consider the relative positions of unknown sample and k neighbors. To solve this problem, Mitani et al. [9] used the local mean vector of k nearest neighbors (LMKNN) to classify unknown samples. On this basis, Pan et al. [10] improved it and proposed a new k-harmonic nearest neighbor classifier based on the multi-local means (MLMKHNN), which not only improved the classification accuracy, but also improved the robustness of k value. However, only one aspect of k value, distance and location distribution are considered in the above schemes.

What's more, the problem of class imbalance has always been a big challenge in classification problems, and it is a problem that needs to be considered in many machine learning algorithms. Because of the existing classification algorithms, the classification results for unknown samples are often biased towards the majority class. For example, the Naive Bayes classifier obtains a classification model by calculating the prior probability and the conditional probability, and then assigns the unknown sample to the class with the largest posterior probability according to the model. According to Bayes' theorem, prior probability is a very important part of calculating posterior probability. The KNN algorithm makes statistic on the number of each class in k training samples closest to the unknown sample, and assigns it to the class that occupies a larger number in the k neighborhoods. Whether it is Naive Bayes, KNN or other machine learning algorithms, although they sometimes seem to be able to achieve a good classification accuracy, they are biased against minority classes for imbalanced datasets.

However, the distribution of classes is often imbalanced in practice. For example, early warning of oil and gas leaks, detection of machine failures and identification of fraudulent calls, etc. In these examples, the amount of data on oil and gas leaks, machine failures, and fraudulent calls are much lower than the amount of data in normal times. However, the traditional machine learning algorithms have the problem of improving the overall classification accuracy by misjudging the samples of minority class. This is very unscientific in practical applications. What we really need is to improve the classification accuracy of each class, especially the minority class (such as those that require early warning samples).

In this paper, we propose a new classification standard. The local distance mean and the centroid distance are combined to serve as the basis for classification. This approach takes into account the distance and position distribution of the training samples relative to the unknown sample. In addition, we propose a new method to deal with the problem of class imbalance. We opt different neighbors from different classes, which does not increase the computational complexity or reduce the sample information. The experimental results show that the proposed classification method perform well in both classes balanced datasets and classes imbalanced datasets, especially for classes imbalanced datasets. The LDMC-KNN algorithm proposed in this paper has a great advantage over the standard KNN algorithm and the latest KNN improved algorithms.

The rest of the paper is organized as follows: Sect. 2 reviews the related works. Section 3 elaborates on the proposed algorithm LDMC-KNN. Our experimental results are presented in Sect. 4 and our conclusion is given in Sect. 5.

2   Related Work

Suppose $T = \{x_n \in R^m\}_{n=1}^N$ is the given m dimensional feature space, while N is the total number of training samples, x_n represents the $n-th$ training sample, R^m is the m dimensional real vector R. $y_n \in \{c_1, c_2, ..., c_N\}$ is the label of the training sample x_n. $T_i = \{x_{ij} \in R^m\}_{j=1}^{N_i}$ represents the collection of $i-th$ class training samples, T_i is a subset of T in feature space. x_{ij} represents the j-th nearest training sample in the i-th class. Suppose the testing sample or unknown sample is represented as x.

2.1   KNN

The basic process of the KNN algorithm is as follows:

The Euclidean distance (Other distance measures can also be used) are calculated from testing sample x to each training samples:

$$dist(x_n, x) = \sqrt{(x_n - x)^\mathrm{T}(x_n - x)}. \tag{1}$$

The distances $dist(x_n, x)$ are sorted from small to large, and the k training samples closest to the testing sample are selected. The number of each class is counted in the k training samples, and the testing sample is classified into the class that accounts for the majority of the k training samples:

$$C_x = \arg\max_{c_i} \sum_{x_n \in X_k} \mathrm{L}(C_{x_n} = C_i). \tag{2}$$

C_x represents the class of x, X_k is the set of k nearest neighbor training samples including x_n. When the class of x_n is the i-th class, $\mathrm{L}(\bullet) = 1$, otherwise, $\mathrm{L}(\bullet) = 0$.

2.2   LMKNN

The basic process of the LMKNN algorithm is as follows:

For a testing sample x, k nearest training samples are selected from each subset T_i (The value of k is less than the training sample number n_{c_i} of each class). The method of distance measurement uses Euclidean distance:

$$dist(x_{ij}, x) = \sqrt{(x_{ij} - x)^{\mathrm{T}}(x_{ij} - x)}. \tag{3}$$

The local mean vectors (i.e. local centroid) are calculated using the k nearest training samples in each class:

$$u_{ik} = \frac{1}{k}\sum_{j=1}^{k} x_{ij}. \tag{4}$$

The distances from the local mean vector of each class to the testing sample are calculated:

$$U_{ik} = \sqrt{(u_{ik} - x)^{\mathrm{T}}(u_{ik} - x)}. \tag{5}$$

Finally, the testing sample x is classified to the class with the shortest distance:

$$C_x = \arg\min_{c_i} U_{ik}. \tag{6}$$

2.3   Imbalance Datasets

For classes imbalanced datasets, the solution can be roughly summarized into two types. The first approach is to pre-process the training set. It generally over-samples the minority class and/or under-samples the majority class to obtain the same number of training samples for each class. One of the most common under-sampling methods is called Random Under-Sampling [11], where majority class samples are randomly discarded until this class contains as many samples as other classes. However, it will lose some information of the training set, thus decreasing the classification accuracy. An over-sampling method is proposed in [12], in which the synthesized samples are introduced along the line segments connecting less than or equal to k minority class nearest neighbors. He et al. proposed a new adaptive synthesis method [13], where different weights are assigned to the different samples of minority classes according to the learning difficulty degree of different minority classes samples. Samples of minority classes that are difficult to learn generate more composite data than samples of minority classes that are easy to learn. However, these over-sampling method will introduce a large number of new samples, increase the computational complexity, and thus prolong the classification time.

The second method is to keep the original datasets unchanged and improve the classifier to relieve the class imbalance. Mullick et al. proposed a class-based global weighting scheme, named Global Imbalance Handling Scheme (GIHS) [6], which takes the ratio of ideal probability and current probability of a class as the global weight related to this class. Zhang et al. [14] proposed k Rare-class Nearest Neighbour (KRNN) classification algorithm, which adjusts the posterior estimation of unknown samples to make it more partial to minority classes. Dubey et al. proposed a modified KNN algorithm [15]. In this method, the weighting factor for each class is calculated by classifying the neighbors of unknown samples using the existing KNN classifier. Li et al. suggested a training stage which exemplar minority class training instances are identified, and the samples of minority classes are extended to a Gaussian sphere [16], this method will make classification more sensitive to minority classes. Liu et al. proposed a class confidence weighting method [17], the samples are weighted by using the probability of attribute values given class labels in KNN algorithm. This approach can correct the preference of traditional KNN algorithm to majority classes. However, the above algorithms either introduce the training stage or need to adjust parameters, which increases the time complexity and eliminates the advantages of KNN algorithm that is simple and easy to implement.

3   Proposed Method

In this section, we propose a new method to eliminate the class imbalance while improving the accuracy of KNN classifier. First, we assume that the distribution of classes is balanced, the number of training samples of each class is the same, and KNN algorithm has no preference for each class. The standard KNN algorithm simply counts the number of classes of k neighbor samples, and does not care about the distance of the k samples. Therefore, under the condition that we guarantee the same number of training samples taken from each class (assuming that k training samples are taken from each class), to calculate the average distance between k training samples in each class and unknown sample.

For an unknown sample x, Its distance to all training samples are calculated using Euclidean distance:

$$dist(x_{ij}, x) = \sqrt{(x_{ij} - x)^{\mathrm{T}}(x_{ij} - x)}. \tag{7}$$

The training samples in each subset T_i are sorted in an increasing order according to their corresponding distances to the unknown sample x. And k nearest training samples are selected from each subset T_i, the corresponding distance $dist(x_{ij}, x), j = 1, ..., k$ are recorded. Then the average distance of the nearest k training samples to the unknown sample are calculated:

$$D_{ik} = \frac{1}{k}\sum_{j=1}^{k} dist(x_{ij}, x). \tag{8}$$

Furthermore, the position distribution of the training samples in each class relative to the unknown sample is considered. The centroid of k nearest training samples are calculated in each class:

$$u_{ik} = \frac{1}{k}\sum_{j=1}^{k} x_{ij}. \tag{9}$$

Then the distance from the centroid of each class to the unknown sample are calculated:

$$U_{ik} = \sqrt{(u_{ik} - x)^{\mathrm{T}}(u_{ik} - x)}. \tag{10}$$

Our ultimate goal is to find a class in which the average distance between k nearest training samples and unknown sample is the shortest (This means that the samples in this class are closer to the unknown sample), and the distance between the centroid of the k nearest training samples and the unknown sample is also the shortest. The shorter the distance between the unknown sample and the centroid, the stronger the enveloping ability of this class of samples to the unknown sample, and the greater the probability that the unknown sample belongs to this class. When the k training samples are uniformly distributed around the unknown sample, the centroid distance is 0.

Therefore, we combined the average distance and centroid distance of k nearest training samples as the basis for judging the class of unknown sample. The final judgment formula is:

$$C_x = \arg \min_{c_i} (U_{ik} + D_{ik}). \tag{11}$$

The above discussion is based on the assumption that the number of samples in each class is balanced. For the imbalanced datasets of classes, the number of training samples of different classes is different. If the same number of nearest neighbors from different classes are opted, it is unfair for the minority classes. Generally speaking, the distribution of samples of minority class is more sparse, the same number of nearest neighbors are opted as the majority class may cause the mean distance between the unknown sample and the nearest neighbors of the minority class to be larger.

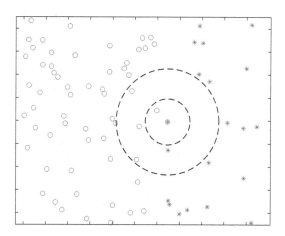

Fig. 1. Sample distribution example of class imbalanced dataset.

In terms of the sample distribution in Fig. 1. The ratio of the sample of the blue circle to the red asterisk is 3:1. It can be seen from the figure that if the standard KNN algorithm is used, the samples of red asterisk close to the classification boundary are easily classified into blue circle class. As far as the samples of red asterisk surrounded by a green circle is concerned, no matter what the k is, it cannot be classified correctly. If we take different number of training samples according to the number of samples in each class. Samples of the majority class need to contribute samples further away from the unknown sample, which is equivalent to giving training samples of the majority class with less weight. The rate of misclassification of minority class samples decreases. In practical applications, it is very important to correctly identify the minority class in the unknown samples

Therefore, we eliminate the class imbalance problem by selecting different numbers of nearest neighbors from different classes. The specific method is as follows:

First, the number of classes $classNum$ and the number of training samples in each class are counted $N = \{n_{c_1}, n_{c_2}..., n_{c_{classNum}}\}$. According to the number of training samples of each class, the number of training samples selected in each class is determined. The class with the smallest training sample is used as a benchmark, and the k nearest training samples are selected from this class. Then the number of training samples selected from other classes is:

$$k_{c_i} = k * round(n_{c_i}/min(N)). \tag{12}$$

Since the number of samples selected must be an integer, $round(\bullet)$ is used to round it. Then, the distance mean and centroid distance of k_{c_i} training samples in each class were calculated. The unknown samples are classified into the class with the shortest combining local distance mean and centroid distance. Note that when the dataset is balanced, the algorithm degenerates to choose k training samples from each class, so the algorithm is equally applicable to the balanced datasets.

We substitute Eqs. (8, 9, 10, 12) into Eq. (11) to get the final judgment formula of the unknown sample:

$$C_x = \arg\min_{c_i} \left(\sqrt{(\frac{1}{k_{c_i}}\sum_{j=1}^{k_{c_i}} x_{ij} - x)^{\mathrm{T}}(\frac{1}{k_{c_i}}\sum_{j=1}^{k_{c_i}} x_{ij} - x) + \frac{1}{k_{c_i}}\sum_{j=1}^{k_{c_i}} \sqrt{(x_{ij} - x)^{\mathrm{T}}(x_{ij} - x)} }\right). \tag{13}$$

The pseudo-code of LDMC-KNN is shown in Algorithm 1.

4   Experiments and Results

4.1   Degree of Imbalance

We use the imbalance ratio (IR) to quantify the imbalanced degree of classes. For the dataset of the two classes, IR is expressed as the ratio of the number of training samples of the majority class and the number of training samples of the minority class. For multi-class datasets, IR is defined as the maximum value of IR

Algorithm 1. The proposed LDMC-KNN classifier

Input: Training sample set T, training sample class set Y, unknown sample x, nearest neighbor number k

Output: The class of the unknown sample

1: Calculate the number of training sample classes $classNum$, and the number of training samples in each class $N = \{n_{c_1}, n_{c_2} ..., n_{c_{classNum}}\}$
2: **for** $i = 1$ to $classNum$ **do**
3:     $k_{c_i} = k * round(n_{c_i}/min(N))$
4: **end for**
5: **for** $i = 1$ to $classNum$ **do**
6:     **for** $j = 1$ to n_{c_i} **do**
7:       $dist(x_{ij}, x) = \sqrt{(x_{ij} - x)^{\mathrm{T}}(x_{ij} - x)}$
8:     **end for**
9:     Sort the distance $dist(x_{ij}, x)$ and take out the first k_{c_i} training samples
10:     $u_{ik} = \frac{1}{k_{c_i}}\sum_{j=1}^{k_{c_i}} x_{ij}$
11:     $U_{ik} = \sqrt{(u_{ik} - x)^{\mathrm{T}}(u_{ik} - x)}$
12:     $D_{ik} = \frac{1}{k_{c_i}}\sum_{j=1}^{k_{c_i}} \sqrt{(x_{ij} - x)^{\mathrm{T}}(x_{ij} - x)}$
13: **end for**
14: $C_x = \arg\min_{c_i} (U_{ik} + D_{ik})$

---

between all two classes. Based on IR values, we divided the datasets into either balanced datasets ($IR \leq 1.15$), mildly imbalanced datasets ($1.15 < IR \leq 3.5$) and highly imbalanced datasets ($IR > 3.5$).

In this section, we use the UCI [18] datasets to demonstrate our proposed approach. The information for the 20 datasets is shown in Table 1. According to the IR value, we can see that the first 3 datasets are either balanced datasets, the middle 12 datasets are mildly imbalanced datasets, and the last 5 datasets are highly imbalanced datasets. (For the Segment, Led7dight, and Glass datasets, one class is used as the minority class, and the others are combined as the majority class, which is the same as in [14,19]). According to the information in Table 1, we can see the datasets used in our experiment is a good example of a wide range of number of instances, from 208 to 7400, and a wide range of number of features, from 3 to 60.

4.2 Indices for Evaluation of Classification Performance

We use the following three indices to evaluate the performances of classifiers:

Accuracy. For a testing set containing M testing samples, it is assumed that the number of correctly classified samples is m. Accuracy is defined as $accuracy = m/M$. The more the unknown samples can be correctly classified, the higher the accuracy is. However, it does not take into account the classification of each class, so it is not suitable to judge the class imbalance data. Therefore, in our experiment, we only use accuracy to evaluate the performance of the classifiers on the class either balanced datasets.

Table 1. Dataset description of 20 real-world datasets from UCI repository.

Dataset	Samples	Classes	Features	Class number ratio	IR
Ringnorm	7400	2	20	3736:3664	1.02
Waveform3	5000	3	21	1657:1647:1696	1.02
Sonar	208	2	60	97:111	1.14
Spambase	4597	2	57	2785:1812	1.54
Cloud	1024	2	10	627:397	1.58
Pima	768	2	8	268:500	1.87
Diabetes	768	2	8	500:268	1.87
Saheart	462	2	9	302:160	1.89
Tictactoc	958	2	9	626:332	1.89
Contraceptive	1473	3	9	629:333:511	1.89
German	1000	2	24	300:700	2.32
Breast	277	2	9	81:196	2.42
Haberman	306	2	3	225:81	2.78
Mammographic	748	2	4	278:570	2.81
Parkinsons	195	2	22	48:147	3.06
Hayesroth	160	2	4	129:31	4.16
Balance	625	3	4	49:288:288	5.88
Segment	2310	2	18	1980:330	6
Led7digit	500	2	7	455:45	10.11
Glass	214	2	9	17:185	10.88

Gmeans. Gmeans is a commonly used evaluation standard for imbalanced datasets. It is based on two classes of confusion matrices. Here, we extend Gmeans to multi-classes problem. We assume that the testing set contains a total of M samples, among which M_c testing samples belong to class c ($c = 1, 2, ..., classNum$), the number of correctly classified in class c is m_c. The calculation method of Gmeans is as follows:

$$Gmeans = (\prod_{c=1}^{classNum} (m_c/M_c))^{1/classNum} \qquad (14)$$

Compared with the accuracy, Gmeans takes into account the classification performance of each class, which is more suitable to be the judgment basis of imbalanced datasets of the class.

Area Under Receiver Operating Characteristics Curve (AUROC). The Receiver Operating Characteristics (ROC) Curve can comprehensively reflect the performance of the classifier, which is also the performance evaluation standard of the class imbalanced classifier. Researchers usually use the area under the

ROC curve, namely AUROC, to further quantify and compare the performance of classifiers. It is calculated as follows [6]:

$$AUROC = ((1 + TPR - FPR)/2), \tag{15}$$

where TPR represents true positive rate and FPR represents false positive rate. Here, minority class is seen as positively labeled. But the AUROC cannot be directly applied to multi-classes scenario, so we only use AUROC as the evaluation standard for two classes of imbalanced problems.

4.3   Experimental Procedure

In practice, in order to avoid the influence of different units and ranges of different dimensional features on the classification, it is necessary to standardize the features first. We use z-score standardization in our experiment

$$Z_i = \frac{X_i - E(X_i)}{\sqrt{D(X_i)}}, \tag{16}$$

where, X_i denotes the original i-dimensional sample feature, Z_i represents the i-th dimensional sample feature after standardization, $E(X_i)$ is the mean of the i-th feature samples, $\sqrt{D(X_i)}$ is the standard deviation of the i-th dimensional feature. Using Eq. (16), the original feature data can be normalized to a mean of zero and a variance of one. It makes data of different magnitudes to be converted to the same magnitude, increasing the comparability of the data. All experiments were conducted on the computer with Intel(R) Core(TM) i7-8700 CPU at 3.20 GHz, 16 GB RAM and Windows 10 64-bit Operating System running with the Matlab R2016b platform-based programs.

In the experiment, the samples are randomly divided into ten, one as the testing set, and the remaining nine as the training set. In order to ensure the fairness of the experiment, the partition of each experimental datasets is performed in the same dataset and is kept unchanged across the different algorithms, to ensure that the testing set and training set used in each algorithm are the same.

Four algorithms are compared in the experiment, which are standard KNN algorithm [4], MLMKHNN algorithm [10], Adaknn2GIHS algorithm [6] and AdaknnGIHS algorithm [6]. These four methods have been briefly introduced in the Sects. 1, 2, where MLMKHNN algorithm is an improvement of KNN algorithm, without taking into account the class imbalance problem. Adaknn2GIHS algorithm and AdaknnGIHS algorithm are proposed for class imbalance datasets to alleviate class imbalance problems, and two methods of adaptive k value are used in these two algorithms to improve the performance of classifiers. In the experiment, for the traditional KNN, the MLMKHNN and the LDMC-KNN proposed by us, the range of k value is 1–20, and each k value is cross-verified ten times to find the optimal k value, and then the corresponding classification performance is compared. For the Adaknn2GIHS algorithm and the AdaknnGIHS algorithm, since they are adaptive to select k value and have a lot of randomness.

Table 2. Comparison of classifiers in terms of Gmeans on imbalance datasets.

Dataset	KNN	LDMC-KNN	MLMKHNN	Adaknn2GIHS	AdaknnGIHS
Glass	0.2158	**0.6550**	0.2158	0.3983	0.4396
Led7digit	0.7966	**0.8945**	0.8765	0.8094	0.8199
Segment	0.9538	**0.9686**	0.9570	0.9388	0.9437
Balance	0.1428	**0.8208**	0.5282	0.5776	0.5246
Hayesroth	0.7371	**0.9786**	0.9628	0.7973	0.8044
Parkinsons	0.9362	**0.9426**	0.9362	0.9087	0.9053
Mammographic	0.6100	**0.6840**	0.5685	0.6575	0.6131
Haberman	0.5159	**0.6138**	0.4934	0.5352	0.5732
Breast	0.5708	**0.6612**	0.5998	0.5849	0.5704
German	0.6404	**0.7050**	0.5910	0.6545	0.6498
Contraceptive	0.4929	**0.5208**	0.4438	0.4750	0.4617
Tictactoc	0.7663	**0.8637**	0.8456	0.7652	0.7511
Saheart	0.5948	**0.6918**	0.6226	0.6498	0.6450
Diabetes	0.6786	**0.7544**	0.7267	0.7119	0.7056
Pima	0.7290	**0.7481**	0.7105	0.7175	0.7108
Cloud	0.9653	**0.9780**	0.9552	0.9572	0.9545
Spambase	0.9082	**0.9281**	0.9267	0.8970	0.9000

Table 3. Comparison of classifiers in terms of AUROC for two classes of imbalance datasets.

Dataset	KNN	LDMC-KNN	MLMKHNN	Adaknn2GIHS	AdaknnGIHS
Glass	0.5679	**0.7036**	0.5567	0.5707	0.6428
Led7digit	0.8523	**0.8976**	0.8854	0.8495	0.8564
Segment	0.9550	**0.9688**	0.9583	0.9394	0.9442
Hayesroth	0.8058	**0.9796**	0.9652	0.8539	0.8543
Parkinsons	0.9391	**0.9436**	0.9391	0.9115	0.9088
Mammographic	0.6503	**0.6897**	0.5792	0.6647	0.6254
Haberman	0.6150	**0.6418**	0.5845	0.5800	0.6004
Breast	0.6153	**0.6703**	0.6335	0.6019	0.5914
German	0.6524	**0.7074**	0.6234	0.6575	0.6543
Tictactoc	0.7905	**0.8712**	0.8551	0.7756	0.7611
Saheart	0.6432	**0.6959**	0.6481	0.6586	0.6548
Diabetes	0.6986	**0.7574**	0.7340	0.7226	0.7096
Pima	0.7336	**0.7517**	0.7093	0.7212	0.7156
Cloud	0.9657	**0.9781**	0.9558	0.9615	0.9550
Spambase	0.9084	**0.9282**	0.9270	0.8970	0.9003

We repeated the experiment ten times, and conducted cross validation ten times for each experiment, then take the average result as the basis for comparison.

Table 2 shows the Gmeans performance for 17 imbalanced datasets. We can find that the algorithm proposed in this paper is always better than and far superior to the other four algorithms on the comparison datasets. Table 3 shows the performance comparison of five classifiers in terms of AUROC for two classes of imbalanced datasets. It can also be seen that our proposed method has obvious advantages. This is because we not only consider the distance and location distribution of each class of samples relative to the unknown samples, but also consider the problem of class imbalance.

Table 4. Comparison of classifiers in terms of accuracy on balance datasets.

Dataset	KNN	LDMC-KNN	MLMKHNN	Adaknn2GIHS	AdaknnGIHS
Sonar	0.9048	**0.9286**	0.9190	0.8476	0.8667
Waveform3	0.8520	**0.8548**	0.8402	0.8436	0.8476
Ringnorm	0.7511	**0.9431**	0.9296	0.6420	0.7286

What's more, to demonstrate that our algorithm is equally applicable to class-balanced datasets, we use three class-balanced datasets for a simple illustration (Because the algorithm proposed in this paper is mainly to solve the classes imbalance problem, we will not discuss the classes balance datasets too much here). Table 4 shows the classification accuracy of five algorithms on three balanced datasets, We can see that for class balanced datasets, although the advantages of our algorithm are not as great as it is for class imbalanced datasets, it is generally superior to the other four methods.

Table 5. The running times(s) of the five algorithms on different datasets.

Dataset	KNN	LDMC-KNN	MLMKHNN	Adaknn2GIHS	AdaknnGIHS
Ringnorm	**3.2252**	5.1621	6.5298	32.4742	32.3622
Waveform3	**1.4002**	2.3725	3.3218	14.5838	15.2613
Sonar	**0.0034**	0.0070	0.0224	0.0853	0.2596
Spambase	**1.3189**	2.0880	2.6676	13.2528	13.9233
Cloud	**0.0601**	0.1032	0.1924	0.8012	0.9646
Pima	**0.0341**	0.0605	0.1255	0.5228	0.7007
Diabetes	**0.0337**	0.0598	0.1252	0.5184	0.6896
Saheart	**0.0127**	0.0240	0.0616	0.2426	0.4188
Tictactoc	**0.0529**	0.0919	0.1761	0.7254	0.8894
Contraceptive	**0.1209**	0.2136	0.4039	1.6684	0.8198
German	**0.0594**	0.1022	0.1890	0.8433	1.0217
Breast	**0.0050**	0.0102	0.0319	0.1231	0.2868
Haberman	**0.0059**	0.0117	0.0352	0.1362	0.3060
Parkinsons	**0.0027**	0.0059	0.0208	0.0851	0.2523
Hayesroth	**0.0020**	0.0052	0.0226	0.0683	0.2367
Balance	**0.0233**	0.0457	0.1194	0.3773	0.5474
Segment	**0.3044**	0.5037	0.7295	3.3785	3.6780
Led7digit	**0.0150**	0.0279	0.0675	0.2579	0.4449
Glass	**0.0032**	0.0069	0.0228	0.0853	0.2701

Finally, we analyze the complexity of the algorithm. Table 5 shows the running times of the five algorithms on different data sets, running time is measured in seconds. As we can see, the running time of our algorithm is only longer than the standard KNN algorithm, and the difference is very small. This is because our algorithm is compared with the standard KNN algorithm, it just has an extra work on the calculation of Eqs. (12) and (13). Although it seems that our algorithm has a loop nesting, it actually splits the entire large training set T into $classNum$ small subset T_i for calculation. Therefore, the amount of computation is not much different from the standard KNN. The running time of the MLMKHNN algorithm is slightly larger because it calculates multiple local mean vectors to calculate the harmonic average distance. The Adaknn2GIHS algorithm and the AdaknnGIHS algorithm introduce a relatively complex training stage. This training phase itself requires running KNN algorithms many times. Therefore, the Adaknn2GIHS algorithm and AdaknnGIHS algorithm require much longer running time.

5   Conclusions

In this paper, we propose an improved KNN algorithm based on combining local distance mean and centroid for imbalanced datasets. This method not only considers the distance from the unknown sample to each class, but also considers the position of the unknown sample in each class. In addition, the problem of class imbalance is solved by taking out different number of samples from different classes.

To evaluate the performance of the proposed LDMC-KNN algorithm, we compare it with the standard KNN and three state-of-the-art KNN-based approaches. The experiment was performed on the datasets of UCI database. Experimental results show that the performance (Gmeans and AUROC) of our proposed algorithm is far better than any of the other four algorithms on the imbalanced datasets. For the balanced datasets, our algorithm is also superior to other algorithms of interest in accuracy. Further, we compared the running times of the five algorithms. The experimental results show that the running time of our algorithm is not much different from the standard KNN algorithm, but it is obviously shorter than any of the other three improved KNN algorithms, demonstrating the advantages of our algorithm.

References

1. Wu, X., Zuo, W., Lin, L., Jia, W., Zhang, D.: F-SVM: combination of feature transformation and SVM learning via convex relaxation. IEEE Trans. Neural Netw. Learn. Syst. **29**(11), 5185–5199 (2018)
2. Safavian, S.R., Landgrebe, D.: A survey of decision tree classifier methodology. IEEE Trans. Syst. Man Cybern. **21**(3), 660–674 (1991)
3. Jiang, L., Zhang, L., Li, C., Wu, J.: A correlation-based feature weighting filter for Naive Bayes. IEEE Trans. Knowl. Data Eng. **31**(2), 201–213 (2019)
4. Cover, T.M., Hart, P.E.: Nearest neighbor pattern classification. IEEE Trans. Inf. Theory **13**(10), 21–27 (1967)
5. Wu, X., et al.: Top 10 algorithms in data mining. Knowl. Inf. Syst. **14**(1), 1–37 (2008)

6. Mullick, S.S., Datta, S., Das, S.: Adaptive learning-based k-nearest neighbor classifiers with resilience to class imbalance. IEEE Trans. Neural Netw. Learn. Syst. **29**(11), 5713–5725 (2018)
7. García-Pedrajas, N., Romero del Castillo, J.A. Cerruela-García, G.: A proposal for local k values for k-nearest neighbor rule. IEEE Trans. Neural Netw. Learn. Syst. **28**(2), 470–475 (2017)
8. Zeng, Y., Yang, Y., Zhao, L.: Pseudo nearest neighbor rule for pattern classification. Pattern Recogn. Lett. **36**(2), 3587–3595 (2009)
9. Mitani, Y., Hamamoto, Y.: A local mean-based nonparametric classifier. Pattern Recogn. Lett. **27**(10), 1151–1159 (2006)
10. Pan, Z., Wang, Y., Ku, W.: A new k-harmonic nearest neighbor classifier based on the multi-local means. Expert Syst. Appl. **67**, 115–125 (2017)
11. Japkowicz, N.: The class imbalance problem: significance and strategies. In: Proceedings of the 2000 International Conference on Artificial Intelligence: Special Track on Inductive Learning, Las Vegas, pp. 111–117 (2000)
12. Chawla, N.V., Bowyer, K.W., Hall, L.O., Philip Kegelmeyer, W.: SMOTE: synthetic minority over-sampling technique. J. Artif. Intell. Res. **16**(1), 321–357 (2002)
13. He, H., Bai, Y., Garcia, E.A., Li, S.: ADASYN: adaptive synthetic sampling approach for imbalanced learning. In: IEEE International Joint Conference on Neural Networks, pp. 1322–1328. IEEE, Hong Kong (2008)
14. Zhang, X., Li, Y., Kotagiri, R., Wu, L., Tari, Z., Cheriet, M.: KRNN: k rare-class nearest neighbour classification. Pattern Recogn. **62**, 33–44 (2017)
15. Dubey, H., Pudi, V.: Class based weighted k-nearest neighbor over imbalance dataset. In: Pei, J., Tseng, V.S., Cao, L., Motoda, H., Xu, G. (eds.) PAKDD 2013. LNCS (LNAI), vol. 7819, pp. 305–316. Springer, Heidelberg (2013). https://doi.org/10.1007/978-3-642-37456-2_26
16. Li, Y., Zhang, X.: Improving k nearest neighbor with exemplar generalization for imbalanced classification. In: Huang, J.Z., Cao, L., Srivastava, J. (eds.) PAKDD 2011. LNCS (LNAI), vol. 6635, pp. 321–332. Springer, Heidelberg (2011). https://doi.org/10.1007/978-3-642-20847-8_27
17. Liu, W., Chawla, S.: Class confidence weighted kNN algorithms for imbalanced data sets. In: Huang, J.Z., Cao, L., Srivastava, J. (eds.) PAKDD 2011. LNCS (LNAI), vol. 6635, pp. 345–356. Springer, Heidelberg (2011). https://doi.org/10.1007/978-3-642-20847-8_29
18. Dua, D., Graff, C.: UCI machine learning repository (2019)
19. Zhang, X., Li, Y.: A positive-biased nearest neighbour algorithm for imbalanced classification. In: Pei, J., Tseng, V.S., Cao, L., Motoda, H., Xu, G. (eds.) PAKDD 2013. LNCS (LNAI), vol. 7819, pp. 293–304. Springer, Heidelberg (2013). https://doi.org/10.1007/978-3-642-37456-2_25

Content Recommendation Algorithm Based on Double Lists in Heterogeneous Network

Jianing Chen$^{(\boxtimes)}$, Xi Li, Hong Ji, and Heli Zhang

Key Laboratory of Universal Wireless Communications,
Ministry of Education, Beijing University of Posts and Telecommunications,
Beijing, People's Republic of China
{chenjianing,lixi,jihong,zhangheli}@bupt.edu.cn

Abstract. Applying recommendation algorithms in mobile edge caching can further improve the utilization of the caching and relieve the pressure of the backhaul links. The key is to capture accurate user preferences which are usually influenced by the user's request record and current request. In this paper, we propose a content recommendation algorithm based on both history request record and current interest. The content, user preferences and user's requests are modeled as vectors from multiple content dimensions. Based on user's request record, we capture the user preferences vector (Pre-Vector) by using the maximum likelihood estimation. The Pre-Vector accurately reflects user preference but has hysteresis. The user current request vector (Req-Vector) can reflect the user's current interest but its accuracy is not stable. We propose the preference-based recommendation list and the request-based recommendation list based on the Pre-Vector and the Req-Vector respectively. In order to ensure the accuracy of the recommendation list, the final recommendation list is generated based on the Pre-Vector and the Req-Vector's cosine similarity. The simulation results show that, the proposed algorithm has improved caching hit rate compared with existing recommendation algorithms.

Keywords: Recommendation algorithm · User preferences · Maximum likelihood estimate · Multiple content dimensions

1 Introduction

Soaring mobile data traffic presents a big challenge for the 5th-generation (5G) mobile communication system. According to the Ericsson Mobile Report 2019 [1], the global average monthly mobile data traffic has reached 29.0 EB in 2019 Q1, and will reach nearly 164.5 EB at the end of 2024. Mobile edge caching [2,3] is one of the promising solutions to solve mobile data traffic congestion. It stores content at the edge of the networks, which shortens the physical distance between users and content, and then alleviates the pressure of the backhaul.

© ICST Institute for Computer Sciences, Social Informatics and Telecommunications Engineering 2020
Published by Springer Nature Switzerland AG 2020. All Rights Reserved
H. Gao et al. (Eds.): ChinaCom 2019, LNICST 313, pp. 140–153, 2020.
https://doi.org/10.1007/978-3-030-41117-6_12

Applying recommendation algorithms in the mobile edge caching is a viable solution to further improve the caching utilization and user experience, and it will also relieve the pressure of the backhaul links. In a heterogeneous network of 5G, in addition to the macro base station (MBS), many small base stations (SBS) [4,5] are densely deployed, which makes the caching space in the network edges much larger compared to the traditional cellular network. This provides more options for content recommendations, which requires an effective algorithm for higher recommendation hit rate.

The research of the recommended algorithm originated from the Internet field in the 1990s. Later, with the prosperity of e-commerce, the research of recommended algorithms has ushered in a boom. Jiang et al. [6] analyzed the key technology related to personalized recommendation in distance education, and proposed multiple recommendation algorithms. Felfernig et al. [7] analyzed the applicability of group recommendation to requirements prioritization, and made the application of group decision heuristics in the context of requirements prioritization. Shaikh et al. [8] listed various limitations of the current recommendation methods and believed that integration of semantic in recommendation techniques could provide better recommendation with proposed system.

In general, the design of the recommendation algorithm inevitably takes into account user preferences [9,10]. Also, many researchers have studied the content recommendation algorithm with additional factors, such as the distance between the user and the content, the user's social relationship, the base station's limited storage space, the association between multiple contents and so on. Wang et al. [11] considered the social relationship of the users, proposed a recommendation system for cached-enabled mobile social network, which could maximize the traffic offloading ratio. Some researchers considered the content association in mobile edge caching recommendation. Kastanakis et al. [12] proposed a content-related approach that enabled joint caching and recommendation in mobile edge caching. Some researchers apply reinforcement learning to the caching recommendation algorithm. Guo et al. [13] developed a Q-learning based algorithm to dynamically replace and recommend the files in the caching of the BS. Yang et al. [14] jointly optimized content caching and recommendation at BSs to maximize the caching gain, and proposed a hierarchical iterative algorithm to solve the optimization problem.

The recommendation algorithm can be classified into two types: the memory recommendation algorithm and the memoryless recommendation algorithm. The memory recommendation algorithm mainly summarizes the user preference based on the user's long-term request record as the recommendation basis. The memoryless recommendation algorithm extracts keywords or key information for the user's current request, and then recommend contents with the similar keywords. Time-varying user preferences make the estimation of user preferences have hysteresis in the condition of only using the memory recommendation algorithm. While only using the memoryless recommendation algorithm to estimate the user preferences has inaccuracy, especially when the user record is very limited. There is very attractive requirement to combine these two types of recommended algorithms to overcome hysteresis and inaccuracy, and then improve the utilization of the caching contents and user experiences.

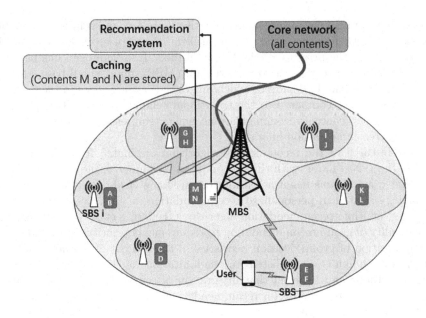

Fig. 1. System model.

In this paper, we investigate the time-varying features of user preference in heterogeneous network, and propose a content recommendation algorithm based on double lists (CRADL) to optimize the recommended hit rate. We assume several SBSs and a MBS collaboratively store and recommend contents to the user in a typical scenario. The optimization problem to maximize the caching recommended hit ratio is analyzed and formulated. The user preference vector (Pre-Vector) is captured by maximum likelihood estimation of user's request record. Then we design the preference-based recommendation list and the request-based recommendation list based on Pre-Vector and the user current request vector (Req-Vector). In order to ensure the accuracy of the recommendation, we need to find a balance between Pre-Vector and Req-Vector. Based on their cosine similarity, we selectively integrate the two lists into one list and recommend to the user. Simulation results show that the proposed algorithm has the better performance in the hit rate compared to the existing caching algorithms in heterogeneous network.

2   System Model

As shown in Fig. 1, we deploy a number of BSs in a region. The MBS located in the middle of the region. The MBS manages these SBSs and knows what content is cached in these SBSs. And we install the recommendation system application in the MBS. We make these BSs collaboratively store the popular content. The MBS manages $m - 1$ SBSs in a the region, all BSs are represented by sets $S = \{s_1, s_2, s_3, s_4, ..., s_m\}$. The user will select the closest BS to access. To simplify, we set the caching space size of each BS is c. The core network has all the contents, assuming that the total number of the contents is k, these contents are represented by $F = \{F_1, F_2, F_3, F_4, ..., F_k\}$. In the case of multiple users, the probability that these contents are requested is subject to the Zipf distribution. The probability P_i of the file ranked i is requested by users is:

$$P_i = \frac{1/i^r}{\sum_{p=1}^{k}(1/p^r)} \tag{1}$$

where r is the zipf index, $r > 0$.

To simplify, we set the size of each content is ξ, the BS j can store l files, the cache space of BS j is always bigger than or equal to the total size of the contents it stores. Then we get a constraint:

$$C1 : \sum^{l} \xi \leqslant c \tag{2}$$

And in reality, the number of cached contents of these m BSs is much smaller than the number of contents of the entire network. We get the another constraint:

$$C2 : mc \leqslant C_{network} \tag{3}$$

where $C_{network}$ is the total number of contents in the core network.

For a single user, we believe that there is a strong connection with the user requests is the user preferences. In order to fully describe user preferences, we intend to measure user preferences from D dimensions, the user preferences vector is represented as: $U = \{u_1, u_2, u_3, u_4, ..., u_D\}$. Similarly, the content F_j vector is modeled as: $F_j = \{f_1, f_2, f_3, f_4, ..., f_D\}$.

3   Problem Formulation

For individual users, the requesting content is more susceptible to their personal preferences. Some users like to listen to Hip-pop, while others like light music and so on. In [15], the author measures a content from multiple dimensions, quantifies the content in each dimension. And the user's request is normally distributed in each dimension. Inspired by [15], we decide to model the user's request as: in the case of unchanging user preferences, the content requested by the user follows a normal distribution in each dimension and the mean of the vectors of these request records is equal to the user preferences vector. Suppose the user sends x requests ($q = \{q_1, q_2, q_3, ..., q_x\}$) with the same user preferences, we get third constraint:

$$C3 : \{u_1, u_2, u_3, u_4, ..., u_D\} = \frac{\sum_{i=1}^{x} q_i}{x}$$
$$= \frac{\sum_{i=1}^{x} \{f_1, f_2, f_3, f_4, ..., f_D\}_i}{x} \tag{4}$$

The user preferences are time-varying. We quantify the user preference duration as the number x of requests, x is a random positive integer value. After the user sends x requests, the user preferences may change to a new random user preferences. The probability that the user preference changes is β, $0 \leqslant \beta \leqslant 1$.

There are two situations that trigger the recommendation system. One is that when the user finishes watching a video or listens to a song, the recommended system in MBS will recommend relevant content to the user. The other is that when the content requested by the user is not stored in the BS and the collaborative BSs, the recommended system will recommend the cached content to the user.

To recommend the user what the user wants, we need to define the similarity between the content. The similarity between content i and content j is defined as:

$$P_{i,j} = \frac{F_i \cdot F_j}{\|F_i\| \cdot \|F_j\|} \tag{5}$$

The user acceptance of recommended content is related to content similarity and content popularity. When the cached content j is recommended to the user, the probability that a user accepts content j is defined as:

$$P_{u,j} = \omega * \left(\frac{U \cdot F_j}{\|U\| \cdot \|F_j\|}\right)^\varphi \tag{6}$$

where ω is the popularity impact coefficient, $\omega = \left(\frac{P_j}{P_1}\right)^\phi$. ϕ is the Popularity impact index, $\phi = 0$ means the user is not affected by popularity. φ is the cosine matching impact index, $\varphi = 0$ means the user is only affected by popularity. $\frac{U \cdot F_j}{\|U\| \cdot \|F_j\|}$ is the user preferences vector and the recommended content vector's cosine matching value.

The recommendation system will recommend z cached contents to the user in the form of a list. In order to conform to human aesthetics, generally 3 to 8 contents are appropriate. Then the probability that the user accepts the recommendation can be expressed as:

$$P_{U_t,list} = 1 - \prod_{i=1}^{z}(1 - p_{ut,i})$$

$$= 1 - \prod_{i=1}^{z}\left[1 - \left(\frac{P_i}{P_1}\right)^\phi * \left(\frac{U_t \cdot F_i}{\|U_t\| \cdot \|F_i\|}\right)^\varphi\right] \tag{7}$$

where U_t is the current user preferences. We hope to maximize the effectiveness of the cached content, that is, to find the recommended hit rate maximum, $max\{P_{U_t,list}\}$.

4   Content Recommendation Algorithm Based on Double Lists

4.1   User Preferences Estimating

To maximize $P_{U_t,list}$, we need to estimate the user preference as accurately as possible from user's records. The estimated user preferences is represented by U_o and it is generated by the user's app, and it is sent to the MBS when a request is sent. Suppose the mobile app counts the user's recent N requests. In any of these D dimensions, the quantized values of these requests are normally distributed. We take the i-th dimension of the N records, denoted by $Q_{N,i} = \{f_{1,i}, f_{2,i}, f_{3,i}, ..., f_{N,i}\}$.

The Maximum Likelihood Estimation (MLE) can be used to estimate the parameters of the model. The goal of MLE is to find a set of parameters that maximize the probability that the model will produce observations:

$$argmax\left\{p(Q_{N,i}; \mu_i, \sigma^2)\right\} \tag{8}$$

where $p(Q_{N,i}; \mu_i, \sigma^2)$ is a likelihood function, indicating the probability of observation data appearing under the parameter μ_i. We assume that each observation is independent and then:

$$p(f_{1,i}, f_{2,i}, f_{3,i}, ..., f_{N,i}; \mu_i) = \prod_{k=1}^{N} p(f_{k,i}; \mu_i, \sigma^2) \tag{9}$$

For convenience, Eq. 9 becomes a logarithmic function form (it obeys normal distribution):

$$p(Q_{N,i}; \mu_i, \sigma^2) = ln(p(Q_{N,i}; \mu_i, \sigma^2))$$
$$= -\frac{Nln(2\pi)}{2} - \frac{Nln(\sigma^2)}{2} - \frac{1}{2\sigma^2}\sum_{k=1}^{N}(f_{k,i} - \mu_i)^2 \tag{10}$$

Find the derivative of Eq. 10 and let it equal 0:

$$\frac{\partial ln(p(Q_{N,i}; \mu_i, \sigma^2))}{\partial \mu} = \frac{1}{2\sigma^2}\sum_{k=1}^{N}(f_{k,i} - \mu_i) = 0 \tag{11}$$

Finally, we get:

$$\mu_i^\star = \overline{Q_{N,i}} = \frac{1}{N}\sum_{k=1}^{N}f_{k,i} \tag{12}$$

Similarly, we can get the values of D dimensions and get the estimated vector μ:

$$\mu = \{\mu_1^\star, \mu_2^\star, \mu_3^\star, ..., \mu_D^\star\} \tag{13}$$

There may be highly deviating requests in this set of data, which would be removed by using the Grubbs criteria. After removing highly deviating requests, calculate μ again, and that is the estimated user preferences U_o (Pre-Vector):

$$U_o = \{\mu_1, \mu_2, \mu_3, ..., \mu_D\} \tag{14}$$

4.2   Content Recommendation Algorithm Based on Double Lists

Now we have U_o (Pre-Vector), and the quantized current request is represented as F_c (Req-Vector). After the MBS obtains the user's request F_c (Req-Vector) and U_o (Pre-Vector), the MBS calculates the cosine similarity degree between U_o and all cached content. According to the descending order of the cosine similarity degree, we can get the preference-based recommendation list (P-list). Similarly, we use the same method to calculate the cosine similarity degree between F_c and all cached content, finally we have the request-based recommendation list (R-list). The two lists is just the initial formation of the recommended lists. When the requested content belongs to hot content, we are not sure whether the user likes the type of content or just the hot content. We introduce popularity to tailor the two lists after matching. The popularity value exists only on the network side and the MBS, and the MBS periodically updates the popularity value of the content cached in the region. The matching degree is calculated as follows:

$$
\begin{aligned}
P - list &: p_{uo,j} = \omega * \left(\frac{U_o \cdot F_j}{\|U_o\| \cdot \|F_j\|}\right)^{\varphi} \\
R - list &: p_{fi,j} = \omega * \left(\frac{F_i \cdot F_j}{\|F_i\| \cdot \|F_j\|}\right)^{\varphi}
\end{aligned}
\tag{15}
$$

After that, we get two lists. We descend the P-list: $\{p_{uo,1}, p_{uo,2}, ...\}$, $P_{uo,1}$ indicates the matching degree of the content with the highest matching degree in P-list. Similarly, we have the R-list: $\{p_{fi,1}, p_{fi,2}, ...\}$.

The cosine similarity between the user preferences vector U_0 and the user's requested content F_i is:

$$q_{uo,fi} = \frac{U_o \cdot F_i}{\|U_o\| \cdot \|F_i\|} \tag{16}$$

If the user preferences vector U_o is similar to the request F_i, $q_{uo,fi}$ is high, we would consider the P-list as a recommended reference. If the user preferences vector U_o is far from the request F_i, $q_{uo,fi}$ would be low, we would consider the R-list as a recommended reference. In order to flexibly recommend caching to users, we need to merge the two lists.

Knowing that a recommended list contains z content, we divide the cosine similarity of U_o and F_i evenly into $z + 1$ levels. In this paper, we assume that a recommendation list contains 4 content, $z = 4$. According to different cosine matching degrees, we take N_{uo} top contents from U-list and N_{fi} top contents from R-list, to form a new recommendation list, where $N_{uo} + N_{fi} = z$.

For example, When the cosine similarity is in level V, $0.8 \leqslant q_{uo,fi} \leqslant 1$, we believe that the user preferences have not changed at this time, and still use the top four contents of P-list as recommendations. As shown in Table 1.

It should be pointed out that in order to avoid duplication, if a content is in the top ranking in both lists, then after the content is taken in U-list, the content is not considered in R-list.

Table 1. The division of $q_{uo,fi}$ ($z = 4$)

Level	Level V	Level VI	Level III	Level II	Level I
$q_{uo,fi}$	$[0.8, 1]$	$[0.6, 0.8)$	$[0.6, 0.4)$	$[0.4, 0.6)$	$[0, 0.2)$
$N_{uo}:N_{fi}$	4:0	3:1	2:2	1:3	0:4

After synthesizing the two lists into one list, we can get the theoretical recommendation acceptance probability:

$$P_{list} = 1 - \prod_{j=1}^{z} (1 - p_{list,j})$$
$$= 1 - [\prod_{j=1}^{N_{uo}} (1 - p_{uo,j})] * [\prod_{k=1}^{N_{fi}} (1 - p_{fi,k})]$$

(17)

5   Simulation Results and Discussions

In this section, we will fully evaluate the performance of the CRADL from different angles. And we will analyze the impact of several important parameters on CRADL performance. For comparison, we also simulate the other three recommended algorithms: the hottest caching recommendation algorithm (Hot-Algorithm), caching recommendation algorithm based on user preference (Pre-Based) and caching recommendation algorithm based on user's current request (Req-Based). The Hot-Algorithm means that the MBS would always recommend the hottest contents to the user. The Pre-Based means that the MBS would recommend contents to the user only based on the user's preference. The Req-Based means that the MBS would recommend contents to the user only based on the user's current request.

We consider setting parameters in the range of $200 * 200$ m: only 1 user, number of BSs $M = 7$, and each BS's default caching capacity $c = 30$ contents. This creates a relatively dense network in which the SBSs are randomly distributed. The core network has all the contents, $C_{network} = 500$ $contents$. The Zipf index is set to $r = 0.9$ by default. The duration of user preference is quantified as: the number of requests to continue in the case of constant preference, the number of requests is random values 1–20. The probability that the user preference changes is $\beta = 0.1$. The Pre-Based algorithm and CRADL consider $N = 10$ user historical requests. We set the Popularity impact index $\phi = 1$ and the cosine matching impact index $\varphi = 1$. And we assume that the user does not move and selects the nearest base station access.

In order to get close to the reality, we followed the qqmusic's classification to the music: electronic music, pop music, Chinese Style Music, ballad, Hip-Hop, country music and so on, a total of 15 categories, which means vector dimension $D = 15$. We assume that the core network has a total of 500 contents, $k = 500$. And we quantified the top 500 songs of qqmusic and got 500 15-dimensional vectors of the top 500 songs. The quantitative criteria are as Table 2 (in terms of a single dimension such as Hip-Hop).

Table 2. The quantitative criteria (Hip-Pop as an example)

Degree	Not Hip-Pop	A little Hip-Pop	Normal Hip-Pop	Very Hip-Pop	Super Hip-Pop
Values	0–0.2	0.2–0.4	0.4–0.6	0.6–0.8	0.8–1

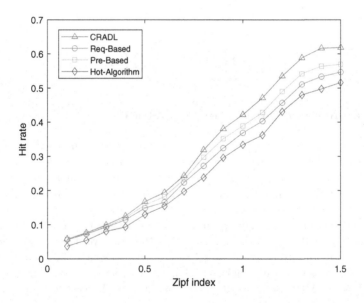

Fig. 2. The recommended hit rate changes as the Zipf index changes.

Figure 2 shows that as the Zipf index changes, the probability that the recommendation list is accepted by the user is on the rise. Because as the Zipf index increases, the probability of users accepting recommended content is also increasing, which results in an increase in the hit rate of the four methods. When calculating user preferences, Pre-Based refers to the user's last 10 requests, while Req-Based simply treats the request content vector (F_c) as a user preference vector. So the user preferences calculated by Pre-Based are closer to real user preferences than Req-Based, thus the Pre-Based's hit rate is higher than the Req-Based's. And CRADL is combines the advantages of the Pre-Based and Req-Based, so CRADL has the highest hit rate.

The Req-Based algorithm takes into account the user's current request, so the acceptance probability of the Req-Based algorithm is larger than the Hot-Algorithm. The Pre-Based algorithm considers the user $N = 10$ historical requests, the Pre-Based algorithm can accurately capture the user's preference, so it has higher hit rate. And CRADL has always the highest hit rate. Because CRADL considers the user's current request and the user preference, the appropriate caching recommendation list can be flexibly generated when the current request differs from the user's preferences.

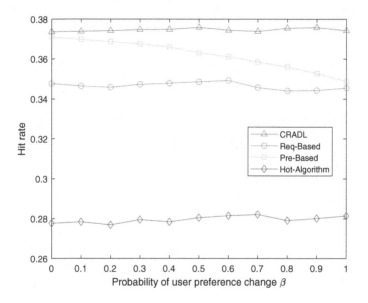

Fig. 3. The recommended hit rate changes as the probability of user preference change β changes.

Figure 3 shows that as the user preference change probability β changes, the probability that the hit rate of the recommended list also changes. Both Req-Based algorithm and Hot-Algorithm are memoryless, so changes in the probability of change in user preference can't affect the performance of Req-Based algorithm and Hot-Algorithm. For the Pre-Based algorithm, as the increase in β means that the user preference changes more frequently, the user preference estimated by the historical request matches the current request less. So the hit rate of Pre-Based algorithm would drop, from 37.1% to 34.8%. CRADL can consider both user preference and the current request, it can adapt to changes in user preference rate and maintain a 37–38% caching recommendation hit rate.

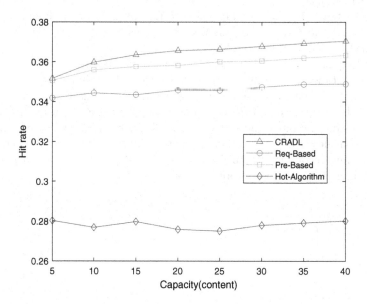

Fig. 4. The recommended hit rate changes as BS's caching capacity c changes.

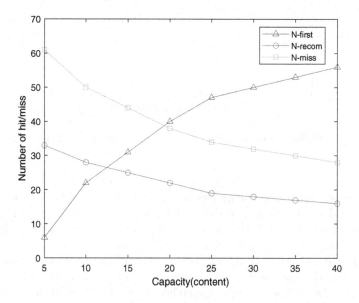

Fig. 5. The caching first hit rate changes as BS's caching capacity c changes.

Figure 4 shows that as BS's caching capacity c changes, the probability that the hit rate of the recommended list changes slowly. In the previous chapters, we know that the probability of acceptance of users is affected by the popularity of the content. For the content at the end of the popularity ranking, even if the cosine matching degree is high, the probability of being accepted is not high because the popularity is too low, so the content with highly popular and highly cosine-matched is easier to accept. That means, even if the caching space of the BSs is increased, the influence of the long tail effect is too small, which makes the recommended hit rate increase little.

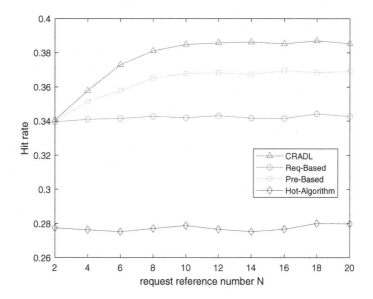

Fig. 6. The recommended hit rate changes as the number of historical records reference N changes.

But as for the number of the caching first hits (when caching recommendation system is not triggered), with the expansion of the BSs' caching space, the number of the caching first hits has a big improvement, as shown in Fig. 5. In each set of tests, the user generated 100 requests. The number of successful recommendations N_{recom} plus the number of recommended failures N_{miss} plus the number of caching first hits N_{first} equals 100, $N_{first} + N_{recom} + N_{miss} = 100$.

Figure 6 shows that as the number of user record N changes, the Pre-Based algorithm and CRADL's recommended hit rate has improved, and then stabilized. Both Req-Based algorithm and Hot-Algorithm are memoryless, so the number of historical records reference N can't affect the performance of Req-Based method and Hot-Algorithm. As can be seen from Fig. 6, when $N < 10$, the Pre-Based algorithm's hit rate and CRADL's hit rate begin to increase. When $N = 10$, the hit rate of CRADL is approximately 38.5% of the saturation value, and the saturation value of the Pre-Based algorithm is 36.9%. It can be determined that in our scenario, the accuracy of the user preference can be estimated when $N > 10$. When $\beta = 0.1$, on average, every time a user sends 10 requests, he will change his preferences once. So when $N > 1/\beta = 10$, the curves for CRADL and Pre-Based are flat.

6   Conclusion

In this paper, we studied the mobile edge caching recommendation system in heterogeneous network. In addition to popularity, the content requested by the users and the probability of the users accepting the recommended cached content were often highly correlated with their own preferences. Based on user preference and popularity, a question of maximizing the caching hit ratio was formulated. And a content recommendation algorithm based on multiple content dimensions was proposed. We quantified the user preferences, content, and requests from multiple dimensions. User preferences vector was derived by maximum likelihood estimation and Grubbs criterion. Then two recommended lists were generated based on user current request vector and user preferences vector. The preference-based recommendation list reflected the recent user preferences, the request-based recommendation list reflected the current user preferences. Finally, we merged two lists based on the two vectors' cosine matching. Compared with the other three recommended methods, the method we proposed could achieve a highest hit rate, whether there was a change in BS's capacity or a change in Zipf index or a change in probability of user preference change. In our scenario, we set the user preference change to be random, but in reality it was not. In the future work, we will explore the impact of $q_{uo,fi}$ division on the hit rate optimization problem, and we will investigate the connection of user preference to popularity, or other elements.

Acknowledgment. This work is jointly supported by National Natural Science Foundation of China (Grant No. 61771070), and the National Natural Science Foundation of China (Grant No. 61671088).

References

1. Ericsson Mobility Report 2019, June 2019. https://www.ericsson.com/en/mobility-report/reports/june-2019
2. Guo, F., Zhang, H., Ji, H., Li, X.: An efficient computation offloading management scheme in the densely deployed small cell networks with mobile edge computing. IEEE/ACM Trans. Netw. **26**(6), 2651–2664 (2018)
3. Parvez, I., Rahmati, A., Guvenc, I., Sarwat, A.I., Dai, H.: A survey on low latency towards 5G: RAN, core network and caching solutions. IEEE Commun. Surv. Tutor. **20**(4), 3098–3130 (2018)
4. Li, J., Chu, S., Shu, F., Wu, J., Jayakody, D.N.K.: Contract-based small-cell caching for data disseminations in ultra-dense cellular networks. **18**(5), 1042–1053 (2019)

5. Liu, Y., Yu, F., Li, A., Ji, H., Zhang, H., Leung, V.: Joint access and resource management for delay-sensitive transcoding in ultra-dense networks with mobile edge computing. In: 2018 IEEE International Conference on Communications (ICC), pp. 1–6 (2018)

6. Jiang, P.R.Y., Zhan, H., Zhuang, Q: Application research on personalized recommendation in distance education. In: 2010 International Conference on Computer Application and System Modeling (ICCASM 2010), vol. 13, pp. 357–360 (2010)

7. Felfernig, A., Ninaus, G.: Group recommendation algorithms for requirements prioritization. In: 2012 Third International Workshop on Recommendation Systems for Software Engineering (RSSE), pp. 59–62 (2012)

8. Shaikh, S., Rathi, S., Janrao, P.: Recommendation system in E-commerce websites: a graph based approached. In: 2017 IEEE 7th International Advance Computing Conference (IACC), pp. 931–934 (2017)

9. Chatzieleftheriou, L.E., Karaliopoulos, M., Koutsopoulos, I.: Caching-aware recommendations: Nudging user preferences towards better caching performance. In: IEEE INFOCOM 2017 - IEEE Conference on Computer Communications, pp. 1–9 (2017)

10. Sermpezis, P., Giannakas, T., Spyropoulos, T., Vigneri, L.: Soft cache hits: improving performance through recommendation and delivery of related content. IEEE J. Sel. Areas Commun. **36**(6), 1300–1313 (2018)

11. Wang, Y., Ding, M., Chen, Z., Luo, L.: Caching placement with recommendation systems for cache-enabled mobile social networks. IEEE Commun. Lett. **21**(10), 2266–2269 (2017)

12. Kastanakis, S., Sermpezis, P., Kotronis, V., Dimitropoulos, X.: CABaRet: leveraging recommendation systems for mobile edge caching. In: 2018 MECOMM, pp. 1–6 (2018)

13. Guo, K., Yang, C., Liu, T: Caching in base station with recommendation via Q-learning. In: 2017 IEEE Wireless Communications and Networking Conference (WCNC), pp. 1–6 (2017)

14. Liu, D., Yang, C.: A learning-based approach to joint content caching and recommendation at base stations. In: 2018 IEEE Global Communications Conference (GLOBECOM), pp. 1–7 (2018)

15. Lee, M., Molisch, A.F., Sastry, N., Raman, A.: Individual preference probability modeling and parameterization for video content in wireless caching networks. IEEE/ACM Trans. Netw. **27**(2), 676–690 (2019)

Research on High Precision Location Algorithm of NB Terminal Based on 5G/NB-IoT Cluster Node Information Fusion

Wei Ju$^{(\boxtimes)}$, Di He$^{(\boxtimes)}$, Xin Chen, Changqing Xu, and Wenxian Yu

Shanghai Key Laboratory of Navigation and Location-Based Services,
Shanghai Jiao Tong University, Shanghai, People's Republic of China
{15121115997,dihe,xin.chen,cqxu,wxyu}@sjtu.edu.cn

Abstract. With the development of the Internet of Things, a large number of connection requirements for sensing and control are generated. However, in wireless positioning, Narrowband Internet of Things (NB-IoT) has poor positioning accuracy which takes the cell-ID positioning method. The further integration of 5G and NB-IoT networks is expected to effectively improve the positioning accuracy of NB-IoT networks. Therefore, the high-precision positioning algorithm for researching converged networks has broad application prospects and academic significance. In order to improve the positioning accuracy of NB-IoT, based on the 5G and NB-IoT heterogeneous positioning framework, we propose to introduce a number of cluster nodes, which have the function of communicating with 5G and NB-IoT networks simultaneously. The signal bandwidth in NB-IoT network is narrow and clock synchronization is difficult to accomplish, so only DOA (Direction of Arrival) and RSSI principles can be considered. In this paper, we firstly use 5G to perform high-precision positioning of cluster nodes according to the principles of TDOA (Time Difference of Arrival). Based on the solution space $(x \pm \varepsilon_x, y \pm \varepsilon_y)$, the NB-IoT terminal is located by the cluster nodes according to the DOA and RSSI fusion method. This method helps reduce the matching time and improve the accuracy of single DOA/RSSI positioning method. Meanwhile, in the case of allowing cluster node errors, higher precision NB-IoT network positioning results can be obtained. Compared to a single NB-IoT network positioning, the final positioning accuracy of NB-IoT terminal can be improved by 80–90%.

Keywords: DOA · RSSI · Fusion positioning

1 Introduction

With the development of the Internet of Things, a large number of connection requirements for sensing and control are generated. This type of demand has low connection rate requirements, but is very sensitive to power consumption and cost, and is widely distributed and large in number. In wireless positioning, Narrowband Internet of Things (NB-IoT) has poor positioning accuracy, and cellular network has relatively high positioning accuracy with the help of TDOA, DOA information and so on. However, the

© ICST Institute for Computer Sciences, Social Informatics and Telecommunications Engineering 2020
Published by Springer Nature Switzerland AG 2020. All Rights Reserved
H. Gao et al. (Eds.): ChinaCom 2019, LNICST 313, pp. 154–167, 2020.
https://doi.org/10.1007/978-3-030-41117-6_13

current 3G/4G network cannot carry a huge number of IoT connections. The fifth generation communication system (5G) is expected to meet the needs of IoT connectivity, and the further integration of 5G and NB-IoT networks is expected to effectively improve the positioning accuracy of NB-IoT networks. Therefore, the high-precision positioning algorithm for researching converged networks has broad application prospects and academic significance.

As a sub-network of LTE, NB-IoT only supports the cell-ID positioning method [1]. The positioning accuracy of this method depends on the size of the cell, and generally exceeds 300 m. The 5G has more precise clock synchronization, ultra-wide bandwidth, and multi-antenna design. It supports TOA, TDOA, DOA and other positioning principles [2], and the positioning accuracy can reach the sub-meter level. However, 5G and NB-IoT belong to different networks. The 5G positioning information cannot be directly applied to the positioning of the NB-IoT terminal.

In order to improve the positioning accuracy of NB-IoT while preserving the low power consumption and low-cost characteristics of NB-IoT, based on the 5G and NB-IoT heterogeneous positioning framework, we propose to introduce a number of cluster nodes, which have the function of communicating with 5G and NB-IoT networks at the same time. The signal bandwidth in NB-IoT network [1] is narrow and clock synchronization is difficult to accomplish, resulting in the poor performance of TDOA algorithm then DOA and RSSI principles can be considered. The multi-antenna design of 5G in cluster nodes will be beneficial to DOA estimation. In traditional method, terminal in NB-IoT network is obtained by Cell-ID positioning method without heterogeneous positioning framework and fusion algorithm. It is believed that more positioning information can obtain more accurate positioning results. Therefore, based on the actual situation of the NB-IoT network and the new feature of the converged network, DOA and RSSI fusion algorithm is used on NB-IoT side to improve single-sided positioning performance and TDOA algorithm is used to obtain the position of cluster nodes. On the other hand, the process of solving the positioning result is a problem of solving multiple linear equations. Step-by-step positioning may result in a local optimal solution. The solution of the cluster node after the first TDOA algorithm has an error, which will affect the positioning result of the second step. In this paper, within the error range of the solution obtained in the first step, the global optimal solution is searched to obtain a more accurate positioning result. From the results, the positioning precision of this method is increased by 90% in the X direction.

The first section of this paper mainly introduces the problems of NB-IoT terminal positioning, main methods and defects, and the improved methods. In Sect. 2 the TDOA positioning model and CHAN algorithm are introduced. In Sect. 3 DOA and RSSI fusion algorithm is introduced and is compared with the single RSSI positioning method. In Sect. 4 the fusion algorithm on both sides with the DOA and RSSI fusion algorithm are compared and analyzed performance.

2 Traditional TDOA-Based Positioning on 5G Side

In this section, TDOA positioning model [3] and a general solution algorithm named CHAN [4] will be illustrated.

2.1 TDOA Positioning Model

The TDOA positioning model estimates the position of the terminal mainly by measuring the transmission time difference of the signal transmitted from the terminal to the positioning reference base station. The distance difference obtained by the transmission time difference is satisfied by a hyperbolic model which focuses on two positioning reference base stations. To get the estimated position of the terminal, it is theoretically only necessary to measure the difference in arrival time between the two groups. The intersection of the two sets of hyperbolic curves obtained is the position of the terminal we are solving. However, in practical applications, the two sets of parameters tend to be poor, so in this experiment four base stations are selected to ensure better positioning performance.

On a 2D plane, there are M base station where M is greater than or equal to 4. The base station coordinates are (x_i, y_i), where $i = 1, 2, \cdots, M$. Supposing that the terminal coordinates to be estimated are (x, y), use the first base station as a reference base station and R_i represents the distance from terminal to base station i. $R_{i,1}$ represents the difference between the distance from terminal to base station i and the distance from terminal to base station 1.

$$R_{i,1} = c\tau_{i,1} = R_i - R_1 \quad i = 2, \ldots M \tag{1}$$

where $R_i = \sqrt{(x_i - x)^2 + (y_i - y)^2}$, $i = 1, 2, \cdots, M$, c is the propagation speed of radio waves in vacuum which equals to $3 * 10^8$ m/s. $\tau_{i,1}$ is the difference between the time from terminal to base station i and the time from terminal to base station 1. The TDOA positioning model can be described as following Fig. 1.

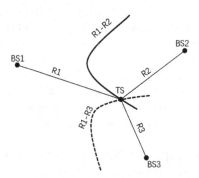

Fig. 1. TDOA positioning model

After applying linearization transform to formula (1), formula (2) is derived as follows:

$$\left(R_{i,1} + R_1\right)^2 = R_{i,1}^2 + 2R_{i,1}R_1 + R_1^2 = x_i^2 + y_i^2 - 2x_ix - 2y_iy + x^2 + y^2 \tag{2}$$

Let $K_i = x_i^2 + y_i^2$, $x_{i,1} = x_i - x_1$, $y_{i,1} = y_i - y_1$, then we get:

$$x_ix + y_iy + R_{i,1}R_1 = \frac{1}{2}\left(K_i - K_1 - R_{i,1}^2\right) \tag{3}$$

In formula (3) x and y are unknown and remain to be solved. Thus it can be thought as a set of linear formulas. The solution of the formulas is the location of the terminal to be estimated.

2.2 CHAN Algorithm

The CHAN algorithm is one of the classic algorithms based on TDOA measurement parameters.

Starting from formula (3), we can change it into linear formula (4)

$$G_a z_a = h \tag{4}$$

where $G_a = - \begin{pmatrix} x_{2,1} & y_{2,1} & R_{2,1} \\ x_{3,1} & y_{3,1} & R_{3,1} \\ x_{4,1} & y_{4,1} & R_{4,1} \end{pmatrix}$, $z_a = (x, y, R_1)^T$, $h = \frac{1}{2} \begin{pmatrix} R_{2,1}^2 - K_2 + K_1 \\ R_{3,1}^2 - K_2 + K_1 \\ R_{4,1}^2 - K_2 + K_1 \end{pmatrix}$. We

define Z_a^0 as the value in the case of zero noise. Then the error vector can be described as:

$$e = h - G_a Z_a^0 \tag{5}$$

Supposing that e is statistically approximate to a Gaussian distribution and its covariance matrix exists, then we can get:

$$\psi = E\left(ee^T\right) = c^2 BQB \tag{6}$$

where $B = \text{diag}\{R_2^0, R_3^0, R_4^0\}$, Q is the covariance matrix of noise vector which obeys Gaussian distribution.

Suppose the elements in z_a are independent of each other. After weighing the error of data in z_a, the problem becomes a weighted least squares problem. The formula to be solved becomes formula (7):

$$\left(G_a^T \psi G_a\right) z_a = G_a^T \psi h \tag{7}$$

The least squares estimate of z is

$$z_a = \left(G_a^T \psi^{-1} G_a\right)^{-1} G_a^T \psi^{-1} h \tag{8}$$

When the distance from terminal to base station is quite long, ψ can be substitute by Q. An approximation of z_a can be obtained as formula (9):

$$z_a \approx \tilde{z}_a = \left(G_a^T Q^{-1} G_a\right)^{-1} G_a^T Q^{-1} h \tag{9}$$

From the $\tilde{z}_a$ calculated by formula (9), the B matrix is recalculated. According to formula (6) ψ is calculated which is unknown before. Now formula (8) is available and the first estimate of z_a is obtained.

Use the first estimate of z_a to construct a set of error formula to obtain the second estimate of z_a as formula (10):

$$\begin{cases} z_{a,1} = x^0 + e_1 \\ z_{a,2} = y^0 + e_2 \\ z_{a,3} = R^0 + e_3 \end{cases} \tag{10}$$

where $z_{a,i}$ is one component of z_a and e_i is the estimate error of z_a. Then the second estimate of z_a is obtained by formula (11):

$$z_{a1} = \left(G_{a1}^T \psi_1^{-1} G_{a1} \right)^{-1} G_{a1}^T \psi_1^{-1} h_1 \tag{11}$$

Where $z_{a1} = \begin{pmatrix} (x - x_1)^2 \\ (y - y_1)^2 \end{pmatrix}$, $G_{a1} = \begin{pmatrix} 1 & 0 \\ 0 & 1 \\ 1 & 1 \end{pmatrix}$, $h_1 = \begin{pmatrix} (z_{a,1} - x_1)^2 \\ (z_{a,2} - y_1)^2 \\ (z_{a,3})^2 \end{pmatrix}$, $\psi_1 = $

$4 B_1 cov(z_a) B_1$, $B_1 = diag\{x^0 - x_1, y^0 - y_1, R_1^0\}$, $cov(z_a) = \left(G_a^{0T} \psi^{-1} G_a^0 \right)^{-1}$.

Finally, the estimate solution of terminal's position is as formula (12):

$$(x, y)^T = \pm \sqrt{z_{a1}} + (x_1, y_1)^T \tag{12}$$

Traditional TDOA-based positioning requires signals with high precision clock resolution and complex clock synchronization and has poor performance at NLOS scene [5–7], which is its drawbacks and limitations. NB-IoT network doesn't support such characteristic without high precision clock or synchronization. That's why DOA and RSSI fusion algorithm [8–10] is used in NB-IoT network rather than TDOA.

3   Novel DOA and RSSI Fusion Method on NB-IoT Side

3.1   DOA Positioning Model

Assuming that there are D signal sources in the far field of the antenna array, all the signal received by the antenna array approximately are plane wave. If the antenna array consists of M omnidirectional antennas and the first element set as the reference element, the ith signal received by the reference element is as follows:

$$s_i(t) = z_i(t) e^{j\omega_0 t}, i = 0, 1, L, D - 1 \tag{13}$$

where $z_i(t)$ is the complex encircled modulating of the i-th signal, which including the information of signal. $e^{j\omega_0 t}$ is the carrier wave of space signal. Due to the narrowband hypothesis condition, the signal with propagation delay τ can be represented as formula (14):

$$s_i(t - \tau) = z_i(t - \tau) e^{j\omega_0(t-\tau)} \approx s_i(t) e^{-j\omega_0 \tau}, i = 0, 1, L, D - 1 \tag{14}$$

Ideally the signal received by the m-th element can be represented as formula (15):

$$x_m(t) = \sum_{i=0}^{D-1} s_i(t - \tau_{mi}) + n_m(t) \tag{15}$$

where τ_{mi} is the time delay of the i-th array element relative to the reference array element when it reaches the m-th array element, $n_m(t)$ is additive noise of the m-th element. Generally, signal received by the whole antenna array is represented as formula (16):

$$X(t) = \sum_{i=0}^{D-1} s_i(t)a_i + N(t) = AS(t) + N(t) \tag{16}$$

where $a_i = \left[e^{-j\omega_0\tau_{1i}}, e^{-j\omega_0\tau_{2i}}, L, e^{-j\omega_0\tau_{Mi}}\right]^T$ is the direction vector of the i-th signal, $A = \left[a_0, a_1, L, a_{D-1}\right]$ is the array manifold, $S(t)$ is the signal matrix and $N(t)$ is the additive noise matrix.

3.2 MUSIC Algorithm

MUSIC algorithm is also known as Multiple Signal Classification algorithm [11]. It can be described as the following steps:

1. Collect signal samples as $X(n)$, $n = 0, 1, L, K-1$, and estimate covariance function as formula (17):

$$\hat{R}_X = \frac{1}{P} \sum_{i=0}^{P-1} XX^H \tag{17}$$

   where P is the number of sampling points.
2. Apply eigenvalue decomposition on $\hat{R}_X$:

$$\hat{R}_X V = \Lambda V \tag{18}$$

   where $\Lambda = \text{diag}(\lambda_0, \lambda_1, L, \lambda_{M-1})$ is eigenvalue diagonal array and is arranged from largest to smallest, V is the corresponding feature vector.
3. According to the number of minimum eigenvalue K we can calculate the number of signal $\hat{D}$ by $\hat{D} = M - K$. Construct the noise subspace as V_N.
4. Define the MUSIC spatial spectrum as:

$$P_{MUSIC}(\theta) = \frac{a^H(\theta)a(\theta)}{a^H(\theta)V_N V_N^H a(\theta)} \tag{19}$$

and then search the spectrum to find $\hat{D}$ peaks, which is the estimate value of DOA.

3.3 RSSI Positioning Model

RSSI is also known as Received Signal Strength Indication [12]. The basic idea is to discretize the area to be located and collect the signal strength information of each discrete point to create a fingerprint information database, which called location fingerprint library. Whenever need to estimate a terminal's position, we find the point in the library that best matches the point to be located. Generally, basic location fingerprint positioning system consists of two parts: offline fingerprint generation and online fingerprint matching. The model can be described as Fig. 2.

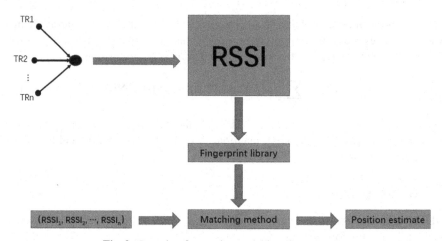

Fig. 2. Location fingerprint model location process

The two parts can be described as follows:

1. Offline fingerprint generation

Usually several transmitters are used to transmit signal continuously, simultaneously a receiver is moved onto different point to measure the signal strength and combine them into a vector to store in the fingerprint database. In the experimental area, some reference point are choses as the transmitters, position of which is precise. The receiver signal strength indication and the actual position is one-to-one mapping. The fingerprint information vector can be described as:

$$d_{(i,j)}(\tau) = \left[d_{1,j}(\tau), \cdots, d_{R,j}(\tau)\right], \tau = 1, 2, 3, \cdots, t, t > 1 \tag{20}$$

where $d_{(i,j)}(\tau)$ is the RSSI value of the j-th reference point at time t from the i-th transmitter, t is the sampling time period and R is the number of transmitters.

2. Online fingerprint matching

In this part the RSSI information of the point to be located need to be matched with the fingerprint information in the library. Firstly, the positioning area should be limited in the area in which the fingerprint information was measured. Then compare the obtained RSSI information with the information in the fingerprint library and find the best match point in the library. Finally, through specific positioning algorithm the final position of the target can be calculated.

3.4 Fusion of DOA and RSSI

Single DOA or RSSI positioning has poor precision and higher time complexity which limited by the principle of positioning. Generally fusion algorithm can combine the advantages of different algorithm [8, 9]. In this paper the DOA and RSSI fusion algorithm is used to improve the positioning accuracy of the NB-IoT network and reduce the matching time of the RSSI positioning algorithm in application.

This paper's idea is to make full use of the measurement parameters of DOA and RSSI and mainly divided into the following steps:

1. Generate an offline fingerprint library for the target area.
2. Assuming that two cluster nodes lie in (x_0, y_0) and (x_1, y_1) which is precisely known, measure the DOA of the terminal to two cluster nodes and mark them as (θ_1, θ_2) with an uncertainty parameter as (δ_1, δ_2).
3. The angle estimated by the DOA algorithm limits the range of the fingerprint information library that needs to be searched to within the range of $(\theta_1 \pm \delta_1, \theta_2 \pm \delta_2)$
4. In the restricted area of the DOA parameter, calculate the matching function for each point in fingerprint library and find best match grid in library. The matching function adapted is MAE (mean-absolute-error). It can be described as follows:

$$f_{mae} = \sum \left(mae(rssi_{i,j}, rssi) + mae(rssi_{i+1,j}, rssi) \right.$$
$$\left. + mae(rssi_{i,j+1}, rssi) + mae(rssi_{i+1,j+1}, rssi) \right) \tag{21}$$

where rssi is the real RSSI value measured in experiment. Function MAE is de fined as formula (22):

$$mae(x, y) = \frac{1}{L} \sum_{i=0}^{L} |x_i - y_i| \tag{22}$$

where L is the length of vector x and y.

5. The solution we find in the fingerprint library is a grid. Then the corresponding coordinates of the four vertices of the grid point are weighted, and the weight is the reciprocal of the MAE value, which is illustrated in formula (23). This method ensures that the smaller the error, the greater the influence on the final positioning result.

$$(x, y) = \sum w_{i,j} * (x_i, y_i) \tag{23}$$

where $w_{i,j} = \frac{1}{mae(rssi_{i,j}, rssi)}$.

The NB-IoT single-side fusion positioning method with DOA and RSSI parameter is shown in Fig. 3.

3.5 Result of DOA and RSSI Fusion Algorithm

In this experiment, RSSI fingerprint library was constructed with a pitch of 5 m in the dimension of x and y. The signal attenuation model is as formula (23) shows:

$$PL = 32.44 + 20 * \log(f_c) + 20 * \log(d) \tag{24}$$

The following Table 1 gives s summary of related parameter configurations.

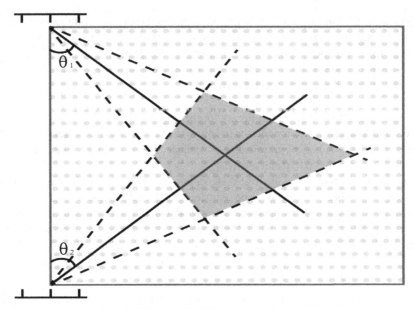

Fig. 3. DOA and RSSI fusion algorithm model

In the specific implementation of this paper, the experimental area is set to a square of 1000 m, the sampling interval of fingerprint library is set as 5 m to avoid excessive calculations and poor accuracy. Currently we consider the DOA and RSSI parameter fusion positioning algorithm of a single node. Two cluster nodes are placed at (1, 1) and (1, 1000), and the target node to be located is put in the experimental area randomly. Firstly, RSSI fingerprint library is established limited in the experimental area. Then two DOA parameters from the target node to the cluster node is measured to generate a DOA region, in which the point meets the constraints of $(\theta_1 \pm \delta_1, \theta_2 \pm \delta_2)$. Then the corresponding area in the RSSI fingerprint library is searched to find the value that minimizes the evaluate function. At last, Weighting the reference points found in the fingerprint library that meet the previous condition, the weight is the reciprocal of the MAE function and normalized. A total of 100 points of data were measured. The experimental results are shown in Figs. 4 and 5.

It can be seen from the data distribution in Fig. 4 that the positioning error of the fusion algorithm is smaller than the mean error of single RSSI positioning algorithm, and the variance is smaller. The mean and standard deviation for the data in the Figs. 4 and 5 is calculated and listed in Table 2.

From the data in Table 2, it can be seen that the average positioning error of the fusion positioning algorithm in the x direction and the y direction is much smaller than that of the single positioning method, which proved my method is effective. The performance of traditional RSSI algorithm is easily affected by interference and has a severe offset from the real position. As a contrast, the fusion Algorithm limits the area of RSSI matching by using DOA information, which reduces the impact of random interference.

Table 1. Parameters configuration

Attribute	Value
Number of cluster nodes	2
Position of cluster nodes	(1 m, 1 m), (1 m, 1000 m)
Sampling interval of fingerprint library	5 m in both x and y dimension
Antenna array	Uniform line array
Number of antennas	8
SNR	20 dB
Snapshot	512
Evaluate function	Mean Absolute Error

4   Fusion Positioning of 5G and NB-IoT

In our fusion positioning scheme, some cluster nodes were introduced to help improve the precision of NB-IoT terminal. Ideally, these cluster nodes have the ability of communicating with the 5G side and the NB-IoT side, and these functions are still in implementation by others. In the previous experiments, assuming that the location of the cluster nodes is precisely known, based on the location of the cluster nodes the DOA and RSSI fusion positioning from the cluster nodes to the NB-IoT terminals is completed. However, in actual situations, the location of the cluster nodes needs to be obtained in advance by other positioning methods, such as TDOA mentioned before.

4.1   Algorithm Description

The problem with this situation is that the error caused by the TDOA positioning of the cluster nodes is further transmitted to the next step of the fusion positioning of the NB-IoT terminals by the cluster nodes, resulting in different degrees of deterioration of the positioning results. In this part we try to reduce this impact by consider the error of cluster node positioning. Specifically, suppose the position solution of the cluster node is (x, y) and the corresponding error is (δ_x, δ_y). For the points in the solution space $(x \pm \delta_x, y \pm \delta_y)$, regard it as the position coordinates of the cluster nodes. Then DOA and RSSI fusion positioning method is used to achieve higher positioning accuracy.

4.2   Result of Fusion Positioning Algorithm

In this part, the fusion algorithm on both sides is compared with the one-side positioning algorithm. For the points in the uncertain regions generated by the cluster nodes due to the error, respectively, the NB-IoT side DOA and RSSI fusion algorithm positioning experiments are performed. The results is showed in Fig. 6 and Table 3.

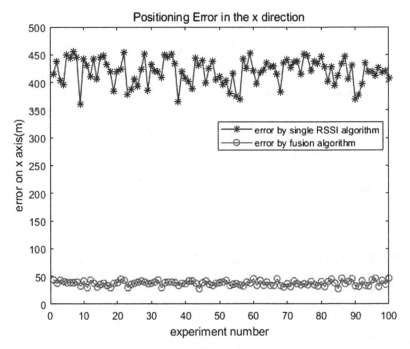

Fig. 4. Positioning Error in the x direction

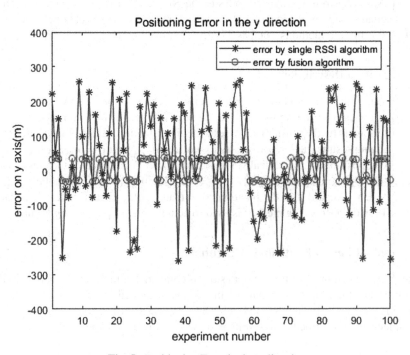

Fig. 5. Positioning Error in the y direction

Table 2. Result analysis

Direction	Algorithm	Mean	Standard Deviation
X	RSSI Algorithm	419.4068(m)	41.6814
	Fusion Algorithm	37.5169(m)	8.2867
Y	RSSI Algorithm	28.6660(m)	289.7484
	Fusion Algorithm	3.9701(m)	57.6721

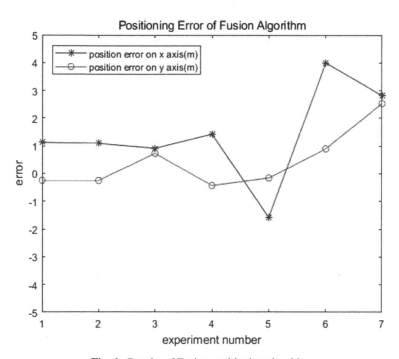

Fig. 6. Results of Fusion positioning algorithm

From the data showed in Fig. 6, we can get a conclusion that the position error is far less than that of the algorithm on NB-IoT side showed in Figs. 4 and 5. The final positioning accuracy in X direction can reach 1 m and 1 m in Y direction. The result proved that the stepwise positioning produces a local optimal solution. In the case of considering the global optimal solution, higher positioning accuracy can be obtained.

Table 3. Result analysis of fusion Algorithm

Condition	X(m)	Y(m)
Real value	482	534
Estimate value	483.1235	533.7515
Real value	517	574
Estimate value	518.0938	573.7508
Real value	487	482
Estimate value	487.9171	482.7340
Real value	558	439
Estimate value	559.4247	438.5715
Real value	466	559
Estimate value	464.4247	558.8438
Real value	570	585
Estimate value	572.8163	587.5350
Real value	574	467
Estimate value	578.0024	467.9018

5 Conclusion

In conclusion, by introducing cluster nodes, the NB-IoT single-side DOA and RSSI fusion positioning algorithm effectively improves the positioning accuracy of the NB-IoT network terminal. The average of final positioning error is less than 40 m in the x direction and less than 10 m in the y direction. In the case of strong noise interference, its performance is much better than single RSSI positioning algorithm.

In the fusion positioning experiment of the whole network, considering the error of the cluster node, the solution closer to the actual position of the point to be estimated can be obtained, and the positioning error is further reduced. In the case of strong noise, the overall solution has a mean error of 1.8504 m in the x direction and an average error of 0.7505 m in the y direction.

Acknowledgement. This research work is supported by the National Natural Science Foundation of China under Grant Nos. 61971278, 61771308, 61871265, 61873163 and 61771302, and the Equipment Pre Research Foundation of China under Grant No. 61404130218, and the Important National Science and Technology Specific Project of China under Grant No. 2018ZX03001020-005, and the Shanghai Science and Technology Committee under Grant No. 17511106300.

References

1. GPP TS 36.211 V15.0.0 (2017-12), "Evolved Universal Terrestrial Radio Access (E-UTRA); Physical channels and modulation", Release 15 (2017)
2. GPP TS 36.355 V15.0.0 (2018-06), "Evolved Universal Terrestrial Radio Access (E-UTRA); LTE Positioning Protocol (LPP)", Release 15 (2018)
3. Liu, C., Yang, J., Wang, F.: Joint TDOA and AOA location algorithm. J. Syst. Eng. Electron. **24**(2), 183–188 (2013)
4. Lin, L., So, H.C., Chan, F.K.W., et al.: A new constrained weighted least squares algorithm for TDOA-based localization. Sig. Process. **93**(11), 2872–2878 (2013)
5. Chen, P.C.: A non-line-of-sight error mitigation algorithm in location estimation. In: IEEE Wireless Communications and Networking Conference, September 1999
6. Wylie, M.P., Holtzman, J.M.: The non-line-of-sight problem in mobile location estimation. In: 1996 5th IEEE International Conference on Universal Personal Communications, Record. IEEE (1996)
7. Hara, S., Yabu, T., et al.: A perturbation analysis on the performance of TOA and TDOA localization in Mixed LOS/NLOS environments. IEEE Trans. Commun. **61**(2), 679–689 (2013)
8. Stefano Maddio, A.C., Manes, G.: RSSI/DoA based positioning systems for wireless sensor network. In: New Approach of Indoor & Outdoor Localization Systems (2012)
9. Bayat, K., Adve, R.S.: Joint TOA/DOA wireless position location using matrix pencil. In: IEEE Vehicular Technology Conference. IEEE (2004)
10. Bnilam, N., Ergeerts, G., Subotic, D., et al.: Adaptive probabilistic model using angle of arrival estimation for IoT indoor localization. In: IEEE 2017 International Conference on Indoor Positioning and Indoor Navigation (IPIN) – Sapporo, 18 October 2017–21 October 2017, pp. 1–7 (2017)
11. Stoica, P., Arye, N.: MUSIC, maximum likelihood, and Cramer-Rao bound. IEEE Trans. Acoust. Speech Sign. Process. **37**(5), 0–741 (1989)
12. Demirbas, M., Song, Y.: An RSSI-based scheme for sybil attack detection in wireless sensor networks. In: 2006 International Symposium on a World of Wireless, Mobile and Multimedia Networks (WoWMoM 2006). IEEE (2006)

A Novel Indoor Positioning Algorithm Based on IMU

Bi He[1], Hui Wang[1(✉)], Minshuo Li[1], Kozyrev Yury[1], and Xu Shi[2]

[1] School of Mathematics and Computer Science,
Zhejiang Normal University, Jinhua 321004, China
hwang@zjnu.cn
[2] School of Physics and Electronic Information Engineering,
Zhejiang Normal University, Jinhua 321004, China

Abstract. Although the Global Positioning System (GPS) can provide more accurate outdoor positioning services, it cannot detect the signals in indoor environments or in densely populated areas. Therefore, indoor positioning service has gradually been paid more attention. Most researchers currently use a nine-axis inertial sensor for indoor positioning. However, when the object is moving fast and frequently, it is obvious that using nine-axis inertial sensor has a large amount of computation. In addition, Kalman filtering algorithm is always cumbersome when data fusion is carried out for inertial sensors. The use of zero-velocity update algorithm (ZVU) to improve double integral can reduce the cumulative error, but the degree is far from enough. This paper mainly completes the following works: Firstly, the six-axis inertial sensor is used for indoor positioning. Then the digital motion processor is used instead of Kalman filter for attitude solution. Lastly, ZVU is optimized. Specifically, in the six-axis inertial sensor, the three-axis accelerometer is used to measure the force of the object, and the three-axis gyroscope is used to detect the current posture of the object. Since the three-axis magnetometer is missing, it is possible to effectively reduce a part of the calculation amount. In addition, the digital motion processor is used instead of the Kalman filter for the attitude solution, which avoids cumbersome filtering and data fusion. Finally, we optimize the ZVU so that the cumulative error is reduced again. The experimental results show that the algorithm proposed in this paper has certain feasibility and practical application value.

Keywords: Inertial sensor · Indoor positioning · Accelerometer · Gyroscope · Zero-velocity update

1 Introduction

Recently, with the continuous development of wireless sensor networks (WSNs), intelligent embedded systems and ubiquitous computing technologies, the demand

Foundation item: Natural Science Foundation of Zhejiang Province, China (No. LY16F020005).

for location services has increased. Although the Global Positioning System (GPS) can provide more accurate outdoor positioning services, it cannot detect the signals in indoor environments or in densely populated areas. Therefore, indoor positioning service has gradually been paid more attention. Indoor positioning refers to the positional positioning in the indoor environment. It mainly integrates various technologies such as wireless communication, base station positioning, and inertial navigation positioning to form an indoor position positioning system, thereby realizing the position monitoring of people and objects in the indoor space.

For indoor positioning technology, the more mature indoor positioning systems are Active Badge [1], LANDMARC [2], Horus [3], AH-Los [4] and so on. In China, the research on this aspect started late, but also achieved some results. For example, the Weyes system of Beihang University [5], and the high-precision indoor positioning achieved by Ultra Wide Band (UWB) by the University of Science and Technology of China [6]. Generally, the above indoor positioning solutions can be classified into the following five categories according to the types of hardware devices: base station based technology, WIFI based technology, wireless sensor based technology, UWB based technology and inertial sensor based technology. Wherein, the base station based technology depends on the base station signal, and the positioning accuracy is low. The indoor positioning method based on WIFI, wireless sensor and UWB has high precision but high cost and is susceptible to the external interference. However, the inertial sensor based positioning technology does not depend on any external information, with good concealment and no external interference. Therefore, this paper adopts the inertial sensor based positioning technology.

So far, researchers have proposed a variety of indoor positioning methods based on inertial sensors, which are mainly divided into two types. One method is to estimate position based on approximate step size and step number. It estimates step size by acceleration and calculates step number to obtain position information. We call this method pedometer method (PM). Although this method avoids the increase of position error caused by double integral of acceleration, its accuracy may be limited by the influence of step size. Another method is based on inertial navigation theory, which estimates the position by transforming coordinate system and calculating double integral of acceleration. We call this method double integral method (DIM). Since the double integral method can pursue higher accuracy, this paper uses the double integral method based on inertial sensor to conduct indoor positioning.

However, most researchers currently use nine-axis inertial sensors for indoor positioning. The nine axes include three-axis accelerometers, three-axis gyroscopes and three-axis magnetometers. When the object is moving fast and frequently, it is obvious that using nine-axis inertial sensor has a large amount of computation. In addition, Kalman filtering algorithm is always cumbersome and computationally intensive when data fusion is carried out for inertial sensors. The usage of zero-velocity update algorithm (ZVU) to improve double integral can reduce the cumulative error, but the degree is far from enough. Therefore, how to reduce the computational complexity of indoor positioning based on inertial sensors and how to reduce the cumulative error caused by double integral method become the key issues of indoor positioning based on inertial sensors.

Therefore, in order to solve the above problem, we use a six-axis inertial sensor for indoor positioning. The six axes include a three-axis accelerometer and a three-axis gyroscope. We also used digital motion processor instead of Kalman filter for attitude solution. In particular, we calibrate the acceleration before using ZVU to further reduce the cumulative error. The main contributions of this paper are summarized as follows:

1. A six-axis inertial sensor is used for indoor positioning. The three-axis accelerometer is used to measure the force of the object, and the three-axis gyroscope is used to detect the current posture of the object. The lack of a three-axis magnetometer can effectively reduce the amount of computation and speed up the reaction when the object moves rapidly and frequently.
2. Based on six-axis inertial sensor, digital motion processor is used instead of the Kalman filter for attitude solution. It can appropriately reduce the workload of the processor and avoid cumbersome filtering and data fusion. In addition, the ZVU is optimized in this paper to reduce the cumulative error again.
3. Finally, based on the indoor positioning algorithm of inertial sensors, a simulation platform is built to verify the algorithm. The experimental results show that the algorithm is feasible and has practical application value.

The structure of the rest of this paper is as follows: in Sect. 2, the working principle of inertial sensor is briefly described, and the accelerometer and gyroscope are introduced respectively. In Sect. 3, the indoor positioning algorithm based on inertial sensor is introduced in details. In Sect. 4, the simulation platform is built for the indoor positioning algorithm described in this paper, and the experimental results are described. In Sect. 5, the full text is summarized.

2   Working Principle of Inertial Sensor

2.1   Accelerometer

The acceleration sensor is to use the inertia force produced by the motion of the object to obtain the acceleration of the object at the current moment. The acceleration sensor is mainly composed of three parts: a mass, an elastic component and a sensitive component. When an object moves, a force is exerted on the mass in one direction. At the same time, the elastic component deforms to a certain extent. The other end of the elastic component is the sensitive component. The sensitive component will detect the current acceleration according to the degree of deformation of the elastic component, so as to complete the acceleration detection [7]. The specific details are shown in Fig. 1, which shows the internal structure of single-axis acceleration sensor. As for the indoor positioning, the three-axis acceleration sensor is basically used. The three axes of the three-axis accelerometer are x, y and z axes respectively. Each coordinate axis direction contains a single-axis accelerometer as shown in Fig. 1. The accelerometer is used to measure the acceleration data in each direction. Its unit is m/s^2. It can be expressed as an acceleration vector. When the object is stationary, it returns the acceleration of gravity, so the acceleration sensor is also called the gravity sensor [8].

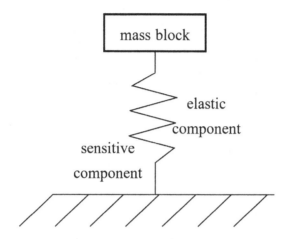

Fig. 1. Internal structure of single-axis acceleration sensor.

2.2 Gyroscope

Traditional mechanical gyroscopes, such as liquid floated gyroscope and electrostatic gyroscope, have high-velocity rotating rotors inside. It uses the mechanical characteristics of gyroscope to measure the angle with high accuracy. Optical gyroscopes, such as laser gyroscopes and fiber optic gyroscopes, use the Sagnac effect of light propagation to calculate the angular velocity of rotation. In this paper, we use a MEMS gyroscope, which is also a mechanical gyroscope. Its working principle is different from these two types of gyroscopes. In particular, the MEMS gyroscope is small in size, and it is difficult to design a gyro rotor with a large moment of inertia and to detect the mechanical properties of the rotor. Therefore, the MEMS gyroscope of the vibration type structure is basically used. It calculates the angular velocity by measuring the Gothic acceleration acting on the vibration components. The specific details are shown in Fig. 2, which shows the internal structure of a single-axis MEMS gyroscope. In the indoor positioning, a three-axis gyroscope sensor is basically used. The three axes of the three-axis gyroscope sensor are x, y and z axes respectively. Each coordinate axis direction contains one of the above single-axis gyroscope sensor. It is used to measure the gyroscope data in each direction. Its unit is rad/s. When a three-axis MEMS gyroscope works, its internal vibration mass block will vibrate in accordance with a certain driving mode. If an axis of the gyroscope generates angular velocity, the angular velocity will be calculated by detecting the Gothic force acting on the vibration mass block [9].

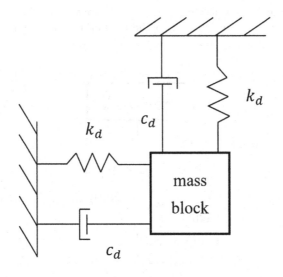

Fig. 2. Internal structure of single-axis gyroscope sensor.

3   Indoor Positioning Algorithm of Inertial Sensor

This paper proposes an indoor positioning algorithm based on inertial measurement unit (IMU). The block diagram of the indoor positioning algorithm is shown in Fig. 3. The upper, middle and lower portions of the figure correspond to four main components of the algorithm, with the lower part of the figure covering two parts. The upper part of the figure describes the algorithm of solving quaternion by digital motion processor (DMP). It is used to directly calculate quaternion q from acceleration measurement value a_b and gyroscope measurement value $gyro_b$. The middle part of the figure describes the coordinate transformation algorithm. It transforms the acceleration measurement a_b of the carrier coordinate system into the acceleration measurement value a_n of the geographic coordinate system by the quaternion q obtained by the DMP solution quaternion algorithm. The lower part of the figure describes the acceleration double integral algorithm and the zero-velocity update algorithm (ZVU). The ZVU algorithm is used in the acceleration double integral algorithm, so they are placed together. The output of this part includes the velocity estimate v and the position estimate p. Each component of the indoor positioning algorithm will be described in details in the following sections.

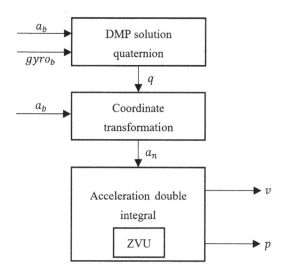

Fig. 3. Block diagram of indoor positioning algorithm.

3.1 DMP Solution Quaternion

The MPU6050 integrates an extensible digital motion processor (DMP). DMP is the unique hardware feature of InvenSense MPU devices. It combines the data of accelerometer and gyroscope, and directly solves the quaternion from it. It can reduce the workload of the main processor, avoid cumbersome filtering and data fusion processing, and reduce the complexity of system operation. Moreover, the main processor only needs to read the data when the DMP processing is completed. During DMP processing, the main processor can handle other tasks. This can improve the efficiency of the processor. In addition, the DMP images are stored on the non-permanent memory of the main processor, and the set data will disappear after power off. Therefore, every time the DMP function is activated on power, it is necessary to initialize the DMP. The flow chart of DMP solution quaternion is shown in Fig. 4:

3.2 Coordinate Transformation

Since the coordinate system of the chip is different from the coordinate system of the object, the sensor data should be transformed between the two coordinate systems. The coordinate systems involved are explained as follows:

1. Geographical Coordinate System
   Commonly used geographic coordinate systems mainly include the "East-North-Sky" coordinate system and the "North-East-Earth" coordinate system. This article uses the "East-North-Sky" coordinate system, also known as the Inertial Cartesian coordinate system. The origin is the center of mass of the carrier, the x axis points east along the direction of the local latitude,

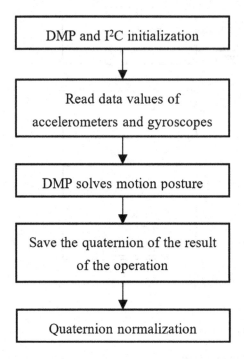

Fig. 4. Flow chart of DMP solution quaternion.

the y axis points north along the direction of the local meridian, and the z axis is determined by the right-hand rule. The geographic coordinate system is usually indicated by the lower corner "n".

2. Carrier Coordinate System

   The carrier coordinate system in this paper is the coordinate system of a certain part of the moving object carrying the inertial measurement unit (IMU). It will change with the movement of the object. The carrier coordinate system is self-defined. It consists of three axes that are orthogonal to each other. The origin of the coordinate system is usually set to the position of the center of gravity of the moving object. The x-axis is directed in the direction of moving forward, the y-axis is perpendicular to the direction of gravity acceleration, and the z-axis is perpendicular to the xoy plane. It follows the right-hand rule. The carrier coordinate system is usually indicated by the lower corner "b".

In the process of moving, the position change of the object is directed at the geographic coordinate system, which reflects the navigation information. The sensor data is relative to the chip itself, i.e. the carrier coordinate system, which reflects the posture information. In order to estimate the position of the object in the geographic coordinate system using the sensor data in the carrier coordinate system, coordinate transformation is needed.

There are many ways to coordinate transformation. In this paper, the quaternion method is used. Specifically, the geographic coordinate system is $ox_ny_nz_n$, and the carrier coordinate system is $ox_by_bz_b$. When the object moves, the measured value in the carrier coordinate system is $a_b(t) = (a_{bx}(t), a_{by}(t), a_{bz}(t))$. After coordinate conversion, the value in the geographic coordinate system is $a_n(t) = (a_{nx}(t), a_{ny}(t), a_{nz}(t))$. The conversion relationship is as follows:

$$a_n(t) = q_m(t) \otimes a_b(t) \otimes q_m^*(t). \tag{1}$$

Among them, $q_m(t)$ is the quaternion at time t obtained by the DMP solution in the previous section. $q_m^*(t)$ is the conjugate quaternion of $q_m(t)$, and $\otimes$ represents the quaternion multiplication. Acceleration vectors $a_b(t)$ and $a_n(t)$ are regarded as pure vector quaternions. When multiplying quaternions, its scalar part is equal to zero.

3.3   Acceleration Double Integral

Through the coordinate transformation of the above section, we can get the acceleration vector $a_n(t)$ of the geographic coordinate system. By subtracting the gravity acceleration $g_n(t)$ from $a_n(t)$, we obtain the acceleration driven by the motion as follows

$$a_n^m(t) = a_n(t) - g_n(t). \tag{2}$$

According to Newton's basic law of inertia, the instantaneous velocity is obtained by integrating the acceleration of the object. The acceleration of the object is double integral and the position of the object is obtained. When the object moves continuously from time 0 to time t, the sampling time is t. The distance is set as $p_n^m(t)$. The instantaneous velocity is set to $v_n^m(t)$, and the acceleration value measured by the accelerometer is $a_n^m(t)$. The relationships between the three are as follows:

$$v_n^m(t) = \int_0^t a_n^m(\tau)\mathrm{d}\tau, \tag{3}$$

$$p_n^m(t) = \int_0^t v_n^m(\tau)\mathrm{d}\tau. \tag{4}$$

Therefore, in the geographic coordinate system, the result of formula (2) is used to integrate the acceleration $a_n^m(t)$ to obtain the three-dimensional velocity vector $v_n^m(t)$. Then, the three-dimensional velocity vector $v_n^m(t)$ is integrated to obtain the position information $p_n^m(t)$.

3.4   Zero-Velocity Update Algorithm

The above method is feasible under the ideal conditions. However, the measured acceleration vector $a_n^m(t)$ has the noise and the drifted errors. If the velocity vector $v_n^m(t)$ is immediately integrated, the position estimation error will be infinitely amplified. The zero-velocity update algorithm (ZVU) came into being.

ZVU is an algorithm that reduces the position estimation error. Its basic idea is that at the beginning and end of the movement, the ideal velocity is zero. If the actual measured velocity is not zero, forcibly set it to zero. The difference between the actual velocity (known as zero) and the velocity obtained by integrating the acceleration is used to correct the acceleration offset error, thereby reducing the position estimation error. The derivation process of the zero-velocity update algorithm is as follows:

$$a_n^m(t) = a_n^a(t) + \varepsilon, t \in [0, T], \tag{5}$$

$$v_n^m(t) = \int_0^t a_n^m(\tau)\mathrm{d}\tau = \int_0^t [a_n^a(\tau) + \varepsilon]\mathrm{d}\tau = \int_0^t a_n^a(\tau)\mathrm{d}\tau + \int_0^t \varepsilon\mathrm{d}\tau = v_n^a(t) + \varepsilon t, \tag{6}$$

$$\varepsilon = \frac{v_n^m(T)}{T}. \tag{7}$$

In the above derivation process, the motion-driven acceleration $a_n^m(t)$ is divided into two parts. $a_n^a(t)$ is the actual acceleration vector. ε is the acceleration offset error. T is a period of the object motion. In a period, ε is considered to be a constant. The initial velocity of a moving object is zero, so the derivation (6) of velocity vector $v_n^m(t)$ can be obtained by substituting formula (5) into formula (3). Among them, $v_n^a(t)$ is the actual velocity vector, and εt is the velocity error caused by acceleration bias error. When the motion of the object ends, i.e. $t = T$, the actual velocity $v_n^a(T)$ is zero. Substituting it into the formula (6), the formula (7) can be obtained. That is, the acceleration bias error ε is obtained. From ε, the position estimation error can be reduced. The optimization of ZVU in this paper is to calibrate the deviation of acceleration before ZVU, so as to improve the indoor positioning accuracy of the algorithm.

4   Simulation of Indoor Positioning Algorithm Based on IMU

In order to verify the effectiveness and positioning accuracy of IMU based on indoor positioning algorithm, this section gives the simulation results of the above algorithm, discusses and analyzes it. First, we collect the data of the MPU6050 six-axis sensor. Then, use the MATLAB simulation platform to analyze and process the collected data. Finally, simulate the zero-velocity update algorithm to verify the effectiveness of the algorithm and test the performance of the improved algorithm.

Among them, the MPU6050 six-axis sensor integrates three-axis accelerometer and three-axis gyroscope. The parameters are shown in the following Table 1.

4.1   Zero Correction Simulation

The z-axis of the chip is put up and stationary horizontally. Theoretically, the acceleration measurement value of x-axis and y-axis is 0 and the acceleration

Table 1. Parameter description.

Name	Parameter
Measurement dimension	Accelerometer: 3D; Gyroscope: 3D
Range	Accelerometer: 2g; Gyroscope: 2000dps

measurement value of z-axis is $9.8 m/s^2$. However, this is not the case in actual measurement. The values of the x and y axes are not zero, and the value of the z axis is also deviated from $9.8 m/s^2$. Figure 5 illustrates only the x-axis as an example. The dotted line represents the acceleration of the x-axis before correction and the solid line represents the acceleration of the x-axis after correction. It can be seen from the dotted line part of Fig. 5. When the sensor is placed horizontally with the z-axis facing upward and in a static state, the measured value of the x-axis acceleration is different from zero. Therefore, it is necessary to calibrate the deviation of the measure value of the sensor. That is, the offset is calculated first and compensated then. The corrected measurements are shown on the solid line of Fig. 5. Compared with the dotted line part of Fig. 5, the acceleration value of the x-axis tends to zero in the static state. By this design, the velocity and position can be obtained more accurately when the acceleration is integrated subsequently.

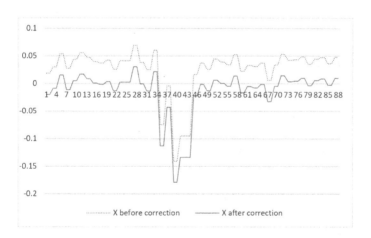

Fig. 5. Comparison of x-axis acceleration before and after correction.

4.2 Zero-Velocity Update Simulation

Similar to the last section, we take the x-axis as an example to illustrate the simulation experiment. Firstly, we assume that if the zero-velocity update algorithm is not adopted, the acceleration can be directly integrated to obtain the uncorrected velocity curve. The dotted line is shown in Fig. 6, where the horizontal axis represents the sampling time, and the vertical axis represents the velocity on the x axis. The unit is m/s. According to the dotted line in Fig. 6, the velocity after the motion is not zero due to the error caused by the integral. On the contrary, if the zero-velocity update algorithm is adopted, we re-integrate the acceleration to obtain the corrected velocity curve, as shown on the solid line in Fig. 6. Obviously, it can be seen from the solid line in Fig. 6 that the velocity at the end of the movement is close to zero after the correction of the zero-velocity update algorithm. Therefore, the zero-velocity update algorithm can effectively reduce the acceleration bias error.

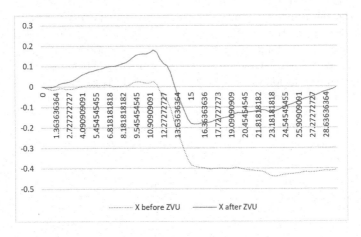

Fig. 6. Comparison of x-axis velocity before and after ZVU.

5 Conclusion

Aiming at the computational complexity and positioning accuracy of indoor positioning, this paper uses the six-axis inertial sensor, and designs the indoor positioning algorithm based on the six-axis inertial sensor. The algorithm includes digital motion processor, coordinate transformation, acceleration double integral and ZVU optimization. The digital motion processor replaces Kalman filter for attitude solution. Coordinate transformation is used for the transformation between geographic coordinate system and carrier coordinate system. The deviation calibration of acceleration before ZVU can make the positioning accuracy higher. The simulation results show that the algorithm has certain feasibility and practical application value.

References

1. Want, R., Hopper, A., Falcao, V., et al.: The active badge location system. ACM Trans. Inf. Syst. (TOIS) **10**(1), 91–102 (1992)
2. Ni, L.M., Liu, Y., Lau, Y.C., et al.: LANDMARC: indoor location sensing using active RFID. In: Proceedings of the First IEEE International Conference on Pervasive Computing and Communications, 2003, (PerCom 2003), pp. 407–415. IEEE (2003)
3. Youssef, M., Agrawala, A.: The horus WLAN location determination system. In: Proceedings of the 3rd International Conference on Mobile Systems, Applications, and Services, pp. 205–218. ACM (2005)
4. Savvides, A., Han, C.C., Strivastava, M.B.: Dynamic fine-grained localization in ad-hoc networks of sensors. In: Proceedings of the 7th Annual International Conference on Mobile Computing and Networking, pp. 166–179. ACM (2001)
5. Victor, L., Xu, K., Gu, C.: A difference model for open WLAN environment based location service. IEEE Infocom (2006, submitted)
6. Yanlong, Z.: Research on Key Technologies of Indoor Positioning. University of Science and Technology of China (2014)
7. Chunbin, G.: Research on indoor positioning technology based on mobile terminal sensor. University of Electronic Science and Technology of China (2015)
8. Hongli, S.: Research and implementation of indoor positioning system based on dead reckoning. University of Electronic Science and Technology of China (2018)
9. Qintuo, Z.: Research on positioning and orientation device based on MEMS inertial sensor. Harbin Engineering University (2008)

Service Delay Minimization-Based Joint Clustering and Content Placement Algorithm for Cellular D2D Communication Systems

Ahmad Zubair, Pengfei Ma, Tao Wei, Ling Wang, and Rong Chai$^{(\boxtimes)}$

Key Lab of Mobile Communication Technology,
Chongqing University of Posts and Telecommunications, Chongqing 400065, China
chairong@cqupt.edu.cn

Abstract. The rapidly increasing content fetching requirements pose challenges to the transmission performance of traditional cellular system. Due to the limited transmission performance of cellular links and the caching capabilities of the base stations (BSs), it is highly difficult to achieve the quality of service (QoS) requirements of multi-user content requests. In this paper, a joint user association and content placement algorithm is proposed for cellular device-to-device (D2D) communication network. Assuming that multiple users located in a specific area may have content requests for the same content, a clustering and content placement mechanism is presented in order to achieve efficient content acquisition. A joint clustering and content placement optimization model is formulated to minimize total user service delay, which can be solved by Lagrange partial relaxation, iterative algorithm and Kuhn-Munkres algorithm, and the joint clustering and content placement strategies can be obtained. Finally, the effectiveness of the proposed algorithm is verified by MATLAB simulation.

Keywords: Cellular network · Device-to-device D2D communication · User association · Content placement · Service delay

1 Introduction

The rapid proliferation of new applications poses great challenges to the traditional cellular systems. To improve user quality of service (QoS) as well as network performance, device-to-device (D2D) communication technology can be applied in cellular systems which allows adjacent user equipments (UEs) communicate with each other in a direct manner without relying on the data forwarding of the base stations (BSs) [1]. Benefited from the improved channel characteristics between D2D peers, D2D communication technology is expected to improve system throughput, reduce transmission delay and power consumption of the devices significantly.

Transmission mode selection and resource allocation problem in cellular D2D communication systems was addressed in previous research work [5–8]. In [6], the authors considered the transmission mode selection problem and presented an energy consumption minimization-based optimal scheme. In [7], the joint transmission mode selection

ⓒ ICST Institute for Computer Sciences, Social Informatics and Telecommunications Engineering 2020
Published by Springer Nature Switzerland AG 2020. All Rights Reserved
H. Gao et al. (Eds.): ChinaCom 2019, LNICST 313, pp. 180–191, 2020.
https://doi.org/10.1007/978-3-030-41117-6_15

and resource allocation problem was formulated as end-to-end sum-rate maximization problem and solved based on BS scheduling method. Considering the constraint on transmission rate, [5] presented a joint transmission mode selection and power control scheme to maximize the energy efficiency of the system. While resource allocation issue was stressed in [5–7], they failed to consider the efficient utilization of resources in the system. Under the assumption of limited resources, the authors in [8] modeled the transmission model selection problem as resource utilization maximization problem, and proposed a channel state-based model selection mechanism to achieve higher resource utilization and D2D transmission gain.

By caching popular contents at the BSs of the cellular system or at certain UEs, the performance of content fetching can be improved significantly. Considering a cellular D2D communication system, the authors in [9] proposed an information-oriented new network architecture enabling wireless network virtualization and D2D communications in order to achieve the maximum revenue of mobile operators. Taking into account various user preference, [10] presented an optimal content delivery strategy which achieves the maximum gain of network offloading.

While user association and content placement have been studied in previous work, the joint design of the two strategies failed to be discussed extensively, thus may result in undesired content fetching performance. Furthermore, while throughput or network revenue were mainly considered in previous work, service delay, which is of particular importance for delay-sensitive users, was not considered for designing joint user association and content placement strategy. In this paper, we consider various content fetching requirements of the users and the content delivery performance in different transmission modes, introducing clustering scheme, and propose a service delay minimization-based joint clustering and content placement algorithm for cellular D2D communication systems.

2 System Model and Proposed Clustering Mechanism

This paper considers a cellular D2D communication system, which is composed of one BS and M content request users (RUs) and M serving users (SUs). Suppose RUs request contents with a certain probability, and the total number of content files required from RUs is denoted by K. Let $P_{i,k}$ denote the preference probability of the ith RU, denoted as RU_i for content k, we obtain $P_{i,k} \in [0,1]$, $0 \leq \sum_{k=1}^{K} P_{i,k} = 1, 1 \leq i \leq M$. The size of content k is denoted by C_k.

In order to achieve efficient content request and reduce content fetching delay, we assume that some popular contents can be cached at the BS or certain SUs, and RUs are allowed to fetch content file in cellular communication mode or D2D transmission mode. More specifically, in cellular communication mode, the RUs access the BS of cellular system to acquire their required content files, while in D2D transmission mode, the RUs interact with their D2D peers, i.e., SUs, to fetch their content files.

For the sake of simplicity, it is assumed that orthogonal frequency division multiple access (OFDMA) scheme is applied for the information interaction in cellular communication mode and D2D transmission mode. As various orthogonal subcarriers are

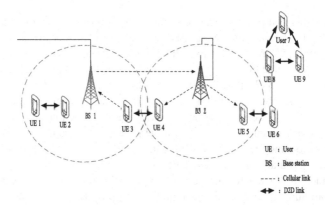

Fig. 1. D2D communication application scenario

allocated for different RUs, there is no transmission interference caused among transmission links. Figure 1 shows the cellular D2D communication system considered in this paper.

Given content file requirements of the RUs and various content fetching performance of the transmission modes, this paper aims to jointly design the transmission mode for the RUs and the content placement strategy for the SUs.

In a cellular D2D communication system, some RUs may need to acquire same content files. By caching some hot contents at certain SUs and employing D2D transmission mode, efficient content access service can be achieved.

Taking into account the diverse content request of RUs and various channel characteristics of the links between users, this paper applies clustering idea and proposes a clustering-based content fetching mechanism. According to network status and user characteristics, the RUs and SUs in the network are dynamically divided into multiple clusters with each cluster consisting of one cluster head (CH) and multiple cluster members (CMs). Without loss of generality, we assume that the CHs are allowed to access the BS directly, while the CMs can only interact with their associated CH.

By suitably choosing SUs as CHs and caching selected content files at the CHs, the CMs may fetch content files through connecting with their CHs in D2D communication mode, In this way, intra-cluster content sharing can be achieved.

Let N_1 denote the maximum number of CHs in the system, and CH_j denote the jth CH, $1 \leq j \leq N_1$. Assuming each CH has a maximum cache capacity for caching content files, we denote $C_j^{\max}$ as the maximum cache capacity of CH_j, $1 \leq j \leq M$. Further assuming that each CH has a limit on the maximum number of associated CMs, we denote N_2 as the maximum number of CMs that associate with one CH.

3   Optimization Problem Formulation

In this paper, we stress the performance of service delay of the RUs, and formulate joint user association and content placement problem as a service delay minimization problem. The detail problem formulation will be discussed in this section.

3.1 User Service Delay Formulation

The total service delay of the users in the system is defined as the sum of intra-cluster D2D communication delay, the delay required for the CHs to fetch contents from the BS, and the content fetching delay in cellular communication mode. We denote the total service delay of the users by D, which can be expressed as

$$D = D^{\text{cm}} + D^{\text{ch}} + D^{\text{b}} \tag{1}$$

where D^{cm} represents the intra-cluster D2D communication delay, D^{ch} denotes the delay required for the CHs to fetch contents from the BS, and D^{b} denotes the delay in cellular communication mode. D^{cm} in (1) can be expressed as

$$D^{\text{cm}} = \sum_{i=1}^{M} \sum_{j=1, j \neq i}^{M} \sum_{k=1}^{K} \delta_{i,j} \beta_{j,k} D_{i,j,k}^{\text{d}} \tag{2}$$

where $\delta_{i,j} \in \{0,1\}$ is the association variable between RUs and the CHs, i.e., $\delta_{i,j} = 1$, if RU_i associates with CH_j, otherwise, $\delta_{i,j} = 0$; $\beta_{j,k}$ denotes content placement variable, i.e., $\beta_{j,k} = 1$, if content k is placed at CH_j, otherwise, $\beta_{j,k} = 0$; $D_{i,j,k}^{\text{d}}$ denotes the service delay when RU_i associates with CH_j and receives content k, $D_{i,j,k}^{\text{d}}$ can be expressed as

$$D_{i,j,k}^{\text{d}} = \frac{C_k}{R_{i,j}^{\text{d}}} \tag{3}$$

where $R_{i,j}^{\text{d}}$ is the transmission rate of the link between RU_i and CH_j.

In (1), D^{ch} can be calculated as

$$D^{\text{ch}} = \sum_{j=1}^{M} \sum_{k=1}^{K} \delta_{j,j} \beta_{j,k} D_{j,k}^{\text{c}} \tag{4}$$

where $\delta_{j,j}$ indicates that RU_j is selected as a CH, $D_{j,k}^{\text{c}}$ represents the corresponding service delay when the BS sends content k to CH_j, and $D_{j,k}^{\text{c}}$ can be computed as

$$D_{j,k}^{\text{c}} = \frac{C_k}{R_j^{\text{c}}} \tag{5}$$

where R_j^{c} is the transmission rate of the link between the BS and CH_j.

In (1), D^{b} is given by

$$D^{\text{b}} = \sum_{i=1}^{M} \sum_{k=1}^{K} \left(1 - \sum_{j=1, j \neq i}^{M} \delta_{i,j} \beta_{j,k} \right) P_{i,k} D_{i,k}^{\text{b}} \tag{6}$$

where $D_{i,k}^{\text{b}}$ is the resulted service delay when RU_i associates the BS to obtain content k, $D_{i,k}^{\text{b}}$ can be expressed as

$$D_{i,k}^{\text{b}} = D_{i,k}^{\text{t}} + D_{i,k}^{\text{w}} \tag{7}$$

where $D_{i,k}^{\text{t}}$ and $D_{i,k}^{\text{w}}$ denote respectively the data transmission delay and queueing delay when RU_i associates with the BS and acquires content k.

3.2 Optimization Model

Under the constraints of user clustering, the cache capacity of CHs, and the minimum transmission rate requirements of the RUs, etc, we formulate joint clustering and content placement problem in cellular D2D communication system as a constrained service delay minimization problem, i.e.,

$$
\min_{\delta_{i,j}, \beta_{j,k}} D
$$

$$
\begin{aligned}
\text{s.t.} \quad & C1 : \delta_{i,j} \in \{0,1\}, \forall i, j \\
& C2 : \beta_{j,k} \in \{0,1\}, \ \forall j, k \\
& C3 : \sum_{j=1}^{M} \delta_{j,j} \leq N_1 \\
& C4 : \sum_{i=1, i \neq j}^{M} \delta_{i,j} \leq N_2, \ \forall j \\
& C5 : \sum_{j=1, j \neq i}^{M} \delta_{i,j} \leq 1, \ \forall i \\
& C6 : \sum_{k=1}^{K} \beta_{j,k} C_k \leq C_j^{\max}, \ \forall j \\
& C7 : R_i \geq R_i^{\min}, \ \forall i
\end{aligned} \tag{8}
$$

where C1 and C2 are the binary condition of the CH association variables and the content placement variables, C3 represents the constraint on the maximum number of the CHs, C4 and C5 are respectively the CH association constraint and the CH selection constraint, and C6 is the maximum cache capacity constraint of the CHs. In C7, R_i and $R_i^{\min}$ denote respectively the achievable transmission rate and the minimum transmission rate requirement of RU$_i$, hence, C7 represents the constraint on the minimum transmission rate requirement of the RUs.

4   Solution to the Optimization Problem

Since the optimization problem given in (8) is a non-convex mixed integer optimization problem, the optimal solution of which is difficult to obtain by the conventional convex optimization algorithm. In this paper, by using the McCormick convex relaxation method [12] and the Lagrangian partial relaxation method [13], the original optimization problem is equivalently converted into three convex optimization subproblems and the modified Kuhn-Munkres (K-M) algorithm [14] is then used to solve the subproblems.

4.1 Reformulation of the Optimization Problem

The optimization problem in (8) contains a number of Boolean variables such as $\delta_{i,j}, \beta_{j,k}$. To tackle the coupling relationship between the variables, we define $\alpha_{i,j,k} = \delta_{i,j}\beta_{j,k}$ and replace $\delta_{i,j}\beta_{j,k}$ by $\alpha_{i,j,k}$ in (8), i.e.,

$$\min_{\delta_{i,j},\beta_{j,k},\alpha_{i,j,k}} \sum_{i=1}^{M}\sum_{j=1}^{M}\sum_{k=1}^{K}\alpha_{i,j,k}D_{j,k}^{c} + \sum_{i=1}^{M}\sum_{j=1,j\neq i}^{M}\sum_{k=1}^{K}\alpha_{i,j,k}D_{i,j,k}^{d}P_{i,k}$$
$$+ \sum_{i=1}^{M}\sum_{k=1}^{K}(1 - \sum_{j=1,j\neq i}^{M}\alpha_{i,j,k})P_{i,k}D_{i,k}^{b} \qquad (9)$$
$$\text{s.t.} \quad C1 - C7$$
$$C8 : \alpha_{i,j,k} = \delta_{i,j}\beta_{j,k}$$

C8 in above problem is a non-convex optimization constraint, which can be equivalently converted to the convex optimization constraints C9–C12 by using the McCormick convex relaxation method.

$$\min_{\delta_{i,j},\beta_{j,k},\alpha_{i,j,k}} \sum_{i=1}^{M}\sum_{j=1}^{M}\sum_{k=1}^{K}\alpha_{i,j,k}D_{j,k}^{c} + \sum_{i=1}^{M}\sum_{j=1,j\neq i}^{M}\sum_{k=1}^{K}\alpha_{i,j,k}D_{i,j,k}^{d}P_{i,k}$$
$$+ \sum_{i=1}^{M}\sum_{k=1}^{K}(1 - \sum_{j=1,j\neq i}^{M}\alpha_{i,j,k})P_{i,k}, D_{i,k}^{b}$$
$$\text{s.t.} \quad C1 - C7, C9 - C12 \qquad (10)$$
$$C9 : \alpha_{i,j,k} \geq 0$$
$$C10 : \alpha_{i,j,k} \geq \delta_{i,j} + \beta_{j,k} - 1$$
$$C11 : \alpha_{i,j,k} \leq \delta_{i,j}$$
$$C12 : \alpha_{i,j,k} \leq \beta_{j,k}$$

To solve the optimization problem in (10), we apply Lagrangian partial relaxation method and relax the constraints C10–C12. In addition, the corresponding Lagrangian multipliers $\eta_{i,j,k}$, $\varphi_{i,j,k}$, $\theta_{i,j,k}$ are introduced and the non-negative constraints on the Lagrangian multipliers are added in the optimization problem, i.e.,

$$\max_{\eta_{i,j,k},\varphi_{i,j,k},\theta_{i,j,k}} \min_{\delta_{i,j},\beta_{j,k},\alpha_{i,j,k}} L(\delta_{i,j},\beta_{j,k},\alpha_{i,j,k},\eta_{i,j,k},\varphi_{i,j,k},\theta_{i,j,k})$$
$$\text{s.t.} \quad C1 - C7, C9$$
$$C13 : \eta_{i,j,k} \geq 0 \qquad (11)$$
$$C14 : \varphi_{i,j,k} \geq 0$$
$$C15 : \theta_{i,j,k} \geq 0$$

Given the Lagrangian multipliers $\eta_{i,j,k}, \varphi_{i,j,k}, \theta_{i,j,k}$, the Lagrangian function can be expressed as

$$L(\delta_{i,j},\beta_{j,k},\alpha_{i,j,k},\eta_{i,j,k},\varphi_{i,j,k},\theta_{i,j,k})$$
$$= f_1(\delta_{i,j}) + f_2(\beta_{j,k}) + f_3(\alpha_{i,j,k}) \qquad (12)$$

Since there is no coupling between the variables in the three functions $f_1(\delta_{i,j})$, $f_2(\beta_{j,k})$ and $f_3(\alpha_{i,j,k})$, the original dual problem can be converted into three subproblems, i.e., user association subproblem SP1, content placement subproblem SP2, and the joint optimization subproblem SP3.

4.2 Iterative Algorithm-Based Solution

Since the optimization variables and the Lagrangian multipliers in the three subproblems are related, in order to obtain the optimal solution of each subproblem, the optimization variables and Lagrangian multipliers should be solved jointly. To this end, we present an iterative algorithm-based method which calculates the optimization variables and the Lagrangian multipliers successively.

Given the maximum number of CHs N_1, we may consider different CH selection possibilities. Let L denote the number of CH selection strategies. For each particular CH selection strategy, we solve the subproblems respectively based on the given Lagrangian multipliers $\eta_{i,j,k}, \varphi_{i,j,k}, \theta_{i,j,k}$, then compare the obtained total service delay corresponding to various CH selection strategies, and select the joint clustering and content placement strategy which offers the smallest total service delay as the global optimal strategy.

K-M Algorithm-Based Solution to the Subproblems. For the lth CH selection strategy, given the Lagrangian multipliers $\eta_{i,j,k}, \varphi_{i,j,k}, \theta_{i,j,k}$, each subproblem is an integer optimization problem containing binary variables, which can be regarded as the matching problem in a bipartite graph. Hence, for individual subproblem, we may set up the bipartite graph with corresponding vertex set, link set and the weight set of links. Then applying the modified K-M algorithm, we can obtain the user association strategy $\delta_{i,j}^{(l,*)}$, the content placement strategy $\beta_{j,k}^{(l,*)}$, and the joint optimization strategy $\alpha_{i,j,k}^{(l,*)}$.

Lagrangian Multiplier Update. Based on the local optimal solution $\delta_{i,j}^{(l,*)}, \beta_{j,k}^{(l,*)}$, $\alpha_{i,j,k}^{(l,*)}$, the gradient iterative algorithm can be used to update the Lagrangian multipliers. The update formula are:

$$\eta_{i,j,k}(t+1) = [\eta_{i,j,k}(t) - \omega_1(\alpha_{i,j,k}^{(l,*)}(t) + 1 - \delta_{i,j}^{(l,*)}(t) - \beta_{j,k}^{(l,*)}(t)]^+ \tag{13}$$

$$\varphi_{i,j,k}(t+1) = [\varphi_{i,j,k}(t) - \omega_2(\delta_{i,j}^{(l,*)}(t) - \alpha_{i,j,k}^{(l,*)}(t))]^+ \tag{14}$$

$$\theta_{i,j,k}(t+1) = [\theta_{i,j,k}(t) - \omega_3(\beta_{j,k}^{(l,*)}(t) - \alpha_{i,j,k}^{(l,*)}(t))]^+ \tag{15}$$

where $\omega_x, x \in \{1, 2, 3\}$ is the step size.

The algorithm proposed in this paper is shown in Table 1.

Table 1. Proposed joint user association and content placement algorithm

---

1. Determine L CH selection strategies;
2. Set the maximum number of iterations T^{max} and the maximum tolerance delay ε;
3. Set $l=1$;
4. Repeat main program
5. Initialize Lagrangian multipliers $\eta_{i,j,k}, \varphi_{i,j,k}, \theta_{i,j,k}$;
6. Solve user association subproblem, obtain local optimal strategy $\delta'_{i,j}$;
   Solve content placement subproblem, obtain local optimal strategy $\beta'_{j,k}$;
   Solve the joint optimization subproblem, obtain local optimal strategy $\alpha'_{i,j,j}$;
7. Update Lagrangian multipliers
$$\eta_{i,j,k}(t+1) = [\eta_{i,j,k}(t) - \omega_1(\alpha'_{i,j,k}(t) + 1 - \delta_{i,j}(t) - \beta'_{j,k}(t)]^+;$$
$$\varphi_{i,j,k}(t+1) = [\varphi_{i,j,k}(t) - \omega_2(\delta_{i,j}(t) - \alpha'_{i,j,k}(t))]^+;$$
$$\theta_{i,j,k}(t+1) = [\theta_{i,j,k}(t) - \omega_3(\beta j, k(t) - \alpha'_{i,j,k}(t))]^+;$$
8. if $\displaystyle\sum_{i=1}^{M}\sum_{j=1}^{M}\sum_{k=1}^{K}(|\eta_{i,j,k}(t+1) - \eta_{i,j,k}(t)| +$
$|\varphi_{i,j,k}(t+1) - \varphi_{i,j,k}(t)| + |\theta_{i,j,k}(t) - \theta_{i,j,k}(t)|) \leq \varepsilon$
9. algorithm converges,
   return $\delta_{i,j}^{(l),*} = \delta'_{i,j}, \beta_{j,k}^{(l),*} = \beta'_{j,k}, \alpha_{i,j,k}^{(l),*} = \alpha'_{i,j,k}$
10. else $t = t + 1$
11. Repeat Steps 6-10 until the algorithm converges or $t = T^{\mathrm{max}}$
12. Set $l = l + 1$,
13. Repeat Steps 5-11 until $l = L$

14. $\{\delta_{i,j}^*, \beta_{j,k}^*, \alpha_{i,j,k}^*\} = \arg\min D^{(l)}(\delta_{i,j}^{(l),*}, \beta_{j,k}^{(l),*}, \alpha_{i,j,k}^{(l),*})$.

---

5   Simulation Results

In this section, we use MATLAB simulation software to evaluate and analyze the performance of the proposed algorithm. The simulation scenario consists of a single BS, multiple RUs and multiple SUs. The BS and users in the network are distributed in an area of 200 m × 200 m. The coordinates of the BS are (100 m, 100 m), and the positions of the users are randomly distributed. The number of users selected in the simulation is 8, the transmit power of the BS 26 dBm, the minimum transmission rate requirement of the RUs is set as 2 Mbit/s, and the power spectral density of the noise is set as −174 dBm/Hz, −160 dBm/Hz and −150 dBm/Hz.

Figure 2 shows the relationship between the total service delay and the number of iterations obtained from the algorithm proposed in this paper. In the simulation, the number of CHs is considered as 2 and 4, and the system transmission performance corresponding to different subchannel bandwidth is considered. It can be seen that the total service delay tends to converge within a small number of iterations, indicating the effectiveness of the proposed algorithm. Comparing the delay performance corresponding to different subchannel bandwidth, we can see the total service delay reduces as the subchannel bandwidth increases. In addition, comparing the service delay performance corresponding to different number of CHs, it can be seen that when the number of CHs increases, the total service delay increases. This is because as the number of CHs increases, the traffic load of the transmission links between the BS and the CHs increases. As in general the link performance between the BS and the CHs may not be as good as the intra-cluster links, thus longer service delay might be resulted.

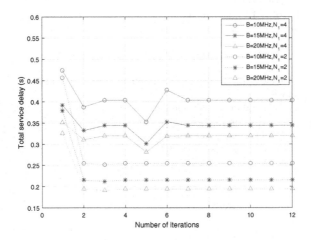

Fig. 2. Total service delay vs the number of iterations

Figure 3 shows the relationship between the total service delay of the users and the arrival rate of the BS obtained from the algorithm proposed in this paper. It can be seen that the total service delay of the users increases as the service arrival rate service increases. The reason is that when the service arrival rate service increases, larger number of packets are required to be transmitted, hence, longer queuing delay is resulted which causes longer total service delay in turn. Comparing the performance obtained from different average service rate, we can see that as the average service rate increases, the total service delay decreases which is benefited from shorter queuing delay. In addition, we can also observe that the increase in the number of CHs leads to an increase in the total service delay.

Figure 4 shows the relationship between total user service delay and traffic arrival rate under different minimum transmission rate limits. It can be seen that for relatively low minimum transmission rate requirement, lower total service delay of the users can be achieved, this is because to meet the minimum transmission rate requirement, a larger number of links might be qualified, thus offering higher flexibility in determining user association strategy and better service delay performance in turn.

Figure 5 shows total service delay versus subchannel bandwidth for different traffic arrival rates. For comparison, we also plot the performance of the algorithm proposed in [15]. It can be seen that given service arrival rate, the total service delay of the users decreases as the subchannel bandwidth increases. This is because the higher subchannel bandwidth offers a higher transmission rate and lower service delay in turn. We can also observe that the total service delay increases as the traffic arrival rate increases

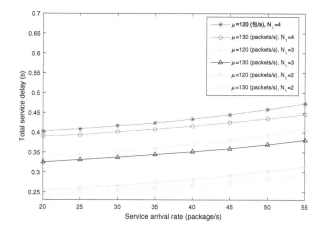

Fig. 3. Total service delay vs service arrival rate (different service rates)

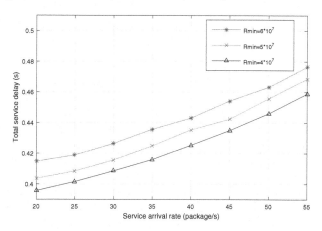

Fig. 4. Total service delay vs service arrival rate (different minimum transmission rate)

as larger amount of service results in longer queuing delay and longer service delay as well. Comparing the service delay performance obtained from our proposed algorithm and the algorithm proposed in [15], we can see that our proposed algorithm offers lower service delay than that proposed in [15]. The reason is that our proposed algorithm addresses joint optimization of user association and content placement and aims to achieve the optimal service delay, while the algorithm proposed in [15] is addressed in algorithm.

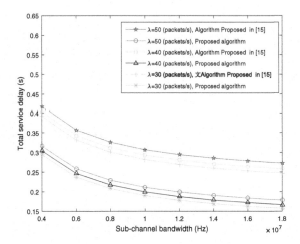

Fig. 5. Total service delay vs subchannel bandwidth

6   Conclusions

For the scenario of single-base cell cellular D2D communication system composed of multiple RUs and multiple SUs, this paper proposes a joint user association and content placement algorithm for cellular D2D communication based on delay optimization. In order to achieve the performance of most users, a clustering mechanism is proposed, which supports SU as the cluster head and supports the sharing of content by RU. Considering the constraints of cluster number, user association cluster head, cluster head cache capacity and transmission rate, a joint user association and content placement optimization model based on user's total service delay is established. In this paper, the Lagrange partial relaxation method is used to convert the original optimization problem into three sub-problems of convex optimization, and an iterative algorithm is proposed to jointly solve the sub-problems to obtain joint clustering optimization strategy and content placement optimization strategy. Finally, the proposed algorithm can realize the optimization of traffic transmission delay by MATLAB simulation.

References

1. Tehrani, M.N., Uysal, M., Yanikomeroglu, H.: Device-to-device communication in 5G cellular networks: challenges, solutions, and future directions. IEEE Commun. Mag. **52**(5), 86–92 (2014)
2. Asadi, A., Wang, Q., Mancuso, V.: A survey on device-to-device communication in cellular networks. IEEE Commun. Surv. Tutorials **16**(4), 1801–1819 (2014)
3. Fodor, G., Dahlman, E., Mildh, G., et al.: Design aspects of network assisted device-to-device communications. IEEE Commun. Mag. **50**(3), 170–177 (2012)
4. Zhu, H.: Radio resource allocation for OFDMA systems in high speed environments. IEEE J. Sel. Areas Commun. **30**(4), 748–759 (2012)

5. Klugel, M., Kellerer, W.: Leveraging the D2D-gain: resource efficiency based mode selection for device-to-device communication. In: IEEE Global Communications Conference (GLOBECOM), Washington, USA, pp. 1–7 (2017)
6. Wen, D., Yu, G., Xu, L.: Energy-efficient mode selection and power control for device-to-device communications. In: IEEE Wireless Communications and Networking Conference (WCNC), Doha, Qatar, pp. 1–7 (2016)
7. Penda, D.D., Liqun, F., Johansson, M.: Mode selection for energy efficient D2D communications in dynamic TDD systems. In: IEEE International Conference on Communications (ICC), London, UK, pp. 5404–5409 (2015)
8. Wang, K., Yu, F., Li, H.: Information-centric virtualized cellular networks with device-to-device communications. IEEE Trans. Veh. Technol. **65**(11), 9319–9329 (2016)
9. Pan, Y., Pan, C., Zhu, H., et al.: On consideration of content preference and sharing willingness in D2D assisted offloading. IEEE J. Sel. Areas Commun. **35**(4), 978–993 (2017)
10. Li, X., Ma, L., Shankaran, R., et al.: Joint mode selection and proportional fair scheduling for D2D communication. In: IEEE 28th Annual International Symposium on Personal, Indoor, and Mobile Radio Communications (PIMRC), Montreal, Canada, pp. 1–6 (2017)
11. Liberti, L., Pantelides, C.C.: An exact reformulation algorithm for large nonconvex NLPs involving bilinear terms. J. Glob. Optim. **36**(2), 161–189 (2006)
12. Boyd, S., Vandenberghe, L.: Convex optimization. Eur. J. Oper. Res. **170**(1), 326–327 (2006)
13. Huang, Y., Nasir, A.A., Durrani, S., et al.: Mode selection, resource allocation, and power control for D2D-enabled two-tier cellular network. IEEE Trans. Commun. **64**(8), 3534–3547 (2016)
14. Jiang, W., Feng, G., Qiu, S.: Optimal cooperative content caching and delivery policy for heterogeneous cellular networks. IEEE Trans. Mob. Comput. **16**(5), 1382–1393 (2017)
15. Ma, R., Xia, N., Chen, H.H., et al.: Mode selection, radio resource allocation, and power coordination in D2D communications. IEEE Wirel. Commun. **24**(3), 112–121 (2017)

T-HuDe: Through-The-Wall Human Detection with WiFi Devices

Wei Zeng$^{(\boxtimes)}$, Zengshan Tian, Yue Jin, and Xi Chen

Chongqing Key Lab of Mobile Communications Technology,
School of Communication and Information Engineering,
Chongqing University of Posts and Telecommunications, Chongqing, China
zengweicq@gmail.com, tianzs@cqupt.edu.cn, jinyue063@gmail.com,
chenxiopr@gmail.com

Abstract. With the rapid development of emerging smart homes applications, the home security systems based on passive detection without carrying any devices has been increasing attention in recent years. Through-The-Wall (TTW) detection is a great challenge since through-the-wall signal can be severely attenuated, and some of the existing TTW-based detection techniques require special equipment or have strict restrictions on placement of devices. Due to the near-ubiquitous wireless coverage, WiFi based passively human detection technique becomes a good solution. In this paper, we propose a robust scheme for device-free Through-the-wall Human Detection (T-HuDe) in TTW with Channel State Information (CSI), which can provide more fine-grained movement information. Especially, T-HuDe utilizes motion information on WiFi signal and uses statistical information of motion characteristics as parameters. To evaluate T-HuDe performance, we prototype it in different environments with commodity devices, and the test results show that human activity detection rate and human absence detection rate of T-HuDe are both above 93% in most detection areas.

Keywords: Through-The-Wall · Active human detection · Channel State Information

1 Introduction

With the rapid development of applications such as smart homes, indoor-based motion detection has recently gained more attention. In order to make a better interactive experience for humans and smart homes, more and more researchers

This work is supported in part by National Natural Science Foundation of China (61771083, 61704015), the Program for Changjiang Scholars and Innovative Research Team in University (IRT1299), Special Fund of Chongqing Key Laboratory (CSTC), Fundamental and Frontier Research Project of Chongqing (cstc2017jcyjAX0380), and University Outstanding Achievement Transformation Project of Chongqing (KJZH17117).

H. Gao et al. (Eds.): ChinaCom 2019, LNICST 313, pp. 192–204, 2020.
https://doi.org/10.1007/978-3-030-41117-6_16

have tapped into device-free sensing, which does not require the target to carry any device. Currently, there are many device-free sensing technologies, such as camera-based, infrared-based, etc. Camera-based motion detection systems have issues of individual privacy, and people behind the wall cannot be detected. Infrared-based motion detection technology has the disadvantage of requiring special equipment support which limits its application scenarios. At the same time, WiFi-based passive human detection can effectively avoid the above disadvantages due to the widely available WiFi signals interacting with objects in the environment.

Recently, using WiFi signals to passively sense the human activity has developed rapidly, including indoor localization [1,2], recognition [3–5], heartbeat detection [6,7], etc. On the one hand, the improvement of technologies such as Orthogonal Frequency Division Multiplexing (OFDM) and Multiple-Input-Multiple-Output (MIMO) enables systems to obtain more fine-grained data using fewer devices. On the other hand, it does not require users to carry any equipment, which is suitable for application of smart home.

Before implementing applications such as device-free passively localization, it is necessary to use device-free sensing technologies to detect whether there are any people in the area of interests without attaching any device [8]. However, there is a wall between the receiver and the transmitter in the home security system, and the TTW signal will be seriously attenuated. Existing techniques that extract statistical features directly from the data, such as PADs [10] and SIED [11], etc., are difficult to apply to complex indoor environments.

In this paper, we leverage Channel State Information (CSI) data between three antennas of the receiver WiFi Network Interface Cards (NIC) to implement device-free Through-the-wall Human Detection (T-HuDe). Our contribution is to use statistical information of motion characteristics, to robustly detect human movement in TTW scenario. Meanwhile, we use Support Vector Machine [13] to detect the active human behind the wall, and test results show that human activity detection rate and human absence detection rate of T-HuDe are both above 93% in most detection areas.

2 Preliminaries

2.1 Channel State Information

Leveraging the off-the-shelf NIC with slight driver modification, $N = 30$ orthogonal subcarrier data can be exported from the CSI data. Taking multipath propagation into consideration, the wireless channel of single carrier can be described as:

$$H(f) = \sum_{m=1}^{M} \alpha_m e^{-j2\pi f \tau_m} \tag{1}$$

where $H(f)$ is a subcarrier with a center frequency of f, and M is the total number of multipath of subcarrier, α_m and τ_m are the complex attenuation and propagation delay for the mth signal path, respectively.

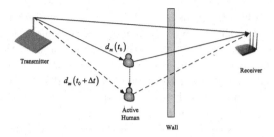

Fig. 1. Reflection path changed by active human.

When there is no object movement the wireless channel in indoor environment is relatively stable, yet it is caused large fluctuation on amplitude and phase of subcarriers that moving human intersect or walk around the transceiver link. Meanwhile, Doppler Frequency Shift (DFS) induced by human movement can introduce additional phase, which can be a key indicator for movement detection.

2.2 Doppler Frequency Shift

The signal is transmitted from the transmitter and experiences through several different paths back to the receiver, and the received signal is a superposition of these different path signals. We can use this multipath components to jointly estimate the DFS [12]. As illustrated in Fig. 1, the path length of the reflection signal changes as the human moves, and produces the DFS. The DFS is given by:

$$f_D = \frac{1}{\lambda} \frac{d_m(t_0 + \Delta t) - d_m(t_0)}{\Delta t} \tag{2}$$

where f_D is the Doppler frequency shift during time Δt, $d_m(t_0)$ is the path length of the human reflection signal at time t_0, λ is the carrier wavelength of the signal.

Active human in the indoor environment will produce DFS, which is difficult to use directly since TTW signal will be severely attenuated. However, we can calculate the trend of the spectrum power corresponding to the DFS of TTW signal, which can well describe the variance of DFS and further describe the changes of human induced channel.

3   Methodology

In this section, we illustrate the design of T-HuDe by real measurements.

3.1   Antenna Selection

The number of antennas on the device increases with the development of MIMO technology. However, different antennas on the same device exhibit different performance, as shown in Fig. 2. Figure 2(a) shows the difference term of the amplitude of each subcarrier of the three antennas, Fig. 2(b) shows the distribution of the amplitude of each subcarrier of the three antennas. The larger the standard deviation, the more likely received signal on an antenna is more sensitive to human movement [15]. Therefore, the strategy for selecting antennas is as follows:

$$ant\_opt = \underset{ant=\{1,2,3\}}{\arg\max} \left\{ \frac{1}{N} \sum_{i \in N} std\left(|H\left(f_i\right)|\right) \right\} \tag{3}$$

where N is the number of subcarriers, and ant is the serial number of the antenna. We consider the variation of all subcarrier data in one antenna, calculate the standard deviation of all subcarrier variations, and the antenna with the largest average standard deviation is the selected antenna.

3.2   Phase Sanitizations

The phase of CSI can be mined some useful characteristics to determine whether there is an active person in the current environment. However, the raw phase has severe random noise, and it is necessary to eliminate the random noise before using the phase information. Combined with the phase information induced by active human, CSI is described by:

$$
\begin{aligned}
H\left(f\right) &= e^{-j2\pi\delta} \sum_{m=1}^{M} \alpha_m e^{-j2\pi f\left(\tau_m + \frac{d_m(t_0+\Delta t)-d_m(t_0)}{c}\right)} \\
&= e^{-j2\pi\delta} \sum_{m=1}^{M} \beta_m e^{-j2\pi f \frac{d_m(t_0+\Delta t)-d_m(t_0)}{c}}
\end{aligned}
\tag{4}
$$

where $\beta_m = \alpha_m e^{-j2\pi f\tau_m}$, δ is random phase offset, c is the propagation speed of the CSI signal in the air. As illustrated in Fig. 1, the signal propagation paths from the transmitter to the receiver can be divided into two categories: some signal propagation paths do not change over time and remain constant, which called static paths; some signal propagation paths change over time, which called dynamic path [14]. Equation (4) can be rewritten as:

$$
H\left(f\right) = e^{-j2\pi\delta} \left(H_S\left(f\right) + \sum_{m \in P_d} \beta_m e^{-j2\pi f \frac{d_m(t_0+\Delta t)-d_m(t_0)}{c}} \right)
\tag{5}
$$

where $H_S(f)$ is vector sum of static paths, P_d is the set of dynamic paths. The distortion phase produced by δ can lead to wrong DFS being estimated. To avoid this phenomenon, we adopt conjugate multiplication to eliminate phase offset.

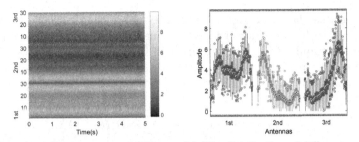

(a) The difference term of different antenna amplitude

(b) The distribution of different antenna amplitudes

Fig. 2. The amplitude in different antenna.

The conjugate multiplication of the antenna is as follows:

$$
\begin{aligned}
|H(f)|^2 &= H(f)\bar{H}(f) \\
&= |H_S(f)|^2 + H_S(f) \sum_{m \in P_d} \beta_m e^{j2\pi f \frac{d_m(t_0 + \Delta t) - d_m(t_0)}{c}} \\
&+ \bar{H}_S(f) \sum_{m \in P_d} \beta_m e^{-j2\pi f \frac{d_m(t_0 + \Delta t) - d_m(t_0)}{c}} \\
&+ \sum_{m_1 \in P_d} \sum_{m_2 \in P_d} \beta_{m_1} \beta_{m_2} e^{-j2\pi f \left(\frac{d_{m_1}(t_0 + \Delta t) - d_{m_1}(t_0)}{c} - \frac{d_{m_2}(t_0 + \Delta t) - d_{m_2}(t_0)}{c} \right)}
\end{aligned}
\tag{6}
$$

We use conjugate multiplication to eliminate the phase offset, but the conjugate multiplied data contains other terms. The product terms among dynamic paths is small and can be ignored, and the value of the conjugate multiplication of static paths is large but regarded as constants in a short time. The product terms of interest are included in the conjugate multiplication of static paths and dynamic paths, which has same value and opposite directions of the DFS [12].

3.3 Filtering

From Eq. (6) we can see that the conjugate multiplication result of an antenna, also known as Channel Frequency Response (CFR) power, can be divided into four parts, of which only two parts contain useful information. The value of the conjugate multiplication of static paths occupies the dominant component and belongs to the zero-frequency component, and considering some low-frequency interference, the lower cutoff frequency of the bandpass filter is set to 2 Hz. Assuming that the speed of the active person is less than 2 m/s and filtering out high frequency components such as some burst noise, the higher cutoff frequency is set to 80 Hz [12].

After using the bandpass filter, a conjugate multiplied component of static paths and dynamic paths can be obtained. In Eq. (6), its component consists

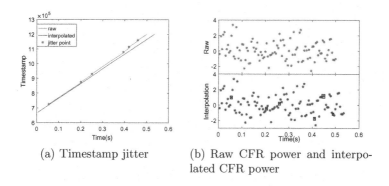

(a) Timestamp jitter

(b) Raw CFR power and interpolated CFR power

Fig. 3. Raw data and interpolated data.

of two parts, which can estimate two Doppler velocities of the same value but opposite directions, but this does not affect the estimation, because only the spectrum power corresponding to the Doppler velocity is concerned instead of the Doppler velocity direction. Based on the above discussion, the subsequent partial default Doppler velocity is positive.

3.4   Linear Interpolation

In general, timestamps are consecutive in adjacent packets. However, data loss is common in data collection and causes sample jitter, while timestamp discontinuities and data loss are related. Since each timestamp corresponds to a filtered CFR power value, we look for the jitter point of the timestamp and use linear interpolation for the corresponding filtered CFR power. As shown in Fig. 3, Fig. 3(a) is the jitter and interpolated timestamp, the timestamp is discrete, and for better description, we draw the timestamps as contiguous, Fig. 3(b) is the jittered and interpolated filtered CFR power. After interpolating the timestamp, a complete filtered CFR power sequence value can be obtained.

3.5   Active Human Detection

Estimated Spectrum Power. In commercial WiFi devices, WiFi signals are transmitted on multiple subcarriers. Countering the frequency selective fading that exists between carriers, we use the MUSIC-based Doppler estimation algorithm [12] with multi-carrier information.

For simplicity, assume that there are K consecutive CSI samples with a sampling interval of microseconds. At the same time, assume that the velocity of K samples is constant during time t_0 and the velocity is $v(t_0) = v(t_0 + \Delta t_k) = \frac{d(t_0 + \Delta t_k) - d(t_0)}{\Delta t_k}$, where Δt_k is the time interval between the kth sample and the first sample at time t_0. If the path is a static path, $v(t_0)$ is zero, and the CSI phase does not change over time. On the contrary, $v(t_0)$ in the dynamic path is non-zero, and the CSI phase changes over time. If there is only a single signal path, the

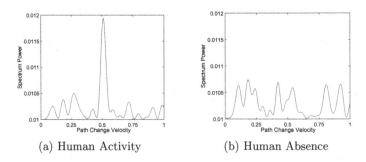

(a) Human Activity   (b) Human Absence

Fig. 4. The spectrum power corresponding to path change velocity in TTW detection.

phase difference between time $t_0 + \Delta t_k$ and time t_0 is $p_{t_0}\left(\Delta t_k\right) = e^{-j2\pi f \frac{v(t_0)\Delta t_k}{c}}$, where f is the carrier frequency. Therefore, the phase difference of the K samples compared to the first sample is as follows:

$$\mathbf{s}\left(v_{t_0}\right) = \left[\, 1\ p_{t_0}\left(\Delta t_2\right)\ p_{t_0}\left(\Delta t_3\right) \ldots p_{t_0}\left(\Delta t_k\right)\right]^T \tag{7}$$

The vector $\mathbf{s}\left(v_{t_0}\right)$ is the steering vector. The received signal matrix composed of M multipath signals is as follows:

$$
\begin{aligned}
\mathbf{X}\left(f\right) &= \left[\, H\left(f,t_0\right)\ H\left(f,t_0 + \Delta t_2\right) \ldots H\left(f,t_0 + \Delta t_K\right)\right]^T \\
&= \begin{bmatrix} 1 & 1 & \cdots & 1 \\ p_{t_0,1}\left(\Delta t_2\right) & p_{t_0,2}\left(\Delta t_2\right) & \cdots & p_{t_0,M}\left(\Delta t_2\right) \\ \vdots & \vdots & \ddots & \vdots \\ p_{t_0,1}\left(\Delta t_K\right) & p_{t_0,2}\left(\Delta t_K\right) & \cdots & p_{t_0,M}\left(\Delta t_K\right) \end{bmatrix} \begin{bmatrix} \beta_1 \\ \beta_2 \\ \vdots \\ \beta_M \end{bmatrix} + \mathbf{N}\left(f\right) \\
&= \left[\, \mathbf{s}\left(v_{t_0,1}\right)\ \mathbf{s}\left(v_{t_0,2}\right) \ldots \mathbf{s}\left(v_{t_0,M}\right)\right] \mathbf{c} + \mathbf{N}\left(f\right) \\
&= \mathbf{Sc} + \mathbf{N}(f)
\end{aligned} \tag{8}
$$

where $p_{t_0,m}\left(\Delta t_k\right)$ is the phase difference of the mth path time $t_0 + \Delta t_k$ and time t_0, $\mathbf{s}\left(v_{t_0,m}\right)$ is the steering vector of the mth path, $\mathbf{N}\left(f\right)$ is noise matrix, and $\mathbf{c} = \left[\, \beta_1\ \beta_2 \ldots \beta_M\right]^T$ is a signal vector. The CSI data contains N subcarriers, and the received CSI data can be written as follows:

$$
\begin{aligned}
\mathbf{Y}\left(f\right) &= \left[\, \mathbf{X}\left(f_1\right)\ \mathbf{X}\left(f_2\right) \ldots \mathbf{X}\left(f_N\right)\right] \\
&= \begin{bmatrix} 1 & 1 & \cdots & 1 \\ p_{t_0,1}\left(\Delta t_2\right) & p_{t_0,2}\left(\Delta t_2\right) & \cdots & p_{t_0,M}\left(\Delta t_2\right) \\ \vdots & \vdots & \ddots & \vdots \\ p_{t_0,1}\left(\Delta t_K\right) & p_{t_0,2}\left(\Delta t_K\right) & \cdots & p_{t_0,M}\left(\Delta t_K\right) \end{bmatrix} \begin{bmatrix} \beta_{1,f_1} & \beta_{1,f_2} & \cdots & \beta_{1,f_N} \\ \beta_{2,f_1} & \beta_{2,f_2} & \cdots & \beta_{2,f_N} \\ \vdots & \vdots & \ddots & \vdots \\ \beta_{M,f_1} & \beta_{M,f_2} & \cdots & \beta_{M,f_N} \end{bmatrix} + \mathbf{N}\left(f\right) \\
&= \left[\, \mathbf{s}\left(v_{t_0,1}\right)\ \mathbf{s}\left(v_{t_0,2}\right) \ldots \mathbf{s}\left(v_{t_0,M}\right)\right] \left[\, \mathbf{c}\left(f_1\right)\ \mathbf{c}\left(f_2\right) \ldots \mathbf{c}\left(f_N\right)\right] + \mathbf{N}\left(f\right) \\
&= \mathbf{SC} + \mathbf{N}\left(f\right)
\end{aligned} \tag{9}
$$

where $\mathbf{c}\left(f_n\right)$ is a vector with carrier frequency f_n, $\mathbf{C} = \left[\, \mathbf{c}\left(f_1\right)\ \mathbf{c}\left(f_2\right) \ldots \mathbf{c}\left(f_N\right)\right]$ is the signal matrix. To estimate the steering vector $\mathbf{s}\left(v_{t_0}\right)$ containing DFS

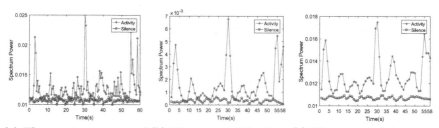

(a) The spectrum power of (b) The mean of the first- (c) The mean of the spec-
raw data   order difference of   the trum power
                              spectrum power

Fig. 5. Activity and silence spectrum power.

information, the MUSIC algorithm is applied to Eq. 9. The correlation matrix
$\mathbf{R_{YY}}$ of the matrix $\mathbf{Y}$ is as follows:

$$\begin{aligned}
\mathbf{R_{YY}} &= \mathrm{E}\left[\mathbf{YY}^{\mathrm{H}}\right] \\
&= \mathbf{S}\mathrm{E}\left[\mathbf{CC}^{\mathrm{H}}\right]\mathbf{S}^{\mathrm{H}} + \mathrm{E}\left[\mathbf{NN}^{\mathrm{H}}\right] \\
&= \mathbf{SR_{CC}S}^{\mathrm{H}} + \sigma^2\mathbf{I}
\end{aligned} \tag{10}$$

where $\mathbf{R_{CC}}$ is the correlation matrix of the signal matrix $\mathbf{C}$, σ^2 is the noise
variance, and $\mathbf{I}$ is the unit matrix. While $\mathbf{R_{CC}}$ is a full rank matrix with K
eigenvalues, including the smallest $K - L$ eigenvalues associated with noise, and
the L eigenvalues associated with the signal. The ith eigenvalue corresponds to
the eigenvector $\mathbf{e}_i$, the noise eigenvector and the signal eigenvector constitute a
noise subspace $\mathbf{E}_N = \begin{bmatrix} \mathbf{e}_1 & \mathbf{e}_2 & \dots & \mathbf{e}_{K-L} \end{bmatrix}$ and a signal subspace, respectively. The
steering vector and the noise subspace $\mathbf{E}_N$ are orthogonal, and the spectrum
function is as follow:

$$P\left(v_{t_0}\right) = \frac{1}{\mathbf{s}^{\mathrm{H}}\left(v_{t_0}\right)\mathbf{E}_N\mathbf{E}_N^{\mathrm{H}}\mathbf{s}\left(v_{t_0}\right)} \tag{11}$$

In which sharp peaks occur at the path change velocity of the signals.

After the above process, we could use Eq. (11) to calculate the path change
velocity spectrum, Fig. 4(a) and (b) depict the path change velocity spectrum
in TTW detection, respectively. In theory, TTW signal path only retains the
dynamic path, and only one peak appears on the spectrum when there is an
active human. The real peak of the spectrum does not appear when active human
absence. In reality, TTW signal will be severely attenuated, which susceptible
to noise, and it is difficult to completely remove all static paths and preserve
the dynamic paths. Therefore, there are multiple peaks in Fig. 4, and we select
the spectrum power of the largest peak to represent the value during this time.
Figure 4(b) shows that there is no active human in the TTW detection, and the
path change speed and its corresponding spectrum power may still have real
peaks. Considering the above situation, it is difficult to directly detect active
human using spectrum power estimated from TTW signal.

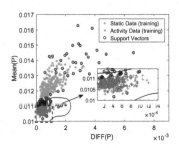

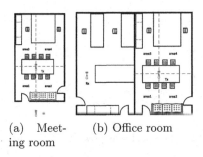

(a) Meet-   (b) Office room
ing room

Fig. 6. The feature distribution of
activity data and static data in TTW
scenario.

Fig. 7. Experiment testbed.

Feature Extraction. As shown in Fig. 5(a), the TTW signal is attenuated
the signal so that the static data is similar to the walk data, and the spectrum
power estimated by the static data and the activity data is similar. Since it is
difficult to directly use the estimated spectrum power, further feature extraction
is required. Although the estimated spectrum power is similar, it can still be
roughly divided into two parts. In this section, we calculate two characteristics
of a period of data, one of which is the mean of the power spectrum power for
a period of time $Mean\,(P) = \frac{1}{W}\sum_{w\in W} P\,(v_w)$, and the other is the mean of the
first-order difference $DIFF\,(P)$:

$$DIFF\,(P) = \frac{1}{W-1}\sum_{w=1}^{W-1} |P\,(v_w) - P\,(v_{w+1})| \tag{12}$$

where W is the length of time. We use the sliding window method to calculate
the mean and the mean of the first-order difference of the spectrum power. As
shown in Fig. 5(b) and (c), the degree of discrimination between the two parts
is improved.

To illustrate the reliability of the selected features, we conduct the SVM [13]
based classification on training data, in which the kernel function is "rbf". As
shown in Fig. 6, the training data can be used for obtaining an effective classifier.

4   Experiment and Evaluation

In this section, we first detail present the experiment settings and methodology.
Then, we evaluate the performance of T-HuDe.

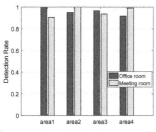
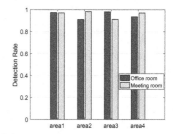

(a) TP rate in different scenarios   (b) TN rate in different scenarios

Fig. 8. Detection rate in different scenarios.

4.1 Experiment Methodology

To evaluate the performance of T-HuDe, we conduct experiments on the mini PC, which is equipped with Intel 5300 WiFi NIC and Ubuntu 10.04 Operating System (OS). CSI measurements are made for each packet using the Linux CSI tool [16]. The mini PC with one antenna is the transmitter, which operates in IEEE 802.11n AP mode at 5.745 GHz with 40 MHz bandwidth, and the mini PC with three antennas is the receiver, which collects 200 packets per second. We collect data in testbed as shown in Fig. 7. The testbed consists of two scenarios, meeting room and office room. In the meeting room scene, one of the AP is placed outside the room, and in the office room scene, the AP is placed in a different room, and all the walls are cement walls. The placement height of AP in all of these scenes are set to 1.1 m.

To test the impact of different areas on the detection rate, we divide the Tx room into 4 areas. The collected data includes two categories: (1) static data: there is no active human in the current environment; (2) activity data: there is an active human in the current environment, and the active human moving around in 4 areas, respectively.

4.2 Performance Evaluation

Evaluation Metric. To evaluate the performance of the T-HuDe system. We use the following two metrics.

– True Positive (TP) Rate: TP rate is the probability that an active human is correctly detected.
– True Negative (TN) Rate: TN rate is the probability that the static environment is correctly detected.

Overall Performance. We first depict TP rate and TN rate of systems working in different experimental cases. To evaluate the overall performance of T-HuDe, we calculate the spectrum power of the Doppler frequency shift with a window size of 0.5 s and calculate the eigenvalues using a parameter setting with a sliding

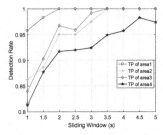 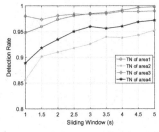

(a) Impact of sliding window on TP rate   (b) Impact of sliding window on TN rate

Fig. 9. Impact of sliding window on detection rate.

window size of 2 s. Figure 8 presents results of four different test areas measured at different places, and shows that the system achieves excellent performance, the TP is higher than 93% in most areas. To make it clear, we compare the static data with the activity data of different areas respectively, and calculate the TN rate of different areas. As shown in Fig. 8(b), in most areas, the TN rate is also higher than 93%. However, the system has different detection rate in different areas, and the detection rate of each area is different. For office room scenarios, area1 and area3 have higher detection rate, and area2 and area4 have lower detection rate. For meeting room scenarios, area1 and area2 have higher detection rate and area3 has lower detection rate. In the higher detection rate areas, the active person is more likely to influence TTW signal, thus having a higher successful detection rate.

Impact of Sliding Window Size. We analyze the effect of sliding window size on TP and TN in different experimental areas. Generally, the detection rates of TP and TN rise as the sliding window size increases. Figure 9 illustrates this conjecture well, with the increase of the size of the sliding window, the detection rate of the system has increased. A reasonable explanation is that the influence of active human motion would be more probably captured when increasing the window size. In Fig. 9(a), the TP rate of most areas is maintained above 95% when the sliding window size exceeds 2.5 s, while the TP tends to be stable when the sliding window is increased to a certain size. When the sliding window size is less than 2 s, the performance of the system is less satisfied, mainly because the sampling time is too short to catch noticeable human movement. The same situation also occurs in Fig. 9(b). It is worth noting that the TP and TN detection rate of area1 are greater than 95% regardless of the sliding window size. The main reason is that area1 is the most sensitive area, and it is easy to detect the motion of the active human.

Compare Other Technologies. To verify the performance of the system, we compare T-HuDe with other systems. To be more specific, we compare T-HuDe with R-TTWD [9], which designed for the TTW human detection with

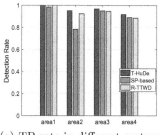

(a) TP rate in different system

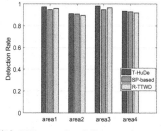

(b) TN rate in different system

Fig. 10. Detection rate in different system.

commodity devices, and relies on amplitude-based features for human detection. To calculate the features, the R-TTWD [9] applies wavelet denoising on the CSI, and performs a Principal Component Analysis (PCA) [17], and then calculates the mean of the first-order difference of the principal components. For fair comparison, we use the antenna selection strategy to select the appropriate single antenna data, and use two eigenvalues in R-TTWD [9], including the mean of the first-order difference of the second principal component and the third principal component. Besides, we also test the detection rate using a fixed threshold based approach to spectrum power, which denoted as "SP-based" in Fig. 10.

Figure 10 shows TP rate and TN rate of systems working in TTW scenarios, and the three detection systems show different detection rate in different areas, which means that the areas have different impact on performance. T-HuDe achieves TP rate and TN above 93% in most areas. SP-based also achieves a good detection rate in most areas, but T-HuDe outperformes SP-based at most places, and SP-based is susceptible to environmental influences, such as TP rate in area 2. In addition, the performance of R-TTWD is acceptable, but it is less satisfied compared to T-HuDe.

5 Conclusion

In this paper, we present an accurate and robustness TTW active human detection system with commodity WiFi devices. Since the different performance of different antennas, we use the antenna selection strategy to select the appropriate antenna and use a bandpass filter to filter out the noise signal. Then, we introduce Doppler-MUSIC to estimate the spectrum power corresponding to the Doppler velocity. Afterwards, we calculate the mean and the mean of the first-order difference of the spectrum power over time to achieve active human detection in TTW. We prototype T-HuDe in two indoor environments, and the experiment results show that the TP rate and TN rate of the system are better than 93% in most areas.

References

1. Xiao, J.: Enhancing WLAN-based indoor localization with channel state information. Hong Kong University of Science and Technology, Hong Kong (2014)
2. Li, X., Li, S., Zhang, D., Xiong, J., Wang, Y., Mei, H.: Dynamic-music: accurate device-free indoor localization. In: Proceedings of the 2016 ACM International Joint Conference on Pervasive and Ubiquitous Computing, pp 196–207 ACM (2016)
3. Duan, S., Yu, T., He, J.: WiDriver: driver activity recognition system based on WiFi CSI. Int. J. Wirel. Inf. Networks 25(2), 146–156 (2018)
4. Wang, H., Zhang, D., Wang, Y., Ma, J., Wang, Y., Li, S.: RT-fall: a real-time and contactless fall detection system with commodity wifi devices. IEEE Trans. Mob. Comput. 16(2), 511–526 (2016)
5. Wang, Y., Wu, K., Ni, L.M.: WiFall: device-free fall detection by wireless networks. IEEE Trans. Mob. Comput. 16(2), 581–594 (2016)
6. Wang, X., Yang, C., Mao, S.: PhaseBeat: exploiting CSI phase data for vital sign monitoring with commodity wifi devices. In: 2017 IEEE 37th International Conference on Distributed Computing Systems (ICDCS), pp. 1230–1239. IEEE (2017)
7. Liu, X., Cao, J., Tang, S., Wen, J., Guo, P.: Contactless respiration monitoring via off-the-shelf wifi devices. IEEE Trans. Mob. Comput. 15(10), 2466–2479 (2015)
8. Youssef, M., Mah, M., Agrawala, A.: Challenges: device-free passive localization for wireless environments. In: Proceedings of the 13th Annual ACM International Conference on Mobile Computing and Networking, pp. 222–229. ACM (2007)
9. Zhu, H., Xiao, F., Sun, L., Wang, R., Yang, P.: R-TTWD: robust device-free through-the-wall detection of moving human with wifi. IEEE J. Sel. Areas Commun. 35(5), 1090–1103 (2017)
10. Qian, K., Wu, C., Yang, Z., Liu, Y., Zhou, Z.: PADS: passive detection of moving targets with dynamic speed using PHY layer information. In: 2014 20th IEEE International Conference on Parallel and Distributed Systems (ICPADS), pp. 1–8. IEEE (2014)
11. Lv, J., Yang, W., Gong, L., Man, D., Du, X.: Robust WLAN-based indoor fine-grained intrusion detection. In: 2016 IEEE Global Communications Conference (GLOBECOM), pp. 1–6. IEEE (2016)
12. Li, X., et al.: IndoTrack: device-free indoor human tracking with commodity wi-fi. Proc. ACM Interact. Mob. Wearable Ubiquit. Technol. 1(3), 72 (2017)
13. Boser, B.E., Guyon, I.M., Vapnik, V.N.: A training algorithm for optimal margin classifiers. In: Proceedings of the fifth Annual Workshop on Computational Learning Theory, pp. 144–152. ACM (1992)
14. Wang, W., Liu, A.X., Shahzad, M., Ling, K., Lu, S.: Understanding and modeling of wifi signal based human activity recognition. In: Proceedings of the 21st Annual International Conference on Mobile Computing and Networking, pp. 65–76. ACM (2015)
15. Qian, K., Wu, C., Zhou, Z., Zheng, Y., Yang, Z., Liu, Y.: Inferring motion direction using commodity wi-fi for interactive exergames. In: Proceedings of the 2017 CHI Conference on Human Factors in Computing Systems, pp. 1961–1972. ACM (2017)
16. Li, Z., Tian, Z., Zhou, M., Jin, Y.: Wi-vision: an accurate and robust LOS/NLOS identification system using Hopkins statistic. In: GLOBECOM 2017–2017 IEEE Global Communications Conference, pp. 1–6. IEEE (2017)
17. Abdi, H., Williams, L.J.: Principal component analysis. Wiley Interdisc. Rev.: Computat. Stat. 2(4), 433–459 (2010)

Legitimate Eavesdropping with Multiple Wireless Powered Eavesdroppers

Qun Li and Ding Xu$^{(\boxtimes)}$

Nanjing University of Posts and Telecommunications, Nanjing, China
xuding@ieee.org

Abstract. This paper considers a suspicious communication network with multiple suspicious source-destination nodes and multiple wireless powered legitimate eavesdroppers, where the legitimate eavesdroppers are assumed to be collusive or non-collusive. A minimum harvested energy constraint is applied at each eavesdropper such that each eavesdropper must harvest a minimum required energy. The legitimate eavesdropping in such a scenario is investigated and our aim is to maximize the average successful eavesdropping probability by optimizing the power splitting ratio at each eavesdropper under the minimum harvested energy constraint. The optimal algorithm is proposed to solve the optimization problem for both collusive eavesdroppers and non-collusive eavesdroppers. Simulation results show that the proposed algorithm achieves the upper bound of the successful eavesdropping probability when the energy harvesting efficiency is large, the required minimum harvested energy is small, or the transmit power of the suspicious source node is high.

Keywords: Legitimate eavesdropping · Wireless powered communication · Successful eavesdropping probability · Collusive eavesdroppers · Non-collusiveeavesdroppers

1 Introduction

Recently, legitimate eavesdropping in physical layer security has attracted a lot of attention due to its ability to legitimately eavesdrop the communication of suspicious users such as terrorists and criminals for government agencies [1–7]. Specifically, in [1], a legitimate eavesdropper was assumed to eavesdrop a point-to-point suspicious communication by proactive jamming to improve eavesdropping performance. In [2], legitimate proactive eavesdropping was investigated for a point-to-point suspicious communication with a multi-antenna legitimate eavesdropper. In [3], legitimate proactive eavesdropping was investigated for a three-node relay-based suspicious communication. In [4], legitimate eavesdropping was investigated for a hybrid automatic repeat request (HARQ) based point-to-point suspicious communication. In [5], legitimate eavesdropping was investigated by assuming that the legitimate eavesdropper can help the suspicious communication for improving the eavesdropping rate. In [6], the legitimate

H. Gao et al. (Eds.): ChinaCom 2019, LNICST 313, pp. 205–215, 2020.
https://doi.org/10.1007/978-3-030-41117-6_17

eavesdropper with the help from a third-party jammer was assumed to eavesdrop a point-to-point suspicious communication. In [7], legitimate eavesdropping was investigated by assuming that a spoofing relay existed for assisting the legitimate eavesdropping. Note that all the above work in [1–7] considered that the legitimate eavesdroppers are powered by conventional energy sources.

Radio frequency (RF) energy harvesting has attracted a lot of attention due to its ability to power devices by harvesting energy from RF signals [8–11]. Therefore, the legitimate eavesdroppers can also be powered by RF energy harvesting. In this respect, very few work investigated legitimate eavesdropping with wireless powered legitimate eavesdroppers. Particularly, in [12], the performance of legitimate eavesdropping in terms of successful eavesdropping probability with a wireless powered legitimate eavesdropper was investigated for a point-to-point suspicious communication. In [13], offline and online proactive jamming algorithms for the legitimate surveillance with a battery-aided full-duplex wireless powered monitor were proposed. In [14], legitimate eavesdropping in a wireless powered suspicious communication network was investigated and four different performance metrics, namely the successful eavesdropping probability, the average eavesdropping rate, the relative eavesdropping rate and the eavesdropping energy efficiency were evaluated. Note that [12–14] considered a point-to-point suspicious communication with only one legitimate eavesdropper.

This paper investigates legitimate eavesdropping in a suspicious communication network with multiple suspicious source-destination nodes and multiple wireless powered legitimate eavesdroppers. Specifically, the legitimate eavesdroppers are assumed to be collusive or non-collusive, and a minimum harvested energy constraint is applied at each eavesdropper such that each eavesdropper must harvest a minimum required energy. Our aim is to maximize the average successful eavesdropping probability by optimizing the power splitting ratio at each eavesdropper under the minimum harvested energy constraint. For both collusive eavesdroppers and non-collusive eavesdroppers, the optimal algorithm is proposed to solve the optimization problem. It is shown that the proposed algorithm outperforms the reference algorithm and achieves the upper bound of the successful eavesdropping probability when the energy harvesting efficiency is large, the required minimum harvested energy is small, or the transmit power of the suspicious source node is high.

The rest of the paper is organized as follows. Section 2 presents the system model and formulates the investigated problem. Section 3 proposes the optimal algorithms. Section 4 verifies the proposed algorithms by simulation results. Section 5 concludes the paper.

2   System Model and Problem Formulation

As shown in Fig. 1, we consider N pairs of suspicious source-destination nodes in presence of M wireless powered legitimate eavesdroppers. Semi-static fading channels are assumed, where channels are constant within a transmission block and may change from block to block. Let h_i denote the channel power gain of

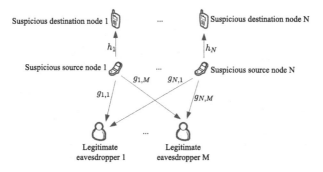

Fig. 1. System model.

the i-th pair of suspicious source-destination nodes and $g_{i,j}$ the channel power gain from the suspicious source node i to the eavesdropper j, respectively. Let p_i denote the transmit power of the suspicious source node i. The achievable rate of the i-th pair of suspicious source-destination nodes is

$$r_0^i = \log_2\left(1 + \frac{p_i h_i}{\sigma^2}\right), \tag{1}$$

where σ^2 denote the noise power. It is assumed that the eavesdroppers are not powered by conventional energy sources and they have to harvest energy for providing enough circuit power. Thus, for the eavesdropper j, a ratio $\rho_{i,j}$ of the receiving power from the suspicious source node i is split for information decoding and the remaining is for energy harvesting. A minimum harvested energy constraint is adopted to guarantee that the eavesdroppers have enough harvested energy, given by

$$\mathbb{E}\left\{\xi \sum_{i=1}^{N}(1 - \rho_{i,j})p_i g_{i,j}\right\} \geq Q_j, j = 1, \ldots, M. \tag{2}$$

where $\mathbb{E}$ is the expectation, ξ is the energy harvesting efficiency and Q_j is the minimum harvested energy requirement for the eavesdropper j. The achievable rate at the eavesdropper j for eavesdropping the suspicious source node i is written as

$$r_1^{i,j} = \log_2\left(1 + \frac{\rho_{i,j}p_i g_{i,j}}{\sigma^2}\right). \tag{3}$$

Two scenario are considered for the eavesdroppers. The first scenario assumes that the eavesdroppers are collusive and the achieved eavesdropping rate for the suspicious source node i is written as

$$r_1^i = \log_2\left(1 + \frac{\sum_{j=1}^{M}\rho_{i,j}p_i g_{i,j}}{\sigma^2}\right). \tag{4}$$

The second scenario assumes that the eavesdroppers are not collusive and the achieved eavesdropping rate for the suspicious source node i is written as

$$r_1^i = \log_2\left(1 + \frac{p_i \max_j \rho_{i,j} g_{i,j}}{\sigma^2}\right). \tag{5}$$

We assume that as long as $r_1^i \geq r_0^i$, the eavesdroppers can successfully eavesdrop the information from the suspicious source node i, and the successful eavesdropping probability for the suspicious source node i is defined as $\Pr(r_1^i \geq r_0^i)$.

Our aim is to maximize the average successful eavesdropping probability by optimizing the power splitting ratio $\{\rho_{i,j}\}$ under the minimum harvested energy constraint. The optimization problem is formulated as

$$(P1): \max_{\{\rho_{i,j}\}} \frac{1}{N} \sum_{i=1}^{N} \Pr(r_1^i \geq r_0^i) \tag{6}$$

$$\text{s.t. } 0 \leq \rho_{i,j} \leq 1, i = 1,\ldots,N, j = 1,\ldots,M, \tag{7}$$

$$\mathbb{E}\left\{\xi \sum_{i=1}^{N}(1 - \rho_{i,j})p_i g_{i,j}\right\} \geq Q_j, j = 1,\ldots,M. \tag{8}$$

3   Proposed Algorithms

In this section, we investigate P1 with collusive eavesdroppers or non-collusive eavesdroppers. P1 may be infeasible due to the constraint in (8). The feasibility condition for P1 is given as follows. If $\mathbb{E}\left\{\xi \sum_{i=1}^{N} p_i g_{i,j}\right\} \geq Q_j$ is satisfied for all $j = 1,\ldots,M$, then P1 is feasible.

To solve P1, we rewrite $\Pr(r_1^i \geq r_0^i)$ as $\Pr(r_1^i \geq r_0^i) = \mathbb{E}\{X_i\}$, where

$$X_i = \begin{cases} 1, & \text{if } r_1^i \geq r_0^i, \\ 0, & \text{otherwise.} \end{cases} \tag{9}$$

We optimally solve P1 using convex optimization theory [15], since the time-sharing condition can be verified to be satisfied by P1 [16]. The Lagrangian of P1 can be written as

$$L(\{\lambda_j\}, \{\rho_{i,j}\}) = \frac{1}{N} \sum_{i=1}^{N} \mathbb{E}\{X_i\}$$

$$+ \sum_{j=1}^{M} \lambda_j \left(\mathbb{E}\left\{\xi \sum_{i=1}^{N}(1 - \rho_{i,j})p_i g_{i,j}\right\} - Q_j\right), \tag{10}$$

where $\lambda_j, j = 1,\ldots,M$ are the non-negative dual variables with respect to the constraint in (8). The dual function $G(\{\lambda_j\})$ is defined as

$$G(\{\lambda_j\}) = \max_{\{\rho_{i,j}\}} L(\{\lambda_j\}, \{\rho_{i,j}\}) \tag{11}$$

$$\text{s.t. } 0 \leq \rho_{i,j} \leq 1, i = 1,\ldots,N, j = 1,\ldots,M. \tag{12}$$

Then, the dual problem to optimize $\{\lambda_j\}$ is given by

$$\max_{\{\lambda_j\}} G(\{\lambda_j\}) \tag{13}$$

$$\text{s.t. } 0 \leq \lambda_j \leq 1, j = 1, \ldots, M, \tag{14}$$

which can be solved with the subgradient method [15]. Thus, what remains is to solve the problem in (11), which is given in what follows.

The problem in (11) can be decoupled into subproblems, each for a suspicious source node in a transmission block as given by

$$\max_{\{\rho_{i,j}\}} \frac{X_i}{N} - \xi p_i \sum_{j=1}^{M} \lambda_j \rho_{i,j} g_{i,j} \tag{15}$$

$$\text{s.t. } 0 \leq \rho_{i,j} \leq 1, j = 1, \ldots, M, \tag{16}$$

for $i = 1, \ldots, N$.

3.1 Collusive Eavesdroppers

For collusive eavesdroppers, we discuss the problem in (15) in the following two cases.

Case 1: $X_i = 1$. In this case, we have to satisfy $\sum_{j=1}^{M} \rho_{i,j} g_{i,j} \geq h_i$ in order to let $X_i = 1$. The problem in (15) is thus rewritten as

$$\max_{\{\rho_{i,j}\}} \frac{1}{N} - \xi p_i \sum_{j=1}^{M} \lambda_j \rho_{i,j} g_{i,j} \tag{17}$$

$$\text{s.t. } 0 \leq \rho_{i,j} \leq 1, j = 1, \ldots, M, \tag{18}$$

$$\sum_{j=1}^{M} \rho_{i,j} g_{i,j} \geq h_i. \tag{19}$$

The above problem belongs to linear programming and thus can be efficiently solved.

Case 2: $X_i = 0$. In this case, we have to satisfy $\sum_{j=1}^{M} \rho_{i,j} g_{i,j} < h_i$ in order to let $X_i = 0$. The problem in (15) is thus rewritten as

$$\max_{\{\rho_{i,j}\}} -\xi p_i \sum_{j=1}^{M} \lambda_j \rho_{i,j} g_{i,j} \tag{20}$$

$$\text{s.t. } 0 \leq \rho_{i,j} \leq 1, j = 1, \ldots, M, \tag{21}$$

$$\sum_{j=1}^{M} \rho_{i,j} g_{i,j} < h_i. \tag{22}$$

It is easy to verify that the optimal solution of the above problem is $\rho_{i,j} = 0, j = 1, \ldots, M$ and the optimal objective function value is 0.

Algorithm 1. Proposed algorithm to solve P1 with collusive eavesdroppers.

1: Initialize: $\lambda_j, j = 1, \ldots, M$.
2: **repeat**
3:    **for** $i = 1$ to N **do**
4:        Obtain $\rho_{i,j}, j = 1, \ldots, M$ by solving the problem in (17) using linear programming and denote its optimal objective function value as O.
5:        **if** $O < 0$ **then**
6:            Set $\rho_{i,j} = 0, j = 1, \ldots, M$.
7:        **end if**
8:    **end for**
9:    Update $\lambda_j, j = 1, \ldots, M$ by the subgradient method.
10: **until** $\lambda_j, j = 1, \ldots, M$ converge to a desired accuracy.

Based on the above discussion on the problem in (15) with collusive eavesdroppers, its optimal solution is obtained by the following steps: Firstly, the problem in (17) is solved with linear programming. Then, if the optimal objective function value in (17) is larger than or equal to 0, the optimal solution the problem in (17) is the optimal solution of the problem in (17). Otherwise, the optimal solution of the problem in (17) is $\rho_{i,j} = 0, j = 1, \ldots, M$.

The algorithm to solve P1 with collusive eavesdroppers is summarized in Algorithm 1.

3.2 Non-collusive Eavesdroppers

For non-collusive eavesdroppers, we discuss the problem in (15) in the following two cases.

Case 1: $X_i = 1$. In this case, we have to satisfy $\max_j \rho_{i,j} g_{i,j} \geq h_i$ in order to let $X_i = 1$. The problem in (15) is thus rewritten as

$$\max_{\{\rho_{i,j}\}} \frac{1}{N} - \xi p_i \sum_{j=1}^{M} \lambda_j \rho_{i,j} g_{i,j} \tag{23}$$

$$\text{s.t. } 0 \leq \rho_{i,j} \leq 1, j = 1, \ldots, M, \tag{24}$$

$$\max_j \rho_{i,j} g_{i,j} \geq h_i. \tag{25}$$

Define the set $\mathbb{J}_i = \{j | \frac{h_i}{g_{i,j}} \leq 1, j = 1, \ldots, M\}$. Suppose that $\rho_{i,j} = \frac{h_i}{g_{i,j}}, j \in \mathbb{J}_i$, then we have $\lambda_j \rho_{i,j} g_{i,j} = \lambda_j h_i$. Thus, the optimal solution of the above problem is

$$\rho_{i,j} = \begin{cases} \frac{h_i}{g_{i,j}}, & j = \arg\min_{k \in \mathbb{J}_i} \lambda_k, \\ 0, & j \neq \arg\min_{k \in \mathbb{J}_i} \lambda_k. \end{cases} \tag{26}$$

The optimal objective function value in (23) is thus $\frac{1}{N} - \xi p_i \lambda_{j^*} h_i$, where $j^* = \arg\min_{k \in \mathbb{J}_i} \lambda_k$.

Algorithm 2. Proposed algorithm to solve P1 with non-collusive eavesdroppers.

1: Initialize: $\lambda_j, j = 1, \ldots, M$.
2: **repeat**
3:     Obtain $\rho_{i,j}, i = 1, \ldots, N, j = 1, \ldots, M$ from (30).
4:     Update $\lambda_j, j = 1, \ldots, M$ by the subgradient method.
5: **until** $\lambda_j, j = 1, \ldots, M$ converge to a desired accuracy.

Case 2: $X_i = 0$. In this case, we have to satisfy $\max_j \rho_{i,j} g_{i,j} < h_i$ in order to let $X_i = 0$. The problem in (15) is thus rewritten as

$$\max_{\{\rho_{i,j}\}} - \xi p_i \sum_{j=1}^{M} \lambda_j \rho_{i,j} g_{i,j} \tag{27}$$

$$\text{s.t. } 0 \leq \rho_{i,j} \leq 1, j = 1, \ldots, M, \tag{28}$$

$$\max_j \rho_{i,j} g_{i,j} < h_i. \tag{29}$$

It is easy to verify that the optimal solution of the above problem is $\rho_{i,j} = 0, j = 1, \ldots, M$ and the optimal objective function value is 0.

Based on the above discussion on the problem in (15) with non-collusive eavesdroppers, its optimal solution is obtained as

$$\rho_{i,j} = \begin{cases} \frac{h_i}{g_{i,j}}, & j = \arg\min_{k \in \mathbb{J}_i} \lambda_k, \\ \frac{1}{N} - \xi p_i \lambda_j h_i \geq 0, \\ 0, & \text{otherwise}, \end{cases} \tag{30}$$

for $j = 1, \ldots, M$.

The algorithm to solve P1 with non-collusive eavesdroppers is summarized in Algorithm 2.

4   Simulation Results

This section provides simulation results to verify the proposed algorithm with collusive eavesdroppers or non-collusive eavesdroppers. In the simulation, all the channel power gains are assumed to follow exponential distribution with unit mean and we set $\sigma^2 = 1$, $N = 2$, $M = 2$ and $p_i = p, i = 1, \ldots, N$. For performance comparison, a reference algorithm which sets $\rho_{i,j} = 0.5$ for all $i = 1, \ldots, N, j = 1, \ldots, M$ is adopted. Besides, an upper bound for the proposed algorithm which ignores the minimum harvested energy constraint and sets $\rho_{i,j} = 1$ for all $i = 1, \ldots, N, j = 1, \ldots, M$ is also adopted.

Figure 2 plots the average successful eavesdropping probability against ξ with $Q = 2\,\text{W}$ and $p = 5\,\text{W}$ for different algorithms. Note that zero average successful eavesdropping probability means P1 is infeasible for the adopted algorithm. It is shown that the average successful eavesdropping probability increases as ξ increases. This is because a higher ξ leads to higher energy harvested by

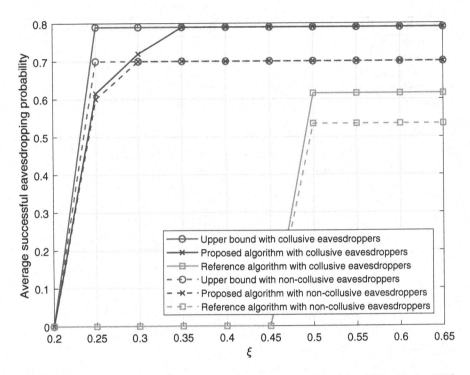

Fig. 2. Average successful eavesdropping probability against ξ ($Q = 2\,\mathrm{W}$ and $p = 5\,\mathrm{W}$).

the eavesdroppers and thus can leave more signal power for information eavesdropping. It is also shown that the average successful eavesdropping probability saturates when ξ is high. This is because in this case, the performance is not restricted by the minimum harvested energy constraint. Besides, it is seen that the average successful eavesdropping probability achieved by the proposed algorithm with collusive eavesdroppers is higher than that with non-collusive eavesdroppers, and the proposed algorithm with collusive/non-collusive eavesdroppers outperforms the reference algorithm with collusive/non-collusive eavesdroppers. It is also seen that the average successful eavesdropping probability achieved by the proposed algorithm with collusive/non-collusive eavesdroppers is lower than the upper bound with collusive/non-collusive eavesdroppers when ξ is small and overlaps with the upper bound with collusive/non-collusive eavesdroppers when ξ is large. This indicates that the proposed algorithm can achieve the upper bound when ξ is large.

Figure 3 plots the average successful eavesdropping probability against Q with $\xi = 0.35$ and $p = 5\,\mathrm{W}$ for different algorithms. It is shown that the average successful eavesdropping probability decreases as Q increases. This is because a higher Q means the eavesdroppers need to harvest more energy and thus leaves less signal power for information eavesdropping. It is also shown that

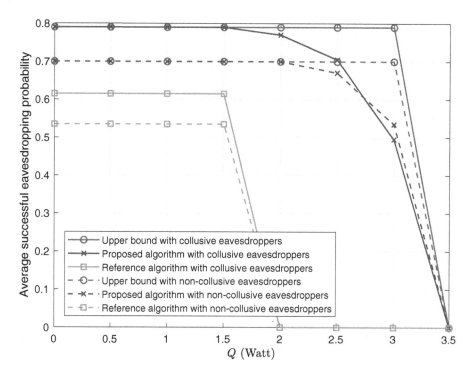

Fig. 3. Average successful eavesdropping probability against Q ($\xi = 0.35$ and $p = 5\,\mathrm{W}$).

the average successful eavesdropping probability is unchanged as Q increases when Q is low. This is because in this case, the performance is not restricted by the minimum harvested energy constraint. Besides, it is seen that the average successful eavesdropping probability achieved by the proposed algorithm with collusive/non-collusive eavesdroppers overlaps with the upper bound with collusive/non-collusive eavesdroppers when Q is small and is lower than the upper bound with collusive/non-collusive eavesdroppers when Q is large. This indicates that the proposed algorithm can achieve the upper bound when Q is small.

Figure 4 plots the average successful eavesdropping probability against p with $\xi = 0.3$ and $Q = 1.5\,\mathrm{W}$ for different algorithms. It is shown that the average successful eavesdropping probability increases as p increases. This is because a higher p leads to higher energy harvested by the eavesdroppers and thus can leave more signal power for information eavesdropping. It is also shown that the average successful eavesdropping probability saturates when p is high. This means the performance is not restricted by the minimum harvested energy constraint when p is high. Besides, it is seen that the average successful eavesdropping probability achieved by the proposed algorithm with collusive/non-collusive eavesdroppers is lower than the upper bound with collusive/non-collusive eavesdroppers when

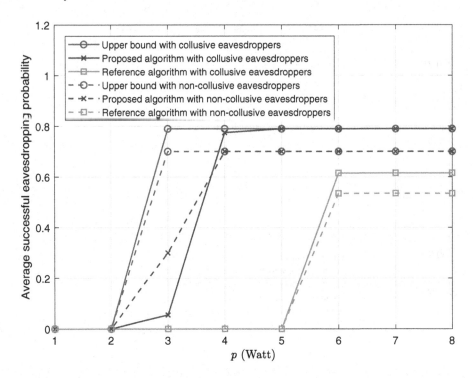

Fig. 4. Average successful eavesdropping probability against p ($\xi = 0.3$ and $Q = 1.5\,\text{W}$).

p is small and overlaps with the upper bound with collusive/non-collusive eavesdroppers when p is large. This indicates that the proposed algorithm can achieve the upper bound when p is large.

5   Conclusions

We investigate legitimate eavesdropping in a suspicious communication network with multiple suspicious source-destination nodes and multiple wireless powered legitimate eavesdroppers, where the legitimate eavesdroppers are assumed to be collusive or non-collusive. The aim is to maximize the average successful eavesdropping probability by optimizing the power splitting ratio at each eavesdropper under the minimum harvested energy constraint. We derive the optimal algorithm to solve the optimization problem for both collusive eavesdroppers and non-collusive eavesdroppers. It is shown that the proposed algorithm achieves the upper bound of the successful eavesdropping probability when the energy harvesting energy is large, the required minimum harvested energy is small, or the transmit power of the suspicious source node is high.

References

1. Xu, J., Duan, L., Zhang, R.: Proactive eavesdropping via cognitive jamming in fading channels. IEEE Trans. Wirel. Commun. **16**(5), 2790–2806 (2017)
2. Zhong, C., Jiang, X., Qu, F., Zhang, Z.: Multi-antenna wireless legitimate surveillance systems: design and performance analysis. IEEE Trans. Wirel. Commun. **16**(7), 4585–4599 (2017)
3. Hu, D., Zhang, Q., Yang, P., Qin, J.: Proactive monitoring via jamming in amplify-and-forward relay networks. IEEE Signal Process. Lett. **24**(11), 1714–1718 (2017)
4. Xu, J., Li, K., Duan, L., Zhang, R.: Proactive eavesdropping via jamming over HARQ-based communications. In: Proceedings of the IEEE Global Communications Conference, pp. 1–6 (2017)
5. Li, B., Yao, Y., Zhang, H., Lv, Y., Zhao, W.: Energy efficiency of proactive eavesdropping for multiple links wireless system. IEEE Access **6**, 26081–26090 (2018)
6. Xu, D., Li, Q.: Proactive eavesdropping through a third-party jammer. IEICE Trans. Fundam. Electron. Commun. Comput. Sci. **101**(5), 878–882 (2018)
7. Zeng, Y., Zhang, R.: Wireless information surveillance via proactive eavesdropping with spoofing relay. IEEE J. Sel. Top. Sign. Process. **10**(8), 1449–1461 (2016)
8. Xu, D., Li, Q.: Resource allocation for secure communications in cooperative cognitive wireless powered communication networks. IEEE Syst. J. **13**(3), 2431–2442 (2019)
9. Zeng, Y., Clerckx, B., Zhang, R.: Communications and signals design for wireless power transmission. IEEE Trans. Commun. **65**(5), 2264–2290 (2017)
10. Xu, D., Zhu, H.: Secure transmission for SWIPT IoT systems with full-duplex IoT devices. IEEE IoT J. **6**, 10915–10933 (2019)
11. Zhang, H., Huang, S., Jiang, C., Long, K., Leung, V.C., Poor, H.V.: Energy efficient user association and power allocation in millimeter-wave-based ultra dense networks with energy harvesting base stations. IEEE J. Sel. Areas Commun. **35**(9), 1936–1947 (2017)
12. Xu, D., Li, Q.: Legitimate surveillance with a wireless powered monitor in rayleigh fading channels. IEICE Trans. Fundam. Electron. Commun. Comput. Sci. **101**(1), 293–297 (2018)
13. Xu, D.: Legitimate surveillance with battery-aided wireless powered full-duplex monitor. IEEE Syst. J. (Accepted for publication)
14. Xu, D., Zhu, H., Li, Q.: Jammer-assisted legitimate eavesdropping in wireless powered suspicious communication networks. IEEE Access **7**, 20363–20380 (2019)
15. Boyd, S., Vandenberghe, L.: Convex Optimization. Cambridge University Press, Cambridge (2004)
16. Yu, W., Lui, R.: Dual methods for nonconvex spectrum optimization of multicarrier systems. IEEE Trans. Commun. **54**(7), 1310–1322 (2006)

WiHlo: A Case Study of WiFi-Based Human Passive Localization by Angle Refinement

Zengshan Tian, Weiqin Yang$^{(\boxtimes)}$, Yue Jin, and Gongzhui Zhang

School of Communication and Information Engineering,
Chongqing University of Posts and Telecommunications,
Chongqing 400065, China
yangweiqin555@gmail.com

Abstract. The emergence of the Internet of Things (IoT) has promoted the interconnection of all things. And the access control of devices and accurate service promotion are inseparable from the acquisition of location information. We propose WiHlo, a passive localization system based on WiFi Channel State Information (CSI). WiHlo directly estimates the human location by refining the angle-of-arrival (AoA) of the subtle human reflection. WiHlo divides the received signals into static path components and dynamic path components, and uses phase offsets compensation and direct wave suppression algorithms to separate out the dynamic path signals. By combining the measured AoAs and time-of-arrivals (ToAs) with Gaussian mean clustering and probability analysis, WiHlo identifies the human reflection path from the dynamic paths. Our implementation and evaluation on commodity WiFi devices demonstrate WiHlo outperforms the state-of-the-art AoA estimation system in actual indoor environment.

Keywords: WiFi · Passive localization · AoA

1 Introduction

Indoor localization systems play an increasingly important role in many emerging applications, such as indoor navigation, body/behavioral analysis, aged care and unobtrusive motion tracking, etc. In the last few decades, indoor localization systems based on mobile phones, wearable devices, and camera have been proposed. However, all of these technologies require the target to be actively involved

This work is supported in part by National Natural Science Foundation of China (61771083, 61704015), the Program for Changjiang Scholars and Innovative Research Team in University (IRT1299), Special Fund of Chongqing Key Laboratory (CSTC), Fundamental and Frontier Research Project of Chongqing (cstc2017jcyjAX0380), and University Outstanding Achievement Transformation Project of Chongqing (KJZH17117).

H. Gao et al. (Eds.): ChinaCom 2019, LNICST 313, pp. 216–229, 2020.
https://doi.org/10.1007/978-3-030-41117-6_18

in the location process in a device-carrying manner, which we call device-based localization [1–3]. The localization method that the target needs to carry devices at all times is actually not feasible in reality. In the scenario where users take the initiative to obtain location information, such as family life track tracking and hospital health monitoring, it is against users' habits to require a person to wear a variety of unfamiliar devices, and even they often forget to wear relevant devices. In the localization of fire rescue, it is impossible for us to require firefighters to carry a large number of professional equipment, and the masses waiting for rescue are usually not carrying any localization equipment. The limitations of the above scenarios lead to the emergence of passive localization, which arouses people's interest in this field.

Passive localization technologies based on ultrasonic, radar, and computer vision have all been studied for years. However, ultrasonic-based localization systems have a small coverage area and significantly reduced performance in a noisy environment [4]. Radar-based systems require very high bandwidth and the costs are expensive [5]. Computer vision-based systems can only work in bright Line-of-sight (LOS) environments and the privacy of users is not protected [6]. With the development of WiFi technology, many indoor scenes can install high-speed and stable WiFi infrastructures. These devices have low cost and large coverage. Compared with other systems, WiFi based passive localization systems have better application prospects.

In this work, we aim to achieve accurate passive human localization using WiFi Channel State Information (CSI). While passive localization with only commodity WiFi infrastructures is challenging. In these systems, the received signals are superposition of direct path signals, static objects reflection signals and moving human reflection signal, and the energy exponent of human reflection signal we care about is far weaker than those strong reflections. And due to the imperfection of the hardware and the non-strict synchronization of the transceivers, there are different offsets in phase measurements. Therefore, it is difficult to extract useful information from the aliasing signal.

We propose WiHlo, which can get an accurate location information of human by angle-of-arrival (AoA) refinement. The main contributions of our work are summarized as follows:

- A Two-dimensional Spatial Smoothing (2D-SS) algorithm is applied to construct a large-scale virtual antenna arrays for super-resolution estimation of time of arrival (ToA) and AoA.
- We separate out the dynamic path signal from the aliasing signal through our dynamic path capture algorithm. And we introduce the Gaussian mean clustering and probability analysis to identify the human reflection path's AoA.
- We conduct comprehensive field studies to evaluate the performance of WiHlo. The experimental results show that WiHlo achieves a median localization error of 0.67 m in actual indoor environment using only two receivers, which is better than the state-of-the-art AoA based system.

The rest of the paper is organized as follows. Section 2 gives the related work. Section 3 describes the system design. Section 4 validates system's performance with the experimental evaluations. The conclusion is drawn in Sect. 5.

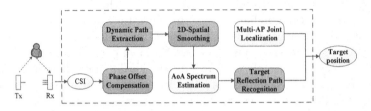

Fig. 1. System architecture: WiHlo consists of four main components. Once we get the AoA measurement on multiple receivers, we can obtain the location of the human using the triangulation algorithm.

2 Related Work

Our work is closely related to the research of indoor localization. We will discuss the related work in following two groups: Non-WiFi-based and WiFi-based approaches.

Non-WiFi-based indoor localization technology mainly includes Zigbee [24,25] and Bluetooth [26,27]. Zigbee is a wireless network protocol based on IEEE 802.15.4 for low-speed and short-distance transmission. It has the advantages of low complexity, short distance, low cost and low power consumption, etc. However, due to the characteristics of its own gateway attribute, the technology has high latency, short distance and other congenital defects when applied to localization work. Bluetooth localization technology (BLE) is also a research hotspot in recent years, especially the low power consumption Bluetooth 4.0 has more advantages of energy saving, low cost, low latency, and long effective connection distance. When the device enters the signal coverage area, the corresponding application will detect the received Bluetooth signal and use it to locate or forward information. BLE is mainly subject to the limited propagation distance, so in order to achieve a wide range of localization requirements, we usually need to deploy a large number of anchor devices.

In order to achieve high bandwidth and high quality Wireless Local Area Network (WLAN) services and make WLAN reach the performance level of Ethernet, experts at home and abroad have been devoting themselves to the research of new standards. The WLAN protocol 802.11n, which is officially approved by the IEEE, is an industry-changing protocol, and its modulation method is orthogonal frequency division multiplexing (OFDM). In the indoor channel research, the channel state information (CSI) of each subcarrier channel can be parsed by this technology, which makes it possible for ordinary academic personnel to conduct finer channel characteristics research through WLAN.

We divide WiFi based indoor localization technologies into the pattern-based and the model-based approaches. The pattern-based approaches work by selecting and learning features. Xiao et al. [20] use the frequency diversity feature of CSI to build a fingerprint database, achieve DFL on commodity WiFi devices by monitoring the CSI feature pattern shift. Seifeldin et al. [21] develop Nuzzer, it builds a passive radio map in the area of interest for large-scale localization. When faced with general perception, pattern-based approach achieves the expected results. However, when the perception task and perception environment are more complex, the performance of these systems declined significantly. The model-based approach is to understand and abstract the mathematical model between the received signal and target location. Li et al. [8] propose MaTrack, it utilizes the CSI subcarrier phase measurements to identify the moving target's angle information, and with only two receivers it achieves a high accuracy. Wang et al. [19] propose LiFS, this system utilizes Fresnel model to improve the accuracy of localization in LOS scenarios. In this work, we aim to use AoA model to achieve passive human localization. To distinguish from prior works, we focus on better extracting the subtle human reflection signals and obtain a refined AoA estimate.

3 System Design

3.1 System Overview

In this section, we present the detailed design of WiHlo. As shown in Fig. 1, our system is composed of four main components, namely Phase Offset Compensation, Dynamic Path Extraction, 2D-Spatial Smoothing, and Target Reflection Path Recognition. In following sections, we will show details of each component.

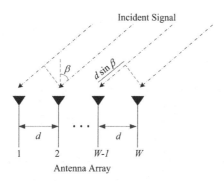

Fig. 2. A linear array with W antennas at the receiver. The incident angle of the signal is β, antenna spacing d is half-wavelength of the signal.

3.2 AoA Estimation Algorithm Based on 2D-SS

As shown in Fig. 2, we place W antennas with the antenna spacing of size d on the receiver, where d is half-wavelength of the signal. Therefore, the distance difference between the two adjacent antennas on the array is $d\sin\beta$. It can be deduced from the distance difference that the phase difference between antennas with W 1 antenna spacing is $-2\pi f (W - 1) d \sin\beta/c$, where f is the signal frequency and c is the speed of light. The introduced phase difference on two adjacent antennas can be written as a function of the AoA

$$\psi_\beta = e^{-j2\pi fd\sin(\beta)/c} \tag{1}$$

To achieve super-resolution estimation of AoA, we do not only introduce phase differences across antennas but also introduce phase differences across subcarriers, as described in [3]. The time differences introduce measurable phase differences across subcarriers, for evenly-spaced subcarriers, the phase difference introduced across two adjacent subcarriers is $-2\pi f_\sigma\tau$, where f_σ is the adjacent subcarrier spacing and τ is the ToA. The introduced phase difference across subcarriers can be written as a function of the ToA of the path:

$$\Theta(\tau_i) = e^{-j2\pi f_\sigma \tau_i} \tag{2}$$

where τ_i is the ToA of the ith propagation path. Thus, for W antennas and K subcarriers, we obtain a total of $W \times K$ virtual sensors. For a path with AoA β and ToA τ, the steering vector can be rewritten as:

$$\mathbf{v}(\beta,\tau) = \left[1,\cdots,\Theta(\tau)^{K-1},\cdots,\psi_\beta{}^{W-1},\cdots,\psi_\beta{}^{W-1}\Theta(\tau)^{K-1}\right]^T \tag{3}$$

Assume there are L incident signals and the received signal of lth path for the first subcarrier of first antenna is $s_l(t)$, the received signal at each sensor is a superposition of all paths and can be expressed as:

$$\mathbf{U}(t) = [u_1(t),\cdots,u_M(t)]^T = \sum_{l=1}^{L}\mathbf{v}(\beta_l)s_l(t) + \mathbf{N}(t) = \mathbf{DS}(t) + \mathbf{N}(t) \tag{4}$$

where β_l represents the AoA of the lth incident signal, $\mathbf{D}$ is the direction matrix, $\mathbf{N}(t)$ is the noise vector. The basic idea of the MUSIC algorithm [7] is eigenstructure analysis of an $W \times W$ correlation matrix $\mathbf{R}_U$ of the W CSI samples. From (4), we represent the covariance matrix as:

$$\mathbf{R}_U = \mathbb{E}\left[\mathbf{UU}^H\right] = \mathbf{D}\mathbb{E}\left[\mathbf{UU}^H\right]\mathbf{D}^H + \mathbb{E}\left[\mathbf{NN}^H\right] = \mathbf{DR}_S\mathbf{D}^H + \sigma^2\mathbf{I} \tag{5}$$

where $\mathbf{R}_S$ is the correlation matrix of the signal vector, $\mathbf{I}$ is an identity matrix and σ^2 is the variance of noise, $(\cdot)^H$ denote conjugate operation.

By doing eigenvalue decomposition on the covariance matrix $\mathbf{R}_U$, we can get W eigenvalues. The largest L eigenvalues correspond to the L path signals and the other W-L eigenvalues correspond to the noise. And we have a eigenvectors corresponding to the smallest W-L eigenvalues called noise subspace

$\mathbf{E}_N = [\overrightarrow{e}_1, \cdots, \overrightarrow{e}_{W-L}]$. Since the signal and the noise subspace are orthogonal, so the AoA spectrum function can be expressed as:

$$P(\beta)_{MUSIC} = \frac{1}{\mathbf{v}^H(\beta)\,\mathbf{E}_N\mathbf{E}_N{}^H\mathbf{v}(\beta)} \tag{6}$$

where v(β) is called the steering vector, in which sharp peaks occur at the AoAs of the target reflective signals.

In indoor environment, there are strong direct and multipath interference signals, and they have coherence with the human reflection signals. To eliminate the interference of the coherent signals and tackle the limitation of insufficient number of antennas, we conduct the 2D-SS [11,12] on $\mathbf{R}_U$ instead of $\mathbf{U}(t)$. 2D-SS is a kind of spatial smoothing technology, it is an effective method to deal with coherent or strongly coherent signals. Its basic idea is to divide the isometric linear array into several overlapping sub-arrays, so that the rank of the antenna array model is only related to the direction of arrival of the signal, but not affected by signal correlation, so as to achieve the purpose of de-correlation. We give a schematic diagram of Fig. 3 to illustrate the application of 2D-SS, the elements in the dashed blue and red boxes construct the covariance matrices of the first and second sub-arrays. Based on the observation that the first elements of the covariance matrices of the first and second sub-arrays are $h_{1,1} \times h_{1,1}$ and $h_{1,2} \times h_{1,2}$, we get the covariance matrices of the existing sub-arrays by increasing the subcarrier ID and antenna index number to $P_2 = 30 - L_{sub2} + 1$, $P_1 = 3 - L_{sub1} + 1$, respectively, $L_{sub1} = 2$ and $L_{sub2} = 15$ are chosen. Then, the number of subarrays and elements in each sub-array equals to $P = P_1 \times P_2$ and $L = L_{sub1} \times L_{sub2}$. Obviously, the smoothed CSI matrix could provide 32 measurement vectors using one CSI reading only, which makes it feasible to calculate the covariance matrix.

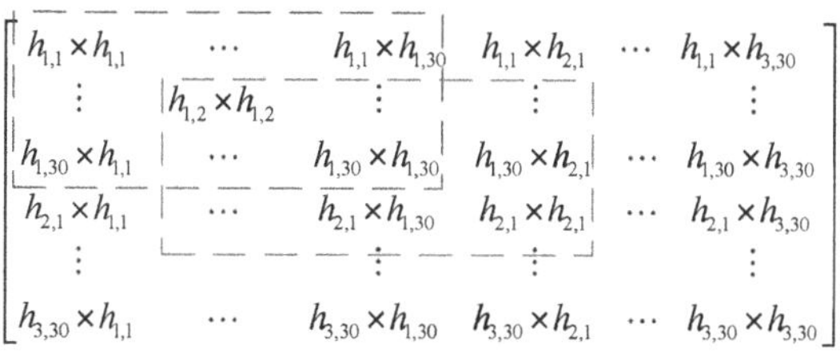

Fig. 3. The virtual array antenna is constructed by Two-dimensional Spatial Smoothing to realize the super resolution estimation of AoA.

The covariance matrix of the CSI after the process of 2D-SS on $\mathbf{R}_U$ is modified into:

$$\mathbf{R}_{2D-SS} = \frac{1}{P_1 \times P_2} \sum_{m=1}^{P_1} \sum_{n=1}^{P_2} \mathbf{R}_{m,n} \tag{7}$$

where $\mathbf{R}_{m,n}$ is the sub-covariance matrix in $\mathbf{R}_U$ with respect to the nth sub-carrier at the mth antenna. Then, we conduct the MUSIC algorithm on the smoothed covariance matrix to obtain the direction vectors, as well as the AoA and ToA with respect to each signal path.

3.3 Phase Offsets Compensation and Dynamic Path Signal Extraction

To identify the signal of human reflection path and estimate corresponding AoA, we must compensate for random phase offsets and suppress these strong signal components. Assume the CSI samples without random phase offsets at mth antenna are represented as:

$$H\left(f,\tau,m\right) = \sum_{i=1}^{L} A_i e^{-j2\pi(f+\Delta f_j)\left(\tau_i+\frac{d\sin\beta_{m,i}}{c}\right)} \tag{8}$$

where L represents the total number of multipath, A_i and τ_i represent the complex attenuation factor and propagation time delay of the ith path, f represents the center frequency and Δf_j represents the frequency difference between jth subcarrier and 0th subcarrier, $\beta_{m,i}$ represents the incident angle of the ith path at mth antenna, c is the speed of light. When phase offsets $e^{-j\phi}$ are introduced, the CSI samples are represented as:

$$\begin{cases} H\left(f,\tau,m\right) = e^{-j\phi}\left(\sum_{i=1}^{L} A_i e^{-j2\pi(f+\Delta f_j)\left(\tau_i+\frac{d\sin\beta_{m,i}}{c}\right)}\right) \\ \phi = 2\pi\left(k(\lambda_p + \lambda_s) + \Delta t_i \varepsilon_f\right) + \zeta \end{cases} \tag{9}$$

where λ_p and λ_s represent packet detection delay (PDD) and sampling frequency offset (SFO), which are all related to the subcarrier frequency, ε_f represents carrier frequency offset (CFO), k and Δt_i represent the subcarrier index and the packet interval time, respectively. ζ is the initial phase offset between the channels of the receiver, which can be manually corrected by a power splitter as described in [2].

By classifying multipath signals into static group P_s and dynamic group P_d, (9) can be converted into:

$$H\left(f,\tau,m\right) = e^{-j\phi}H_S\left(f\right) + e^{-j\phi}\sum_{i\in P_d} A_i e^{-j2\pi(f+\Delta f_j)\left(\tau_i+\frac{d\sin\beta_{m,i}}{c}\right)} \tag{10}$$

In (10), $f\tau_i$ is the same for all measurements, so it can be merged into the complex attenuation A_i. And $\Delta f_j \tau_i$ (close to 0.0003125) is small enough to be ignored. After omitting the two terms, we have:

$$H\left(f,\tau,m\right) = e^{-j\phi}H_S\left(f\right) + e^{-j\phi}\sum_{i\in P_d} A_i e^{-j2\pi\left(\Delta f_j \tau_i + f\frac{d\sin\beta_{m,i}}{c}\right)} \tag{11}$$

In non-cooperative radar [13], the time domain interference cancellation algorithm, such as batch version of extensive cancellation algorithm (ECA-B), is used to eliminate the direct wave and multipath interference in received signal. The key to this kind of system is to select an independent antenna as a reference antenna to obtain direct wave signals. In Intel 5300 Network Interface Card (NIC) there still contains multiple antennas, and the time-variant random phase offsets are the same across different antennas on a WiFi card [8,10]. To remove random phase offsets, we use the method mentioned in [14,15,22] to calculate the conjugate multiplication of CSI of one pair of antennas. Assume that the reference antenna is the nth one, we get the product of conjugate multiplication:

$$
\begin{aligned}
H_c\left(f, \tau_i\right) = {} & H\left(f, \tau, m\right) * \overline{H}\left(f, \tau, n\right) \\
= {} & \underbrace{H_S\left(f, m\right) \overline{H}_S\left(f, n\right)}_{\text{static term}} + \underbrace{H_S\left(f, m\right) \sum_{l \in Q_d} \overline{B}_l e^{j 2\pi\left(\Delta f_j \tau_l + f \frac{d \sin \beta_{n,l}}{c}\right)}}_{\text{target term}} \\
& + \underbrace{\overline{H}_S\left(f, n\right) \sum_{i \in P_d} A_i e^{-j 2\pi\left(\Delta f_j \tau_i + f \frac{d \sin \beta_{m,i}}{c}\right)}}_{\text{target term}} \\
& + \underbrace{\sum_{i \in P_d, l \in Q_d} A_i \overline{B}_l e^{-j 2\pi\left(\Delta f_j(\tau_i - \tau_l) + f \frac{d\left(\sin \beta_{m,i} - \sin \beta_{n,l}\right)}{c}\right)}}_{\text{cross term}}
\end{aligned}
\tag{12}
$$

where $H\left(f, \tau, m\right)$ is the CSI of the mth antenna, $\overline{H}\left(f, \tau, n\right)$ is the conjugate of CSI of the reference antenna, P_d and Q_d are the sets of dynamic paths at mth antenna and reference one, $\overline{(\cdot)}$ denotes conjugate operation.

More interesting, we find the product (12) can be divided into three categories, named static term, target term and cross term, where the first summation term is static term with lower frequency, which can be treated as a constant in a short time period and can be almost filtered by a high-pass filter. The cross term is only product of dynamic parts on two antennas, which is orders weaker than the others, and can be omitted. The rest is the target term and residual static term, which keep the human location information we care about. In this work, according to a person's normal walking speed (0.3 m/s–2 m/s), we use a bandpass filter to separate out the target term and set the lower and upper cutoff frequencies to 2 Hz and 80 Hz.

We run benchmark experiments to verify the above-mentioned method. We choose a meeting room with a size of 9.0 m × 7.7 m, which is a typical indoor multipath environment. By carefully selecting some test points, it is ensured that the angle of direct path between transceiver is 0° and the resulting reflection path's AoA are located near 45° and 60°. A person spins slightly at these positions to produce reflection signals. We can clearly see in Fig. 5(a) and (d), without the direct wave suppression and de-coherence, the energy peak of the AoA spatial spectrum will appear near around 0°, and the target reflection path's

AoA cannot be detected. While in Fig. 5(b) and (e), after suppressing the direct wave, the AoA of target reflection path appears, but without de-coherence, the spectrum is still blurred. By integrating direct wave suppression and 2D-SS, we can accurately identify the human reflection path's AoA, as shown in Fig. 5(c) and (f). We also introduce Gaussian mean clustering [9] to show the results of multiple experiments, plot in Fig. 4(a) and (b).

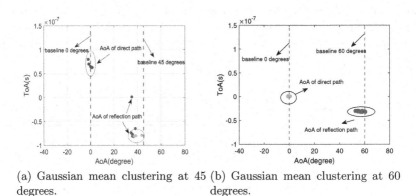

(a) Gaussian mean clustering at 45 degrees.

(b) Gaussian mean clustering at 60 degrees.

Fig. 4. We perform continuous estimation of AoA and plot the clustering result.

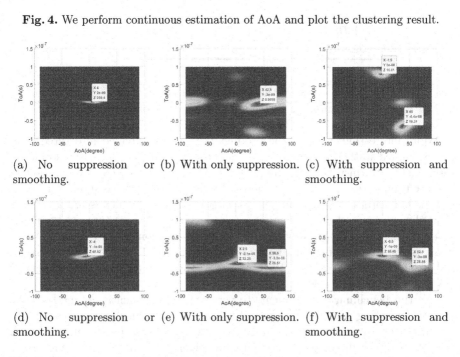

(a) No suppression or smoothing.

(b) With only suppression.

(c) With suppression and smoothing.

(d) No suppression or smoothing.

(e) With only suppression.

(f) With suppression and smoothing.

Fig. 5. We run benchmark experiments to verify the super-resolution AoA estimation method. Experimental results show the AoA of reflection path can be accurately captured after direct wave suppression and spatial smoothing.

3.4   Target Reflection Path Recognition

The last reflector of the dynamic path is not always the target, we need to separate the human reflection path from all dynamic paths. The AoA of moving human has a larger fluctuation range than other paths in a short time measurement. Similar to the ideas of [3] and [23] and benefit from their inspiration, we believe that the human reflection signal should be the shortest direct dynamic signal with the minimum ToA measurement. Therefore, we rely on the probabilistic analysis to assign a likelihood value to each dynamic path. The likelihood value of each path is calculated by incorporating the number of peak points with the variance of the AoA and ToA.

$$l_k = 1/\left(1 + \exp\left(-\left(\omega_k p_k + \omega_\beta \varsigma_{\beta_k} + \omega_\tau \varsigma_{\tau_k}\right)\right)\right) \tag{13}$$

where p_k, ς_{β_k}, and ς_{τ_k} are the number of peak points and the variance of the AoA and ToA in the cluster corresponding to the kth dynamic path. ω_k, ω_β and ω_τ are the weights of the number of peak points and the variance of the AoA and ToA.

3.5   Target Location Estimation

In this work, human localization is achieved by combining multiple receivers' target AoA information. It is assumed that there are R receivers. Given the receiver locations (x_1, y_1), (x_2, y_2), $\cdots$, (x_R, y_R) and the estimated AoA at each receiver $\beta_1{}^{target}$, $\beta_2{}^{target}$, $\cdots$, $\beta_R{}^{target}$, we need to identify the location $p = (x_p, y_p)$ of the target.

To minimize the deviation between actual values and the observed, we use the least square (LS) criterion [16] and solve the optimal location by minimizing the objective function below.

$$minimize \sum_{i=1}^{R} l_i * d_i{}^2$$

$$subject\ to \ \sin(\beta_{it}) = \frac{|x_t - x_i|}{\sqrt{(x_t - x_i)^2 + (y_t - y_i)^2}} \tag{14}$$

$$d_i = e^{j2\pi d \sin(\beta_i{}^{target}) f/c} - e^{j2\pi d \sin(\beta_{it}) f/c}$$

where the weighting factor l_i is the likelihood value of most likely candidate for the direct human reflection path from ith dynamic path. The basic idea of formulating this optimization problem is searching through all the possible values of the target location and find one that gives the minimum distance from the estimated AoA values. We refer to the method mentioned in [17] and use the modified metric $e^{j2\pi d \sin(\beta_{it}) f/c}$ instead of β_{it}, because it is tolerant to these large errors as the value of the metric remains close even when AoA gets miscalculated from $-90°$ to $90°$.

4   Experimental Evaluation

In this section, we evaluate the performance of WiHlo. We first describe the system implementation and evaluation setup. Then we present detailed experimental results covering overall localization performance, AoA estimation performance and discussion on several factors. Further more, we compare with a typical AoA based system.

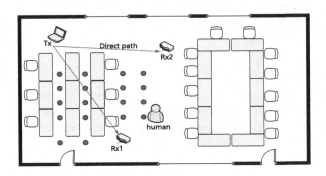

Fig. 6. Meeting room floorplan

4.1   Experimental Methodology

We use a laptop with an omnidirectional antenna to broadcast packets over the air, and two minPCs running Ubuntu 10.04 with an Intel 5300 network interface card (NIC) as receivers. Every receiver has three antennas, forming a uniform linear array. We install the CSI toolkit developed by Halperin [18] on these miniPCs to obtain CSI information for each received packet. Our experiments are conducted in the 5 GHz frequency band with 40 MHz bandwidth, the transmission rate of packets is set to 1 kHz. The processing computer is an ordinary Dell laptop, and processes CSI data using MATLAB. We evaluate system performance in a meeting room, as shown in Fig. 6. The size of the meeting room is 9.0 m× 7.7 m, and there are many chairs and desks which make it a rich multipath scenario. We let a person spin around at those predetermined points noted as red dots in Fig. 6 and use the absolute difference between the measured value and the real one as an indication of error evaluation.

4.2   Localization Performance and AoA Estimation Accuracy

To validate the localization performance of WiHlo, we compare it with MaTrack [8]. Figure 7(a) illustrate the cumulative distribution functions (CDFs) of the localization errors, from the results, we can see that our system outperforms the MaTrack system, specifically, we are able to achieve a median localization error of 0.67 m in the meeting room, while MaTrack's localization accuracy greatly deviates from the real value, because in this scenario, MaTrack fails to take into account the suppression of strong path signals, resulting in serious inaccurate AoA estimation. Figure 7(b) gives the average AoA estimation performances of WiHlo and the MaTrack, when test in the meeting room, WiHlo achieves a median angle error of 7.5°, such good performance benefits from our phase offsets compensation and direct wave suppression operations.

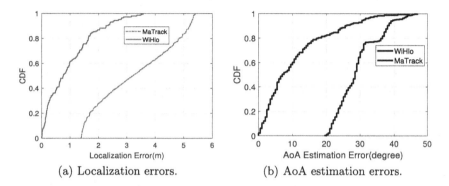

(a) Localization errors.

(b) AoA estimation errors.

Fig. 7. We demonstrate the localization accuracy and AoA estimation error of WiHlo and MaTrack.

4.3   Performance Analysis and Discussion

Impact of the Distance Between Transceivers. The distance between the transmitter and receiver affect the system performance, and when the target is in a certain position, the signal-to-noise-ratio (SNR) at a longer distance will be lower. We choose three different distances to verify the impact of the distance between transceivers. Specifically, as shown in Fig. 8(a), the localization error under the transceiver distance of 6 m much larger than 4 m and 2 m. Therefore, we need to select an appropriate transceiver distance according to the size of the monitoring range to ensure the accuracy.

Impact of Packet Rate. In our previous experiment, the packet rate was set at 1 kHz, which put forward high requirements for our WiFi devices since the increase in the packet rate means that the cost and power consumption of the equipment will also increase. In order to verify the effect of different size of packet rate to perception sensitivity, we select several groups of packet rate from small to large to conduct experiments. Figure 8(b) shows the results: Before reaching 500 Hz, the localization accuracy of WiHlo has been improved with the increase of the packet rate. Continuing to improve the packet rate to 2000 Hz has a limited effect on improving the accuracy. Therefore, in order to reduce the requirement for equipment hardware and ensure sufficient accuracy, we can also choose to set the packet rate to 500 Hz.

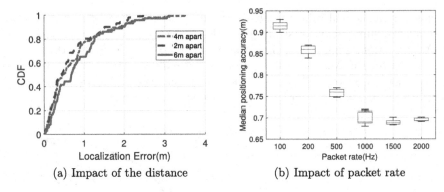

(a) Impact of the distance   (b) Impact of packet rate

Fig. 8. We discuss the effects of two factors on localization performance. (a) is the impact of the distance between transceivers; (b) is the impact of packet rate.

5 Conclusion

In this work, we achieve passive localization on commodity WiFi infrastructures. Using the phase offsets compensation and direct wave suppression methods, we separate out the dynamic path. Combining Gaussian mean clustering and probability analysis, we get the AoA of the human reflection path. The experimental results show that our system achieves an average median AoA estimation accuracy of 7.5°, and an average median localization error of 0.67 m under indoor environment, which is better than the existing system.

References

1. Bahl, P., Padmanabhan, V.N.: RADAR: an in-building RF-based user location and tracking system. In: INFOCOM Nineteenth Joint Conference of the IEEE Computer & Communications Societies. IEEE (2000)
2. Xiong, J., Jamieson, K.: ArrayTrack: a fine-grained indoor location system. In: USENIX Conference on Networked Systems Design & Implementation (2013)
3. Kotaru, M., Joshi, K., Bharadia, D., Katti, S.: SpotFi: decimeter level localization using WiFi. ACM SIGCOMM Comput. Commun. Rev. **45**(4), 269–282 (2015)
4. Mao, W., He, J., Qiu, L.: CAT: high-precision acoustic motion tracking. In: International Conference on Mobile Computing & Networking (2016)
5. Adib, F.M., Kabelac, Z., Katabi, D., Miller, R.C.: 3D tracking via body radio reflections (2014)
6. Xu, C., Gao, M., Firner, B., Zhang, Y., Li, J.: Towards robust device-free passive localization through automatic camera-assisted recalibration. In: SenSys (2012)
7. Schmidt, R.: Multiple emitter location and signal parameter estimation. IEEE Trans. Antennas Propag. **34**(3), 276–280 (1986)
8. Li, X., Li, S., Zhang, D., Xiong, J., Wang, Y., Mei, H.: Dynamic-MUSIC: accurate device-free indoor localization. In: ACM International Joint Conference on Pervasive & Ubiquitous Computing (2016)
9. Güngör, E., Özmen, A.: Distance and density based clustering algorithm using Gaussian kernel. Expert Syst. Appl. **69**, 10–20 (2017)

10. Xie, Y., Li, Z., Li, M.: Precise power delay profiling with commodity WiFi. IEEE Trans. Mobile Comput. **PP**(99), 1 (2015)

11. Shan, T.J., Wax, M., Kailath, T.: On spatial smoothing for direction-of-arrival estimation of coherent signals. IEEE Trans. Acoust. Speech Sign. Process. **33**(4), 806–811 (1985)

12. Tian, Z., Li, Z., Zhou, M., Jin, Y., Wu, Z.: PILA: sub-meter localization using CSI from commodity Wi-Fi devices. Sensors **16**(10), 1664 (2016)

13. Wang, J., Wang, H.T., Zhao, Y.: Direction finding in frequency-modulated-based passive bistatic radar with a four-element Adcock antenna array. IET Radar Sonar Navig. **5**(8), 807–813 (2011)

14. Wang, W., Liu, A. X., Shahzad, M., Ling, K., Lu, S.: Understanding and modeling of WiFi signal based human activity recognition. In: International Conference on Mobile Computing & Networking (2015)

15. Qian, K., Wu, C., Zhou, Z., Zheng, Y., Yang, Z., Liu, Y.: Inferring motion direction using commodity Wi-Fi for interactive exergames. In: CHI Conference (2017)

16. Wang, S., Jackson, B.R., Inkol, R.: Hybrid RSS/AOA emitter location estimation based on least squares and maximum likelihood criteria. In: Communications (2012)

17. Bharadia, D., Joshi, K.R., Kotaru, M., Katti, S.: BackFi: high throughput WiFi backscatter. ACM SIGCOMM Comput. Commun. Rev. **45**(5), 283–296 (2015)

18. Halperin, D., Hu, W., Sheth, A., Wetherall, D.: Tool release: gathering 802.11n traces with channel state information. ACM SIGCOMM Comput. Commun. Rev. **41**(1), 53 (2011)

19. Wang, J., Jiang, H., Xiong, J., Jamieson, K., Xie, B.: LiFS: low human-effort, device-free localization with fine-grained subcarrier information. In: International Conference on Mobile Computing & Networking (2016)

20. Xiao, J., Wu, K., Yi, Y., Wang, L., Ni, L.M.: Pilot: passive device-free indoor localization using channel state information (2013)

21. Seifeldin, M., Youssef, M.: Nuzzer: a large-scale device-free passive localization system for wireless environments. IEEE Trans. Mobile Comput. **12**(7), 1321–1334 (2013)

22. Qian, K., Wu, C., Zhang, Y., Zhang, G., Yang, Z., Liu, Y.: Widar2.0: passive human tracking with a single Wi-Fi link. In: Proceedings of the 16th Annual International Conference on Mobile Systems, Applications, and Services (MobiSys 2018), pp. 350–361. ACM, New York (2018). https://doi.org/10.1145/3210240.3210314

23. Zhang, L., Gao, Q., Ma, X., Wang, J., Yang, T., Wang, H.: DeFi: robust training-free device-free wireless localization with WiFi. IEEE Trans. Veh. Technol. **67**(9), 8822–8831 (2018). https://doi.org/10.1109/TVT.2018.2850842

24. Niu, J., Wang, B., Lei, S., Duong, T.Q., Chen, Y.: ZIL: an energy-efficient indoor localization system using ZigBee radio to detect WiFi fingerprints. IEEE J. Sel. Areas Commun. **33**(7), 1431–1442 (2015)

25. Habaebi, M.H., Khamis, R.O., Zyoud, A., Islam, M.R.: RSS based localization techniques for ZigBee wireless sensor network. In: International Conference on Computer & Communication Engineering (2014)

26. Zhu, J., Luo, H., Chen, Z., Li, Z.: RSSI based Bluetooth low energy indoor positioning. In: International Conference on Indoor Positioning & Indoor Navigation (2015)

27. Rida, M.E., Liu, F., Jadi, Y., Algawhari, A.A.A., Askourih, A.: Indoor location position based on Bluetooth signal strength. In: International Conference on Information Science & Control Engineering (2015)

An Integrated Processing Method Based on Wasserstein Barycenter Algorithm for Automatic Music Transcription

Cong Jin[1], Zhongtong Li[1], Yuanyuan Sun[1], Haiyin Zhang[2], Xin Lv[3(✉)],
Jianguang Li[4], and Shouxun Liu[4]

[1] School of Information and Communication Engineering,
Communication University of China, Beijing 100024, China
{jincong0623,lizhongtong}@cuc.edu.cn
[2] School of Computer and Cyberspace Security, Communication University of China,
Beijing 100024, China
hynn0633@outlook.com
[3] School of Animation and Digital Arts, Communication University of China,
Beijing 100024, China
lvxincuc@163.com
[4] Communication University of China, Beijing 100024, China
{lijianguang,sxliu}@cuc.edu.cn

Abstract. Given a piece of acoustic musical signal, various automatic music transcription (AMT) processing methods have been proposed to generate the corresponding music notations without human intervention. However, the existing AMT methods based on signal processing or machine learning cannot perfectly restore the original music signal and have significant distortion. In this paper, we propose a novel processing method which integrates various AMT methods so as to achieve better performance on music transcription. This integrated method is based on the entropic regularized Wasserstein Barycenter algorithm to speed up the computation of the Wasserstein distance and minimize the distance between two discrete distributions. Moreover, we introduce the proportional transportation distance (PTD) to evaluate the performance of different methods. Experimental results show that the precision and accuracy of the proposed method increase by approximately 48% and 67% respectively compared with the existing methods.

Keywords: Automatic Music Transcription · Machine learning · Wasserstein Barycenter · Ensemble · NMF

Supported by the National Natural Science Foundation of China (NSFC) under Grant Nos. 61631016, National Key Research and Development Plan of Ministry of Science and Technology No. 2018YFB1403903 and the Fundamental Research Funds for the Central Universities No. CUC2019E002, CUC19ZD003.

H. Gao et al. (Eds.): ChinaCom 2019, LNICST 313, pp. 230–240, 2020.
https://doi.org/10.1007/978-3-030-41117-6_19

1   Introduction

Famous audio researchers Moore [1], Pitztalski and Galler [2] proposed the term "Automatic Music Transcription" (AMT) firstly in 1977. These audio researchers believed that by programming computers, they can manage to analyze digital records of music, so that they could detect the pitch of melodies and chord patterns as well as the rhythm of percussion instruments. In music transcription system, a musical acoustic signal can be transformed to the format of music notation like a MIDI file [3]. As a basic problem in Music Information Retrieval (MIR), a complete AMT system would resolve the pitch, timing, and instrument of the sound events.

Various research groups of polyphonic pitch detection used different techniques for music transcriptions. Yeh [4] presented a cross pitch estimation algorithm based on the score function of a pitch candidate set. Nam et al. [5] posed a transcription approach which uses deep belief networks to calculate a midlevel time-pitch representation. Duan et al. [6] and Emiya et al. [7] proposed a model of spectral peak, non-peak region and the residual noise via Maximum Likelihood (ML) Methods. More recently, Peeling and Godsill [8] raised a F0 estimation function and an inhomogeneous Poisson in the frequency domain. In spectrogram factorization-based multi-pitch detection, resulting in harmonic and inharmonic NMF, Vincent et al. [9] merged harmonic constraints in the NMF model. Bertin et al. [10] presented a Bayesian model based on NMF, and each pitch in harmonic positions is treated as a model of Gaussian components. Fuentes et al. [11] modeled each note as a weighted amount of narrowband log spectrum, and switched to log frequency with the convoluted PLCA algorithm. Abdallah and Plumbley [12] combined machine learning and dictionary learning via non-negative sparse coding.

In this paper, we propose a converged method based on Earth Mover's Distance and Wasserstein Barycenter, to compare our experimental result of music transcription with the ground truth. In Sect. 2, we introduce the algorithm of Earth Mover's Distance and Wasserstein Barycenter. In Sect. 3, we present an experiment including data preparation, music transcription with NMF, data trimming, merging and evaluation. At last, we conclude that our crowdsourcing method improves the robustness and accuracy of transcription result.

2   Algorithm

Our idea of music transcription ensemble is inspired by the recent study on Earth Mover's Distance and Wasserstein Barycenter in the area of machine learning. Here, we introduce their formal definitions first.

Definition 1 (Earth Mover's Distance (EMD) [13,14]). *Let $X = \{x_1, x_2, \cdots, x_{n_1}\}$ and $Y = \{y_1, y_2, \cdots, y_{n_2}\}$ be two sets of weighted points in $\mathbb{R}^d$ with non-negative weights α_i and β_j for each $x_i \in X$ and $y_j \in Y$ respectively, and W_X and W_Y be their corresponding total weights. The Earth Mover's Distance between X and Y is $\mathcal{EMD}(X, Y)$*

$$= \frac{1}{\min\{W_X, W_Y\}} \min_F \sum_{i=1}^{n_1} \sum_{j=1}^{n_2} f_{ij} ||x_i - y_j||^2, \tag{1}$$

where $F = \{f_{ij}\}$ *is a feasible flow from* X *to* Y, *i.e., each* $f_{ij} \geq 0$, $\sum_{i=1}^{n_1} f_{ij} \leq \beta_j$, $\sum_{j=1}^{n_2} f_{ij} \leq \alpha_i$, *and* $\sum_{i=1}^{n_1} \sum_{j=1}^{n_2} f_{ij} = \min\{W_X, W_Y\}$.

Roughly speaking, EMD is an example of the least cost and maximum flow problem in Euclidean space $\mathbb{R}^d$. Therefore, the problem of computing EMD can be solved by linear programming [15]. In addition, several faster algorithms have been proposed by using the techniques developed in computational geometry [16–18]. Following EMD, we have the definition of Wasserstein Barycenter.

Definition 2 (Wasserstein Barycenter (WB) [19]**).** *Given a set of point sets* $X_1, X_2, \cdots, X_k \subset \mathbb{R}^d$, *where each* X_j *has the same total weight, the problem of Wasserstein Barycenter is to build a new point set* Q, *such that the total EMDs* $\sum_{j=1}^k \mathcal{EMD}(X_j, Q)$ *is minimized.*

Intuitively, the WB Q can be treated as the representation of all the given patterns $X_1, X_2, \cdots, X_k$. As mentioned in [14], WB has extensive applications in practical areas. For example, it can be applied to compute the average of a large set of images, so as to obtain a robust pattern or compress the image dataset. Prior works include [19–25]. Recently, researchers also use WB to handle Bayesian inference problem [26].

In theory, Ding and Liu have systematically studied the problem of WB (they call it as geometric prototype in the paper) [14]. Given an instance of geometric prototype problem, they show that a small core-set, which is independent of any geometric prototype algorithm, can be effectively computed. That is, one can achieve a similar result via running any available black box algorithm on the core-set. The benefit of computing the core-set is that the data size can be significantly reduced and thus the existing algorithms can run much faster. The reader can find more details about core-set in [27, 28].

In this paper, we adopt the method from [22] for computing WB. For the sake of completeness, we briefly describe their algorithm below.

In Ye's paper [22], they have developed an improved Bregman ADMM (B-ADMM) method to optimize the centroid of big clusters. With the calculation of centroid distribution, clustering has a serious expandability problem, and they introduced the Wasserstein barycenter algorithm, which can calculate the sum of least squared distances with cluster members.

Suppose a set of discrete distributions $\{Q^{(1)}, ..., Q^{(N)}\}$, N stands for the size of a Wasserstein barycenter's computation. They intend to get a centroid Q: $\{(\omega_1, x_1), ..., (\omega_m, x_m)\}$, such that

$$\min_Q \frac{1}{N} \sum_{n=1}^N W^2(Q, Q^{(n)}) \tag{2}$$

where includes the weights of the centroids $\{\omega_i \in \mathbb{R}+\}$, the supporting points $\{x_i \in \mathbb{R}^d\}$, and the optimum coupling between Q and $Q^{(n)}$ for each n, expressed as $\{\pi_{i,j}^{(n)}\}$.

Clustering in B-ADMM method optimizes $\{\omega_i\}$ and $\{\pi_{i,j}^{(n)}\}$ in turn, n = $1, 2, \ldots, N$, versus $\{x_i\}$. Δ_n is defined a Probabilistic simplex of n dimensions. To solve the optimal transport issue, they have introduced two sets of variables $\pi_{(n,1)} = (\pi_{i,j}^{(n,1)}), i \in L', j \in L_n$, and $\pi_{(n,2)} = (\pi_{i,j}^{(n,2)}), i \in L', j \in L_n$, for n = $1, 2, \cdots, N$ the constraints as follows. Let

$$\Delta_{n,1} := \{\pi_{i,j}^{(n,1)} \geqslant 0 : \sum_{i=1}^{m} \pi_{i,j}^{(n,1)} = \omega_j^{(n)}, j \in L_n\} \tag{3}$$

$$\Delta_{n,2}(\omega) := \{\pi_{i,j}^{(n,2)} \geqslant 0 : \sum_{j=1}^{m} \pi_{i,j}^{(n,2)} = \omega_i, i \in L'\} \tag{4}$$

then $\pi^{(n,1)} \in \Delta_{n,1}$ and $\pi^{(n,2)} \in \Delta_{n,2}(\omega)$.

3   Experiment

In this section, we start to describe training data and experimental settings, and then conduct the state-of-the-art method to merge different transcription results. In this experiment, we employ anaconda3 and python3.5 to perform the transcription, and sklearn toolbox to deal with data; while adopted pycharm to merge the data of different transcription results.

3.1   Data Preparation in Different Scenes

In data preparation period, the instrumental sound records in studio were described as dry source, however, most of scenes were not ideal. For a large amount of ground noises would be added to dry source during recording due to the sound card device or background. What's more, some instrumental sounds were recorded in different scenes and added different noises. We chose three classical music pieces by Bach, Mozart and Beethoven and preprocessed them with filter noise, distortion noise, reverb noise and dynamic noise.

3.2   Experimental Settings and Transcription

In this paper, we first proposed a method based on non-negative matrix factorization. Non-negative matrix factorization (NMF) algorithm is utilized as a tool for music transcription [29]. The NMF model in its simplest form decomposes an input spectrogram $A \in \mathbb{R}_+^{X \times Y}$ with X frequency bins and Y frames as:

$$A \approx FT \tag{5}$$

where R $\ll$ X,Y; $F \in \mathbb{R}_+^{X \times Y}$ contains the spectral cardinality of each R tone component; and $T \in \mathbb{R}_+^{X \times Y}$ is the matrix of pitch activity across time.

Then we employed a fresh and simple Time-frequency representation, using the effectiveness of spectral features when highlighting the start time of notes. In addition, we adopted the NMF model to input the proposed features. In our system, we used different audio signals recorded in different scenes with a sample rate of 48 kHz. We split the frame with a hamming window of 8192 samples and a jump size of 1764 samples. The 16384-point DFT was calculated on every frame via double zero padding. Smoothing the spectrum through a median filter covered 100 ms. The algorithms is updated and iterated 50 times. Each row of the transcription results showed: onset time, offset time, notations of Midi are as followed in Fig. 1.

```
[[ 0.7   1.64 60.  ]
 [ 1.18  1.82 63.  ]
 [ 1.62  2.26 64.  ]
 [ 2.08  2.66 65.  ]
 [ 2.5   3.4  80.  ]
 [ 2.52  3.12 68.  ]
 [ 2.94  3.8  81.  ]
 [ 2.94  3.58 69.  ]
 [ 3.4   3.94 70.  ]
 [ 3.4   3.86 82.  ]
 [ 3.82  4.4  79.  ]
```

Fig. 1. The transcription result

3.3   Data Trimming with Random Forest

When we conducted the transcription experiment, we found that the results had some differences in dimensions of matrixes and maybe some data were lost or added when transcription was performing. In order to obtain a better merging result, we applied Random Forest Regression to complete data trimming through inserting the predicted value or removing the large deviation. Random forest is an integrated algorithm of decision tree. Random forests contain multiple decision trees to reduce the risk of over-fitting.

Random forests train is a series of decision trees, so the training process is analogical. Due to the addition of random processes to the algorithm, there is a small difference among each decision tree. By combining the prediction results of each tree, the variance of the prediction is reduced and the performance on the test set is improved. Random representation:

1. At each iteration, the original data are subsampled to obtain different training data.
2. For each tree node, considering different random feature subsets as split.
3. The training process of decision making is the same as that of decision tree.

We first made an initial guess at the missing value, such as filling it with mean/median, then sorting it from small to large according to the missing rate of variable. Using Random Forest Regression to fill in the missing value of variable first, and then iterating it until the latest and final filling result no longer change (with little change). As is shown in Fig. 2, according to Random Forest Regression which we can obtain the predict value and then by comparing with true value, the result is great.

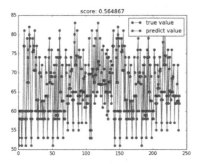

Fig. 2. Data prediction with Random Forest Regression (red line stands for predict value and green line stands for true value) (Color figure online)

3.4 Ensemble and Comparison

In this section, we used transcribed data sets adding four kinds of noises to see the properties of the ensemble method through the Wasserstein Barycenter algorithm which we described above. In ensemble experiments, we examined the conditions under which ensemble method could estimate clusters of transcription data. In comparison experiments, we compared the ensemble method with single transcription method in four scenes through Proportional Transportation Distance (PTD) to see the advantages of the ensemble method.

(i) Ensemble. Firstly, we examined data sets in four scenes (adding filter noise, distortion noise, reverb noise and dynamic noise) under which we could get reasonable clusters. Then, we employed the Wasserstein Barycenter algorithm as our ensemble method to obtain results. For example, as is shown in Fig. 3, we put forward the transcription data with reverb noises before ensemble. It can be seen that there is a large gap between unmerged data and raw data.

While, we generated the 10 transcription data adding with different reverb noises and then merged them through Wasserstein means algorithm. The comparison between merged data and raw data is shown in Fig. 4.

(ii) Comparison. We show that ensemble method is more robust than single transcription method in four scenes through Proportional Transportation Distance (PTD). The experimental results are evaluated objectively by using PTD

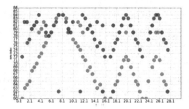

Fig. 3. The raw data and unmerged data with reverb noises. (The blue dots represent the raw data) (Color figure online)

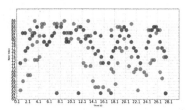

Fig. 4. The raw data and merged data with reverb noises. (The blue dots represent raw data) (Color figure online)

described above. The PTD is computed by first dividing each point's weight by the total weight of its point set, and then the EMD of resulting point sets is calculated [30]. According to the EMD and PTD method, we present notation as sets of weighted points. The weight represents note duration. Each note stands for a point distributed in the x and y coordinates, representing the start time and pitch, respectively. We use the Euclidean distance as the ground distance. Thus, the distance between two notes with the coordinates (x_i, y_i) and (x_j, y_j) is

$$d_{ij} = \sqrt{(x_i - x_j)^2 + (y_i - y_j)^2}$$

Then it is used to calculate the EMD of the two audio matrices. At last, we switch the EMD to PTD as the comparison of merged and unmerged data. The result is shown in Fig. 5.

We selected three classical music pieces by Bach, Mozart and Beethoven in four scenes by adding different noises including filter noise, distortion noise, reverb noise and dynamic noise. We calculate the PTD between unmerged data and ground truth (or raw data), and then between merged data and ground truth. The PTD comparison of merged and unmerged data in four scenes are shown in Tables 1, 2, 3 and 4.

From these tables we can see that the transcription has a more robust result after merging. By comparing the PTD between merged and unmerged data, we can find that the merged data are already very close to the ground truth, and the PTD of merged data decreased more than 3 times compared with unmerged data.

Fig. 5. The PTD Comparison. (The middle blue dot represents the raw data, the black dots represent the merged data, and other points represent the unmerged data.) (Color figure online)

Table 1. The PTD comparison in scene1 with filter noises. (Filter 1–5 are unmerged data, mix are merged data)

PTD	Filter1	Filter2	Filter3	Filter4	Filter5	Mix
Bach	4.9777	4.1040	4.9818	4.7306	3.9892	0.3624
Beethoven	3.6474	3.4409	2.9725	2.9948	2.9216	0.7622
Mozart	1.8165	2.2874	1.8099	1.7664	1.7765	0.5321

Table 2. The PTD comparison in scene2 with reverb noises. (Reverb 1–5 are unmerged data, mix are merged data)

PTD	Reverb1	Reverb2	Reverb3	Reverb4	Reverb5	Mix
Bach	1.8228	1.9929	2.4563	2.4874	3.4708	0.4978
Beethoven	3.0975	3.2011	4.3783	3.1690	2.9124	0.4137
Mozart	2.4403	2.0241	1.8956	1.8765	1.8224	0.4167

Table 3. The PTD comparison in scene3 with dynamic noises. (Dynamic 1–5 are unmerged data, mix are merged data)

PTD	Dynamic1	Dynamic2	Dynamic3	Dynamic4	Dynamic5	Mix
Bach	2.3392	3.0378	2.8648	2.6319	2.4494	0.3909
Beethoven	2.4482	2.8423	2.4436	2.4857	2.9649	0.7432
Mozart	1.9077	1.9662	1.9327	1.8483	1.8813	0.6417

Table 4. The PTD comparison in scene4 with distortion noises. (Distortion 1–5 are unmerged data, mix are merged data)

PTD	Distortion1	Distortion2	Distortion3	Distortion4	Distortion5	Mix
Bach	3.2819	3.8431	3.1133	2.8937	2.2559	0.6667
Beethoven	4.2782	4.3418	3.5581	5.0861	2.7737	0.4621
Mozart	2.6864	2.6495	2.5223	2.1681	1.9183	0.8932

3.5   Evaluation and Performance

We employed the evaluation by calculating precision ($P = \frac{N_{tp}}{N_{tp}+N_{fp}}$), recall ($R = \frac{N_{tp}}{N_{tp}+N_{fn}}$), F-measure ($F = \frac{2PR}{P+R}$) and accuracy ($A = \frac{N_{tp}}{N_{tp}+N_{fp}+N_{fn}}$), where N_{tp}, N_{fp} and N_{fn} are the values of true positives, false positives and false negatives, respectively. If the pitch is correct and its starting time is within 50ms of the ground truth, we computed the notes as true positives [31].

The results are shown in Table 5. First of all, we averaged precision, recall, F-measure and accuracy of unmerged data from three composers in four scenes. Then, we compared the values of them in four scenes with those of merged data. It can be seen that the ensemble method is better than single transcription method in four scenes and the rates of precision, recall, F-measure and accuracy are obviously higher than those of unmerged data. It has increased nearly 2 times in F-measure and accuracy and 1.5 times in precision and recall.

Table 5. Performance comparison on the real date set

	Precision	Recall	F-measure	Accuracy
Filter	0.4321	0.6667	0.3766	0.3232
Reverb	0.4405	0.6829	0.3841	0.3927
Dynamic	0.4272	0.6977	0.3385	0.3431
Distortion	0.4137	0.6914	0.3278	0.3703
Mix	0.6421	0.9231	0.7371	0.6642

4   Conclusion

In this paper we showed that Wasserstein Barycenter is effective in multiple scenes ensemble in machine learning. In different scenes and pieces of music, we presented their effectiveness in ensemble results, as well as in improving the robustness and accuracy of music transcriptions. We also proposed an objective evaluation to measuring the differences between music notation transcriptions in different scenes and the ground truth scores. Finally, we drew a conclusion that our crowdsourcing method is very useful in improving the robustness and accuracy of transcription results.

References

1. Moorer, J.A.: On the transcription of musical sound by computer. Comput. Music J. 1(4), 32–38 (1977)
2. Piszczalski, M., Galler, B.A.: Automatic music transcription. Comput. Music J. 1(4), 22–31 (1977)

3. Duan, Z., Benetos, E.: Automatic music transcription. In: Proceedings of the International Society for Music Information Retrieval Conference, Malaga, Spain (2015)

4. Chunghsin, Y.: Multiple fundamental frequency estimation of polyphonic recordings (2008)

5. Nam, J., Ngiam, J., Lee, H., Slaney, M.: A classification-based polyphonic piano transcription approach using learned feature representations (2011)

6. Duan, Z., Pardo, B., Zhang, C.: Multiple fundamental frequency estimation by modeling spectral peaks and non-peak regions. IEEE Trans. Audio Speech Lang. Process. **18**(8), 2121–2133 (2010)

7. Emiya, V., Badeau, R., David, B.: Multipitch estimation of piano sounds using a new probabilistic spectral smoothness principle. IEEE Trans. Audio Speech Lang. Process. **18**(6), 1643–1654 (2010)

8. Peeling, P.H., Godsill, S.J.: Multiple pitch estimation using non-homogeneous poisson processes. IEEE J. Sel. Top. Signal Process. **5**(6), 1133–1143 (2011)

9. Vincent, E., Bertin, N., Badeau, R.: Adaptive harmonic spectral decomposition for multiple pitch estimation. IEEE Trans. Audio Speech Lang. Process. **18**(3), 528–537 (2010)

10. Bertin, N., Badeau, R., Vincent, E.: Enforcing harmonicity and smoothness in Bayesian nonnegative matrix factorization applied to polyphonic music transcription. IEEE Trans. Audio Speech Lang. Process. **18**(3), 538–549 (2010)

11. Fuentes, B., Badeau, R., Richard, G.: Adaptive harmonic time-frequency decomposition of audio using shift-invariant PLCA. In: IEEE International Conference on Acoustics, Speech and Signal Processing, pp. 401–404 (2011)

12. Abdallah, S.M., Plumbley, M.D.: Polyphonic transcription by non-negative sparse coding of power spectra. In: Proceedings of the International Society for Music Information Retrieval Conference (2004)

13. Rubner, Y., Tomasi, C., Guibas, L.J.: The earth mover's distance as a metric for image retrieval. Int. J. Comput. Vis. **40**(2), 99–121 (2000)

14. Ding, H., Liu, M.: On geometric prototype and applications. In: 26th Annual European Symposium on Algorithms, pp. 1–15 (2018)

15. Ahuja, R.K., Magnanti, T.L., Orlin, J.B.: Network Flows: Theory, Algorithms, and Applications. Prentice Hall, Upper Saddle River (1993)

16. Agarwal, P.K., Fox, K., Panigrahi, D., Varadarajan, K.R., Xiao, A.: Faster algorithms for the geometric transportation problem. In: 33rd International Symposium on Computational Geometry, pp. 1–16 (2017)

17. Cabello, S., Giannopoulos, P., Knauer, C., Rote, G.: Matching point sets with respect to the Earth Mover's Distance. Comput. Geom. **39**(2), 118–133 (2008)

18. Arthur, D., Vassilvitskii, S.: k-means++: the advantages of careful seeding. In: Proceedings of the Eighteenth Annual ACM-SIAM Symposium on Discrete Algorithms, pp. 1027–1035 (2007)

19. Cuturi, M., Doucet, A.: Fast computation of Wasserstein Barycenters. In: International Conference on Machine Learning, pp. 685–693 (2014)

20. Baum, M., Willett, P., Hanebeck, U.D.: On Wasserstein Barycenters and MMOSPA estimation. IEEE Signal Process. Lett. **22**(10), 1511–1515 (2015)

21. Gramfort, A., Peyré, G., Cuturi, M.: Fast optimal transport averaging of neuroimaging data. In: Ourselin, S., Alexander, D.C., Westin, C.-F., Cardoso, M.J. (eds.) IPMI 2015. LNCS, vol. 9123, pp. 261–272. Springer, Cham (2015). https://doi.org/10.1007/978-3-319-19992-4_20

22. Ye, J., Wu, P., Wang, J.Z., Li, J.: Fast discrete distribution clustering using Wasserstein Barycenter with sparse support. IEEE Trans. Signal Process. **65**(9), 2317–2332 (2017)

23. Benamou, J.-D., Carlier, G., Cuturi, M., Nenna, L., Peyré, G.: Iterative Bregman projections for regularized transportation problems. SIAM J. Sci. Comput. **37**(2), 1111–1138 (2015)
24. Ding, H., Berezney, R., Xu, J.: k-prototype learning for 3d rigid structures. In: Advances in Neural Information Processing Systems, pp. 2589–2597 (2013)
25. Ding, H., Xu, J.: Finding median point-set using earth mover's distance. In: Twenty Eighth AAAI Conference on Artificial Intelligence (2014)
26. Staib, M., Claici, S., Solomon, J., Jegelka, S.: Parallel streaming Wasserstein Barycenters. In: Advances in Neural Information Processing Systems, pp. 2647–2658 (2017)
27. Phillips, J.M.: Coresets and sketches. Comput. Res. Repos. (2016)
28. Agarwal, P.K., Har-Peled, S., Varadarajan, K.R.: Geometric approximation via coresets. Comb. Comput. Geom. **52**, 1–30 (2005)
29. Smaragdis, P., Brown, J.C.: Non-negative matrix factorization for polyphonic music transcription. In: IEEE Workshop on Applications of Signal Processing to Audio and Acoustics, pp. 177–180 (2003)
30. Typke, R., Veltkamp, R.C., Wiering, F.: Searching notated polyphonic music using transportation distances. In: Proceedings of the 12th Annual ACM International Conference on Multimedia, pp. 128–135 (2004)
31. Gao, L., Su, L., Yang, Y.H., Tan, L.: Polyphonic piano note transcription with non-negative matrix factorization of differential spectrogram. In: IEEE International Conference on Acoustics, Speech and Signal Processing, pp. 291–295 (2017)

Spinal-Polar Concatenated Codes in Non-coherent UWB Communication Systems

Qianwen Luo, Zhonghua Liang[(✉)], and Yue Xin

School of Information Engineering, Chang'an University,
Xi'an 710064, People's Republic of China
956829305@qq.com, lzhxjd@hotmail.com, 342996436@qq.com

Abstract. Non-coherent ultra-wideband (UWB) systems have attracted great attention due to their low complexity, and without the need of channel estimation. In order to improve the transmission reliability, polar codes were recently introduced into non-coherent UWB systems because of their capability of approaching the Shannon channel capacity, and their low complexity in both coding and decoding. In the case of polar codes with medium and short length, the bit error rate (BER) performance of coded incoherent UWB systems is limited to incompletely channel polarization, poor Hamming distance and the sensitivity of successive cancellation (SC) decoding resulting in error propagation. In order to improve the performance of coded systems using polar codes with medium and short length, Spinal-Polar codes were recently presented, in which inner codes and outer codes are complementary, and the outer codes have good pseudo-random characteristics and error correction performance in the case of short length. Therefore, in this paper, the interleaved Spinal-Polar codes are introduced into the non-coherent UWB systems. Simulation results show that the interleaved Spinal-Polar codes can effectively improve the BER performance of the coded non-coherent UWB systems using polar codes with medium and short code length.

Keywords: UWB · Non-coherent reception · Spinal coding · Polar coding · Concatenated coding

1 Introduction

Ultra-wideband (UWB) is a short-range wireless communication technology that uses spectrum overlap technology to make full use of spectrum resources. UWB technology has good coexistence and confidentiality characteristics, strong multipath resolution and fine positioning accuracy. The incoherent UWB systems

This work was supported in part by the National Natural Science Foundation of China under Grant 61271262 and Grant 61572083, and in part by Joint Fund of Ministry of Education of China (Grant No. 6141A02022610).

H. Gao et al. (Eds.): ChinaCom 2019, LNICST 313, pp. 241–251, 2020.
https://doi.org/10.1007/978-3-030-41117-6_20

have been widely studied for its low cost, low complexity and without the need of precise synchronization while achieving suboptimal bit error rate (BER) performance. However, many key technologies need to be developed for UWB communication systems, and these key technologies are of great significance to improve the performance of systems. Among them, channel coding is investigated to guarantee reliability.

At present, some forward error correction FEC codes have been introduced into incoherent UWB systems to improve the BER performance of the systems [1–4]. Polar codes were also recently introduced into non-coherent UWB systems due to their capability of approaching the Shannon channel capacity, and complexity in both coding and decoding [5]. In the case of polar codes with medium and short length, the performance is inferior to that of Turbo codes and low density parity check (LDPC) codes. Several typical concatenated polar coding schemes were studied to improve the performance of polar codes with medium and short length at present. The traditional Reed Solomon (RS)-Polar codes can reduce the frame error rate (FER), however, it is hard to implement because the length of outer codes increases exponentially with the increase of the length of inner codes [6]. In the interleaved RS-Polar codes, the efficiency of the concatenated codes is higher as the coding length increases [7]. The LDPC-Polar codes was proposed to overcome the incompletely polarization of polar codes with medium and short length [8]. The BCH-Polar codes and the Convolutional-Polar codes were proposed, in which the decoding scheme of outer codes is relatively complex [9]. In order to solve the problem of pairwise bit error resulted from SC decoding, interleaved LDPC-Polar codes were proposed [10]. However, LDPC codes can obtain better error correcting ability only when the coding length is long enough. Moreover, it has high encoding complexity, therefore, the encoding complexity of the concatenated codes will increase. Each of these concatenated codes improves the performance of polar codes, but also suffers from the problem that the error correction capability of outer codes is affected by the coding length. The interleaved Spinal-Polar codes were proposed in [11], and it can significantly improve the performance of polar codes in acceptable complexity [11]. In the interleaved Spinal-Polar codes, the information sequence is divided into many data streams before interleaving operation. Therefore, we can make full use of the performance of Spinal codes with short code length. The joint iterative decoding corresponding to interleaved coding can alleviate the problem of error derivation in SC decoding [12].

Based on the discussions above, in this paper, the interleaved Spinal-Polar codes are used to improve the BER performance of the coded incoherent UWB systems using polar codes with medium and short length. The information sequence is coded by Spinal coding scheme firstly, and then the second layer of protection is obtained by polar coding.

The rest of this paper is organized as follows. Section 2 introduces the signal and channel models for the coded non-coherent UWB systems. Section 3 introduces interleaved Spinal-Polar codes and joint iterative decoding. Section 4 gives some simulation results. Finally, Sect. 5 provides the concluding remarks.

2   Signal and Channel Model

2.1   NC-PPM Signaling

PPM is a modulation method that uses data signal to change the pulse position in one symbol period. According to the IEEE 802.15.4a standard, PPM-UWB signal is formed by evenly spaced double pulses to meet the FCC mask requirements. The PPM-UWB signal is [4]

$$s(t) = \sqrt{\frac{E_b}{2N_s}} \sum_{i=0}^{N-1} v_i (t - iT_s) \tag{1}$$

where $v_i(t) \triangleq [1 - c_n(i)] s(t) + c_n(i) s\left(t - \frac{T_s}{2}\right)$, information bit $c_n(i)$ determines the location of $s(t)$ throughout the symbol period, N indicates the length of the original information transmitted, E_b represents the average energy of each symbol, N_s represents the pulse pairs in each symbol, and T_s represents the symbol period.

2.2   TR Signaling

Assuming the information bit stream is $c_n \in \{0, 1\}$, it is expressed as symbol sequence $b_n \in \{-1, 1\}$ after BPSK modulation. In the TR transmission scheme, the basic unit of the transmitted signal is a pulse pair containing a data pulse and a reference pulse, and the reference pulse is transmitted before the modulated data pulse. The TR signaling is [13]

$$\hat{s}_{TR}(t) = \sum_{n=-\infty}^{\infty} \sum_{i=0}^{N_s-1} g(t - nT_s - iT_f) + b_n g(t - nT_s - iT_f - T_d) \tag{2}$$

where $g(t)$ represents the UWB pulse, T_f represents the duration of each frame, T_d represents the interval between two pulses in a pulse pair, $T_s = N_s T_f$ is the bit period, and b_n is the n information bit. $\tau_{\max}$ and T_p represent maximum channel spread time and pulse width respectively, to avoid inter-pulse interference (IPI), taking $T_d \geq \tau_{\max} + T_p$, and taking $T_f \geq 2T_d$ to avoid inter-frame interference (IFI). Compares to TR-UWB systems, the TRPC-UWB systems have smaller interval between the data pulse and the reference pulse. In this paper, the simulation of the BER performance of TRPC-UWB systems, assuming $T_d = T_p$.

2.3   Channel Model

The channel impulse response of the UWB multipath channel model given by the IEEE 802.15.4a standard is [14]

$$h(t) = \sum_{l=1}^{L} \alpha_l \delta(t - \tau_l) \tag{3}$$

where L represents the total number of multipaths, α_l and τ_l represent complex amplitude and spread delay of the l-th path.

3   Interleaved Spinal-Polar Coding Scheme for Non-coherent UWB Systems

3.1   Interleaved Spinal-Polar Coding Scheme

The coding process of coded non-coherent UWB systems using interleaved Spinal-Polar codes is described as follows. Firstly, the information sequence is coded by Spinal codes, next the interleaving process is operated, and then polar coding is parallel implemented. The specific Spinal coding process is referred to in reference [15]. Polar coding is represented by four parameters (N, k, A, u_{A^c}), the specific coding process is referred to reference [16]. Two important steps in polar coding are generating matrix and selecting bit sub-channel index of transmission information. When selecting the bit sub-channel index of transmission information, the channel noise is obtained by training sequence in non-coherent UWB systems, the specific process is referred to reference [5]. When the interleaved Spinal-Polar coding is performed, it is assumed that the number of channels is P, and each row of the matrix W has P Spinal code-words. Table 1 shows the specific procedure of the interleaved Spinal-Polar coding, where the channel number is P [11], m represents the length of each Spinal code-word and n represents the length of each polar code-word.

Algorithm 1. Interleaved Spinal-Polar coding procedure

Initialization:

Divide the information sequence M into r block data streams, each block contains m' bits, m'bits are divided into m'/k part;

Set the channel number parameter P in the outer Spinal coding;

Define the concatenated encoding matrix X with size $mP \times n$.

for $i \leftarrow 1$ to m'/k do

    for $j \leftarrow 1$ to r do

        $W\left(j, (i-1)\,mk/m'p + 1 : imk/m'p\right) = Spinalencoder(\bar{m}_i, P)$;

    end for

    $W' = W^t$;

    $X\left((i-1)\,mk/m' + 1, imk/m'\right) = Polarencoder\,(W', n)$;

end for

End Obtain the interleaving Spinal-Polar coding matrix $X_{mP \times n}$.

3.2   Joint Iterative Decoding for Interleaved Spinal-Polar Codes

The coded NC-PPM, TR and TRPC signaling using interleaved Spinal-Polar codes pass through the channel firstly, then the channel transmission sequence pass through the receiving filters. The signals are expressed as follows [5]

$$r\,(t) = \tilde{s}\,(t) * h\,(t) + n\,(t) \tag{4}$$

where $*$ denotes a linear convolution, $n(t)$ represents a complex additive white Gaussian noise.

The autocorrelation operation is performed on the filtered TR and TRPC signaling, and the output decision variable by the receiver is [4]

$$D = \int_{mT_s+T_1}^{mT_s+T_2} \tilde{r}(t)\tilde{r}(t-T_d)\,dt \tag{5}$$

where $T_1 = T_d + T_l$, $T_2 = T_d + 2(N_f-1)T_d + T_h + T_p = (2N_f-1)T_d + T_h + T_p$, T_l and T_h represent the starting and ending points of the integral respectively, T_l usually approaches the arrival time of the first path, integral interval $[T_1, T_2]$ will affect the detection effect, so the choice of T_1 and T_2 should make the autocorrelation operation cover as many meaningful multipath channels as possible. The specific determination algorithm can be referred to reference [17], and finally the receiver output information [17]

$$\tilde{b} = \frac{\text{sgn}(D-d_0)+1}{2} \tag{6}$$

In TR-UWB systems, d_0 in (6) is taked as 0. However, in TRPC-UWB systems, it is generally assumed that the pulse interval is approximately equal to the pulse width. This will inevitably lead to inter-pulse interference, so it results in the deviation of the decision threshold. Therefore, "0" isn't the appropriate decision threshold for TRPC-UWB systems any more. In the process of simulating the BER performance of the coded TRPC-UWB systems, we assume that $T_d = T_p$ and use the optimized decision threshold d_0, and the specific acquisition method is referred to reference [17].

The coded NC-PPM signaling passing through the filter is detected by a square-law detector firstly, and then the signal passing through the square-law detector is fed into the energy integrator with different integration windows. The decision variable is from the different energy value of the energy integrator with different integration windows. The signal energy collected corresponding to different integration length is [4]

$$D_0 = \int_{T_1}^{T_2} \tilde{r}(t)^2\,dt \tag{7}$$

$$D_1 = \int_{T_1+\frac{T_s}{2}}^{T_2+\frac{T_s}{2}} \tilde{r}(t)^2\,dt \tag{8}$$

Among them, the starting and ending moments of the integral T_1 and T_2 are determined in reference [4]. The final decision variable $D = D_1 - D_0$. The receiver output decision information [4]

$$\tilde{b} = \frac{\text{sgn}(D)+1}{2} \tag{9}$$

where $\text{sgn}(x) = \begin{cases} +1, & x > 0 \\ -1, & x < 0 \end{cases}$.

In the coded non-coherent UWB systems, the decision variable is used as the output of the receiver, to obtain the decoded decision variable. In this paper, the joint iterative decoding algorithm [12] is applied, where, SC decoding for inner codes [16] and FSD decoding for outer codes [18] are used, respectively. Algorithm 2 shows the process of the joint iterative decoding algorithm.

Algorithm 2. Joint iterative decoding algorithm

Initialization:

Define the decoding auxiliary matrix y^t and decoding matrix $\hat{W}$;

for $i \leftarrow 1$ to r **do**

    for $j \leftarrow 1$ to mP **do**

        $y^t (1 : mP, i) = Polardecoder(n, A, y (1 : mP, i))$;

    end for

    $\hat{W} (1 : m, i) = FSDdecoder \left(P, y^t (1 : m, i), B, k\right)$;

    //update information obtained from Spinal decoder back to the SC

decoder

    $y' (1 : mP, i) = Spinalencoder \left(\hat{W} (1 : m, i), P\right)$;

end for

End the decoding matrix $\hat{W}_{m \times r}$ is get.

---

4   Simulation Results and Discussions

4.1   Parameter Setting for Outer Codes

In order to realize the complementary advantages between inner and outer codes in interleaved Spinal-Polar codes, it is necessary to reasonably design the code length of Spinal codes and polar codes, that is, to reasonably set the values of k and r of Spinal codes and the values n of polar codes. In simulation, the parameter setting of the outer codes mainly includes the Hash function and the number of channel. In addition, the outer codes are applied at a fixed coding rate, so it is also necessary to set the coding form.

A. Hash Function

In order to reduce the collision probability of different information segments through hash function and ensure the efficiency of identifying the original information sequence correctly, it is needed to adopt hash function with a long state length as much possible. However, in order to balance hardware requirements and the performance of concatenated codes, the one-at-a-time hash function with 32 bits length is adopted in this paper.

B. Coding Form

Due to the sequential nature of Spinal coding, the information data stream m_i has nothing to do with the coding symbol according to the information data stream $m_{i-1}, m_{i-2}, \cdots, m_1$, so the information data stream in former coded by

Spinal codes can be better protected. That is, the error correction performance of Spinal codes cannot be improved by increasing the coding length [19]. Therefore, the BER of the coding form $S(n, k, P)$ (where $n \neq k$) is greater than that of the coding form $S(k, k, P)$, that is $P_e > \varepsilon_D$, where ε_D is the BER of the coding form $S(k, k, P)$ of spinal codes.

C. Channel Number Settings

The BER calculation formula for the Spinal codes in the AWGN channel is given in [20]

$$P_e(i) = 2^{-\Theta\left(iPC^2/k\right)} \tag{10}$$

In the formula (10), i represents the index of the block information, P represents the number of channels, and C represents the channel capacity. It can be seen that the error correction performance of the Spinal codes increases with the increase of the number of channels. Therefore, a number of channels greater than 1 is set in the simulation process.

4.2   Simulation Results

In this paper, simulation is carried out under CM1 and CM8 channel models, and the final BER data are obtained from an average of 100 channels, including coded NC-PPM, TR and TRPC systems using interleaved Spinal-Polar codes. CM1 is the channel environment of residential line-of-sight and CM8 channel is the channel environment of factory non-line-of-sight. The uncoded TRPC systems have better BER performance compared to uncoded TR systems. The NC-PPM systems are one kind of non-coherent UWB systems, which have different modulation modes at the transmitter and detection methods at receiving end. In the case of outer codes with single channel, there are two cases of concatenated coding rate, 1/4 and 1/8, and the corresponding coding length are 512, 1024.

Figure 1 shows the BER performance of the coded TR-UWB systems using interleaved Spinal-Polar codes in the CM1 channel model. The results show that the coded systems have better performance. When the coding rate is the same, the interleaved Spinal-Polar codes can improve the BER performance of the coded systems using polar codes with medium and short length. For example, when the code length is 512 and $BER = 1 \times 10^{-3}$, the coded TR-UWB systems using interleaved Spinal-Polar codes achieve a performance gain of 0.5 dB compared to the coded TR-UWB systems using polar codes. When the code length is 1024 and $BER = 1 \times 10^{-4}$, the coded TR-UWB systems using interleaved Spinal-Polar codes achieve a performance gain of 1.3 dB compared to the coded TR-UWB systems using polar codes.

Figure 2 shows the BER performance of the coded TRPC-UWB systems using interleaved Spinal-Polar codes in the CM1 channel model.

As can be seen from Fig. 2, the coded systems have better performance as the coding rate decreases. For example, when $BER = 1 \times 10^{-4}$, compared to the coded systems with the coding rate 1/4, the coded systems with coding rate 1/8

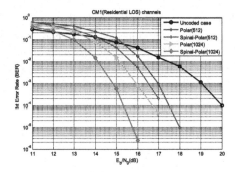

Fig. 1. BER performance of the coded TR-UWB systems using interleaved spinal-polar codes in CM1 channels.

achieves a performance gain of approximately 1.5 dB. When the coding rate is the same, the coded TRPC-UWB systems using interleaved Spinal-Polar codes improve the BER performance of the coded TRPC-UWB systems using polar codes. For example, when the code length is 512 and $BER = 1 \times 10^{-5}$, the coded TRPC-UWB systems using concatenated codes achieves a performance gain of approximately 0.9 dB.

Figure 3 gives the BER simulation of the coded TRPC-UWB systems interleaved Spinal-Polar coding scheme in the CM8 channel model.

The simulation result in Fig. 3 shows that the interleaved Spinal-Polar coded systems under this channel model have better BER performance as the coding rate decreases. For example, when $BER = 1 \times 10^{-5}$, the concatenated coding systems with a coding rate 1/8 obtain a performance gain of nearly 2.0 dB compared with the concatenated coding systems with a coding rate 1/4. At the same coding rate, the BER performance of the coded TRPC-UWB systems using interleaved Spinal-Polar coding scheme is better than that of the coded TRPC-UWB systems using polar coding scheme. For example, when the codes

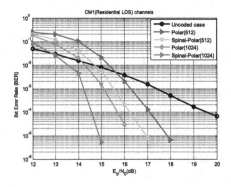

Fig. 2. BER performance of the coded TRPC-UWB systems using interleaved spinal-polar codes in CM1 channels.

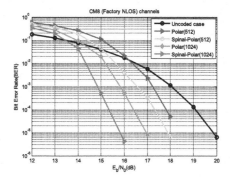

Fig. 3. BER performance of the coded TRPC-UWB systems using interleaved spinal-polar codes in CM8 channels.

length is 1024, the coded systems using the concatenated coding scheme obtain a performance gain of 1.1 dB.

Figure 4 shows the BER performance simulation of the coded NC-PPM system using interleaved Spinal-Polar codes in the CM1 channel model. As can be seen from Fig. 4, the Spinal-Polar interleaved coded systems achieve better performance gain than polar coded systems at the same coding rate. For example, when $BER = 1 \times 10^{-4}$, the concatenated coding systems with the coding rate 1/4 and 1/8 obtain the performance gains of 0.4 dB and 0.6 dB compared with the coded systems using polar codes alone. The BER performance of the coded systems using concatenated codes get better as the coding rate decreases. For example, when $BER = 1 \times 10^{-4}$, the concatenated coding systems with the coding rate 1/8 obtain a performance gain of nearly 1 dB compared with the concatenated coding systems with the coding rate 1/4.

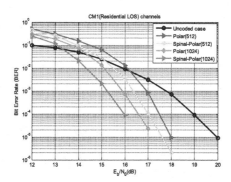

Fig. 4. BER performance of the coded NC-PPM systems using interleaved spinal-polar codes in CM1 channels.

4.3   Complexity Comparison

Table 1. Complexity comparison

	Interleaved Spinal-Polar concatenated codes	Polar codes
Coding	$O\left\{\frac{m'}{k}P\left[r\left(v+k\right)+n\right]\right\}$	$O\left(N\right)$
Decoding	$O\left(rmB\cdot 2^{k}\left(v+k+\log B\right)+N\log n\right)$	$O\left(N\log N\right)$

Table 1 shows the time complexity of the interleaved Spinal-Polar codes and the polar codes. Where the massage sequence is divided into r blocks, the state length of Hash function for Spinal coding is v, the number of channels is P, each of information blocks is divided into m'/k parts, the length of spinal code-word is m. The length of polar code-word is n. The main time cost is the Hash function acts on the information in Spinal coding, that is $O\left(v+k\right)$.

5   Conclusions

In this paper, the coded non-coherent UWB systems using interleaved Spinal-Polar codes are evaluated under CM1 and CM8 channels. Theoretical analysis and simulation results show the interleaved Spinal-Polar coding scheme can effectively improve the BER performance of the coded non-coherent UWB systems using polar codes with the medium and short length.

References

1. Liang, Z., Dong, X., Gulliver, T.A.: Performance of coded transmitted reference pulse cluster UWB systems. In: Proceedings of IEEE Asilomar Conference on Signals, Systems, and Computers, October 2008, pp. 1990–1995 (2008)
2. Liang, Z., Dong, X., Gulliver, T.A., Liao, X.: Performance of transmitted reference pulse cluster ultra-wideband systems with forward error correction. Int. J. Commun. Syst. **27**, 265–276 (2014)
3. Zang, J., Liang, Z., Liu, J., Li, P., Yang, X.: Performance of transmitted reference pulse cluster UWB communication systems using LDPC codes. In: IEEE International Symposium on Personal, October 2015, pp. 585–589 (2015)
4. Liang, Z., Zang, J., Yang, X., Dong, X., Song, H.: Low-density parity-check codes for noncoherent UWB communication systems. China Commun. **14**, 1–11 (2017)
5. Ma, L., Liang, Z., Liu, D.: Performance of polarized channel coding in TRPC-UWB communication systems. In: IEEE International Conference on Cyber-Enabled Distributed Computing and Knowledge Discovery (CyberC), pp. 466–470 (2017)
6. Bakshi, M., Jaggi, S.: Concatenated polar codes. In: IEEE International Symposium on Information Theory, pp. 918–922 (2010)
7. Mahdavifar, H., El-Khamy, M., Lee, J., Kang, I.: Performance limits and practical decoding of interleaved Reed-Solomon polar concatenated codes. IEEE Trans. Commun. **62**, 1406–1417 (2014)

8. Guo, J., Qin, M., Fabregas, A.G., Siegel, P.H.: Enhanced belief propagation decoding of polar codes through concatenation. In: IEEE International Symposium on Information Theory, pp. 2987–2991 (2014)
9. Wang, Y., Narayanan, K., Huang, Y.: Interleaved concatenations of polar codes with BCH and convolutional codes. IEEE J. Sel. Areas Commun. **34**, 267–277 (2016)
10. Meng, Y., Li, L., Hu, Y.: A novel interleaving scheme for polar codes. In: IEEE 84th Vehicular Technology Conference, pp. 1–5 (2017)
11. Dong, D., Wu, S., Jiang, X., Jiao, J., Xhang, Q.: Towards high performance short codes: concatenated with the spinal codes. In: IEEE 28th Annual International Symposium on Personal, Indoor, and Mobile Radio Communications (PIMRC), pp. 1–5 (2017)
12. Xu, X., Wu, S., Dong, D., Jiao, J., Zhang, Q.: High performance short polar codes: a concatenation scheme using spinal codes as the outer code. IEEE Access **6**(99), 70644–70654 (2018)
13. Dong, X., Lee, A., Xiao, L.: A new UWB dual pulse transmission and detection technique. In: IEEE International Conference on Communications, pp. 2835–2839 (2005)
14. Molisch, A., et al.: IEEE 802.15.4a channel model-final report. IEEE 802.15-04-0662-02-004a (2005)
15. Perry, J., Balakrishnan, H., Shah, D.: Rateless spinal codes. In: ACM Workshop on Hot Topics in Networks, pp. 1–6 (2011)
16. Arikan, E.: Channel polarization: a method for constructing capacity-achieving codes for symmetric binary-input memoryless channels. IEEE Trans. Inf. Theory **55**, 3051–3073 (2009)
17. Dong, X., Jin, L., Orlik, P.: A new transmitted reference pulse cluster system for UWB communications. IEEE Trans. Veh. Technol. **57**(5), 3217–3224 (2008)
18. Yang, W., Li, Y., Yu, X., Li, J.: A low complexity sequential decoding algorithm for rateless spinal codes. IEEE Commun. Lett. **19**(7), 1105–1108 (2015)
19. Yang, H.: Design and analysis of cascaded Spinal codes (2018)
20. Balakrishnan, H., Iannucci, P., Perry, J., Shah, D.: De-randomizing Shannon: the design and analysis of a capacity-achieving rateless code (2012). https://arxiv.org/abs/1206.0418

Dynamic Programming Based Cooperative Mobility Management in Ultra Dense Networks

Ziyue Zhang[1,2], Jie Gong[3], and Xiang Chen[1,2(✉)]

[1] School of Electronics and Information Technology, Sun Yat-sen University,
Guangzhou 510006, China
chenxiang@mail.sysu.edu.cn
[2] Key Lab of EDA, Research Institute of Tsinghua University in Shenzhen (RITS),
Shenzhen 518075, China
[3] School of Data and Computer Science, Sun Yat-sen University,
Guangzhou 510006, China

Abstract. In ultra dense networks (UDNs), base stations (BSs) with mobile edge computing (MEC) function can provide low latency and powerful computation to energy and computation constrained mobile users. Meanwhile, existing wireless access-oriented mobility management (MM) schemes are not suitable for high mobility scenarios in UDNs. In this paper, a novel dynamic programming based MM (DPMM) scheme is proposed to optimize delay performance considering both wireless transmission and task computation under an energy consumption constraint. Based on markov decision process (MDP) and dynamic programming (DP), DPMM utilizes statistic system information to get a stationary optimal policy and can work in an offline mode. Cooperative transmission is further considered to enhance uplink data transmission rate. Simulations show that the proposed DPMM scheme can achieve close-to-optimal delay performance while consume less energy. Moreover, the handover times are effectively reduced so that quality of service (QoS) is improved.

Keywords: Mobile edge computing · Mobility management · Cooperative transmission · Markov decision process · Dynamic programming

1 Introduction

With the increasing requirements of massive access and multimedia service in future radio access networks, ultra dense networks (UDNs) [5] and mobile edge

Supported in part by Science, Technology and Innovation Commission of Shenzhen Municipality (No. JCYJ20170816151823313), NSFC (No. 61771495), States Key Project of Research and Development Plan (No. 2017YFE0121300-6), Guangdong Provincial Special Fund For Modern Agriculture Industry Technology Innovation Teams (No. 2019KJ122), the Science and Technology Program of Guangzhou under Grant (No. 201707010166).

H. Gao et al. (Eds.): ChinaCom 2019, LNICST 313, pp. 252–263, 2020.
https://doi.org/10.1007/978-3-030-41117-6_21

computing (MEC) [6] are urgently required in 5G mobile communication systems. UDN aims at satisfying high data rate requirements to enhance the overall network capacity. In MEC, cloud computing and storage resources are placed at the network edge, so that mobile users experience lower latency, higher reliability and reduced computing power. However, due to the intensive deployment of base stations (BSs) in the UDN network and the high mobility of users, handover among BSs may frequently occur during data transmission or task computing. Frequent handover among BSs causes additional time delay and reduces the quality of service. Therefore, mobility management (MM) needs to be taken care of to guarantee low-latency and reliable service.

Mobile edge computing has drawn increasing attentions recently. The existing works mainly focus on task offloading policies and resource management schemes, i.e., how and when to offload a computation task from a mobile device to the edge or cloud systems. Ref. [8] proposed a partial computation offloading policy by comprehensively considering cloud computing and MEC in Internet of Things (IoTs), but the resources of MEC are not limited, which is unrealistic. Moreover, the user's mobility was not considered. Some other works consider service migration due to user's mobility, which is a key component of MM in MEC. With the consideration of the complex dynamics of UDN and the low mobility of users, a non-stochastic online-learning approach was proposed in [10] to reduce unnecessary handover. However, the high mobility of users makes the mobility management policy ineffective.

Due to the mobility of users and the change of wireless environment, the information obtained will be inaccurate, which brings challenges to wireless transmission and computation offloading. A Q-learning based MM was proposed in [13] to handle the information uncertainties, considering the wireless transmission and computation offloading. An energy efficient mobility scheme was designed in [15] to improve computation delay performance while satisfying communication energy constraint. Ref. [15] proposed a method to solve the optimization task using Lyapunov optimization and Multi-armed Bandits. Different from [15], a user-oriented energy-aware MM policy was proposed in [11] considering handover cost and the BSs' random ON/OFF. However, all these works are online-learning approachs which do not take advantage of user mobility statistics. In addition, inter-BS cooperation is not considered.

There are a few works considering cooperation to improve communication and computation performance. A joint computation and communication cooperation approach was proposed in [1] by using the helper user as a relay. In practice, using another BS as a relay would cause more access problems. Ref. [4] proposed a scalable BS switching strategy, which applied cooperative communications and power control, to extend the network coverage to the service areas of the switched-off BSs. However, the cooperative data transmission among BSs has not been considered in those works.

In this paper, an MM scheme considering both user's high mobility and BS cooperation is proposed. A high mobility user is guided to connect to delay-optimal BSs and performs handover if necessary. By utilizing the statistic information of user mobility and edge servers' status, the MM problem is formulated as a Markov decision process (MDP) and solved by the dynamic programming (DP) algorithm. Simulations show that delay performance can be greatly enhanced by using cooperative data transmission. Moreover, the proposed algorithm can effectively reduce handover times compared with the benchmark algorithm to guarantee UE's quality of service (QoS).

2   System Model and Problem Formulation

In this section, we will introduce the system model. The user mobility model, task generation and computation are first introduced. Then, the cooperative data transmission, the time delay and energy consumption model, the handover cost are described in detail. Finally, the mobility management problem is formulated.

2.1   System Overview

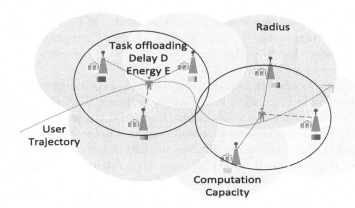

Fig. 1. Illustration of the considered mobility management in UDN with MEC-enabled BSs. A mobile UE with random walk trajectory offloads tasks to two of the candidate BSs via cooperative data transmission. The blue curve is the walk trajectory. The green lines mean connections between the UE and its serving BSs while the red lines mean possible connections between the UE and the candidate BSs. Moreover, the red/green colored bar below each BS refers to BS's computation status (red: heavy loaded, green: idle or lightly loaded). (Color figure online)

As shown in Fig. 1, the system, which is considered as a UDN environment, is running a set of MEC-enabled BSs which denoted as $\mathcal{S}_N = \{1, 2, \ldots, N\}$. A high mobility user equipment (UE) moves randomly in the network, which is modeled as a two-dimensional Brown motion, generating totally M tasks to be offloaded to the BSs for computing. Let $L_m \in \mathcal{S}_L$ denoting the UE's location where task m is generated. Due to the UDN environment, there are always several candidate service BSs $\mathcal{S}_A(L_m) \subseteq \mathcal{S}_N$, where $\mathcal{S}_A(L_m)$ is the set of candidate BSs in location L_m.

2.2   Task Computation

The computation task m is characterized using a two-parameter model [7]: input data of size λ_m bits that needs to be offloaded and computation intensity μ indicating how many CPU cycles are required to compute one bit input data. Without loss of generality, we assume that tasks are all of equal size λ. The following analysis can be extended to the cases where the data sizes are not equal. Moreover, the CPU frequency distribution of BSs is uniform.

Each BS $n \in \mathcal{S}_N$ is equipped with an MEC server of CPU frequency $f \in \mathcal{S}_F$ and supports cooperative data reception with the other BS. A UE who needs task offloading can choose one BS or two BSs according to the candidate BSs and time delay. Once the task is offloaded to two BSs via cooperation, it can be computed jointly by the two BSs. The equivalent CPU frequency is modeled as the sum of the two serving BSs' CPU frequency for simplicity. If BS n_1 and BS n_2 are selected to task computation, the computation delay is

$$d^c_{m,n_1,n_2} = \frac{\mu\lambda}{f_{m,n_1} + f_{m,n_2}}, \tag{1}$$

where f_{m,n_1} and f_{m,n_2} are the CPU frequencies that BS n_1 and BS n_2 can provide to task m respectively. If the UE selects one BS to compute tasks, the computation delay is

$$d^c_{m,n_1} = \frac{\mu\lambda}{f_{m,n_1}}, \tag{2}$$

where f_{m,n_1} is the CPU frequency of BS n_1.

2.3   Cooperative Data Transmission

Maximal ratio combining (MRC) is one of diversity merging technologies [14]. Compared with selection combining (SC) and equal gain combining (EGC), MRC can get the best performance by getting a higher signal noise ratio (SNR). According to Ref. [12], the SNR can be calculated as follows:

$$\mathrm{SNR}_{m,n_1,n_2} = \frac{P_t(H_{m,n_1} + H_{m,n_2})}{\sigma^2}, \tag{3}$$

where H_{m,n_1} and H_{m,n_2} represent the channel power gain at task m between the UE and the serving BSs n_1 and n_2 respectively. σ^2 denotes the noise power and P_t denotes the transmitted power.

Compared to the non-cooperative transmission model's SNR:

$$\mathrm{SNR}_{m,n_1} = \frac{P_t H_{m,n_1}}{\sigma^2}. \tag{4}$$

The transmission diversity of MRC can greatly improve data transmission rate by increasing SNR.

2.4   Time Delay and Energy Consumption

The task is offloaded to the serving BSs through the wireless uplink channel. Assume that the SNR of uplink channel is constant during task transmission. The uplink transmission rate is represented as follows:

$$r_{m,n_1,n_2} = W\log_2\left(1 + \text{SNR}_{m,n_1,n_2}\right),$$ (5)

where SNR_{m,n_1,n_2} is the equivalent SNR using MRC while connecting to BS n_1 and BS n_2. W is the channel bandwidth. The transmission delay sending the task data of size λ to BS n_1 and BS n_2 is

$$d_{m,n_1,n_2}^t = \frac{\lambda}{r_{m,n_1,n_2}}.$$ (6)

The energy consumption of uplink transmission is

$$e_{m,n_1,n_2}^t = \frac{P_t\lambda}{r_{m,n_1,n_2}}.$$ (7)

Meanwhile, cooperative data transmission also brings extra energy consumption

$$e_{m,n_1,n_2}^{cop} = \frac{P_{cop}\lambda}{r_{m,n_1,n_2}},$$ (8)

where P_{cop} is the energy consumption per second.

Obviously, if the UE only connects to one BS, the uplink transmission rate between task m and serving BS n_1 is

$$r_{m,n_1} = W\log_2\left(1 + \text{SNR}_{m,n_1}\right).$$ (9)

The transmission delay sending the task data of size λ to BS n_1 is

$$d_{m,n_1}^t = \frac{\lambda}{r_{m,n_1}}.$$ (10)

And the energy consumption of uplink transmission is

$$e_{m,n_1}^t = \frac{P_t\lambda}{r_{m,n_1}}.$$ (11)

2.5   Handover Cost

For each task m, it must be computed in the same one BS or two BSs according to the communication conditions. Due to the high mobility of the UE, different tasks may be offloaded to different BSs for a lower time delay. When handover is executed, there is an additional delay cost.

Let c_m be one-time handover cost for task m and $a_m \in \mathcal{S}_A(L_m)$ be the set of the index of serving BSs for task m, the overall handover cost is

$$D_h = c_m \sum_{m=1}^{M-1} d_m^h = c_m \sum_{m=1}^{M-1} \mathbb{I}\{a_m \neq a_{m+1}\},$$ (12)

where d_m^h is the handover delay of task m. $\mathbb{I}\{x\}$ is an indicator function with $\mathbb{I}\{x\} = 1$ if x is true and $\mathbb{I}\{x\} = 0$ otherwise.

2.6   Problem Formulation

In this paper, we consider the problem of minimizing the average delay under the constraint of average energy consumption, to determine which BSs serve the user and calculate the task. For task m, the overall delay is

$$D_{m,a_m} = d^c_{m,a_m} + d^t_{m,a_m} + d^h_{m,a_m}, \tag{13}$$

consisting of computing delay d^c_{m,a_m}, transmission delay d^t_{m,a_m} and handover delay d^h_{m,a_m}. As we focus on the user's energy, the overall energy consumption for task m is

$$E_{m,a_m} = e^t_{m,a_m} + e^{cop}_{m,a_m}. \tag{14}$$

We formulate the problem as an infinite horizon problem and an average cost problem. Therefore, the problem is formulated as follows:

$$\begin{aligned}
&\min_{a_1,a_2,\dots} \quad \lim_{M\to+\infty} \frac{1}{M} \sum_{m=1}^{M} D_{m,a_m} \\
&s.t. \quad \lim_{M\to+\infty} \frac{1}{M} \sum_{m=1}^{M} E_{m,a_m} \leq \alpha B \\
&\qquad\qquad\qquad a_m \in \mathcal{S}_A(L_m), \quad \forall m.
\end{aligned} \tag{15}$$

where B is the battery capacity and $\alpha \in (0,1]$ indicates the desired energy consumption for all tasks.

3   Proposed Mobility Management Scheme

In this section, a dynamic programming algorithm is proposed to make decision based on statistic information. Handover and cooperative data transmission are considered. Moreover, a benchmark algorithm with full information is given for comparison.

3.1   Cooperative Mobility Management with DP

Dynamic programming is used to solve the MM problem. Firstly, the problem (15) can be formulated as an MDP consisting of state set $\mathcal{S}$, action set $\mathcal{A}$, state transition probability P and reward function R. The parameters of the DP-based cooperative mobility management (DPMM) scheme are defined as follows:

(1) **Agent:** The agent is a UE who decides to select BSs to ensure task computation with the shortest delay.
(2) **State:** The state is defined as $s = ((n_i, n_j), l, (f_i, f_j))$, where n_i and n_j represent the service BSs of the previous task. l represents the location of UE. The available computing power of service BSs is denoted by f_i and f_j respectively. If the UE only connects to a single BS, set n_2 and f_2 equal to 0. Then, the state space can be expressed as

$$\begin{aligned}
\mathcal{S} = \{s = ((n_i, n_j), l, (f_i, f_j)) \mid n_i \in \mathcal{S}_N, n_j \in \mathcal{S}_N \cup \{0\}, \\
l \in \mathcal{S}_L, f_i \in \mathcal{S}_F, f_j \in \mathcal{S}_F \cup \{0\}\}.
\end{aligned} \tag{16}$$

(3) **Action:** The action is a decision to select one or two BSs as the service BSs for the current task. The set of action per state is defined as

$$\mathcal{A} = \{a = (n_i, n_j) \mid n_i \in \mathcal{S}_N, n_j \in \mathcal{S}_N \cup \{0\}\}. \tag{17}$$

By selecting a set that consists of two elements at each state, the UE can use cooperative data transmission method which is MRC as introduced in Sect. 2.3 to get the improvement of transmission rate. If only one BS is selected, we have $n_j = 0$.

(4) **Reward:** The reward for executing an action a at state s is the negative execution time of each task, which is defined as $R_{s,a} = -D_m$.

(5) **State Transition Probability:** The state transition probability $P \in \mathbb{R}^{s \times s \times a}$ is generated according to the statistic information of the random walk trajectory model and BSs' CPU frequency distribution.

To generate the state transition probability P, we need to know the state set, the random walk trajectory model and the BSs' CPU frequency distribution. As the two-dimensional Brown motion is continuous, the probability of UE's each location is zero. To directly calculate the state transition probability, network areas need to be discretized, resulting in discretization errors. Therefore, we propose a simulation based method to calculate P.

In this method, all states are initialized firstly and then the next state of each state is counted. Each experiment needs to be done until termination, or until it has been done a relatively large number of times. After these experiments, the state transition probability P can be concluded using following formula:

$$P_{ss'}^a = \frac{T_{ss'}^a}{T_s^a}, \tag{18}$$

where $P_{ss'}^a$ is the state transition probability of turning to state s' after the user takes action a at state s. $T_{ss'}^a$ is the number of times when the user takes action a at state s and then turns to state s'. T_s^a is the number of times that the user takes action a at state s.

By using DP algorithm, the optimal value function is calculated by value iteration algorithm [2]. Each state-action pair (s, a) corresponds to an action-value function, the action-value function can be defined as follows:

$$q_\pi(s, a) = R_s^a + \sum_{s' \in \mathcal{S}} P_{ss'}^a \nu_\pi(s'), \tag{19}$$

where π is the action selection policy. $\nu(s)$ is the value function of state s defined as follows:

$$\nu_\pi(s) = \sum_{a \in \mathcal{A}} \pi(a|s) q_\pi(s, a). \tag{20}$$

The i-stage value function is defined as

$$\nu_{i+1}(s) = \max_a R_s^a + \sum_{s' \in \mathcal{S}} P_{ss'}^a \nu_i(s'), \tag{21}$$

and the differential utility is defined as $v_i(s) = \nu_i(s) - \nu_i(s_0)$, where s_0 is some fixed state. Then Bellman equation [2] can be given as follows:

$$\gamma^* + v^*(s) = \max_a \left[R_s^a + \sum_{s' \in \mathcal{S}} P_{ss'}^a v^*(s') \right], \tag{22}$$

where γ^* is the optimal average utility. The differential utility $v_i(s)$ represents the maximum difference between the expected utility from state s to a given state s_0 and the utility if the utility of each stage is γ^* [3]. In value iteration algorithm, we first calculate

$$\gamma_{i+1}(s_0) = \max_a \left[R_{s_0}^a + \tau \sum_{s' \in \mathcal{S}} P_{s_0 s'}^a v_i(s') \right]. \tag{23}$$

Then we calculate the differential utility as

$$v_{i+1}(s) = (1 - \tau)v_i(s) + \max_a \left[R_s^a + \tau \sum_{s' \in \mathcal{S}} P_{ss'}^a v_i(s') \right] - \gamma_{i+1}(s_0). \tag{24}$$

Then the optimal policy $\pi^*(s)$ can be found by calculating the optimal $v^*(s)$.

Algorithm 1. DP-based Mobility Management

1: Generate the set of state $\mathcal{S}$, the set of action $\mathcal{A}$, the reward of state-action pair $R(s, a)$, and state transition probability P accord ing to the known models.
2: Initialize the differential utility $v_0(s) = 0$, the initial policy π_0 and parameter τ.
3: Choose a fixed state s_0.
4: **repeat**
5:     **for** every s **do**
6:       $v_{i+1}(s) = (1 - \tau)v_i(s) + \max_a \left[R_s^a + \tau \sum_{s' \in \mathcal{S}} P_{ss'}^a v_i(s') \right] - \gamma_{i+1}(s_0).$
7:     **end for**
8: **until** $v_{i+1} = v_i$
9: **output** $\pi^*(s)$

Note that the parameter $\tau \in (0, 1)$ is used to guarantee the convergence of relative value iteration and does not change the optimal value [2]. Since the optimal average utility is irrelative with the initial state, $\gamma_{i+1}(s_0)$ converges to γ^*.

The proposed DPMM scheme with statistic information is summarized in **Algorithm 1**. The MDP parameters are generated at first. Then the differential utility, the policy and a fixed state are initialized. Line 4 to line 9 is the value iteration algorithm to get the optimal policy according to the known models. The iteration will stop when the maximal differential utility does not increase.

3.2 Mobility Management with Greedy Strategy

For comparison, a delay optimal greedy strategy (DOGS) is proposed as a base-line. In this strategy, the UE simply selects its serving BSs with minimum delay, without considering energy consumption and handover. The algorithm is summarized in **Algorithm 2**.

Algorithm 2. Delay Optimal Greedy Strategy (DOGS)

1: **if** $\exists$ task m **then**
2:    **input** L_m, $\mathcal{S}_A(L_m)$, λ, μ and $\forall n \in \mathcal{S}_A(L_m)$, $f_{m,n}$, $H_{m,n}$ at the beginning of task m.
3:    Calculate the expected delay for each BS or each two BSs as in (13);
4:    Select one BS or two BSs with the shortest expected delay.
5: **end if**

---

4 Simulations

In this section, we evaluate the average delay performance and the average energy consumption of the proposed DPMM scheme and the DOGS scheme. Moreover, the times of handover is an important indicator to ensure the quality of service. Simulations are run to show the performance of the proposed scheme.

As shown in Fig. 2, a $300\,\mathrm{m} \times 300\,\mathrm{m}$ square area with four densely deployed BSs is simulated. The UE can associate with BSs within a distance of $100\,\mathrm{m}$. The trajectory of UE is generated by the classic random walk model with speed $v \subset [5, 10]\,\mathrm{m/s}$. The wireless channel gain is modeled as $H_{m,n} = 127 + 30 \times \log_{10} d$ as suggested in [9]. The cooperative power $P_{cop} = 0.2W$. Other simulation parameters are based on [11,15], including channel bandwidth $W = 20\,\mathrm{Mhz}$, noise power $\sigma^2 = 2 \times 10^{-13}W$, transmit power $P_t = 0.5W$. We consider a video stream analysis with some tasks generated during the whole moving process. The size of every task is $\lambda = 100\,\mathrm{Mbits}$ and the computation intensity is $\mu = 20$ cycles/bit referring to [11]. The available CPU computation frequency is $f_{m,n} \in [\frac{1}{2}F, F]$, where $F = 25\,\mathrm{GHz}$.

Figure 3(a) and (b) compare the average delay performance and the average energy consumption of DPMM and DOGS over M tasks, respectively. It can be seen that although the DPMM scheme sacrifices about 10% of the delay performance, the energy consumption can be reduced. More importantly, the DPMM scheme can greatly reduce handover times compared with DOGS as shown in Fig. 4, which significantly reduces signalling cost for handover. This is because in order to effectively control the handover times, the DPMM algorithm will select the service BSs according to the average reward of the long-term state. As a result, the single selection of BSs in a certain state is not optimal.

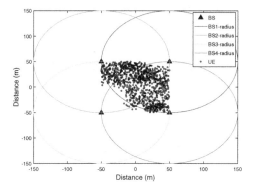

Fig. 2. Network topology

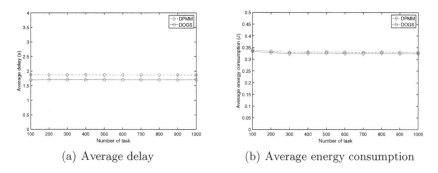

(a) Average delay   (b) Average energy consumption

Fig. 3. Performance of DPMM compared with DOGS.

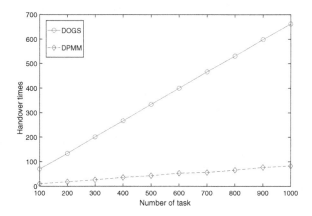

Fig. 4. Handover times

To show the benefits of cooperation, we also compare the DP algorithms with and without MRC. The result is shown in Fig. 5(a). It can be seen that by using MRC, the average delay is reduced by 50% due to the increased data transmission

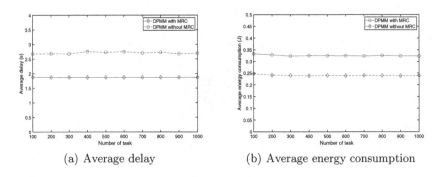

(a) Average delay   (b) Average energy consumption

Fig. 5. DPMM with MRC and without MRC

rate. Figure 5(b) shows that the energy consumption of DPMM with MRC is 20% higher than the energy consumption of DPMM without MRC. This is because the transmission diversity of MRC can greatly improve data transmission rate by increasing SNR. However, it will consume extra energy. Therefore, by sacrificing a certain amount of energy, the delay performance can be greatly improved.

Finally, DPMM algorithm is an offline algorithm, which means that it only needs to use the current statistics information to calculate once. Then it can get the optimal mobility management strategy. Considering that the statistical information of the BSs side and the user side will not change frequently, the computational complexity of the algorithm will not affect the user's long-term experience.

5   Conclusions

In this paper, we investigated the problem of MM based on BS cooperation. The DPMM scheme was proposed to make MM decision based on statistic information, taking UDN environment and high mobility of user into consideration. Simulations show that the proposed algorithm has greatly reduced handover times. At the same time, compared with greedy algorithm, it has similar delay performance. Furthermore, a cooperative data transmission scheme was proposed, which used the cooperation of BSs to improve data transmission rate. Through cooperative data transmission, the delay performance can be significantly improved. Future researches will include designing MM schemes for multiple users scenarios where the users may compete for transmission and computing resources.

References

1. Cao, X., Wang, F., Xu, J., Zhang, R., Cui, S.: Joint computation and communication cooperation for energy-efficient mobile edge computing. IEEE Internet Things J. **6**(3), 4188–4200 (2019)

2. Dimitri, P.B.: Dynamic Programming and Optimal Control, vol. 2, 3rd edn. Athena Scientific, Belmont (2005)
3. Gong, J., Zhou, S., Zhou, Z.: Networked MIMO with fractional joint transmission in energy harvesting systems. IEEE Trans. Commun. **64**(8), 3323–3336 (2016)
4. Han, F., Safar, Z., Lin, W.S., Chen, Y., Liu, K.J.R.: Energy-efficient cellular network operation via base station cooperation. In: 2012 IEEE International Conference on Communications (ICC), pp. 4374–4378 (2012)
5. Kamel, M., Hamouda, W., Youssef, A.: Ultra-dense networks: a survey. IEEE Commun. Surv. Tutor. **18**(4), 2522–2545 (2016)
6. Mach, P., Becvar, Z.: Mobile edge computing: a survey on architecture and computation offloading. IEEE Commun. Surv. Tutor. **19**(3), 1628–1656 (2017)
7. Mao, Y., You, C., Zhang, J., Huang, K., Letaief, K.B.: A survey on mobile edge computing: the communication perspective. IEEE Commun. Surv. Tutor. **19**(4), 2322–2358 (2017)
8. Ning, Z., Dong, P., Kong, X., Xia, F.: A cooperative partial computation offloading scheme for mobile edge computing enabled internet of things. IEEE Internet Things J. **6**(3), 4804–4814 (2019)
9. Niu, C., Li, Y., Hu, R.Q., Ye, F.: Fast and efficient radio resource allocation in dynamic ultra-dense heterogeneous networks. IEEE Access **5**, 1911–1924 (2017)
10. Shen, C., Tekin, C., van der Schaar, M.: A non-stochastic learning approach to energy efficient mobility management. IEEE J. Sel. Areas Commun. **34**(12), 3854–3868 (2016)
11. Sun, Y., Zhou, S., Xu, J.: EMM: energy-aware mobility management for mobile edge computing in ultra dense networks. IEEE J. Select. Areas Commun. **35**(11), 2637–2646 (2017)
12. Tse, D., Viswanath, P.: Fundamentals of Wireless Communication. Cambridge University Press, Cambridge (2005)
13. Wang, J., Liu, K., Ni, M., Pan, J.: Learning based mobility management under uncertainties for mobile edge computing. In: 2018 IEEE Global Communications Conference (GLOBECOM), pp. 1–6 (2018)
14. Zhang, X., Beaulieu, N.C.: SER of threshold-based hybrid selection/maximal-ratio combining in correlated nakagami fading. IEEE Trans. Commun. **53**(9), 1423–1426 (2005)
15. Xu, J., Sun, Y., Chen, L., Zhou, S.: E2m2: energy efficient mobility management in dense small cells with mobile edge computing. In: 2017 IEEE International Conference on Communications (ICC), pp. 1–6 (2017)

Low-Latency Transmission and Caching of High Definition Map at a Crossroad

Yue Gu[✉], Jie Liu, and Long Zhao

Wireless Signal Processing and Network (WSPN) Lab, Key Laboratory of Universal Wireless Communication, Ministry of Education, Beijing University of Posts and Telecommunications (BUPT), Beijing 100876, China
guyue0929@bupt.edu.cn

Abstract. High definition (HD) map attracts more and more attention of researchers and map operators in recent years and has become an indispensable part for autonomous or assistant driving. Different from existing navigation map, HD map has the features of high precision, large-volume data and real-time update. Therefore, the real-time HD map transmission to the vehicles becomes one main challenge in vehicular networks. This paper considers the scenario that a RSU at the crossroad caches and transmits HD maps to its covered vehicles in four directions. To reduce the average delay of HD map delivery, the transmission power allocation for vehicles and the cache allocation for HD maps of different road segments are optimized by leveraging the traffic density and vehicle positions. Simulation results indicate that the proposed scheme has lower latency than that of equal power allocation scheme based on real traffic data.

Keywords: Vehicle networks · High definition map · Cache · Delay

1 Introduction

High definition (HD) maps are lane-level maps within 10 cm precision and real-time updated maps. Usually, HD map can be divided into three layers, including static layer, dynamic layer and analysis layer [1]. Ordinary navigation map is about 1 kb per kilometer, while HD map data is much larger than that of the ordinary navigation map. Levinson and Thrun employed data compression technology to store 20,000 miles map data in 200 GB of memory, which is equivalent to 6 MB per kilometer [2]. Momenta claimed that they used a monocular camera to generate HD semantic maps, which could be compressed to 10 kb/km. TomTom's HD map named road DNA is founded with 25 kb/km in average [3]. In conclusion, the HD map has larger data per kilometer than the normal maps and needs to be updated in real time [4], therefore the on-board unit is not suitable for pre-caching the entire city map for driving. How to transmit HD maps to vehicles in a mobile environment timely and effectively becomes a challenge for automatic driving.

This work was supported by the China Natural Science Funding under Grant 61601044.

H. Gao et al. (Eds.): ChinaCom 2019, LNICST 313, pp. 264–277, 2020.
https://doi.org/10.1007/978-3-030-41117-6_22

In vehicular networks, V2I communications are helpful to take proactive management in order to avoid traffic jam or transmit entertainment contents [5]. Some schemes have been studied in the literature. An intelligent traffic management system based on V2I communications is proposed aiming to coordinate traffic in a limited urban area, including different driving scenarios [6, 7]. In [8], RSU transmits cycle information of traffic light to coming vehicles, then the vehicles can collaboratively optimize their speeds and other appropriate actions in order to pass crossroad within a shortest time. Caching based infrastructure is another research point, it usually focuses on minimizing the delay or resolving contents caching scheme with limited memory. Considering both RSU caches and vehicle caches in a single-directional highway scenario, the minimum latency has been studied in [9]. In vehicular content centric networks, based on the prediction results of mobile nodes' probability of reaching different hot areas according to their past trajectories, vehicles can be chosen as caching nodes which stay more time in a hot area and provide more services [10]. Considering the trajectory and dwell time of vehicles passing several RSUs on a single-directional road, the contents caching problem at the RSU has been studied based on aggregate statistics about the distribution of the dwell time under each cache nodes [11]. Moreover, the DDPG, a method of deep reinforcement learning, is also employed to find the proactive caching strategy of RSU on the road [12]. However, the features of transmission contents and the mobility of vehicles are less utilized in the aforementioned researches. This paper considers the requirement features of HD map and the mobility of vehicles in order to further reduce the latency of HD map transmission.

In this paper, we consider a scenario of vehicular networks at a crossroad. Located in the center of the crossroad, the RSU is in charge of caching and transmitting map sections of surrounding roads to the covered vehicles. The goal of this paper is to minimize the average delay of HD map delivery to the vehicles, where both the transmission delays and backhaul delays are primarily considered. Based on the mobility features of vehicles and requirement features of HD map, a transmission power allocation scheme and a caching allocation scheme are proposed, which can effectively reduce the transmission delay and the backhaul delay, respectively.

The rest of this paper is organized as follows. Section 2 introduces the system model and formulates the considered problem. The formulated problem is solved in Sect. 3, where the optimal power allocation and cache allocation schemes are proposed. Section 4 gives the simulation results and analysis. Section 5 concludes this paper in the end.

2 System Model and Problem Formulation

2.1 System Model

As shown in Fig. 1, we consider a scenario of vehicular networks, where the RSU with the storage capacity C and M antennas at the crossroad caches the HD maps of four directions and transmits them to K single-antenna vehicles within its coverage. The available system bandwidth is B, the coverage radius is L and the vehicles are uniformly distributed on the covered road segments.

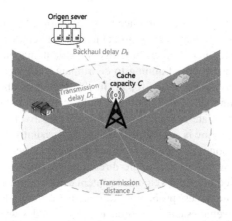

Fig. 1. HD map transmission scenario at the crossroad.

Channel Model

The channel vector from the RSU to the kth vehicle can be obtained by the uplink pilot transmission and channel estimation, which can be expressed as

$$\mathbf{g}_k^{\mathrm{H}} = [g_{k1}, g_{k2}, \ldots, g_{kM}], \tag{1}$$

where $g_{ki} = \sqrt{\phi \xi_k d_k^{-\alpha}} h_{ki}$, ϕ is a constant related to antenna gain, shadow fading variable ξ_k follows the log-normal distribution $10 \log_{10} \xi_k \sim \mathbb{N}(0, \sigma_{\mathrm{SF}}^2)$, d_k denotes the distance between the kth vehicle and the RSU, and α represents path loss exponent. Small-scale fading variables $h_{ki} \sim \mathbb{CN}(0, 1)(k = 1, 2, \cdots, K; i = 1, 2, \cdots, M)$.

Transmission Model

When the number of antennas becomes large, matched filtering (MF) has been proved to be the asymptotically optimal precoder, therefore it is employed in this paper. The MF precoding vector of the kth vehicle is $\mathbf{w}_k = \mathbf{g}_k / \|\mathbf{g}_k\| (k = 1, 2, \ldots, K)$. Denoting s_k as transmitted modulation symbol of the kth vehicle with $\|s_k\| = 1$, then the received signal of the ith vehicle is given by

$$y_i = \sqrt{\frac{p_i}{M}} \mathbf{g}_i^{\mathrm{H}} \mathbf{w}_i s_i + \mathbf{g}_i^{\mathrm{H}} \sum_{k=1, \neq i}^{K} \sqrt{\frac{p_k}{M}} \mathbf{w}_k s_k + n_i, \tag{2}$$

where $\mathbf{p}/M = [p_1, p_2, \cdots, p_K]/M$ denotes the power allocation vector, $n_i \sim \mathbb{CN}(0, N_0 B)$ is the complex white Gaussian noise (AWGN) at the ith vehicle with the noise power spectral density N_0.

Then, the signal-to-interference-plus-noise ratio of the ith vehicle can be written as

$$\gamma_i(p_i) = \frac{\frac{p_i}{M} \|\mathbf{g}_i\|^2}{N_0 B + \sum_{k=1, \neq i}^{K} \frac{p_k}{M} \frac{|\mathbf{g}_i^{\mathrm{H}} \mathbf{g}_k|^2}{\|\mathbf{g}_k\|^2}}. \tag{3}$$

According to [13], the channel hardening and asymptotic orthogonality effects are valid for large M, i.e., $\mathbf{g}_i^H \mathbf{g}_i / M \rightarrow \phi \xi_i d_i^{-\alpha}$ and $\mathbf{g}_k^H \mathbf{g}_i / M \rightarrow 0 (i \neq k)$. Substituting them into (3) gives rise to

$$\gamma_i(p_i) = \frac{\phi \xi_i d_i^{-\alpha} p_i}{N_0 B}. \tag{4}$$

According to Shannon's formula, the transmit rate of the ith vehicle can be expressed as

$$R_i(p_i) = B \log_2 \left[1 + \gamma_i(p_i) \right]. \tag{5}$$

Caching Model and Delay Model

We assume that m_x and $M_x (x \in \{n,s,e,w\})$ denote the map data cached at the RSU and the road map data of the x direction, therefore $\eta_x = m_x / M_x (x \in \{n,s,e,w\})$ represents the ratio of x-direction road data cached at the RSU. The total delay of HD map transmission mainly consists of downlink transmission delay and backhaul delay, while the processing delay and queuing delay are ignored in this paper.

Transmission Delay

Supposing that m bit data of HD map is requested by each vehicle at each time, the transmission delay of the kth vehicle can be expressed as

$$d_{Tk}(p_k) = \frac{m}{R_k(p_k)}, \tag{6}$$

and the total transmission delay of all vehicles is given by

$$D_T(\mathbf{p}) = \sum_{k=1}^{K} \frac{m}{R_k(p_k)}. \tag{7}$$

Backhaul Delay

If the requested map data was not cached at the RSU, the RSU should request it from the data center, which generates the backhaul delay and it can be expressed as

$$d_{Bk} = \frac{m}{R'}, \tag{8}$$

where R' represents the transmit rate from the data center to the RSU.

As the path planning of automatic driving has been determined in advance, the RSU knows the number of vehicles requesting the map of x-direction, denoted by n_x and $\sum_{x \in \{n,s,w,e\}} n_x = K$. Then, the total backhaul delay of all vehicles can be written as

$$D_B(\eta) = \sum_{x \in \{n,s,w,e\}} n_x (1 - \eta_x) \frac{m}{R'}, \tag{9}$$

where $\eta = [\eta_n, \eta_s, \eta_e, \eta_w]$ and η_x is equivalent to the probability that the RSU has stored the requested map segments.

Average Delay

Based on the transmission delay in (7) and backhaul delay in (9), the average delay of each vehicle is given by

$$D(\boldsymbol{\eta}, \mathbf{p}) = \frac{1}{K}D_B(\boldsymbol{\eta}) + \frac{1}{K}D_T(\mathbf{p}) = \frac{1}{K}\sum_{k=1}^{K}\frac{m}{R_k(p_k)} + \frac{1}{K}\sum_{x \in \{n,s,w,e\}} n_x(1 - n_x)\frac{m}{R'}.$$

(10)

2.2 Problem Formulation

Assuming that the total transmit power of the RSU is P/M, the objective of this paper is to minimize the average delay of each vehicle, while satisfying the constraints of the total transmit power and RSU storage capacity, i.e., the problem can be formulated by

$$\min_{\mathbf{p}, \boldsymbol{\eta}} \{D(\boldsymbol{\eta}, \mathbf{p})\}$$

$$\text{s.t.} \sum_{k=1}^{K} p_k \leq P,$$

$$\sum_{x \in \{n,s,e,w\}} \eta_x M_x \leq C,$$

$$0 \leq \eta_x \leq 1, \quad x \in \{n,s,e,w\}.$$

(11)

3 Caching and Transmission Schemes of HD Map

The average delay expression (10) can be divided into two independent parts. One part is the backhaul delay influenced by storage capacity and the traffic flow on each road, which can be reduced by optimizing the cache allocation at the RSU. Another part is the transmission delay, which can be minimized by power allocation at the RSU. Therefore, problem (11) can be divided into caching allocation problem and power allocation problem, i.e.,

$$\min_{\boldsymbol{\eta}} \{D_B(\boldsymbol{\eta})\}$$

$$\text{s.t.} \sum_{x \in \{n,s,e,w\}} \eta_x M_x \leq C,$$

$$0 \leq \eta_x \leq 1, \quad x \in \{n,s,e,w\},$$

(12)

and

$$\min_{\mathbf{p}} \{D_T(\mathbf{p})\}$$

$$\text{s.t.} \sum_{k=1}^{K} p_k \leq P.$$

(13)

The problems (12) and (13) will be solved respectively in the following subsections.

3.1 Optimal Cache Allocation Scheme

The objective function in problem (12) can be transformed into

$$D_B(\eta) = -\frac{m}{R'}\left(\frac{n_n}{M_n}\eta_n M_n + \frac{n_s}{M_s}\eta_s M_s + \frac{n_e}{M_e}\eta_e M_e + \frac{n_w}{M_w}\eta_w M_w\right) + \frac{mK}{R'}, \quad (14)$$

and problem (12) can be rewritten as

$$\max\left(\frac{n_n}{M_n}\eta_n M_n + \frac{n_s}{M_s}\eta_s M_s + \frac{n_e}{M_e}\eta_e M_e + \frac{n_w}{M_w}\eta_w M_w\right), \quad (15)$$

$$\text{s.t.} \quad \eta_1 M_1 + \eta_2 M_2 + \eta_3 M_3 + \eta_4 M_4 - C = 0. \quad (16)$$

Based on (15) and (16), it is easy to know that more cache capacity of RSU should be allocated for the map with larger n_x / M_x. Therefore, we obtain Algorithm 1 to allocate η_x in order to minimize the backhaul delay.

Algorithm 1 Optimal Caching Allocation Algorithm

Step 1: Initialize C, M_x, n_x, $x \in \{n,s,w,e\}$.

Step 2: Calculate n_x/M_x, sort them in descending order.

Step 3: Denote $n_1/M_1 \geq n_2/M_2 \geq n_3/M_3 \geq n_4/M_4$ as the order, then
   For i=1:4
      If $C - M_i \geq 0$, then $\eta_i = 1, C = C - M_i$;
      Else $C - M_i < 0$, then $\eta_i = C/M_i$, $C = 0$, break.
   End.

3.2 Optimal Power Allocation Scheme

Proposition 1: With the fixed number of vehicles K, the minimum transmission delay is given by

$$D_T = \frac{m}{B}\sum_{k=1}^{K}\log_2^{-1}\left[1 + \frac{\phi\xi_k q_k(\lambda)}{N_0 B}\right], \quad (17)$$

where

$$q_k(\lambda) = \frac{N_0 B}{\phi\xi_k}\left\{\exp\left[2W_0\left(\frac{1}{2}\sqrt{\frac{m\phi\xi_k \ln 2}{N_0 B^2 \lambda d_k^{-\alpha}}}\right)\right] - 1\right\}, \quad (18)$$

and $W_0(\cdot) : [-e^{-1}, +\infty) \to [-1, +\infty)$ is the first real branch of the Lambert W function satisfying $W_0(x)e^{W_0(x)} = x$. And λ is the Lagrange multiplier, which can be calculated by a bi-section algorithm.

Proof. Let $q_k = d_k^{-\alpha} p_k$, the transmit rate of the kth vehicle can be rewritten into $R_k(q_k) = B \ln(1 + \phi \xi_k q_k / N_0 B) / \ln 2$ and the total power constraint in problem (13) becomes $\sum_{k=1}^{K} q_k d_k^{\alpha} \leq P$. Then, the objective is to allocate q_k in order to minimize the average transmission delay.

The problem (13) can be solved by Lagrange multiplier method. Denoting $\mathbf{q} = [q_1, q_2, \cdots, q_K]^{\mathrm{T}}$, the Lagrange function of problem (13) can be written as

$$L(\mathbf{q}, \lambda) = D_{\mathrm{T}}(\mathbf{p}) + \lambda \left(\sum_{k=1}^{K} p_k - P \right) = \frac{m \ln 2}{B} \sum_{k=1}^{K} \ln^{-1} \left(1 + \frac{\phi \xi_k q_k}{N_0 B} \right)$$
$$+ \lambda \left(\sum_{k=1}^{K} q_k d_k^{\alpha} - P \right). \tag{19}$$

According to KKT conditions, we have

$$\frac{\partial L(\mathbf{q}, \lambda)}{\partial q_k} = \frac{-m \phi \xi_k \ln 2}{N_0 B^2 \left(1 + \frac{\phi \xi_k q_k}{N_0 B} \right) \ln^2 \left(1 + \frac{\phi \xi_k q_k}{N_0 B} \right)} + \lambda d_k^{\alpha} = 0, \tag{20}$$

and

$$\sum_{k=1}^{K} q_k d_k^{\alpha} - P = 0. \tag{21}$$

Solving (20) leads to

$$\left(1 + \frac{\phi \xi_k q_k}{N_0 B} \right) \ln^2 \left(1 + \frac{\phi \xi_k q_k}{N_0 B} \right) = \frac{m \phi \xi_k \ln 2}{N_0 B^2 \lambda d_k^{\alpha}}. \tag{22}$$

Let $\Phi = m \phi \xi_k \ln 2 / N_0 B^2 d_k^{\alpha}$ and $\alpha = \ln(1 + \phi \xi_k q_k / N_0 B) / 2$, Eq. (22) can be transformed into

$$\alpha \exp(\alpha) = \frac{1}{2} \sqrt{\frac{\Phi}{\lambda}}. \tag{23}$$

Equation (23) is a transcendental equation with two roots, i.e., $\alpha_1 = W_0(\sqrt{\Phi/\lambda}/2)$ and $\alpha_2 = W_0(-\sqrt{\Phi/\lambda}/2)$. Because $\alpha > 0$ based on (23), then we can obtain $\alpha = \alpha_1 = W_0(\sqrt{\Phi/\lambda}/2)$, and $q_k(\lambda)$ can be written as

$$q_k(\lambda) = \frac{N_0 B}{\phi \xi_k} \left\{ \exp \left[2W_0 \left(\frac{1}{2} \sqrt{\frac{m \phi \xi_k \ln 2}{N_0 B^2 \lambda d_k^{\alpha}}} \right) \right] - 1 \right\}. \tag{24}$$

In order to determine λ, we substitute (24) into (21) and have

$$\sum_{k=1}^{K} \frac{N_0 B}{\phi \xi_k} \left[\exp\left(2W_0 \left(\frac{1}{2} \sqrt{\frac{m\phi \xi_k \ln 2}{N_0 B^2 \lambda d_k^{\alpha}}} \right) \right) - 1 \right] d_k^{\alpha} - P = 0. \tag{25}$$

Defining

$$f(\lambda) = \sum_{k=1}^{K} \frac{N_0 B}{\phi \xi_k} \left[\exp\left(2W_0 \left(\frac{1}{2} \sqrt{\frac{m\phi \xi_k \ln 2}{N_0 B^2 \lambda d_k^{\alpha}}} \right) \right) - 1 \right] d_k^{\alpha} - P, \tag{26}$$

Function $f(\lambda)$ is a monotonically decreasing function with respect to λ. When $\lambda \to 0$, $f(\lambda)$ tends to infinity; while $f(\lambda)$ is less than 0 when $\lambda \to +\infty$. Therefore, equation $f(\lambda) = 0$ has a unique solution and can be obtained by bi-section method, which is given in Algorithm 2.   □

The complexity of Algorithm 2 can be approximated by $\lceil \log_2 [(\lambda_U - \lambda_L)/\varepsilon] \rceil$, where $\lceil \ \rceil$ denotes rounding up to an integer.

Algorithm 2 Bi-Section Algorithm for Minimum Transmission Delay.

Step 1: Initialize λ_L and λ_U with $f(\lambda_L) > 0$ and $f(\lambda_U) < 0$, toleration error $\varepsilon > 0$.

Step 2: Let $\lambda = (\lambda_L + \lambda_U)/2$ and calculate $f(\lambda)$.

If $|f(\lambda)| > \varepsilon$, go to step 3;

Else go to step 4.

Step 3: If $f(\lambda) > 0$, then $\lambda_L = \lambda$;

Else $f(\lambda) < 0$, then $\lambda_U = \lambda$.

Go to step 2.

Step 4: Substituting λ into (24) results in q_k and therefore we obtain the minimum delay D_T using (17).

---

4 Simulation and Analysis

In this section, the backhaul delay and transmission delay of the proposed scheme are first evaluated with respect to different system parameters in contrast to the equal cache or power allocation scheme. Then, the average delay of HD map delivery for each vehicle is given based on real traffic data in Beijing.

4.1 Simulation Setup

In the simulation, the distance from the kth vehicle to the RSU, d_k, follows uniform distribution within the RSU's coverage, i.e., $[10, L]$ m. The other default parameters are listed in Table 1.

Table 1. Simulation parameters.

Parameters	Values	Parameters	Values
L	300 m	R'	10 Mbps
Number of vehicles K	100	Bandwidth B	500 kHz
σ_{SF}	8 dB	Total transmit power P	25 dBm
α	3	Constant ϕ	0.001
N_0	−174 dBm/Hz	C	100 kb
$M_x, x \in \{n,s,w,e\}$	50 kb	Map segment size m	1 kb
Free flow speed v_F	50 m/s	Jamming density ρ_J	1 vehicle/m

4.2 Backhaul Delay

The backhaul delay is mainly affected by the total number of vehicles and cache. An equal cache allocation scheme is used for comparison, where the cache is equally divided into four parts to store maps of four directions, respectively.

Figure 2 shows the backhaul delay of 20 vehicles distributed in four directions. The horizontal axis denotes the number of vehicles in the north-direction road while the other vehicles are equally distributed in other three roads. Table 2 enumerates the numbers of vehicles in four-direction roads. From Fig. 2, the backhaul delay of the proposed scheme first increases and then decreases with the number of vehicles increases in the north-direction road, because the vehicle numbers of four directions first tends to the same and then the number of north-direction dominates the total number; meanwhile the RSU first tends to equally allocate the cache capacity and then prefers to cache the north-direction map. Moreover, the total backhaul delay of the proposed scheme is lower than that of the equal cache allocation scheme.

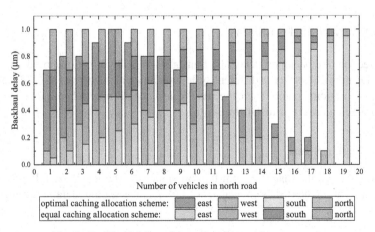

Fig. 2. Backhaul delay of four directions at the crossroad.

Table 2. Enumeration of vehicle distribution in four direction

Horizontal axis	1	2	3	4	5	6	7	8	9	10
North	1	2	3	4	5	6	7	8	9	10
South	7	6	6	6	5	5	5	4	4	4
West	6	6	6	5	5	5	4	4	4	3
East	6	6	5	5	5	4	4	4	3	3
Horizontal axis	11	12	13	14	15	16	17	18	19	20
North	11	12	13	14	15	16	17	18	19	20
South	3	3	3	2	2	2	1	1	1	0
West	3	3	2	2	2	1	1	1	0	0
East	3	2	2	2	1	1	1	0	0	0

4.3 Transmission Delay

Figure 3 shows the error, upper bound and lower bound of $f(\lambda)$ in each iteration in order to verify the convergence of the bi-section algorithm with the initialization values $\lambda_L = 10^{-7}$ and $\lambda_U = 10^{-5}$. We can see that the upper bound decreases and the lower bound increases with the increasing number of iterations. Both bounds and the error tend to zero, which validates the convergence of the proposed bi-section algorithm.

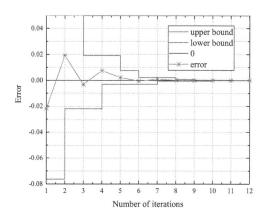

Fig. 3. Error v.s. the number of iterations in bi-section algorithm.

Figure 4 or 5 shows the relationship between the average transmission delay and the system bandwidth or total transmit power. With the same bandwidth, the average transmission delay of the optimal power allocation is lower than that of equal power allocation in Fig. 4; with the same transmission power, the average transmission delay of the optimal power allocation performs better than the equal power allocation in Fig. 5. Therefore, both Figs. 4 and 5 validate the proposed power allocation algorithm. Besides, the delay gap between the optimal power allocation and equal power allocation decreases with the increasing total transmit power.

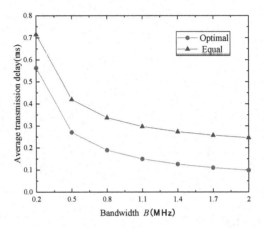

Fig. 4. Average transmission delay v.s. bandwidth.

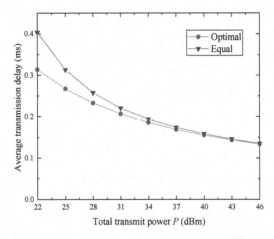

Fig. 5. Average transmission delay v.s. total transmission power.

4.4   Average Delay Based on Real Traffic Data

Next, the real traffic data of one day is employed to simulate the change of content requirements at the RSU. The origin data contains the vehicle speed samples on the Jianguomen Bridge in Beijing on October 2018. In order to obtain the traffic numbers of four-direction roads, the following relationship between average vehicle speed and traffic density is employed [14]

$$\bar{v} = v_\mathrm{F}(1 - \rho/\rho_\mathrm{J}), \tag{27}$$

where the constant v_F is the free flow speed and the constant ρ_J denotes the jamming density. Then, the traffic density and the numbers of vehicles on the four-direction roads can be calculated. Table 3 lists the calculated numbers of vehicles of 24 h in four-direction roads.

Table 3. The numbers of vehicles in four-direction roads.

Time in one day (hour)	1	2	3	4	5	6	7	8	9	10	11	12
North	80	95	72	72	57	76	141	148	137	131	126	116
South	45	30	15	26	4	11	53	95	92	95	90	81
West	101	92	75	56	44	64	51	88	110	103	105	106
East	117	139	121	111	105	99	109	102	114	111	111	114
Time in one day (hour)	13	14	15	16	17	18	19	20	21	22	23	24
North	106	111	120	130	136	143	145	117	99	107	83	83
South	72	71	83	84	84	112	120	116	107	85	67	56
West	107	106	107	94	100	119	135	117	105	98	108	83
East	101	113	109	105	108	125	121	122	132	113	103	112

Figure 6 shows the cache allocation change of one day with $M_n = M_w = 45$ kb and $M_e = M_s = 35$ kb. The vertical axis represents the cache proportions of four-direction roads, and the horizontal axis denotes the time of 24 h. It can be seen from Fig. 6, the caching proportions of four-direction maps are related to not only the numbers of vehicles on four directions but also the map sizes of four directions, i.e., $n_x / M_x (x \in \{e,s,w,n\})$.

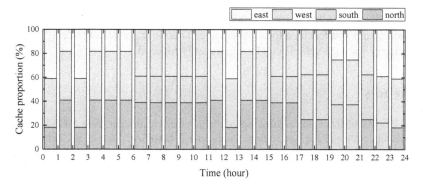

Fig. 6. Cache proportion at the RSU of one day based on real traffic data.

Figure 7 shows the average delay of each vehicle based on the numbers of vehicles in Table 3 and cache allocation in Fig. 6. The average delay of the proposed scheme is lower than that of the equal power and cache allocation scheme. Besides, we can observe that the average delay becomes smallest at 4:00 am and highest at around 6:00 pm, which is the evening rush hour in Beijing.

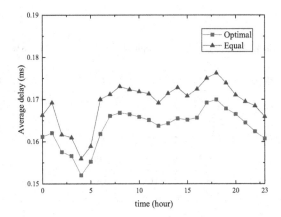

Fig. 7. Average delay of one day based on real traffic data.

5   Conclusion

This paper considered the problem of caching HD map at the RSU and transmitting it to vehicles at a crossroad. The objective of this paper is to minimize the average delay of HD map delivery for each vehicle with both the total transmit power and cache capacity constraints at the RSU. According to the vehicle mobility, we proposed the transmission power allocation and cache allocation scheme in order to minimize the average delay of HD map delivery. Simulation results indicate that the proposed power or cache allocation scheme can reduce the transmission or backhaul delay compared with the equal power/cache allocation scheme. Therefore, the average delay of the HD map delivery for each vehicle can be significantly reduced.

References

1. Jiao, J.: Machine learning assisted high-definition map creation. In: 2018 IEEE 42nd Annual Computer Software and Applications Conference (COMPSAC), Tokyo, pp. 367–373 (2018)
2. Li, W., Meng, X., Wang, Z., Fang, W., Zou, J., Li, H., et al.: Low-cost vector map assisted navigation strategy for autonomous vehicle. In: 2018 IEEE Asia Pacific Conference on Circuits and Systems (APCCAS), pp. 536–539, Chengdu (2018)
3. GPS Business News. https://gpsbusinessnews.com/TomTom-Road-DNA-Precise-Location-Tech-for-Driverless-Cars_a5470.html. Accessed 15 May 2015
4. Papp, Z., Brown, C., Bartels, C.: World modeling for cooperative intelligent vehicles. In: Intelligent Vehicles Symposium, Eindhoven, pp. 1050–1055. IEEE (2008)
5. Zheng, K., Hou, L., Meng, H., Zheng, Q., Lu, N., Lei, L.: Soft-defined heterogeneous vehicular network: architecture and challenges. IEEE Netw. **30**(4), 72–80 (2016)

6. Milanes, V., Villagra, J., Godoy, J., Simo, J., Perez, J., Onieva, E.: An intelligent V2I-based traffic management system. IEEE Trans. Intell. Transp. Syst. **13**(1), 49–58 (2012)
7. Chen, S., Hu, J., Shi, Y., Zhao, L.: LTE-V: A TD-LTE-based V2X solution for future vehicular network. IEEE Internet Things J. **3**(6), 997–1005 (2016)
8. Djahel, S., Jabeur, N., Barrett, R., Murphy, J.: Toward V2I communication technology-based solution for reducing road traffic congestion in smart cities. In: 2015 International Symposium on Networks, Computers and Communications (ISNCC), Hammamet, pp. 1–6 (2015)
9. Ma, J., Wang, J., Liu, G., Fan, P.: Low latency caching placement policy for cloud-based VANET with both vehicle caches and RSU caches. In: 2017 IEEE Globecom Workshops (GC Wkshps), pp. 1–6, Singapore (2017)
10. Yao, L., Chen, A., Deng, J., Wang, J., Wu, G.: A cooperative caching scheme based on mobility prediction in vehicular content centric networks. IEEE Trans. Veh. Technol. **67**(6), 5435–5444 (2018)
11. Mahmood, A., Casetti, C., Chiasserini, C.F., Giaccone, P., Harri, J.: Mobility-aware edge caching for connected cars. In: 2016 12th Annual Conference on Wireless on-demand Network Systems and Services (WONS), Cortina d'Ampezzo, pp. 1–8 (2016)
12. Zhang, Z., Yang, Y., Hua, M., Li, C., Huang, Y., Yang, L.: Proactive caching for vehicular multi-view 3D video streaming via deep reinforcement learning. IEEE Trans. Wireless Commun. **18**(5), 2693–2706 (2019)
13. Ngo, H.Q., Larsson, E.G., Marzetta, T.L.: Energy and spectral efficiency of very large multiuser MIMO systems. IEEE Trans. Commun. **61**(4), 1436–1449 (2013)
14. Zhao, L., Wang, F., Zheng, K., Riihonen, T.: Joint optimization of communication and traffic efficiency in vehicular networks. IEEE Trans. Veh. Technol. **68**(2), 2014–2018 (2019)

Gradient-Based UAV Positioning Algorithm for Throughput Optimization in UAV Relay Networks

Xiangyu Li$^{(\boxtimes)}$ ⓘ, Tao Peng, and Xiaoyang Li

Wireless Signal Processing and Networks Laboratory (WSPN),
Key Laboratory of Universal Wireless Communications, Ministry of Education,
Beijing University of Posts and Telecommunications, Beijing, China
{lixymiracle,pengtao,lixiaoyang111}@bupt.edu.cn

Abstract. Under natural disaster or other emergency situations, the fixed communication infrastructures are unavailable, which brings great inconvenience to information interaction among people. In this paper, we design a UAV relay network, using a small-scale UAV fleet serves as communication relays of a team of ground users performing collaborate tasks. Aiming at the user's requirement for high communication capacity for multi service transmission, we present a distributed gradient-based algorithm of finding the optimal positions of UAV in UAV relay network to improve the network average end-to-end throughput in real-time. The system optimization objective is formulated by using Shannon-Hartley Theorem and received signal-to-noise ratio (SNR) that incorporates with UAV positions and ground user positions. Due to the non-smoothness of the objective function, we use generalized gradient instead. Each UAV moves along the generalized gradient direction of objective function to optimize the target locally, and finally, all UAV convergence to stable positions of optimizing the network throughput. Simulation results show the effectiveness of our method in improving the network average end-to-end throughput.

Keywords: UAV relay network · Throughput optimization · Gradient-based positioning

1 Introduction

Recently, the application of unmanned aerial vehicles (UAVs) has attracted increasing research interest. Small-scale UAV fleet is a practical choice for commercial applications due to their ease of deployment, low cost and hovering ability. Such aerial vehicles are suitable for natural disaster rescue, environmental

This work is supported in part by the National Natural Science Foundation of China (No. 61631004) and the National Science and Technology Major Project of China under Grant 2016ZX03001017.

H. Gao et al. (Eds.): ChinaCom 2019, LNICST 313, pp. 278–291, 2020.
https://doi.org/10.1007/978-3-030-41117-6_23

monitoring, delivery of goods and outdoor tourism. The using of single or multiple UAVs as communication relays or aerial base stations for ground users' communications in emergency situations and for public safety has been of particular interest because of their mobility and large coverage capabilities. Meanwhile, the development of wireless and mobile communication technologies has changed all aspects of our lives. The demand for high-capacity, high-reliability, low-latency wireless communication is increasing. In a UAV relay network, the locations of UAV affect various network performance metrics, including throughput, connectivity and coverage. The positions of ground nodes can usually be obtained by GPS or other navigation system, one practical way to optimize above metrics is positioning UAVs based on the nodes positions and network topology.

Many existing works have studied UAV relay network and its optimization. Rasario et al. [1] proposed a mechanism for the placement of UAV relays to support the transmission of high-quality live videos. [2] proposed an algorithm for the performance optimization of the ground-to-relay link of a UAV relay network by controlling the UAV heading angle. Zeng et al. [3] addressed the throughput maximization problem in a UAV relaying systems by optimizing the source/relay transmit power along with the relay trajectory. The paper [4] investigated a particle swarm optimization (PSO) based method of finding the optimal positions of unmanned aerial vehicles functioning as a communication relays to improve the network connectivity and communication performance of a team of ground nodes. Dixon et al. [5,6] presented a decentralized mobility control algorithm for optimizing the end-to-end communication capacity of a UAV relay chain system. The chaining controller drives the location of a virtual control point, using estimates of the communication objective function gradient calculated by stochastic approximation techniques, to locations of improving the relay performance. In [7], a centralized heuristic algorithm was proposed for positioning UAV to maximize the throughput of a software-defined disaster area UAV communication network. [8] developed a distributed controller to position a team of aerial vehicles in a configuration that optimizes communication link quality, to support a team of ground vehicles performing a collaborative task. They presented a gradient-based control approach where the agent locally minimizes a physically motivated cost function.

UAV deployment algorithm can be divided into three categories: heuristic algorithm [4,7], gradient based search [5,6,8] and others [2,3]. Heuristic algorithm has strong global search ability, which can obtain good UAV positions in given iterations. Gradient based search has continuous search trajectory, which is attractive in real-time optimization system. Other algorithm, such as UAV heading angle control, is applicable to specific UAV network.

There are some limitations in above works. The work [1,3,5,6] only consider one end-to-end transmission link, which is impractical for scenarios of multi-team collaboration, while paper [2] did not consider the actual available end-to-end communication capacity for ground users. The methods in [4] and [7] are centralized and time-consuming, causing poor network invulnerability, and not suitable for real-time optimization system. In [8], the objective function lacks physical meanings.

In view of the shortcomings of above literature, in this paper, we design a distributed UAV relay network according to the search and rescue scenario, supporting multi-users end-to-end communication. We propose a novel decentralized UAV positioning algorithm to optimize the average end-to-end throughput of the network in real-time. We consider the flow-pipe (FP) end-to-end communication capacity model [5], and generate the system optimization target by Shannon-Hartley Theorem based on the received signal-to-noise ratio (SNR). We design a gradient-based controller, driving the UAV moves along the gradient flow to maximize the target. Due to the non-smoothness of our objective function, the generalized gradient theory is introduced. We utilize the stochastic approximation to estimate the generalized gradient, and the convergence of the objective function to local maxima is proved by using the non-smooth stability analysis literature [9]. The optimization effectiveness is validated by simulation experiments. By contrast with PSO, this optimization result is global maxima.

The remainder of this paper is organized as follows. Section 2 describes the system model and optimization objective. Section 3 provides the detailed description of the proposed positioning algorithm. Section 4 shows the result of simulation experiments. In Sect. 5, we conclude this work.

2   System Model and Problem Formulation

In disaster or other emergency situations. The field is usually partitioned in several isolated regions and the fixed communication infrastructures are unavailable. The team members performing collaborate tasks in different regions cannot communicate directly with each other. The use of multiple UAV as communication relays for this scenario is feasible because of their mobility and large coverage capabilities. In this paper, we consider a distributed UAV mesh network.

2.1   UAV Relay Network Model

As shown in Fig. 1, a small-scale UAV fleet is employed as aerial base stations to serve a group of ground users. The network is designed as decentralized structure to reduce the dependency to control center which has high risk of being destroyed in complicated environment. All UAV play the same role and construct a top-layer network, their motions are self-controlled and in the same fixed altitude. Further, each UAV forms a sub-network with certain number of users and provides communication relay service for them. The motion of ground users is uncontrolled in their regions. For this model and optimization problem, we make following assumptions:

- The users are distributed in isolated areas, cannot communicate directly with other users without relays. The UAV communication range can cover the deployment area, and UAV can communicate with each other directly.
- UAV equips with multi-radios which occupy different channels, while ground users have one. Users in the same sub-network share a communication channel by time division multiple access (TDMA), while the air-to-air links using independent radio. No communication interference is considered in this work.

- Ground users can report their positions obtained by GPS to UAV in real-time. UAV shares these information with each other through interactions that occupy seldom communication bandwidth.
- The ground user has the willingness to communicate continuously with all other users in the network.

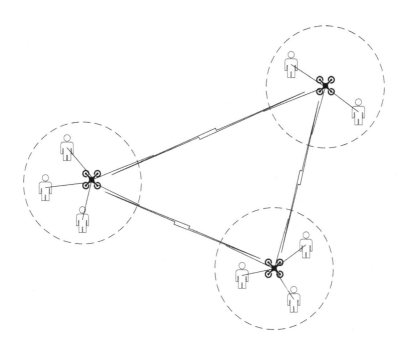

Fig. 1. System model of UAV relay network.

On a given area, a group of N UAV flying at height H are deployed as communication relays to serve K users. Let $\mathcal{N} = \{n_1, n_2, ..., n_N\}$ with $|\mathcal{N}| = N$ be the set of sub-networks of the system, the corresponding identifier of UAV is represented as $\mathcal{A} = \{a_1, a_2, ..., a_N\}$ with horizontal coordinates $\mathcal{P}_a = \{p_1, p_2, ..., p_N\}$, $p_i \in \mathbb{R}^2$. Let $\mathcal{K} = \{k_1, k_2, ..., k_N\}$ with $|\mathcal{K}| = K$ presents the number of ground users in each sub-network. For sub-network n_i, the corresponding users set can be expressed as $\mathcal{U}_i = \{u_{i1}, u_{i2}, ..., u_{ik_i}\}$ with horizontal positions $\mathcal{P}_{iu} = \{p_{i1}, p_{i2}, ..., p_{ik_i}\}$ where $p_{ij} \in \mathbb{R}^2$, the horizontal distance between these users and the host UAV is $\mathcal{D}_i = \{d_{i1}, d_{i2}, ..., d_{ik_i}\}$. The user u_{ij} in n_i is willing to communicate continually with all other users in the network.

2.2 SNR Field and Communication Capacity

Communication quality can be characterized by received signal-to-noise ratio (SNR). Denote the transmit power of node as P, and the received additive white

Gaussian noise (AWGN) power is σ^2, the available SNR between user u_{ij} and UAV a_i is given as

$$SNR_{ij} = \frac{PG_{ij}}{\sigma^2} \tag{1}$$

where G_{ij} is the channel power gain. We assume that the channel power gain from the UAV to users follows the free-space path loss model, which can be expressed as

$$G_{ij} = \frac{\rho_0}{d_{ij}^\alpha} \tag{2}$$

where ρ_0 denotes the channel power gain at the reference distance $d = 1m$, α represents the path-loss exponent and $d_{ij} = (H^2 + \|p_i - p_{ij}\|^2)^{\frac{1}{2}}$ is the distance between the user u_{ij} and UAV a_i. Further, the SNR between these two nodes can be written as

$$SNR_{ij} = \frac{\gamma_0}{d_{ij}^\alpha} \tag{3}$$

where $\gamma_0 = P\rho_0/\sigma^2$ denotes the reference received signal-to-noise ratio (SNR) at $d = 1m$. The capacity of communication link between any two nodes is a function of the channel bandwidth and the SNR of received signal. We use the Shannon-Hartley Theorem, the unit bandwidth maximum achievable rate in bps/Hz can be expressed as

$$\begin{aligned} r_{ij} &= \log_2(1 + SNR_{ij}) \\ &= \log_2(1 + \frac{\gamma_0}{d_{ij}^\alpha}) \end{aligned} \tag{4}$$

2.3 UAV Relay Network Average End-to-End Throughput

We assume the capacity of a single link is divided equally by communications carried by the link. The flow-pipe (FP) model [5] is implemented in end-to-end throughput calculation, it equals to the capacity of the worst link of all links in an end-to-end communication.

For an air-to-ground link, the theoretical capacity between user u_{ij} and UAV a_i is r_{ij}. The rate is firstly divided because the channel is shared by TDMA within the sub-network, and each user can get $1/k_i$ time slot in a unit time. We get the real link rate

$$r'_{ij} = \frac{r_{ij}}{k_i} \tag{5}$$

The link carries the number of $2(K-1)$ communications, including up-link and down-link transmissions. And for each communication, the available average rate is

$$\bar{r}_{ij} = \frac{r_{ij}}{2k_i(K-1)} \tag{6}$$

With regard to air-to-air links, the link capacity between UAV a_m and UAV a_n is R_{mn}, the link undertakes the cross sub-networks transmission with the number of $2k_m k_n$ and for each communication, the available rate is

$$\bar{R}_{mn} = \frac{R_{mn}}{2k_m k_n} \tag{7}$$

For a communication between u_{ni} and u_{nj} in sub-network n, the end-to-end throughput can be expressed as

$$\min(\bar{r}_{ni}, \bar{r}_{nj}) \tag{8}$$

Respectively, the sum of end-to-end throughput and communication amounts in sub-networks are

$$\sum_{n\in\mathcal{N}}\sum_{i\in\mathcal{U}_n}\sum_{j\in\mathcal{U}_n, j\neq i}\min(\bar{r}_{ni}, \bar{r}_{nj}),\ \sum_{n\in\mathcal{N}} k_n(k_n-1) \tag{9}$$

For a communication between $u_{n_1 i}$ in sub-network n_1 and $u_{n_2 j}$ in sub-network n_2, the throughput can be expressed as

$$\min(\bar{r}_{n_1 i}, \bar{R}_{n_1 n_2}, \bar{r}_{n_2 j}) \tag{10}$$

Respectively, the sum of end-to-end throughput and amounts of cross sub-network communication are

$$\sum_{n_1\in\mathcal{N}}\sum_{n_2\in\mathcal{N}, n_2\neq n_1}\sum_{i\in\mathcal{U}_{n_1}}\sum_{j\in\mathcal{U}_{n_2}}\min(\bar{r}_{n_1 i}, \bar{R}_{n_1 n_2}, \bar{r}_{n_2 j}),\ \sum_{n_1\in\mathcal{N}}\sum_{n_2\in\mathcal{N}, n_2\neq n_1} k_{n_1} k_{n_2} \tag{11}$$

The system average end-to-end throughput of the UAV relay network can be defined as

$$J = \frac{\displaystyle\sum_{n\in\mathcal{N}}\sum_{i\in\mathcal{U}_n}\sum_{j\in\mathcal{U}_n, j\neq i}\min(\bar{r}_{ni}, \bar{r}_{nj}) + \sum_{n_1\in\mathcal{N}}\sum_{n_2\in\mathcal{N}, n_2\neq n_1}\sum_{i\in\mathcal{U}_{n_1}}\sum_{j\in\mathcal{U}_{n_2}}\min(\bar{r}_{n_1 i}, \bar{R}_{n_1 n_2}, \bar{r}_{n_2 j})}{\displaystyle\sum_{n\in\mathcal{N}} k_n(k_n-1) + \sum_{n_1\in\mathcal{N}}\sum_{n_2\in\mathcal{N}, n_2\neq n_1} k_{n_1} k_{n_2}} \tag{12}$$

where J is a function of all nodes positions p due to the definition of link rate r and R.

2.4 Problem Formulation

As can be seen above, the system average end-to-end throughput associates with the positions of all nodes. Ground users are moving in corresponding areas and uncontrollable while UAV are self-controlled and can adjust their positions dynamically. Our goal is real-timely maximizing (12) by distributed adaptive deployment of UAV. Namely, to determine

$$p^* = arg\max_{p\in\mathbb{R}^{2\cdot N}}(J) \tag{13}$$

where p^* presents a group of positions of UAV.

3 Gradient-Based UAV Positioning Algorithm

This section describes a distributed gradient-based controlling algorithm to optimize the system average end-to-end throughput. We design a gradient controller for each UAV, driving the UAV moves along the gradient direction of global objective function. The target is optimized locally in these movement process. We lead into the generalized gradient due to the locally non-differentiable of the objective function. Furthermore, we prove the stability of the controller by non-smooth analysis.

3.1   Generalized Gradient Controller

Gradient ascent (decent) is a general method in solving various engineering optimization problems. Consider the problem of maximizing a continuous differentiable function $J(p)$ where $p \in \mathbb{R}^d$, which is equivalent to find p^* that maximizing $J(p)$ such that the gradient at p^*

$$g(p^*) = \nabla J(p^*) = \frac{\partial J}{\partial p}(p^*) = 0 \tag{14}$$

using gradient ascent, the iteration optimization process can be expressed as

$$p_{k+1} = p_k + \lambda g(p_k) \tag{15}$$

where p_k is the variable at the kth iteration, $\lambda > 0$ is the iteration movement step and $g(p_k)$ indicates the normalized gradient of the objective function at p_k. Following the direction of gradient flow in each iteration, the objective function will converge to local maxima finally.

Owing to the existence of minimum functions in (12) lead to locally non-differentiable at points where the elements in minimum function are equal, gradient ascent method has theoretical defects. We must instead use the generalized gradient.

The generalized gradient and its properties are studied in discontinuous dynamic systems [9]. For a locally Lipschitz function J, $\mathbb{R}^d \to \mathbb{R}$, and $\Omega_J \in \mathbb{R}^d$ denotes the set of points where J fails to be differentiable. The generalized gradient ∂J at a non-differentiability point p, can be expressed as the convex hull of all possible limits of the gradient at neighboring points where the function J is differentiable [9], written as

$$\partial J(p) = co \left\{ \lim_{i \to \infty} \nabla J(p_i) : p_i \to p, p_i \notin S \cup \Omega_J \right\} \tag{16}$$

where co denotes convex hull. If function J is continuously differentiable at p, then the generalized gradient $\partial J(p) = \nabla J(p)$. Moreover, the generalized gradient vector field [9] $Ln\partial(J)$, $\mathbb{R}^d \to \mathbb{R}$, where $Ln : \mathcal{B}(\mathbb{R}^d) \to \mathcal{B}(\mathbb{R}^d)$ is a set-valued map that associates to each subset S of $\mathbb{R}^d$ the set of least-norm elements of its closure $\overline{S}$. Furthermore, $Ln(\partial J/\partial p)$ is a direction of ascent of J at $p \in \mathbb{R}^d$.

We then design a generalized gradient controller. For UAV i, the controller can be expressed as

$$\dot{p}_i = Ln(\partial J)(p_i) \tag{17}$$

where $Ln(\partial J)$ is the generalized gradient vector field of J, and p_i is the position of UAV i.

Calculating the generalized gradient of (12) is a difficult task. The method of stochastic approximation for estimating the generalized gradient of non-smooth function and the appropriate conditions for convergence has been studied in [10]. In this paper, we apply a stochastic approximation approach named least squares gradient estimation (LSGE) mentioned in [5] (Fig. 2).

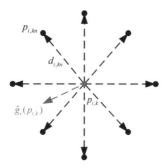

Fig. 2. An example of sample points and sample vectors around a control point.

The LSGE algorithm uses the least square method to fit the objective function and provides the least-square estimate of the gradient of the target point. We take n sample points $\{p_{i,k_1}, p_{i,k_2}, ..., p_{i,k_n}\}$ around the position of UAV i at $p_{i,k}$ (defined as control point) of time k with sample angle $2\pi/n$ and define the sample vector

$$d_{i,k_n} = p_{i,k_n} - p_{i,k} \tag{18}$$

where $d_{i,k_n} = h\boldsymbol{v}_{i,k}$, $\boldsymbol{v}_{i,k}$ with $\|\boldsymbol{v}_{i,k}\| = 1$ is the vector direction and $h > 0$ is the length of sample vector. Define the sample matrix $H_{i,k}$ used by the LSGE algorithm [5]

$$H_{i,k} = \begin{bmatrix} 1 & d_{i,k_1} \\ \vdots & \vdots \\ 1 & d_{i,k_n} \end{bmatrix} \tag{19}$$

then the LSGE method is given by

$$\begin{bmatrix} \hat{J}(p_{i,k}) \\ \hat{g}_i(p_{i,k}) \end{bmatrix} = (H_{i,k}^T H_{i,k})^{-1} H_{i,k}^T \begin{bmatrix} J(p_{i,k_1}) \\ \vdots \\ J(p_{i,k_n}) \end{bmatrix} \tag{20}$$

where $\hat{J}(p_{i,k})$ is an estimate value of the objective function at $p_{i,k}$, $J(p_{i,k_n})$ denotes the measurement of objective function at sample point p_{i,k_n}, which can be precisely calculated as the positions of all other nodes can be obtained in real time. $\hat{g}_i(p_{i,k})$ is the estimation of generalized gradient of UAV i at $p_{i,k}$. The error and variance analysis of this method in estimating the generalized gradient is presented in [11].

As the generalized gradient provide the movement direction, the position iteration process for UAV i can be expressed as

$$p_{i,k+1} = p_{i,k} + \lambda \hat{g}_i(p_{i,k}) \tag{21}$$

3.2 Non-smooth Analysis of the Controller

In this section, we present the stability analysis of generalized gradient controller. We achieve this by non-smooth analysis in discontinuous dynamic system [9].

The existence of generalized gradient vector field of the objective function depends on the fact that the function is locally Lipschitz and regular. A function $f : \mathbb{R}^d \to \mathbb{R}^m$ is locally Lipschitz at $x \in \mathbb{R}^d$ if there exist a L_x, $\varepsilon \in (0, \infty)$ such that

$$\|f(y) - f(y')\|_2 \leq L_x \|y - y'\|_2 \tag{22}$$

for all y, $y' \in B(x, \varepsilon)$ where $B(x, \varepsilon)$ is a ball centered at x of radius ε.

A function is said to be regular when its right directional derivative $f'(x; v)$ is equal to its generalized directional derivative $f^0(x; v)$ [9], where

$$f'(x; v) = \lim_{h \to 0^+} \frac{f(x + hv) - f(x)}{h} \tag{23}$$

$$f^0(x; v) = \lim_{h \to 0^+} \sup_{y \to x} \frac{f(y + hv) - f(y)}{h} \tag{24}$$

With regard to the locally Lipschitz and regular function, various results are available to facilitate the computation of generalized gradient [9]. Followings are the two properties for conserving the locally Lipschitz and regular property of our objective function.

Sum Rule: If f_1, f_2: $\mathbb{R}^d \to \mathbb{R}$, are locally Lipschitz and regular at $x \in \mathbb{R}^d$, s_1, $s_2 \in \mathbb{R}$, then the function $s_1 f_1 + s_2 f_2$ is locally Lipschitz and regular at x and the generalized gradient $\partial(s_1 f_1 + s_2 f_2)(x) = s_1 \partial f_1 + s_2 \partial f_2$.

The Minimum (Maximum) of A Finite Set of Continuous Differentiable Functions is Locally Lipschitz and Regular: For $k \in \{1, 2, ..., m\}$, let $f_k : \mathbb{R}^d \to \mathbb{R}$ be locally Lipschitz at $x \in \mathbb{R}^d$, and define the functions f_{max}, f_{min}: $\mathbb{R}^d \to \mathbb{R}$ by

$$f_{max} = max\{f_k(x) : k \in \{1, 2, ..., m\}\} \tag{25}$$

$$f_{min} = min\{f_k(x) : k \in \{1, 2, ..., m\}\} \tag{26}$$

f_{max}, f_{min} are locally Lipschitz and regular.

We combine the two rules above to valid the property of our objective function and utilize Proposition 11 in [9] to prove the stability of our controller (16) as Theorem 1.

Theorem 1. UAV follows the generalized gradient vector field of J such that $\dot{p}_i = Ln(\partial J/\partial p_i)$ will asymptotically converge to the critical points of J where the strongly stable critical points are local maxima of J.

Proof: On account of the continuous differentiability of functions (6) and (7), (8) and (10) are locally Lipschitz and regular using the second rule above. Then, consider the objective function J, which is an algebraic composition of a series of minimum functions, by applying the sum rule, we conclude that J is a locally Lipschitz and regular. According to Proposition 11 in [9], the strict maximizer of J are strongly equilibria of the non-smooth gradient flow of J. Further, we find a compact and strongly invariant set for this dynamic system follow the example of [8]. If the UAV flies out of the ground user field, it will fail to communicate with other nodes which leads to the generalized gradient $\partial J/\partial p_i$ for agent i goes to zero. So the ground user field is a strongly invariant set that with any initial conditions, the UAV will converge to the set of critical points of J. Then our distributed generalized gradient controller can be expressed as

$$\dot{p}_i = Ln(\frac{\partial J}{\partial p_i})$$

$$= Ln(\frac{\partial(\sum\limits_{n\in\mathcal{N}}\sum\limits_{a\in\mathcal{U}_n}\sum\limits_{b\in\mathcal{U}_n,a\neq b}\min(\bar{r}_{na},\bar{r}_{nb}) + \sum\limits_{n_1\in\mathcal{N}}\sum\limits_{n_2\in\mathcal{N},n_2\neq n_1}\sum\limits_{a\in\mathcal{U}_{n_1}}\sum\limits_{b\in\mathcal{U}_{n_2}}\min(\bar{r}_{n_1 a},\bar{R}_{n_1 n_2},\bar{r}_{n_2 b}))}{\partial p_i \cdot (\sum\limits_{n\in\mathcal{N}}k_n(k_n-1) + \sum\limits_{n_1\in\mathcal{N}}\sum\limits_{n_2\in\mathcal{N},n_2\neq n_1}k_{n_1}k_{n_2})})$$

$$= \hat{g}_i(p_i)$$

$$(27)$$

where $\hat{g}_i(p_i)$ is the generalized gradient estimation value.

4 Simulation Experiences

In this section, we show the performance of our algorithm in optimizing the UAV relay network average end-to-end throughput. We consider a group of users distribute in a $3000 * 3000\,\text{m}^2$ area, and a small-scale of UAV fleet provides communication relay service. Each UAV forms a sub-network with several users and their users are unchanged during the optimization process. We assume UAV can gain the positions of all nodes through information interaction.

The algorithm is implemented using MATLAB. The simulation parameters are provided in Table 1. The iteration step size λ can affect the stability of

Table 1. Simulation parameters

Parameter term	Value	Unit
UAV flight height (H)	100	m
Node transmit power (P)	0.1	W
Channel power gain at reference distance $= 1\,\text{m}$ (ρ_0)	-50	dB
Received noise power (σ^2)	-110	dBm
Path-loss exponent (α)	2	n/a
Length of sample vector (h)	10	m
Iteration step size (λ)	8	m

controller around convergence positions of objective function, if the value is too big. We use 8 in following simulations.

Figure 3(a) presents a two-uav four-user scenario, user1 (500, 1200), user2 (500, 2200), user3 (2500, 1200) and user4 (2500, 2200) are plotted with hollow circles, and uav1 starts at (600, 2800) serving user1-2 and uav2 starts at (1500, 2800) serving user3-4. The controller drives the UAV along the generalized gradient flow and stops at positions marked out with stars. The change of system average end-to-end throughput during the optimization process is shown is Fig. 4, increasing from 0.4363 bps/Hz to 0.6884 bps/Hz. We choose different start positions for UAV, the final convergence positions are same.

A scenario of three-uav and six-user is shown in Fig. 3(b). The positions of nodes, the sub-networks partition and the UAV optimization trajectory is plotted with different colors. From the blue line in Fig. 4, we see a significant increase

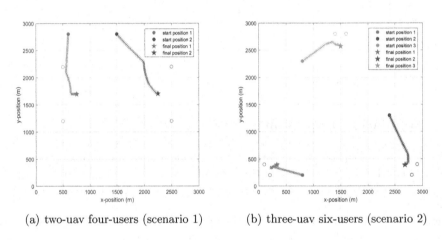

(a) two-uav four-users (scenario 1)   (b) three-uav six-users (scenario 2)

Fig. 3. The optimization of two sample scenarios.

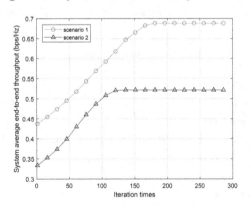

Fig. 4. Variation of throughput versus iteration times.

in system throughput, from 0.3330 bps/Hz to 0.5221 bps/Hz. The convergence positions of UAV instruct that the air-to-air link rates are the bottleneck of the end-to-end communications, causing UAV moves closer to get higher link rates. Different UAV start positions get the same optimization result.

Particle swarm optimization (PSO) [4] is a heuristic iteration algorithm, which can obtain global optimal solution by multiple particles joint searching solution space. As the searching process is random in each iteration, UAV can fly only if getting the final result. Let P_{num} be the particle number, N denotes the UAV number, I denotes the iteration times. For PSO, in each optimization, the total computation times of fitness function is $P_{num}I$. And in a distributed network, each UAV need to executes PSO algorithm to obtain its target position. Therefore, the total computation times is $NP_{num}I$ in each movement. In general, dozens of particles need be used in large-scale optimization problems and hundreds of iteration is necessary. This cause long computation time and is difficult to meet the real-time requirements if ground users are moving in their regions. While for our algorithm, the iteration process is continuous, UAV can fly in each iteration which has very little computation as described in Sect. 3. If users are moving, the UAV can adjust their flight direction in real-time.

Although PSO is not feasible to tackle this problem, it has great global search capability. We implement PSO with high iteration times and view the result of PSO as the optimal optimization result to validate the effectiveness of

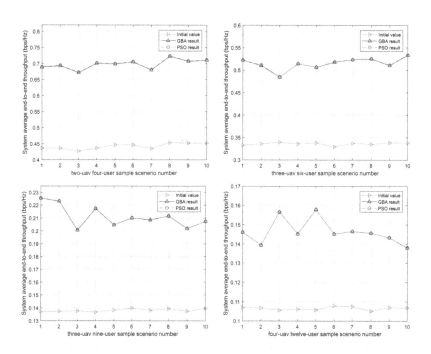

Fig. 5. Variation of throughput versus iteration times.

our method. We let the locations of a group of UAV as a particle, and using (12) as the fitness function.

We take 40 sample simulation scenarios and apply the gradient-based algorithm (GBA) and PSO to optimize the system average end-to-end throughput, respectively. The optimization result is presented in Fig. 5.

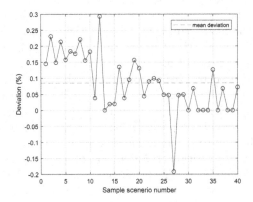

Fig. 6. Variation of throughput versus iteration times.

We can observe a great improvement in system average end-to-end throughput by using GBA. The final results of our method approximate the PSO result closely, illustrating that our algorithm can obtain optimal solution in theory. And the local maxima is global maxima in these scenarios of users distributing in isolated areas. In other scenarios, multi local maxima may exist, different UAV starting positions may converge to different local maxima. For this system, local maxima is also acceptable because the optimization is in real-time. The deviation (shown in Fig. 6) between our result and optimal value comes from gradient estimation.

In these 40 sample scenarios, the average deviation of network average end-to-end throughput of GBA with respect to optimal value is 0.085%.

5   Conclusions

In this paper, we designed a pragmatic UAV relay network to provide communication relays for ground users in emergency situations. The optimization of system average end-to-end throughput has been formulated and addressed to satisfy users' demand for communication capacity. To tackle this problem, we proposed a novel gradient-based UAV positioning algorithm. Using the generalized gradient controller, the UAV deploys adaptively to maximize the optimization target in real-time, making the network have high communication capacity at all times. We have proved the convergence and stability of this method by applying the relative theories of discontinuous dynamic system. The effectiveness of our method has been demonstrated by simulation experiments, whose results approximate closely to the optimal values obtained by PSO.

References

1. Rosário, D., Filho, J.A., Rosário, D., Santosy, A., Gerla, M.: A relay placement mechanism based on UAV mobility for satisfactory video transmissions. In: 2017 16th Annual Mediterranean Ad Hoc Networking Workshop (Med-Hoc-Net), Budva, pp. 1–8 (2017). https://doi.org/10.1109/MedHocNet.2017.8001638
2. Zhan, P., Yu, K., Swindlehurst, A.L.: Wireless relay communications with unmanned aerial vehicles: performance and optimization. IEEE Trans. Aerosp. Electron. Syst. **47**(3), 2068–2085 (2011). https://doi.org/10.1109/TAES.2011. 5937283
3. Zeng, Y., Zhang, R., Lim, T.J.: Throughput maximization for UAV-enabled mobile relaying systems. IEEE Trans. Commun. **64**(12), 4983–4996 (2016). https://doi. org/10.1109/TCOMM.2016.2611512
4. Ladosz, P., Oh, H., Chen, W.: Optimal positioning of communication relay unmanned aerial vehicles in urban environments. In: 2016 International Conference on Unmanned Aircraft Systems (ICUAS), Arlington, VA, pp. 1140–1147 (2016). https://doi.org/10.1109/ICUAS.2016.7502562
5. Dixon, C., Frew, E.W.: Optimizing cascaded chains of unmanned aircraft acting as communication relays. IEEE J. Sel. Areas Commun. **30**(5), 883–898 (2012). https://doi.org/10.1109/JSAC.2012.120605
6. Dixon, C.: Controlled mobility of unmanned aircraft chains to optimize network capacity in realistic communication environments. Ph.D. dissertation, University of Colorado (2010)
7. ur Rahman, S., Kim, G., Cho, Y., Khan, A.: Positioning of UAVs for throughput maximization in software-defined disaster area UAV communication networks. J. Commun. Netw. **20**(5), 452–463 (2018). https://doi.org/10.1109/JCN.2018.000070
8. Gil, S., Schwager, M., Julian, B.J., Rus, D.: Optimizing communication in air-ground robot networks using decentralized control. In: 2010 IEEE International Conference on Robotics and Automation, Anchorage, AK, pp. 1964–1971 (2010). https://doi.org/10.1109/ROBOT.2010.5509622
9. Cortes, J.: Discontinuous dynamical systems. IEEE Control Syst. Mag. **28**(3), 36–73 (2008). https://doi.org/10.1109/MCS.2008.919306
10. Bartkutė, V., Sakalauskas, L.: Simultaneous perturbation stochastic approximation of nonsmooth functions. Eur. J. Oper. Res. **181**(3), 1174–1188 (2007). https://doi. org/10.1016/j.ejor.2005.09.052. ISSN 0377-2217
11. Brekelmans, R., Driessen, L., Hamers, H., Hertog, D.D.: Gradient estimation schemes for noisy functions. J. Optim. Theory Appl. **126**(3), 529–551 (2005). https://doi.org/10.1007/s10957-005-5496-2

DISA Workshop

Workshop Summary on Data-Intensive Services Based Application (DISA 2019)

Honghao Gao[1], Ying Li[2], and Yuyu Yin[3]

[1] Computing Center, Shanghai University, China
gaohonghao@shu.edu.cn
[2] College of Computer Science and Technology, Zhejiang University, China
yingli.zju@gmail.com
[3] School of Computer Science, Hangzhou Dianzi University, China
yinyuyu@hdu.edu.cn

The data-intensive services based application (DISA) is considered as a collection of related structured activities or tasks (services) that produce a specific result. There are huge data sets exchanged between several loosely coupled services in such a data-intensive application. The Workshop DISA 2019 is in conjunction with 14th EAI International Conference on Communications and Networking in China (Chinacom 2019). On behalf of the organization committee, I would like to say thanks to Chinacom 2019 to give a platform to encourage academic researchers and industry practitioners to present and discuss all methods and technologies in a broad spectrum of data-intensive services based applications.

The paper titled 'Accompaniment Music Separation Based on 2DFT and Image Processing' presents how single-channel music manifests in the 2D Fourier Transform spectrum. In the image domain, the position of periodic peak energy is determined by image filtering. Then the masking matrix is constructed by a rectangular window to extract the constituent of the accompaniment music.

The paper titled 'Average Speed Based Broadcast Algorithm for Vehicular Ad Hoc Networks' shows an improved algorithm based on Speed Adaptive Probabilistic Flooding (SAPF), to solve the problem of the broadcast storm and broadcast unreliability in Vehicular Ad Hoc Networks (VANET) on highways. This approach alleviates the network load and reduces the complexity of implementation.

The paper titled 'Secure k-Anonymization Linked with Differential Identifiability' defines (k,ρ)-anonymization that achieves a secure k-anonymization notion linked with differential identifiability under the condition of privacy parameter ρ. It can make k-anonymization perform securely, while (k,ρ)-anonymization achieves the relaxation of the notion of differential identifiability, which can avoid a lot of noise and help obtain better utility for certain tasks.

The paper titled 'Multi-convex Combination Adaptive Filtering Algorithm Based on Maximum Versoria Criterion' proposes a multi-convex combination MVC (MCMVC) algorithm, aiming at the contradiction between the convergence rate and steady-state mean square error of adaptive filter based on Maximum Versoria Criterion (MVC).

The paper titled 'Energy management strategy based on battery capacity degradation in EH-CRSN' proposes an optimal adaptive sampling rate control algorithm

(ASRC), which can adaptively adjust the sampling rate according to the battery level and effectively manage energy use.

The paper titled 'Multipath and distorted detection based on multicorrelator' discusses the model of multipath signal and distorted signal. The multi-correlator range setting method is proposed considering the characteristics of the correlation functions of these two models, and the appropriate detection values are selected, which can effectively distinguish signals at the relevant peak levels.

The paper titled 'Delay Optimization-based Joint Route Selection and Resource Allocation Algorithm for Cognitive Vehicular Ad Hoc Networks' first proposes a candidate link selection method that selects the transmission links satisfying the link lifetime constraint. Then stressing the importance of transmission delay, the author formulates the joint route selection and resource allocation problem as an end-to-end transmission delay minimization problem.

The paper titled 'Energy Efficiency Optimization-based Joint Resource Allocation and Clustering Algorithm for M2M Communication Networks' considers an M2M communication network and formulate the joint resource allocation and clustering problem as system EE maximization problem. The author decomposes it into two subproblems, mainly power allocation and clustering, and uses Lagrange dual method and modified K-means algorithm to handle these problems.

The paper, titled 'Latency-reliability Analysis for Multi-antenna System' investigates the relationship between the latency and reliability of the diversity system. Diversity systems adopted with maximal ratio combining and selection combining techniques are analyzed, respectively.

The paper titled 'Cost Function Minimization-based Joint UAV Path Planning and Charging Station Deployment' considers joint UAV path planning and CS deployment problem. The author formulates the problem as a cost function minimization problem, that heuristic algorithms are used, including A* algorithm, K-shortest path algorithm, and genetic algorithm (GA).

The paper titled 'Energy Efficient Computation Offloading for Energy Harvesting-Enabled Heterogeneous Cellular Networks' considers a MEC-enabled heterogeneous cellular network (HCN) consisting of one macro base station (MBS), one small base station (SBS) and several users. The author proposes a hotbooting Q-learning-based algorithm to obtain the optimal strategy.

The paper titled 'Wi-Fi Gesture Recognition Technology Based on Time-Frequency Features' proposes a device-free gesture recognition system based on channel state information. First, the DWT-PCA combined denoising method is adopted for extracting useful gesture signals in complex environments. Then, the frequency domain characteristics of the gesture signal are constructed by using the STFT of the processed CSI amplitude signal. The features are trained and classified using the SVM classification method.

The paper titled 'DPTM: A UAV Message Transmission Path Optimization Method under Dynamic Programming' proposes a UAV message transmission path optimization method under dynamic programming named DPTM. It obtains the optimal object of message transmission, and then obtains the optimal path of messages to the destination node, to reduce ping-pong effect ratio and delay.

Acknowledgments

We want to thank EAI and Chinacom 2019 to provide this opportunity to let us organize Workshop DISA 2019. We also thank you for the support from the National Natural Science Foundation of China (NSFC) under Grant No. 61902236.

Multi-convex Combination Adaptive Filtering Algorithm Based on Maximum Versoria Criterion (Workshop)

Wenjing Wu, Zhonghua Liang$^{(\boxtimes)}$, Yimeng Bai, and Wei Li

School of Information Engineering, Chang'an University,
Xi'an 710064, People's Republic of China
lzhxjd@hotmail.com

Abstract. Aiming at the contradiction between the convergence rate and steady state mean square error of adaptive filter based on Maximum Versoria Criterion (MVC), this paper introduces the multi-convex combination strategy into MVC algorithm, and proposes a multi-convex combination MVC (MCMVC) algorithm. Simulation results show that compared with the existing MVC algorithm, MCMVC algorithm can select the best filter more flexibly under different weight change rates, and thus it has faster convergence speed and stronger tracking ability. Moreover, compared with the existing multi-convex combination maximum correntropy criterion (MCMCC) algorithm, MCMVC algorithm not only ensures the tracking performance, but also has lower exponential computation and steady-state error.

Keywords: Maximum Versoria Criterion (MVC) · Multi-convex combination · Multi-convex combination maximum correntropy criterion (MCMCC) · Steady-state error

1 Introduction

At present, adaptive filters have been widely used in signal processing and machine learning. With the development of linear adaptive filters, many linear adaptive filtering algorithms have been proposed, the most common of which are: least mean square (LMS) algorithm [1], affine projection algorithm (APA) [2] and recursive least squares (RLS) algorithm [3]. Although the above algorithms have the advantage of good performance in Gaussian noise environment, there is still a problem of performance degradation under non-Gaussian noise.

Therefore, many linear adaptive filtering algorithms against non-Gaussian noise have been proposed, such as least mean fourth (LMF) algorithm based on

This work was supported in part by the National Natural Science Foundation of China under Grant 61271262 and Grant 61871314, and in part by the Fundamental Research Funds for the Central Universities, CHD under Grant 300102249303 and Grant 300102249107.

H. Gao et al. (Eds.): ChinaCom 2019, LNICST 313, pp. 297–306, 2020.
https://doi.org/10.1007/978-3-030-41117-6_24

gradient [4], least mean p-power (LMP) algorithm [5] and recursive least p-norm (RLP) algorithm [6]. In recent years, the concepts of entropy, mutual information and correntropy in information theory have been applied in the field of adaptive filtering, among which the maximum correntropy criterion (MCC) algorithm [7] and minimum error entropy (MEE) algorithm [8] have attracted wide attention due to their strong robustness to non-Gaussian environments. The common point of MCC and MEE algorithms is that when the error is outliers, the superposition of weight updating is almost zero, which makes the algorithm resistant to non-Gaussian impulse noise.

However, since the default Gaussian kernel function in the MCC algorithm is not the optimal, Chen et al. proposed generalized maximum correntropy criterion (GMCC) by using generalized Gaussian density function as cost function in [9]. GMCC algorithm can be used in various non-Gaussian noise environments and it includes the original correntropy with a Gaussian kernel as a special case. Later, in [10], Huang et al. proposed maximum versoria criterion (MVC) algorithm in which the versoria function is used as cost function. Compared with GMCC algorithm, MVC algorithm not only avoids the high exponential function, but also has lower steady-state error and stronger resistance to non-Gaussian interference. However, MVC algorithm with invariable step-size has the contradiction between the convergence rate and steady state mean square error.

Therefore, this paper introduces the multi-convex combination strategy into MVC algorithm, and proposes a multi-convex combination adaptive filtering algorithm under non-Gaussian noise, namely MCMVC algorithm. Different from the traditional multi-convex combination strategy [11], the proposed MCMVC algorithm uses MVC to update the mixing factor indirectly, so it has strong robustness against various non-Gaussian noises.

In addition, in order to improve the convergence speed of MCMVC algorithm, the corresponding weight transfer scheme for non-Gaussian noise is presented. Simulation results show that in non-stationary system identification scenarios the proposed algorithm not only has good performance in the presence of non-Gaussian noise, but also has better tracking performance and convergence performance.

2   Adaptive Filtering Algorithm Based on Maximum Versoria Criterion

Considering the system identification model, the unknown system is modeled as a linear finite length unit impulse response filter. Therefore, the ideal output signal for an unknown system is

$$d(i) = \mathbf{u}(i)^T W_0 + v(i), \tag{1}$$

where $v(i)$ is noise interference, i represents the number of iterations, superscript T represents the vector transpose operation, $\mathbf{u}(i) \in R^m$ represents the input vector of the unknown system, usually defined as: $\mathbf{u}(i) \in [u(i), u(i-1), \ldots,$ $u(i+m-1)]^T$, m represents the filter length, and W_0 represents the unknown weight vector to be estimated.

The system output error is defined as

$$e(i) = d(i) - \mathbf{u}(i)^T W(i-1), \tag{2}$$

where $W(i-1)$ is the weight vector for the $i-1$-th iteration.

The generalized versoria function as a cost function can be expressed as [10]

$$J(W(i-1)) = E[\frac{1}{1 + \tau|e(i)|^p}], \tag{3}$$

where E represents the expectation operation, $p > 0$ represents the shape parameter of the generalized versoria function, $\tau = (2\alpha)^{-p}$, and $\alpha > 0$ represents the radius of the circle generated by versoria function. From (3), the gradient of the cost function of the generalized versoria function can be obtained as

$$\nabla J(W(i-1)) = \tau p \frac{1}{(1 + \tau|e(i)|^p)^2}|e(i)|^{p-1}sign(e(i))\mathbf{u}(i). \tag{4}$$

According to the random positive gradient principle of the adaptive algorithm, the weight coefficient update formula based on maximum versoria criterion is [10]

$$W(i) = W(i-1) + \eta_1 \frac{1}{(1 + \tau|e(i)|^p)^2}|e(i)|^{p-1}sign(e(i))\mathbf{u}(i), \tag{5}$$

where $\eta_1 = \tau p$ is the step-size. When $p = 2$, the weight update formula of the standard MVC algorithm can be obtained

$$W(i) = W(i-1) + \eta_1 \frac{1}{(1 + \tau e^2(i))^2}e(i)\mathbf{u}(i). \tag{6}$$

3   Multi-convex Combination Maximum Versoria Criterion Algorithm

According to Eq. (6), the overall weight vector and output of MCMVC algorithm can be expressed as

$$W_{eq}(i) = \sum_{k=1}^{L} v_k(i)W_k(i), \tag{7}$$

$$y_{eq}(i) = \sum_{k=1}^{L} v_k(i)y_k(i), \tag{8}$$

where $v_k(i)$ represents the mixing factor and satisfies $\sum_{k=1}^{L} v_k(i) = 1$, $y_k(i) = \mathbf{u}(i)^T W_k(i)$, $k = 1, 2 \ldots L$ represents the output of the partial filter, $W_k(i)$ represents the weight of the k-th partial filter, namely

$$W_k(i) = W_k(i-1) + \mu_k \frac{1}{(1 + \tau e_k{}^2(i))^2} e_k(i)\mathbf{u}(i), \qquad (9)$$

where μ_k represents the step size of the k-th partial filter.

In MCMVC algorithm, the setting of the mixing factor $v_k(i)$ uses a softmax activation function that enhances the stability of the multi-convex combination filter, namely

$$v_k(i) = \frac{\exp(\alpha_k(i))}{\sum_{j=1}^{L} \exp(\alpha_j(i))}, k = 1, 2 \cdots L, \qquad (10)$$

where $\alpha_k(i)$ is updated by maximizing the versoria function. The updated expression of improved $\alpha_k(i)$ is as follows

$$
\begin{aligned}
\alpha_k(i+1) &= \alpha_k(i) + \frac{\mu_\alpha}{2\tau} \frac{\partial f(e_{eq}(i))}{\partial \alpha_k(i)} \\
&= \alpha_k(i) + \frac{\mu_\alpha}{2\tau} \frac{\partial f(e_{eq}(i))}{\partial v_k(i)} \frac{\partial v_k(i)}{\partial \alpha_k(i)}, \\
&= \alpha_k(i) + \mu_\alpha v_k(i)(y_k(i) - y_{eq}(i)) \frac{e_{eq}(i)}{(1 + \tau e_{eq}{}^2(i))^2}
\end{aligned} \qquad (11)
$$

where $f(e_{eq}(i) = \frac{1}{1 + \tau e_{eq}{}^2(i)})$ is the expression of versoria function, μ_α is the update step of $\alpha_k(i)$, and $\mu_\alpha \gg \mu_1$. In (11), in order to prevent MCMVC algorithm from stopping, limit the range of $\alpha_k(i)$ to $[-\varepsilon, \varepsilon]$, where $\varepsilon = \frac{1}{2}ln(101 - L)$.

In MCMVC algorithm, this paper proposes a weight transfer scheme suitable for non-Gaussian noise environment, which accelerates the convergence performance of the combined filter. The weight transfer scheme transfers a part of the weight coefficient of the combined filter to the filter which is worse than the combined filter. The weight of the improved k-th partial filter can be expressed as

$$W_k(i+1) = \beta W_k(i) + \mu_i \frac{1}{(1 + \tau e_k{}^2(i))^2} e_k(i)\mathbf{u}(i) + (1 - \beta)W_{eq}(i), \qquad (12)$$

where β is the smoothing factor. The use condition of Eq. (12) is that the combined filter is obviously superior to the partial filter, and its judgment is based on the versoria estimator of the filter. Therefore, this paper defines the versoria estimator of partial filters and combined filters as follows

$$ver(e_k(i)) = 0.9ver(e_k(i-1)) + 0.1 \frac{1}{1 + \tau e_k{}^2(i)}, \qquad (13)$$

$$ver(e_{eq}(i)) = 0.9ver(e_{eq}(i-1)) + 0.1 \frac{1}{1 + \tau e_{eq}{}^2(i)}. \qquad (14)$$

When $ver(e_{eq}(i))/ver(e_k(i)) \geq \gamma_k$ and $\gamma_k > 1$, the weight coefficient transfer can be performed using Eq. (12). Through a lot of experiments, when γ_k and β take 2 and 0.8 respectively, the algorithm achieves the best transfer effect. Then, the implementation process of the MCMVC algorithm is shown in Algorithm 1.

Algorithm 1. Implementation Process of MCMVC Algorithm

Initialization:

Parameter: μ_α, ε, β, τ, L, γ_k, μ_k, $k = 1, 2, \cdots, L$.

Initialization: $\alpha_k(0) = 0$, $v_k(0) = 1/L$, $W_k(0) = 0$, $k = 1, 2, \cdots, L$, $ver(e_k(0)) = 0$, $ver(e_{eq}(0)) = 0$.

Computation:

while $i \geq 1$ do

(1) Compute partial filter output: $y_k(i) = W_k^T(i)\mathbf{u}(i)$, $k = 1, 2 \cdots L$;

(2) Compute partial filter error: $e_k(i) = d(i) - y_k(i)$, $k = 1, 2 \cdots L$;

(3) Compute combined filter output: $y_{eq}(i) = \sum\limits_{k=1}^{L} v_i(i)y_i(i)$;

(4) Compute combined filter error: $e_{eq}(i) = d(i) - y_{eq}(i)$;

(5) Compute versoria estimator of the filter:

$ver(e_k(i)) = 0.9ver(e_k(i-1)) + 0.1\frac{1}{1+\tau e_k{}^2(i)}$, $k = 1, 2 \cdots L$;

$ver(e_{eq}(i)) = 0.9ver(e_{eq}(i-1)) + 0.1\frac{1}{1+\tau e_{eq}{}^2(i)}$;

(6) Update partial filter weight vector:

if $\gamma_k \leq ver(e_{eq}(i))/ver(e_k(i))$

$W_k(i+1) = \beta W_k(i) + \mu_i\frac{1}{(1+\tau e_k{}^2(i))^2}e_k(i)\mathbf{u}(i) + (1-\beta)W_{eq}(i)$;

else

$W_k(i+1) = W_k(i) + \mu_k\frac{1}{(1+\tau e_k{}^2(i))^2}e_k(i)\mathbf{u}(i)$;

(7) Update mixing factor:

$\alpha_k(i+1) = \alpha_k(i) + \mu_\alpha v_k(i)(y_k(i) - y_{eq}(i))\frac{e_{eq}(i)}{(1+\tau e_{eq}{}^2(i))^2}|_{-\varepsilon}^{\varepsilon}$;

$v_k(i+1) = \frac{\exp(\alpha_k(i+1))}{\sum_{j=1}^{L}\exp(\alpha_j(i+1))}$, $k = 1, 2 \cdots L$;

(8) Update combined filter weight vector: $W_{eq}(i+1) = \sum_{k=1}^{L} v_k(i+1)W_k(i+1)$.

End

---

4   Simulation

In this section, the convergence and tracking performance of MCMVC algorithm are analyzed and compared with MVC and MCMCCC algorithms [12] via simulations of non-stationary linear system identification. In the simulation, the length of the identification system and the length of the adaptive filter are both set to 32; the input signal is a Gaussian white noise sequence with zero mean and variance 1. For noise $v(i)$, this paper uses mixed noise model to simulate non-Gaussian noise with impulse noise, which can be expressed as

$$v(i) = (1 - \varsigma(i))A(i) + \varsigma(i)B(i), \tag{15}$$

where $\varsigma(i)$ is 0.04, $B(i)$ is a Gaussian noise with zero mean and variance 15, and four different noises are considered for $A(i)$ as follows: (1) Gaussian noise with zero mean and variance 0.25; (2) Uniform noise distributed in $\{-0.5, 0.5\}$; (3) Laplacian noise with zero mean and variance 1; (4) Binary distribution noise distributed in $\{-0.5, 0.5\}$ with equal-probability, that is $p(x = 0.5) = p(x = 0.5) = 0.5$.

This paper introduces different weight vector change rates through the random walk model. The random walk model can be expressed as

$$W_0(i+1) = W_0(i) + q(i), \tag{16}$$

where the initial value of ideal weight $W_0(i)$ is generated randomly within the range of $[-1, 1]$, $q(i)$ represents the random zero mean vector with independent and identical distribution, its positive definite auto-correlation matrix is $Q = E[q(i)q^T(i)]$. $Tr(Q)$ is the measurement of the velocity of weight vector. In addition, $q(i)$ is considered to be an independent gaussian distribution.

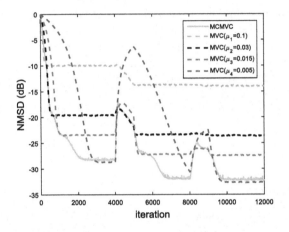

Fig. 1. Performance of different algorithms when $A(i)$ is Uniform noise

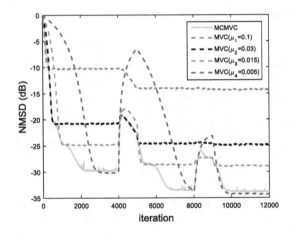

Fig. 2. Performance of different algorithms when $A(i)$ is Gaussian noise

Figures 1, 2, 3 and 4 show the tracking performance comparison between MCMVC algorithm and MVC algorithm with corresponding step size under four non-Gaussian noise environments. The number of combined filters in MCMVC algorithm is $L = 4$, the step size parameters are $\mu_1 = 0.1$, $\mu_1 = 0.03$, $\mu_1 = 0.015$ and $\mu_1 = 0.005$, the parameter μ_α is 5, and the parameter τ is 0.12. In addition, when the number of iterations are $4000 \le i \le 5000$ and $8000 \le i \le 9000$, weight vectors are added to $Tr(Q_1) = 10^{-6}$ and $Tr(Q_1) = 10^{-7}$ respectively.

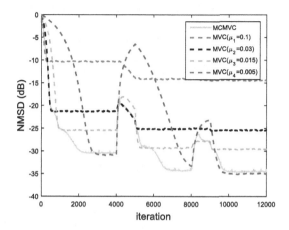

Fig. 3. Performance of different algorithms when $A(i)$ is Laplacian noise

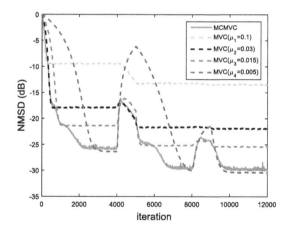

Fig. 4. Performance of different algorithms when $A(i)$ is Binary noise

According to Fig. 5, when the noise $A(i)$ is uniform noise, the change process of the four mixing factors of MCMVC algorithm can be seen. At different weight change rates, MCMVC algorithm can adaptively select partial adaptive filters with optimal performance, so that the performance of the algorithm shows the performance of the optimal filter. For example, after the weight vector $Tr(Q_1)$

is added, MCMVC algorithm first selects the adaptive filter with the optimal performance step size μ_2, then selects the adaptive filter with the optimal performance step size μ_3 to play the main role, finally, when the stable state is reached, the adaptive filter with the optimal performance step size μ_4 plays the main role.

Figure 6 shows performance comparison of weight transfer method for MCMVC algorithm when $A(i)$ is uniform noise. It can be seen from the graph that in the convergence stage and the convergence stage after the weight vector changes, the MCMVC algorithm with $\beta = 1$ has faster tracking speed than the MCMVC algorithm with $\beta = 0.8$. The weight transfer method transfers part of the weight of the combined filter to the filter with worse performance than the combined filter, so the convergence speed of the multi-convex combined filter is further improved.

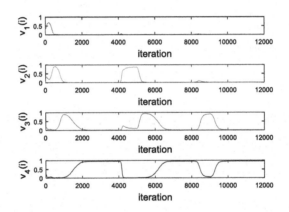

Fig. 5. Four mixing factors of MCMVC algorithm when $A(i)$ is Uniform noise

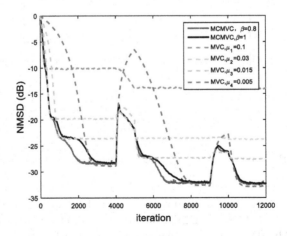

Fig. 6. Performance comparison of weight transfer method for MCMVC algorithm

Figure 7 shows the performance comparison between MCMCC algorithm and MCMVC algorithm when $A(i)$ is uniform noise. Among them, the step parameters of MCMCC algorithm are $\mu_1 = 0.1$, $\mu_2 = 0.03$, $\mu_3 = 0.015$ and $\mu_4 = 0.005$. The step parameters of MCMVC algorithm are $\mu_1 = 0.03$, $\mu_2 = 0.01$, $\mu_3 = 0.005$ and $\mu_4 = 0.001$. In all the algorithms, parameter μ_α is taken as 5. In addition, when the number of iterations is $8000 \leq k \leq 9000$, the weight vector $Tr(Q_1) = 10^{-6}$ is added to the weight change rate. As can be seen from Fig. 7, MCMVC algorithm is composed of MVC algorithms with low steady-state error and no exponential operation. Therefore, compared with MCMCC, MCMVC algorithm has lower steady-state error and exponential computation.

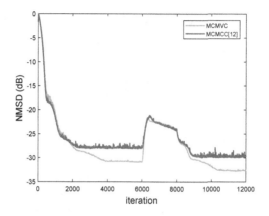

Fig. 7. Performance comparison between MCMVC and MCMCC algorithms when A(i) is Uniform noise

5   Conclusions

In this paper, the multi-convex combination strategy is combined with MVC algorithm, and MCMVC algorithm is proposed to overcome the contradiction between the convergence speed and the steady-state error of MVC algorithm. Simulation results show that compared with MVC algorithm, MCMVC algorithm can adaptively select the optimal performance filter under different weight change rates, and therefore has faster convergence speed and stronger tracking ability. At the same time, compared with MCMCC algorithm, MCMVC algorithm has lower exponential computation and steady-state error while guaranteeing tracking performance.

References

1. Sayed, A.H.: Adaptive Filters, pp. 139–209. Wiley, Hoboken (2008)
2. Ozeki, K., Umeda, T.: An adaptive filtering algorithm using an orthogonal projection to an affine subspace and its properties. Electron. Commun. Jpn. **67**(5), 19–27 (1984)
3. Gao, Y.: An adaptive filtering algorithm based on least square criterion. J. Guangzhou Univ. 32–34 (2001)
4. Walach, E., Widrow, B.: The least mean fourth (LMF) adaptive algorithm and its family. IEEE Trans. Inf. Theory **30**(2), 275–283 (1984)
5. Pei, S.C., Tseng, C.C.: Least mean p-power error criterion for adaptive FIR filter. IEEE J. Sel. Areas Commun. **12**(9), 1540–1547 (1994)
6. Zha, D.F., Qiu, T.S.: Adaptive generalized recursive least p-norm filtering algorithm based on minimum dispersion criterion. J. Electron. Inf. Technol. 54–58 (2007)
7. Singh, A., Principe, J.C.: Using correntropy as a cost function in linear adaptive filters. In: International Joint Conference on Neural Networks (IJCNN), pp. 2950–2955 (2009)
8. Principe, J.C.: Information Theoretic Learning: Renyi's Entropy and Kernel Perspectives. Springer, New York (2010). https://doi.org/10.1007/978-1-4419-1570-2
9. Chen, B., Xing, L., Zhao, H., et al.: Generalized correntropy for robust adaptive filtering. IEEE Trans. Sig. Process. **64**(13), 3376–3387 (2016)
10. Huang, F., Zhang, J., Zhang, S.: Maximum versoria criterion-based robust adaptive filtering algorithm. IEEE Trans. Circuits Syst. II Express Briefs **64**(10), 1252–1256 (2017)
11. Arenas-Garcia, J., Gomez-Verdejo, V., Figueiras-Vidal, A.R.: New algorithms for improved adaptive convex combination of LMS transversal filters. IEEE Trans. Instrum. Meas. **54**(6), 2239–2249 (2005)
12. Wu, W., Liang, Z., Luo, Q., Li, W.: Tracking performance of improved convex combination adaptive filter based on maximum correntropy criterion. In: Liu, X., Cheng, D., Jinfeng, L. (eds.) ChinaCom 2018. LNICST, vol. 262, pp. 184–193. Springer, Cham (2019). https://doi.org/10.1007/978-3-030-06161-6_18

Secure k-Anonymization Linked with Differential Identifiability (Workshop)

Zheng Zhao$^{1(\boxtimes)}$, Tao Shang^2, and Jianwei Liu^2

^{1} School of Electronic and Information Engineering, Beihang University, Beijing 100083, China
zhaozheng1000@163.com

^{2} School of Cyber Science and Technology, Beihang University, Beijing 100083, China
shangtao@buaa.edu.cn

Abstract. Most k-anonymization mechanisms that have been developed presently are vulnerable to re-identification attacks, e.g., those generating a generalized value based on input databases. k-anonymization mechanisms do not properly capture the notion of hiding in a crowd, because they do not impose any constraints on the mechanisms. In this paper, we define (k, ρ)-anonymization that achieves secure k-anonymization notion linked with differential identifiability under the condition of privacy parameter ρ. Both differential identifiability and k-anonymization limit the probability that an individual is re-identified in a database after an adversary observes the output results of the database. Furthermore, differential identifiability can provide the same strong privacy guarantees as differential privacy. It can make k-anonymization perform securely, while (k, ρ)-anonymization achieves the relaxation of the notion of differential identifiability, which can avoid a lot of noise and help obtain better utility for certain tasks. We also prove the properties (k, ρ)-anonymization under composition that can be used for application in data publishing and data mining.

Keywords: Differential identifiability · k-anonymization · Privacy preservation

1 Introduction

Privacy-preserving notions for data publishing and data mining have achieved many advances with the increase of collected data that is used for various data analysis. Many privacy definitions and applications for releasing data securely have been introduced in the literatures (see [16] and [20] for surveys). k-anonymity was proposed by Sweeny and Samarati [17–19] to protect the content of released data records. Some follow-up notions include l-diversity [15] and t-closeness [13]. The most prominent is k-anonymity. Its basic idea is to ensure that each quasi-identifier group has at least k tuples in order that individuals cannot be uniquely re-identified. The notion of k-anonymity tries to work on the attributes of quasi-identifiers, which is exposed to some subtle but effective attacks. Even the k-anonymity that treats all attributes as quasi-identifiers

H. Gao et al. (Eds.): ChinaCom 2019, LNICST 313, pp. 307–316, 2020.
https://doi.org/10.1007/978-3-030-41117-6_25

does not provide sufficient privacy preservation against re-identification attacks [9]. In addition, k-anonymization mechanisms that satisfy k-anonymity have weaknesses, because they do not properly capture the notion of hiding in a crowd. Thus it is necessary to solve such problem and define a new notion of k-anonymization that is secure without related weaknesses.

A privacy notion that is widely accepted is differential privacy (DP) developed by a series of works [1–5]. The basic idea is that any individual in a database has only a limited influence on the output of the database to hide the contribution of any single individual. Since privacy is a social notion with many facets, research fields examine various facets of privacy to understand strength and weakness. In 2011, Kifer and Machanavajjhala [11] argued that differential privacy is not robust to arbitrary background knowledge and impossible to provide privacy and utility without the assumption of data. Gehrke et al. [8] introduced zero-knowledge to provide sufficient protection when an individual may be strongly correlated with other individuals. In 2012, Lee and Clifton [12] considered that differential privacy does not match legal definitions of privacy, which is required to protect individually identifiable data. As a result, they proposed differential identifiability (DI). The privacy parameter ρ limits the probability estimate that is the contribution of an individual to the output results.

Although privacy definitions have some differences, both differential identifiability and differential privacy provide strong privacy guarantees. In fact, such strong privacy definitions are not suitable for all scenarios. Some mechanisms may add a lot of noise to satisfy the given privacy definition, thus reducing the utility of released data. For differential privacy, some relaxation notions have been proposed. In 2012, Li et al. [14] proposed the definition of differential privacy under sampling that captures the adversary's uncertainty about the input database. The results showed that sampling is a powerful tool that can greatly benefit differential privacy when sampling is used correctly. Gehrke et al. [7] introduced crowd-blending privacy that can achieve better utility and strictly relax the notion of differential privacy. However, for differential identifiability, there does not exist any relaxation or even properties on it for application in data publishing and data mining. So the new notion of k-anonymization should be able to achieve the relaxation of the notion of differential identifiability.

In order to provide sufficient privacy guarantees, we further study k-anonymization privacy preservation mechanisms and its link with differential identifiability. Both differential identifiability and k-anonymization limit the probability that an individual is re-identified in a database after an adversary observes the output results of the database. In this paper, we define a new notion of (k, ρ)-anonymization that makes k-anonymization linked with differential identifiability to properly capture the notion of hiding in a crowd. The new notion can make k-anonymization perform securely and achieve the relaxation of the notion of differential identifiability. Furthermore, we prove the properties of (k, ρ)-anonymization under composition that can allow us to apply it for complex privacy preservation issues in data mining and data publishing. Taken together, the results can provide basis for practical application of differential identifiability.

2 Preliminaries

A database D can be considered a finite multiset. Each attribute value is a fixed value in the universe U. Each entry in U can correspond to an individual in the database that privacy should be protected. $I(t)$ denotes the identity of the individual corresponding to the entry t in U. $\mathcal{I}_D = \{I(t)|t \in D\}$ denotes the set of individuals which belong to D. $D' \subset D$ is a database having one less individual than D, i.e., $|D'| = |D| - 1$.

Lee and Clifton [12] argued that differential privacy limits how much one individual can affect an output, not how much information can be leaked about an individual. This does not match legal definitions of privacy, which is required to protect individually identifiable data. Thus they proposed the definition of ρ-differential identifiability that can provide the same guarantees as differential privacy, but ρ limits the probability estimate that an individual belongs to the input database. The definition is:

Definition 1 *(ρ-differential identifiability [12]). A randomized mechanism M is said to satisfy ρ-differential identifiability if for all databases D, any $D' = D - t^*$, for any entry $t \in U - D'$:*

$$Pr[I(t) \in \mathcal{I}_D|M(D) = R, D'] \leq \rho. \tag{1}$$

The definition of ρ-differential identifiability limits the identifiability risk of any individual in the universe U, thus the posterior probability that any individual t belonging to the database is less than or equal to ρ after an adversary observes the output response R. In order to calculate the posterior probability, it is necessary to assume prior beliefs that an adversary may have.

To measure the adversary's confidence in making an inference, the proposed definition assumes that there exists a *possible worlds model* [12] in which the adversary considers the set of all possible databases. Given the adversary's prior knowledge $\mathcal{L} = \langle U, D', \mathcal{I}_D' \rangle$, the set of all possible databases Ψ is

$$\Psi = \{D' \cup \{t\}|t \in U \wedge t \notin D'\}.$$

Every possible world $\omega \in \Psi$ is equally likely to be D. Only one of the databases in Ψ is the true database which generates the output response R. In other words, only one individual is uncertain, and this individual must be drawn uniform from $m = |\Psi| = |U| - |D'|$ possible individuals with the probability between 0 and 1. At the same time, Lee and Clifton have experimentally proved that when the value of ρ is close to the correct probability of a random guess, the output response is barely utility and the privacy goal is also violated. Thus ρ-differential identifiability will be useful when $\rho > \frac{1}{m}$.

3   New Secure k-Anonymization Notion Linked with Differential Identifiability

Both differential identifiability and differential privacy provide strong privacy guarantees. For some data analysis tasks, some mechanisms may add a lot of noise to satisfy the given privacy definition while reducing the utility of released data. Furthermore, such strong privacy guarantees may be too restrictive for specific data analysis. We may require a privacy definition that can be strictly relaxed. In this section, we focus on a new k-anonymization notion linked with differential identifiability, which can relax the notion of differential identifiability and be more secure than classical k-anonymization.

3.1   Classical k-Anonymization

k-anonymity [19] is a privacy definition specifically for protecting data records of tables. A published table satisfies k-anonymity if each quasi-identifier (QID) group has at least k records in the table to reduce the probability of identification. k-anonymity requires the separation of all attributes into quasi-identifiers (QIDs) and sensitive attributes (SAs). The adversary is assumed to only know QIDs. Such separation is very hard to achieve in practice. And any separation between QIDs and SAs based on the adversary's background knowledge can be easily violated. There may exist an adversary that knows sensitive information on some individuals. If these individuals can be re-identified based on these information, it is still a privacy leak.

The literature [14] makes a clear distinction between k-anonymity and k-anonymization algorithms. k-anonymization aims to generate the anonymized output of the given input dataset which satisfies k-anonymity. Intrinsically, the notion of k-anonymity is very weak. Then classical k-anonymization based on k-anonymity is also vulnerable to re-identification attacks when some individuals have extreme values. For example, we assume that the input dataset contains the monthly income of individuals in a town. The adversary has known that only one individual's monthly income has been over $200\,K$ in this town. When $k(=15)$-anonymization generates the output dataset which contains one group taking $[50\,K, 210\,K]$ as the generalized value of monthly income, the adversary can conclude the individual is in the group and the individual's monthly income is $210\,K$. The adversary can re-identify the individual with a probability that is over $1/15$.

Most classical k-anonymization that computes generalization values according to the input dataset is sensitive to extreme values, thus leaking private information.

3.2 (k, ρ)-Anonymization

Classical k-anonymization does not provide sufficient privacy preservation. We consider that it does not properly capture the notion of hiding in a k crowd, because it does not impose any constraints on the mechanism used to generate generalized outputs, just as also mentioned in [14] and [7]. We aim to develop a new secure k-anonymization privacy definition whose mechanism used does not overly depend on an individual in the input dataset, i.e., it can achieve the notion of hiding in a k crowd.

In Definition 1, $I(t) \in \mathcal{I}_D$ can be denoted by $t \in D$. For convenience, we use $\mathbf{t}$ to denote $t \in D$, $M(D)$ to denote $M(D) = R$. Then Eq. 1 can be written $Pr[\mathbf{t}|M(D)] \leq \rho$.

Definition 2. *For all databases D, an individual $t \in D$ ρ-hides in a k crowd in D with respect to a mechanism M if $Pr[\mathbf{t}|M(D)] \leq \rho$ and $\rho \leq \frac{1}{k}$.*

Definition 3 ((k, ρ)-*anonymization*). *A mechanism M is (k, ρ)-anonymization if for any database D and each individual $t \in D$, t ρ-hides in a k crowd in the database D.*

(k, ρ)-anonymization requires that for each individual $t \in D$, t hides in a k crowd in D. Individual t is indistinguishable from at least other $k - 1$ individuals by means of the mechanism M regardless of what the database D is, i.e., an adversary can re-identify t with a probability less than $\rho \leq \frac{1}{k}$. Thus the attribute value of the individual t can be changed to the value of any other individuals in the k crowd. The mechanism M does not release any re-identifying privacy information on the individual t except the common information in a k crowd.

Many mechanisms achieving k-anonymization generalize a value in the input database by means of replacing specific values with general values, such as replacing a specific monthly income with monthly income range. As described in Sect. 3.1, if it is not used carefully, the privacy information may be leaked. Most of these mechanisms do not satisfy (k, ρ)- anonymization. If the data can be generalized appropriately, it is possible to achieve (k, ρ)-anonymization.

(k, ρ)-anonymization is not sufficiently strong privacy preservation method in all scenarios. It is crucial for relaxing the notion of differential identifiability that an adversary may observe some common information on the individual t when the adversary knows every individual in a k crowd except the individual t. In a sense, this can be viewed as a privacy leak that is not allowed in differential identifiability. We consider that the leaked information on t is non-sensitive information, because it is shared by a k crowd. Such relaxation is needed in some scenarios that sacrifice non-sensitive information for improved utility while the individual t is not re-identified with a probability over $\frac{1}{k}$.

(k, ρ)-anonymization can be viewed as the relaxation of the notion of differential identifiability, thus there is a relationship between (k, ρ)-anonymization and differential identifiability.

Proposition 1. *A mechanism M satisfies ρ-differential identifiability. Then M is (k, ρ)-anonymization for $\rho \leq \frac{1}{k}$ (any integer $k \geq 2$) and any database D of size at least k.*

Proof. If the mechanism M satisfies ρ-differential identifiability, for any database D of size at least k and every individual $t \in D$, we can know

$$Pr[I(t) \in \mathcal{I}_D | M(D) = R]$$
$$= Pr[t \in D | M(D) = R]$$
$$< \rho.$$

According to Definition 1, t is re-identified in D with a maximum probability of $\rho(\leq \frac{1}{k})$, i.e.,

$$Pr[\mathbf{t} | M(D)] \leq \rho,$$

so the individual t can ρ-hide in a k crowd in the database D. The mechanism M is (k, ρ)-anonymization.

Proposition 2. *For any mechanism M, any database D of size at least k and each individual $t \in D$, the mechanism M satisfies ρ-differential identifiability if and only if for any integer $k \geq 2$ and $\rho = \frac{1}{k}$, t ρ-hides in a k crowd in the database D, i.e., M is (k, ρ)-anonymization.*

Proof. The "only if" direction can refer to Proof 3.2. If the mechanism M satisfies ρ-differential identifiability,

$$Pr[I(t) \in \mathcal{I}_D | M(D) = R]$$
$$= Pr[t \in D | M(D) = R]$$
$$= Pr[\mathbf{t} | M(D)]$$
$$\leq \rho = \frac{1}{k}.$$

t can ρ-hide in a k crowd in the database D that satisfies (k, ρ)-anonymization.

For the "if" direction, the mechanism M is (k, ρ)-anonymization. The individual t ρ-hides in a k crowd in the database D. Assume that the mechanism M does not satisfy ρ-differential identifiability for the sake of contradiction, then there exists

$$Pr[I(t) \in \mathcal{I}_D | M(D) = R]$$
$$= Pr[t \in D | M(D) = R]$$
$$> \rho.$$

Then for any database D of size at least k and each individual $t \in D$, t is re-identified in D with a probability over $\rho = \frac{1}{k}$, i.e.,

$$Pr[\mathbf{t} | M(D)] > \rho.$$

Thus the individual t does not hide in a k crowd, which contradicts the fact that M is (k, ρ)-anonymization.

3.3 Privacy Axiom

Kifer and Lin [10] considered that the questions such as what makes a good privacy definition and how the data publisher should choose one must be addressed axiomatically. They presented the two axioms, namely the Privacy Axiom of Choice and the Transformation Invariance. The former allows us to randomly choose a privacy mechanism as long as this decision is not influenced by input database. It is a fundamental axiom which is required for any application of statistical privacy. The latter states that postprocessing sanitized data maintains privacy as long as the postprocessing mechanism does not deal with the sensitive information directly. We now show that the notion of (k, ρ)-anonymization also satisfies the two axioms.

Proposition 3. *Given two mechanisms M_1 and M_2 that both are (k, ρ)-anonymization, for any $p \in [0, 1]$, M_p is the mechanism that outputs M_1 with probability p and M_2 with probability $1 - p$ on input database D, then M_p is also a privacy mechanism that satisfies (k, ρ)-anonymization.*

Proof. Since both M_1 and M_2 are (k, ρ)-anonymization, for any database D and each individual $t \in D$, we have

$$
\begin{aligned}
Pr[\mathbf{t}|M_p(D)] &= pPr[\mathbf{t}|M_1(D)] + (1 - p)Pr[\mathbf{t}|M_2(D)] \\
&\leq p \cdot \rho + (1 - p) \cdot \rho \\
&= \rho \\
&\leq \frac{1}{k}.
\end{aligned}
$$

Therefore, the mechanism M_p also is (k, ρ)-anonymization.

Proposition 4. *Let M_1 be (k, ρ)-anonymization. For a randomized M_2 whose input space is the output space of M_1, $M(\cdot) = M_2(M_1(\cdot))$ also is (k, ρ)-anonymization.*

Proof. The randomness in M_2 is independent of both the data and the randomness in the mechanism M_1. We have

$$
\begin{aligned}
&Pr[\mathbf{t}|M_2(M_1(D))] \\
&= Pr[t \in D|M_2(M_1(D)) = R] \\
&= \frac{Pr[D = D' \cup \{t\}] \cdot Pr[M_2(M_1(D' \cup \{t\})) = R]}{Pr[M_2(M_1(D)) = R]} \\
&= \frac{Pr[D = D' \cup \{t\}] \cdot Pr[M_1(D' \cup \{t\}) = S]Pr[M_2(S) = R]}{Pr[M_1(D) = S]Pr[M_2(S) = R]} \\
&\leq \rho \\
&\leq \frac{1}{k}.
\end{aligned}
$$

We know that $M(\cdot) = M_2(M_1(\cdot))$ also is (k, ρ)-anonymization.

3.4   Composition Axiom

(k, ρ)-anonymization can show that an adversary only know some common information shared by a k crowd, which can be viewed as the relaxation of differential identifiability. Thus (k, ρ)-anonymization takes advantage of the adversary's uncertainty about the input database, i.e., the definition does not assume the adversary's background knowledge about database. Inevitably, there exists some weaknesses. It has appeared in [6,7,14] that any privacy definition which exploits the adversary's uncertainty. Let M_1 and M_2 be (k, ρ)-anonymization. Since the two crowds generated by M_1 and M_2 for an individual t may be basically disjoint, the new crowd generated by the combination of M_1 and M_2 includes the individual t and can be very small. The adversary can re-identify individual t with a probability over $\frac{1}{k}$. Thus (k, ρ)-anonymization can release the output of a database in the non-interactive model only once.

Although (k, ρ)-anonymization mechanism is not robust under composition, we expect that it can compose (k, ρ_1)-anonymization mechanism with ρ_2-differential identifiability mechanism to obtain a (k, ρ)-anonymization mechanism, while ρ is a function of ρ_1 and ρ_2. Such composition can be useful in certain scenario. Given the anonymized output database that satisfies (k, ρ)-anonymization, one can release the database in the interactive model and meanwhile answer the queries that use the mechanisms satisfying ρ-differential identifiability.

Proposition 5. *Assume that mechanism M_1 is (k, ρ_1)-anonymization and M_2 is a mechanism that satisfies ρ_2-differential identifiability, then the mechanism $M = (M_1, M_2)$ is $(k, \rho_1\rho_2 m)$-anonymization.*

Proof. Let D be any database and t be any individual in D. The mechanism M_1 is (k, ρ_1)-anonymization making

$$Pr[\mathbf{t}|M_1(D)] = Pr[t \in D|M_1(D)]$$
$$\leq \rho_1.$$

M_2 is a ρ_2-differential identifiability mechanism making

$$Pr[I(t) \in \mathcal{I}_D|M_2(D) = R] = Pr[t \in D|M_2(D)]$$
$$\leq \rho_2.$$

We have

$$
\begin{aligned}
Pr[\mathbf{t}|M(D)] &= Pr[\mathbf{t}|(M_1(D), M_2(D))] \\
&= Pr[t \in D|(M_1(D), M_2(D))] \\
&= \frac{Pr[D = D' \cup t]Pr[M_1(D' \cup t), M_2(D' \cup t)]}{Pr[M_1(D), M_2(D)]} \\
&= \frac{Pr[D = D' \cup t]Pr[M_1(D' \cup t)]Pr[M_2(D' \cup t)]}{Pr[M_1(D)]Pr[M_2(D)]} \\
&= \frac{Pr[D = D' \cup t]Pr[M_1(D' \cup t)]}{Pr[M_1(D)]} \cdot \frac{Pr[M_2(D' \cup t)]}{Pr[M_2(D)]} \\
&\leq \rho_1\rho_2 m.
\end{aligned}
$$

When the values of ρ_1 and ρ_2 are taken carefully, it can make $\rho_1\rho_2 m \leq \frac{1}{k}$. Thus the individual t can $\rho_1\rho_2 m$-hides in a k crowd with respect to M in the database D.

It is normal that privacy level degrades as more information is leaked. As mentioned in the proof, we must control the values of ρ_1 and ρ_2 in a good way to satisfy $(k, \rho_1\rho_2 m)$-anonymization. Note that when the value of m is too large, the values of ρ_1 and ρ_2 will become very small to satisfy $\rho_1\rho_2 m \leq \frac{1}{k}$ which introduces too much noise. Furthermore, an adversary may conclude with high confidence that the individual t is not in the database D after observing query results and considering the values of ρ_1 and ρ_2 are very small. It is evident that the composition between differential identifiability mechanism and other weaker mechanism should be used in a well-controlled way.

4   Conclusions

In this paper, we proved the properties of differential identifiability under composition that can allow us to apply differential identifiability for complex privacy queries in data mining and data publishing. We identified the weaknesses of the k-anonymization methods and provided the notion of (k, ρ)-anonymization. (k, ρ)-anonymization can avoid the vulnerabilities existing in classical k-anonymization and achieve the relaxation of the notion of differential identifiability. We also studied the power and the potential weaknesses under composition. The results show that it is important to control the privacy parameters to prevent privacy information leaked when (k, ρ)-anonymization is used in the interactive model. Our achievements provide basis for practical application of differential identifiability and will facilitate the development of practical privacy-preserving data mining algorithms supporting differential identifiability.

Acknowledgment. This project was supported by the National Key Research and Development Program of China (No. 2016YFC1000307) and the National Natural Science Foundation of China (No. 61571024, 61971021) for valuable helps.

References

1. Blum, A., Dwork, C., McSherry, F., Nissim, K.: Practical privacy: the SuLQ framework. In: Proceedings of the Twenty-Fourth ACM SIGMOD-SIGACT-SIGART Symposium on Principles of Database Systems, PODS 2005, pp. 128–138. ACM Press, New York (2005)
2. Dinur, I., Nissim, K.: Revealing information while preserving privacy. In: Proceedings of the Twenty-Second ACM SIGMOD-SIGACT-SIGART Symposium on Principles of Database Systems, PODS 2003, pp. 202–210. ACM Press, New York (2003)
3. Dwork, C.: Differential privacy. In: Bugliesi, M., Preneel, B., Sassone, V., Wegener, I. (eds.) ICALP 2006. LNCS, vol. 4052, pp. 1–12. Springer, Heidelberg (2006). https://doi.org/10.1007/11787006_1

4. Dwork, C., McSherry, F., Nissim, K., Smith, A.: Calibrating noise to sensitivity in private data analysis. In: Halevi, S., Rabin, T. (eds.) TCC 2006. LNCS, vol. 3876, pp. 265–284. Springer, Heidelberg (2006). https://doi.org/10.1007/11681878_14

5. Dwork, C., Nissim, K.: Privacy-preserving datamining on vertically partitioned databases. In: Franklin, M. (ed.) CRYPTO 2004. LNCS, vol. 3152, pp. 528–544. Springer, Heidelberg (2004). https://doi.org/10.1007/978-3-540-28628-8_32

6. Ganta, S.R., Kasiviswanathan, S.P., Smith, A.: Composition attacks and auxiliary information in data privacy. In: Proceedings of the 14th ACM SIGKDD International Conference on Knowledge Discovery and Data Mining, KDD 2008, pp. 265–273. ACM Press, New York (2008)

7. Gehrke, J., Hay, M., Lui, E., Pass, R.: Crowd-blending privacy. In: Safavi-Naini, R., Canetti, R. (eds.) CRYPTO 2012. LNCS, vol. 7417, pp. 479–496. Springer, Heidelberg (2012). https://doi.org/10.1007/978-3-642-32009-5_28

8. Gehrke, J., Lui, E., Pass, R.: Towards privacy for social networks: a zero-knowledge based definition of privacy. In: Ishai, Y. (ed.) TCC 2011. LNCS, vol. 6597, pp. 432–449. Springer, Heidelberg (2011). https://doi.org/10.1007/978-3-642-19571-6_26

9. He, Y., Naughton, J.F.: Anonymization of set-valued data via top-down, local generalization. Proc. VLDB Endow. **2**(1), 934–945 (2009)

10. Kifer, D., Lin, B.R.: Towards an axiomatization of statistical privacy and utility. In: Proceedings of the Twenty-Ninth ACM SIGMOD-SIGACT-SIGART Symposium on Principles of Database Systems, PODS 2010, pp. 147–158. ACM Press, New York (2010)

11. Kifer, D., Machanavajjhala, A.: No free lunch in data privacy. In: Proceedings of the 2011 ACM SIGMOD International Conference on Management of Data, SIGMOD 2011, pp. 193–204. ACM Press, New York (2011)

12. Lee, J., Clifton, C.: Differential identifiability. In: Proceedings of the 18th ACM SIGKDD International Conference on Knowledge Discovery and Data mining, KDD 2012, pp. 1041–1049. ACM Press, New York (2012)

13. Li, N., Li, T., Venkatasubramanian, S.: t-closeness: privacy beyond k-anonymity and l-diversity. In: 22nd International Conference on Data Engineering, ICDE 2007, pp. 106–115. IEEE Computer Society Press, Los Alamitos (2007)

14. Li, N., Qardaji, W., Su, D.: On sampling, anonymization, and differential privacy or, k-anonymization meets differential privacy. In: Proceedings of the 7th ACM Symposium on Information, Computer and Communications Security, ASIACCS 2012, pp. 32–33. ACM Press, New York (2012)

15. Machanavajjhala, A., Gehrke, J., Kifer, D., Venkitasubramaniam, M.: l-diversity: privacy beyond k-anonymity. In: 22nd International Conference on Data Engineering, ICDE 2006, p. 24. IEEE Computer Society Press, Los Alamitos (2006)

16. Mendes, R., Vilela, J.P.: Privacy-preserving data mining: methods, metircs, and applications. IEEE Access **5**, 10562–10582 (2017)

17. Samarati, P.: Protecting respondents identities in microdata release. IEEE Trans. Knowl. Data Eng. **13**(6), 1010–1027 (2001)

18. Sweeny, L.: Achieving k-anonymity privacy protection using generalization and suppression. Int. J. Uncertain. Fuzziness Knowl.-Based Syst. **10**(5), 571–588 (2002)

19. Sweeny, L.: k-anonymity: a model for protecting privacy. Int. J. Uncertain., Fuzziness Knowl.-Based Syst. **10**(5), 557–570 (2002)

20. Yu, S.: Big privacy: challenges and opportunities of privacy study in the age of big data. IEEE Access **4**, 2169–3536 (2016)

Energy Management Strategy Based on Battery Capacity Degradation in EH-CRSN (Workshop)

Errong Pei[1(⊠)], Shan Liu[1], and Maohai Ran[2]

[1] School of Communication and Information Engineering,
Chongqing University of Posts and Telecommunications, Chongqing 400065, China
peier@cqupt.edu.cn
[2] Chongqing Electric Power College, Chongqing 400053, China

Abstract. Energy Harvesting Cognitive Wireless Sensor Network (EH-CRSN) is a novel network which introduces cognitive radio (CR) technology and energy harvesting (EH) technology into traditional WSN. Most of the existing works do not consider that battery capacity of the sensor is limited and will decay over time. Battery capacity degradation will reduce the lifetime of the sensor and affect the performance of the network. In this paper, in order to maximize the network utility of the energy harvesting sensor node in its life cycle, we are concerned with how to determine the optimal sampling rate of sensor node under the condition of battery capacity degradation. Therefore, we propose an optimal adaptive sampling rate control algorithm (ASRC), which can adaptively adjust the sampling rate according to the battery level and effectively manage energy use. In addition, the impact of link capacity on network utility is further investigated. The simulation results verify the effectiveness of the algorithm, which shows that the algorithm is more realistic than the existing algorithm. It can maximize the network utility and improve the overall performance of the network.

Keywords: Energy management · Cognitive radio · Battery degradation · Sampling rate control

1 Introduction

In order to alleviate the spectrum shortage of unlicensed frequency bands and prolong the network lifetime, energy harvesting cognitive wireless sensor network (EH-CRSN) has been proposed and developed. In EH-CRSN, sensor nodes can opportunistically access the vacant licensed channels which can provide a spectrum-efficient, energy-efficient, and long-lived wireless networking solution in the coming era of the Internet of Things (IoTs) [1]. In RF-powered CRSNs, sensor nodes can harvest energy from dedicated RF power sources and ambient RF signals (e.g., WiFi signals, TV, and microwave radio)

This work was supported in part by the Chongqing Basic and Cuttingedge Project under Grant cstc2018jcyjAX0507 and cstc2017jcyjBX0005, National Natural Science Foundation of China under Grant 61671096 and 61379159.

H. Gao et al. (Eds.): ChinaCom 2019, LNICST 313, pp. 317–327, 2020.
https://doi.org/10.1007/978-3-030-41117-6_26

[2], and store them in batteries for later use. However, the lifetime of battery is closely related to the charging and discharging cycles. Frequent battery charging and discharging operations can cause irreversible battery capacity degradation and endanger the lifetime of sensor nodes.

Existing works hardly consider the degradation of battery capacity and link constraint, which is not practical. Reference [3] studies the network utility maximization problem in static route rechargeable sensor networks. however, the impact of battery capacity degradation is neglected. Reference [4] proposes a fast sampling rate control algorithm based on RF energy harvesting wireless sensor networks. However, it considers that the energy consumption rate does not exceed the energy harvesting rate. Reference [5] proposes a distributed solution called QuickFix, to compute the optimal sampling rate and routing path. However, insufficient battery capacity would result in the loss of recharging opportunities. Reference [6] does not consider the link capacity constraint for congestion control. Reference [7] proposes a double-threshold policy under channel fading conditions. Reference [8] studies random Markov chain framework to capture the degradation status of battery capacity. However, it does not consider the issue of maximizing network utility.

In this paper, we propose an adaptive sampling rate control algorithm (ASRC) which can adaptively determine the sampling rate of each RF-powered cognitive wireless sensor node under the condition of battery capacity degradation. Our algorithm achieves the goal of maximizing the overall utility of the network.

The rest of the paper is organized as follows: Sect. 2 establishes the system model and the mathematical model of optimization problem; Sect. 3 proposes the optimization strategy and algorithm to solve the problem; Sect. 4 gives the simulation results; Sect. 5 summarizes the relevant conclusions.

2 System Model and Problem Formulation

2.1 Network Model

We consider a static-routing RF-powered CRSN with N sensor nodes (excluding the sink node), each sensor node only has a unique link to the next hop. Figure 1 is illustration of an RF-powered CRSN. All sensor nodes are equipped with CR module and EH module. They can opportunistically access the licensed spectrum of the PU and transmit the data collected from the environment to the sink node.

2.2 Energy Harvesting Model

We consider sensor nodes can harvest energy from dedicated RF sources to ensure a stable supply of energy. The amount of energy harvested by sensor node depends on the transmission power of RF energy source, the distance, and the propagation characteristics of the environment. In the terrestrial environment, the energy harvest rate of the node i from the uth energy source can be expressed as [9]:

$$E_{i,u} = \delta \frac{G_u G_i \lambda_u^\alpha}{4\pi d_{i,u}^\alpha} \cdot P_u \qquad (1)$$

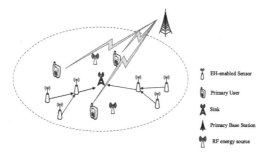

Fig. 1. Illustration of an RF-powered CRSN

Where δ is the energy conversion efficiency, G_u and G_i are the antenna gain of the uth energy source and the ith sensor node respectively; α is the path loss exponent; the RF signal wavelength, the energy collection efficiency; d is the distance between the node and the energy source; P_u is the transmission power of each energy source.

2.3 Energy Consumption Model

We consider the time cycle of energy harvesting is divided into a set $T = \{1, \cdots, T\}$, and T represents the length of the cognitive wireless sensor life cycle. Let r_i^t represent the sampling rate of the node i at the time slot t. Each sensor node consumes additional energy due to the cognitive radio module, so the energy consumption rate of the whole node can be expressed as:

$$\omega(r^t) = e_\tau + (e_i^s + e_i^t)r_i^t + (e_i^r + e_i^t) \sum_{j \in A(i)} r_j^t \tag{2}$$

Where $r^t = [r_1^t, \cdots, r_N^t]^T$ is the sampling rate vector. Let e_i^s, e_i^r and e_i^t denote the energy consumption per bit of the sensor node data sensing, receiving and transmitting respectively; e_τ denote the energy consumed by spectrum sensing, and $A(i)$ denote a group of sensor nodes using the sensor node i as a relay node.

2.4 Battery Capacity Degradation Model

The number of charge and discharge cycles of the battery is related to the battery discharge depth (D). The discharge depth is denoted as the ratio of the amount of battery discharges to the battery capacity. Considering the exponential decay model of the battery energy level [8], the decay rate of battery capacity at the time slot t is:

$$q_i = \lambda e^{\theta(1 - \frac{B_i^t}{B_0})} \tag{3}$$

Where q_i denote the amount of battery degradation of node i at the time slot t. B_i^t denote the battery energy level of node i at the time slot t; B_0 denote the initial capacity of the battery; the battery constant $\lambda > 0$, $\theta > 0$. Since the energy decay model is an exponential decay model which is only related to the current battery energy level, the node's current battery energy level can be expressed as:

$$B_i^t = \left[B_i^{t-1} + E_{i,u}\Delta t - \omega(r^t)\Delta t \right]_0^{B_i^c} \tag{4}$$

Where B_i^c denote the battery capacity of node i at the current time slot, Δt denote time interval of time slot t. Equation (4) can be recursively calculated by

$$B_i^t = B_i^0 + \sum_{k=1}^{t} E_{i,u}\Delta t - \sum_{k=1}^{t} \omega(r_i^t)\Delta t \tag{5}$$

The current battery capacity of the node can be expressed as:

$$B_i^c = B_0 - \sum_{k=1}^{t} \lambda e^{\theta(1-\frac{B_i^t}{B_0})} \tag{6}$$

When $B_i^c \leq D_{\min}B_0$ and $B_0 = 0$, the remaining storage space of the battery cannot maintain the continuously operation of sensor node, and the life cycle of the cognitive wireless sensors is over. $D_{\min}$ denote the ratio of the minimum discharge space for maintaining the operation of the wireless sensor to the initial battery capacity.

2.5 Problem Formulation

We establish a mathematical model and propose an optimal adaptive sampling rate control algorithm (ASRC) to manage battery energy. Assuming that adjacent nodes operate on orthogonal channels, the utility function is assumed to be increasing and strictly concave. For example, let $U(r_i^t) = \log(1 + r_i^t)$, which is known to guarantee the fairness of each sensor nodes [10]. The network utility maximization problem in RF-powered CRSN with link and battery capacity constraints can be expressed as:

$$\max_{r_i^t} \sum_{t \in T} \sum_{i \in N} U(r_i^t)$$

$$s.t \begin{cases} r_i^t + \sum_{j \in A_i} r_j^t \leq c_i^t \\ B_i^t \leq B_i^c \\ B_i^t \geq B_i^c - B_0 D \\ B_i^t \geq 0 \end{cases} \tag{7}$$

Constraint 1 indicates that the flow over one link should not exceed the link capacity to avoid link congestion. Constraint 2 indicates that the battery energy level should be within the current battery capacity range. Constraint 3 indicates that the battery energy level must be within the discharge space to avoid excessive battery discharge. Constraint 4 indicates that the battery level must be greater than zero. We can decouple the original optimization problem into separable subproblems and then solve it locally by dual decomposition [6].

3 Optimal Adaptive Sampling Rate Control Algorithm

3.1 Introducing Lagrange

We introduce the Lagrangian multipliers $\lambda_i^t, u_i^t, \alpha_i^t \geq 0$ for each sensor node at each time slot, and $\lambda = [\lambda_i^t]_{i \in N, t \in T}, u = [u_i^t]_{i \in N, t \in T}, \alpha = [\alpha_i^t]_{i \in N, t \in T}$ are the Lagrangian multiplier matrixes. The Lagrangian function for our optimization problem is:

$$L(R, \lambda, u, \alpha, \beta) = \sum_{t \in T} \sum_{i \in N} U(r_i^t) + \sum_{t \in T} \sum_{i \in N} [\lambda_i^t(c_i^t - (r_i^t + \sum_{j \in A_i} r_j^t))$$
$$+ u_i^t(B_i^c - B_i^t) + \beta_i^t(B_i^t - (B_i^c - B_0 D)) + \alpha_i^t B_i^t] \qquad (8)$$

We define the intermediate variables as follows, these equations can be proved through expansion of both sides and mathematical induction.

$$\begin{cases} \zeta_i^t = \sum_{k=t}^{T} (u_i^t - \alpha_i^t - \beta_i^t) \\ \sigma_i^t = [\zeta_i^t(e_i^s + e_i^t) + \sum_{j \in R(i)} \zeta_j^t(e_j^r + e_j^t)]\Delta t \\ \eta_i^t = \lambda_i^t + \sum_{j \in R(i)} \lambda_j^t \end{cases} \qquad (9)$$

Thus, the Lagrangian is:

$$L(R, \lambda, u, \alpha, \beta) = \sum_{t \in T} \sum_{i \in N} [U(r_i^t) - r_i^t \eta_i^t + r_i^t \sigma_i^t + (\beta_i^t - u_i^t) \sum_{k=1}^{t} q_i]$$
$$+ \sum_{t \in T} \sum_{i \in N} [\lambda_i^t c_i^t + (u_i^t - \beta_i^t)B_0 + \beta_i^t B_0 D - \zeta_i^t(B_i^0 + \sum_{k=1}^{T} E_{i,u} \Delta t)] \qquad (10)$$

Through the Lagrangian function, the original optimization problem can be decomposed, and the subproblem is:

$$P(\lambda, u, \alpha, \beta) = \max_{r_i^t \geq 0} \sum_{t \in T} \sum_{i \in N} [U(r_i^t) - r_i^t \eta_i^t + r_i^t \sigma_i^t + (\beta_i^t - u_i^t) \sum_{k=1}^{t} q_i] \qquad (11)$$

It is not difficult to judge that the subproblem is also a convex optimization problem, and the optimal solution satisfy the KKT optimization condition:

$$\frac{1}{r_i^t} + (\sigma_i^t - \eta_i^t) + (\beta_i^t - u_i^t)\frac{\theta}{C_0}(e_i^s + e_i^t)\Delta t \sum_{k=1}^{t} q_i = 0 \qquad (12)$$

The slackness conditions are as follows:

$$\begin{cases} u_i^t(B_i^c - B_i^t) = 0 \\ \beta_i^t(B_i^t - (B_i^c - B_0 D)) = 0 \\ \alpha_i^t B_i^t = 0 \end{cases} \qquad (13)$$

So, the sampling rate can be obtained from Eq. (12):

$$r_i^t = [U'^{-1}(\eta_i^t - \sigma_i^t + (u_i^t - \beta_i^t)g_i)]^+ \tag{14}$$

Where

$$g_i = \frac{\theta}{C_0}(e_i^y + e_i^t)\Delta t \sum_{k=1}^{t} q_i \tag{15}$$

3.2 Dual Problem

From the sampling rate formula (14), the Lagrangian multipliers in the equation can be solved by the dual problem of the optimization problem. The dual problem can be expressed as:

$$\min_{\lambda,u,\alpha,\beta} P(\lambda, u, \alpha, \beta)$$
$$s.t \quad \lambda_i^t, u_i^t, \alpha_i^t, \beta_i^t \geq 0 \tag{16}$$

The optimal solution to the dual problem can be solved iteratively by the subgradient method. The Lagrangian multipliers is updated in the opposite direction of the subgradient of the dual function:

$$\begin{cases} \lambda_i^{t,k+1} = [\lambda_i^{t,k} - v_\lambda(c_i^t - (r_i^t + \sum_{j \in A(i)} r_j^t))]^+ \\ u_i^{t,k+1} = [u_i^{t,k} - v_u(B_i^c - B_i^t)]^+ \\ \beta_i^{t,k+1} = [\beta_i^{t,k} - v_\beta(B_i^t - (B_i^c - B_0D))]^+ \\ \alpha_i^{t,k+1} = [\alpha_i^{t,k} - v_\alpha B_i^t]^+ \end{cases} \tag{17}$$

3.3 Battery Management Strategy

It can be seen from the sampling rate formula (14) that the sampling rate is related to the battery level under the condition of battery degradation and limited discharge space. We demonstrate the following lemma, which optimizes the sampling rate of nodes at different battery energy levels to maintain a reasonable energy level. Theoretical estimation of the life cycle of cognitive wireless sensors is also solved.

Lemma 1: When $B_i^c - B_0D > 0$, if the battery energy level meet $B_i^c - B_0D \leq B_i^t \leq B_i^c$, $r_i^t = 1/\eta_i^t$. If the battery energy level is equal to $B_i^c - B_0D$, then $r_i^t = [U'^{-1}(\eta_i^t - \sigma_i^t - \beta_i^t)g_i)]^+$, if the battery energy level is equal to B_i^c, then $r_i^t = [U'^{-1}(\eta_i^t - \sigma_i^t + u_i^t)g_i)]^+$.

When $B_i^c - B_0D \leq 0$, if the battery energy level meet $0 \leq B_i^t \leq B_i^c$, then $r_i^t = 1/\eta_i^t$. If the battery energy level is equal to 0, then $r_i^t = [1/(\eta_i^t - \sigma_i^t)]^+$, if the battery energy level is equal to B_i^c, then $r_i^t = [U'^{-1}(\eta_i^t - \sigma_i^t + u_i^t)g_i)]^+$.

Proof: When $B_i^c - B_0 D > 0$, if the battery energy level meet $B_i^c - B_0 D \leq B_i^t \leq B_i^c$, it is easy to know by the slackness conditions (13): $u_i^t = 0, \alpha_i^t = 0, \beta_i^t = 0$, from sampling rate formula (14): $r_i^t = 1/\eta_i^t$. Also, if the battery energy level is equal to $B_i^c - B_0 D, \beta_i^t > 0, u_i^t = 0, \alpha_i^t = 0$, via calculation, $r_i^t = [U'^{-1}(\eta_i^t - \sigma_i^t - \beta_i^t)g_i)]^+$, if the battery energy level is equal to $B_i^c, u_i^t > 0, \beta_i^t = 0, \alpha_i^t = 0$, via calculation, $r_i^t = [U'^{-1}(\eta_i^t - \sigma_i^t + u_i^t)g_i)]^+$.

When $B_i^c - B_0 D \leq 0$, if the battery energy level meet $0 \leq B_i^t \leq B_i^c$, it is Easy to know by slackness conditions (13): $u_i^t = 0, \alpha_i^t = 0, \beta_i^t = 0$, from sampling rate formula (14): $r_i^t = 1/\eta_i^t$. Also, if the battery energy level is equal to 0, $\alpha_i^t > 0, u_i^t = 0, \beta_i^t = 0$, via calculation, $r_i^t = [1/(\eta_i^t - \sigma_i^t)]^+$, if the battery energy level is equal to $B_i^c, u_i^t > 0, \beta_i^t = 0, \alpha_i^t = 0$, via calculation, $r_i^t = [U'^{-1}(\eta_i^t - \sigma_i^t + u_i^t)g_i)]^+$.

According to the Eq. (3), the relationship between the battery discharge space and the sensor network life cycle can be approximated. We denote C_{T_n} as the battery capacity of the nth charge and discharge cycle, t_n is the length of the nth charge and discharge cycle, the amount of battery degradation in the nth time slot: $\Delta q = C_{T_n} - C_{T_{n-1}}$ and D_{min} is the minimum discharge space. It can be expressed as:

$$D_{min} B_0 = w(r_{min}^t)t_n \tag{18}$$

Where

$$\omega(r_{min}^t) = e_\tau + e_i^s r_{min}^t \tag{19}$$

The amount of battery capacity degradation during the nth charge and discharge cycle is:

$$\Delta q = \int_0^{t_n} \lambda e^{\theta(1-\frac{B_L^t}{B_0})} dt \tag{20}$$

The number of charge and discharge cycles during the sensor life cycle $N_{cyc}(D)$ is:

$$N_{cyc}(D) = \int_{D_{min} B_0}^{B_0} \frac{1}{\Delta q} dB \tag{21}$$

So, the life cycle of the sensor approximately is:

$$T \cong \sum_{n=1}^{N_{cyc}(D)} t_n \tag{22}$$

The detailed steps of the proposed algorithm are as follows:

Adaptive sampling rate control algorithm (ASRC)

Input: network topology configuration, energy consumption rate, energy harvesting rate, link capacity, initial battery level, depth of discharge, life cycle T.

Output: Network utility $U(r_i^t)$.

Initialization: let the number of iteration k=1, each node starts with an arbitrary Lagrangian multiplier ;

Repeat

    for each node i=1,...,N **do**

Each node sends $\lambda_i^t, u_i^t, \beta_i^t, \alpha_i^t$ to the sensor node $j, j \in A(i)$, collecting and forwarding information from neighboring nodes, and calculate $\eta_i^t, \sigma_i^t, \zeta_i^t$ according to the intermediate variable Eq. (9);

    for each time slot t=1,...,T **do**

The node battery level state is updated, according to the battery level state, each node adaptively adjust sampling rate by the Lemma 1;

Each node locally updates the Lagrangian multiplier according to Eq. (17);

End

k=k+1;

until λ, u, σ converge within a small range;

---

4 Simulation Results and Analysis

In this section, simulation results are provided to demonstrate the performance of the proposed ASRC algorithm and are compared with QuickFix in [5]. Figure 2 shows the simple network topology. All the results are obtained by MATLAB.

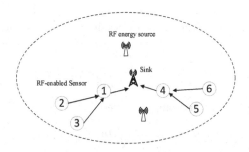

Fig. 2. Network topology

We consider the 20*20 m area, 6 sensor nodes are equipped with RF energy harvesting capability and cognitive function. For calculation conveniently, it is assumed that the sensor nodes are symmetrically distributed around the sink. Transmission power is 3 W. The energy consumption rate for sampling, transmitting and receiving are 100nJ/bit, 150nJ/bit, 158nJ/bit, respectively [4], and the energy consumed by spectrum sensing is 0.1 mJ/s. The link capacity is 2 kbps, Table 1 shows other detailed simulation parameters.

Table 1. Simulation parameters

Parameter	Value
RF harvesting band	900 MHz
Initial battery capacity	10 J
Initial battery level	0 J
Battery degradation parameter λ, θ	0.035, 2
Harvesting efficiency	0.9
Antenna gain G_s, G_r	8, 2
Path loss factor	2

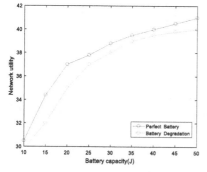

Fig. 3. Battery capacity impact on network utility

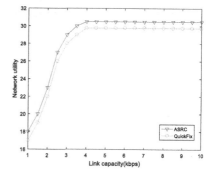

Fig. 4. Link capacity impact on network utility

In Fig. 3, we compare the impact of perfect battery and battery degradation on network utility. The ASRC algorithm considers the exponential decay model, so the perfect battery has better utility. But ASRC algorithm can adaptively adjust the sampling rate according to the battery level. It is more practical for those nodes in harsh environments.

In Fig. 4, we evaluate the impact of link capacity on network utility. Compared with QuickFix algorithm, ASRC effectively improves the network utility. Because the energy constraint of QuickFix algorithm only considers the node consumption rate not exceeding the energy harvesting rate. The excess energy collected cannot save the battery for later use, so it cannot be flexibly use in the time range.

Figure 5 shows that depth of discharge (D) impact on network utility. When D = 0.1 to D = 0.4, the network utility is improved which can also increase the accuracy of environmental monitoring. When D = 0.4 to D = 1, the network utility cannot be continuously improved due to the node link capacity is fixed. When D < 0.036, the battery discharge space does not guarantee the minimum communication requirements of the sensor node, so it is not considered.

Figure 6 shows that the curve of life cycle with depth of discharge. The two curves are very close. It can be seen that the life cycle of the theoretical calculation and the

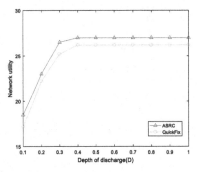

Fig. 5. Depth of discharge (D) impact on network utility

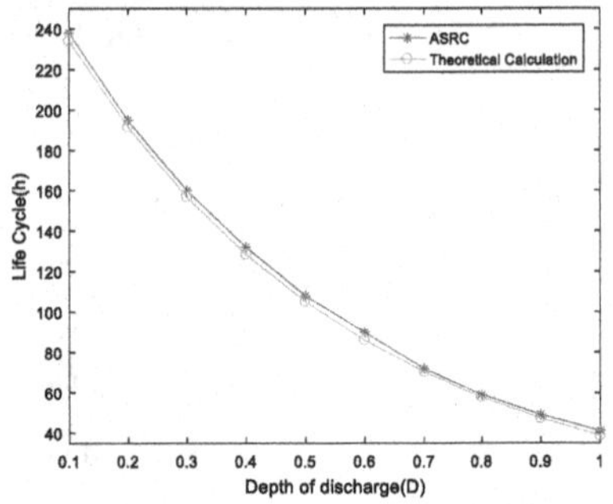

Fig. 6. Depth of discharge (D) impact on the life cycle

ASRC algorithm are almost same under the same discharge space, indicating that depth of discharge determines the life cycle of the wireless sensor.

5   Conclusion

In this paper, a novel cognitive wireless sensor network based on RF energy harvesting is considered. We have proposed a sampling rate control algorithm called ASRC for maximizing network utility under battery capacity degradation to manage battery energy. Also, we take the node link constraints into account. The results indicate that the proposed algorithm is more practical as compared to the existing algorithm for energy management in EH-CRSN. In future, we will jointly optimize sample rate and routing based on the characteristics of battery degradation to maximize network utility.

References

1. Aslam, S., Ejaz, W., Ibnkahla, M.: Energy and spectral efficient cognitive radio sensor networks for Internet of Things. IEEE Internet Things J. **5**(4), 3220–3233 (2018)
2. Ren, J., Hu, J., Zhang, D., Guo, H., Zhang, Y., Shen, X.: RF energy harvesting and transfer in cognitive radio sensor networks: opportunities and challenges. IEEE Commun. Mag. **56**(1), 104–110 (2018)
3. Deng, R., Zhang, Y., He, S., Chen, J., Shen, X.: Maximizing network utility of rechargeable sensor networks with spatiotemporally coupled constraints]. IEEE J. Sel. Areas Commun. **34**(5), 1307–1319 (2016)
4. Zhao, C., Chen, S., Wu, C., Chen, F., Ji, Y.: Accelerated sampling optimization for RF energy harvesting wireless sensor network. IEEE Access **6**, 52161–52168 (2018)
5. Liu, R.S., Sinha, P., Koksal, C.E.: Joint energy management and resource allocation in rechargeable sensor networks. In: 2010 Proceedings IEEE INFOCOM, pp. 1–9. IEEE, March 2010
6. Zhang, Y., He, S., Chen, J., Sun, Y., Shen, X.S.: Distributed sampling rate control for rechargeable sensor nodes with limited battery capacity. IEEE Trans. Wireless Commun. **12**(6), 3096–3106 (2013)
7. Tutuncuoglu, K., Yener, A., Ulukus, S.: Optimum policies for an energy harvesting transmitter under energy storage losses. IEEE J. Sel. Areas Commun. **33**(3), 467–481 (2015)

8. Michelusi, N., Badia, L., Carli, R., Corradini, L., Zorzi, M.: Energy management policies for harvesting-based wireless sensor devices with battery degradation. IEEE Trans. Commun. **61**(12), 4934–4947 (2013)
9. Lu, X., Wang, P., Niyato, D., Kim, D.I., Han, Z.: Wireless networks with RF energy harvesting: a contemporary survey. IEEE Commun. Surv. Tutor. **17**(2), 757–789 (2014)
10. Ren, J., Zhang, Y., Deng, R., Zhang, N., Zhang, D., Shen, X.S.: Joint channel access and sampling rate control in energy harvesting cognitive radio sensor networks. IEEE Trans. Emerg. Top. Comput. **7**(1), 149–161 (2016)

Multipath and Distorted Detection Based on Multi-correlator (Workshop)

Rongtao Qin[1,2(✉)]

[1] BeiHang University, XueYuan Road No.37, HaiDian District, Beijing, China
504932624@qq.com
[2] Hefei Innovation Research Institute, BeiHang University, Hefei, Anhui, China

Abstract. With the advent of new Global Navigation Satellite Systems (GNSS) and signals, the signal quality monitoring techniques for navigation signals also need to be updated. In the traditional satellite signal integrity detection, the multi-correlator processing method is commonly used in signal quality monitoring to detect if a signal is distorted. This method often assumes that multipath signals have been eliminated, avoiding multipath signals from interfering with the detection results. However, if there is a multipath signal that has not been eliminated, since the correlation functions of the multipath signal and the distorted signal have a certain similarity, if the detection method without considering the multipath effect is used, here is a case where the multipath signal is erroneously detected as a distorted signal. Since the influence of the multipath signal and the distorted signal on the positioning result is very different, it is necessary to distinguish the two signals during the detection process. In this paper, the model of multipath signal and distorted signal is discussed for the new generation GNSS signal (BOC signal). Based on the characteristics of the correlation functions of these two models, a multi-correlator range setting method is proposed, and the appropriate detection values are selected, which can effectively distinguish multipath signals and distorted signals at the relevant peak levels.

Keywords: Multi-correlator · Multipath signal · Distorted signal

1 Introduction

The quality of satellite navigation signals is directly related to the user's positioning, navigation, and timing service performance. When the satellite fails for some reason, the navigation signal will be distorted in the time domain. At this time, the receiver needs to inform the user of the availability of the satellite signal in time. As an effective detection mechanism, signal quality monitoring (SQM) technology has received extensive attention. SQM is favored by multipath signals and distorted signals for its simplicity and efficiency. It is highly autonomous and does not require external dependencies [1].

For distorted signals, the International Civil Aviation Organization (ICAO) proposed a 2nd-Order Step (20S) threat model for GNSS signals [2, 3]. The model describes the anomalous waveform, or evil waveform (EWF), as the combination of a second-order

H. Gao et al. (Eds.): ChinaCom 2019, LNICST 313, pp. 328–337, 2020.
https://doi.org/10.1007/978-3-030-41117-6_27

ringing (analog failure mode) and/or a lead/lag of the pseudorandom noise code (PRN) chips. In SQM, it is important to detect the distorted signal.

The multipath signal refers to the reproduction of the original signal after the signal is reflected and scattered by the obstacle. The model of the multipath signal in the time domain is discussed in [4]. Multipath signals also have an impact on positioning. [5] discusses the effects of multipath signals on receiver performance. Usually in SQM, it is often assumed that multipath signals have been suppressed. However, if there is a multipath signal that is not suppressed and eliminated, it may interfere with the detection of the distorted signal by SQM. Therefore, it is necessary to distinguish the distorted signal and the multipath signal in SQM.

Multi-correlator technology is a commonly used signal quality monitoring method. The principle is to use the multi-correlator output information of the correlation peak to determine whether the satellite signal is distorted. Multi-correlator technology was originally used for multipath suppression. Narrow Early-minus-Late (E-L), introduced in [6], and Double Delta (DD), introduced in [7, 8], are two applications of multi-correlator technology in multipath suppression. Subsequently, multi-correlator technology has also been widely used in SQM, and the application of multi-correlator technology in SQM is discussed in [9, 10].

Based on the multipath and distorted model of the new generation GNSS signal, the multi-correlator processing method is used to monitor the satellite signal quality. Aiming at the characteristics of BOC modulation, a multi-correlator range setting method is proposed, and the appropriate detection values are selected to distinguish between normal signal, distorted signal and multipath signal.

2 Multipath and Distorted Model of New Generation GNSS Signal

2.1 New Generation GNSS Signal Model

The BOC (binary offset carrier) modulation can be regarded as the product of the baseband signal and a square wave subcarrier. BOC(m,n) is a simplified representation of BOC modulation from a square wave subcarrier of m × 1.023 MHz frequency and a pseudo code of n × 1.023 MHz chip rate.

The standard BOC modulation process can be expressed in the time domain as:

$$x(t) = s(t)\text{sgn}(\sin(2\pi f_{sc}t)) \tag{1}$$

Where t is the time, f_{sc} is the frequency of the subcarrier, $s(t)$ is the baseband signal, $\sin(2\pi f_{sc}t)$ is the sinusoidal square wave subcarrier.

When BOC modulation is used, the autocorrelation curve of the signal is no longer a unimodal case, but changes due to the values of m and n. The autocorrelation function of the BOC modulation has a plurality of peaks, and the width of the main peak is n/m chips, and the number of positive peaks is $L = 2m/n - 1$.

Since the autocorrelation main peak width of BOC modulation is narrower than that of traditional BPSK, the correlation function is better, so signal quality monitoring is easier.

2.2 Distorted Signal Model

The distorted of satellite signals is mainly caused by the abnormality of the signal generator hardware in the analog or digital part. According to the difference between analog and digital domain distorted, the typical distorted models are mainly divided into three categories: digital circuit fault (TMA), analog circuit fault (TMB) and a combination of the two (TMC). This model is also identified by the International Civil Aviation Organization (ICAO). In the distorted model defined by ICAO, there are three key parameters. Δ (chip): used to describe the leading or trailing edge of the signal than the normal position; damped oscillation frequency f_d (MHz): describes the frequency of ringing phenomenon at the edge of the signal; Damping coefficient σ (MNerpers/s): describes the attenuation factor of ringing phenomenon at the edge of the signal.

The TMA model can be modeled as the sum of a normal sequence and a Δ sequence, which is the difference between the normal sequence and its cyclically shifted sequence, expressed as:

$$x_{TMA} = x(t) + x_\Delta(t) \tag{2}$$

$$x_\Delta(t) = \begin{cases} \max[x(t - \Delta) - x(t), 0] \ \Delta \geq 0 \\ \min[x(t + \Delta) - x(t), 0] \quad else \end{cases} \tag{3}$$

The TMB model can be represented by a 2nd-Order Step system response, expressed as:

$$x_{TMB} = x(t)h_{(\sigma, f_d)}(t) \tag{4}$$

Where $h_{(\sigma, f_d)}(t)$ is the step response of the code edge, which can be expressed as:

$$h_{(\sigma, f_d)}(t) = \begin{cases} 0 & t < 0 \\ 1 - e^{-\sigma t}\left[\cos(2\pi f_d t) + \frac{\sigma}{2\pi f_d}\sin(2\pi f_d t)\right] & t \geq 0 \end{cases} \tag{5}$$

The TMC model is a hybrid model of TMA and TMB, which can be expressed as:

$$x_{TMC} = [x(t) + x_\Delta(t)]h_{(\sigma, f_d)}(t) \tag{6}$$

The ICAO model parameters that have been recognized by ICAO are given in Annex 6, Volume 10 of the International Civil Aviation Convention

2.3 Multipath Signal Model

Multipath signals are generated by the refraction and reflection of the direct signals. The multipath signal can be described by three parameters of amplitude attenuation, propagation delay and phase variation. For the sake of discussion, consider the presence of only one multipath signal. Since this paper only studies the effect of multipath effects on correlation peaks, it is only necessary to use amplitude attenuation and delay parameters to represent multipath signals (phase changes do not affect correlation peaks). The multipath signal can be expressed as:

$$x_m(t) = x(t) + \sigma_m x(t - T) \tag{7}$$

Where σ_m is the amplitude attenuation of the signal, T is the propagation delay of the signal. In general, the multipath signal amplitude is smaller than the direct signal. So, there should be $\sigma_m < 1$.

3 Multi-correlator Signal Quality Monitoring

3.1 Multi-correlator Technology

The multi-correlator technology uses a number of different interval correlators to process the received data, and judges the state of the received data according to the output of each correlator. This method can not only monitor the multipath signals contained in the input data. It also provides a more practical method for monitoring distorted waveforms.

Multi-correlator technology has a large number of applications in signal quality monitoring technology, but there is no specific standard for the range setting of multi-correlator. Moreover, when performing signal quality monitoring of a distorted signal, it is often assumed that the multipath signal has been suppressed and eliminated. If the multipath signal is not suppressed and eliminated, it may interfere with the result of signal quality monitoring and cause false alarm. To solve this problem, we propose a multi-correlator range setting method for BOC signals. On this basis, the detection values are selected to distinguish between multipath signals and distorted signals.

3.2 Multi-correlator Range Setting and Detection Values Selection

For the distorted signal model, the TMC model is a mixture of TMA model and TMB mode, so only the TMC model is considered. When $\Delta = 0.07$ $f_d = 10$ $\sigma = 2$, the correlation function of the distorted signal and the normal signal is shown as follows:

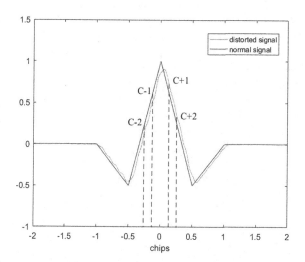

Fig. 1. The correlation function of the distorted signal and the normal signal

Figure 1 shows that the correlation function of the distorted signal oscillates compared with the normal signal, and the correlation peak appears flat, causing the symmetry of the correlation peak and the stability of the slope to be destroyed.

For the multipath signal model, when $T = 0.15$ $\sigma_m = 0.5$, the correlation function of the multipath signal and the normal signal is shown as follows:

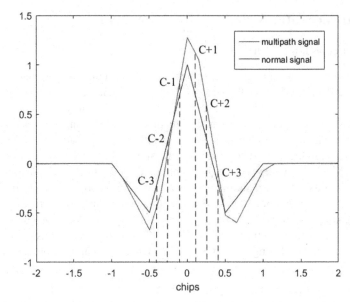

Fig. 2. The correlation function of the multipath signal and the normal signal

Figure 2 shows that the correlation function of the multipath signal is the sum of the correlation functions of the normal signal and the normal signal with delay and attenuation. The correlation peaks are no longer symmetrical, and a sudden change in slope occurs on both the rising and falling edges of the main peak.

Different from BPSK modulation, since the correlation function of the BOC modulation signal has multiple positive and negative peaks, the influence of the multipath signal based on the BOC modulation signal is more complicated. The interval between every two positive or negative peaks of the BOC signal's correlation function is n/m chips. After the attenuation and delay, these peak points are also the point at which the slope of the multipath signal's correlation function is abrupt. Since the multi-correlator is usually placed on the main peak, only the mutation points falling within the main peak range are considered. Since the distance between the two mutation points is $n/2m$, there are only two mutation points in the main peak range at the same time. There are three cases at this time:

(1) Multi-correlator range does not contain mutation points. Setting the correlators according to Fig. 2, which range is C_{-1} to C_1. Within the correlation detection range, the unilateral slopes of both sides have not been abrupt.
(2) The multi-correlator range contains one mutation point. Setting the correlators according to Fig. 2, which range is C_{-2} to C_2. Within the detection range of the correlator, there has been a sudden change in the unilateral slope of one side.
(3) The multi-correlator range contains two mutation points. Setting the correlators according to Fig. 2, which range is C_{-3} to C_3. Within the detection range of the correlator, the unilateral slopes on both sides have been abrupt.

Since the symmetry of the correlation peak and the stability of the slope of the distorted signal and the multipath signal are both destroyed, there is a possibility that the multipath signal is misjudged as a distorted signal. In order to be able to detect multipath signals, it is necessary to set the correlator range so that it must contain only one transition point. The correlator range $C_- \sim C_+$ needs to satisfy:

$$\forall T, C_+ \geq T \text{ and } C_- \geq T - \frac{n}{2m} \text{ and } C_- = -C_+ \tag{8}$$

Or

$$\forall T, C_+ \leq T \text{ and } C_- \leq T - \frac{n}{2m} \text{ and } C_- = -C_+ \tag{9}$$

If and only if $C_+ = n/4m$, the above formula holds. Therefore, when the correlator range is set to $-n/4m - n/4m$, there must be only one mutation point in the correlator range.

After setting the range of multiple correlators according to the above method, it is necessary to find a detection values to distinguish between multipath signals and distorted signals. The following detection amount is considered:

$$\Delta_i = \left| \frac{I_{-i} - I_i}{I_0} \right| i = 1, 2 \ldots n \tag{10}$$

$$R_i = I_i - I_{i+1} \, i = 1, 2 \ldots n - 1 \tag{11}$$

$$R_{-i} = I_{-i} - I_{-i-1} \, i = 1, 2 \ldots n - 1 \tag{12}$$

Where Δ_i is the Δ detection value, R_i and R_{-i} are bilateral slope detection value, I_i and I_{-i} are the output of the correlator pair which number is i. The mean and variance of Δi reflect the symmetry of the correlation peak. The mean of R_i or R_{-i} reflects whether the slope is normal. The variance of R_i or R_{-i} reflects whether the slope is abrupt.

Theoretically for normal signals, due to the symmetry of the correlation peaks, the mean and variance of Δ_i should be zero, and the mean of R_i or R_{-i} is related to the number and interval of correlators, and the variance of R_i or R_{-i} should be zero. For distorted signals, the mean and variance of Δ_i should be much larger than the normal value, and the mean of R_i or R_{-i} should be different from the normal value, and both the variances of R_i and R_{-i} should be much larger than the normal value. For multipath signals, the mean and variance of Δ_i should be much larger than the normal value, and the mean of R_i or R_{-i} should be different from the normal value, and one of the variances of R_i and R_{-i} should be much larger than the normal value, while another one should be similar to the normal value.

Assume that the detection values of the normal signals are Δ_{normal_mean}, Δ_{normal_var}, $R_{+normal\_var}$, $R_{-normal\_var}$, representing the mean of Δ_i, the variance of Δ_i, the variance of R_i, the variance of R_{-i}. The detection process can be expressed as:

$$\begin{aligned} det1 = \left| \Delta_{mean} - \Delta_{normal\_mean} \right| \quad det2 = \left| \Delta_{var} - \Delta_{normal\_var} \right| \\ det3 = \left| R_{+var} - R_{+normal\_var} \right| \quad det4 = \left| R_{-var} - R_{-normal\_var} \right| \end{aligned} \tag{13}$$

Where Δ_{mean} is the mean of the detected Δ_i, Δ_{var} is the variance of the detected Δ_i, R_{+var} is the variance of the detected R_i, R_{-var} is the variance of the detected R_{-i}. By comparing the values of the above four equations and the thresholds, the type of signal can be determined. When all four values are smaller than the thresholds, it can be considered as a normal signal. When all four values are larger than the thresholds, it can be considered as a distorted signal. When three values are larger than the thresholds and one value is smaller than the threshold, it can be considered as a multipath signal.

4 Multi-correlator Simulation Analysis

4.1 Multipath Signal Simulation Analysis

For the convenience of discussion, it is assumed that the normal signal is the BOC(1,1) signal.

For the multipath signal model, the correlation peak of the multipath signal can be obtained by taking different parameters, as follows (Fig. 3):

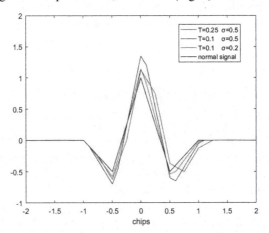

Fig. 3. Multipath signal correlation function

According to the multi-correlator range setting method proposed in Sect. 3.2, set the number of correlator pairs to 10 pairs, whose unilateral range is $n/40m–n/4m$ chips and interval is $n/40m$ chips.

For the normal signal model and the multipath signal model under different parameters, the mean and variance of the detection values are shown in the following table:

Table 1 shows that the mean and variance of Δ_i of multipath signals are significantly higher than those of normal signals. The mean of R_i and R_{-i} of multipath signals are significantly different from those of normal signals. The variance of R_{-i} of multipath signals is similar to that of normal signals. And the variance of R_i of multipath signals is significantly higher than that of normal signals.

Table 1. Detection values of normal signal and the multipath signal

Detection values	Normal signal	$T = 0.125$ $\sigma_m = 0.5$	$T = 0.2$ $\sigma_m = 0.5$	$T = 0.2$ $\sigma_m = 0.2$
Mean of Δ_i	1.67×10^{-17}	0.2285	0.3249	0.1444
Variance of Δ_i	1.26×10^{-33}	0.0065	0.0240	0.0047
Mean of R_i	0.0750	0.0791	0.0541	0.0666
Variance of R_i	8.30×10^{-33}	0.0014	9.72×10^{-4}	1.56×10^{-4}
Mean of R_{-i}	0.0750	0.1125	0.1125	0.0900
Variance of R_{-i}	1.24×10^{-32}	2.81×10^{-32}	2.42×10^{-32}	2.82×10^{-32}

4.2 Distorted Signal Simulation Analysis

Because the GPS system uses BPSK modulation, the GLONASS system uses BOC modulation, so the parameter range is selected according to the GLONASS system from the ICAO model parameters.

For the distorted signal model, the correlation peak of the distorted signal can be obtained by taking different parameters, as follows (Fig. 4):

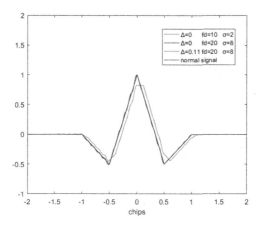

Fig. 4. Distorted signal correlation function

Also set the number of correlator pairs to 10 pairs, whose unilateral range is $n/40m-n/4m$ chips and interval is $n/40m$ chips.

For the normal signal model and the distorted signal model under different parameters, the mean and variance of the two detection values are shown in the following table:

Table 2 shows that the mean and variance of Δ_i of distorted signals are significantly higher than those of normal signals. The variances of R_i and R_{-i} of multipath signals are significantly higher than that of normal signals. When Δ is very large, f_d and σ are

Table 2. Detection values of normal signal and the distorted signal

Detection values	Normal signal	$\Delta = 0.11$ $f_d = 10$ $\sigma = 2$	$\Delta = 0.05$ $f_d = 15$ $\sigma = 5$	$\Delta = 0$ $f_d = 20$ $\sigma = 8$
Mean of Δ_i	1.67×10^{-17}	0.3557	0.1668	0.0112
Variance of Δ_i	1.26×10^{-33}	0.0125	5.97×10^{-4}	6.07×10^{-5}
Mean of R_i	0.0750	0.0778	0.0744	0.0747
Variance of R_i	8.30×10^{-33}	4.43×10^{-4}	1.75×10^{-5}	5.70×10^{-6}
Mean of R_{-i}	0.0750	0.452	0.685	0.0765
Variance of R_{-i}	1.24×10^{-32}	0.0019	5.28×10^{-4}	1.80×10^{-4}

very small, the means of R_i and R_{-i} of distorted signals are significantly different from those of normal signals. However, when Δ is very small, f_d and σ are very large, the means of R_i and R_{-i} of distorted signals are similar to those of normal signals.

4.3 Multipath and Distorted Signal Comparison

As can be seen from the above, both multipath and distorted signals have an effect on the correlation peak, causing the detection values to change.

In the usual signal quality monitoring, the main purpose is to detect the distorted signal. As can be seen from the analysis in Sect. 3.2, if set the threshold of the mean of Δ_i, the variance of Δ_i and the variances of R_i and R_{-i}, we can accurately distinguish between the distorted signal and the normal signal.

According to the steps in Sect. 3.2, the $det1$ $det2$ $det3$ $det4$ values of the multipath signal and the distorted signal are calculated separately, shown in the following table:

Table 3 shows that the multipath signals under each parameter have three values that are significantly greater than zero, while the other value is almost equal to zero. The four values of the distorted signals under each parameter are significantly greater than zero. This is consistent with our theoretical value, which can be used to determine whether the signal is a multipath signal or a distorted signal.

Table 3. Det values of multipath signal and the distorted signal

Det values	Multipath $T = 0.125$ $\sigma_m = 0.5$	Multipath $T = 0.2$ $\sigma_m = 0.5$	Multipath $T = 0.2$ $\sigma_m = 0.2$	Distorted $\Delta = 0.11$ $f_d = 10$ $\sigma = 2$	Distorted $\Delta = 0.05$ $f_d = 15$ $\sigma = 5$	Distorted $\Delta = 0$ $f_d = 20$ $\sigma = 8$
det1	0.2285	0.3249	0.1444	0.3557	0.1668	0.0112
det2	0.0065	0.0240	0.0047	0.0125	5.97×10^{-4}	6.07×10^{-5}
det3	0.0014	9.72×10^{-4}	1.56×10^{-4}	4.43×10^{-4}	1.75×10^{-5}	5.70×10^{-6}
det4	1.57×10^{-32}	1.18×10^{-32}	1.58×10^{-32}	0.0019	5.28×10^{-4}	1.80×10^{-4}

In the actual situation, due to the various noises, the correlation curve is not as ideal as the simulation. Therefore, when setting the threshold, it is necessary to count the detection value of the normal signal multiple times under actual conditions. The threshold is set according to the statistical characteristics of the detection values, so that the false alarm and the missed alarm probability meet the requirements.

5 Conclusion

In this paper, for the new generation GNSS Signal, the model of multipath signal and distorted signal are discussed. In order to be able to distinguish these kinds of signals using multi-correlator technology, according to the characteristics of these kinds of signal correlation functions, a multi-correlator range setting method for BOC signals is proposed. Based on this method, we have selected several suitable detection values. By analyzing the detection characteristics of the three signals, we can effectively distinguish the three signals. Finally, the model of multipath signal and distorted signal is simulated and verified. The simulation results show that the multipath correlator range setting method and the selected detection value can be used to distinguish the multipath signal and the distorted signal effectively.

References

1. Sun, C., Cheong, J.W., Dempster, A., Demicheli, L., Cetin, E., Zhao, H.: Performance assessment of multi-metric joint detection technique for anti-spoofing. In: IGNSS, pp. 1–15, February 2018
2. Phelts, R.E.: Multicorrelator techniques for robust mitigation of threats to GPS signal quality. Ph.D. thesis, Stanford University, CA (2001)
3. Phelts, R.E., Akos, D.M., Enge, P.K.: Robust Signal Quality Monitoring and Detection of Evil Waveforms, ION-GPS-2000, Salt lake City, UT, USA (2000)
4. Kaplan Elliott, D., Hegarty Christopher, J.: Understanding GPS Principles and Applications, 2nd edn. Publishing House of Electronics Industry, Beijing (2007)
5. Liu, L., Amin, M.G.: Tracking performance and average error analysis of GPS discriminators in multi-path. Signal Process. **89**, 1224–1239 (2009)
6. Van Dierendonck, A.J., et al.: Theory and performance of narrow correlator spacing in a GPS receiver. Navig. J. US Inst. Navig. **39**(3), 265–283 (1992)
7. McGraw, G.A., Braasch, M.S.: GNSS Multipath mitigation using gated and high resolution correlator concepts. In: Proceedings of the US Institute of Navigation NTM, Nashville, USA (1999)
8. Garin, L., Rousseau, J.-M.: Enhanced strobe correlator – multipath rejection for code and carrier. In: Proceedings of the US Institute of Navigation GPS, USA (1997)
9. Akos, D.M., Phelts, R.E., Mitelman, A., Pullen, S., Enge, P.: GPS-SPS signal quality monitoring (SQM). In: Position Location and Navigation Symposium, Conference Proceedings Addendum, IEEE PLANS (2000)
10. Phelts, R.E., Akos, D., Enge, P.: Signal quality monitoring validation. ICAO, GNSSP WG-B, WP/29, Seattle, WA (2000)

Delay Optimization-Based Joint Route Selection and Resource Allocation Algorithm for Cognitive Vehicular Ad Hoc Networks (Workshop)

Changzhu Liu$^{(\boxtimes)}$, Rong Chai, Shangxin Peng, and Qianbin Chen

Key Lab of Mobile Communication Technology,
Chongqing University of Posts and Telecommunications, Chongqing 400065, China
1039410361@qq.com, {chairong,chenqb}@cqupt.edu.cn,
1585975437@qq.com

Abstract. Cognitive vehicular ad-hoc networks (CVANETs) are expected to improve spectrum utilization efficiently and offer both infotainment and safety services for vehicles. In this paper, the joint route selection and resource allocation problem is considered for CVANETs. Taking into account the lifetime of transmission links, we first propose a candidate link selection method which selects the transmission links satisfying the link lifetime constraint. Then stressing the importance of transmission delay, we formulate the joint route selection and resource allocation problem as an end-to-end transmission delay minimization problem. As the formulated optimization problem is a complicated integer nonlinear problem, which cannot be solved conveniently, we equivalently transform the original problem into two subproblems, i.e., resource allocation subproblem for candidate links and route selection subproblem. Solving the two optimization subproblems by applying the K shortest path algorithm and the Dijkstra algorithm, respectively, we can obtain the joint route selection and resource allocation strategy. Simulation results demonstrate the effectiveness of the proposed algorithm.

Keywords: Cognitive vehicular ad hoc networks · Route selection · Resource allocation · Channel allocation · Time-frequency resource block

1 Introduction

Cognitive vehicular ad hoc networks (CVANETs) have received considerable attention from both academia and industry in recent years. In CVANETs, cognitive vehicles (CVs) equipped with onboard units are allowed to share the spectrum resource of primary vehicles (PVs) in an opportunistic manner, and transmitting both infotainment and safety related information through interacting with roadside units and other vehicles [1,2].

In CVANETs, in the case that the direct connection between one cognitive source vehicle (CSV) and cognitive destination vehicle (CDV) pair is inaccessible, multi-hop cognitive relay vehicles (CRVs) can be applied to forward the data packets for the CSV

© ICST Institute for Computer Sciences, Social Informatics and Telecommunications Engineering 2020
Published by Springer Nature Switzerland AG 2020. All Rights Reserved
H. Gao et al. (Eds.): ChinaCom 2019, LNICST 313, pp. 338–350, 2020.
https://doi.org/10.1007/978-3-030-41117-6_28

so that the successful information interaction between the CSV and CDV pair can be achieved. It is apparent that various route selection and resource allocation strategies may result in different user quality of service (QoS) as well as network transmission performance.

Some recent research works address the problem of route selection in CVANETs [3–5]. The authors in [3] study the route selection problem in software-defined vehicular networks and propose a cognitive routing protocol which aims to achieve the maximal end-to-end link lifetime. In [4], the authors present a software defined cognitive network framework of the Internet of vehicles and propose a reinforcement learning (RL)-based algorithm which selects the route selection strategies to maximize the rewards of the vehicles overtime. A cognitive anypath vehicular routing protocol is proposed in [5]. By jointly considering the geographical location information and the perceived channel information of various vehicles, the candidate vehicles which have available channel resources and are located close to the destination vehicles are selected as the relay vehicles.

Resource allocation problem in CVANETs is considered in [6–8]. In [6], the vehicles are categorized into primary providers (PPs) that intend to transmit safety-related messages and secondary providers (SPs) with non-safety information to be delivered. A prioritized optimal channel allocation approach is proposed to improve channel utilization and an optimal channel-hopping and channel allocation strategy is designed for the SPs to achieve the maximum throughput.

The authors in [7] study the problem of reliable adaptive resource management for CVANETs and design a distributed and adaptive resource management controller, which allows the optimal exploitation of cognitive radio and data fusion in the networks. The resource management problem is formulated as a constrained stochastic network utility maximization problem and the optimal cognitive resource manager is designed to dynamically allocate the access time windows at the serving roadside units, together with the access rates and traffic flows at the served vehicular clients. The problem of resource allocation for video streaming in CVANETs is studied in [8]. A semi-Markov decision process-based resource allocation scheme is proposed to facilitate video streaming application. By jointly considering the states of background users and vehicle users, and the availability of cognitive bands, an optimal resource allocation algorithm is proposed to improve the video streaming quality while guaranteeing the call-level performance of the background users.

Route selection problem or resource allocation problem in CVANETs has been studied independently in [3–8]. In this paper, we jointly consider route selection and resource allocation problem in CVANETs. Taking into account the link lifetime, we first propose a candidate link selection method which selects the candidate links satisfying the link lifetime constraints. Then stressing the importance of data transmission delay, we characterize the end-to-end data transmission delay of the CSV and CDV pair, and formulate the joint route selection and resource allocation problem as an end-to-end transmission delay minimization problem. Since the formulated optimization problem is a complicated nonlinear integer optimization problem which cannot be solved conveniently using traditional optimization tools, we transform the original problem into two subproblems, i.e., route selection subproblem of candidate links and resource allocation subproblem and solve the two subproblems by means of the K shortest path algorithm and the Dijkstra algorithm, respectively.

The remainder of this paper is organized as follows. Section 2 describes the system model considered in this paper. In Sect. 3, we propose a candidate link selection method. In Sect. 4, the optimization problem formulation is presented. The solution to the formulated optimization problem is described in Sect. 5 and the simulation results are described in Sect. 6. Finally, we conclude the paper in Sect. 7.

2 System Model

In this paper, we consider a CVANET consisting of L PVs and a number of CVs, where a CSV intends to transmit data packets to a CDV through a number of CRVs. For convenience, we let V_i denote the ith CRV, $1 \leq i \leq M$, where M denotes the number of the CRVs in the network, let V_0 and V_{M+1} denote respectively the CSV and the CDV. Figure 1 shows the network model considered in this paper.

We assume that each PV is allocated one licensed channel, and different licensed channels are allocated to various PVs so as to avoid the interference among the PVs. We denote the set of the licensed channels of the PVs as $C = \{C_1, C_2, ..., C_L\}$, where C_l denotes the licensed channel of the lth PV, $1 \leq l \leq L$. We further assume that the overlay spectrum sharing mode is applied between the PVs and the CVs. More specifically, the CVs are allowed to access the idle channels which are not occupied by the PVs. In the case that one PV initializes a data transmission on its allocated channel, the CVs transmitting on the channel should terminate the communications, wait on the channel or switch to other available channels in order to avoid causing interference to the PV.

In this paper, we assume that the data transmission of both the PVs and the CVs is in the unit of time slots with fixed time duration. More specifically, a number of continuous time slots are assigned to the PVs and the CVs for conducting data transmission. It is also assumed that by applying efficient spectrum prediction mechanism, the channel occupancy status of the PVs during a certain period of time can be obtained. Let $\alpha_{l,t} \in \{0, 1\}$ denote the time-frequency resource block (RB) identifier occupied by the lth PV, i.e., $\alpha_{l,t} = 1$, if the lth PV occupies the lth channel at the tth time slot, otherwise, $\alpha_{l,t} = 0$, $1 \leq l \leq L$, $1 \leq t \leq N_0$, where N_0 denotes the total number of time slots.

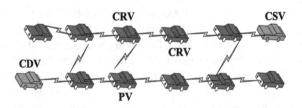

Fig. 1. System model

3   Candidate Link Selection Method

The rapid movement of the vehicles may result in communications link failure in the CVANET. To characterize the stability of transmission links connecting two vehicles, we introduce the concept of link lifetime which is defined as the time duration from connection establishment to link disconnection.

Let $L_{i,j}^0$ denote the link between V_i and V_j, x_i and y_i denote the position of V_i on horizontal direction and vertical axis, respectively, $v_{i,x}$ and $v_{i,y}$ denote the speed of V_i at the corresponding direction, D_i^t and D_i^r denote the transmission range and receiving range of V_i, respectively, and $T_{i,j}$ denote the lifetime of $L_{i,j}^0$. Denote $D_{i,j}^{(1)}$ as the distance between V_i and V_j at current time slot, we obtain

$$D_{i,j}^{(1)} = \sqrt{(x_i - x_j)^2 + (y_i - y_j)^2}. \tag{1}$$

Assuming at current time slot, V_i is capable of transmitting data packet to V_j directly, i.e., $D_{i,j}^{(1)} \leq \min\{D_i^t, D_i^r\}$.

Denote $D_{i,j}^{(2)}$ as the distance between V_i and V_j after time slot t, we obtain [9]

$$D_{i,j}^{(2)} = \sqrt{\Delta x_{i,j}^2 + \Delta y_{i,j}^2} \tag{2}$$

where $\Delta x_{i,j}$ and $\Delta y_{i,j}$ are given by

$$\begin{aligned}
\Delta x_{i,j} &= x_i + v_{i,x}t - x_j - v_{j,x}T_{i,j}, \\
\Delta y_{i,j} &= y_i + v_{i,y}t - y_j - v_{j,y}T_{i,j}.
\end{aligned} \tag{3}$$

The life time of $L_{i,j}^0$ can be expressed as

$$T_{i,j} = \max\{t : D_{i,j}^{(2)} \leq \min\{D_i^t, D_i^r\}\}. \tag{4}$$

To ensure stable transmission, we can select the transmission links of which the lifetime is larger than a given minimum lifetime threshold. Let $T_i^{\min}$ denote the minimum link lifetime of V_i, the candidate link set of V_i can be expressed as

$$\Psi_i = \left\{ L_{i,j}^0 | T_{i,j} \geq T_i^{\min}, 0 \leq i, j \leq M + 1, i \neq j \right\}. \tag{5}$$

Let $L_{ij} \in \Psi_i$, $0 \leq i, j \leq M + 1, i \neq j$ denote the candidate link of V_i, among all the candidate links of V_i, the links offering the optimal transmission performance will be selected and the corresponding optimal resource allocation strategy will be designed, as discussed in following sections.

4   Optimization Problem Formulation

In this paper, to jointly design route selection and resource allocation algorithm for CSV and CRVs in the CVANET, we examine the end-to-end transmission delay of the candidate routes between the CSV and the CDV and formulate the joint optimization problem as an end-to-end transmission delay minimization problem.

4.1 Objective Function Formulation

The end-to-end transmission delay of the candidate routes between the CSV and the CDV can be expressed as

$$D = \sum_{i=0}^{M} \sum_{j=1,j\neq i}^{M+1} \tau \beta_{i,j} N_{i,j} \tag{6}$$

where τ denotes the duration of the time slot, $\beta_{i,j}$ is the binary route selection variable, $\beta_{i,j} = 1$ indicates that $L_{i,j}$ is selected to transmit the data packets for the CSV; otherwise, $\beta_{i,j} = 0$, and $N_{i,j}$ is the minimum number of the time slots required to successfully transmit the data packets of the CSV through $L_{i,j}$. Let S denote the size of the data packets of the CSV, $N_{i,j}$ should meet the following constraints:

$$\sum_{l=1}^{L} \sum_{t=1}^{N_{i,j}-1} \tau \delta_{i,j,l,t} R_{i,j,l} < S, \tag{7}$$

$$\sum_{l=1}^{L} \sum_{t=1}^{N_{i,j}} \tau \delta_{i,j,l,t} R_{i,j,l} \geq S \tag{8}$$

where $\delta_{i,j,l,t}$ denotes the resource allocation variable of $L_{i,j}$, i.e., $\delta_{i,j,l,t} = 1$ if the lth channel is allocated to $L_{i,j}$ at the tth time slot, otherwise, $\delta_{i,j,l,t} = 0$, and $R_{i,j,l}$ denotes the data rate of $L_{i,j}$ when transmitting data packets on the lth channel, which can be expressed as

$$R_{i,j,l} = B_l \log_2 \left(1 + \frac{P_i h_{i,j,l}^2}{\sigma^2} \right) \tag{9}$$

where B_l is the bandwidth of the lth channel, P_i is the transmit power of V_i, $h_{i,j,l}$ denotes the channel gain of $L_{i,j}$ on the lth channel and σ^2 is the power of channel noise.

Let $R_{i,j}$ denote the data rate of $L_{i,j}$, we can express $R_{i,j}$ in terms of $R_{i,j,l}$ as follows

$$R_{i,j} = \sum_{l=1}^{L} \sum_{t=1}^{N_{i,j}} \delta_{i,j,l,t} R_{i,j,l}. \tag{10}$$

4.2 Optimization Constraints

To design the optimal joint route selection and resource allocation strategies which minimizes the total end-to-end transmission delay, we should consider a number of optimization constraints.

Flow Conservation Constraints. While the data packets of the CSV may transmit via various CRVs, route selection constraints should be satisfied at the CSV, the CDV and the CRVs, i.e.,

$$C1 : \sum_{j=1}^{M+1} \beta_{0,j} = 1, \tag{11}$$

$$C2 : \sum_{i=0}^{M} \beta_{i,M+1} = 1, \tag{12}$$

$$C3 : \sum_{i=0,i\neq j}^{M} \beta_{i,j} = \sum_{i'=1,i'\neq j}^{M+1} \beta_{j,i'}, 1 \leq j \leq M. \tag{13}$$

Time Slot Allocation Constraints. In the case that $L_{i,j}$ is assigned to V_i, at least one time-frequency RB should be allocated to $L_{i,j}$, hence, we obtain the following constraint:

$$C4 : \beta_{i,j} \leq \sum_{l=1}^{L} \delta_{i,j,l,t}. \tag{14}$$

As it is assumed that continuous time slots should be allocated to the CSV or the CRVs, we obtain

$$C5 : \prod_{t=1}^{t'-1} \left(\sum_{i=0}^{M} \sum_{j=1,j\neq i}^{M+1} \sum_{l=1}^{L} \delta_{i,j,l,t} \right) = 1, \text{ if } \delta_{i,j,l,t'} = 1. \tag{15}$$

To avoid causing interference to the PVs, the CSV and the CRVs are only allowed to occupy the time-frequency RBs which are not used by the PVs, i.e.,

$$C6 : \delta_{i,j,k,t} \leq \alpha_{k,t}. \tag{16}$$

Both the number of time slots and the resource allocation variables should meet the conditions given in (7) and (8), for convenience, we rewrite the constraints as follows

$$C7 : \sum_{l=1}^{L} \sum_{t=1}^{N_{i,j}-1} \tau \delta_{i,j,l,t} R_{i,j,l} < S, \tag{17}$$

$$C8 : \sum_{l=1}^{L} \sum_{t=1}^{N_{i,j}} \tau \delta_{i,j,l,t} R_{i,j,l} \geq S. \tag{18}$$

Considering the practical implementation of CVs, we assume that each CV can only send data packets to at most one neighboring CV at one time slot, and can only receive data packets from at most one neighboring CV, i.e.,

$$C9 : \sum_{i=0}^{M} \delta_{i,j,l,t} + \sum_{i'=1}^{M+1} \delta_{j,i',l,t} \leq 1. \tag{19}$$

Maximum Handoff Number Constraint. As frequent handoff of CSV and CRVs may cause high signaling cost and transmission performance degradation which are highly undesired. In this paper, we assume that the number of handoff on each link should subject to a maximum number of handoff, denoted by $H^{\max}$, i.e.,

$$C10 : \sum_{t=1}^{N_{i,j}} \sum_{l=1}^{L} \sum_{l'=1,\ l'\neq l}^{L} \delta_{i,j,l,t}\delta_{i,j,l',t+1} \leq H^{\max}. \tag{20}$$

Minimum Data Rate Constraint. We assume that the data transmission of CSV should meet a minimum data rate requirement. Let $R^{\min}$ denote the minimum data rate requirement of the CSV, the actual data rate on $L_{i,j}$, denoted by $R_{i,j}$ should meet

$$C11 : R_{i,j} \geq R^{\min}. \tag{21}$$

4.3   Optimization Model

According to the aforementioned optimization objective and constraints, the optimization problem can be formulated as

$$\min_{\beta_{i,j},\delta_{i,j,l,t}} \quad D \\ \text{s.t.} \quad C1 - C11. \tag{22}$$

5   Solution to the Optimization Problem

The optimization problem formulated in (22) is a complicated nonlinear integer optimization problem that is difficult to be solved conveniently. However, by considering the lack of coupling between the resource allocation problem of one particular route and the route selection problem in the network, the original optimization problem can be equivalently transformed into two subproblems, namely, the resource allocation subproblem of candidate links and the route selection subproblem, and the two subproblems can then be solved successively.

5.1   Solution to the Resource Allocation Subproblem

In this subsection, we first assume that $L_{i,j}$ is allocated to the CSV for data transmission, i.e., $\beta_{i,j} = 1$, and simplify the joint route selection and resource allocation problem into the resource allocation subproblem of $L_{i,j}$, which can then be solved by applying the K shortest path algorithm [10].

Resource Allocation Subproblem Formulation. Under the assumption of $\beta_{i,j} = 1$, the transmission delay of $L_{i,j}$ can be calculated as

$$D_{i,j} = \sum_{l=1}^{L} \sum_{t=1}^{N_{i,j}} \tau \delta_{i,j,l,t} \frac{S}{R_{i,j,l}}, \tag{23}$$

the resource allocation subproblem of $L_{i,j}$ can be formulated as

$$\min_{\delta_{i,j,l,t}} D_{i,j} \tag{24}$$

$$\text{s.t } C4 - C11 \text{ in } (22).$$

As both τ and S are given constants, the above optimization problem is equivalent to the following problem

$$\min_{\delta_{i,j,l,t}} \sum_{l=1}^{L} \sum_{t=1}^{N_{i,j}} \delta_{i,j,l,t} \frac{1}{R_{i,j,l}} \tag{25}$$

$$\text{s.t } C4 - C11 \text{ in } (22).$$

To illustrate the resource allocation subproblem of $L_{i,j}$, we show one simple example in Table 1. Consider the case $L = 3$ and $N_{i,j} = 7$, Table I plots the unit transmission delay which is defined as the reciprocal of the data rate corresponding to particular time-frequency RBs. In Table 1, T_t denotes the tth time slot, $1 \le t \le 7$. Since PVs may initialize data transmission at certain time-frequency RBs, the CSV and CRVs cannot occupy these RBs for data transmission. For simplicity, we define the transmission delay of the CSV and CRVs at these time-frequency RBs as ∞. Since $N_{i,j}$ can be calculated based on (7) and (8), it is apparent that to solve the above optimization problem is equivalent to finding the combination of RBs within time interval between $t = 1$ and $N_{i,j}$, which offering the minimum transmission delay under the given conditions.

Table 1. Unit transmission delay of various time-frequency RBs

	T_1	T_2	T_3	T_4	T_5	T_6	T_7
C_1	$\frac{1}{R_{i,j,1}}$	∞	∞	$\frac{1}{R_{i,j,1}}$	$\frac{1}{R_{i,j,1}}$	$\frac{1}{R_{i,j,1}}$	∞
C_2	∞	$\frac{1}{R_{i,j,2}}$	$\frac{1}{R_{i,j,2}}$	∞	$\frac{1}{R_{i,j,2}}$	∞	$\frac{1}{R_{i,j,2}}$
C_3	$\frac{1}{R_{i,j,3}}$	$\frac{1}{R_{i,j,3}}$	$\frac{1}{R_{i,j,3}}$	$\frac{1}{R_{i,j,3}}$	∞	$\frac{1}{R_{i,j,3}}$	$\frac{1}{R_{i,j,3}}$

Graph Theory-Based Problem Formulation. In this subsection, we apply the graph theory, map the problem of resource allocation for $L_{i,j}$ into the route selection problem in a weighted graph and determine the optimal solution by means of the K shortest path algorithm [10].

Applying the graph theory to solve the resource allocation subproblem of $L_{i,j}$, we create a weighted directed graph, $G_0 = (V_0, E_0, W_0)$, where $V_0 = \{X_s, X_{l,t}, X_d\}$ are vertices in the graph, X_s and X_d are the introduced super source node and super destination node, respectively, $X_{l,t}, 1 \leq l \leq L, 1 \leq t \leq N_{i,j}$, denotes the time-frequency RB identifier of the lth channel at the tth time slot; $E_0 = \{E_s, E_r, E_d\}$ is the set of the connected edges between channels in adjacent time slots, $E_s = \{(X_s, X_{l,1})\}$ denotes the set of the edges connecting X_s and $X_{l,1}$, $E_r = \{(X_{l,t-1}, X_{l',t})\}$ denotes the set of edges connecting $X_{l,t-1}$ and $X_{l',t}$, $1 \leq l, l' \leq L, 2 \leq t < N_{i,j}$, $E_d = \{(X_{l,N_{i,j}-1}, X_d)\}$ denotes the set of edges connecting $X_{l,N_{i,j}-1}$ and X_d. It should be noticed that in the case of $\alpha_{l,t} = 0$, there does not exist an edge between $X_{l',t-1}$ and $X_{l,t}$, and between $X_{l,t}$ and $X_{l',t+1}$. $W_0 = \{D_{s,l}, D_{l_1,l_2,t}, D_{l,d}\}$ is the weight set of the edges, $1 \leq l_1, l_2 \leq L, 1 \leq t \leq N_{i,j}$, where $D_{s,l}$ and $D_{l,d}$ are constants representing the weight of the links between X_s and $X_{l,1}$, and the weight of the links between $X_{l,N_{i,j}}$ and X_d, respectively, $D_{l_1,l_2,t} = \frac{1}{R_{i,j,l_1-1}}$ is the unit transmission delay of the link between $X_{l_1,t-1}$ and $X_{l_2,t}$.

Figure 2 shows a graphical representation of resource allocation subproblem of $L_{i,j}$.

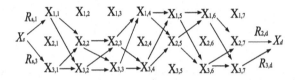

Fig. 2. Graphical representation of resource allocation subproblem.

K Shortest Path Algorithm-Based Resource Allocation Strategy. The K shortest path algorithm can be applied to find the K end-to-end routes offering the minimum weight between a source node and a destination node in a weighted directed graph.

The steps of solving the resource allocation subproblem in G_0 based on the K shortest path algorithm can be summarized as follows:

Step 1: Initialization phase
Initialize K, calculate $R_{i,j,l}$ and $T_{i,j}$ based on (7), (8) and (9).
Step 2: Find the K shortest paths
Determining the K shortest paths from X_s to X_d based on the K shortest path algorithm. Denote P_k as the kth path obtained, $1 \leq k \leq K$ and $\Phi = \{P_k, 1 \leq k \leq K\}$ as the set of the K shortest paths.
Step 3: Check handoff number condition
Calculating the number of handoff along P_k, $1 \leq k \leq K$. If P_k fails to meet the constraint C11 in (22), remove P_k from Φ.
Step 4: Find the optimal path
If $\Phi = \emptyset$, set $N_{i,j} = N_{i,j} + 1$, repeat step 1 to 3; elseif Φ only contains one path, set the path as the optimal path; else, among all the paths in Φ, select the one with the minimum delay as the optimal path.
Step 5: Determine the optimal resource allocation strategy
For the selected optimal path, map the path strategy to the optimal resource allocation strategy. More specifically, if $(X_s, X_{l,1})$ is contained in the optimal path, then

set $\delta_{i,j,l,1}^* = 1$; if $(X_{l,t-1}, X_{l,t})$ is contained in the optimal path, then set $\delta_{i,j,l,t}^* = 1$; similarly, if $(X_{l,N_{i,j}-1}, X_{\mathrm{d}})$ is contained in the optimal path, then $\delta_{i,j,l,N_{i,j}}^* = 1$.

According to the obtained resource allocation strategy, the transmission delay of $L_{i,j}$ can be calculated as

$$D_{i,j}^* = \sum_{l=1}^{L} \sum_{t=1}^{N_{i,j}} \tau \delta_{i,j,l,t}^* \frac{S}{R_{i,j,l}}. \tag{26}$$

5.2 Solution to the Route Selection Subproblem

For given resource allocation strategies of $L_{i,j}$, $1 \leq i,j \leq M, i \neq j$, we can then solve the route selection problem of the CSV. To this end, we model the CVANET as a weighted graph, and solve the optimal route selection problem between the CSV and the CDV by means of Dijkstra's Algorithm [11].

Route Selection Subproblem Formulation. Based on the obtained optimal resource allocation strategy and the minimum transmission delay of the candidate links, the corresponding end-to-end transmission delay between the CSV and the CDV can be calculated as

$$D^{\mathrm{tot}} = \sum_{i=0}^{M} \sum_{j=1, j \neq i}^{M+1} \beta_{i,j} D_{i,j}^*. \tag{27}$$

The route selection subproblem which minimizes the end-to-end transmission delay can be formulated as

$$\min_{\beta_{i,j}} D^{\mathrm{tot}} \tag{28}$$

$$\text{s.t } \mathrm{C1} - \mathrm{C4} \text{ in } (22).$$

The optimization problem (28) is the problem of determining the shortest path between two points in a given network model. By modeling the CVANET considered in this paper as a weighted directed graph in graph theory, Dijkstra's algorithm can be used to obtain the optimal route with the minimum end-to-end transmission delay [11].

Dijkstra's Algorithm-Based Optimal Route Selection Strategy. Dijkstra's algorithm is widely used to solve the shortest path problem in a weighted directed graph. In order to apply the Dijkstra's algorithm to solve the optimization problem formulated in (28), the network topology of the CVANET is modeled as a weighted directed graph $G = (V, E, W)$, where V denotes the set of CVs, i.e., $V = \{V_0, V_1, \cdots, V_{M+1}\}$, E is the candidate link set, $E = \{L_{i,j}\}$, $W = \{D_{i,j}^*\}$ is the weight set of $L_{i,j}$.

According to the Dijkstra's algorithm, the CVs in graph G are divided into unlabeled nodes and labeled nodes. All nodes are unmarked nodes at the initialization phase.

Let U^u and U^l represent the unlabeled nodes and the labeled nodes respectively, and η_i denote the optimal transmission delay between V_0 and V_i, $1 \le i \le M + 1$, we set $\eta_0 = 0$. Let $\Pr(V_i)$ denote the predecessor node of V_i, i.e., the last hop node of V_i along the path from the CSV to the CDV.

The steps to determine the shortest path between the CSV and the CDV based on Dijkstra's algorithm are as follows:

Step 1: Initialization phase
Let $\eta_i = \infty$, $1 \le i \le M + 1$. If V_i and V_j are not single-hop neighbor nodes, then $D^*_{i,j} = \infty$. Let $U^u = \{V_i, 1 \le i \le M + 1\}$, $U^l = \{V_0\}$ and $V_t = V_0$.
Step 2: Search one-hop shortest CRV of V_i
If V_i is a one-hop neighbor of V_t, calculate η_i. If $\eta_t + D^*_{t,i} < \eta_i$, then $\eta_i = \eta_t + D^*_{t,i}$. For all one-hop neighbor nodes of V_t, select the one with the shortest distance between V_t, which can be denoted as V_x, i.e.,

$$V_x = \arg\min_{L_{t,i} \in E}\{\eta_i\}, \tag{29}$$

then $\Pr(V_x) = V_t$, $U^u = U^u - \{V_x\}$, $U^l = U^l \cup \{V_x\}$, and $V_t = V_x$.
Step 3: Determine the optimal route
Repeat step 2 until $V_t = V_{M+1}$, the algorithm terminates, and the optimal route can be determined by searching $\Pr(V_x)$ in reverse order. As a result, the route with the minimum end-to-end transmission delay between the CSV and the CDV can be obtained, i.e., $\beta^*_{i,j} = \arg\min_{\beta_{i,j}}\{D^{tot}\}$.

6   Simulation Results

In this section, MATLAB simulation software is used to evaluate the performance of the proposed joint route selection and resource allocation algorithm. In the simulation, it is assumed that all the CVs are randomly distributed on a $1000\,m \times 15\,m$ road section. Simulation parameters are shown in Table 2.

In the simulation, our proposed algorithm is compared with the route selection algorithm proposed in [3] and the random channel allocation algorithm. To examine the performance of the route selection algorithm proposed in [3], we first apply our proposed resource allocation strategy on the candidate links, and then determine the optimal route selection strategy based on the algorithm proposed in [3]. To examine the performance of the random channel allocation algorithm, we first randomly select the available channel for the CSV and the CRVs and then apply our proposed end-to-end transmission delay minimization-based route selection algorithm to obtain the optimal route selection strategy.

Figure 3 shows the end-to-end transmission delay versus the number of channels. It can be seen from the figure that as the number of channels increases, the end-to-end transmission delay gradually decreases for our proposed algorithm and the algorithm proposed in [3]. This is because the diversity of channel selection results in better transmission performance. Comparing the transmission performance obtained from three algorithms, we can see that our algorithm outperforms the other two algorithms. The

Table 2. Simulation parameter list

Parameter	Value
The maximum communication range of CSV and CRVs	300 m
Number of CRVs	40
Speed of CSV, CRVs and CDV	60–80 km/h
Packet size	1280 bits
Length of time slot	5 ms
Number of channels	3–12
Channel bandwidth	1 MHz
Transmission power of CSV and CRVs	0.1–1 W
Noise power	−136 dBm
Center frequency of channels	1 GHz

reason is that the route selection algorithm proposed in [3] aims at maximizing the transmission data rate, which may result in suboptimal end-to-end transmission delay. Furthermore, as the random channel allocation algorithm randomly selects the transmission channel, thus may offer undesired transmission performance.

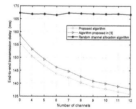

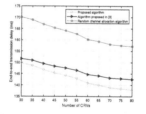

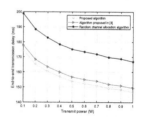

Fig. 3. End-to-end transmission delay versus the number channels.

Fig. 4. End-to-end transmission delay versus the number of CRVs.

Fig. 5. End-to-end transmission delay versus the transmit power of CSV and CRVs

Figure 4 shows the end-to-end transmission delay versus the number of CRVs. From the figure we can see that as the number of CRVs increases, the end-to-end transmission delay decreases. This is because the larger number of CRVs may offer the increased number of available transmission links and transmission routes in turn, resulting in better transmission performance. It can also be observed that compared with the other two algorithms, our proposed joint optimization algorithm enjoys desired transmission performance.

Figure 5 shows the end-to-end transmission delay versus the transmit power of the CSV and the CRVs. We can see from the figure that the end-to-end transmission delay decreases as the transmit power of the CVs increases. This is because larger transmit power offers better transmission data rate and smaller transmission delay in turn. In addition, we can also observe that the proposed joint optimization algorithm achieves the smallest end-to-end transmission delay compared with the other two algorithms.

7   Conclusions

In this paper, the problem of joint route selection and resource allocation in CVANETs is addressed. We first examine the stability of the transmission links in the network and propose a candidate link selection method which selects the transmission links satisfying the link lifetime constraint. We then formulate the joint route selection and resource allocation problem as an end-to-end transmission delay minimization problem. By equivalently transforming the original problem into two subproblems, i.e., resource allocation subproblem for candidate links and route selection subproblem and solving the two optimization subproblems by applying the K shortest path algorithm and the Dijkstra's algorithm, respectively, the optimal joint route selection and resource allocation strategy can be obtained. To examine the performance of our proposed algorithm, we compare it with the route selection algorithm proposed in [3] and the random channel allocation algorithm. Simulation results demonstrate the effectiveness of the proposed algorithm.

References

1. Jiang, C., Chen, Y., Liu, K.R.: Data-driven optimal throughput analysis for route selection in cognitive vehicular networks. IEEE J. Sel. Areas Commun. **32**, 2149–2162 (2014)
2. Miao, P., Li, P., Fang, Y.: Cooperative diversity in wireless networks: efficient protocols and outage behavior. IEEE J. Sel. Areas Commun. **30**, 760–768 (2012)
3. Ghafoor, H., Koo, I.: CR-SDVN: a cognitive routing protocol for software-defined vehicular networks. IEEE Sens. J. **18**(4), 1761–1772 (2018)
4. Wang, C., Zhang, L., Li, Z., Jiang, C.: SDCoR: software defined cognitive routing for Internet of vehicles. IEEE Internet Things J. **5**, 3513–3520 (2018)
5. Kim, W., Oh, S.Y., Gerla, M., Lee, K.C.: CoRoute: a new cognitive anypath vehicular routing protocol. Wirel. Commun. Mob. Comput. **11**(12), 1588–1602 (2011)
6. Chu, J.H., Feng, K.T., Lin, J.S.: Prioritized optimal channel allocation schemes for multi-channel vehicular networks. IEEE Trans. Mob. Comput. **14**(7), 1463–1474 (2015)
7. Cordeschi, N., Amendola, D., Baccarelli, E.: Reliable adaptive resource management for cognitive cloud vehicular networks. IEEE Trans. Veh. Technol. **64**(6), 2528–2537 (2015)
8. He, H., Shan, H., Huang, A., Sun, L.: Resource allocation for video streaming in heterogeneous cognitive vehicular networks. IEEE Trans. Veh. Technol. **65**(10), 7917–7930 (2016)
9. Qian, J., Jing, T., Huo, Y., Zhou, W., Li, Z.: A next-hop selection scheme providing long path life-time in VANETs. In: IEEE International Symposium on Personal, Indoor, and Mobile Radio Communications (PIMRC), pp. 1929–1933 (2015)
10. Liu, H., Jin, C., Yang, B., Zhou, A.: Finding top-K shortest paths with diversity. IEEE Trans. Knowl. Data Eng. **30**(3), 488–502 (2018)
11. Cormen, T.H., Leiserson, C.E., Ronald, R.L., Stein, C.: Introduction to Algorithms, 2nd edn, pp. 595–601. MIT Press and McGraw-Hill, London and New York (2001). Section 24.3: Dijkstra's Algorithm

Energy Efficiency Optimization-Based Joint Resource Allocation and Clustering Algorithm for M2M Communication Networks (Workshop)

Changzhu Liu[✉], Ahmad Zubair, Rong Chai, and Qianbin Chen

Key Lab of Mobile Communication Technology,
Chongqing University of Posts and Telecommunications, Chongqing 400065, China
1039410361@qq.com, ahmadcqupt@qq.com,
{chairong,chenqb}@cqupt.edu.cn

Abstract. In recent years, machine-to-machine (M2M) communications have attracted great attentions from both academia and industry. In M2M communication networks, machine type communication devices (MTCDs) are capable of communicating with each other intelligently under highly reduced human interventions. In this paper, we address the problem of joint resource allocation and clustering for M2M communications. By defining the system energy efficiency (EE) as the sum of the EE of MTCDs, the joint resource allocation and clustering problem is formulated as a system EE maximization problem. As the original optimization problem is a nonlinear fractional programming problem, which cannot be solved conveniently, we transform it into two subproblems, i,e., power allocation subproblem and clustering subproblem, and solve the two subproblems by means of Lagrange dual method and modified K-means algorithm, respectively. Numerical results demonstrate the effectiveness of the proposed algorithm.

Keywords: Machine to machine (M2M) communications · Clustering · Resource allocation · Energy efficiency (EE)

1 Introduction

Machine to machine (M2M) communications have been considered as one of the promising technologies to realize the Internet of Things (IoT) in future 5th generation network [1]. In M2M, machine type communication devices (MTCDs) are capable of communicating with each other intelligently under highly reduced human interventions. In some practical M2M applications, i.e., smart home, smart wearable device [2], massive access requests from MTCDs pose challenges and difficulties to the random access and resource allocation schemes of the traditional access networks.

In past few years, resource allocation problem has been studied for M2M communications [3–5]. In [3], the authors proposed a preamble allocation method which maximized system throughput and provides effective QoS differentiation across various random access loads. The authors in [4] studied joint resource blocks (RBs) scheduling and power allocation issues for M2M communications in long term evolution-advanced (LTE-A) networks and proposed a sum-throughput maximization-based optimal resource allocation scheme for the MTCDs. In [5], the authors studied resource

H. Gao et al. (Eds.): ChinaCom 2019, LNICST 313, pp. 351–363, 2020.
https://doi.org/10.1007/978-3-030-41117-6_29

allocation problem of energy harvesting cognitive radio sensor networks and developed an aggregate network utility optimization framework to achieve efficient resource management.

It has been demonstrated that resource allocation strategies can be jointly designed with clustering schemes to enhance the transmission performance of the MTCDs in M2M communication systems. In [6], energy efficient clustering and medium access control (MAC) problem was investigated for cellular-based M2M communication systems. To achieve the tradeoff between energy efficiency (EE), transmission delay, and spectral efficiency, and prolong the lifetime of the M2M system, the authors proposed an optimal clustering and MAC scheme. The authors in [7] proposed an energy efficient power control, user pairing and time scheduling algorithm to achieve the minimum energy consumption in non-orthogonal multiple access (NOMA)-based M2M communication systems. In [8], to accommodate massive access for MTCDs in cellular systems, relaying and resource partitioning schemes were designed for the MTCDs under the consideration of the signaling overhead in the cellular systems.

In this paper, we address the joint resource allocation and clustering problem for M2M communications. By defining system EE as the sum of the EE of MTCDs, the joint resource allocation and clustering problem is formulated as an EE maximization problem. As the original optimization problem is a nonlinear fractional programming problem, which cannot be solved conveniently, we transform it into two subproblems, i,e., power allocation subproblem and clustering subproblem, and solve the two subproblems by means of Lagrange dual method and modified K-means algorithm, respectively.

The rest of this paper is organized as follows. The system model is presented in Sect. 2. In Sect. 3, the optimization problem is formulated. Section 4 discusses the solution of the optimization problem. Section 5 analyzes the simulation results. Finally, we make a conclusion in Sect. 6.

2   System Model

In this paper, we consider the uplink transmission scenario of an M2M communication network consisting of a single base station (BS) and multiple MTCDs. Let M denote the number of MTCDs. We assume that the BS is deployed in the network center and the MTCDs are randomly deployed within the coverage area of the BS. We further assume that the MTCDs need to transmit their data packets to the BS and may apply direct transmission mode in which the MTCDs transmit their data packets the BS directly. On the other hand, to achieve highly efficient data transmission, we assume that the cluster head (CH) forwarding mode is available. More specifically, the MTCDs may form various clusters with each cluster having one CH and a number of cluster members (CMs). While the CHs in each cluster may transmit their data packets to the BS in direct transmission mode, the CMs may apply CH forwarding mode, i.e., sending their data packets to the associated CHs, which then forward the received data packets to the BS on behalf of the CMs.

We further assume that there are a number of channels with equal bandwidth. Let B denote the bandwidth of each channel. For simplicity, it is assumed that enough bandwidth resources are available and all the transmission links can be allocated with one channel, hence, no transmission interference among transmission links exists. Figure 1 shows the system model.

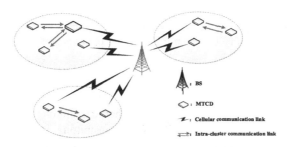

Fig. 1. System model.

3 Optimization Problem Formulation

In this section, we define system EE as the total EE of the MTCDs and formulate the joint resource allocation and clustering problem as system EE maximization problem.

3.1 Objective Function

Considering the performance of all the MTCDs, we define system EE as the sum of EE of the MTCDs, which can be expressed as

$$\eta = \sum_{i=1}^{M} \eta_i \tag{1}$$

where η_i denotes the EE of the ith MTCD. For simplicity, we denote the ith MTCD as MTCD_i. The expression of η_i is given by

$$\eta_i = \delta_i^{\mathrm{d}} \eta_i^{\mathrm{d}} + \sum_{j=1}^{M} \delta_{i,j}^{\mathrm{c}} \eta_{i,j}^{\mathrm{c}} \tag{2}$$

where $\delta_i^{\mathrm{d}} \in \{0,1\}$ is the association variable of MTCD_i in direct transmission mode, i.e., if $\delta_i^{\mathrm{d}} = 1$, MTCD_i transmits data packets to the BS directly, otherwise, $\delta_i^{\mathrm{d}} = 0$, $1 \leq i \leq M$, η_i^{d} denotes the EE of MTCD_i in direct transmission mode. The expression of η_i^{d} can be defined as follows:

$$\eta_i^{\mathrm{d}} = \frac{R_i^{\mathrm{d}}}{p_i^{\mathrm{d}} + p_{\mathrm{cir}}} \tag{3}$$

where p_{cir} is the circuit power consumption of MTCD_i, p_i^{d} denotes the transmit power of MTCD_i when transmitting data packets to the BS directly, R_i^{d} denotes the transmit rate of MTCD_i in direct transmission mode, which can be expressed as

$$R_i^{\mathrm{d}} = B \log_2 \left(1 + \frac{p_i^{\mathrm{d}} h_i^{\mathrm{d}}}{\sigma^2} \right) \tag{4}$$

where h_i^d denotes the channel gain of the link between MTCD$_i$ and the BS, σ^2 denotes the noise power.

In (2), $\delta_{i,j}^c$ is the association variable of MTCD$_i$ and the jth CH in CH forwarding mode, i.e., if $\delta_{i,j}^c = 1$, MTCD$_i$ chooses jth CH to forward its data packets to the BS, otherwise, $\delta_{i,j}^c = 0$, $1 \leq i \neq j \leq M$, for simplicity, let CH$_j$ represent the jth CH, $\eta_{i,j}^c$ denotes the EE of MTCD$_i$ when transmitting data packets to CH$_j$, which can be expressed as

$$\eta_{i,j}^c = \frac{R_{i,j}^c}{p_{i,j}^c + p_{cir}} \tag{5}$$

where $p_{i,j}^c$ is the transmit power of MTCD$_i$ when transmitting data packets to CH$_j$, $R_{i,j}^c$ denotes the transmit rate of MTCD$_i$ when transmitting data packets to CH$_j$. The expression of $R_{i,j}^c$ is given by

$$R_{i,j}^c = B \log_2 \left(1 + \frac{p_{i,j}^c h_{i,j}^c}{\sigma^2} \right) \tag{6}$$

where $h_{i,j}^c$ denotes the channel gain of the link between MTCD$_i$ and CH$_j$.

3.2 Optimization Constraints

The optimal design of the joint resource allocation and clustering strategy should be subject to a number of constraints including maximum number of CHs, maximum number of MTCDs in clusters, etc.

Maximum Number of CHs. Let $\delta_{j,j}^c = 1$ denote the CH identifier, i.e. if $\delta_{j,j}^c = 1$, MTCD$_j$ acts as a CH, otherwise, $\delta_{j,j}^c = 0$, $1 \leq j \leq M$. Denote the maximum number of CHs in the network as N_{max}, we may express the constraint on the maximum number of CHs as:

$$C1 : \sum_{j=1}^{M} \delta_{j,j}^c \leq N_{max}, \forall i. \tag{7}$$

Maximum Number of MTCDs in Clusters. Assuming that the number of MTCDs that one CH can associate is at most K, hence, we obtain the following constraint:

$$C2 : \sum_{i=1, i \neq j}^{M} \delta_{i,j}^c \leq K, 1 \leq j \leq M. \tag{8}$$

CH Association Constraint. Assuming each MTCD can choose at most one CH for association, i.e.,

$$C3 : \sum_{j=1, i \neq j}^{M} \delta_{i,j}^c \leq 1, 1 \leq i \leq M. \tag{9}$$

Mode Selection Constraint. Assume that each MTCD can either choose direct transmission mode or CH forwarding mode, i.e.,

$$C4 : \delta_i^{\mathrm{d}} + \sum_{j=1,j\neq i}^{M} \delta_{i,j}^{\mathrm{c}} \leq 1,\ 1 \leq i \leq M. \tag{10}$$

Maximum Transmit Power Constraints. As the transmit power of each MTCD must be less than the maximum transmit power, we obtain

$$C5 : p_i^{\mathrm{d}} \leq p_i^{\mathrm{max}},\ 1 \leq i \leq M, \tag{11}$$

$$C6 : p_{i,j}^{\mathrm{c}} \leq p_i^{\mathrm{max}},\ 1 \leq i \neq j \leq M \tag{12}$$

where p_i^{max} denotes the maximum transmit power of MTCD_i.

Transmit Rate Constraint. Considering the various QoS requirements of different MTCDs, we assume that there is a minimum rate requirement for each MTCD. The transmit rate of the MTCDs should be higher than the minimum transmit rate, i.e.,

$$C7 : R_i \geq R_i^{\mathrm{min}},\ 1 \leq i \leq M \tag{13}$$

where R_i^{min} is the minimum transmit rate, R_i denotes the actual transmit rate of $\mathrm{MTCD}_i,\ 1 \leq i \leq M$, which can be expressed as

$$R_i = \delta_{i,j}^{\mathrm{d}} R_i^{\mathrm{d}} + \sum_{j=1,j\neq i}^{M} \delta_{i,j}^{\mathrm{c}} R_{i,j} \tag{14}$$

where $R_{i,j} = \min \left\{ R_{i,j}^{\mathrm{c}}, R_j^{\mathrm{d}} \right\}$.

3.3 Optimization Problem

Considering the aforementioned objective function and optimization constraints, we formulate the EE maximization-based joint resource allocation and clustering problem as

$$\max_{\delta_i^{\mathrm{d}},\delta_{i,j}^{\mathrm{c}},p_i^{\mathrm{d}},p_{i,j}^{\mathrm{c}}} \eta \tag{15}$$

$$\text{s.t.}\quad C1 - C7$$

$$C8 : \delta_i^{\mathrm{d}} \in \{0,1\},\ 1 \leq i \leq M,$$

$$C9 : \delta_{i,j}^{\mathrm{c}} \in \{0,1\},\ 1 \leq i \neq j \leq M.$$

4 Solution of the Optimization Problem

The optimization problem in (15) is a nonlinear fractional programming problem, which cannot be solved conveniently, however, it can be demonstrated that given the clustering strategy, the power allocation strategy of the MTCDs in various transmission modes can be designed independently. Hence, we may transform the optimization problem formulated in (15) into two subproblems, i.e., power allocation subproblem and clustering subproblem.

4.1 Power Allocation Subproblem

In this subsection, we suppose $MTCD_i$ transmits its data packets to CH_j in CH forwarding mode, i.e., $\delta_{i,j}^c = 1, 1 \leq i \neq j \leq M$, the power allocation subproblem of $MTCD_i$ can be expressed as

$$\max_{\eta_{i,j}^c} \quad \eta_{i,j}^c \tag{16}$$

$$\text{s.t.} \quad \text{C1} : p_{i,j}^c \leq p_i^{\max}, 1 \leq i \leq M, i \neq j,$$

$$\text{C2} : R_{i,j}^c \geq R_i^{\min}, 1 \leq i \leq M, i \neq j$$

Iterative Algorithm-Based Energy Efficiency Maximization. The optimization problem formulated in (16) is a non-convex problem with the objective function being a nonlinear fractional function, which cannot be solved directly using traditional optimization tools. In this subsection, we apply an iterative algorithm to solve the optimization problem.

To transform the objective function of the optimization problem defined in (16), we denote q as the EE of $MTCD_i$, i.e., $q = \dfrac{R_{i,j}^c}{p_{i,j}^c + p_{\text{cir}}}$, q^* is the maximum EE, and $p_{i,j}^{c,*}$ as the optimal power allocation strategy of $MTCD_i$, i.e.,

$$q^* = \frac{R_{i,j}^c \left(p_{i,j}^{c,*}\right)}{p_{i,j}^{c,*} + p_{\text{cir}}} = \max_{p_{i,j}^c} \frac{R_{i,j}^c}{p_{i,j}^c + p_{\text{cir}}}. \tag{17}$$

It can be proved that the maximum EE q^* is achieved if and only if the following condition meets:

$$R_{i,j}^c \left(p_{i,j}^c\right) - q^* \left(p_{i,j}^c + p_{\text{cir}}\right) = 0. \tag{18}$$

Thus, the optimization problem formulated in (16) can be transformed into the following problem:

$$\max_{q, p_{i,j}^c} \quad R_{i,j}^c - q \left(p_{i,j}^c + p_{\text{cir}}\right) \tag{19}$$

$$\text{s.t.} \quad \text{C1} : p_{i,j}^c \leq p_i^{\max}, 1 \leq i \leq M, i \neq j,$$

$$\text{C2} : R_{i,j}^c \geq R_i^{\min}, 1 \leq i \leq M, i \neq j.$$

While the objective function in the above optimization problem is a nonlinear function of q and $p_{i,j}^c$, which cannot be solved directly, it can be observed that given q, the optimization problem in terms of local power allocation strategy can be obtained based on which the value of q can be updated and the local power allocation strategy can be re-designed.

Applying iterative algorithm, the optimal EE q^* and power allocation strategy $p_{i,j}^{c,*}$ can be obtained. The problem solving process can be summarized briefly: starting from an initial value of q, the locally optimal power allocation strategy can be obtained through applying traditional convex optimization tools, then the EE q can be updated based on the obtained power solution. Then given the updated q, the power allocation process can be re-conducted to obtained power allocation strategy, the process continues until the algorithm converges, i.e., $\left|R_{i,j}^c \left(p_{i,j}^c\right) - q \left(p_{i,j}^c + p_{\text{cir}}\right)\right| \leq \varepsilon_0$, where ε_0 denotes the maximum tolerance.

Lagrange Dual Method-Based Power Allocation Algorithm. For a given value of q, the power allocation subproblem can be expressed as follows:

$$\max_{p_{i,j}^c} \quad R_{i,j}^c - q\left(p_{i,j}^c + p_{\text{cir}}\right) \tag{20}$$

$$\text{s.t.} \quad \text{C1}: p_{i,j}^c \leq p_i^{\max}, 1 \leq i \leq M, i \neq j,$$
$$\text{C2}: R_{i,j}^c \geq R_i^{\min}, 1 \leq i \leq M, i \neq j.$$

The optimization problem formulated in (20) is a constrained convex optimization problem which can be solved by applying Lagrange dual method. The Lagrange function can be formulated as [9]

$$L\left(\varphi, \mu, p_{i,j}^c\right) = R_{i,j}^c - q\left(p_{i,j}^c + p_{\text{cir}}\right) - \varphi\left(p_{i,j}^c - p_i^{\max}\right) - \mu\left(R_i^{\min} - R_{i,j}^c\right) \tag{21}$$

where φ, μ are Lagrange multipliers.

The optimization problem in (20) can then be transformed into Lagrange dual problem:

$$\min_{\varphi, \mu} \max_{p_{i,j}^c} L\left(\varphi, \mu, p_{i,j}^c\right) \tag{22}$$

$$\text{s.t.} \quad \varphi \geq 0, \ \mu \geq 0.$$

The optimization problem formulated in (22) consists of two subproblems, i.e., internal maximum subproblem and external minimum subproblem, which can be solved iteratively. For a set of fixed Lagrange multipliers, the internal maximum subproblem can be solved to obtain the locally optimal power allocation strategy, which can then be applied to solve the external minimum subproblem to obtain the updated Lagrange multipliers.

The locally optimal power allocation strategy can be obtained by calculating the derivative of formulated Lagrange function with respect to $p_{i,j}^c$ and let the computed derivative equal to zero, i.e.,

$$\frac{\partial L\left(\varphi, \mu, p_{i,j}^c\right)}{\partial p_{i,j}^c} = \frac{(1+\mu)\,Bh_{i,j}^c}{\ln 2\left(\sigma^2 + p_{i,j}^c h_{i,j}^c\right)} - q - \varphi = 0, \tag{23}$$

we can obtain

$$p_{i,j}^{c,*} = \left[\frac{(1+\mu)\,B}{(q+\varphi)\,ln2} - \frac{\sigma^2}{h_{i,j}^c}\right]^+ \tag{24}$$

where $[x]^+ = \max\{x, 0\}$, denote $\eta_{i,j}^{c,*}$ as the optimal EE of MTCD_i obtained from $p_{i,j}^{c,*}$.

To solve the external minimum subproblem, we apply gradient descent algorithm to calculate the Lagrange multipliers, i.e.,

$$\varphi\left(t_1 + 1\right) = \left[\varphi\left(t_1\right) - \omega_1\left(p_i^{\max} - p_{i,j}^c\right)\right]^+, \tag{25}$$

$$\mu\left(t_1 + 1\right) = \left[\mu\left(t_1\right) - \omega_2\left(R_{i,j}^c - R_i^{\min}\right)\right]^+ \tag{26}$$

where t_1 denotes the iteration index, ω_1 and ω_2 are step size. The proposed Lagrange dual method-based power allocation algorithm is shown in Algorithm 1. The above

---

Algorithm 1. Lagrange Dual Method-based Power Allocation Algorithm

---

1: Set the maximum number of iterations T_1, and the maximum tolerance ε_1
2: Initialize the Lagrange multipliers $\varphi(t_1)$, $\mu(t_1)$ for $t_1 = 0$
3: **repeat**
4:     Compute the power allocation strategy
       $$p_{i,j}^{c,*} = \left[\frac{(1+\mu)f_i B}{(\varphi+\varphi)\ln 2} - \frac{\sigma^2}{h_{i,j}^c} \right]^+$$
5:     Update the Lagrange multipliers:
       $$\varphi(t_1 + 1) = \left[\varphi(t_1) - \omega_1 \left(p_i^{\max} - p_{i,j}^c \right) \right]^+$$
       $$\mu(t_1 + 1) = \left[\mu(t_1) - \omega_2 \left(R_{i,j}^c - R_i^{\min} \right) \right]^+$$
6:     **if** $|\varphi(t_1 + 1) - \varphi(t_1)| + |\mu(t_1 + 1) - \mu(t_1)| \leq \varepsilon_1$ **then**
7:         The algorithm terminates
8:         Convergence = **true**
9:         **return** $p_{i,j}^{c,*}$
10:    **else**
11:        $t_1 = t_1 + 1$
12:    **end if**
13: **until** Convergence = **true** or $t_1 = T_1$

---

algorithm can be extended to the case that MTCD$_i$ communicates with BS in direct transmission mode, let $p_i^{d,*}$ denote the optimal value of p_i^d, $\eta_i^{d,*}$ denotes the optimal EE corresponding to $p_i^{d,*}$.

4.2   Clustering Subproblem

In this subsection, based on the optimal power allocation strategy obtained from previous subsection, we address the clustering subproblem and solve the subproblem by means of the modified K-means algorithm.

Direct Transmission Mode Selection. It can be understood easily that one MTCD may tend to transmit its data packets to the BS directly provided that it achieves the maximum EE in direct transmission mode compared to CH forwarding mode. Hence, we may first assign the direct transmission mode to the MTCDs simply by comparing the EE of the MTCDs obtained at different transmission modes.

In Table 1, we plot the optimal EE of the MTCDs obtained in different transmission modes. As we can see from the table, different rows in the table represent the EE of different MTCDs, and different columns correspond to different transmission modes of the MTCDs. In particular, in CH forwarding modes, we consider the case that any MTCD can be selected as the CH of other MTCDs. For simplicity, we define the EE of MTCD$_i$ as 0 when the MTCD selects itself as CH for data forwarding, i.e., $\eta_{i,i}^{c,*} = 0$, $1 \leq i \leq M$.

Table 1. EE of the links between BS and MTCDs and between MTCDs

	Direct transmission mode	CH forwarding mode			
		$MTCD_1$	$MTCD_2$	$\cdots$	$MTCD_M$
$MTCD_1$	$\eta_1^{d,*}$	0	$\eta_{1,2}^{c,*}$	$\cdots$	$\eta_{1,M}^{c,*}$
$MTCD_2$	$\eta_2^{d,*}$	$\eta_{2,1}^{c,*}$	0	$\cdots$	$\eta_{2,M}^{c,*}$
$\cdots$	$\cdots$	$\cdots$	$\cdots$	$\cdots$	$\cdots$
$MTCD_M$	$\eta_M^{d,*}$	$\eta_{M,1}^{c,*}$	$\eta_{M,2}^{c,*}$	$\cdots$	0

Examining Table 1, we can see that in the case that $MTCD_i$ achieves the maximum EE when forwarding data packets to $MTCD_j$ (CH_j), i.e., $\eta_i^{d,*} \geq \eta_{i,j}^{c,*}$, $\forall \, 1 \leq j \neq i \leq M$, we should assign direct transmission mode to $MTCD_i$, i.e., $\delta_i^{d,*} = 1$. Let Φ_d denote the set of MTCDs which are assigned direct transmission mode, i.e., $\Phi_d = \left\{ MTCD_i \middle| \delta_i^{d,*} = 1, \, 1 \leq i \leq M \right\}$. It should be mentioned that $MTCD_i \in \Phi_d$ cannot be the CM of any clusters, however, it may act as CH for other CMs. Let Φ denote the set of all the MTCDs, i.e., $\Phi = \{MTCD_i, 1 \leq i \leq M\}$.

Candidate CH Selection. To reduce the computation complexity of the clustering scheme, we propose a candidate CH selection scheme which selects the qualified CHs based on the transmission performance of the MTCDs.

Since the selected CHs should forward data packets for their associated CMs within the clusters, the characteristic of the link between the CHs and the BS, i.e., the direct transmission link of the CHs, is of particular importance as it may affect the transmission performance of data packets significantly. To avoid selecting the MTCDs with highly limited transmission performance, we set a threshold on the EE of the direct transmission link of the MTCDs and set the MTCDs with the EE of the direct transmission link being greater than the threshold as the candidate CHs.

Let η_{min} denote the EE threshold of the direct transmission link of the MTCDs, $MTCD_i$ can be set as a candidate CH provided that $\eta_i^{d,*} \geq \eta_{min}, 1 \leq i \leq M$. Denoting Φ_0 as the set of the candidate CHs, we obtain

$$\Phi_0 = \{MTCD_i | \eta_i^{d,*} \geq \eta_{min}, \, 1 \leq i \leq M\}. \tag{27}$$

Let K_0 denote the number of candidate CHs, i.e., $K_0 = |\Phi_0|$, where $|x|$ represents the number of elements in set x.

Modified K-Means Algorithm-Based Clustering Scheme. The K-means algorithm is commonly used for solving clustering problems [10]. In this paper, we propose a modified K-means algorithm to solve the clustering problem of the MTCDs.

The basic idea of the proposed algorithm can be summarized briefly. We first set the initial number of CHs, i.e., $K_1 = \min \{N_{max}, K_0\}$, then, select the CHs which offer the highest EE of both the direct link and the association links with other MTCDs. Given the initial CHs, associate the CMs with the CH offering the maximum EE of the association links. Within each cluster, the CH selection and association processes are repeated until the algorithm achieves convergence.

The steps of modified K-means algorithm-based clustering scheme are as follows:

(a) *Initialization*: Set the maximum number of iterations T', the maximum tolerance Δ, set $t' = 1$, and determine the number of CHs, i.e., $K_1 = \min\{N_{\max}, K_0\}$.

(b) *Initial CH selection*: For MTCD$_i \subset \Phi$, $1 \le i \le M$, calculate the sum of EE of both the direct link and the association links with other MTCDs, denoted as ψ_i, i.e.,

$$\psi_i = \eta_i^{d,*} + \sum_{j=1, j \neq i}^{M} \eta_{i,j}^{c,*}, \ 1 \le i \le M.$$

Select K_1 MTCDs which offer the largest EE as the CHs. More specifically, ordering MTCD$_i \in \Phi$ according to ψ_i, i.e.,

$$\psi_{i_1} \ge \psi_{i_2} \ge \cdots \ge \psi_{i_k} \ge \cdots \ge \psi_{i_{K_0}}, \forall \, \text{MTCD}_{i_k} \in \Phi.$$

The first K_1 MTCDs will be selected as the CHs. Let Φ_{ch} denote the set of CHs, we set

$$\Phi_{\text{ch}} = \{\text{MTCD}_{i_k} \mid 1 \le k \le K_1, \ \text{MTCD}_{i_k} \in \Phi\}.$$

Let Φ_{cm} denote the set of CMs, we obtain

$$\Phi_{\text{cm}} = \{\text{MTCD}_i \mid \text{MTCD}_i \in \Phi, \ \text{MTCD}_i \notin \{\Phi_{\text{ch}} \cup \Phi_{\text{d}}\}\}.$$

(c) *Initial CH Association*: For MTCD$_i \in \Phi_{\text{cm}}$, compute the EE of the links between MTCD$_i$ and MTCD$_j \in \Phi_{\text{ch}}$, and choose the CH which offers the largest EE as the associated CH. Let MTCD$_{j'}$ denote the associated CH of MTCD$_i$, we obtain

$$\text{CH}_{j'} = \arg\max_{\text{MTCD}_j \in \Phi_{\text{ch}}} \left\{\eta_{i,j}^{c,*}\right\}, \ \text{MTCD}_i \in \Phi_{\text{cm}}.$$

Accordingly, we set $\delta_{i,j'}^c = 1$.

(d) *System EE calculation*: Update the set of direct transmission MTCDs by removing those MTCDs which are selected as CHs, denote $\Phi_{\text{d}'}$ as the updated set of direct transmission MTCDs, we express $\Phi_{\text{d}'}$ as

$$\Phi_{\text{d}'} = \{\text{MTCD}_i \mid \text{MTCD}_i \in \Phi_{\text{d}}, \ \text{MTCD}_i \notin \Phi_{\text{ch}}\}.$$

For MTCD$_i \in \Phi_{\text{d}'}$, set the direct transmission mode selection variable $\delta_i^{d,*} = 1$. Based on the obtained transmission mode selection and clustering strategy, we calculate system EE denoted by $\eta_{t'}$, i.e.,

$$\eta_{t'} = \sum_{\text{MTCD}_i \in \Phi_{\text{d}'}} \eta_i^{d,*} + \sum_{\text{MTCD}_i \in \Phi_{\text{ch}}} \eta_i^{d,*} + \sum_{\text{MTCD}_i \in \Phi_{\text{cm}}} \sum_{\text{MTCD}_{j'} \in \Phi_{\text{ch}}} \eta_{i,j'}^{c,*} \quad (28)$$

(e) *CH reselection*: Assuming MTCD$_{j'} \in \Phi_{\text{ch}}$ is selected as one CH, we let $\Phi_{j'}$ denote the set of the CMs which are associated with MTCD$_{j'}$, i.e.,

$$\Phi_{j'} = \{\text{MTCD}_i \mid \text{MTCD}_i \in \Phi_{\text{cm}}, \ \delta_{i,j'}^c = 1\}.$$

For $\forall$ MTCD$_i$ $\in$ $\Phi_{j'}$, compute the sum of EE of the direct link between MTCD$_i$ and the BS, the link between MTCD$_i$ and MTCD$_{j'}$, and the links between MTCD$_i$ and MTCD$_{i'}$ $\in$ $\Phi_{j'}$, $i \neq i'$. Let ζ_i denote the EE performance of MTCD$_i$ $\in$ $\Phi_{j'}$, we express ζ_i as

$$\zeta_i = \eta_i^{\mathrm{d},*} + \eta_{i,j'}^{\mathrm{c},*} + \sum_{\mathrm{MTCD}_{i'} \in \Phi_{j'}, i' \neq i} \eta_{i,i'}^{\mathrm{c},*}$$

and choose MTCD$_i$ $\in$ $\Phi_{j'}$ which offers the largest EE as the updated CH, i.e.,

$$\mathrm{CH}_i = \underset{\{\mathrm{MTCD}_{j'}\} \cup \Phi_{j'}}{\arg\max} \{\zeta_i\}.$$

Accordingly, update the set of Φ_{ch} and Φ_{cm}.

(f) *CH reassociation*: For MTCD$_i$ $\in$ Φ_{cm}, compute the EE of the link between MTCD$_i$ and MTCD$_j$ $\in$ Φ_{ch}, and choose the CH which offers the largest EE as the associated CH.

(g) *System EE update*: Re-calculate the system EE based on (28), denoted by $\eta_{t'+1}$.

(h) *Algorithm convergence*: If $|\eta_{t'+1} - \eta_{t'}| \leq \Delta$ or $t' = T'$, then algorithm stops, the corresponding clustering strategy can be obtained, otherwise, set $t' = t' + 1$, return to Step (e).

Table 2. Simulation parameters

Parameters	Value
Number of MTCDs	15
Small scale fading distribution	Rayleigh fading with unit variance
Channel path loss model	$128.1 + 37.6 \log(d)$ dB
Bandwidth of one RB	180 KHz
Maximum transmit power	0.15 W
Noise power	-104 dBm
Circuit power consumption	0.3 W

5 Simulation Result Analysis

In this section, simulation results are presented to show the performance by our proposed scheme. For comparison, we also examine the performance of the previously proposed algorithm in [4] via simulation. In the simulation, we consider an M2M communication network consisting of one BS and M MTCDs. The size of the simulation region is set as $500\,\mathrm{m} \times 500\,\mathrm{m}$, and the MTCDs are randomly located in the simulation area. Unless otherwise mentioned, the simulation parameters are listed in Table 2.

Figure 2 shows system EE versus maximum transmit power for different circuit power consumption. From the figure, we can see that for small p_i^{max}, the EE increases with the increase of $p_i^{\max}$ for both schemes, indicating that a larger power threshold is desired for achieving the maximum EE. However, as the maximum transmit power reaches to a certain value, the EE obtained from our proposed scheme converges to a constant while the EE obtained from the scheme proposed in [4] decreases as the power increases. This is because the scheme proposed in [4] aims to achieve the maximum transmit rate, thus may require higher power consumption, resulting in undesired EE. It can also be observed from the figure that the EE obtained from both algorithms decreases with the increase of circuit power consumption. Comparing the curves in the graph, we can see that the proposed algorithm offers higher EE than that of previously proposed scheme.

In Fig. 3, we examine system EE versus maximum transmit power for different noise power. From the figure, we can see that the EE decreases with the increase of noise power. This is because larger noise power results in reduced transmission performance and lower EE in turn. Comparing the results obtained from two algorithms, we can see that our proposed scheme offers better performance compared with [4].

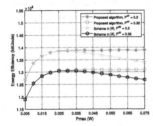

Fig. 2. Energy efficiency versus maximum transmit power (different circuit power).

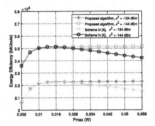

Fig. 3. Energy efficiency versus maximum transmit power (different noise power).

In Fig. 4, we plot system EE versus the number of MTCDs for different circuit power consumption. We set the number of MTCDs from 10 to 55 in the simulation. It can be see from the figure that the EE obtained from both algorithms decreases with the increase of circuit power consumption. As the number of MTCDs increases, the EE obtained from both algorithms increases accordingly. This is due to the fact that as the number of MTCDs increases, the increased amount of data flows are transmitted through the system, resulting in an increased EE. In addition, we can observe that our proposed scheme is more energy efficient than other algorithm.

Figure 5 shows system EE versus the number of MTCDs for different noise power. From the figure, we can see that the EE decreases with the increase of noise power and increases as the number of MTCDs increase. This is because larger noise power results in worse transmission performance and lower EE in turn. In addition, we can see that our proposed algorithm offers outperforms the other scheme.

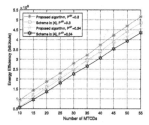
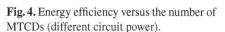
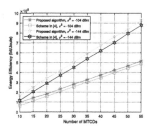

Fig. 4. Energy efficiency versus the number of MTCDs (different circuit power).

Fig. 5. Energy efficiency versus the number MTCDs (different noise power).

6   Conclusion

In this paper, we consider an M2M communication network and formulate the joint resource allocation and clustering problem as system EE maximization problem. As the formulated optimization problem is a nonlinear fractional programming problem, which cannot be solved directly, we decompose it into two subproblems, i.e., power allocation subproblem and clustering subproblem, and solve the two subproblems by means of Lagrange dual method and modified K-means algorithm, respectively. Numerical results show that our proposed algorithm outperforms previously proposed algorithm.

References

1. Dawy, Z., Saad, W., Ghosh, A., Andrews, J.G., Yaacoub, E.: Toward massive machine type cellular communications. IEEE Wirel. Commun. **24**(1), 120–128 (2017)
2. Sun, W., Liu, J., Zhang, H.: When smart wearables meet intelligent vehicles: challenges and future directions. IEEE Wirel. Commun. **24**(3), 58–65 (2017)
3. Han, H., Guo, X., Li, Y.: A high throughput pilot allocation for M2M communication in crowded massive MIMO systems. IEEE Trans. Veh. Technol. **66**(10), 9572–9576 (2017)
4. Ghavimi, F., Lu, Y., Chen, H.: Uplink scheduling and power allocation for M2M communications in SC-FDMA-based LTE-a networks with QoS guarantees. IEEE Trans. Veh. Technol. **66**(7), 6160–6170 (2017)
5. Zhang, D., Chen, Z., Awad, M.K., Zhang, N., Zhou, H., Shen, X.S.: Utility-optimal resource management and allocation algorithm for energy harvesting cognitive radio sensor networks. IEEE J. Sel. Areas Commun. **34**(12), 3552–3565 (2016)
6. Miao, G., Azari, A., Hwang, T.: E^2-MAC: energy efficiency medium access for massive M2M communications. IEEE Trans. Commun. **64**(11), 4720–4735 (2016)
7. Yang, Z., Xu, W., Pan, Y., Pan, C., Chen, M.: Energy efficiency resource allocation in machine-to-machine communications with multiple access and energy harvesting for IoT. IEEE Internet Things J. **5**(1), 229–245 (2018)
8. Tefek, U., Lim, T.J.: Relaying and radio resource partitioning for machine-type communications in cellular networks. IEEE Trans. Wirel. Commun. **16**(2), 1344–1356 (2017)
9. Boyd, S., Vandenberghe, L.: Convex Optimization. Cambridge University Press, Cambridge (2004)
10. Kaufman, L., Rousseeuw, P.J.: Finding groups in data: an introduction to cluster analysis. In: DBLP (2009)

Latency-Reliability Analysis
for Multi-antenna System (Workshop)

Zhichao Xiu$^{(\boxtimes)}$, Hang Long, and Yixiao Li

Wireless Signal Processing and Network Lab, Key Laboratory of Universal
Wireless Communication, Ministry of Education, Beijing University of Posts
and Telecommunications, Beijing, China
xiuzhichao@bupt.edu.cn

Abstract. The relationship between the latency and reliability of multi-
antena diversity system is investigated in this paper. The system performance of diversity system is analysed with the outage probability chosen
as the reliability metric. Two combining techniques are considered in the
diversity system. It is proved that the latency-reliability trade-off degree
(LRTD), i.e., the slope of the latency-outage curves with logarithmic
scales, equals the number of the diversity order. In addition, the diversity
system with considering system overhead is investigated. Golden section
search algorithm and a simplified iterative method can be used to obtain
the optimum diversity order of multiple-input and single-output (MISO)
system adopted with maximal ratio combining and section combining
techniques, respectively.

Keywords: Latency-reliability trade-off degree · Multi-antenna ·
Overhead

1 Introduction

In the emerging fifth wireless communication systems, there are several crucial
performance requirements and targets including the data rate, the number of
connected devices, device battery life, end-to-end latency, and reliability of communication [1]. The use case with low latency and high reliability is a very important application scenario [2]. For example, in vehicular network applications,
data transmission latency below 5 ms and very high reliability of packet error
rations $< 10^{-6}$ are expected [2]. Other application scenarios of low-latency and
high-reliability communications include future factory applications, distributed
utility grid protection, autonomous driving and so on [3].

Some solutions are proposed to meet the low latency target such as: employing shorter transmission time interval (TTI), cooperative communications, and
massive multiple-input multiple-output (MIMO) [1]. Simultaneously, in-depth

Supported by China Unicom Network Technology Research Institute and project
61302088 which was supported by National Natural Science Foundation of China.

theoretical analyses among the solutions for low-latency and high-reliability communications are necessary. In [4], the fundamental trade-off between the outage capacity, system bandwidth, and the latency requirement for ultra-reliable and low-latency systems is demonstrated by system-level simulations. In [5], the relationship among reliability, throughput, and given latency requirement is shown. Given the existing studies in the literature, a generalized analysis on the relationship among latency, reliability and other performance metrics is much needed.

The relay technique has been used to meet the reliability and latency requirements. Cooperative communication based relaying schemes are discussed in [6], which can provide ultra-high reliability while meeting the latency requirement at moderate SNR. The low-latency and high-reliability communications in multi-relay systems have been considered, and a new metric termed latency-reliability trade-off degree (LRTD) is proposed in [7], which can also be analysed in other communication systems.

At the same time, diversity technique can also be used for low-latency and high-reliability communications. The ultra-reliable and low-latency communication can be supported through high diversity, transmission with shared diversity resources is proposed in [8]. Diversity technique can result in significant increase in system performance. Simultaneously, more system elements are cost for system overhead [5], which is important and not ignorable in low-latency frame structures. The reliability constraints on control information are studied in [9], and some enhancement techniques are proposed. Reference [10] characterizes the trade-off between the training sequence length and data code length. It is important to consider the system overhead in the low-latency and high-reliability communications.

In this study, the relationship between latency and reliability in multi-antenna diversity systems is analysed. The relationship between latency and reliability has been investigated in [7]. For spatial diversity systems, the slope of the logarithmic scaled latency-reliability curve in diversity systems is proven to be equivalent to the number of diversity order. In addition, the system overhead is considered. In the multi-antenna diversity system with overhead, the reliability increases because of the diversity gain at first, and decreases at last because of the system overhead. With considering the system overhead, the optimum number of diversity number is investigated. Golden section search algorithm is used to find the optimum diversity order for the multiple-input and single-output (MISO) system adopted with maximal ratio combining. A simple iterative method is used for the MISO system adopted with selection combining.

The remainder of this paper is organized as follows. In Sect. 2, the relationship between latency and reliability of spatial diversity system is analysed. Section 3 investigates the optimum number of diversity order for MISO system, where the system overhead is considered. Section 4 concludes this study.

2   Latency-Reliability Analysis of Diversity System

To improve the performance of the communication systems, we consider the adoption of diversity technique. There are several diversity techniques can be applied to wireless communication systems. In time diversity, the same data is transmitted at different time slots, which is difficult to achieve in low latency scenario. The channel gain in frequency diversity is related to the bandwidth and transmitted signal. In this paper, we focus on spatial diversity when describing diversity systems and the different combing techniques.

Multiple antennas can be installed at the transmitter or/and at the receiver to achieve spatial diversity. In spatial diversity at the receive side, the receiver is employed with multiple antennas. Consider a single-input and multiple-output (SIMO) system, the multiple received signals can be combined by maximum ratio combining (MRC), selection combing (SC), or equal gain combing (EGC) [11].

For transmit diversity, consider a MISO system. Under the assumption that the channel state information (CSI) is available to both the transmitter and receiver, the transmit diversity design is quite similar to receive diversity with MRC. The detailed analysis of maximum ratio transmission (MRT) scheme has been presented in [12]. Similarly, the analysis for SC under transmit diversity is the same as under receiver diversity. That is to say, the system performance analyses of SIMO and MISO systems can be described by the same formulas.

In this section, latency-reliability analyses of diversity systems are investigated, while MRC and SC combining techniques are applied respectively. In diversity systems, the fading paths are assumed to be independent and identical distributed (i.i.d.) Rayleigh fading channels.

Similar to the system model described in [7], the system performance can be analysed as follows. Data packets of length of C bits are transmitted over a system bandwidth of B Hz. The required latency is L in the unit of seconds. The outage probability is chosen as the system reliability metric. The instantaneous received signal-to-noise ratio (SNR) is defined as ρ, which is considered as a variable due to channel fading. According to the Shannon capacity theorem, the system spectral efficiency can be shown as a function of ρ, i.e., $\log_2(1 + \rho)$ bits/symbol. In the ideal system without any overhead, the number of time and frequency resource elements of the spatial diversity system is BL. In this section, we take a SIMO system as a reference, which consists of one antenna for transmission and N_R antennas for reception. The system outage probability can be shown as

$$P_{out} = \Pr\left[BL\log_2(1 + \rho) < C\right] = \Pr\left[\rho < \rho_{\text{th}}\right], \tag{1}$$

where

$$\rho_{\text{th}} = 2^{\frac{C}{LB}} - 1 \tag{2}$$

is the SNR threshold.

Rayleigh fading is assumed for the multiple wireless channels. Each channel has the same average SNR. As such, the instantaneous SNR ρ_i of each channel is an exponentially distributed variable

$$p(\rho_i) = \frac{1}{\gamma} e^{-\frac{\rho_i}{\gamma}}, \tag{3}$$

where $\gamma = E(\rho_i)$ is the average SNR. According to the probability density function (PDF) of the instantaneous SNR in (3), the system outage probability in (1) can be attained as

$$P_{out} = \int_0^{\rho_{th}} p(\rho)\mathrm{d}\rho. \tag{4}$$

The instantaneous received SNR ρ is a function of the multiple SNRs of the independent fading channels, which depends on the combining technique and the number of diversity channels.

2.1 Diversity System with MRC

Considering of combining the multiple receive signals by MRC technique, the received SNR is seen as the sum of the SNR of each antenna as follows [11]

$$\rho = \sum_{i=1}^{N_R} \rho_i, \tag{5}$$

where ρ_i is the received SNR of the i-th antenna. We can rewrite (4), the outage probability of diversity system adopted with MRC technique for any N_R can be obtained as

$$P_{out}(N_R) = \int_{\rho_1+\cdots+\rho_{N_R}<\rho_{th}} \int\cdots\int p(\rho_1)p(\rho_2)\cdots p(\rho_N)\mathrm{d}\rho_1\mathrm{d}\rho_2\cdots\mathrm{d}\rho_{N_R}$$
$$= 1 - e^{-\frac{\rho_{th}}{\gamma}} \sum_{i=0}^{N_R-1} \frac{\rho_{th}^i}{i!\gamma^i}. \tag{6}$$

The outage probability in (6) can also be viewed as a function of latency L. The outage probability results with $N_R = 1, 2, 3$ are plotted against the latency in Fig. 1. The outage probability and the required latency are both plotted with the logarithmic scale. Obviously, the outage probability is a monotonically decreasing function of L. The latency and reliability of a system have their own constraints and cannot be improved simultaneously. Therefore, the latency-reliability trade-off should be analysed. As can be seen from Fig. 1, the curves with different average SNRs are nearly parallel.

As it is well known, the slope of the SNR-outage probability curve amounts to the diversity order, that is,

$$d = -\lim_{\gamma\to\infty} \frac{\log P_{out}}{\log \gamma} = N_R. \tag{7}$$

The relationship between latency and reliability can be derived by analyzing the latency-reliability trade-off degree defined in [7]. Similar to the diversity order, the LRTD can be derived as follows. First, we define

$$f = \frac{\rho_{th}}{\gamma} = \frac{a^{\frac{1}{t}} - 1}{\gamma}. \tag{8}$$

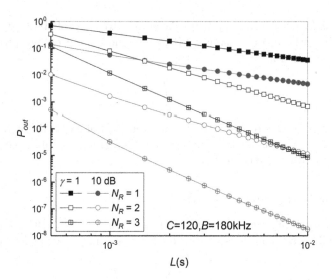

Fig. 1. Outage probability vs. latency with logarithmic scale in a diversity system with MRC

Then we have

$$
\begin{aligned}
d_{LR} &= -\lim_{L \to \infty} \frac{\log P_{out}(N_R)}{\log L} \\
&= \lim_{x \to 0} \frac{\log \left(1 - e^{-f} \sum_{i=0}^{N_R-1} \frac{f^i}{i!} \right)}{\log x} \\
&= \lim_{x \to 0} \frac{x f' e^{-f} \frac{f^{N_R-1}}{(N_R-1)!}}{1 - e^{-f} \sum_{i=0}^{N_R-1} \frac{f^i}{i!}} \\
&= \lim_{x \to 0} \frac{f'}{(N_R-1)!} \frac{x f^{N_R-1}}{1 - e^{-f} \sum_{i=0}^{N_R-1} \frac{f^i}{i!}} \\
&= \lim_{x \to 0} \frac{f'}{(N_R-1)!} \frac{x f^{N_R-2} f'(N_R-1) + f^{N_R-1}}{e^{-f} \frac{f^{N_R-1}}{(N_R-1)!} f'} \\
&= 1 + \lim_{x \to 0} \frac{x f'(N_R-1)}{f} = 1 + N_R - 1 \\
&= N_R.
\end{aligned}
\tag{9}
$$

As can be seen from (9), the result does not depend on particular values of f. It only requires that

$$
\lim_{x \to 0} f = 0,
\tag{10}
$$

the derivative of f,

$$f' = \frac{\partial f}{\partial x} \tag{11}$$

exits, and

$$\lim_{x \to 0} f' \neq 0. \tag{12}$$

As can be seen in (9), in a diversity system with MRC, the LRTD is the same as the system diversity order, which can also be seen from the slopes of the outage probability-latency curves in Fig. 1.

2.2   Diversity System with SC

Considering of combining the multiple receive signals by SC technique, the diversity antenna with the maximum SNR is chosen to receive the signal as follows

$$i_c = \arg\max_{i \in [1,\, 2,\, ...,\, N_R]} \rho_i, \tag{13}$$

where ρ_i is the received SNR of the i-th antenna. Therefore, the outage probability of the diversity system adopted with SC technique for any N_R can be obtained as

$$\begin{aligned} P_{out}(N_R) &= \Pr\left[\ \max(\rho_i) < \rho_{\text{th}}\right] \\ &= \Pr\left[\rho_1 < \rho_{\text{th}}, \rho_2 < \rho_{\text{th}}, \cdots, \rho_N < \rho_{\text{th}}\right]. \end{aligned} \tag{14}$$

For each diversity channel, the outage probability can be derived as

$$P_{out}(1) = \Pr[\rho_i < \rho_{th}] = \int_0^{\rho_{\text{th}}} p(\rho_i)\mathrm{d}\rho_i = 1 - \mathrm{e}^{-\frac{\rho_{\text{th}}}{\gamma}}. \tag{15}$$

The diversity antennas are independent and have the identical distributed channels. Then (14) can be rewritten as

$$P_{out}(N_R) = \prod_{i=1}^{N_R} \Pr\left[\rho_i < \rho_{th}\right] = [P_{out}(1)]^{N_R}. \tag{16}$$

The outage probability results with $N_R = 1, 2, 3$ are plotted against the latency in Fig. 2. As can be seen, similar to Fig. 1, the curves with different average SNRs are nearly parallel.

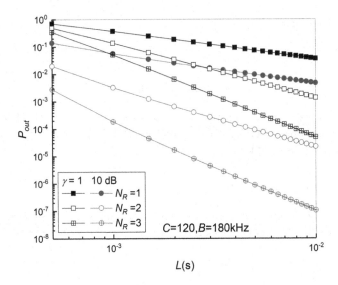

Fig. 2. Outage probability vs. latency with logarithmic scale in a diversity system with SC

Similar to the analysis in (9), we analysis the LRTD with any N_R. We have

$$
\begin{aligned}
d_{LR} &= -\lim_{L\to\infty}\frac{\log P_{out}(N_R)}{\log L} \\
&= \lim_{x\to 0}\frac{\log P_{out}(N_R)}{\log x} \\
&= \lim_{x\to 0}\frac{xP'_{out}(N_R)}{P_{out}(N_R)} \\
&= 1 + \lim_{x\to 0}\frac{xP''_{out}(N_R)}{P'_{out}(N_R)} \\
&= 1 + \lim_{x\to 0}(N_R - 1)\frac{xP'_{out}(1)}{P_{out}(1)} + \lim_{x\to 0}\frac{xP''_{out}(1)}{P'_{out}(1)} \\
&= 1 + N_R - 1 \\
&= N_R.
\end{aligned}
\tag{17}
$$

As can be seen in (17), in a diversity system with SC technique, the LRTD is the same as the system diversity order, which can also be seen from the slopes of the outage probability-latency curves in Fig. 2.

In this section, spatial diversity with multiple antennas is applied to the low-latency and high-reliability communications. The latency-reliability trade-off of the diversity system is analysed. The above analysis indicates that the slope of the P_{out}-L curve is the same as the diversity order. That is, the SNR scaling is similar to the latency scaling. The conclusion remains the same when the diversity system is applied with different combining techniques. Therefore, we can replace L with γ in (9) and (17) while the conclusion remains the same. In other words, the latency and reliability can be improved with diversity techniques.

3   System Overhead Analysis in Diversity System

In a diversity system, the SNR received from each diversity channel ρ_i should be known at receive or transmit side for the purpose of combining. We can assume that the system overhead ratio of all the resource elements for a reference signal is α. In a SIMO system with one transmitting antenna and N_R receiving antennas, one reference signal is required at the transmit side. Hence, the number of resource elements for overhead is constant. With the diversity antennas increase, the SIMO system performance gets better. However, in a MISO system with N_T transmitting antennas and one receiving antenna, the required reference signals have the linear relation with the number of diversity antennas N_T. That is, when the transmitter is equipped with N_T antennas, the number of resource elements for the overhead is $N_T \alpha BL$, and the number of resource elements left for data transmission is $BL(1 - N_T \alpha)$.

In consideration of the system overhead for reference signals, (2) can be rewritten as

$$\rho_{\text{th}} = 2^{\frac{C}{LB(1 - N_T \alpha)}} - 1. \tag{18}$$

As can be seen, ρ_{th} is a monotonically increasing function of N_T in consideration of the overhead, which affects the relationship between latency and reliability as we discuss in more detail as follows.

3.1   MISO System with MRC

Without considering the overhead, as shown in (6), the outage probability of the multi-antenna diversity system with MRC is a monotonically decreasing function of N_T. In the case of considering the overhead, integrating (18) into (6), we have the outage probability of the MISO system with MRC as a function of N_T.

In order to analysis the trend of outage probability with the growth of N_T, we can first analysis how the SNR threshold ρ_{th} affects the outage probability. Using the properties of incomplete gamma function [13], the outage probability in (6) can be written as

$$P_{out}(N_T) = 1 - e^{-\frac{\rho_{\text{th}}}{\gamma}} \sum_{i=0}^{N_T-1} \frac{\left(\frac{\rho_{\text{th}}}{\gamma}\right)^i}{i!}$$
$$= \frac{1}{(N_T - 1)!} \int_0^{\frac{\rho_{\text{th}}}{\gamma}} t^{N_T-1} e^{-t} dt. \tag{19}$$

As can be seen from (19), the outage probability of the MISO system is a monotonically increasing function of ρ_{th}. In (18), ρ_{th} is a monotonically increasing function of N_T in consideration of the overhead. Therefore, in the multi-antenna diversity system with overhead, with the increase of N_T, the outage probability will initially decrease due to the diversity gains. Then, too many system resource elements are occupied due to the system overhead. The system outage probability will increase at last. There exists an optimum number of diversity order to achieve the lowest outage probability.

As plotted in Fig. 3 using the parameter $\alpha = 0.05$ [7], the outage probability is a discrete unimodal distribution function of the diversity order N_T, which is in accordance with the previous theoretical derivation. It can be seen from Fig. 3 that the optimum number is $N_T = 9$. We can use greedy search to find the optimum N_T, but the optimum number is very large when α is small.

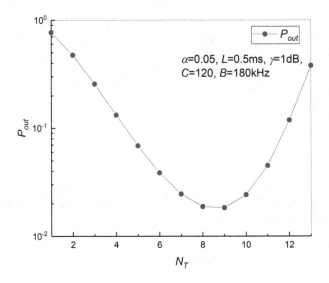

Fig. 3. Outage probability vs. diversity order in the system with MRC

In order to reduce the number of calculations, we propose to use the Golden Section Search (GSS) algorithm for finding the optimum diversity order N_T which leads to the minimum value of P_{out} [14]. Compared with the Binary Search algorithm, the benefit of GSS is that the function value is calculated additionally once more instead of two times at each iteration. GSS is usually adopted for finding the extremum of a unimodal continuous function, but in this problem, P_{out} is a discrete function. The initial search interval of N_T is $[1, \lfloor 1/\alpha \rfloor]$. In the algorithm, the search interval is narrowed down by the golden section ratio $r = 0.618$ after each iteration. The searching process using GSS algorithm is shown in Algorithm 1.

In the GSS algorithm described above, we have $1/r = r/1 - r$ as shown in Fig. 4. Therefore, one new point is selected and one more function value is calculated at each iteration. The number of diversity order N_T is discrete, so that the iteration of the golden section search can terminate when the size of search range is less than or equal to 2, i.e., $b - a \leq 2$. Then, the optimum number is $N_T = \lceil (a + b)/2 \rceil$.

Algorithm 1. GSS algorithm for finding the optimum diversity order N_T

Input: function value P_{out}, parameter α
Output: optimum diversity order N_T
1: initial $a = 1, b = floor(1/\alpha), r = 0.618, left = 1, right = 1$
2: **repeat**
3:     **if** $left$ **then**
4:         $x1 = floor(b - r(b - a)), f1 = P_{out}(x1)$
5:     **end if**
6:     **if** $right$ **then**
7:         $x2 = ceil(a + r(b - a)), f2 = P_{out}(x2)$
8:     **end if**
9:     **if** $f1 > f2$ **then**
10:         $a = x1, x1 = x2, f1 = f2, left = 0, right = 1$
11:     **else**
12:         $b = x2, x2 = x1, f2 = f1, right = 0, left = 1$
13:     **end if**
14: **until** $(b - a \leq 2)$
15: **return** $N_T = ceil((a + b)/2)$

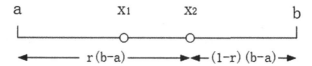

Fig. 4. Division of interval in GSS algorithm

As shown in Fig. 3, when the latency $L = 0.5\,ms$, the optimum number of diversity order is $N_T = 9$. Using the GSS algorithm, when $\alpha = 0.05$, the initial search interval is $[1, 20]$, the result is also $N_T = 9$. As shown in Fig. 5(a), when $\alpha = 0.05$, the GSS algorithm gives the same results as greedy search algorithm. When $\alpha = 0.04$, more results are plotted in Fig. 5(b). The reason for calculation error of GSS algorithm is that the outage probability is a discrete unimodal distribution function of the diversity order N_T. At each iteration, the new point selected by golden ratio should be rounded up or down to the nearest integer. The search range cannot be narrowed down any more when $b - a = 1$ or 2. Therefore, there could be an error by using GSS algorithm. As shown in Fig. 5(a) and (b), with the increase of L, the optimum number of diversity order N_T increases. Comparing Fig. 5(a) with (b), it can be seen that, with the decrease of α, the optimum N_T increases.

The results of optimum number by using GSS algorithm and greedy search algorithm are compared in Fig. 5(a) and (b). The GSS algorithm gives smaller results of N_T than the greedy search algorithm. The error is less than or equal to 1. Moreover, the GSS algorithm needs less number of calculations than the greedy search algorithm, especially when α is small. Therefore, when the outage probability is a discrete unimodal distribution function of the diversity order, the GSS algorithm can be used to find the optimum diversity order N_T.

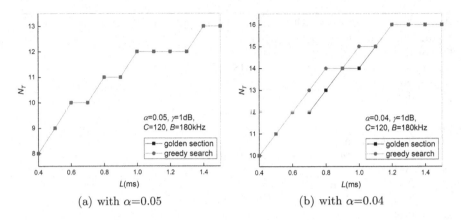

(a) with α=0.05   (b) with α=0.04

Fig. 5. Optimum number of diversity order with the GSS and greedy search algorithm

3.2   MISO System with SC

Without considering the overhead, as shown in (16), the outage probability of the multi-antenna diversity system with SC is a monotonically decreasing function of the diversity order. In the case of considering the overhead, integrating (18) into (16), we have the outage probability of the MISO system with SC as a function of N_T.

As can be seen from (15), the outage probability is a monotonically increasing function of ρ_{th}. In (18), ρ_{th} is a monotonically increasing function of N_T in consideration of the systems overhead. Therefore, in the MISO system with SC with overhead, with the increase of N_T, the outage probability of the diversity system will initially decrease due to the diversity gains. Then, because of the overhead, the system outage will increase at last. Therefore, there exist an optimum number of diversity order to achieve the lowest outage probability. The outage probability considered of system overhead with $L = 1\,\mathrm{ms}$ and $\alpha = 0.05$ is plotted as a function of N_T in Fig. 6.

The outage probability of the MISO system with SC is similar to the outage probability of multi-relay system modeled in [7]. To obtain the optimum diversity order, we can use the simplified iterative method proposed in [7], which is much simpler than greedy search method. The optimum number of diversity order can be obtained taking the derivative of the outage probability in (16), then we have

$$P_1 \log P_1 + N \frac{\partial P_1}{\partial N_T} = 0, \tag{20}$$

where $P_1 = P_{out}(1)$. Because that the number of antenna N_T should be an integer, the result should round down to the nearest integer. According to the LRTD analysis in (17), when considering the system overhead, we have an approximate fitting function

$$P_1 \approx \frac{b}{L(1 - N_T \alpha)}, \tag{21}$$

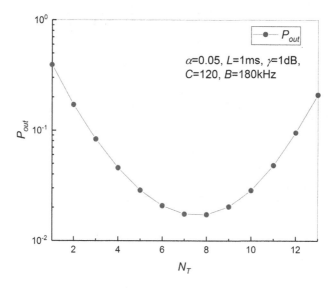

Fig. 6. Outage probability vs. diversity order in the system with SC

where b is a constant, which can be obtained by fitting the outage probability curve indicated by the black square symbol in Fig. 2, $b = 0.0003694$.

Integrating (21) into (20), we have

$$\frac{L}{b}x = e^{(1-x)/x}, \tag{22}$$

where

$$x = 1 - N_T\alpha. \tag{23}$$

Equation (22) can be rewritten as

$$x = \frac{1}{1 + \log\left(\frac{L}{b}x\right)}. \tag{24}$$

It can be proved that the two functions in (22) have a single intersection point in the interval of $x \in [0, 1]$. That is, there is an optimum diversity order.

Therefore, the sole root of (24) can be calculated by the iterative method. The iteration start from $x = 1$. The iteration process to obtain the optimum diversity order N_T is shown in Algorithm 2.

As shown in Fig. 6, the optimum number of diversity order is $N_T = 8$. The simplified iterative method in Algorithm 2 gives the result $N_T = 7$.

The results of optimum number by using simplified iterative method and greedy search method are compared in Fig. 7. The simplified iterative method gives smaller results of N_T than the greedy search method. The error is not large. Simultaneously, the error of the lower bound of the outage probability due to inaccurate N_T is small. The iterative method can be used to find the optimum diversity order N_T with simpler and less calculations.

Algorithm 2. A simplified iterative method for finding the optimum N_T

Input: function parameter α, the required latency L
Output: optimum diversity order N_T
 1: initial $b = 0.0003694, x = 1, n = 1$
 2: **while** $n = 1$ or $|N - N0| > 0.1$ **do**
 3:     $x0 = x$
 4:     $x = 1/\left(1 + \log(Lx/b)\right)$
 5:     $N = (1 - x)/\alpha$
 6:     $N0 = (1 - x0)/\alpha$
 7:     $n = n + 1$
 8: **end while**
 9: **return** $N_T= \text{floor}(N)$

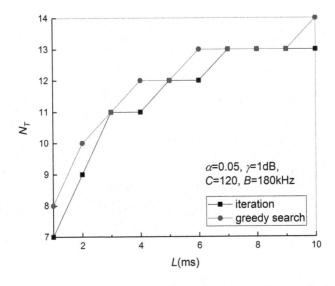

Fig. 7. Optimum number of diversity order with the iteration method and greedy search method with $\alpha = 0.05$

4   Conclusion

In this paper, the relationship between the latency and reliability of diversity system is investigated. Diversity systems adopted with maximal ratio combining and selection combining techniques are analysed respectively. The LRTD is proved to be the same as the number of the diversity order whichever combining technique is adopted. For the MISO system considered of system overhead, the trade-off between diversity gains and the system overhead is analysed. For system with MRC, golden section search algorithm for discrete function is proposed to obtain the optimum number of diversity order. For system with SC, the optimum diversity order is obtained with a simplified iterative method which is much simpler than greedy search method.

References

1. Osseiran, A., Boccardi, F., Braun, V., Kusume, K., Marsch, P., Maternia, M., et al.: Scenarios for 5G mobile and wireless communications: the vision of the metis project. IEEE Commun. Mag. **52**(5), 26–35 (2014)
2. METIS D1.5, Updated scenarios, requirements and KPIs for 5G mobile and wireless system with recommendations for future investigations. ICT-317669-METIS/D1.5, Deliverable D1.5 (2015)
3. Li, Z., Uusitalo, M.A., Shariatmadari, H., Singh, B.: 5G URLLC: design challenges and system concepts. In: 2018 15th International Symposium on Wireless Communication Systems (ISWCS), Lisbon, Portugal, pp. 1–6 (2018)
4. Li, C.-P., Jiang, J., Chen, W., Ji, T., Smee, J.: 5G ultra-reliable and low-latency systems design. In: 2017 European Conference on Networks and Communications (EuCNC), Oulu, Finland, pp. 1–5 (2017)
5. Soret, B., Mogensen, P., Pedersen, K.I., Aguayo-Torres, M.C.: Fundamental trade-offs among reliability, latency and throughput in cellular networks. In: 2014 IEEE Globecom Workshops (GC Wkshps), Austin, TX, USA, pp. 1391–1396 (2014)
6. Swamy, V.N., Suri, S., Rigge, P., Weiner, M., Ranade, G., Sahai, A., et al.: Cooperative communication for high-reliability low-latency wireless control. In: 2015 IEEE International Conference on Communications (ICC), London, UK, pp. 4380–4386 (2015)
7. Long, H., Xiang, W., Sun, Y.: Low-latency and high-reliability performance analysis of relay systems. IET Commun. **12**(5), 627–633 (2018)
8. Kotaba, R., Navarro Manchón, C., Balercia, T., Popovski, P.: Uplink transmissions in URLLC systems with shared diversity resources. IEEE Wirel. Commun. Lett. **7**(4), 590–593 (2018)
9. Shariatmadari, H., Li, Z., Iraji, S., Uusitalo, M.A., Jäntti, R.: Control channel enhancements for ultra-reliable low-latency communications. In: 2017 IEEE International Conference on Communications Workshops (ICC Workshops), Paris, France, pp. 504–509 (2017)
10. Schiessl, S., Al-Zubaidy, H., Skoglund, M., Gross, J.: Delay performance of wireless communications with imperfect CSI and finite-length coding. IEEE Trans. Commun. **66**(12), 6527–6541 (2018)
11. Aloi, G.: Wireless Communications. Cambridge University Press, Cambridge (2007)
12. Lo, T.K.Y.: Maximum ratio transmission. IEEE Trans. Commun. **47**(10), 1458–1461 (1999)
13. Telatar, E.: Capacity of multi-antenna Gaussian channels. Eur. Trans. Telecommun. **10**(6), 585–595 (1999)
14. Cheney, W., Kincaid, D.: Numerical Mathematics and Computing. Cole Publishing Company, Pacific Grove (2007)

Cost Function Minimization-Based Joint UAV Path Planning and Charging Station Deployment (Workshop)

Tao Wei[✉], Rong Chai, and Qianbin Chen

Key Lab of Mobile Communication Technology,
Chongqing University of Posts and Telecommunications, Chongqing 400065, China
1192417369@qq.com, {chairong,chenqb}@cqupt.edu.cn

Abstract. The rapid development of automatic control, wireless communication and intelligent information processing promotes the prosperity of unmanned aerial vehicles (UAVs) technologies. In some applications, UAVs are required to fly from given source places to certain destinations for task execution, a reasonable path planning and charging stations (CSs) strategy can be designed to achieve the performance enhancement of task execution of the UAVs. In this paper, we consider joint UAV path planning and CS deployment problem. Stressing the importance of the total time of the UAVs to perform tasks and the cost of deploying and maintaining CSs, we formulate the joint path planning and CS deployment problem as a cost function minimization problem. Since the formulated optimization problem is an NP-hard problem which cannot be solved easily, we propose a heuristic algorithm which successively solves two subproblems, i.e, path planning subproblem and destination path selection subproblem by applying the A* algorithm, K-shortest path algorithm and genetic algorithm (GA), respectively. Simulation results validate the effectiveness of the proposed algorithm.

Keywords: UAV · Path planning · Charging station deployment · Cost function

1 Introduction

The rapid development of automatic control, wireless communication and intelligent information processing promotes the prosperity of unmanned aerial vehicles (UAVs) technologies. Being capable of flying under certain commands and executing specific tasks without a human pilot on board, UAVs have been commonly applied in public and military fields [1].

In some applications [2–5], UAVs are required to fly from given source places to certain destinations for task execution, a reasonable path planning strategy for the UAV should be designed. Furthermore, due to the limited battery capacity of the UAVs, long-distance continuous flying might be difficult. To tackle this problem, various charging stations (CSs) can be deployed, i.e., deploying multiple CSs in the flying area of the UAVs, can be an efficient and practical approach. By charging at the CSs, long distance flight for UAVs might be possible.

© ICST Institute for Computer Sciences, Social Informatics and Telecommunications Engineering 2020
Published by Springer Nature Switzerland AG 2020. All Rights Reserved
H. Gao et al. (Eds.): ChinaCom 2019, LNICST 313, pp. 378–390, 2020.
https://doi.org/10.1007/978-3-030-41117-6_31

In recent years, researchers have carried out studies on UAV path planning and CS deployment. The algorithm in [6] studied the path planning problem of UAVs and proposed an A* algorithm-based heuristic search method to obtain the shortest flight time. Aiming to minimize the flight time, the authors in [7] proposed a path planning method based on A* algorithm and Dubins path strategy. Considering the flight constraints of the UAVs during the planning process, the authors in [8] modeled the threat regions as points and proposed a K-shortest path algorithm-based strategy with the objective of minimizing the total flight time. To determine the paths with the shortest flight time, the authors in [9] discussed any-angle path planning algorithm that are variants of classical A* algorithm. Through propagating information along the edges of the flight grid, the shortest paths can be determined. In [10], the authors proposed a path planing algorithm which aims to minimize the flight time of UAVs.

The problem of CS deployment was considered when planing paths for UAVs [11, 12]. In [11], the authors studied the problem of determining a path for an energy-limited UAV to visit a set of sites, and presented an algorithm aiming to find the shortest time for UAVs and the optimal locations to place CSs. The authors in [12] consider deploying mobile CSs for the UAVs, and proposed a joint UAV path planning and CS deployment algorithm to obtain the optimal UAVs flight path and require the shortest time for the CSs reach the charging points.

In this paper, we study joint UAV path planning and CS deployment problem. Stressing the importance of the total time of the UAVs to perform tasks and the cost of deploying the CSs, we formulate the joint path planning and CS deployment problem as a cost function minimization problem. Since the formulated optimization problem is an NP-hard problem which cannot be solved easily, we propose a heuristic algorithm which successively solves two subproblems, i.e, path planning subproblem and destination path selection subproblem by applying the A* algorithm, K-shortest path algorithm and genetic algorithm (GA), respectively.

The rest of this paper is organized as follows. Section 2 describes the system model considered in this paper and the discrete processing of the UAV flight area. Section 3 presents the formulation of the cost function minimization problem. The solution to the optimization problem is described in Sect. 4. Section 5 presents the numerical results. The conclusion is drawn in Sect. 6.

2   System Model and Discrete Processing of the Flight Area

In this paper, we consider the scenario that multiple UAVs are required to perform tasks in a rectangular area. We denote X, Y respectively as the length and the width of the area, U_l as the lth UAV, $1 \leq l \leq L$, L is the total number of UAVs. Let S = $\{S_1, S_2, \ldots, S_L\}$ denote the set of task sources and D = $\{D_1, D_2, \ldots, D_L\}$ denote the set of task destinations of the UAVs, where S_l, D_l denote respectively the task source and destination of U_l.

Due to the limited endurance of the UAVs, they may not perform long-distance tasks, thus should be charged during the flight. We assume that CSs can be deployed in the flight area of UAVs, let C = $\{C_1, C_2, \ldots, C_M\}$ denote the set of CSs, where C_m denotes the mth CS, $1 \leq m \leq M$, M is the total number of CSs. We further assume that there are some threats in the flight area and the CSs can only be deployed in the area without obstacles. Figure 1 shows the system model considered in this paper. For simplicity, we conduct two-dimensional discrete processing over the flight region of the UAVs, more specifically, we model the flight area of the UAVs as a two-dimensional grid. Let Δ_x and Δ_y respectively be the distance between the adjacent grids in row and columns, let $N_x^{\max}$ and $N_y^{\max}$ be the maximum number of the grids in row and column, respectively, where $N_x^{\max} = [\frac{X}{\Delta_x}]$, $N_y^{\max} = [\frac{Y}{\Delta_y}]$. $N_{i,j}$ denotes the node in the ith row and the jth column, $0 \leq i \leq N_x^{\max}, 0 \leq j \leq N_y^{\max}$. Let N_l^s denote the source grid of U_l and N_l^d denotes the destination grid of U_l, we obtain $N_l^s = \arg\min\{|S_l - N_{i,j}|^2\}$, $N_l^d = \arg\min\{|d_l - N_{i,j}|^2\}$.

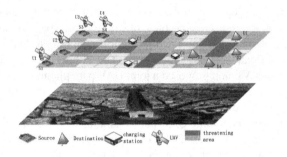

Fig. 1. System model

Let $y_{i,j,m}$ denote CS deployment variable, if C_m is deployed at $N_{i,j}$, $y_{i,j,m} = 1$, otherwise, $y_{i,j,m} = 0$. We denote $x_{l,m}$ as the charging variable of the UAVs, if U_l charges at C_m, $x_{l,m} = 1$, otherwise, $x_{l,m} = 0$. The flight path of the UAVs might be subject to certain types of threats, i.e., atmospheric threats, terrain threats, etc., we denote $G_{i,j}$ as the threats indicator of $N_{i,j}$, that is, if $N_{i,j}$ is the threatening area, $G_{i,j} = 1$, otherwise, $G_{i,j} = 0$. Figure 2 shows the two-dimensional discretization of the flight area of the UAVs.

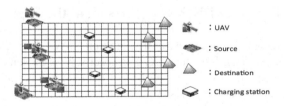

Fig. 2. System model

3   Optimization Problem Formulation

In this section, we examine the overall cost of the UAVs performing tasks and formulate the joint UAV path selection and CS deployment problem as a cost function minimization problem.

3.1   Objective Function

Stressing the importance of the total time required for the UAVs to perform missions and the cost of deploying the CSs, we define the cost function, denoted by Q as

$$Q = T + \lambda F \tag{1}$$

where T denotes the time required for the UAVs to perform the tasks, F denotes the cost of deploying the CSs, and λ denotes the weighting factor. T can be computed as

$$T = \sum_{l=1}^{L} T_l \tag{2}$$

where T_l denotes the time required for U_l to fly from N_l^s to N_l^d, and can be calculated as

$$T_l = T_l^t + T_l^c \tag{3}$$

where T_l^t denotes the flight time required for U_l to reach the destination, and can be expressed as

$$T_l^t = \sum_{i_1=0}^{N_x^{max}} \sum_{j_1=0}^{N_y^{max}} \sum_{i_2=0}^{N_x^{max}} \sum_{j_2=0}^{N_y^{max}} z_{l,i_1,j_1,i_2,j_2} T_{l,i_1,j_1,i_2,j_2} \tag{4}$$

where z_{l,i_1,j_1,i_2,j_2} denotes path planing variable. If U_l reaches N_{i_2,j_2} via N_{i_1,j_1}, then $z_{l,i_1,j_1,i_2,j_2} = 1$, otherwise, $z_{l,i_1,j_1,i_2,j_2} = 0$, T_{l,i_1,j_1,i_2,j_2} denotes the flight time required for U_l to fly from N_{i_1,j_1} to N_{i_2,j_2}, which can be computed as

$$T_{l,i_1,j_1,i_2,j_2} = \frac{D_{i_1,j_1,i_2,j_2}}{v_l} \tag{5}$$

where v_l denotes the flight speed of U_l, D_{i_1,j_1,i_2,j_2} denotes the flight distance between N_{i_1,j_1} and N_{i_2,j_2}, in the case no threatening area between N_{i_1,j_1} and N_{i_2,j_2}, D_{i_1,j_1,i_2,j_2} can be expressed as

$$D_{i_1,j_1,i_2,j_2} = \sqrt{(i_1 - i_2)^2 \Delta_x^2 + (j_1 - j_2)^2 \Delta_y^2}. \tag{6}$$

However, in the case that there exists threatening area between N_{i_1,j_1} and N_{i_2,j_2}, D_{i_1,j_1,i_2,j_2} should be calculated as discussed in later subsections.

T_l^c in (3) denotes the charging time of U_l during the flight from N_l^s to N_l^d, and can be expressed as

$$T_l^c = \sum_{i_2=0}^{N_x^{max}} \sum_{j_2=0}^{N_y^{max}} \sum_{m=1}^{M} T_{l,i_1,j_1,i_2,j_2}^m x_{l,m} y_{i_2,j_2,m} \tag{7}$$

where T^m_{l,i_1,j_1,i_2,j_2} denotes the charging time of U_l at C_m when flying from N_{i_1,j_1} to N_{i_2,j_2}, which can be computed as

$$T^m_{l,i_1,j_1,i_2,j_2} = \frac{W_{l,i_1,j_1,i_2,j_2}}{P_m} \tag{8}$$

where P_m denotes the charging power of C_m, W_{l,i_1,j_1,i_2,j_2} denotes the energy consumption of U_l when flying from N_{i_1,j_1} to N_{i_2,j_2}. The energy consumption of the UAV is related to the flight distance, and can be expressed as

$$W_{l,i_1,j_1,i_2,j_2} = W_l D_{i_1,j_1,i_2,j_2} \tag{9}$$

where W_l denotes the unit energy consumption of U_l.

F in (1) can be expressed as

$$F = \sum_{i=0}^{N_x^{\max}} \sum_{j=0}^{N_y^{\max}} \sum_{m=1}^{M} F_{i,j,m} y_{i,j,m} \tag{10}$$

where $F_{i,j,m}$ denotes the cost of C_m at node $N_{i,j}$, and is given by

$$F_{i,j,m} = F^o_{i,j,m} + F^c_{i,j,m} \tag{11}$$

where $F^o_{i,j,m}$ denotes the cost for deploying C_m at node $N_{i,j}$, $F^c_{i,j,m}$ denotes the cost required for maintaining C_m at node $N_{i,j}$. In this paper, we assume that both $F^o_{i,j,m}$ and $F^c_{i,j,m}$ are given constants.

3.2 Optimization Constraints

To achieve efficient path planning and CS deployment, the following constraints must be considered.

Charging Station Deployment Constraints. In this paper, we assume that at most one CS can be deployed at any node, i.e.,

$$C1 : \sum_{m=1}^{M} y_{i,j,m} \leq 1. \tag{12}$$

In addition, we assume that each CS can at most be deployed at one node, hence, the constraint can be expressed as

$$C2 : \sum_{i=0}^{N_x^{\max}} \sum_{j=0}^{N_y^{\max}} y_{i,j,m} \leq 1 \tag{13}$$

UAV Path Planing Constraints. Through flying from the sources to the destinations, the following path planning constraints must be considered.

$$C3 : \sum_{i_2=0}^{N_x^{\max}} \sum_{j_2=0}^{N_y^{\max}} z_{l,i_1,j_1,i_2,j_2} = 1, \text{ if } N_{i_1,j_1} = S_l,$$

$$(i_2, j_2) \neq (i_1, j_1) \tag{14}$$

$$C4 : \sum_{i_1=0}^{N_x^{\max}} \sum_{j_1=0}^{N_y^{\max}} z_{l,i_1,j_1,i_2,j_2} = 1, \text{ if } N_{i_2,j_2} = D_l$$

$$(i_2, j_2) \neq (i_1, j_1) \tag{15}$$

$$C5 : \sum_{i_1=0}^{N_x^{\max}} \sum_{j_1=0}^{N_y^{\max}} z_{l,i_1,j_1,i_2,j_2} = \sum_{i_3=0}^{N_x^{\max}} \sum_{j_3=0}^{N_y^{\max}} z_{l,i_2,j_2,i_3,j_3},$$

$$\text{if } N_{i_2,j_2} \neq \{S_l, D_l\} \tag{16}$$

Maximum Flight Distance Constraint. The path between two adjacent nodes can be selected for the UAVs only if the distance between two points is less than the maximum flight distance of the UAVs, hence, we can express the maximum flight distance constraint as

$$C6 : z_{l,i_1,j_1,i_2,j_2} = 0, \text{ if } D_{i_1,j_1,i_2,j_2} > D_l^{\max} \tag{17}$$

where $D_l^{\max}$ denotes the maximum flight distance of U_l.

Maximum Number of UAVs Constraint. We assume that limited by the charging power of the CSs, the constraint on the maximum number of UAVs must be considered, i.e.,

$$C7 : \sum_{i_1=0}^{N_x^{\max}} \sum_{j_1=0}^{N_y^{\max}} \sum_{l=1}^{L} z_{l,i_1,j_1,i_2,j_2} y_{i_2,j_2,m} x_{l,m} \leq N_m \tag{18}$$

where N_m denotes the maximum number of UAVs allowed to charge at C_m.

Flight Area Constraint. As the UAVs cannot fly over the threaten areas, the constraint can be expressed as

$$C8 : z_{l,i_1,j_1,i_2,j_2} = 0, \text{ if } G_{i_2,j_2} = 1 \tag{19}$$

Maximum Task Execution Time Constraint. Let $T_l^{\max}$ denote the maximum allowable time for U_l to reach the destination, the maximum task execution time constraint can be expressed as

$$C9 : T_l \leq T_l^{\max} \tag{20}$$

3.3 Optimization Problem

Considering the objective function and optimization constraints, we formulate the joint UAV path planning and CS deployment problem as

$$\min_{x_{l,m}, y_{i,j,m}, z_{l,i_1,i_2,j_1,j_2}} Q$$

$$\text{s.t.} \quad \text{C1} - \text{C9}. \tag{21}$$

Through solving above optimization problem, we can obtain the joint path planning, CS deployment strategy.

4   Solution to the Optimization Problem

The optimization problem formulated in (21) is an NP-hard problem which cannot be solved easily using traditional convex optimization tools. In this section, we propose a heuristic algorithm which successively solves two subproblems, i.e, path planning subproblem and destination path selection subproblem by applying the A* algorithm, K-shortest path algorithm and genetic algorithm (GA), respectively.

4.1   Path Planning Subproblem

In this subsection, for simplicity, we assume that CS deployment strategy is given, i.e., $y_{i,j,m} = 1, 0 \leq i \leq N_x^{\max}, 0 \leq j \leq N_y^{\max}, 1 \leq m \leq M$. As $F_{i,j,m}$ is a given constant, the path planing process of different UAVs is relatively independent, hence, the optimization problem formulated in (21) reduces to a set of path planning subproblems. For U_l, the path planning subproblem can be formulated as

$$\min_{x_{l,m}, z_{l,i_1,i_2,j_1,j_2}} T_l$$

$$\text{s.t.} \quad \text{C3} - \text{C9 in (21).} \tag{22}$$

K-shortest Paths Algorithm-Based Path Planning Strategy. To solve the optimization problem in (22), we model the system model as a weighted graph $G = (V, E, W)$, where $V = \{N_l^s\} \cup \{N_l^d\} \cup \{N_{i,j}\}, 1 \leq l \leq L, 1 \leq m \leq M, 0 \leq i \leq N_x^{\max}, 0 \leq j \leq N_y^{\max}$. Let V_i denote the ith vertex in V, $1 \leq i \leq |V|$, $|a|$ denotes the number of elements in set a, $E = \{E_{i,j}, 1 \leq i, j \leq N, i \neq j\}$ denotes the link set, where $E_{i,j}$ represents the link between V_i and V_j, and $W = \{W_{i,j}, 1 \leq i, j \leq I, i \neq j\}$ denotes the weight set of links, $W_{i,j}$ denotes the weight of $E_{i,j}$. Let V_i and V_j represent N_{i_1,j_1} and N_{i_2,j_2}, respectively, $W_{i,j}$ can be computed as

$$W_{i,j} = T_{l,i_1,j_1,i_2,j_2} + \sum_{m=1}^{M} T_{l,i_1,j_1,i_2,j_2}^m y_{i_2,j_2,m} \tag{23}$$

Given $W_{i,j}$, we apply the K-shortest paths algorithm to obtain the K candidate paths offering the minimum cost. Let P_l denote the set of the K candidate paths of U_l, p_l^k denote the kth candidate path of U_l, we may express P_l as $P_l = \{p_l^1, p_l^2, \ldots p_l^k, \ldots p_l^K\}$.

It should be noticed that to calculate $W_{i,j}$ based on (23), the distance between V_i and V_j, denoted by D_{l,i_1,j_1,i_2,j_2} should be calculated. However, since various types of threats might exist along the flight path between V_i and V_j, the flight distance may not exactly equal to the length of the directly connected link between the two positions. In next subsection, we apply A* algorithm to calculate the optimal D_{l,i_1,j_1,i_2,j_2}.

A* Algorithm-Based Flight Distance Determination. A* algorithm is commonly used to solve the problem of path planning in the scenario consisting of threat areas or obstacles. The basic idea of A* algorithm is that given start position and destination position, a cost function is defined, and a feasible path from start position to destination position is obtained through determining the intermediate nodes successively. To determine individual intermediate nodes, we select the one offering the smallest cost function.

Let s and d denote respectively the start position and destination position, the process of determining the optimal path between s and d based on A* algorithm can be summarized as follows:

(1) Initialization
Set $\Psi_1 = \{s\}$ and $\Psi_2 = \Phi$, where Φ denotes the empty set.
(2) Calculating cost function
Let x denote the reachable node of s, update Ψ_1 as $\Psi_1 = \Psi_1 \cup \{x\}$. Let $C(x)$ denote the cost of selecting x as the next-hop node, $C(x)$ can be calculated as

$$C(x) = ag(x) + bh(x) \tag{24}$$

where $g(x)$ denotes the cost required for routing from the start position s to x, $h(x)$ denotes the estimated cost due to flying from x to the destination position d, a and b are weighting parameters.
(3) Determining one hop reachable nodes of s
Select the reachable node of s which offers the smallest cost as the next-hop node, i.e., $x^* = \arg \min C(x)$.
(4) Update Ψ_1 and Ψ_2, and s
Remove x^* from Ψ_1, i.e., set $\Psi_1 = \Psi_1 \setminus \{x^*\}$ and add x^* to Ψ_2, i.e., $\Psi_2 = \Psi_2 \cup \{x^*\}$, set $s = x^*$.
(5) Algorithm termination condition
If $x^* = d$, the algorithm completes, otherwise, back to Step (2).

Applying the A* algorithm, we will be able to determine the optimal flight strategy between any two nodes V_i and V_j in G, and obtain the optimal flight distance denoted by D^*_{l,i_1,j_1,i_2,j_2}.

4.2 Destination Path Selection Subproblem

While each UAV may fly according to the obtained K candidate paths strategy, i.e., P_l, $1 \leq l \leq L$, considering the possible sharing on CSs and the various deployment cost of the CSs, it is highly possible that the overall cost might be reduced by selecting suitable candidate path for individual UAVs. More specifically, among K candidate paths, we may select one candidate path for each UAV so as the achieve the total cost minimization.

It can be demonstrated that given the K candidate paths set of all the UAVs, the problem of selecting one candidate path for each UAV can be formulated as an optimization problem. Let $T^*_{l,k}$ denote the cost of U_l when choosing the kth candidate path, $y_{i,j,m,l,k}$ denote the CS deployment strategy of U_l on the kth candidate path. That is, if C_m is deployed at $N_{i,j}$, which is selected as the intermediate node of the kth candidate path of U_l, $y_{i,j,m,l,k} = 1$, otherwise, $y_{i,j,m,l,k} = 0$. Notice that given the candidate path selection strategy P_l, $y_{i,j,m,l,k}$ is a known constant.

Redefine the cost function Q as Q', we obtain

$$Q' = \sum_{l=1}^{L} \sum_{k=1}^{K} \alpha_{l,k} T_{l,k} * - \sum_{m=1}^{M} \sum_{l=1}^{L} \sum_{k=1}^{K} \sum_{i=0}^{N_x^{\max}} \sum_{j=0}^{N_y^{\max}} \frac{\alpha_{l,k} y_{i,j,m,l,k} F_{i,j,m}}{A_m} \quad (25)$$

where $\alpha_{l,k}$ is the destination path selection variable, i.e., $\alpha_{l,k} = 1$, if U_l chooses the kth candidate path, $\alpha_{l,k} = 0$, otherwise. A_m is the number of UAVs which share C_m, and can be expressed as

$$A_m = \sum_{l=1}^{L} \sum_{k=1}^{K} \sum_{i=0}^{N_x^{\max}} \sum_{j=0}^{N_y^{\max}} \alpha_{l,k} y_{i,j,m,l,k}. \quad (26)$$

The destination path selection problem can be formulated as

$$\min_{\alpha_{l,k}} Q'$$

$$\text{s.t.} \sum_{k=1}^{K} \alpha_{l,k} = 1. \quad (27)$$

where the constraint indicates that one UAV can only select one candidate path as its destination path.

The formulated optimization problem in (27) is an nonlinear integer optimization problem, which can be solved via the extensive search method for the scenario with small number of UAVs and relatively small path planning area of the UAVs. However, the computation complexity becomes prohibitive as the size of the problem increases. In this subsection, we model the optimization problem as a biological evolution process and propose a low-complexity GA-based destination path search strategy.

Defining the combination of the candidate paths selected for various UAVs as population, and choosing Q' in (25) as fitness function, we can solve the problem based on GA [13].

The steps for obtaining the GA-based destination path search strategy can be summarized as follows.

(1) Initialization

Set generation counter $t = 1$, denote population size by N and $p_{l,t,n}$ as the candidate path of UAV$_l$ of the nth individual in the tth generation, i.e., $p_{l,t,n} = p_l^{k_l}$,

Table 1. Simulation parameters

Parameters	Value
The flight speed of UAVs (v_k)	10 km/h
The cost for deploying and maintaining CSs ($F_{i,j,m}$)	10,000.0
Number of iterations $T_{\max}$	100.0
Chromosome mutation probability (P_{mut})	0.2
Weighting factor (λ)	1.0/1.5
Number of candidate paths K	8
Number of UAVs n	4, 6
Number of threaten areas	10

$1 \leq k_l \leq K, 1 \leq n \leq N, 1 \leq t \leq T_{\max}$ where N and $T_{\max}$ denote respectively the maximum number of individuals and generations. Defining the population of the nth individual in the tth generation as

$$R_{t,n} = \left(p_{1,t,n,}, p_{2,t,n}, \cdots, p_{L,t,n}\right)^{\mathrm{T}}, \tag{28}$$

and denoting R_t as the population in the tth generation, we express the initial population as

$$R_1 = \left(R_{1,1}, R_{1,2}, \cdots, R_{1,N}\right)^{\mathrm{T}}. \tag{29}$$

(2) Fitness function evaluation
Substitute $R_{t,n}$ into the fitness function Q', the corresponding fitness value can be obtained.

(3) Gene selection
Through a fitness proportionated-based process [13], the fitness function assigns each fitness value a probability of selecting individuals. The probability of selecting $R_{t,n}$ can be defined as

$$P(R_{t,n}) = \frac{Q'(R_{t,n})}{\sum_{n=1}^{N} Q'(R_{t,n})}. \tag{30}$$

Selecting individuals with high $P(R_{t,n})$ from the population R_t, and conducting reproduction, we can obtain the reproduced population $R_t^{(1)}$.

(4) Crossover process
Randomly select two parent individuals R_{t,n_1}, R_{t,n_2} from $R_t^{(1)}, 1 \leq n_1, n_2 \leq N$, crossover the two parent individuals to form two children individuals R'_{t,n_1}, R'_{t,n_2} of the next generation through applying crossover-based method.

(5) Mutation process
Based on Gaussian mutation process, mutating the two children individuals R'_{t,n_1}, R'_{t,n_2} with certain mutation rate P_{mut}, and collecting the resulting individuals $R_{t,n}$, we can obtain the next generation:

$$R'_t = (R'_{t,1}, R'_{t,2}, \ldots, R'_{t,N}). \tag{31}$$

(6) Termination condition

If $|Q'(R'_t) - Q'(R_t)| \leq Q_{\text{th}}$, where Q_{th} denotes the threshold of Q', the algorithm terminates and the obtained R'_t offers the feasible destination path selection solution. If $t = T_{\max}$, the process terminates and the destination path selection algorithm fails, else set $R_{t+1} = R'_t$, $t = t + 1$, go to Step (3).

5   Simulation and Result Analysis

In this section, we examine the performance of the proposed joint path planning and CS deployment algorithm via simulation. In the simulation, we consider a square region with the size being 50 km × 50 km where a number of UAVs perform tasks from source position to destination position. We assume that threaten areas are randomly located in the region. Other parameters used in the simulation are summarized in Table 1. Simulation results are averaged over 100 independent processes involving different simulation parameters.

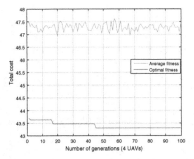

Fig. 3. Total cost versus number of generations (4 UAVs).

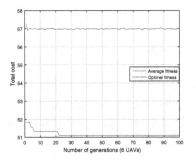

Fig. 4. Total cost versus number of generations (6 UAVs).

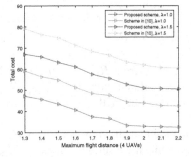

Fig. 5. Total cost versus maximum flight distance (4 UAVs).

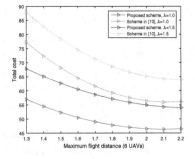

Fig. 6. Total cost versus maximum flight distance (6 UAVs)

In Figs. 3 and 4, we plot the total cost of UAVs versus the number of generations of GA. The number of UAVs is set as 4 and 6 in Figs. 3 and 4, respectively. It can be seen from the figure that the total cost converges to a constant, demonstrating the effectiveness of the applied GA.

Figures 5 and 6 show the total cost versus the maximum flight distance of the UAVs with different weighting factor. The number of UAVs is set as 4 and 6 in Figs. 5 and 6. For comparison, we plot the total cost of the UAVs obtained from our proposed scheme and the scheme proposed in [10]. We can see from the figures that the total cost decreases with the increase of the maximum flight distance of the UAVs. This is because as the maximum flight distance of the UAVs increases, the number of the CSs required to be deployed will decrease, which will result in the decrease of the total cost in turn. It can also be observed from the figures that, for both schemes, the total cost increases with the increase of weighting factor. Comparing the results obtained from our proposed scheme and the scheme proposed in [10], we can see that our proposed algorithm outperforms the scheme proposed in [10]. The reason is that our proposed scheme aims at minimizing the total cost, while the scheme proposed in [10] mainly considers the minimization of the flight time of UAVs and fails to consider the deploy time of the UAVs, thus may result in undesired total time.

6 Conclusions

In this paper, we jointly investigate UAV path planning and CS deployment algorithm. To stress the importance of the total time of the UAV to perform tasks and the cost of deploying and maintaining CSs, we formulate the joint optimization problem as a total cost minimization problem. Since the formulated optimization problem is an NP-hard problem, which cannot be solved easily, we transform the problem into two subproblems, i.e., path planning subproblem and destination path selection subproblem, and solve the two subproblems by applying the A* algorithm, K-shortest path algorithm and GA, respectively. The simulations demonstrate the effectiveness of the proposed algorithm.

References

1. Gupta, L., Jain, R., Vaszkun, G.: Survey of important issues in UAV communication networks. IEEE Commun. Surv. Tutor. **18**(2), 1123–1152 (2016). Second Quarter
2. Michael, N., Stump, E., Mohta, K.: Persistent surveillance with a team of MAVs. In: 2011 IEEE/RSJ International Conference on Intelligent Robots and Systems, pp. 2708–2714 (2011)
3. Liu, P., et al.: A review of rotorcraft unmanned aerial vehicle developments and applications in civil engineering. Smart Struct. Syst **13**(6), 1065–1094 (2014)
4. Özaslan, T., Shen, S., Mulgaonkar, Y., Michael, N., Kumar, V.: Inspection of penstocks and featureless tunnel-like environments using micro UAVs. In: Mejias, L., Corke, P., Roberts, J. (eds.) Field and Service Robotics. STAR, vol. 105, pp. 123–136. Springer, Cham (2015). https://doi.org/10.1007/978-3-319-07488-7_9
5. Dunbabin, M., Marques, L.: Robots for environmental monitoring: significant advancements and applications. IEEE Robot. Autom. Mag. **19**(1), 24–39 (2012)

6. Rnzhou, Y., Yong, D., Chengguo, Z.: Application of improved A* algorithm based on DTW in track planning. Electro-Opt. Control **23**(6), 5–10 (2016)
7. Song, X., Hu, S.: 2D path planning with Dubins-path-based A* algorithm for a fixed-wing UAV. In: Proceedings of the ICCSSE, pp. 69–73, August 2017
8. Chen, X., Li, G., Chen, X.: Path planning and cooperative control for multiple UAVs based on consistency theory and Voronoi diagram. In: 2017 29th Chinese Control and Decision Conference (CCDC), pp. 881 886 (2017)
9. Nash, A., Koenig, S.: Any-angle path planning. AI Mag. **34**, 85–107 (2013)
10. Liu, Y., Luo, Z., Liu, Z., Shi, J., Cheng, G.: Cooperative routing problem for gound vehicle and unmanned aerial vehicle: the application on intelligence, surveillance, and reconnaissance missions. IEEE Access **7**, 63504–63518 (2019)
11. Yu, K., Budhiraja, A.K., Tokekar, P.: Algorithms for routing of unmanned aerial vehicles with mobile recharging stations. In: 2018 IEEE International Conference on Robotics and Automation (ICRA), pp. 1–5 (2018)
12. Zhang, B., Liu, C.H., Tang, J., Xu, Z., Ma, J., Wang, W.: Learning-based energy-efficient data collection by unmanned vehicles in smart vities. IEEE Trans. Ind. Inform. **14**(4), 1666–1676 (2018)
13. Mitchell, M.: An Introduction to Genetic Algorithms. MIT Press, London (1998)

Energy Efficient Computation Offloading for Energy Harvesting-Enabled Heterogeneous Cellular Networks (Workshop)

Mengqi Mao$^{(\boxtimes)}$, Rong Chai, and Qianbin Chen

School of Communication and Information Engineering,
Chongqing University of Posts and Telecommunications, Chongqing 400065, China
maomengqii@163.com, {chairong,chenqb}@cqupt.edu.cn

Abstract. Mobile edge computing (MEC) is regarded as an emerging paradigm of computation that aims at reducing computation latency and improving quality of experience. In this paper, we consider an MEC-enabled heterogeneous cellular network (HCN) consisting of one macro base station (MBS), one small base station (SBS) and a number of users. By defining workload execution cost as the weighted sum of the energy consumption of the MBS and the workload dropping cost, the joint computation offloading and resource allocation problem is formulated as a workload execution cost minimization problem under the constraints of computation offloading, resource allocation and delay tolerant, etc. As the formulated optimization problem is a Markov decision process (MDP)-based offloading problem, we propose a hotbooting Q-learning-based algorithm to obtain the optimal strategy. Numerical results demonstrate the effectiveness of the proposed scheme.

Keywords: Mobile edge computing · Heterogeneous cellular network · Computation offloading · Resource allocation · Hotbooting Q-learning

1 Introduction

Mobile edge computing (MEC) is regarded as an emerging paradigm of computation that aims at reducing computation latency and improving quality of experience through pushing mobile computing, network control and storage to the network edges of cellular networks [1]. On the other hand, to improve the transmission performance of the cellular users, heterogeneous cellular networks (HCNs) which consist of macro base stations (MBSs) and various heterogeneous small BSs (SBSs) have demonstrated promising advantages. By deploying high performance MEC servers at the MBS or the SBSs of the HCNs, MEC-enabled HCNs are expected to offer flexible network access and enhanced computation capability for the users.

In recent years, considerable efforts have been dedicated to studying the computation offloading schemes of the MEC-enabled HCNs [2,3]. In [2], computation offloading schemes were considered for MEC-enabled HCNs. Aiming to minimize the overall computation overhead of all the users, the authors formulated the computation offloading problem as a non-cooperative game model and demonstrated the existence of Nash

H. Gao et al. (Eds.): ChinaCom 2019, LNICST 313, pp. 391–401, 2020.
https://doi.org/10.1007/978-3-030-41117-6_32

equilibrium point. In [3], a two-tier computation offloading framework was proposed for HCNs. By formulating task execution problem as an energy consumption minimization problem, and solving the problem by means of separable semi-definite program and quadratically constrained quadratic program, an efficient joint user association and computation offloading algorithm strategy was obtained.

Energy harvesting (EH) technology can also be applied to reduce the on-grid energy consumption of the MEC servers. The authors in [4] considered the task offloading problem in an EH-powered MEC system. The task offloading problem was formulated as a system cost minimization problem and solved by using the Lyapunov optimization optimization technique. Specifically, the emerging EH-SBSs, which are equipped with EH devices (like solar panels or wind turbines) and exploit renewable energy as supplementary or alternative power sources, have received great attentions from both academia and industry. The possibility and reliability of self-powered cellular networks were investigated in [5]. In [6], a dynamic computation offloading framework was proposed for an EH-enabled MEC system. By examining the weighted sum of task execution delay and task dropping cost, the task execution problem was formulated as average weighted sum minimization problem and the optimal offloading strategy were obtained by solving the optimization problem.

The problem of task offloading and resource allocation can be jointly designed to further enhance task execution performance. In [7], the problem of task offloading and resource allocation was considered for MEC systems and an optimal joint design scheme was proposed to achieve the minimization of system-wide computation overhead. The authors in [8] addressed the problem of joint task offloading and resource allocation problem in an MEC-enabled HCN and proposed a joint optimal scheme to achieve the minimum energy consumption of the users.

In this paper, we consider the computation offloading and resource allocation problem in an MEC-enabled HCN. By defining workload execution cost as the weighted sum of the energy consumption of MBS and workload dropping cost, the joint computation offloading and resource allocation problem is formulated as a workload execution cost minimization problem. As the original optimization problem is a Markov decision process (MDP) problem, traditional Q-learning-based algorithm and hotbooting Q-learning-based algorithm are proposed to solve the problem.

2   System Model

In this paper, we consider an MEC-enabled HCN consisting of one MBS, one SBS and a number of users where the users are allowed to access both the MBS and the SBS through wireless links, and the SBS may also access the MBS via wireless link. To facilitate edge computation, we assume that both the MBS and the SBS are equipped with an MEC server, which are capable of executing user workloads. It is further assumed that the MBS is powered solely by on-grid power, while the SBS is equipped with an EH component and powered purely by the harvested renewable energy. The considered system model is plotted in Fig. 1.

We consider the computation offloading and resource allocation problem during a relatively long time duration. For convenience, the time duration is divided into equal-length slots with the length of each time slot being τ. We assume that at each time

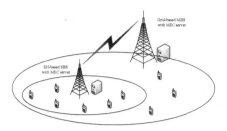

Fig. 1. System model

slot, the computation workloads may arrive at the SBS randomly, and the arrival of the workload follows a Poisson process with the average amount of the workload being λ. Let λ_k denote the amount of the workload arriving at the beginning of the kth time slot, we set $E[\lambda_k] = \lambda$, $k = 1, 2, 3, \cdots$, where $E[x]$ denotes the expectation value of x. At each time slot, upon receiving the workload from the users, the SBS may conduct local computing or offload the workload to the MBS. In addition, due to highly limited energy supply at the SBS, the SBS may also drop the workload. Let $x_k^m \in \{0, 1\}$ and $x_k^s \in \{0, 1\}$ denote respectively the computation offloading variable of the MBS and the SBS at the kth time slot, i.e., $x_k^m = 1$, if the computation workload requested at the kth time slot is offloaded to the MBS, otherwise, $x_k^m = 0$; $x_k^s = 1$, if the computation workload requested at the kth slot is executed at the SBS, otherwise, $x_k^s = 0$. We further define the binary variable of workload dropping. Let $x_k^d \in \{0, 1\}$ denote the workload dropping variable at the kth time slot, i.e., $x_k^d = 1$, if the workload requested at the kth time slot is dropped, otherwise, $x_k^d = 0$.

In the case that the workload is executed locally at the SBS at the kth time slot, the SBS may allocate a portion of computation capability of the MEC server to the workload. Let f_k^s denote the computation capability of the SBS allocated for executing the workload at the kth time slot, we have $0 \le f_k^s \le f_{\max}$, where $f_{\max}$ denotes the maximum computation capability of the MEC server deployed at the SBS.

3   Problem Formulation

In this section, we define the average long-term execution cost of the workloads and formulate the joint computation offloading and resource allocation problem as a workload execution cost minimization problem.

3.1   Objective Function

We define the average long-term execution cost of the workloads as

$$C = \lim_{T \to \infty} \frac{1}{T} E \left[\sum_{k=0}^{T-1} C_k \right] \tag{1}$$

where C_k denotes the execution cost of the workload at the kth time slot. Jointly considering the energy consumption of the MBS and the workload dropping cost, we formulate C_k as

$$C_k = x_k^{\mathrm{m}} E_k^{\mathrm{m}} + \phi \psi_k \tag{2}$$

where E_k^{m} is the energy consumption of the MBS at the kth time slot, ψ_k denotes the workload dropping cost at the kth time slot and ϕ is the weight of the workload dropping cost. We formulate E_k^{m} as

$$E_k^{\mathrm{m}} = \delta^{\mathrm{m}} (f^{\mathrm{m}})^2 W_k \tag{3}$$

where δ^{m} is the energy consumption coefficient of the MBS, f^{m} is the computation capability of the MBS. ψ_k in (2) can be calculated as

$$\psi_k = x_k^{\mathrm{d}} \lambda_k. \tag{4}$$

3.2   Optimization Constraints

To design the optimal joint computation offloading and resource allocation strategy which minimizes the execution cost of the workloads, we should consider following optimization constraints.

Workload Processing Constraint. In this paper, we assume that the SBS can only choose one of the two computation offloading modes for the workloads or drop the workloads, thus, we can express the workload processing constraint as

$$C1: \quad x_k^{\mathrm{m}} + x_k^{\mathrm{s}} + x_k^{\mathrm{d}} = 1. \tag{5}$$

Resource Allocation Constraints. The computing resource constraints of the SBS can be expressed as

$$C2: \quad 0 \le f_k^{\mathrm{s}} \le f_{\max}, \tag{6}$$

$$C3: \quad 0 \le P_k \le P_{\max} \tag{7}$$

where P_k denotes the transmit power of the SBS when transmitting the workload to the MBS at the kth time slot and $P_{\max}$ denotes the maximum transmit power of the SBS.

Delay Tolerant Constraint. In this paper, we consider delay-sensitive applications and assume that the execution latency of the workloads should be less the length of time slot, i.e.,

$$C4: \quad D_k \le \tau \tag{8}$$

where D_k denotes the workload execution latency at the kth time slot, which can be expressed as

$$D_k = x_k^{\mathrm{m}} D_k^{\mathrm{m}} + x_k^{\mathrm{s}} D_k^{\mathrm{s}} \tag{9}$$

where D_k^{m} and D_k^{s} denote respectively the workload execution latency in MBS offloading mode and SBS computing mode at the kth time slot. D_k^{m} can be formulated as

$$D_k^{\mathrm{m}} = D_k^{\mathrm{m,t}} + D_k^{\mathrm{m,e}} \qquad (10)$$

where $D_k^{\mathrm{m,t}}$ denotes the transmission latency required for SBS to offload its workload to the MBS and $D_k^{\mathrm{m,e}}$ denotes the workload computation latency at the MBS. $D_k^{\mathrm{m,t}}$ is given by

$$D_k^{\mathrm{m,t}} = \frac{\lambda_k}{R_k} \qquad (11)$$

where R_k denotes the achievable data rate of SBS when transmitting to the MBS at the kth time slot and can be expressed as

$$R_k = B\log_2\left(1 + \frac{P_k g_k}{\sigma^2}\right) \qquad (12)$$

where B denotes the bandwidth of the link between the SBS and the MBS, P_k denotes the transmit power of the SBS when offloading to the MBS at the kth time slot, g_k and σ^2 denote respectively the channel gain and the noise power of the link between the SBS and the MBS at the kth time slot. $D_k^{\mathrm{m,e}}$ can be computed as

$$D_k^{\mathrm{m,e}} = \frac{W_k}{f^{\mathrm{m}}} \qquad (13)$$

where W_k denotes computation resource required for workload execution. W_k can be calculated as

$$W_k = \rho\lambda_k \qquad (14)$$

where ρ denotes the number of CPU cycles required to process one bit. D_k^{s} in (9) can be formulated as

$$D_k^{\mathrm{s}} = \frac{W_k}{f_k^{\mathrm{s}}}. \qquad (15)$$

It should be noticed that without loss of generality, we assume that the output of the computation execution at the MBS is of small size, hence, we may omit the transmission latency for sending the result back to the SBS.

Energy Causality Constraint. At each time slot, the energy consumed by the SBS will not exceed its battery level, i.e., the energy causality constraint must be satisfied, which can be expressed as

$$\mathrm{C5}: \quad E_k^{\mathrm{s}} \leq B_k \qquad (16)$$

where E_k^{s} denotes the energy consumption of the SBS at the kth time slot, and B_k denotes the residual battery level at the beginning of the kth time slot. E_k^{s} can be calculated as the sum of basic energy consumption, the energy consumption resulted from executing the workload locally and that for transmitting the workload to the MBS, hence, can be expressed as

$$E_k^{\mathrm{s}} = E_k^{\mathrm{s,0}} + x_k^{\mathrm{s}} E_k^{\mathrm{s,e}} + x_k^{\mathrm{m}} E_k^{\mathrm{m,t}} \qquad (17)$$

where $E_k^{s,0}$ denotes the basic energy consumption of the SBS, $E_k^{s,e}$ denote the energy consumption of the SBS for executing the workload, and $E_k^{m,t}$ denotes the energy consumption required for the SBS to transmit the workload to the MBS. $E_k^{s,e}$ can be formulated as

$$E_k^{s,e} = \delta^s (f_k^s)^2 W_k \tag{18}$$

where δ^s is the energy consumption coefficient of the SBS. $E_k^{m,t}$ is given by

$$E_k^{m,t} = P_k D_k^{m,t}. \tag{19}$$

The battery energy level B_k in (16) evolves according to the following equation:

$$B_{k+1} = \min\left\{ B_k + E_k^h - E_k^s, B_{max} \right\} \tag{20}$$

where E_k^h denotes the harvested energy of the SBS at the kth time slot, and B_{max} denotes the battery capacity of the SBS. To capture the intermittent and unpredictable nature of the EH process, we model it as successive energy packet arrivals, i.e., at the beginning of the kth time slot, energy packets with the amount of energy being $E_k^h \leq E_{max}$ arrives at the SBS and then will be harvested and stored in the battery. Then, from the $(k + 1)$th time slot, the stored energy will be available for computation and communication. We further assume that E_k^h, $k \geq 1, 2, \cdots$ is i.i.d. with the maximum value being E_{max}.

3.3   Optimization Problem

To minimize the long-term average execution cost subject to the constraints, we formulate the optimization problem as follows:

$$\min_{x_k^m, x_k^s, x_k^d, f_k^s, P_k} \lim_{T \to \infty} \frac{1}{T} E\left[\sum_{k=0}^{T-1} C_k \right] \tag{21}$$

$$\text{s.t.} \quad C1 - C5$$

4   Solution of the Optimization Problem

It can be shown that the optimization problem formulated in (21) can be regarded as an infinite-horizon MDP problem and solved by using reinforcement learning method.

4.1   MDP-Based Offloading Problem Formulation

The problem of making an offloading decision for the SBS can be formulated as a finite MDP which can be characterized by four elements, i.e., state space, action space, reward function and policy.

State Space. The state of the MDP at any particular slot can be characterized by three metrics, i.e., the residual battery level of the SBS, the channel gain of the link between the SBS and the MBS, and the amount of the workloads arriving at each time slot. Let S denote the state space of the MDP and $s_k \in S$ denote the state at the kth time slot, we obtain $s_k = \{B_k, g_k, \lambda_k\}$.

Action Space. The action of the MDP taken at any time slot can be characterized by the computation offloading and resource allocation strategy made at the time slot. Let A denote the action space of the MDP and $a_k \in A$ denote the action taken at the kth time slot, we may express $a_k = \{x_k^m, x_k^s, x_k^d, f_k^s, P_k\}$.

Reward Function. In the case that the MDP is at state s_k, various actions can be taken under the constraints C1–C5, immediate reward will be resulted accordingly. We define the immediate reward function of taking action a_k at state s_k as follows:

$$r(s_k, a_k) = \begin{cases} -E_k^m, & \text{if } x_k^m = 1 \\ -\phi\psi_k, & \text{if } x_k^d = 1 \\ 0, & \text{if } x_k^s = 1 \end{cases} \tag{22}$$

Policy. The policy of the formulated MDP at the kth time slot is defined as a mapping $\pi : s_k \rightarrow a_k$. Given initial state $s_0 \in S$, we focus on optimizing the policy to maximize the expected long-term system reward, the expected discounted long-term system reward is defined as

$$V^\pi(s_0) = \mathrm{E}\left(\sum_{k=0}^{\infty} \gamma^k r(s_k, a_k) | s_0\right) \tag{23}$$

where $\gamma \in (0, 1)$ is a constant discount factor. The discounted cumulative reward $V(s_k)$ of state s_k can be expressed as

$$V(s_k) = r(s_k, a_k) + \gamma \sum_{\tilde{s}_k \in S} p(\tilde{s}_k | s_k, a_k) V(\tilde{s}_k) \tag{24}$$

where $p(\tilde{s}_k | s_k, a_k)$ is the transition probability from s_k to $\tilde{s}_k$ when choosing action a_k. The optimal policy π^* can be obtained when the total discounted expected reward is maximal according to the Bellman's theory, i.e.,

$$V^*(s_k) = \max_{a_k \in A} V(s_k) \tag{25}$$

where $V^*(s_k)$ is the expected optimal reward of s_k.

4.2 Traditional Q-Learning-Based Method

Examining (23)–(25), we can see that given the transition probability $p(\tilde{s}_k | s_k, a_k)$, the optimal policy can be derived by solving the Bellman equation. However, in many practical scenarios, it can be very different or computationally prohibitive to obtain these probability distributions. To tackle this problem, model-free reinforcement learning method such as Q-learning method can be employed to derive the optimal policy.

Applying Q-learning method to solve the joint computation offloading and resource allocation problem formulated in (21), we define Q value denoted by $Q(s_k, a_k)$ for state-action pair (s_k, a_k). Given an initial value of $Q(s_k, a_k)$, for $\forall (s_k, a_k)$, $Q(s_k, a_k)$ can be updated according to the following formula:

$$Q(s_k, a_k) = (1 - \alpha) Q(s_k, a_k)$$
$$+ \alpha \left(r(s_k, a_k) + \gamma \max_{a_k' \in \Lambda} Q\left(s_k', a_k'\right) \right) \tag{26}$$

where $0 \leq \alpha \leq 1$ is the learning rate. Once $Q(s_k, a_k)$ achieves convergence for $\forall (s_k, a_k)$ pair, the optimal action a_k^* taken at state s_k can be determined, and the optimal joint computation offloading and resource allocation strategy can be obtained.

It should be noticed that to achieve the tradeoff between exploring the new actions and exploitating the existing actions, ε-greedy policy can be applied. More specifically, although with a high probability $(1 - \varepsilon)$, the action which maximizes the reward function will be selected; with a relatively small probability ε, one action is randomly selected to avoiding the algorithm converging to the local maximum.

4.3   Hotbooting Q-Learning-Based Method

For simplicity, applying traditional Q-learning algorithm to solve engineering problem, we may set the initial Q value as zero for $\forall (s_k, a_k)$ pair, however, this may require relative long time for the algorithm to achieve convergence, which is highly undesired. To solve this problem, hotbooting technique can be applied. In particular, instead of initializing Q value as zero, we may obtain a set of training data in advance from large-scale experiments conducted in similar scenarios, then set the initial Q value based on the training data. In this manner, as the training data and initial Q value can be relatively close to the optimal value, the time required for the algorithm to achieve convergence can be reduce significantly. The proposed hotbooting Q-learning-based method for solving the joint computation offloading and resource allocation problem is summarized in Algorithm 1.

Algorithm 1. Hotbooting Q-learning based offloading decision

1: Initialization α, γ and B_0
2: Set $\mathbf{Q} = \mathbf{Q^*}$ according to the hotbooting technique
3: **for** $k = 1, 2, 3, \dots$ **do**
4:     Observe the channel condition g_k, workload size λ_k
        and the current battery level B_k
5:     Select $a_k = \{x_k^m, x_k^s, x_k^d, f_k^s, P_k\}$ via ε-greedy policy
6:     Evaluate the energy consumption, workload drop rate
        and the execution cost
7:     Update $Q(s_k, a_k)$ via (26)
8: **end for**

---

5 Simulation Results

In this section, simulation results are provided to evaluate the proposed Hotbooting Q-learning-based algorithm. For comparison, we also examine the performance of two benchmark algorithms, i.e., Q-learning-based algorithm and greedy algorithm. To conduct Greedy algorithm, At each time slot, the joint computation offloading and resource allocation strategy was designed with the aim of minimizing the instantaneous workload execution cost. The parameters used in the simulation are given in Table 1.

Table 1. Simulation parameters

Parameters	Value
Channel bandwidth B	10 MHz
Noise power σ^2	-95 dBm
Battery capacity $B_{\max}$	100 J
Maximum transmit power $P_{\max}$	2 W
Circuit power consumption $E_k^{s,0}$	20 J
Time slot length τ	1 s
Bit/CPU conversion coefficient ρ	1000

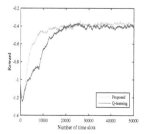

Fig. 2. Reward vs number of time slots

Fig. 3. Workload drop rate vs average size of the workload

Figure 2 shows the system reward versus number of time slots. From the figure, we can see that the Q-learning algorithm can almost achieve the same reward as the proposed Hotbooting Q-learning algorithm, the time required for the Q-learning algorithm to reach convergence is much longer, demonstrating the effectiveness of the proposed hotbooting Q-learning algorithm. This is because the hotbooting technique can formulate the emulated experiences in dynamic radio environments to effectively reduce the exploration trials and thus significantly improve the convergence speed of Q-learning.

In Fig. 3 shows workload drop rate versus the average size of the computation workload. It is shown in the figure that the workload drop rate increases with the increase of the average size of the computation workload for both our proposed scheme and the

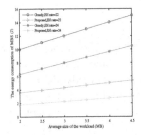

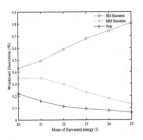

Fig. 4. The energy consumption of MBS vs average size of the workload

Fig. 5. Workload execution vs mean of harvested energy

greedy scheme. This is because larger workload size requires larger energy consumption for completing workload computation, thus resulting in larger workload drop rate due to insufficient residual energy of the SBS's battery.

In Fig. 4, we can see that the energy consumption of MBS increases with the increase of the average size of the computation workload for the proposed scheme and the greedy scheme. This is because larger workload size results in larger energy consumption for completing workload computation, thus the algorithm prefers to execute workload at the MBS for energy savings. Comparing the results obtained from our proposed scheme and the greedy scheme, we can see that our proposed scheme outperforms the greedy scheme.

In Fig. 5, it is shown in the figure that the ratio of the workload being executed at the SBS increases with the increase of the mean of harvested energy, while the ratio of the workload being executed at the MBS and that being dropped decrease with the increase of the mean of harvested energy. It is because that the SBS tends to execute the workloads for high rewards in the case that the energy of the SBS is relatively sufficient.

6   Conclusion

In this paper, we consider an MEC-enabled HCN system and formulate the joint computation offloading and resource allocation as an optimization problem which minimizes the long-term execution cost of the workloads. As the formulated optimization problem is MDP-based offloading problem, we propose a Q-learning-based algorithm and a hot-booting Q-learning-based algorithm. Numerical results demonstrate the effectiveness of the proposed algorithms.

References

1. Mao, Y., You, C., Zhang, J., Huang, K., Letaief, K.B.: A survey on mobile edge computing: the communication perspective. IEEE Commun. Surv. Tutor. **19**(4), 2322–2358 (2017)
2. Guo, H., Liu, J., Zhang, J.: Efficient computation offloading for multi-access edge computing in 5G HetNets. In: Proceedings of the IEEE International Conference on Communication (ICC), Kansas City, MO, pp. 1–6 (2018)

3. Dai, Y., Xu, D., Maharjan, S., Zhang, Y.: Joint computation offloading and user association in multi-task mobile edge computing. IEEE Trans. Veh. Technol. **67**(12), 12313–12325 (2018)
4. Wu, H., Chen, L., Shen, C., Wen, W., Xu, J.: Online geographical load balancing for energy-harvesting mobile edge computing. In: Proceedings of the IEEE International Conference on Communication (ICC), pp. 1–6, May 2018
5. Dhillon, H.S., Li, Y., Nuggehalli, P., Pi, Z., Andrews, J.G.: Fundamentals of heterogeneous cellular networks with energy harvesting. IEEE Trans. Wirel. Commun. **13**(5), 2782–2797 (2014)
6. Mao, Y., Zhang, J., Letaief, K.B.: Dynamic computation offloading for mobile-edge computing with energy harvesting devices. IEEE J. Sel. Areas Commun. **34**(12), 3590–3605 (2016)
7. Pham, Q., Le, L.B., Chung, S., Hwang, W.: Mobile edge computing with wireless backhaul: joint task offloading and resource allocation. IEEE Access **7**, 16444–16459 (2019)
8. Song, Z., Liu, Y., Sun, X.: Joint radio and computational resource allocation for NOMA-based mobile edge computing in heterogeneous networks. IEEE Commun. Lett. **22**(12), 2559–2562 (2018)

Wi-Fi Gesture Recognition Technology Based on Time-Frequency Features (Workshop)

Zengshan Tian, Mengtian Ren[✉], Qing Jiang, and Xiaoya Zhang

School of Communication and Information Engineering,
Chongqing University of Posts and Telecommunications,
Chongqing 400065, China
rmt812@126.com

Abstract. With the rapid development of artificial intelligence, gesture recognition has become the focus of many countries for research. Gesture recognition using Wi-Fi signals has become the mainstream of gesture recognition because it does not require additional equipment and lighting conditions. Firstly, how to extract useful gesture signals in a complex indoor environment. In this paper, after de-noising the signal by Discrete Wavelet Transform (DWT) technology, Principal Component Analysis (PCA) is used to eliminate the problem of signal redundancy between multiple CSI subcarriers, further to remove noise. Secondly, the frequency domain features of the gesture signal are constructed by performing Short-Time Fourier Transform (STFT) on the denoised CSI amplitude signal. Then, the time domain features are combined with the frequency domain features, and the features are trained and classified using the Support Vector Machine (SVM) classification method to complete the training and recognition of gesture. The experimental results show that this paper can effectively identify gestures in complex indoor environments.

Keywords: Dynamic gesture recognition · Discrete Wavelet Transform · Principal Component Analysis · Time-frequency domain features

1 First Section

With the rapid development of science and technology in the 21st century and the popularity of computers, human-computer interaction technology has become the object of attention and research in many countries [1]. Gesture as one of the basic features of vision, it is the simplest way to interact with nature. And it plays an important role in many fields such as smart home and auxiliary car control system. Therefore, gesture recognition has gradually become an important research direction of human-computer interaction.

At present, the previous works are mainly based on wearable sensors [2], computer vision [3], and radiofrequency signals [4]. Among them, the gesture

© ICST Institute for Computer Sciences, Social Informatics and Telecommunications Engineering 2020
Published by Springer Nature Switzerland AG 2020. All Rights Reserved
H. Gao et al. (Eds.): ChinaCom 2019, LNICST 313, pp. 402–413, 2020.
https://doi.org/10.1007/978-3-030-41117-6_33

recognition system based on wearable devices and computer vision started earlier, has been very mature so far and achieved gratifying precision. However, the wearable sensors system requires the user to wear a sensing device such as a data glove or an armband to obtain response parameters, it is inconvenient for the user; the computer vision system cannot be used in dark or smoke environments. Compared with them, the Wi-Fi signal-based gesture recognition system does not require a piece of wearable equipment and the condition of light. It only needs to use software upgrades and updates, so it gradually becomes the mainstream of gesture recognition.

In the Wi-Fi based gesture recognition system, most systems currently use Received Signal Strength Indications (RSSI) to capture a signal. However, RSSI has poor stability under uncertain noise and indoor multipath conditions, therefore RSSI does not provide sufficient reliability. As the pursuit of reliability becomes higher and higher, Channel State Information (CSI) gradually appears in everyone's field of vision. In this paper, we realized a gesture recognition system based on CSI which is collected from commercial wireless devices. It does not require additional sensors, is resilient to changes within the environment and can operate in non-line-of-sight scenarios. The basic idea is to leverage the amplitude of CSI to complete the gesture recognition. There are several challenges, however, that need to be addressed to realize our system including handling the noisy and extracting the feature of different gestures. To address these challenges, the main contributions of this paper are as follows:

1. How to extract gesture signals from complex indoor environments? First, the least variance method is used to segment the gesture. Then, we use the Discrete Wavelet Transform-Principal Component Analysis (DTW-PCA) to extract useful gesture signals in a complex environment.
2. How to extract features of different gestures for classification? We propose a method that combines time domain and frequency domain feature information to complete classification.

The rest of this paper is organized as follows. We first summarize the related work in Sect. 2, followed by Sect. 3, which is a brief introduction to the gesture recognition system. Then in Sect. 4 we illustrate the detailed system design and methodology. We show the experimental results and evaluation of the performance in Sect. 5. Finally, we will conclude this work and list our future work in Sect. 6.

2   Related Work

In this section, we introduce the state-of-the-artwork of gesture recognition systems, which are related to our work. These systems are mainly divided into the following two categories.

(1) Device-Based Gesture Systems: These technologies include wearable sensors and computer vision: As mentioned earlier, the wearable based methods usually need gloves or external sensors attached to a user for gesture capture.

These methods can capture the gestures more precisely, but the process is invasive, as the user needs to wear sensors around him. For example, Wang et al. [5] describe a system using data glove for gesture recognition, which can measure the change of hand joints' angles and the motion state of the hand. And PhonePoint Pen [6] recognizes handwriting by holding a mobile phone in hands; The other type is camera-based systems, the camera based method uses the camera to capture user gesture behavior, which relies on high-resolution video or images and cannot be used in non-light conditions for example darkness. [7] proposes a camera-based hand gesture that can achieve a higher average recognition rate and better distinguishes the confusion gesture. The Xbox Kinect [8] and Leap Motion [9] also can be the typical successful examples of applications.

(2) Device-Free Gesture Systems: Nowadays, Kellogg et al. [4] can use Radio-frequency identification (RFID) to identify gestures and it can achieve high precision, but the system only works with RFID transmissions whose costs are high. In the device-free systems, the wireless signal-based method has a low expanse and is easy to deploy. In 2015, Abdelnasser et al. proposed WiGest [10], which performs gesture recognition by analyzing the rising and falling edges of RSSI signal changes. The accuracy is 87.5% in the case of a single access point when there are three access points. the accuracy rate is 96%. But the RSSI is lack of stable in complex indoor environments. The system WiGeR [11] leverages the fluctuation of the amplitude of CSI caused by the gesture to complete the recognition. But the pattern recognition such as dynamic time warping (DTW) takes a lot of time so that it is not practical.

All of these systems contain some weaknesses which make it hard to be further popularized, though most of them can achieve an impressive estimation accuracy.

3   System Overview

In this section, we first briefly introduce the background knowledge of CSI value which is the foundation of our system, then give an overview of the system.

3.1   Channel State Information

The indoor environment is complex and changeable, and there are interferences of multipath effects, such as static reflections on walls, sofas, tables and so on. The model diagram is shown in Fig. 1.

According to Fig. 1, the CSI data received by the receiver is a superposition of multiple path signals, which can be expressed as

$$
\begin{aligned}
H\left(f_i, t\right) &= \left|H\left(f_i, t\right)\right| \times \arg\left(H\left(f_i, t\right)\right) \\
&= e^{-j2\pi ft} \sum_{k=1}^{N} a_k\left(f_i, t\right) e^{-j2\pi f_i \tau_k(t)} + n
\end{aligned}
\tag{1}
$$

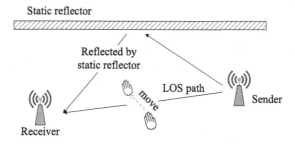

Fig. 1. Indoor environment diagram.

where $|H(f_i,t)|$ and $\arg(H(f_i,t))$ are the amplitude and phase of the i sub-carrier at the t moment, f_i is the frequency of the subcarrier, $e^{-j2\pi ft}$ is phase shift due to phase error, N is the number of multipath, $a_k(f_i,t)$ is the propagation attenuation of the first multipath, $e^{-j2\pi f_i \tau_k(t)}$ is the phase shift due to propagation delay, n is noise vector.

The literature [12] derives the square formula of the CSI amplitude according to formula (1) as follows

$$
\begin{aligned}
|H(f_i,t)|^2 &= \sum_{k \in P_d} 2|H_s(f_i) a_k(f_i,t)| \cos\left(\frac{2\pi \nu_k t}{\lambda} + \frac{2\pi d_k(0)}{\lambda} + \varphi_{sk}\right) \\
&+ |H_s(f_i)|^2 + \sum_{k \in P_d} |a_k(f_i,t)|^2 \\
&+ \sum_{\substack{k,l \in P_d \\ k \neq l}} |a_k(f_i,t) a_l(f_i,t)| \cos\left(\frac{2\pi(\nu_k - \nu_l)t}{\lambda} + \frac{2\pi(d_k(0) - d_l(0))}{\lambda} + \varphi_{kl}\right)
\end{aligned}
\tag{2}
$$

It can be obtained from formula (2) that the square of the CSI amplitude is composed of some constant and cosine functions, which can accurately reflect the jitter of the target motion. Therefore, this paper considers the feature information of CSI amplitude to complete the training and recognition of the gesture.

3.2 Overview

As shown in Fig. 2, our gesture recognition system consists of three modules: CSI data preprocessing, feature extraction of gesture and gesture recognition. In the CSI data preprocessing, we use the DWT to remove noise, and PCA is also used to reduce the data dimension as well as remove noise further. After CSI data preprocessing, we combine time domain and frequency domain features information to extract the features such as event duration, interquartile range, spectral entropy and so on. At last, these features be used for classification in gesture recognition.

4 System Design

In this section, we elaborate on the methodology of our system relied on three blocks as mentioned before.

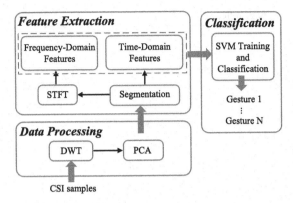

Fig. 2. Overview of system.

4.1 Data Preprocessing

As can be seen from Fig. 1, the CSI data received by the receiver is a superposition of multiple path signals, and there are interferences from static reflections such as walls, tables and chairs. So how to extract the signal changes caused by the user's gesture movement in a complex indoor environment is a huge challenge.

In response to this problem, first, this paper uses the Discrete Wavelet Transform (DWT) technique to effectively remove the noise and smooth the CSI data. The core thought is three steps: decomposition, noise removal and reconstruction. Firstly, DWT decomposes the signal into detail coefficients $\{\beta^1 f \beta^2 f \cdots f \beta^J\}$ (with $J = 5$) and approximation coefficients α^J. Then we apply hard thresholding to denoise the 1–3 layer detail coefficients. Finally, we combine the approximation coefficient and the denoised detail coefficient to reconstruct the CSI signal.

Second, since the CSI signal has 30 subcarriers, the information carried by the 30 subcarriers is redundant and the number of all subcarriers increases the computational complexity. Therefore, we use the Principal Component Analysis (PCA) to effectively reduce the data, and further achieve the denoising. PCA is a mathematical transformation method that converts a given set of related variables into another set of unrelated variables by a linear transformation. These new variables are arranged in descending order of variance. In the mathematical transformation, the total variance of the variables is kept constant, so that the first variable has the largest variance, which is called the first principal component, and the variance of the second variable is the second largest, and is not related to the first variable, and is called the second principal component, and so on. According to the literature [13], the first principal component after the dimension reduction contains almost all the information of the gesture motion signal.

Figure 3 shows the result of noise filtering. It shows the DWT-PCA method can extract the signal from the complex indoor environment. Figure 4 compares the first three principal components for the same activity when de-noising is applied before PCA. It also shows that a jority of the gesture activity induced variation is concentrated in the first and second principal components, but in the third principal component (and onwards) the noise level begins to have a higher influence [13].

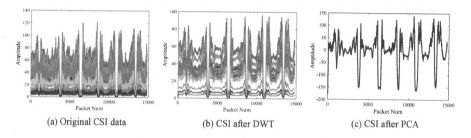

(a) Original CSI data   (b) CSI after DWT   (c) CSI after PCA

Fig. 3. Channel State Information (CSI) preprocessing.

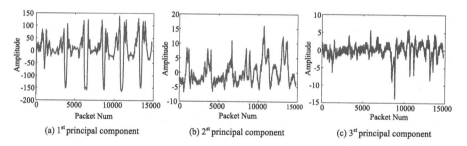

(a) 1st principal component   (b) 2st principal component   (c) 3st principal component

Fig. 4. Comparison of the resultant first three PCs after wavelet de-noising and then PCA. First and second PCs are less noisy, yet in the third PC, the noise level has a higher influence.

4.2   Segment Algorithm

The CSI data is a continuous-time series. To complete feature extraction and classification of gestures, segmentation of the received time series is required. To solve this problem, we divide the continuous-time series by the smallest variance segment algorithm.

In the segmented algorithm, we use two windows on the CSI time series to segment it. Firstly, The first window corresponds to the beginning of the time series, and the beginning of the second window corresponds to the end of the first window; Secondly, the width W is initialized to $W_{\min}$, the first window is $P_{frist} = (P_1, P_2, \cdots, P_w)$ and the second window is $P_{\sec ond} = (p_{w+1}, p_{w+2}, \cdots, p_{2w})$; Thirdly, we calculate the variance difference between the two windows; Then, we make $w = w+1$ and repeat the second step to calculate the variance difference of the two windows until the width of the window reaches $W_{\max}$. We can get $W_{\max} - W_{\min} + 1$ pairs of (w, d). The window width W corresponds to the minimum d is the final window width. Finally, repeat the previous steps unless there is not enough time series. Figure 5 shows the result of gesture segmentation, we can see from Fig. 5 the algorithm can segment the gesture more accurately. The results of 5 kinds of gesture segmentation are shown in Fig. 6.

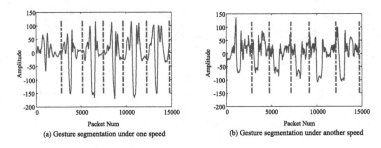

(a) Gesture segmentation under one speed   (b) Gesture segmentation under another speed

Fig. 5. The segmentation graph of Wave gesture.

4.3 Time Frequency Analysis

After CSI data collection and preprocessing, a transformation to the time-frequency domain is necessary to perform the feature extraction. For the time-frequency analysis, there are various linear and non-linear techniques. Among them, the non-linear methods tend to distort the frequency components generated by movement. Therefore, we selected Short-Time Fourier Transform (STFT) for our time-frequency analysis.

In STFT, the time resolution and frequency resolution are inversely proportional, so it is necessary to find an optimal window size to obtain satisfactory time resolution and frequency resolution. Since each person completes a gesture action for 1 to 4 s, the time is short and requires sufficient time resolution. For this problem, we opt for an FFT window size of 256 samples at a sampling rate of 1000 pkts/s. We chose the overlap size of two windows to be 250 samples. So, the selected parameters provide us with a frequency resolution of $\frac{sample\ rate}{FFT size} \approx 4\,\mathrm{Hz}$ and a time resolution of $\frac{window - overlap}{sample\ rate} \approx 0.006\,\mathrm{s}$. Figure 6 shows the STFT of five gestures.

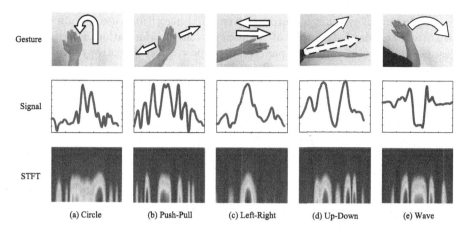

Fig. 6. Time domain signal diagram and spectrum diagram corresponding to the five gestures.

4.4 Feature Extraction

Although the time domain signal and the frequency domain signal can well reflect the characteristics of different gesture motions, most of the pattern recognition methods are not feasible due to the inconsistency of time series. The time-series-inconsistent recognition method, for example, Hidden Markov Model has a large time expenditure and is not suitable for practical application scenarios. Therefore, we propose to select useful features for training and classification. The selected features are shown in Table 1.

Table 1. Selected eigenvalue

Time domain	Frequency domain
Standard deviation	Spectral entropy of 1–10 Hz
Interquartile range	Spectral entropy of 10–20 Hz
Event duration	Spectral entropy of 20–30 Hz

The literature [14] uses the mean, standard deviation, and interquartile range of time-domain features to identify the gesture but due to the small amplitude of gestures, these statistical feature values are not representative. In response to this problem, we choose the standard deviation, interquartile range and duration of each gesture motion are used as the time-domain feature. The standard deviation can well reflect the degree of dispersion of the gesture signal based on the mean, which is more representative than the mean; The interquartile range reflects the degree of dispersion of 50% of the data in the middle of the signal, and is not affected by the extreme value; Since the time of each action is different, the duration of each action obtained by segmentation is also used as the feature.

For frequency-domain features, conventional algorithms use feature such as mean and standard deviation of frequency domain information as criteria for gesture classification. In this paper, we propose spectral entropy in different frequency ranges as the feature. This is a normalized feature and measures the textural properties of a gesture (randomness in the distribution of energy in a spectrogram). The calculation formula is as follows

$$\begin{cases} H = -\sum_{i=k_l}^{k_u} p\left(n_i\right) \ln p\left(n_i\right) \\ p\left(n_i\right) = \frac{\hat{p}(n_i)}{\sum \hat{p}(n_i)} \\ \hat{p}\left(n_i\right) = |S|^2 \end{cases} \quad (3)$$

where $\hat{p}\left(n_i\right)$ is the of spectrum amplitude, $p\left(n_i\right)$ is the normalized power spectral density. k_l and k_u are lower and upper frequency bounds. H is the spectral entropy in the corresponding frequency range.

5 Experimental Evaluation

In this section, we will describe the relevant experimental setup and analyze the result of our experiments.

5.1 Lab Environment

The proposed gesture system contains a transmitter and a receiver both equipped with the Intel 5300 wireless NIC and CSI toolkit, and the parameters setting is shown in Table 2. All the experiments are conducted in a typical indoor environment with the size for 70 square meters, surrounded by meeting tables, chairs and other furniture. During the experiments, five gestures shown in Fig. 6 are designed to verify the effectiveness of the proposed system.

Table 2. Parameter setting

Parameters	Transmitting AP	Receiving AP
Mode	Injection	Monitor
Channel number	Default = 149 5.745 GHz	
Bandwidth	Default = 40 MHz	
Number of subcarriers	30	
Index of subcarriers	$[-58, -54, \ldots, 54, 58]$	
Transmit power	15 dBm	

5.2   Result

Classification Accuracy. This paper first verifies the effectiveness of the algorithm. Five groups of 100 gestures each with 500 groups to build classifiers and test samples, and used 3 times cross-validation and SVM classifier to calculate classification accuracy. Figure 7 is the confusion matrix diagram.

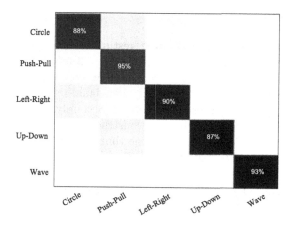

Fig. 7. Confusion matrix diagram at 1000 sampling rate.

The results of Fig. 8 show that the classification accuracy of the five gestures in the method of extracting time domain features and frequency domain features is {88%, 95%, 90%, 87%, 93%}, and the overall average accuracy of the five gestures is 90.6%. Among them, the gestures Push-Pull and Wave have higher recognition accuracy, while the Circle and Up-Down gesture recognition accuracy is relatively low, because the Push-Pull and Wave gestures have a greater impact on the direct link, and the features are more obvious.

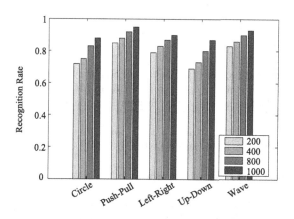

Fig. 8. Recognition accuracy under different sampling rates.

Impact of Sample Rate. As can be seen from Fig. 8, the increase of the sampling rate improves the recognition rate of the system. If the sampling rate is increased to 2000 packet/s, the recognition accuracy will be higher, but it will also reduce the performance of the device and the operating efficiency of the system, so the sampling rate of this paper is 1000 Hz.

6   Conclusion

In this paper, we propose a device-free gesture recognition system based on channel state information. First, the DWT-PCA combined denoising method is adopted for extracting useful gesture signals in complex environments, after denoising by DWT, PCA solves the problem of signal redundancy between multiple CSI subcarriers to further remove noise; Secondly, the frequency domain characteristics of the gesture signal are constructed by using the STFT of the processed CSI amplitude signal; Then, the time domain features are combined with the frequency domain features, and the features are trained and classified using the SVM classification method. The experimental results show that this paper can effectively recognize gestures in complex indoor environments. The average recognition rate reached 90.6%.

References

1. Zhou, Y., Jiang, G., Lin, Y.: A novel finger and hand pose estimation technique for real-time hand gesture recognition. Pattern Recogn. **49**, 102–114 (2016)
2. Sturman, D.J., Zeltzer, D.: A survey of glove-based input. IEEE Comput. Graphics Appl. **14**(1), 30–39 (1994)
3. He, Y., Yang, J., Shao, Z., Li, Y.: Salient feature point selection for real time RGB-D hand recognition. In: 2017 IEEE International Conference on Real-time Computing and Robotics (RCAR), pp. 103–108. IEEE (2017)
4. Kellogg, B., Talla, V., Gollakota, S.: Bringing gesture recognition to all devices. In: 11th fUSENIXg Symposium on Networked Systems Design and Implementation (fNSDIg 2014), pp. 303–316 (2014)
5. Wang, X., Sun, G., Han, D., Zhang, T.: Data glove gesture recognition based on an improved neural network. In: Proceedings of the 29th Chinese Control Conference, pp. 2434–2437. IEEE (2010)
6. Agrawal, S., Constandache, I., Gaonkar, S., Roy Choudhury, R., Caves, K., DeRuyter, F.: Using mobile phones to write in air. In: Proceedings of the 9th International Conference on Mobile Systems, Applications, and Services, pp. 15–28. ACM (2011)
7. Wu, X., Mao, X., Chen, L., Xue, Y.: Trajectory-based view-invariant hand gesture recognition by fusing shape and orientation. IET Comput. Vision **9**(6), 797–805 (2015)
8. Microsoft kinect. http://www.microsoft.com/en-us/kinectforwindows
9. Leap motion. https://www.leapmotion.com
10. Abdelnasser, H., Youssef, M., Harras, K.A.: WiGest: a ubiquitous wifi-based gesture recognition system. In: 2015 IEEE Conference on Computer Communications (INFOCOM), pp. 1472–1480. IEEE (2015)

11. Al-qaness, M., Li, F.: WiGeR: WiFi-based gesture recognition system. ISPRS Int. J. Geo-Inf. **5**(6), 92 (2016)

12. Wang, W., Liu, A.X., Shahzad, M., Ling, K., Lu, S.: Understanding and modeling of WiFi signal based human activity recognition. In: Proceedings of the 21st Annual International Conference on Mobile Computing and Networking, pp. 65–76. ACM (2015)

13. Palipana, S., Rojas, D., Agrawal, P., Pesch, D.: FallDeFi: Ubiquitous fall detection using commodity Wi-Fi devices. Proc. ACM Interact. Mob. Wearable Ubiquit. Technol. **1**(4), 155 (2018)

14. He, W., Wu, K., Zou, Y., Ming, Z.: WiG: WiFi-based gesture recognition system. In: 2015 24th International Conference on Computer Communication and Networks (ICCCN), pp. 1–7. IEEE (2015)

Accompaniment Music Separation Based on 2DFT and Image Processing (Workshop)

Tian Zhang[✉], Tianqi Zhang, and Congcong Fan

Chongqing University of Posts and Telecommunications, Chongqing, China
284148541@qq.com, zhangtq@cqupt.edu.cn, 2669432120@qq.com

Abstract. For the difficulty of separation of accompaniment from mono music, image filtering was applied into a novel approach to separate accompaniment music. Our approach presents how single channel music manifests in the 2D Fourier Transform spectrum. In image domain, the position of periodic peak energy was determined by image filtering, and then masking matrix was constructed by rectangular window to extract the constituent of the accompaniment music. We find that our system is more robust and very simple to describe. The simulation experiments show that the method in this work has an advantage over other separation algorithm.

Keywords: Accompaniment separation · 2 dimension fourier transform · Time-frequency mask · Image processing

1 Introduction

In the information age, the demand for music signal processing technologies such as music annotation, retrieval, and identification, under massive digital music is growing. However, the correlation between accompaniment music and human voice makes it difficult for accompaniment and vocals to be extracted separately, which brings huge obstacles to music processing. The separation of vocal accompaniment in the music signal, as a pre-treatment of these techniques, has drawn increasing attention and has important research value.

In recent years, many experts have conducted in-depth research on music separation. Li and Hsu et al. used pitch estimation [1–3] to generate a sound music template, and Li used amplitude and phase information to further estimate the pitch [2] to generate a more accurate template, and then used the template to extract singing voice from the mixed music.

Using the sparseness of the vocal signal and the low rank property of the music accompaniment, Huang separates the mixed signal amplitude spectrum into a sparse matrix and a low rank matrix [4], and then uses the binary mask to realize the separation of music. REPET used the beat spectrum to extract background music, based on the priori knowledge of musical accompaniment with a certain periodicity [5–8]. Raffi based on local self-similarity of the accompaniment music, proposed adaptive method [9]. And

H. Gao et al. (Eds.): ChinaCom 2019, LNICST 313, pp. 414–424, 2020.
https://doi.org/10.1007/978-3-030-41117-6_34

similar matrixes [10] are used to extract the model of the repeated background music, which further improves the accuracy of the separation. The separation methods studied by the above scholars can separate the accompaniment music to a certain extent, but the robustness of the algorithm is poor, and the separation effect of different music segments is different.

In music information retrieval, 2DFT (2 Dimension Fourier Transform) has been used for song recognition [11, 12] and music segmentation [13]. Stöter and Fabian Robert [14] and others used 2DFT transform as input for sound source separation. Pishdadian et al. [15] used a multi-resolution 2D patches instead of a fixed-size 2D patches to further improve this separation method. Both approaches focus on distinguishing different characteristics of the sound source (such as vibrato, etc.), to separate sources with the same fundamental frequency from one to another in short audio. Both need to create more complex multi-resolution filter banks using 2DFT. At present, most scholars use the sparseness and periodicity of signals to separate music while few scholars use 2DFT transform to separate the accompaniment music.

Based on the above analysis, we explored a novel accompaniment separation method using image processing based on 2DFT. Our system is with high robustness and very easy to describe and implement and competitive to existing music separation method.

2 Proposed Method

2.1 The 2D Fourier Transform on Single Channel Musical Signals

The 2DFT, like the IDFT in music analysis, is a popular technique in digital image processing, and is used for image denoising and compression, among other things, but 2DFT cannot be applied on single channel audio. By taking the magnitude of the 2DFT on the STFT (Short-Time Fourier Transform), we obtain a key-invariant representation of the audio.

Let $\mathbf{X}_{\omega,\tau}$ denote the constant Q transform (CQT) of the music signal $f(t)$, $\mathbf{W}_{\omega,\tau} = |\mathbf{X}_{\omega,\tau}|$ is its amplitude spectrum, where and are variables representing frequency and time respectively. The 2D Fourier transform is expressed as follows

$$F(u,v) = \frac{1}{MN} \sum_{\omega=0}^{M-1} \left[\sum_{\tau=0}^{N-1} W_{\omega,\tau} exp(-j2\pi v\tau/N) \right] \exp(-j2\pi u\omega/M) \quad (1)$$

The vertical dimension and horizontal dimension of 2DFT domain are called scale and rate. These terms are borrowed from studies of the auditory system in mammals [16–18]. Figure 1 presents 2DFT spectrum of different music signals.

It can be seen from Fig. 1(b) that the energy of the pure singing voice mainly concentrates on the central region of the 2DFT transform spectrum, while the energy of the singing voice is striped from the center of the 2DFT transform spectrum to the two sides as shown in Fig. 1(c). The 2DFT transform spectrum of mixed music is a superposition of pure vocal and pure music spectra as shown in Fig. 1(a). If the 2DFT transform spectrum of the mixed music can be separated into the forms of the two figures (b) and (c) of Fig. 1, the accompaniment and the singing voice can be separated.

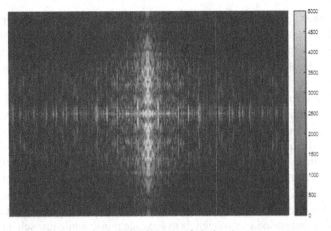

(a) The 2DFT spectrum of mixed music

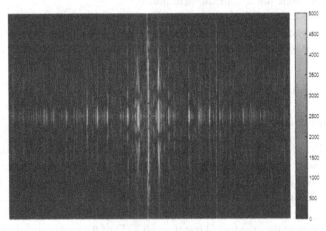

(b) The 2DFT spectrum of pure singing

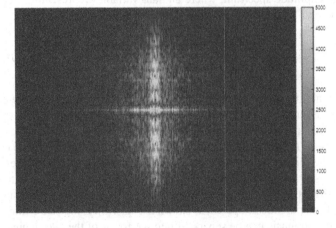

(c) The 2DFT spectrum of pure accompaniment

Fig. 1. 2DFT spectrum of different music signals

2.2 Accompaniment Music Separation

We separate accompaniment music by constructing time-frequency masking. In 2DFT spectrum, we set 1 to the position of bright stripe, and 0 otherwise. By this way, we obtain time-frequency masking. To pick bright stripe positions, we compare the difference between the maximum and minimum magnitude values over a neighborhood surrounding each point in the scale-rate domain with a certain threshold. When the difference is greater than the threshold, the maximum point existing in the neighborhood is recorded. This means there is a sharp increase in energy compared to other points.

In this work, we design our neighborhood shape to be a rectangle whose size along the scale is 1. The size of our rectangle neighborhood along the rate axis varies from 15 to 50. If the neighborhood is too large, the singing will be easily leaked into the accompaniment. On the contrary, the separated accompaniment will be more easily leaked into the singing voice.

We denote the center point of our rectangle neighborhood by $C = (s_C, r_C)$, and represent the length of the neighborhood. Set the standard deviation γ of $W_{\omega,\tau}$ for the threshold and α for the difference between the maximum and minimum magnitude values over a neighborhood, that is

$$\alpha = \max_N |F(s,r)| - \min_N |F(s,r)| \tag{2}$$

The vocal masking matrix can be derived from the following formula:

$$M_{\mathrm{fg}}(s_C, r_C) = \begin{cases} 1 & \alpha > \gamma \quad |F(s,r)| = \max_N |F(s,r)| \\ 0 & otherwise \end{cases} \tag{3}$$

Figure 2 shows the masking matrix of the singing voice.

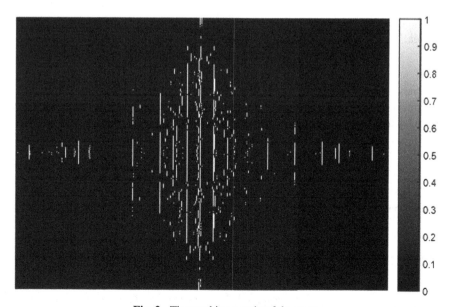

Fig. 2. The masking matrix of the song

It can be seen in Fig. 2, the positions of the value 1 are basically consistent with the positions of the singing value in mixed music matrix. Comparing masking matrix and 2DFT spectrum in Fig. 1, we find the energy of accompaniment music is mainly concentrated in the position of the center of the spectrum, and the vocal energy at this position is relatively low. Therefore, the masking matrix is processed to remove the center. The masking matrix after processing is shown in Fig. 3.

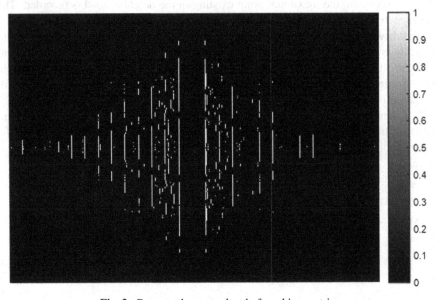

Fig. 3. Remove the center band of masking matrix

The masking matrix of accompaniment music can be calculated by the following formula:

$$M_{bg}(s, r) = 1 - M_{fg}(s, r) \tag{4}$$

Where represents inverse 2D Fourier transform, and denotes element-by-element multiplication. The time-frequency masking can obtain by comparing the magnitude spectrogram of accompaniment and singing.

$$M_{bg}(\omega, \tau) = \begin{cases} 1 & |X_{bg}(\omega, \tau)| = |X_{fg}(\omega, \tau)| \\ 0 & otherwise \end{cases} \tag{5}$$

The short-time Fourier spectrum of the accompaniment can be obtained by the two-dimensional inverse Fourier transform by the masking matrix of the singing voice and the 2DFT transform spectrum of the mixed music.

Finally, the time domain signal of the accompaniment can be obtained by time-frequency masking $M_{bg}(\omega, \tau)$ and the time-frequency spectrogram $X(\omega, \tau)$ of the mixed signal.

$$x_{bg}(t) = ICQT\{M_{bg}(\omega, \tau) \cdot X(\omega, \tau)\} \tag{6}$$

Where $ICQT\{\cdot\}$ is the inverse constant Q transform.

3 Evaluations

The music data set in the experiment uses the music data set MIR-1 K [19] published by Hsu Lab. The data set consists of 1,000 song clips in the form of split stereo WAVE files sampled at 16 kHz, extracted from 110 karaoke Chinese pop songs, performed mostly by amateurs, with the music and voice recorded separately on the left and right channels, respectively. The duration of the clips ranges from 4 to 13 s.

In order to quantitatively evaluate the separation effect of the method in this work, the Févotte Blind Source Separation Evaluation (BSS_EVAL) [20] was used to measure the performance of the improved algorithm. The toolbox provides a set of measures that intend to quantify the quality of the separation between the source signal and its estimate. The principle is to decompose the estimated signal as follows:

$$\hat{s}(t) = s_{t\,arg\,et}(t) + e_{\mathrm{interf}}(t) + e_{artif}(t) + e_{noise}(t) \tag{7}$$

Where $s_{t\,arg\,et}(t)$ is the portion of the estimated signal that belongs to the source signal, and $e_{\mathrm{interf}}(t)$ is the estimated error caused by the other signal source, that is, the portion of the estimated signal that is a mixed signal but does not belong to the source signal. $e_{artif}(t)$ represents the system noise error due to the algorithm itself, and denotes the noise interference error contained in the observed signal.

Since the effects of noise can be ignored in most music separations, $e_{noise}(t)$ can be omitted directly. Therefore, we use the following performance indicators, namely source-to-interference ratio (SIR) and source-to-artifacts ratio (SAR), which are defined as follows:

$$SIR = 10\lg\left[\frac{\left\|s_{t\,arg\,et}(t)\right\|^2}{\left\|e_{\mathrm{interf}}(t)\right\|^2}\right] \tag{8}$$

$$SAR = 10\lg\left[\frac{\left\|s_{t\,arg\,et}(t) + e_{\mathrm{interf}}(t)\right\|^2}{\left\|e_{artif}(t)\right\|^2}\right] \tag{9}$$

SIR represents the resolution of the algorithm, SAR represents the robustness of the algorithm, and the higher the values of SIR and SAR, the better the performance of the algorithm.

3.1 Comparative Results

A piece of music (geniusturtle_5_01.wav) in MIR-1 K was randomly selected, and the accompaniment was separate by the method in this work. Waveforms comparison before and after separation are shown in Fig. 4.

It can be seen from Fig. 4 that the waveforms of the separated accompaniment and the original accompaniment are basically the same in shape, but the amplitude of the separated accompaniment waveform is reduced, which is caused by the neighborhood length being too small. It can be improved by adjusting the length of the rectangular neighborhood.

After verifying that the method can effectively separate the accompaniment music, the advantages of the method are explained. Five pieces of music in the MIR-1 K

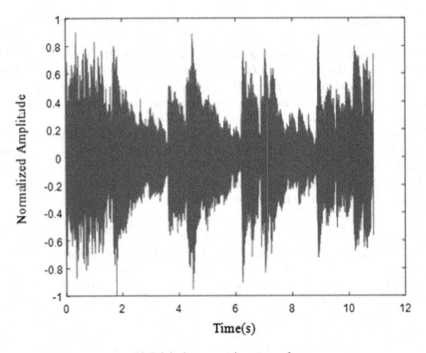

(a) Original accompaniment waveform

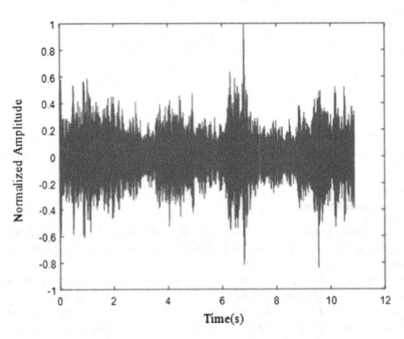

(b) Separated accompaniment with neighborhood is 15.

Fig. 4. Comparison of waveforms before and after separation

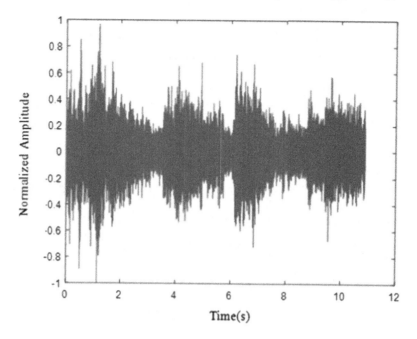

(c) Separated accompaniment with neighborhood is 35.

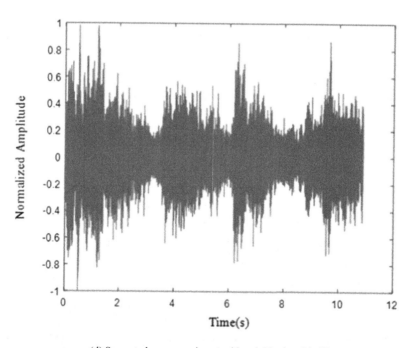

(d) Separated accompaniment with neighborhood is 50.

Fig. 4. (*continued*)

dataset are randomly selected and separated, and the SIR and SAR values are calculated. The extracted segment is 'Ani_1_05.wav. ', 'jmzen_3_05.wav', 'leon_6_07.wav', 'annar_1_06.wav', 'fdps_3_05.wav'), the result is shown in Fig. 5.

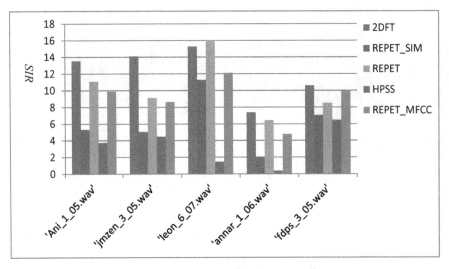

(a)Accompaniment separation indicator SIR (dB) contrast diagram

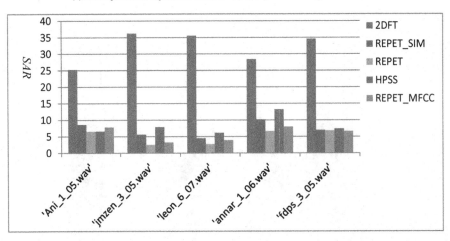

(b) Accompaniment separation indicator SAR (dB) contrast diagram

Fig. 5. Comparison diagram of random 5 music segment separation performance indexes

It can be seen from Fig. 5, our approach is superior to HPSS and REPET and its improved algorithm in separating indicators SIR and SAR when separating music accompaniment. In this work, proposed method has at least 2 dB improvement on SIR compared with other traditional algorithms. In SAR, our method keeps about 30 dB, which is at least 15 dB better than other algorithms.

The 500 pieces of music in MIR-1 K were separated by the 2DFT algorithm, and the SIR and SAR averages were calculated and compared with HPSS algorithm, REPET and its improved algorithm. The results are shown in Table 1.

Table 1. Separation performance (Average result)

Method	Accompaniment	
	SIR(dB)	SAR(dB)
HPSS	4.989	8.078
REPET	8.121	4.572
REPET-SIM	4.672	6.068
REPET-MFCC	7.346	5.278
2DFT	9.290	31.177

It can be seen from Table 1 that the 2DFT algorithm in this paper is about 4 dB higher than HPSS in SIR when separating accompaniment. Compared with REPET and its improved algorithm, SIR is improved by about 0.9–4 dB. In terms of SAR, the SAR of this algorithm is 27 dB. Better than other algorithms.

4 Conclusion

Aiming at the accompaniment separation in music separation, we proposed an accompaniment separation approach based on 2DFT transform. The method firstly transforms the single-dimensional music signal into a two-dimensional domain by 2D Fourier transform, and then uses the image filtering method to process the spectrogram. Thus we used the rectangular neighborhood to pick the position of the energy peak, and constructed the masking matrix to extract the music accompaniment component. Finally time-domain accompaniment was recovered by inverse transformation. Simulation experiments show that the music accompaniment separation method based on 2DFT does not need to create a complex filter bank and very easy to implement. We find that our system is competitive with existing unsupervised music separation approaches that leverage similar assumptions.

References

1. Li, Y., Wang, D.L.: Separation of singing voice from music accompaniment for monaural recordings. IEEE Trans. Audio Speech Lang. Process. **15**(4), 1475–1487 (2007)
2. Li, Y., Woodruff, J., Wang, D.L.: Monaural musical sound separation based on pitch and common amplitude modulation. IEEE Trans. Audio Speech Lang. Process. **17**(7), 1361–1371 (2009)
3. Hsu, C.L., Jang, J.S.R.: On the improvement of singing voice separation for monaural recordings using the MIR-1 K dataset. IEEE Trans. Audio Speech Lang. Process. **18**(2), 310–319 (2010)

4. Huang, P.S., Chen, S.D., Smaragdis, P.: Singing-voice separation from monaural recordings using robust principal component analysis. In: 2012 IEEE International Conference on Acoustics, Speech and Signal Processing (ICASSP), pp. 57–60 (2012)

5. Rafii, Z., Pardo, B.: A simple music/voice separation method based on the extraction of the repeating musical structure. In: 2011 IEEE International Conference on Acoustics, Speech and Signal Processing (ICASSP), pp. 221–224 (2011)

6. Rafii, Z., Pardo, B.: Repeating pattern extraction technique (REPET): a simple method for music/voice separation. IEEE Trans. Audio Speech Lang. Process. 21(1), 73–84 (2013)

7. Zhang, T., Xu, X., Wu, W.: Music/vice separation based on the multi-repeating structure of mel-frequence cepstrum coefficients. Acta Acustica 2016(1), 134–142 (2016). (in Chinese)

8. Rafii, Z., Pardo, B.: Online REPET-SIM for real-time speech enhancement. In: IEEE International Conference on Acoustics, Speech and Signal Processing. IEEE (2016)

9. Liutkus, A., Rafii, Z., Badeau, R.: Adaptive filtering for music/voice separation exploiting the repeating musical structure. In: 2012 IEEE International Conference on Acoustics, Speech and Signal Processing (ICASSP), pp. 53–56 (2012)

10. Rafii, Z., Pardo, B.: Music/voice separation using the similarity matrix. In: 13th International Society for Music Information Retrieval(ISMIR), pp. 583–588 (2012)

11. Seetharaman, P., Rafii, Z.: Cover song identification with 2D fourier transform sequences. In: 2017 IEEE International Conference on Acoustics, Speech and Signal Processing (ICASSP), pp. 616–620 (2017)

12. Bertin-Mahieux, T., Ellis, D.P.: Large-scale cover song recognition using the 2D Fourier transform magnitude. In: 13th International Society for Music Information Retrieval Conference (2012)

13. Nieto, O., Bello, J.P.: Music segment similarity using 2D-fourier magnitude coefficients. In: 2014 IEEE International Conference on Acoustics, Speech and Signal Processing (ICASSP), pp. 664–668 (2014)

14. Stöter, F.-R., Liutkus, A., Badeau, R., et al.: Common fate model for unison source separation. In: IEEE International Conference on Acoustics Speech and Signal Processing (ICASSP). IEEE, pp. 126–130 (2016)

15. Pishdadian, F., Pardo, B., Liutkus, A.: A multi-resolution approach to common fate-based audio separation. In: 2017 IEEE International Conference on Acoustics, Speech and Signal Processing (ICASSP), pp. 566–570 (2017)

16. Chi, T., Ru, P., Shamma, S.A.: Multiresolution spectrotemporal analysis of complex sounds. J. Acoust. Soc. Am. 118(2), 887–906 (2005)

17. Patterson, R.D., Allerhand, M.H., Giguere, C.: Time-domain modeling of peripheral auditory processing: a modular architecture and a software platform. J. Acoust. Soc. Am. 98(4), 1890–1894 (1995)

18. Ru, P., Shamma, S.A.: Representation of musical timbre in the auditory cortex. J. New Music Res. 26(2), 154–169 (1997)

19. http://sites.google.com/site/unvoicedsoundseparation/mir-1k[OL]

20. Vincent, E., Gribonval, R., Fevotte, C.: Performance measurement in blind audio source separation. IEEE Trans. Audio Speech Lang. Process. 14(4), 1462–1469 (2006)

Average Speed Based Broadcast Algorithm for Vehicular Ad Hoc Networks (Workshop)

Qichao Cao[✉], Yanping Yu, and Xue Su

College of Information and Electronic Engineering, Zhejiang Gongshang University,
Hangzhou 310018, China

2731491712@qq.com, yuyanping@zjgsu.edu.cn, 2865287037@qq.com

Abstract. In order to solve the problem of broadcast storm and broadcast unreliability in Vehicular Ad Hoc Networks (VANET) on highways, an improved algorithm based on Speed Adaptive Probabilistic Flooding (SAPF) [1], which is referred to as Average Speed Based Broadcast (ASBB), is proposed. Since the average speed of vehicles in the vicinity reflects the network congestion around the current node more accurately, ASBB dynamically calculates the forwarding probability according to the average speed of the current node and the corresponding neighbor nodes. To obtain the speed of neighbor nodes, each node encapsulates its speed into the header of packets it transmits, instead of employing new types of packet for exchanging speed. This approach alleviates the network load and reduces the complexity of implementation. Meanwhile, only the nodes located behind the current node may participate in the forwarding of the broadcast packet, which reduces the number of nodes participating in the forwarding and further mitigates the broadcast storm and improves the broadcast reliability. The simulation results show that ASBB performs well in terms of suppressing broadcast storms, increasing the reachability and reducing the end-to-end delay.

Keywords: Vehicular Ad Hoc Networks · Broadcast storm · Broadcast reliability · Probability based broadcast algorithms · Average speed based broadcast algorithms

1 Introduction

On highway, many accidents are usually caused by slow detection of rear vehicles to the accidents in front of them [2]. Vehicular Ad Hoc Networks (VANETs) [3] are a type of network in which self-organizing technology is applied to the inter-vehicle communication. It can rapidly and automatically form a network providing communication between vehicles. Hazard warning applications in VANETs can extend the vision of drivers, allowing drivers to know the accidents in advance and take steps to avoid traffic accidents. The problem faced by VANETs in this scenario is how to quickly and reliably transmit emergency warning messages to other vehicles.

Broadcasting is the technique by which a source node transmits a broadcast packet to all other nodes in a network. After receiving a broadcast packet, a node may forward

© ICST Institute for Computer Sciences, Social Informatics and Telecommunications Engineering 2020
Published by Springer Nature Switzerland AG 2020. All Rights Reserved
H. Gao et al. (Eds.): ChinaCom 2019, LNICST 313, pp. 425–435, 2020.
https://doi.org/10.1007/978-3-030-41117-6_35

it to the nodes within its coverage. Therefore, a message is disseminated throughout the network quickly.

Flooding is the simplest broadcast algorithm in VANETs [4]. By flooding, each node forwards the packet received after receiving it for the first time. When the node distribution is sparse, it achieves high broadcast coverage and low latency. However, when the node distribution is dense, it is easy to cause serious broadcast storm due to a large number of redundant transmissions. Redundant transmission may also result in unreliable broadcast and longer end-to-end delay which seriously deteriorate the performance of emergency information transmission. In addition, since the topology of VANETs changes rapidly, traditional broadcast algorithms are not able to be applied to VANETs directly. Therefore, it is desirable to design efficient, reliable broadcast algorithms which are suitable to VANETs.

To address the broadcast storm problem of VANETs, many algorithms have been proposed. Basically, they can be categorized into single-hop broadcast algorithms and multi-hop broadcast algorithms [5–8]. The single-hop broadcast is referred to as the approach by which the source nodes only transmit the broadcast packets to the nodes within its one-hop coverage, and the broadcast packet cannot be transmitted throughout the entire network. In contrast, by the multi-hop broadcast, the broadcast packets are forwarded throughout the entire network. Since the coverage of the multi-hop broadcast is larger, it is more suitable for the highway scenario. The multi-hop broadcast algorithm in VANETs can be further divided into probability based broadcast algorithms, delay based broadcast algorithms, location based broadcast algorithms, cluster based broadcast algorithms and hybrid broadcast algorithms.

By the probability based broadcast algorithms, the node that receives a certain broadcast packet for the first time calculates the forwarding probability according to a predetermined rule, then the node forwards the broadcast packet according to the forwarding probability. The forwarding probability is calculated based on local or global parameters, such as distance, density, speed, and so on. Such algorithms have the advantages of its simplicity to be implemented. The SAPF [1] algorithm is one of representative algorithms by which each node calculates its forwarding probability according to the speed of the vehicle. The higher the speed, the larger the forwarding probability. However, when calculating the forwarding probability, only its own speed of the current node is considered. By observing the fact that the speed of only one node cannot well reflect the node density in its vicinity, the calculation of its forwarding probability in SAPF is not reasonable enough.

In the delay based broadcast algorithms, each node in the network sets a different waiting delay before forwarding the broadcast packet. Generally, the delay is set according to the distance between the transceiver nodes. The farther the distance, the shorter the delay. The node whose delay count down to zero first forwards the broadcast packet first. If the other nodes that is still deferring receive the broadcast packet again, they stop the delay and no longer participate in the forwarding process. This type of algorithms achieves low broadcast packet redundancy. However, when the node density is heavy, the nodes whose distances to the upstream node are close have almost identical delay.

Hence, their delay timers expire and then those nodes start to transmit almost simultaneously which result in more redundant broadcast packets [9]. Moreover, according to [10], the optimal forwarding node may suffer from the longest waiting delay.

In location based broadcast algorithms, the forwarding nodes are selected according to the location and the direction of the nodes. Generally, the node that is the farthest from the source node is selected as the forwarding node. In this way, the number of nodes participating in forwarding is reduced. The main drawback of this category of broadcast algorithms is that GPS or other positioning devices are generally required to obtain the position. There are some representative algorithms such as BPAB (Binary-Partition-Assisted Broadcast) [11], improved BPAB, UVMBP (Urban VANET Multi-hop Broadcast Protocol), UMBP (Urban Multi-hop Broadcast Protocol) [10], and 3P3B (Trinary Partitioned Black-burst-based Broadcast) [12]. The core idea behind these algorithms is to use the dichotomy or the trichotomy to select the farthest effective area. Then, the nodes in the farthest effective area compete to forward broadcast packets. These algorithms can select the optimal forwarding node faster, with low delay. However, the complexity of selecting the forwarding node is high.

In the cluster based broadcast algorithms, each cluster is composed of cluster head nodes, gateway nodes, and member nodes. The cluster head is responsible for transmitting the message to the member nodes in the cluster, and the gateway node is responsible for realizing communication between the clusters. This type of algorithms reduces the redundancy of transmission. However, because the topology of VANETs changes rapidly, the cluster based broadcast algorithms have large maintenance overhead. Also, they have longer delay.

The aforementioned types of broadcast algorithms are able to suppress the broadcast storm and provide the broadcast reliability to some extent. However, they suffer from one problem or another. Therefore, some hybrid broadcast algorithms are proposed with the aim to perform better. However, hybrid broadcast algorithms still have many problems, e.g. high redundant broadcast packets and low reliability. They may not meet the requirements for low delay [13, 14] and high reliability [15] under highway scenario.

From the above discussion, the following conclusions can be drawn for the highway scenario. Firstly, the fewer nodes participating in the broadcast, the more favorable to mitigate the broadcast storm. Secondly, the fewer the number of packets forwarded, the better the suppression effect on the broadcast storm. Thirdly, the broadcast algorithm must accurately reflect the situation of surrounding nodes, thereby improving the reliability of the algorithm. An improved algorithm based on SAPF, Average Speed Based Broadcast algorithm (ASBB), is proposed.

In ASBB, each relay node calculates the forwarding probability based on the average speed of the current node and the neighbor nodes, and then forwards the broadcast packet according to the probability. First of all, the algorithm is a probability based broadcast algorithm, which is simple and easy to be implemented and can effectively suppress broadcast storm. Secondly, the average speed of the current node and the neighbor nodes is used as a parameter for dynamically calculating the forwarding probability, which can accurately reflect the network congestion in the vicinity of the current node. In addition, the speed and location of the neighbors are carried by the broadcast packet header, so it is not required to periodically exchange additional new type of packets to acquire the speed of the neighbor nodes. Consequently, the network load is reduced, possible congestion is alleviated and the broadcast storm is mitigated. As a result, the broadcast reliability is not deteriorated. Furthermore, only the nodes located behind the immediate upstream nodes may be selected as the forwarding nodes, which further reduce the number of forwarding nodes and suppress the broadcast storm.

The rest of this paper is organized as follows. The introduction is given in Sect. 1. Section 2 describes ASBB in detail. The simulation scenario and simulation results are given in Sect. 3. Conclusions are drawn in Sect. 4.

2 Description of ASBB

Firstly, density of nodes distribution is relevant to the velocity of nodes [1]. However, we argue that the average speed nodes can better reflect the nearby density of nodes. Thus, the forwarding probability of each relay node is determined according to the average speed of the current node and the neighbor nodes.

The following strategies are adopted in ASBB. (1) Each node in the network obtains the speed and location of its neighbors by extracting from the headers of the packets received and calculates the average speed of the current node and its neighbors. (2) Calculate the forwarding probability according to the average speed of the current node and the neighboring nodes and forward the broadcast packet according to the forwarding probability. (3) The speed and location information of the neighbor nodes are carried in the broadcast packet headers. (4) Nodes located behind the immediate upstream node may be selected as the forwarding nodes.

2.1 Table Maintaining

In ASBB, each node in a network needs to maintain a neighbor information table (NIT) and a table recording the broadcast packets received (TRBPR).

A node establishes or updates the corresponding entry in NIT which is consisted of upon receiving a broadcast packet. The NIT includes the IP address of the current node j and entries of neighbor nodes. The entry of the qth neighbor node of node j is consisted of the IP address of the qth neighbor node of node j, the speed v_{jq} of the qth neighbor node of node j, and overtime value T_1 of the corresponding entry. So after running for a period of time, each node has the speed values of its neighbor nodes. If the overtime of an entry is expired, this entry should be canceled since the entry has not been updated by the corresponding nodes.

2.2 Calculate the Forwarding Probability

The basic idea behind ASBB is that a node forwards a packet received according to the forwarding probability of the node which varies with the average speed of the node and its own neighbor nodes. The higher the average speed, the higher the broadcast probability, and vice versa. Therefore, calculating the broadcast forwarding probability is the key step of ASBB. Before that, it is required to determine the average speed of a node.

The average speed $\bar{v}_j$ of the node j and its surrounding area is calculated as the Eq. (1):

$$\bar{v}_j = \frac{1}{n+1}\left(v_j + \sum_{q=1}^{n} v_{jq}\right) \tag{1}$$

Where n is the number of neighbor nodes of node j recorded in NIT of node j, v_j denotes the speed of the current node j, and v_{jq} denotes the speed of the qth neighbor node of node j.

The forwarding probability P_j of node j is calculated as in Eq. (2):

$$P_j = \begin{cases} 0.08 & \bar{v}_j < 15\,\text{km/h} \\ \frac{2}{\pi}sin^{-1}\frac{\bar{v}_j}{120} & 15\,\text{km/h} \leq \bar{v}_j \leq 110\,\text{km/h} \\ 0.738 & \bar{v}_j > 110\,\text{km/h} \end{cases} \tag{2}$$

When $\bar{v}_j < 15$ km/h, the traffic on the road is close to saturation, which means the network reaches a very high density. So, the forwarding probability of node j is set as $P_j = \frac{2}{\pi}sin^{-1}\frac{15}{120} \approx 0.08$. When $15\,\text{km/h} \leq \bar{v}_j \leq 110\,\text{km/h}$, calculate the forwarding probability of node j according to $P_j = \frac{2}{\pi}sin^{-1}\frac{\bar{v}_j}{120}$. When $\bar{v}_j > 110$ km/h, the network density is sparse. In order to improve the broadcast coverage, the forwarding probability is set as $P_j = \frac{2}{\pi}sin^{-1}\frac{110}{120} \approx 0.738$, which is a relatively high probability. It can be seen from Eq. (2) that P_j is monotonically increased with $\bar{v}_j$. Apparently, $P_j \in [0.08, 0.738]$.

2.3 Source Node Sends a Broadcast Packet

Assuming that node i is a source node in the Vehicular Ad Hoc Network, the steps for the source node i to send a broadcast packet are as in Algorithm 1.

Algorism 1 Source node sends a broadcast packet.	
1	the source node i generates a broadcast packet with sequence number z; establishes the broadcast packet entry in TRBPR; sets an overtime value T_2; records that the broadcast packet has been received;
2	node i obtains the speed v_i of the current node;
3	encapsulates the IP address of the source node i, the broadcast packet sequence number, the IP address of the current node i, the broadcast destination IP address, the speed and location information of the node i into the broadcast packet header;
4	transmits the broadcast packet;
5	end;

2.4 Relay Node Receives and Forwards Broadcast Packets

All nodes in the network can act as relay nodes. Assume that node j is a relay node in the Vehicular Ad Hoc Network. Node j receives a broadcast packet with sequence number z from its previous hop neighbor nodes h. The steps are shown as in Algorithm 2.

Algorism 2 Relay node receives and forwards a broadcast packet.

1   node j receiving a broadcast packet with sequence number z from its previous hop neighbor node h;

2   **if** node j receives the broadcast packet from node h for the first time **then**

3 | establish a new entry for node h in NIT; record the speed v_{jq} of the node h; set the overtime value T_1;

4   **else**

5 | update the speed v_{jq} in the corresponding entry of the node h in NIT; update the overtime value T_1;

6   **if** there is an entry of the broadcast packet in TRBPR of node j **then**

7 | directly discards the broadcast packet (the node j does not receive the broadcast packet for the first time);

8 | end;

9   obtain the position (x_h, y_h) of the last hop neighbor node h in the broadcast packet header; obtain the position (x_h, y_h) of the current node j, and compare the values of x_j and x_h;

10   **if** $x_j > x_h$ **then**

11 | directly discarding the broadcast packet (it is indicated that node j is located in front of the previous hop node h);

12 | end;

13   establish a new entry of the broadcast packet in TRBPR of node j; set the overtime value T_2; add the record that the broadcast packet has been received;

14   Obtain the speed v_j of the current node j; calculate the average speed $\bar{v}_j$ of the current node j and its neighbors according to $\bar{v}_j = \frac{1}{n+1}\left(v_j + \sum_{q=1}^n v_{jq}\right)$;

15   calculate the forwarding probability P_j of the node j according to the equation (2); generate a random number σ which is uniformly distributed over [0-1];

16   **if** $\sigma > P_j$ **then**

17 | directly discarded the broadcast packet;

18   **else**

19 | node j encapsulates the broadcast packet received in the format of the broadcast packet; forwards the broadcast packet;

20   end;

3 Simulation

To evaluate the performance of ASBB, we conducted a series of simulations over a diverse range of network conditions. To compare the performance, Flooding and SAPF are taken as references. In the simulation, a highway whose size is 1.0 km * 9.0 km has three lanes in each direction. Initially, nodes in a network are randomly and uniformly distributed on the road according to the node density set before the simulation. The initial velocity of vehicles is uniformly distributed over [60, 120] km/h. Each node adaptively adjusts the speed according to its distance from the front node. According to the 80th entry of the Enforcement Regulations of the People's Republic of China Road Traffic Safety Law, a vehicle should maintain a distance of more than 100 m from the immediate front vehicle of the same lane when the vehicle speed exceeds 100 km/h. The distance can be shortened appropriately, but the shortest distance is 50 m when the vehicle speed is lower than 100 km/h. In this case, the speed of the vehicle should be maintained constant. When the distance between the two closest nodes on the same lane is less than 50 m, the deceleration starts at an acceleration speed of -5 m/s^2. The acceleration starts at 5 m/s^2 when the distance is greater than 100 m. The maximum speed is no more than 120 km/h. Each node remains in the same lane when moving forward and will not change lanes during driving. All vehicles use an omni-directional antenna and moves in the same direction. A source node in the network transmits at Constant Bit Rate (CBR). Detailed parameter setting is shown in Table 1.

Table 1. Simulation parameters

Parameters	Value	
Wireless interface rate (Mb/s)	11	
MAC layer protocol	IEEE802.11DCF	
Antenna	Omni-directional antenna	
Node wireless coverage radius (m)	300	
Road length (km)	9.0	
Number of lanes (lane)	3	
Lane width (m)	3.75	
Broadcast packet size (bytes)	1024	
Simulation time (s)	200	
Change parameters		
Node density (vehicles/km/lane)	10/15/20/25/30	20
CBR (Packets/s)	1	0.5/1/1.5/2

The node density and CBR are set as follows.

Scenario 1: The node density in the network is set to 10, 15, 20, 25, 30 vehicles/km/lane, while CBR of a source node is 1 Packet/s.

Scenario 2: The node density in the network is set to 20 vehicles/km/lane while a source node varies CBR from 0.5, 1, 1.5, to 2 Packets/s.

The performance of Flooding, SAPF and ASBB are compared in terms of ratio of forwarding nodes, reachability and average end-to-end delay.

Ratio of forwarding nodes is the result of the number of forwarding nodes over the number of all nodes in a network. Figure 1 shows the ratio of forwarding nodes versus the node densities. Figure 2 shows the ratio of forwarding nodes versus the CBR rates. It can be seen that, in most cases, the ASBB algorithm has the lowest ratio of forwarding nodes,

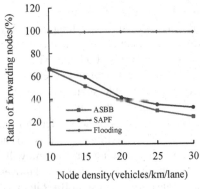

Fig. 1. The ratio of forwarding nodes versus different node densities

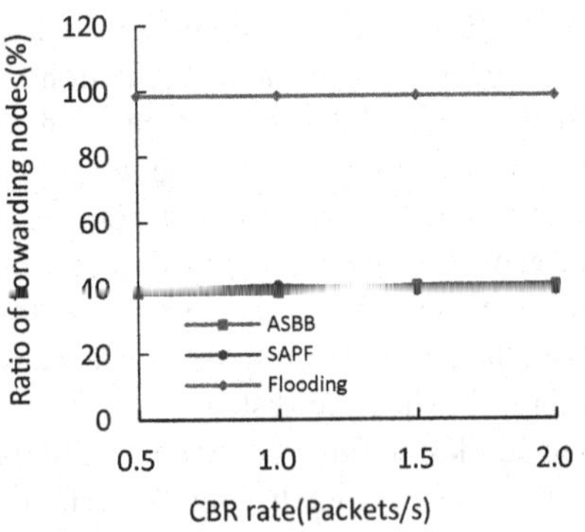

Fig. 2. The ratio of forwarding nodes versus CBR rates

followed by SAPF, Flooding, respectively. The reasons are given as follows. According to Eq. (2), the forwarding probability is calculated based on the average speed of the current node and the neighbor nodes in ASBB. The average speed of the current node and the neighbor nodes can better reflect the network congestion around the current node. While in SAPF, the forwarding probability is calculated only according to the speed of the current node which cannot accurately reflect the traffic situation around the current node. Thus, the selected forwarding node may not be reasonable. For example, when the nodes on the same lane are densely distributed on a highway, there may be several nodes moving fast, which leads to a higher forwarding probability and then more nodes are involved in forwarding. However, if the ASBB algorithm is adopted the forwarding probability that is calculated according to the average speed of the current node and its neighbor nodes is lower than that of SAPF. So less nodes are involved in forwarding, which directly leads to the lower ratio of forwarding nodes. For Flooding, all nodes participate in the forwarding of broadcast packets, so the ratio of forwarding nodes is the highest.

The lower the ratio of forwarding nodes, the better the broadcast storm suppression effect. Therefore, the ASBB algorithm suppresses broadcast storm best among the above three broadcast algorithms.

Reachability is the number of packets received in the entire network over the number of packets should be received. Figure 3 shows the reachability versus the node densities and Fig. 4 shows the reachability versus CBR rates. We can observe that Flooding has the best performance in terms of reachability, followed by ASBB, and SAPF respectively. This can be explained as follows. In Flooding, all the nodes participate in the forwarding of broadcast packets. Intuitively, the reachability flooding is the highest. In SAPF, sometimes the case that one node is of low speed which leads to low forwarding probability while its neighbors are of high speed exists. The node with low forwarding probability may not participate in the forwarding of broadcast packets, which may lead to network fragmentation. In this case, the broadcast packet will not be received by all nodes. As a result, the reachability decreases. If the ASBB algorithm is adopted however, the forwarding probability that is calculated according to the average speed

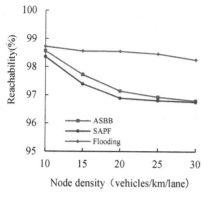

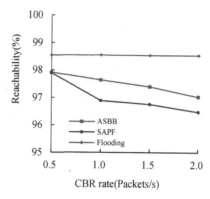

Fig. 3. The reachability versus node densities   **Fig. 4.** The reachability versus CBR rates

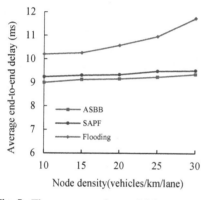

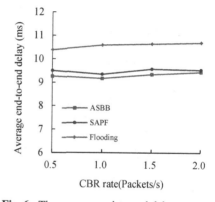

Fig. 5. The average end-to-end delay versus node densities

Fig. 6. The average end-to-end delay versus CBR rates

of the current node and its neighbor nodes is higher than that of SAPF. More nodes are involved in forwarding, which directly increases the reachability.

The higher the reachability of the broadcast packet, the higher the reliability of the broadcast algorithm. In summary, ASBB is more reliable than SAPF.

Average end-to-end delay is defined as the averaged time duration from the time when a packet is sent from a source to the time when the packet reaches a destination. Figure 5 shows the average end-to-end delay versus the node densities. Figure 6 shows the average end-to-end delay versus the CBR rates. It is evident that ASBB maintains the lowest average end-to-end delay, followed by SAPF and Flooding respectively. While the fewer the number of forwarding nodes, the smaller the probability of the channel contending, the smaller the collision probability between broadcast packets. Thus, the simulation results can be explained as follows. In ASBB, the forwarding probability is adaptively adjusted according to the average speed of the current node and its neighbor nodes which is more reasonable than SPAF. As a result, fewer forwarding nodes are involved in forwarding in ASBB than that in SPAF. Intuitively, the forwarding nodes involved in Flooding are the most, which lead to the highest end-to-end delay.

4   Conclusions

In this paper, to mitigate the broadcast storm and to provide reliability, an average speed based broadcast algorithm ASBB is proposed. The simulation results show that the performance of ASBB algorithm is better than that of SAPF in terms of ratio of forwarding node, reachability and average end-to-end delay. Therefore, ASBB algorithm can effectively suppress broadcast storm, providing higher reliability and short end-to-end delay at the same time. It can be well applied to VANETs on highway.

References

1. Mylonas, Y., Lestas, M., Pitsillides, A., Ioannou, P.G., Papadopoulou, V.: Speed adaptive probabilistic flooding for vehicular ad-hoc networks. IEEE Trans. Veh. Technol. **64**(5), 1973–1990 (2015)
2. Biswas, S., Tatchikou, R., Dion, F.: Vehicle-to-vehicle wireless communication protocols for enhancing highway traffic safety. IEEE Commun. Mag. **44**(1), 74–82 (2006)
3. Hartenstein, H., Laberteaux, L.P.: A tutorial survey on vehicular ad hoc networks. IEEE Commun. Mag. **6**(6), 164–171 (2008)
4. Tseng, Y.C., Ni, S.Y., Chen, Y.S., Sheu, J.P.: The broadcast storm problem in a mobile ad hoc network. Wireless Netw. **8**(2/3), 153–167 (2002)
5. Mussa, S.A.B., Manaf, M., Ghafoor, K.Z.: Beaconing and transmission range adaptation approaches in vehicular ad hoc networks: trends and research challenges. In: International Conference on Computational Science and Technology 2014, Kota Kinabalu, Malaysia, pp. 1–6. IEEE (2014)
6. Kumar, R., Dave, M.: A review of various VANET data dissemination protocols. Int. J. U-E-Serv. Sci. Technol. **5**(3), 27–44 (2012)
7. Pramuanyat, N., Nakorn, K.N., Rojviboonchai, K.: Preliminary study of reliable broadcast protocol on 802.11p public transport testbed. In: International Conference on Electrical Engineering/Electronics, Computer, Telecommunications and Information Technology 2015, Hua Hin, Thailand, pp. 1–6. IEEE (2015)
8. Lee, S., Lim, A.: Reliability and performance of IEEE 802.11n for vehicle networks with multiple nodes. In: International Conference on Computing, Networking and Communications 2012, Maui, HI, USA, pp. 252–256. IEEE (2012)
9. Li, D., Huang, H., Li, X., et al.: A distance-based directional broadcast protocol for urban vehicular ad hoc network. In: International Conference on Wireless Communications, Networking and Mobile Computing 2007, Shanghai, China, pp. 1520–1523. IEEE (2007)
10. Korkmaz, G., Ekici, E.: Urban multi-hop broadcast protocol for inter-vehicle communication systems. In: ACM International Workshop on Vehicular Ad Hoc Networks 2004, Philadelphia, PA, USA, pp. 76–85. ACM (2004)
11. Sahoo, J., Wu, E.H.K., Sahu, P.K., et al.: BPAB: binary partition assisted emergency broadcast protocol for vehicular ad hoc networks. In: International Conference on Computer Communications and Networks 2009, San Francisco, CA, USA, pp. 1–6. IEEE (2009)
12. Suthaputchakun, C., Dianati, M., Sun, Z.: Trinary partitioned black-burst-based broadcast protocol for time-critical emergency message dissemination in VANETs. IEEE Trans. Veh. Technol. **63**(6), 2926–2940 (2014)

13. Lima, D.S., Paula, M.R.P., Robert, F.M., et al.: ProbT: a temporal probabilistic protocol to mitigate the broadcast storm problem in VANETs. In: International Conference on Information Networking 2015, Cambodia, pp. 7–12. IEEE (2015)
14. Al-Dubai, A.Y., Khalaf, M.B., Gharibi, W., et al.: A new adaptive probabilistic broadcast protocol for vehicular networks. In: IEEE Vehicular Technology Conference 2015, Glasgow, UK, pp. 1–5. IEEE (2015)
15. Alotaibi, M.M., Mouftah, H.T.: Probabilistic area-based dissemination for heterogeneous transmission ranges in vehicular ad-hoc networks. In: IEEE International Conference on Computer and Information Technology, Liverpool, UK, pp. 1101–1108. IEEE (2015)

Author Index

Ai, Bo I-579, II-113

Bai, Yimeng II-297

Cai, Wen-Yu I-498
Cao, Qichao II-425
Chai, Rong I-129, II-180, II-338, II-351,
　II-378, II-391
Chen, Chen I-607
Chen, Dongfeng I-669
Chen, Huifang I-316, I-483
Chen, Jianing II-140
Chen, Jing I-642
Chen, Liang I-43
Chen, Nan I-368
Chen, Peijie II-29
Chen, Qianbin I-129, I-283, I-385, II-338,
　II-351, II-378, II-391
Chen, Xi II-192
Chen, Xiang II-252
Chen, Xin II-154
Cheng, Wei I-269
Cui, Guonan I-143
Cui, Jingjing I-693
Cui, Mingxin I-549

Dai, Cui-Qin I-283, I-385
Deng, Pingyu I-167
Ding, Lianghui I-331, I-607
Ding, Peng I-741
Ding, Yuemin I-117
Dong, Yangze I-207
Du, Yifan I-679
Duan, Hongda I-316
Duan, Yu I-729

Fan, Bo I-43
Fan, Congcong II-414
Fan, Wenjin I-246
Fan, Yaqing I-402
Fan, Zifu I-589
Fang, Bing I-564
Fang, Chao I-417

Feng, Hao I-642
Feng, Wenquan I-537
Fu, Biao I-385
Fu, Luoyi I-77
Fu, Peipei I-549

Gan, Xiaoying I-77
Gao, Wenjing I-707
Gilani, Syed Mushhad Mustuzhar I-619
Gong, Jie II-252
Gu, Yue II-264
Guo, Chang I-331
Guo, Shuo II-113
Guo, Wenbin I-707
Guo, Zhe I-331, I-607

He, Bi II-168
He, Di II-154
He, Wenxi I-258, I-679
He, Xiandeng I-368, I-457
Hu, Jianling I-193, I-356
Hu, Junshi I-102
Hu, Tianze I-316
Huang, Guimin I-402
Huang, Jun I-693
Huang, Kai I-402

Ji, Hong I-102, II-140
Jiang, Qing II-402
Jin, Cong II-230
Jin, Yue II-192, II-216
Ju, Wei II-154
Justo, Godfrey Njulumi I-66

Kuang, Ling I-720

Lan, Bo I-220
Lei, Weijia I-433
Li, ChunLin I-471
Li, Huayu I-579
Li, Jianguang II-230
Li, Jin I-301
Li, Juan I-669

Li, Kui   I-143, I-167
Li, Lanhui   I-3
Li, Lingxia   II-95
Li, Lixuan   I-537
Li, Minshuo   II-168
Li, Qian   II-62
Li, Quanqi   I-509
Li, Qun   I-525, II-205
Li, Shanshan   I-631, I-707
Li, Wei   II-297
Li, Xi   I-102, II-140
Li, Xiangyu   II-278
Li, Xiaohui   I-117
Li, Xiaoyang   II-278
Li, Yang   I-43
Li, Yixiao   II-364
Li, Yong   I-269
Li, Yonggang   I-445
Li, Youming   I-659
Li, Yuanjiang   I-33
Li, Zhaohui   I-433
Li, Zhenzhen   I-549
Li, Zhongtong   II-230
Liang, Zhonghua   II-241, II-297
Liao, Guangyan   I-283
Lin, Hai   I-417
Liu, Biao   I-509
Liu, Changzhu   II-338, II-351
Liu, Danpu   I-91
Liu, Dian   II-82
Liu, Erwu   I-53, I-344
Liu, Hongqing   II-20
Liu, Jianwei   II-307
Liu, Jie   II-264
Liu, Junkai   I-207
Liu, Liang   I-143
Liu, Pingshan   I-402
Liu, Qian   I-509
Liu, Qixu   I-509
Liu, Shan   II-317
Liu, Shouxun   II-230
Liu, Wei-Lun   I-269
Liu, Xingcheng   II-126
Liu, Yan   I-642
Liu, Yang   I-720
Liu, Yu   I-246
Liu, Zhanjun   I-720
Liu, Zhenxing   I-117

Liu, Zi-Qiang   I-498
Long, Hang   I-258, I-679, II-62, II-364
Lu, Zhufei   I-331, I-607
Luo, Jiamei   II-37
Luo, Qianwen   II-241
Luo, Zhen   II-20
Lv, Tiejun   I-3
Lv, Xin   II-230
Lyu, Junyi   I-91

Ma, Chaochen   I-77
Ma, Pengfei   II-180
Mao, Mengqi   II-391
Massawe, Libe Valentine   I-66
Mathiopoulos, P. Takis   I-283
Meng, Huan   II-20
Ming, Chunqiang   I-445
Muwumba, Abel Mukakanya   I-66

Ngubiri, John   I-66
Ning, MeiJun   I-235

Pei, Errong   II-317
Peng, Min   I-417
Peng, Shangxin   II-338
Peng, Tao   I-220, I-235, I-707, II-47, II-278
Piao, Dongming   I-356

Qin, Qi   I-344
Qin, Rongtao   II-328
Qin, Zhida   I-77
Qiu, Yifan   I-368, I-457
Quan, QingYi   I-235

Ran, Maohai   II-317
Ren, Haoqi   I-741
Ren, Mengtian   II-402
Ren, Yanling   I-33

Shang, Tao   II-307
Shao, Wei   I-564
Shi, Fanwei   I-193, I-356
Shi, Minyan   I-53
Shi, Ruoqi   I-193, I-356
Shi, Xu   II-168
Song, Chao   I-483
Song, Kening   I-33

Song, Xia   I-129
Su, Xue   II-425
Sun, Chao   I-537
Sun, Hua   I-537
Sun, Xiaolei   I-33
Sun, Xin   II-3
Sun, Yinghao   I-659
Sun, Yuanyuan   II-230

Tan, Bin   II-37, II-82
Tan, Xin   I-117
Tan, Xinrui   I-720
Tang, Jian   I-193
Tang, Mingwei   II-62
Tang, Pei   I-579
Tian, Shuangfei   II-73
Tian, Zengshan   II-95, II-192, II-216, II-402

Wan, Xiaoyu   I-589
Wang, Bicheng   I-193, I-356
Wang, Chengfei   II-29
Wang, Fang   I-258
Wang, Gang   I-659
Wang, Huahua   I-669
Wang, Hui   II-168
Wang, Kuang   I-316
Wang, Ling   II-180
Wang, Longchao   I-457
Wang, Longwei   I-53, II-29
Wang, Lusheng   I-417
Wang, Min   II-37
Wang, Ning   I-43
Wang, Qingcai   I-368, I-457
Wang, Rui   I-15, I-53, I-344, II-29, II-82
Wang, Shuhao   I-445
Wang, Wanwan   I-729
Wang, Wenbo   I-220
Wang, Yumei   I-246
Wang, Zhengqiang   I-589
Wang, Zhiqiang   I-509
Wei, Tao   II-180, II-378
Weng, Zhihui   I-33
Wu, Jun   I-15, I-741, II-82
Wu, Wenjing   II-297

Xie, Lei   I-316, I-483
Xie, Zhibin   I-33
Xin, Yue   II-241
Xiong, Lei   I-579, II-113
Xiu, Zhichao   II-364

Xu, Changqing   II-154
Xu, Chuan   I-619
Xu, Ding   I-525, II-205
Xu, Pengfei   I-179
Xu, YueQing   I-235
Xu, Zhixin   I-53

Yang, Feng   I-331, I-607
Yang, Mingyi   II-73
Yang, Tao   I-509
Yang, Weiqin   II-216
Yang, Xiaoxia   I-589
Yao, Dongping   II-113
Yao, Heping   I-368, I-457
Yin, Fangfang   I-91
Yu, Jun   I-15
Yu, Wenxian   II-154
Yu, Yanping   II-425
Yury, Kozyrev   II-168

Zeng, Bo   I-631
Zeng, Minyin   I-91
Zeng, Wei   II-192
Zhang, Chao   I-179, I-301
Zhang, Gangqiang   I-207
Zhang, Gege   I-631
Zhang, Gongzhui   II-216
Zhang, Haiyin   II-230
Zhang, Heli   I-102, II-140
Zhang, Hongjia   I-589
Zhang, Jianyi   I-509
Zhang, Junqing   I-207
Zhang, Mei-Yan   I-498
Zhang, Tian   II-414
Zhang, Tianqi   II-414
Zhang, Wei   II-73
Zhang, Wenru   I-741
Zhang, Xiaoya   II-95, II-402
Zhang, Yating   II-47
Zhang, Yuan   I-43
Zhang, Zhengyu   I-579, II-113
Zhang, Zhifeng   I-741
Zhang, Zhilong   I-91
Zhang, Zhixue   I-631
Zhang, Zhizhong   I-445, I-729
Zhang, Ziyue   II-252
Zhao, Guofeng   I-619
Zhao, Hang   II-82
Zhao, Hongbo   I-537

Zhao, Lei   I-707
Zhao, Long   II-264
Zhao, Songyuan   II-82
Zhao, Yingying   II-126
Zhao, Zheng   II-307
Zheng, Bo   I-269
Zheng, Xiaoyan   I-483
Zhou, Jun   II-3
Zhou, Mo   I-619

Zhou, Qing   I-143, I-167
Zhou, Yi   II-20
Zhou, Ziqiao   I-642
Zhu, Feifei   I-167
Zhu, Fusheng   I-741
Zobary, Firas Fawzy   I-471
Zou, Qin   II-37
Zubair, Ahmad   II-180, II-351
Zuo, PeiLiang   I-220

Printed in the United States
By Bookmasters